MCSE Guide to
Planning a Microsoft® Windows® Server 2003 Network, Enhanced

Byron Wright
Brian McCann

D1309430

THOMSON
™
COURSE TECHNOLOGY

Australia • Canada • Mexico • Singapore • Spain • United Kingdom • United States

THOMSON

COURSE TECHNOLOGY

MCSE Guide to Planning a Microsoft® Windows® Server 2003 Network, Enhanced

is published by Course Technology

Managing Editor:
William Pitkin III

Product Manager:
Nick Lombardi

Development Editor:
Jill Batistick

Associate Production Manager:
Christine Freitas

Production Editor:
Daphne E. Barbas

Manufacturing Coordinator:
Melissa Hulse

Quality Assurance/Technical Edit:
Marianne Snow
Danielle Shaw
Christian Kunciw

Marketing Manager:
Guy Baskaran

Associate Product Managers:
Mirella Misiaszek
David Rivera
Sarah Santoro

Editorial Assistant:
Jenny Smith

Cover Design:
Steve Deschene

Text Designer:
GEX Publishing Services

Compositor:
GEX Publishing Services

ISBN- 13: 978-0-619-21754-9
ISBN- 10: 0-619-21754-5

\underset{\text{BRIEF}}{\text{Contents}}

BRIEF
Contents

TABLE OF

Contents

Introduction

Welcome to *MCSE Guide to Planning a Microsoft Windows Server 2003 Network, Enhanced*. This book offers you real-world examples, interactive activities, and many hands-on projects that reinforce key concepts and help you prepare for a career in Microsoft network management and pass the Microsoft 70-293 exam. This book provides in-depth study of configuring, administering, and troubleshooting the services available within a Microsoft Windows Server 2003 network infrastructure. Throughout the book, we provide pointed review questions to reinforce the concepts introduced in each chapter. In addition to the review questions, we provide detailed hands-on projects that let you experience firsthand the processes involved in Windows Server 2003 network configuration and management. Finally, to put a real-world slant on the concepts introduced in each chapter, we provide case studies to prepare you for situations that must be managed in a live networking environment.

Intended Audience

MCSE Guide to Planning a Microsoft Windows Server 2003 Network, Enhanced is intended for people who have some experience administering and supporting Windows Server 2003 network and directory services. To best understand the material in this book, you should have background in Windows Server 2003 and general networking concepts. Ideally you have worked with the material presented in Course Technology's *MCSE Guide to Managing a Microsoft Windows Server 2003 Network, Enhanced* and *MCSE Guide to Managing a Microsoft Windows Server 2003 Environment, Enhanced*.

New to This Edition

- Appendix B provides detailed lab setup instructions to assist instructors in preparing their labs for class.

- Appendix C features expanded and more comprehensive chapter summaries to assist students in reviewing the material covered in each chapter.

- Two new Practice Exams are provided. One is located in the back of the textbook and is printed on perforated pages so that it can be handed in as a homework assignment or test. The second is posted on *www.course.com* in the password protected Instructor's Resource section, along with the Solutions to both exams. The questions on these Practice Exams are modeled after the type of questions students will see on the actual

MCSE 70-293 certification exam. In addition to helping students review what they have learned, they have the added benefit of preparing them for the certification exam.

■ Our CoursePrep ExamGuide content is now included in PDF format on the CD that accompanies this textbook. This content features key information, bulleted memorization points, and review questions for every exam objective in an easy-to-follow two-page-spread layout. This is an excellent resource for self-study before taking the 70-293 certification exam.

Chapter Descriptions

Chapter 1, "Overview of Planning a Windows Server 2003 Network," provides an overview of network services, Windows Server 2003 editions, and how to plan a network infrastructure.

Chapter 2, "TCP/IP Architecture," outlines what TCP/IP is and how the different components of the TCP/IP protocol stack communicate. The purpose of each component is explored, including what each is used for.

Chapter 3, "Planning Network Data Flow," describes different types of network traffic and how each is affected by the physical components of a network. Monitoring, optimizations, and troubleshooting network traffic are also explored.

Chapter 4, "Planning and Configuring Routing and Switching," explains how to configure routers, demand-dial connections, virtual LANs, network address translation, Internet connection sharing, and an Internet connection firewall.

Chapter 5, "Planning, Configuring, and Troubleshooting DHCP," provides a framework for planning and implementing DHCP including authorization, superscopes, backups, and logging.

Chapter 6, "Planning, Configuring, and Troubleshooting WINS," describes what WINS is, how it works, and how to implement it in various situations.

Chapter 7, "Planning a DNS Strategy," explains the functions of DNS and the strategies that can be used for implementation. Topics include primary zones, secondary zones, Active Directory integrated zones, Dynamic DNS, and integration with WINS.

Chapter 8, "Managing and Troubleshooting DNS," focuses on the configuration of DNS servers and DNS zones including security, DNS server roles, root hints, and zone replication.

Chapter 9, "Planning and Managing Certificate Services," explains the role of cryptography in network services including how it relates to Public Key Infrastructure. The chapter also explains how to use Windows Server 2003 as a certification authority to create and distribute certificates, perform authentication, encrypt data, and create digital signatures.

Chapter 10, "Planning and Managing IP Security," outlines how the IPSec protocol can be used to provide data security on a network. It also describes how to enable and configure IPSec using IPSec policies.

Chapter 11, "Planning Network Access," describes how to configure Windows Server 2003 as both a dial-up server and virtual private network (VPN) server, as well as control user access. This chapter also outlines how to configure Windows Server 2003 to act as a Remote Authentication Dial-In User Service (RADIUS) server using Internet Authentication Service (IAS).

Chapter 12, "Planning and Implementing Server Availability and Scalability," shows how to implement and manage Windows Server 2003 as a server cluster for higher availability or as a network load balancing cluster for higher scalability.

Chapter 13, "Planning Server and Network Security," identifies types of security and how to enhance security for various server roles. Implementing security for wireless networks is also covered.

Chapter 14, "Problem Recovery," explores a number of issues related to server recovery and management. File backup and recovery, recovery tools, remote management, and imaging are also covered.

Features and Approach

MCSE Guide to Planning a Microsoft Windows Server 2003 Network, Enhanced differs from other networking books in its unique hands-on approach and its orientation to real-world situations and problem solving. To help you comprehend how Microsoft Windows network management concepts and techniques are applied in real-world organizations, this book incorporates the following features:

- **Chapter Objectives**—Each chapter begins with a detailed list of the concepts to be mastered. This list gives you a quick reference to the chapter's contents and is a useful study aid.

- **Activities**—Hands-on Activities are incorporated throughout the text, giving you practice in setting up, managing, and troubleshooting a network system. The activities give you a strong foundation for carrying out network administration tasks in the real world. Because of the book's progressive nature, completing the hands-on activities in each chapter is essential before moving on to the end-of-chapter projects and subsequent chapters.

- **Chapter Summary**—Each chapter's text is followed by a summary of the concepts introduced in that chapter. These summaries provide a helpful way to recap and revisit the ideas covered in each chapter.

- **Key Terms**—All of the terms within the chapter that were introduced with boldfaced text are gathered together in the Key Terms list at the end of the chapter. This provides you with a method of checking your understanding of all the terms introduced.

- **Review Questions**—The end-of-chapter assessment begins with a set of review questions that reinforce the ideas introduced in each chapter. Answering these questions will ensure that you have mastered the important concepts.

- **Case Projects**—Finally, each chapter closes with a section that proposes certain situations. You are asked to evaluate the situations and decide upon the course of action to be taken to remedy the problems described. This valuable tool will help you sharpen your decision-making and troubleshooting skills, which are important aspects of network administration.

- **Tear-Out Practice Exam**—A 50 question tear-out exam is included in the back of the text. The questions are modeled after the actual MCSE certification exam and the exam is on perforated pages so students can hand it in as an assignment or an exam. The answers to the Practice Exam are included as part of the Instructor Resources.

- **On the CD-ROM**—The CD-ROM includes CoursePrep® test preparation software, which provides sample MCSE exam questions mirroring the look and feel of the MCSE exams. The CD also contains a complete CoursePrep ExamGuide workbook in PDF format. It devotes an entire two-page spread for every exam objective, featuring bulleted memorization points and review questions for self-study before exam day.

Text and Graphic Conventions

Additional information and exercises have been added to this book to help you better understand what's being discussed in the chapter. Icons throughout the text alert you to these additional materials. The icons used in this book are described below.

Tips offer extra information on resources, how to attack problems, and time-saving shortcuts.

Notes present additional helpful material related to the subject being discussed.

The Caution icon identifies important information about potential mistakes or hazards.

Each hands-on Activity in this book is preceded by the Activity icon.

CASE PROJECTS

Case project icons mark the end-of-chapter case projects, which are scenario-based assignments that ask you to independently apply what you have learned in the chapter.

Instructor's Resources

The following supplemental materials are available when this book is used in a classroom setting. All of the supplements available with this book are provided to the instructor on a single CD-ROM.

Electronic Instructor's Manual. The Instructor's Manual that accompanies this textbook includes Additional instructional material to assist in class preparation, including suggestions for classroom activities, discussion topics, and additional projects.

Solutions are provided for the end-of-chapter material, including Review Questions, and where applicable, Activities and Case Projects. Solutions to the Practice Exams are also included.

ExamView®. This textbook is accompanied by ExamView, a powerful testing software package that allows instructors to create and administer printed, computer (LAN-based), and Internet exams. ExamView includes hundreds of questions that correspond to the topics covered in this text, enabling students to generate detailed study guides that include page references for further review. The computer-based and Internet testing components allow students to take exams at their computers and also save the instructor time by grading each exam automatically.

Practice Exam. A second 50 question Practice Exam is included as part of the Instructor Resources. Like the Tear-Out Practice Exam in the text, the questions are modeled after the actual MCSE certification exam. The answers to this exam are also included as part of the Instructor Resources.

PowerPoint presentations. This book comes with Microsoft PowerPoint slides for each chapter. These are included as a teaching aid for classroom presentation, to make available to students on the network for chapter review, or to be printed for classroom distribution. Instructors, please feel at liberty to add your own slides for additional topics you introduce to the class.

Figure files. All of the figures and tables in the book are reproduced on the Instructor's Resource CD, in bitmap format. Similar to the PowerPoint presentations, these are included as a teaching aid for classroom presentation, to make available to students for review, or to be printed for classroom distribution.

Minimum Lab Requirements

- Hardware:

Hardware Component	Requirement
CPU	Pentium III 533 or higher
Memory	256 MB RAM
Disk Space	Minimum 2GB (3GB if storing the installation files on local hard drive)
Drives	CD-ROM Floppy Disk
Networking	All labs assume a single instructor server acting as a domain controller. Two network cards are recommended to allow isolation from other networks. All student servers will be configured in pairs and must have two network cards to complete all of the exercises. The first network card is connected to the classroom network with the instructor server. The second network card is connected via crossover cable or hub to the other student server in the pair. Make sure to have Windows Server 2003-compatible network adapters. A connection to the Internet via some sort of NAT or Proxy server is assumed.

- Software:

Windows Server 2003 Enterprise Edition for each computer

The latest Windows Server 2003 Service Pack (if available)

- Set Up Instructions:

To successfully complete the lab exercises, set up classroom computers as listed below:

1. The instructor computer should initially be installed with default configuration options. The name of the server should be *Instructor*. The initial password should be *Password!*.

2. After installation, rename one of the network connections as *Classroom* with an IP address of 192.168.1.10, a subnet mask of 255.255.255.0, and 192.168.1.10 as the DNS server. Rename the other connection as *External* and configure it with the appropriate IP address, subnet mask, and default gateway to allow access to the Internet. Configure routing and remote access and network address translation (if necessary) to allow access to the Internet. If network address translation is configured on this server then Classroom will be the internal interface, and External will be the external interface. For more information on how to configure network address translation please see Chapter 4.

3. Configure the Instructor computer as a domain controller for the domain *Arctic.local*. When asked to create an Administrator password for the domain, use *Password!*. Allow the Active Directory installation wizard to automatically install

DNS and create the domain. If the server does not detect Internet connectivity during the installation of Active Directory it will create a root DNS domain on the instructor server. This prevents the server from performing Internet DNS lookups. Delete the root DNS domain if it is created.

4. Install IIS on the Instructor computer and enable the processing of ASP scripts. This is required for an exercise in Chapter 4. The final exercise in Chapter 4 contains step-by-step instructions on how to enable ASP scripts.

5. After IIS is installed, create the file **C:\inetpub\wwwroot\default.asp**. The contents of this file should be:

```
<html>
<body>

<p>Source IP address = <%=Request.ServerVariables("REMOTE_ADDR")%>
<p>Source TCP Port = <%=Request.ServerVariables("REMOTE_PORT")%>

<p>Server IP address = <%=Request.ServerVariables("LOCAL_ADDR")%>
<p>Server TCP Port = <%=Request.ServerVariables("SERVER_PORT")%>

</body>
</html>
```

6. Student servers are installed by the students in Chapter 1. No initial software configuration is required.

7. Connect each pair of student computers with a crossover cable. Alternatively, they can be connected using straight cables and a hub or switch. During the course activities, each pair of computers is assigned a group number. For example, Student01 and Student02 are group 1, and Student03 and Student04 are group 2.

8. To make identification easier for students consider placing a paper label on the monitor of each server indicating the name of the server and the group number for that pair of computers.

9. It is important to remember that when performing the activities included in this book that the student logs in as the Administrator for the Arctic.local domain. The local Administrator accounts on the student member servers do not have enough privileges to complete some of the activities.

ACKNOWLEDGMENTS

I would like to thank my wife Tracey for her ongoing support and her patience when I let my responsibilities at home slide. As well, I would like to thank my business partner in Conexion Networks, Darrin, who kept the rest of the company afloat while I completed this book.

I would also like to thank the following reviewers for their insight and help as this book was written: Patty Gillilan, Sinclair Community College; John Hagle, Texas State Technical College; and Neal Zimmerman, CHI Institute.

1

Overview of Planning a Windows Server 2003 Network

After reading this chapter, you will be able to:

♦ Understand the process of installing Windows Server 2003

♦ Understand which platforms support upgrades to Windows Server 2003

♦ Describe the components in the Windows Server 2003 networking architecture

♦ List the networking services available in Windows Server 2003

♦ Describe the different editions of Windows Server 2003

♦ Plan a Windows Server 2003 network infrastructure project

Computer networks are an essential part of running a business today. It is impossible to conceive of organizations running without shared files, printers, and other resources. To build networks that are reliable and scalable, proper planning is essential.

INSTALLING WINDOWS SERVER 2003

Windows Server 2003 is as easy to install as any of the more common desktop Windows operating systems such as Windows 2000 or Windows XP. However, the default installation settings for Windows Server 2003 are radically different from Windows 2000.

In Windows 2000, the default file system permissions gave Full Control to the Everyone group. Although this made it easy for even unknowledgeable people to install a functional Windows 2000 server, this was very poor security. Most administrators removed the permissions for the Everyone group and replaced it with the Administrators group. Windows 2003 gives the Everyone group no permissions to the file system and gives the Users group Read access.

Another major security issue in Windows 2000 was the installation of Internet Information Services (IIS) by default. Many security flaws that affected Windows 2000 were based on IIS. Windows Server 2003 does not install IIS by default.

The most common way to install Windows Server 2003 is by booting from CD-ROM. However, you can also install from a share across the network using a network boot disk. This is useful if you install servers often and do not want to be concerned with missing CD-ROMs. In addition, you can copy the \I386 directory from the installation CD-ROM and install directly from the hard drive.

ACTIVITY

Activity 1-1: Installing Windows Server 2003

Time Required: 60 to 90 minutes

Objective: Install Windows Server 2003 as a member server in a domain.

Description: In this activity, you install Windows Server 2003 and join the Arctic.local domain as a member server. In addition, you rename each of your two network connections to be more descriptive. The network connection that is attached to the instructor computer through the classroom hub will be renamed Classroom. The network connection that connects directly to your partner via a crossover cable will be renamed Private. This activity assumes that the BIOS of your workstation has been configured to boot from CD-ROM.

1. Insert the Windows Server 2003, Enterprise Edition CD-ROM in your computer and reboot the system.

2. When the message "Press any key to boot from CD" appears, press a key on the keyboard. A blue screen appears and begins loading drivers. The drivers being loaded are shown in the white bar at the bottom of the screen.

3. A "Welcome to Setup" message appears on the screen. Press **Enter** to begin installing Windows Server 2003, Enterprise Edition.

4. Press **F8** to agree to the license agreement.

5. If your server has a previous installation of Windows Server 2003, you may be prompted to repair the existing installation. If given this option, press the **Esc** key to install a fresh copy of Windows without repairing.

6. Delete all partitions on your system to begin the fresh install. If only Unpartitioned space is shown, skip to Step 7. Otherwise, for each existing partitions, complete the following steps:

   a. Use the arrow keys to highlight the partition you want to delete.

   b. Press **D** to delete the selected partition.

   c. Press **Enter** to confirm the deletion of this partition.

   d. Press **L** to reconfirm the deletion of this partition.

   e. Repeat steps a to d for each remaining partition.

7. Press **C** to create a new partition.

8. In the Create partition of size (in MB): text box, type **4096** and press **Enter**. This creates a 4 GB partition to install Windows Server 2003. It is a good practice to keep the operating system on a separate partition from data and applications. This ensures that if a data or application partition runs out of disk space, the operating system will be unaffected.

9. Ensure that **C: Partition1[New (Raw)]** is selected and press **Enter** to install Windows Server 2003 on that partition.

10. Ensure that **Format the partition using the NTFS file system** is selected and press **Enter**. Wait while the new partition is formatted. This takes about five minutes, depending on the speed of your hard drive. Installation files are then copied to the hard drive. This takes 5 to 10 minutes depending on the speed of your hard drive and CD-ROM drive.

11. After the file copy is finished, you will be prompted to remove your CD-ROM and the system will reboot. Remove your CD-ROM and allow the system to reboot. If you accidentally leave your CD-ROM in the system, be sure not to press a key when the message "Press any key to boot from CD" appears.

12. When the system reboots, a graphical installation screen appears. On the Regional Language and Options screen, click **Next** to accept the default language setting of English (United States) and the default text input language and method of the U.S. keyboard layout.

13. In the Name text box, type your name. In the Organization text box, type **Arctic University** and click **Next**.

14. In the Product Key text box, enter the product key that came with your course materials. If you cannot find this product key, your instructor will provide one for you. Click **Next** to continue.

15. Confirm that the licensing mode selected is **Per Server**. In the Number of concurrent connections text box, type **50**, and then click **Next**.

16. In the Computer name text box, type **STUDENT*xx***, where *xx* is a student number assigned to you by your instructor.

17. In the Administrator password text box, type **Password!**. In the Confirm password text box, type **Password!**, and click **Next**.

18. Ensure that the date, time, and time zone are correct, and then click **Next**.

19. On the Network Settings screen, ensure that **Typical Settings** is selected. This automatically detects and installs the network drivers for your network cards. Each card will be configured to obtain an IP address automatically. You will configure these cards later in the activity. Click **Next** to continue.

20. On the Workgroup or Computer Domain screen, select **No, this computer is not on a network, or is on a network without a domain**, if necessary. You will join the Arctic.local domain later in the activity. Click **Next** to continue. The remainder of the installation takes 20 to 40 minutes, depending on the speed of your server.

21. After your server reboots, log on as **Administrator**.

22. The first time you log on to your server, the Manage Your Server window appears. Click **Don't display this page at logon** and close the Manage Your Server window.

23. Rename your network connections to be more descriptive:
    a. To help determine which network card is which, disconnect the crossover cable that connects your server to your partner's server.
    b. Click **Start**, point to **Control Panel**, and double-click **Network Connections**. There will be two network connections. One of them shows the status of Network cable unplugged. This is the private connection between your server and your partner's server. The network connection with the status Enabled is connected to the classroom network.
    c. Right-click the network connection with the status Enabled and click **Rename**, type **Classroom**, and press **Enter**.
    d. Right-click the network connection with the status Network cable unplugged and click **Rename**, type **Private**, and press **Enter**.

24. Configure the IP address on your Classroom connection:
    a. Right-click **Classroom** and click **Properties**.
    b. Click **Internet Protocol (TCP/IP)** and click the **Properties** button.
    c. Click **Use the following IP address**.
    d. In the IP address text box, type **192.168.1.1*xx***, where *xx* is the student number assigned to you by your instructor.
    e. In the Subnet mask text box, type **255.255.255.0**.
    f. In the Default gateway text box, type **192.168.1.10**, unless given an alternative gateway by your instructor. This may vary depending on how your classroom accesses the Internet.

    g. In the Preferred DNS server text box, type **192.168.1.10** and click **OK**.

    h. Click **Close**.

    i. Close the Network Connections window.

25. Reconnect the crossover cable that connects your server to your partner's server.

26. Copy the \I386 folder from your Windows Server 2003 installation CD-ROM to your hard drive. This will make it easier to add Windows components throughout the remainder of the course.

27. Join the Arctic.local domain:

    a. Click **Start**, right-click **My Computer**, and click **Properties**.

    b. Click the **Computer Name** tab.

    c. Click the **Change** button.

    d. Click **Domain**, type **Arctic.local** in the Domain text box, and then click **OK**.

    e. To join the domain, you must enter the user name and password of a user that has permissions to add computers to the domain. In this instance, log on as the Administrator of the domain. In the User name text box, type **Administrator**; in the Password text box, type **Password!**, and click **OK**.

    f. Click **OK** to close the Computer Name Changes window.

    g. Click **OK** to the notification about restarting your server.

    h. Click **OK**, and click **Yes** to restart your server.

UPGRADING TO WINDOWS SERVER 2003 FROM OTHER PLATFORMS

Not all Windows operating systems can be upgraded to Windows Server 2003. Upgrades are not supported from any Windows desktop operating system, including Windows 9x, Windows NT Workstation, Windows 2000 Professional, and Windows XP.

Supported platforms for upgrades are:

- Windows NT 4.0 Server with Service Pack 5
- Windows NT 4.0 Terminal Server Edition with Service Pack 5
- Windows 2000 Server

INTRODUCING WINDOWS SERVER 2003 NETWORK ARCHITECTURE

Windows Server 2003 is the latest **network operating system (NOS)** from Microsoft. A network operating system is an operating system that is designed for network servers. The network architecture used by Windows Server 2003 is fundamentally the same as the network architecture used by Windows NT, Windows 2000, and Windows XP.

The network architecture used by Windows Server 2003 is so flexible that it can be used in a wide variety of situations from a small office to a large, multinational corporation. Small offices use Windows Server 2003 on a **local area network (LAN)**, which consists of only a single physical location. Larger companies with multiple offices implement Windows Server 2003 on a **wide area network (WAN)**, which consists of multiple physical locations.

There are four major software components in networking: client, service, protocol, and adapter. **Client** software makes requests for resources on the network. **Service** software responds to requests from client software and provides access to resources. To communicate, the client and service software use a common **protocol**, which defines the language that the client and service use. The **adapter** is the driver for the network card.

The operating system uses the network driver to communicate with the network card. Windows Server 2003 has two interfaces to make it easier for developers to create clients, services, protocols, and adapter software. The **Network Driver Interface Specification (NDIS)** is a programming interface that resides between protocols and the adapter software. The **Transport Driver Interface (TDI)** is a programming interface that resides between clients and protocols as well as between services and protocols. Figure 1-1 shows how the networking components relate to NDIS and TDI.

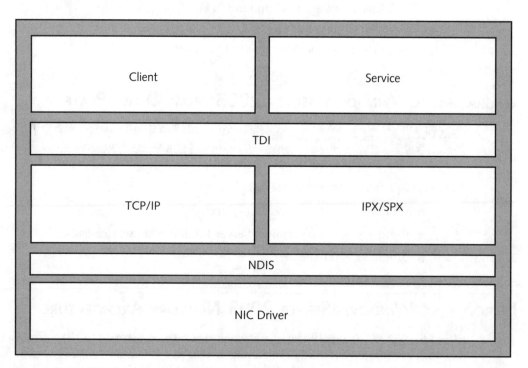

Figure 1-1   Windows Server 2003 networking architecture

NDIS

NDIS is a specification created by Microsoft and 3Com to speed the development of device drivers and enhance networking capabilities. Before a standard interface was defined, the developers of network card drivers had to write code to interact with each protocol being used by each hardware device to which the network card was attached.

Now with a standard specification in place, the developers of network card drivers write code that communicates with NDIS, and protocol developers also write code that communicates with NDIS. Neither the developers of network card drivers nor protocol developers need to be aware of what the other is doing. NDIS acts as an intermediary for all communication between the protocol and the network card driver.

When a protocol is configured to use an adapter, it is referred to as a binding. Bindings between protocols and adapters are controlled by NDIS. A single adapter can be bound to multiple protocols. A single protocol can also be bound to multiple adapters. This is very important in a computer that is acting as a router or a server that communicates with clients using multiple protocols.

Windows Server 2003 uses NDIS version 5.1. Network drivers written for NDIS 4.0 or later are also supported. In Windows 9x operating systems, NDIS 4.0 was included, starting with Windows 95 OSR2. Windows NT 4.0 was the first NT-based operating system to support NDIS 4.0. Network drivers written for these operating systems or later versions should function properly in Windows Server 2003.

TDI

The TDI layer provides clients and services with access to network resources. Applications talk to the TDI layer and the TDI layer passes on the requests to the protocols.

TDI emulates two network access mechanisms: Network Basic Input/Output System (NetBIOS) and Windows Sockets (WinSock). Network Basic Input/Output System **(NetBIOS)** is an older network interface that is used by Windows 9x and Windows NT to access network resources. **Windows Sockets (WinSock)** is used by Internet applications such as Internet Explorer and Outlook Express to access network resources. Starting with Windows 2000, WinSock can also be used by Windows to access **Active Directory**-based resources. **Windows Sockets Direct (WinSock Direct)** is a new enhancement to WinSock that is used to access resources on system area networks.

Developers write services and clients that communicate with NetBIOS or WinSock to access network resources. The applications communicate with the TDI layer, which emulates these interfaces. Developers creating protocols code them to communicate with the TDI layer. For a client and service to communicate, they must both be using the same network access mechanism and protocol.

Activity 1-2: Researching Networking Architecture

Time Required: 5 minutes

Objective: Find further information about NDIS and TDI.

Description: You want to be sure you understand the difference between the TDI layer and NDIS. In this activity, you use the Help and Support utility to find more information.

1. If necessary, start your server and log on as **Administrator**.
2. Click **Start**, and then click **Help and Support**.
3. Click the **Index** button.
4. Type **glossary** in the Type in the keyword to find text box.
5. Double-click the **main glossary** item.
6. Click the **N** button in the browser pane.
7. Scroll the browser pane to **Network Driver Interface Specification (NDIS)**, and read the description.
8. Click the **T** button in the browser pane.
9. Scroll the browser pane to **Transport Driver Interface (TDI)**, and read the description.
10. Close the Help and Support Center window.

Network Protocols

Four major protocols are supported in Windows Server 2003: Internet Protocol version 4 (IPv4), Internet Protocol version 6 (IPv6), Internetwork Packet eXchange/ Sequenced Packet eXchange (IPX/SPX), and **AppleTalk**.

Internet Protocol version 4 (IPv4) is the most common networking protocol used today. Most network components either require it or support using it, and it is also required for connecting to the Internet. IPv4 is normally referred to as TCP/IP without referencing a version number.

Internet Protocol version 6 (IPv6) is a newer version of TCP/IP and offers a number of enhancements. The most obvious enhancement is the expansion of the address space to alleviate a shortage of IP addresses on the Internet. It is not commonly in use yet, but will be in the next 5 to 10 years. This is new in Windows Server 2003.

Internetwork Packet eXchange/Sequenced Packet eXchange (IPX/SPX) is used primarily for backward compatibility with older networks running Novell NetWare. Some older applications also require IPX/SPX. **AppleTalk** is used to communicate with Apple Macintosh computers.

Windows Server 2003 does not support the NetBEUI protocol. NetBEUI was supported in all previous versions of Windows.

NOTE

ACTIVITY

Activity 1-3: Viewing Available Protocols

Time Required: 10 minutes

Objective: Verify the protocols available for installation.

Description: You need to verify the protocols that are available for Windows Server 2003 as part of the planning process for network services. In this activity, you view the list of available protocols in the properties of a network connection.

1. If necessary, turn on your server and log on as **Administrator**.

2. To open the properties of your local area network connection, click **Start**, point to **Control Panel**, point to **Network Connections**, right-click **Classroom**, and then click **Properties**.

3. Notice that TCP/IP is already installed.

4. Click the **Install** button.

5. Click **Protocol** and click **Add**.

6. Notice that TCP/IP is not in the list because it is already installed.

7. Click **Cancel** to close the Select Network Protocol window.

8. Click **Cancel** to close the Select Network Component Type window.

9. Click **Cancel** to close the Classroom Properties window.

UNDERSTANDING NETWORK SERVICES

Windows Server 2003 can perform in a wide variety of roles from file server to application server. This level of flexibility is due to the wide variety of services that run on Windows Server 2003. Each service allows the server to perform a different role.

Default Services

Very few network services are installed on Windows Server 2003 by default. This is essential for a secure network. One of the primary strategies used by hackers is to exploit the default configuration settings of services that were unintentionally installed during the operating system installation.

Windows Server 2003 default network services include:

- *Automatic Updates*—This service monitors the availability of operating system patches. When a patch is available, you are notified and are given the option to download and install it.

- *Background Intelligent Transfer Service (BITS)*—This service ensures that file transfers do not overwhelm the capacity of the server. For example, downloads from Windows Update are controlled by BITS to ensure that regular file access has a higher priority than the download from Windows Update. BITS is only used by applications that have been designed for it.

- *Computer Browser*—This service maintains the list of computers that appears in My Network Places.

- *DHCP Client*—This service enables Windows Server 2003 to obtain an IP address dynamically from a **Dynamic Host Configuration Protocol (DHCP)** server. A DHCP server automatically distributes IP addresses and other IP configuration information to DHCP clients.

- *Distributed File System (DFS)*—This service allows file shares on multiple servers to be viewed as a single logical structure. If **Distributed File System (DFS)** is disabled, then this server cannot access shares through DFS.

- *Distributed Transaction Coordinator (DTC)*—This service is used by programs to coordinate transactions that occur on multiple servers. It ensures that all parts of a transaction are completed.

- *DNS Client*—This service enables Windows Server 2003 to resolve host names to IP addresses by contacting a **Domain Name System (DNS)** server. It is also responsible for caching previous DNS resolution requests. DNS servers are responsible for resolving host names to IP addresses and answering queries for domain services.

- *Error Reporting Service*—This service collects operating system errors and sends them to Microsoft across the Internet.

- *IPSec Services*—This service controls how Windows Server 2003 uses **IP Security (IPSec)** to encrypt data transferred across the network. By default, network traffic is not encrypted.

- *Network Connections*—This service allows you to view and manage the network connections in Control Panel. If this service is disabled, you cannot manage network, **virtual private network (VPN)**, and dial-up connections.

- *Network Location Awareness (NLA)*—This service makes it easier for developers to track network information when they write applications.

- *Remote Procedure Call (RPC)*—This service is used by application developers to communicate with services on remote computers. If this service is stopped, many applications will not function properly.

- *Remote Registry*—This service allows remote editing of the registry. If this service is stopped, all registry edits must be performed on the local computer.

- *Server*—This service is used to share file and print services. If it is disabled, shared files and printers will not be available. In addition, it allows the use of named pipes, which are used by some applications.

- *TCP/IP NetBIOS Helper*—This service is required to support NetBIOS services when using TCP/IP. If it is disabled, pre-Windows 2000 clients will not be able to log on to a **domain controller** or access shared file and print resources. A domain controller authenticates users logging on to the network.

- *Terminal Services*—This service is required for **Remote Desktop**, **Remote Assistance**, and **terminal server**. If this service is disabled, the remote management through Remote Desktop is not possible, and the system may become unstable.

- *Windows Time*—This service enables time synchronization between computers in an Active Directory forest.

- *Wireless Configuration*—This service manages the configuration of wireless networks based on the **802.11** standard, as defined by the Institute of Electrical and Electronics Engineers (IEEE). It provides the ability to roam easily from one wireless network to another. This is not normally required on servers.

- *Workstation*—This service is used to access file and print services on Windows servers across the network. It is also required by some applications that access resources across the network.

Services Added to a Domain Controller

A domain controller holds a copy of Active Directory information. This information is used to authenticate users and configure network resources. As a consequence, additional services are required.

Additional network services running on domain controllers include:

- *Background Intelligent Transfer Service (BITS)*—This service is disabled on domain controller.

- *File Replication Service*—This service synchronizes the contents of the netlogon share between domain controllers. If it is disabled, logon scripts and Group Policy objects will not be properly synchronized between domain controllers.

- *Intersite Messaging*—This service is used to synchronize Active Directory information between sites in an Active Directory forest.

- *Kerberos Key Distribution Center*— This service performs the authentication and distributes Kerberos keys to clients. **Kerberos** is an authentication mechanism used by Windows 2000 and newer clients.

- *Net Logon*—This service is responsible for providing authentication services and registering service information in DNS. If this service is stopped, authentication will be disabled and DNS records will not be properly created. If DNS records are not created, workstations may be unable to find the domain controller.

Optional Network Services and Features

Windows Server 2003 has a wide variety of network services that are optional. These allow Windows Server 2003 to perform many tasks. These services can be combined onto a single server if required.

- **Certificate services** is used to issue and manage certificates that are used in the certificate issuing and control structure know as **Public Key Infrastructure (PKI)**. **Certificates** can be used for authentication, smart cards, file encryption, securing Web traffic, and digital signatures.

- **Clustering** allows greater fault tolerance for applications. If a service or application fails, it can be started on another server with minimal disruption to client computers.

- DHCP is an automated mechanism used to assign IP addresses to client computers. Automating this process saves hours of work for a network administrator. In addition to assigning the IP address, DHCP can also provide IP configuration options, such as subnet masks, the default gateway, and DNS servers.

- DNS is a service that converts host names to IP addresses. Client computers require this to access resources through a host name. Active Directory uses DNS to store service location information.

- **Internet Authentication Service (IAS)** allows a company to use Active Directory for centralized authentication of remote access clients on many different remote access servers. A company using IAS can have remote users dial in to an ISP and use the user ID and password of their Active Directory account for authentication. In addition, IAS can centralize the logging of internal dial-up servers.

- **Internet Connection Firewall (ICF)** provides basic firewall protection for small businesses. It works with LAN, dial-up, and VPN connections. If a firewall is already in place, then ICF is not required.

- **Internet Connection Sharing (ICS)** is an automated way to set up DHCP, NAT, and a DNS proxy for small networks. DHCP automatically provides IP addresses and configuration options that define the ICS server as both the default gateway and the DNS server. The DNS proxy takes client DNS requests and forwards them to the DNS server it is configured to use. NAT allows all of the client computers to share a single IP address from an ISP. This service was not available in Windows 2000 Server and is new in Windows Server 2003.

1

- **Internet Information Services (IIS) 6.0** provides support for **Hypertext Transfer Protocol (HTTP)**, which is used for web connectivity, and **File Transfer Protocol (FTP)**, which is used for file transfers. The default configuration for IIS 6.0 is locked down to be more secure. In addition, it offers enhanced scalability and improved load balancing.

- Load balancing has been added as a standard feature to all versions of Windows Server 2003. In high-traffic environments, a single server may not be able to keep up with the level of service that is required. This is particularly likely for Web-based applications that may be available to thousands of users. **Load balancing** transparently spreads the traffic between two or more servers. From the client perspective, it appears as if there is still only one server.

- **Network Address Translation (NAT)** allows an entire office of computers to share a single IP address when accessing the Internet. If Windows Server 2003 is used as a router to connect with an ISP, only a single IP address is required. As packets are routed through the server running NAT, packet headers are modified to look as if the router created them. When response packets return, the router delivers them to the proper host on the internal network.

- Network bridging allows Windows Server 2003 to be used as a **bridge** to allow multiple network segments to communicate without introducing the complexity of routing. This was not available in Windows 2000 Server and is a new feature in Windows Server 2003.

- **Point-to-Point Protocol over Ethernet (PPPoE)** is used by many high-speed **Internet service providers (ISPs)** to control traffic on their networks. ISPs sell access to the Internet. Windows Server 2003 can access these networks without installing third-party client software. This was not available in Windows 2000 Server and is a new feature in Windows Server 2003.

- **Routing and Remote Access Service (RRAS)** allows Windows Server 2003 to act as a router, VPN server, and dial-in server. Windows Server 2003 can route IPv4, IPv6, IPX/SPX, and AppleTalk packets. **Point-to-Point Tunneling Protocol (PPTP)** and **Layer Two Tunneling Protocol (L2TP)**/IPSec connections are supported for VPN access. The L2TP/IPSec VPN has been improved to allow connections through NAT. A dial-in server allows remote users to connect to office networks using a modem and phone line.

- **Services for Macintosh** allows Macintosh computers to communicate with Windows Server 2003.

- Services for UNIX allows UNIX and **Linux** computers to communicate with Windows Server 2003.

- **Web Distributed Authoring and Versioning (WebDAV)** allows documents to be shared and managed using HTTP.

- Windows Server 2003 includes native support for XML Web services. **Web services** are a standardized way to develop application components that can be accessed across the Internet, and use Internet standards such as **Extensible Markup Language (XML)**, **Simple Object Access Protocol (SOAP)**, **Universal Description, Discovery and Integration (UDDI)**, and **Web Services Description Language (WSDL)**.

- **Windows Internet Naming Service (WINS)** acts as a central registry of NetBIOS name and service information. WINS is required on large networks with pre-Windows 2000 clients.

- **Windows Media Services** provides streaming audio and video. This is used in combination with Windows Media Player on the client computers.

Activity 1-4: Viewing Installed Services

Time Required: 5 minutes

Objective: Identify installed network services.

Description: You are having trouble connecting to one of the test servers in your office. Because other staff have also been configuring the server, you think that Internet Connection Firewall may be installed and configured. In this activity, you verify that ICF is not running.

1. If necessary, start your server and log on as **Administrator**.

2. Click **Start**, point to **Administrative Tools**, and click **Services**.

3. Double-click the **Internet Connection Firewall (ICF)/Internet Connection Sharing (ICS) service**.

4. Verify that the status of the service is stopped and the Startup type is disabled. This means that the service is not currently running and will not start when the server is rebooted.

5. Click **Cancel** to close the Internet Connection Firewall (ICF)/Internet Connection Sharing (ICS) Properties window.

6. Close the Services window.

Activity 1-5: Viewing Available Services

Time Required: 5 minutes

Objective: Verify the network services that are available for installation.

Description: For your planning process, you need to verify the network services that are available for Windows Server 2003. In this activity, you go through the process of installing new Windows components to see which network services are available.

1. If necessary, start your server and log on as **Administrator**.

2. Click **Start**, point to **Control Panel**, and click **Add or Remove Programs**.

1

3. Click **Add/Remove Windows Components**.

4. Scroll through the list to see which services are available.

5. Click **Networking Services**, and click the **Details** button.

6. View the networking services, and then click **Cancel** to close the Networking Services window.

7. Click **Cancel** to close the Windows Components Wizard.

8. Close the Add or Remove Programs window.

SELECTING THE OPERATING SYSTEM FOR THE ENTERPRISE

As with Windows 2000, there are multiple versions (or editions) of Windows Server 2003. Each version is designed to meet the needs of certain market segments that Microsoft has targeted. The four versions are: Web Edition, Standard Edition, Enterprise Edition, and Datacenter Edition. No matter which version of Windows Server 2003 you implement, some features are available only with specific clients, such as Windows 2000 or Windows XP. That specificity is discussed in the last subsection of this part of the chapter.

Web Edition

Windows Server 2003, Web Edition, is a lower-cost version of Windows Server 2003 that is optimized to be a dedicated Web server. This version is meant to counter Linux in the market for utility servers. Windows Server 2003, Web Edition, provides the easy manageability and performance of Windows without the complexity of Linux.

Some unique features of Web Edition are listed here:

- Windows Server 2003 Web Edition must be a **member server** or **standalone server**. A member server is a server that does not contain a copy of Active Directory but is integrated into the domain security structure. A standalone server is not integrated into the security structure of a domain.

- Load balancing is supported.

- Clustering is not supported.

- VPN support is limited.

- Services for Macintosh are not supported.

- Internet Authentication Service is not supported.

- **Remote Installation Services** is not supported. Remote Installation Services is used to install operating systems remotely.

- Windows Media Services are not supported.

- Terminal Services are not supported.

The hardware requirements for Windows Server 2003, Web Edition, are listed in Table 1-1.

Table 1-1   Hardware requirements for Windows Server 2003, Web Edition

Hardware	Minimum System Requirements	Recommended System Requirements
CPU speed	133 MHz	550 MHz
RAM	128 MB	256 MB
Disk space for setup	1.5 GB	N/A
Maximum RAM	2 GB	N/A
Maximum processors	2	N/A
Cluster nodes	N/A	N/A

Standard Edition

Windows Server 2003, Standard Edition, is the version most likely to be used as a departmental file and print server or application server. It has a wide variety of available services such as Remote Installation Services (RIS) and application deployment through **Group Policy**. Group Policy is a mechanism used to centrally deploy software and control desktops through Active Directory.

Some unique features of Standard Edition are listed here:

- Windows Server 2003 Standard Edition can be a domain controller, member server, or standalone server.
- Load balancing is supported.
- Clustering is not supported.
- Full VPN support is available.
- Services for Macintosh are supported.
- Windows Media Server is supported.
- Terminal Services are supported.

The hardware requirements for Windows Server 2003, Standard Edition, are listed in Table 1-2.

Table 1-2   Hardware requirements for Windows Server 2003, Standard Edition

Hardware	Minimum System Requirements	Recommended System Requirements
CPU speed	133 MHz	550 MHz
RAM	128 MB	256 MB
Disk space for setup	1.5 GB	N/A
Maximum RAM	4 GB	N/A
Maximum processors	4	N/A
Cluster nodes	N/A	N/A

Enterprise Edition

Windows Server 2003, Enterprise Edition, is designed to enable large enterprises to deliver highly available applications and Web services. It is available in 32-bit and 64-bit editions. This version of Windows Server 2003 is the logical upgrade from Windows 2000 Advanced Server for enterprises that are implementing Web services using the **Common Language Runtime (CLR)**.

Some unique features of Enterprise Edition are listed here:

- Windows Server 2003 Enterprise Edition can be a member server, domain controller, or standalone server.
- Load balancing is supported.
- Clustering is supported.
- **Metadirectory Services** are supported. Metadirectory Services integrates multiple directory services.
- 64-bit processing is supported on **Itanium** processors.
- Hot add memory is supported.
- **Non-Uniform Memory Access (NUMA)** is supported. NUMA is a memory architecture used for multiprocessor servers.

The hardware requirements for Windows Server 2003, Enterprise Edition, are listed in Table 1-3.

Table 1-3 Hardware requirements for Windows Server 2003, Enterprise Edition

Hardware	Minimum System Requirements	Recommended System Requirements
CPU speed	133 MHz for 32-bit processors 733 MHz for Itanium	550 MHz for 32-bit processors 733 MHz for Itanium
RAM	128 MB	256 MB
Disk space for setup	1.5 GB for 32-bit processors 2.0 GB for Itanium	N/A
Maximum RAM	32 GB for 32-bit processors 64 GB for Itanium	N/A
Maximum processors	8	N/A
Cluster nodes	8	N/A

Datacenter Edition

Windows Server 2003, Datacenter Edition, is designed for mission-critical applications that require the highest levels of availability and scalability. It is available in 32-bit and 64-bit editions.

Unlike other versions of Windows Server 2003, Datacenter Edition cannot be bought as retail software. It can only be bought through qualified Microsoft partners. Most of the Microsoft partners are original equipment manufacturers (OEMs). Microsoft partners submit a server and drivers to Microsoft for testing. Only after Microsoft has approved the hardware and driver combination can it be sold to customers.

A team from Microsoft and the Microsoft partner provide support. Only this team is allowed to install and support Datacenter Edition. The customer can add users and make application adjustments, but cannot add, update, or remove drivers and hardware.

Some unique features of Datacenter Edition are listed here:

- Windows Server 2003 Datacenter Edition can be a member server, domain controller, or standalone server.
- Load balancing is supported.
- Clustering is supported.
- 64-bit processing is supported on Itanium processors.
- Hot add memory is supported.
- Non-Uniform Memory Access (NUMA) is supported.
- The Datacenter program is required.
- Internet Connection Firewall (ICF) is not supported.

The hardware requirements for Windows Server 2003, Datacenter Edition, are listed in Table 1-4.

Table 1-4 Hardware requirements for Windows Server 2003, Datacenter Edition

Hardware	Minimum System Requirements	Recommended System Requirements
CPU speed	400 MHz for 32-bit processors 733 MHz for Itanium	550 MHz for 32-bit processors 733 MHz for Itanium
RAM	512 MB	1 GB
Disk space for setup	1.5 GB for 32-bit processors 2.0 GB for Itanium	N/A
Maximum RAM	64 GB for 32-bit processors 512 GB for Itanium	N/A
Maximum processors	8 minimum 32 maximum for 32-bit processors 64 maximum for Itanium	N/A
Cluster nodes	8	N/A

How Client Operating Systems Use Windows Server 2003 Services

Windows Server 2003 provides a variety of different services. For instance, SMB signing and secure channel encryption and signing are used by newer Windows clients. In addition, the Active Directory client for Windows 9x and Windows NT adds the capability to access Active Directory features. Further details on these services are contained in the following subsections.

Performing SMB Signing

Server Message Block (SMB) is the protocol used by Windows Server to share files and printers. All Windows Server 2003 domain controllers use **SMB signing** as a mechanism to ensure that communication between clients and servers is legitimate. SMB signing places a digital signature on each packet. This prevents the modification of packets in transit.

Windows for Workgroups is not capable of performing SMB signing. The **Active Directory client** is software that can be installed on Windows 9x or Windows NT clients to allow them to use some Active Directory Services. Windows 95 can use SMB signing if the Active Directory client is installed. However, Microsoft recommends that Windows 95 be upgraded to a newer version of operating system. Windows NT supports SMB signing if Service Pack 3 is installed. Windows 2000/XP and Windows 98 fully support SMB signing.

It is possible to disable SMB signing for Windows Server 2003 domain controllers, but it is not recommended.

NOTE

Securing Channel Encryption and Signing

Secure channels are used for communication between Windows clients and servers that have a trust relationship. All Windows NT, Windows 2000, Windows XP, and Windows Server 2003 systems that are part of a domain use secure channels. Windows Server 2003 requires that secure channels be encrypted or signed to ensure that communication is legitimate.

Windows NT supports secure channel encryption and signing if Service Pack 4 is installed. Windows 2000/XP support secure channel encryption and signing by default. This is not relevant for Windows 9x and earlier Windows clients.

It is possible to disable secure channel encryption and signing, but it is not recommended.

NOTE

Accessing Active Directory Features

The Active Directory client is available for Windows 9x and Windows NT. It adds support for Active Directory features that Windows 9x and Windows NT does not natively understand.

Features of the Active Directory client:

- *Site Awareness*—Allows clients to log on to the closest domain controller.

- *Active Directory Service Interfaces (ADSI)*—Allows programmers to access Active Directory. **Active Directory Services Interfaces (ADSI)** can also be used by administrators to manage Active Directory via scripts.

- *Distributed File System (DFS)*—Allows clients to access shares through DFS.

- *NTLM version 2 Authentication*—Allows Windows 9x clients to use NTLMv2 for authentication. NTLMv2 is more secure than the original NTLM protocol. Windows NT does not require the Active Directory client to support NTLMv2. Service Pack 4 for Windows NT adds NTLMv2 support.

- *Active Directory Searching*—Adds the ability to search Active Directory to the Start menu.

Windows 2000 and Windows XP natively support these features. There is no Active Directory client for Windows 2000/XP.

ACTIVITY

Activity 1-6: Comparing Windows 2000 Server and Windows Server 2003

Time Required: 15 minutes

Objective: Explain the new features of Windows Server 2003.

Description: Arctic University is composed of several campus locations scattered through-out the far north. All faculties use basic file and print services. In addition, services such as DNS, DHCP, and WINS are used to facilitate basic network communication. Finally, some professors access network resources remotely via dial-up connections, and others take files home on laptops.

As the new administrator of network services for Arctic University, you will be educating faculty members about the benefits and features of Windows Server 2003. Because each faculty controls its own purchases, it is essential that you be able to convince the faculties of the benefits of moving to Windows Server 2003. The best place to start learning about new features is in the Help and Support utility.

1. If necessary, start your server and log on as **Administrator**.

2. Click **Start**, and then click **Help and Support**.

3. Type **new features** in the Search text box, and press **Enter**.

4. In the Search Results box, under the Help Topics heading, click the topic **Feature comparison: Windows NT, Windows 2000, and the Windows Server 2003 family: Getting Started**.

5. Click the **+** (plus symbol) beside the **Windows 2000 to the Windows Server 2003 family** option.

6. Browse through the features you are interested in and that you think may be relevant to Arctic University.

7. Close the Help and Support Center window.

Activity 1-7: Viewing the Current Edition of Windows Server 2003

Time Required: 5 minutes

Objective: Find the edition of Windows Server 2003 that is installed on a running server.

Description: You are getting settled in your new office. As you requested when you were hired, there are several servers in the office that you can use for testing software. One of them seems to have Windows Server 2003 installed, but you are not sure which edition it is. In this activity, you identify the edition of Windows Server 2003 that is running.

1. If necessary, start your server and log on as **Administrator**.

2. Click the **Start** button, and click **Manage Your Server**.

3. In the Tools and Updates box, click **Computer and Domain Name Information**.

4. Click the **General** tab.

5. Observe the version of Windows Server 2003 that is installed.

6. Close all windows.

Activity 1-8: Viewing the Features of Datacenter Edition

Time Required: 10 minutes

Objective: Identify the unique features of Windows Server 2003, Datacenter Edition.

Description: To evaluate whether Arctic University requires Windows Server 2003, Datacenter Edition, you decide to do some further research. In this activity, you use the Microsoft Web site to find more information.

1. If necessary, start your server and log on as **Administrator**.

2. Click the **Start** button, point to **All Programs**, and click **Internet Explorer**. If this is the first time Internet Explorer has been started, a warning window appears. In the warning window, click the **In the future, do not show this message** checkbox, and click **OK**.

3. Type **www.microsoft.com/windowsserver2003** in the Address bar, and press **Enter**. If this is the first Web site you are visiting, you will receive a warning about blocked content. In the warning window, click **Continue to prompt when Web site content is blocked** to deselect it, and click **Close**.

4. Click the **Product Information** link.

5. Click the **Product Overviews** link.

6. Click the **Windows Server 2003, Datacenter Edition Overview** link.

7. Review the information and close Internet Explorer when you are finished.

PLANNING A WINDOWS SERVER 2003 NETWORK INFRASTRUCTURE

The success of any information technology (IT) project is based on good planning. Although there are many methodologies for creating a good plan, all of them must consider the following:

- Choosing the members of the team
- Identifying the goals of the team
- Documenting the existing situation
- Defining objectives and tasks
- Testing the project
- Rolling out the project

The Team

The people planning a project are essential to its success. Contrary to the opinion of many technical professionals, technology is not the only or most important consideration in a project. A well-balanced team will find all of the important keys for success.

A project team should have representatives from all areas of the IT Department, affected business units, and at least one representative that can liaise with upper management. Each of these representatives can ensure that the interests of their own area are taken into account.

Many areas of IT are impacted by new projects. Network infrastructure support staff can judge the impact of the project on the overall network. Operating system support staff can determine if any operating system patches need to be applied or if there are licensing issues. Application support staff can determine if there are conflicts between new and existing applications. Training departments can help develop time frames for user training on new software.

It is important to remember that technology is used to support business goals. Representatives for business units are the most knowledgeable about business goals and can help ensure that they are met.

There needs to be a defined project manager. The **project manager** is responsible for ensuring that the resources to complete the project are available, and that the project is completed on time. In addition, a project manager needs to liaise with other areas of the company to ensure that this project is supported. This ensures that resources are available when required.

Goals

Any IT project should begin with a set of business goals. No technology should be implemented purely for the sake of the technology. There must be a measurable benefit or the project is simply a waste of money. Goals are used to define the project. One example of a goal may be "To upgrade the network infrastructure to support new cutting edge communication technology such as IP telephony and video conferencing."

Goals should be clearly defined and obtainable. A clearly defined goal is one that all team members can understand. If the team members cannot understand a goal, they are unlikely to achieve it. Goals must be attainable or there is no point attempting the project. It is doomed to fail before it even begins.

One of the keys when setting project goals is to avoid **scope creep**. The scope of a project is the range of issues that the project will address. Initially, this is usually a fairly small list. However, inevitably someone on the project team will begin a statement with "I wish" or "Wouldn't it be cool if...". These two phrases along with many variations are the beginning of scope creep, the process by which a small project becomes a big one, and a big project becomes enormous.

The problem with scope creep is that projects can become unmanageable when they are too large and the resources may not be there to complete them. In the worst situations, some of the original project goals may be compromised by the newer and sometimes frivolous goals. One effective method to prevent scope creep is to implement projects in phases. Then, new goals can be added to later phases and will not affect the project immediately at hand.

Having the proper project team goes a long way toward defining a useful goal because wide representation among business units results in all points of view being considered. However, interviews with an even wider range of staff in the company can help raise issues that may be missed by the individual representatives on the project team. If you choose to conduct interviews as part of the goal definition process, be sure to have a defined range of issues with which you are willing to work. Nothing can sabotage a project faster than raising the expectations of users only to disappoint them.

Documentation

The overall purpose of a network project is to take the network from its existing state and improve it in a specific way defined by the goal. It is impossible to reach a goal without understanding the existing situation. For example, how can you understand how to increase network speed if you do not know the type of traffic that is on the network, or even the type of cabling that is being used?

When new network projects are implemented, a set of documentation is usually created as well. This gives you the state of the network at the point it was implemented. Everyone in the computer industry knows that proper documentation is something that should be done whenever changes are made to the network. Unfortunately, many times another crisis comes along and the documentation is never upgraded. Because it is easy to not complete, you should take great care to ensure that existing documentation is up-to-date. To ensure that existing documentation is up-to-date, you can employ a number of strategies, including site surveys, interviews, and research.

Site Surveys

A site survey is visiting a site to either create new documentation or confirm existing documentation. Performing a site survey is an essential part of any network project that includes new cabling, routers, switches, or any other physical component. Many projects have been significantly impacted by problems that would have been foreseen with a simple site survey. For example, a project plan may call for the installation of several new servers at a location, but the location may not have the physical space to hold the new servers, or there may be no switch ports available into which to plug the servers. In the case of lacking physical space, there may be weeks of delay expanding or building a server room. However, the lack of switch ports may be fixed in a few days by ordering an additional switch.

Interviews

Interviews are useful to confirm the validity of existing documentation. Often, interviews are done as part of a site survey. Many relevant pieces of information may be revealed as a local network technician takes you on a site tour.

Research

Even if documentation of an existing network is accurate, you may need to do significant research to understand the capabilities of some network components. For example, the documentation may indicate that a particular brand of remote access server is being used. If so, you need to understand how that component will, or will not, fit into any potential network changes. Research will aid this understanding.

The easiest place to start researching components is by reading the manuals that came with them. Most vendors offer documentation on their Web sites, as well as additional support information. Finally, Web-based discussion groups on the Internet can be useful. However, be cautious when using information from support forums because information can occasionally be unreliable.

Objectives and Tasks

The objectives of a project are how the goals will be accomplished. The defining characteristic of an objective is that it is measurable so that you can tell when it has been achieved. Based on the goal "To upgrade the network infrastructure to support new cutting edge communication technology such as IP telephony and video conferencing," one objective might be to raise network backbone capacity to 1 Gbps.

NOTE   Objectives are often based on requirements for security and data capacity.

Tasks are how the objectives will be implemented. Often, there are many different ways to attain an objective. The project team must decide how the objective will be attained based on issues such as risks, cost, and time to implement. Tasks required to raise backbone capacity to 1 Gbps may include installing fiber optic cabling, buying new routers and switches, and buying new gigabit network cards for servers.

Testing

IT projects need to be properly tested in a lab environment before they are rolled out to users. Testing in an isolated environment ensures that, in the early stages of implementation, the project will not adversely affect the network. During the testing process, you may find that your original solution is unworkable. If this is the case, it can be redesigned and retested.

The test lab should be used to simulate all conceivable situations and factors that may affect the project. In addition, average users should be involved in the testing process. Average users use new software in ways that an experienced IT person would never dream of. These are the potential problems you want to avoid during the roll out.

Roll Out

The roll out of an IT project is the actual implementation of new software and services. Proper preparation for the roll out is essential to the success of the project.

Proper preparation for a roll out includes training for users and the help desk. Users need to be trained on how to use new software before they are required to use it. In addition, help desk staff need to be trained on new software before they can support it. Administrators need to be trained before they can implement new technology. Ideally, training is timed just before the roll out so that the news skills can be used before they are forgotten.

Everyone affected by the roll out, or potentially affected by the roll out, should be informed it is happening. The help desk needs to know what is happening so that they can understand what may be happening if user problems begin to occur. Users are much more tolerant of network problems if they understand ahead of time that a project is being implemented.

Most successful projects are phased in rather than being completed in one step. Implementation phases may be completing one floor or building at a time. Rolling out a project this way limits the number of users affected by unforeseen difficulties at any given time, and makes it easier to perform appropriate training.

Activity 1-9: Researching Project Planning

Time Required: 15 minutes

Objective: Become familiar with the premiere organization in the project planning industry.

Description: To ensure the success of your projects, you perform further research into best practices for project planning.

1. If necessary, start your server, and log on as **Administrator**.

2. Click the **Start** button, point to **All Programs**, and click **Internet Explorer**. If this is the first time Internet Explorer has been started, a warning window appears.

3. Type **www.pmi.org** in the Address Bar, and press **Enter**. This is the Web site for the Project Management Institute. They have developed a project management body of knowledge that is a guide to best practices for project management and offer certification as a project manager. Read any information you are interested in.

4. Type **http://consultingacademy.com/a07.shtm** in the Address Bar, and press **Enter**. Read the story about the painter. Do you see how this could be relevant to you?

5. Type **http://www.microsoft.com/windowsserver2003/techinfo/ reskit/deploykit.mspx** in the Address Bar, and press **Enter**. Microsoft has a wide variety of project planning documents here. Review some of the information.

6. Close Internet Explorer.

CHAPTER SUMMARY

- The network architecture of Windows Server 2003 is composed of four main networking components: clients, services, protocols, and network adapters.

- The TDI layer resides between clients and protocols or between services and protocols. It emulates NetBIOS and WinSock.

- NDIS is responsible for binding protocols to network adapters. It also makes the development of protocols and network drivers easier by providing a consistent interface.

- Four protocols are supported by Windows Server 2003: IPv4, IPv6, IPX/SPX, and AppleTalk.

❑ Windows Server 2003 installs a limited number of services by default. When a server is promoted to be a domain controller, several network services are added, including File Replication Service, Intersite Messaging, Kerberos Key Distribution Center, and Net Logon.

❑ Many network services are available in Windows Server 2003, including DHCP, DNS, WINS, RRAS, IAS, NAT, ICS, ICF, IPSec, and PKI.

❑ The Web Edition of Windows Server 2003 is designed to be a Web server only and cannot be a domain controller. Up to two processors and 2 GB of RAM are supported.

❑ The Standard Edition of Windows Server 2003 is designed to be a departmental server that provides file, print, and other services. Standard Edition can be configured as a domain controller, but does not support clustering and is not available in a 64-bit version. Up to four processors and 4 GB of RAM are supported.

❑ The Enterprise Edition of Windows Server 2003 is designed to be a highly available enterprise application server supporting up to eight node clusters. Up to eight processors are supported with 32 GB of RAM for 32-bit versions and 64 GB of RAM for 64-bit versions.

❑ The Datacenter Edition of Windows Server 2003 is designed for mission-critical applications supporting up to eight node clusters. A minimum of eight processors is required, up to 32 processors are supported in the 32-bit version, and 64 processors are supported in the 64-bit version. In the 32-bit version, a maximum of 64 GB of RAM is supported and 128 GB of RAM are supported in the 64-bit version.

❑ A successful Windows Server 2003 network infrastructure plan always takes into account the team, goals, testing, and roll out. The team should contain representatives from all affected departments. Goals should define what is done in the project. Testing should be isolated from the production network. The roll out should minimize impact on the existing network.

KEY TERMS

802.11 — A standard for wireless communication created by the Institute of Electrical and Electronics Engineers (IEEE). The most common variant of wireless LAN is 802.11b.

Active Directory — A directory service for Windows 2000 Server and Windows Server 2003 that stores information about network resources.

Active Directory client — The software for Windows 9x and Windows NT clients to let them use some Active Directory services such as sites.

Active Directory Service Interfaces (ADSI) — The interfaces used by programmers to access Active Directory. ADSI can also be used by administrators to manage Active Directory via scripts.

adapter — The networking component that represents the network interface card and driver.

AppleTalk — A protocol that is used when communicating with Apple Macintosh computers.

binding — The process of configuring a network protocol to use a network adapter.

bridge — A network component that controls the movement of packets between network segments based on MAC addresses.

certificate services — A service that allows Windows Server 2003 to create and manage certificates used in PKI.

certificates — A certificate for PKI that is a combination of public and private keys that can be used to encrypt or digitally sign information.

client — A networking component that is installed on computers requesting network services. Client software communicates with a corresponding service.

clustering — The process of combining a group of computers to coordinate the provision of services. When one computer in a cluster fails, others take over its services.

Common Language Runtime (CLR) — A common component that runs code developed for the .NET Framework regardless of the language in which it is written.

Distributed File System (DFS) — A service that makes file shares stored on multiple servers appear as a single logical structure for users. It can also replicate content between servers for fault tolerance.

domain controller — A server running Windows 2000 Server or Windows Server 2003 that holds a copy of the Active Directory information for a domain.

Domain Name System (DNS) — A service used by clients running TCP/IP to resolve host names to IP addresses. Active Directory uses DNS to store service location information.

Dynamic Host Configuration Protocol (DHCP) — A service used by the Windows operating system to automatically assign IP addressing information to clients.

Extensible Markup Language (XML) — A simple text-based mechanism to define content. It uses tags similar to HTML, but unlike HTML, developers can define their own tags.

File Transfer Protocol (FTP) — A protocol that is used on the Internet to transfer files. By default, it uses TCP ports 20 and 21.

Group Policy — An Active Directory-based mechanism to apply centrally defined configuration information out to client computers.

Hypertext Transfer Protocol (HTTP) — The protocol used by Web browsers and Web servers. By default, it uses TCP port 80.

Internet Authentication Service (IAS) — The Microsoft implementation of a RADIUS server. It allows distributed authentication for remote access clients.

Internet Connection Firewall (ICF) — A simple firewall suitable for home use or small offices when connecting to the Internet.

Internet Connection Sharing (ICS) — An automated way to configure DHCP, NAT, and DNS proxy to share a single IP address and configuration information from an ISP.

Internet Information Services (IIS) — A popular suite of Internet services that includes a Web server and FTP server.

Internet Protocol version 4 (IPv4) — The version of the Internet Protocol (IP) that is used on the Internet. It is the IP part of TCP/IP.

Internet Protocol version 6 (IPv6) — An updated version of Internet Protocol that uses 128-bit addresses and provides many new features.

Internet service providers (ISPs) — A company that sells Internet access.

Internetwork Packet eXchange/Sequenced Packet eXchange (IPX/SPX) — The protocol required to communicate with servers running Novell NetWare 4 and earlier.

IP Security (IPSec) — A service used with IPv4 to prevent eavesdropping on communication and to prevent data from being modified in transit.

Itanium — A 64-bit processor family manufactured by Intel.

Kerberos — An authentication mechanism used to verify the validity of user information when Windows 2000 and newer clients log on to Active Directory.

Layer Two Tunneling Protocol (L2TP) — A protocol that places packets inside an L2TP packet to move them across an IP-based network. This can be used to move IPX or AppleTalk packets through a network that is not configured to support them.

Linux — An open source operating system that is very similar to UNIX.

load balancing — The act of two or more computers sharing a single IP address to provide a service to clients. The load balanced computers share the responsibility of providing the service.

local area network (LAN) — A computer network that is contained within a single building. A LAN usually has a minimum speed of 10 Mbps.

member server — A Windows server that is part of a domain but is not a domain controller.

Metadirectory Services — A service in Windows that synchronizes Active Directory content with other directories and databases.

Network Address Translation (NAT) — A service that allows multiple computers to access the Internet by sharing a single public IP address.

Network Basic Input/Output System (NetBIOS) — An older interface used by programmers to access network resources.

Network Driver Interface Specification (NDIS) — An interface for developers that resides between protocols and adapters. It controls the bindings between protocols and adapters.

network operating system (NOS) — An operating system that is optimized to act as a server rather than a client.

Non-Uniform Memory Access (NUMA) — A memory architecture for servers with multiple processors. It adds a third level of cache memory on motherboards.

Point-to-Point Protocol over Ethernet (PPPoE) — A protocol used by some high-speed ISPs to authenticate and control IP traffic on their network.

Point-to-Point Tunneling Protocol (PPTP) — A protocol that can be used to provide VPN connectivity between a Windows client and VPN server. PPTP is supported by Windows 95 and later.

project manager — The leader of a project team who ensures a project is completed on time and on budget.

protocol — The language that two computers use to communicate on a network. Two computers must use the same protocol to communicate.

Public Key Infrastructure (PKI) — A system to create and manage public keys, private keys, and certificates.

Remote Assistance — A system that allows users to request that a support person take remote control of their computer. This allows support personnel to demonstrate tasks to users or fix errors.

Remote Desktop — A method to remote manage Windows Server 2003. When Remote Desktop is used, an administrator or other authorized user can view the server desktop from a workstation and run applications.

Remote Installation Services — A service in Windows that automates the installation of Windows 2000 Professional or Windows XP Professional on client workstations.

Routing and Remote Access Service (RRAS) — A service in Windows that controls routing, dial-in access, and VPN access on a Windows Server 2003 machine.

scope creep — A term that refers to the expansion of a project beyond its original goals.

secure channels — The communication channels used by Windows NT/2000/XP/2003 computers that are members of a domain.

Server Message Block (SMB) — The protocol used by Windows servers for file and printer sharing.

service — A networking component that provides information to network clients. Each service communicates with corresponding client software.

Services for Macintosh — A service that allows Macintosh clients to access file and print services on Windows servers.

Simple Object Access Protocol (SOAP) — A standardized XML-based mechanism to access Web services using HTTP, SMTP, and MIME.

SMB signing — A mechanism to ensure that SMB packets are not tampered with while in transit on the network.

stand-alone server — A Windows server that is not a member of a domain.

terminal server — A system that allows many users to view a remote desktop on a server. This is normally used to provide access to a line of business applications. Each user gets their own version of the desktop.

Transport Driver Interface (TDI) — A software layer that exists between client or service software and protocols. Clients and services use this layer to access network resources.

Universal Description, Discovery and Integration (UDDI) — A worldwide database of businesses and the Web services that they offer.

virtual private network (VPN) — The encrypted communications across a public network.

Web services — The platform-independent services that are available across the Internet or an IP network.

Web Services Description Language (WSDL) — A standardized, XML-formatted mechanism to describe Web services. WSDL is used by UDDI to describe available services.

1

Web Distributed Authoring and Versioning (WebDAV) — A protocol that allows documents to be shared using HTTP.

wide area network (WAN) — A network consisting of more than one physical location. Connectivity between physical locations is usually slower than 10 Mbps.

Windows Internet Naming Service (WINS) — A service used to resolve NetBIOS names to IP addresses as well as to store NetBIOS service information.

Windows Media Services — A service that provides streaming audio and video to clients.

Windows Sockets (WinSock) — A programming interface used by developers to access TCP/IP-based services.

Windows Sockets Direct (WinSock Direct) — An extension of the WinSock programming interface that allows developers to access resources on a system area network.

REVIEW QUESTIONS

1. Which of the following editions of Windows Server 2003 cannot be bought as retail software?

   a. Web Edition

   b. Standard Edition

   c. Enterprise Edition

   d. Datacenter Edition

2. Which of the following editions of Windows Server 2003 support clustering? (Choose all that apply.)

   a. Web Edition

   b. Standard Edition

   c. Enterprise Edition

   d. Datacenter Edition

3. Which of the following features are available in Windows Server 2003, Standard Edition? (Choose all that apply.)

   a. IIS 6.0

   b. ICS

   c. load balancing

   d. 64-bit processing

4. Which of the following new features of Windows Server 2003 allows servers to connect to high-speed Internet service providers without adding third-party software?

   a. wireless support

   b. PPPoE

   c. Internet Connection Firewall (ICF)

   d. Windows Media Services

5. The TDI layer allows multiple protocols to be bound to a network adapter. True or False?

6. Which of the following versions of Windows Server 2003 cannot be a domain controller?

   a. Web Edition

   b. Standard Edition

   c. Enterprise Edition

   d. Datacenter Edition

7. What is the maximum number of processors supported by Windows Server 2003, Enterprise Edition?

   a. 2

   b. 4

   c. 8

   d. 16

   e. 32

8. What is the maximum amount of RAM that can be used in Windows Server 2003, Standard Edition?

   a. 2 GB

   b. 4 GB

   c. 32 GB

   d. 128 GB

9. What is the maximum number of cluster nodes supported by Windows Server 2003, Web Edition?

   a. 0

   b. 2

   c. 4

   d. 8

10. Which of the following network components requests services across the network?

    a. client

    b. service

    c. protocol

    d. NDIS

    e. TDI

11. Which of the following network components emulates NetBIOS?

    a. client

    b. service

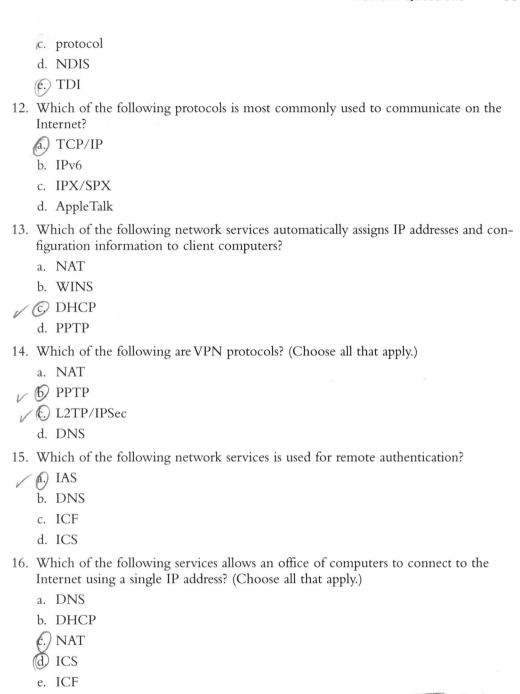

c. protocol

d. NDIS

e. TDI

12. Which of the following protocols is most commonly used to communicate on the Internet?

   a. TCP/IP

   b. IPv6

   c. IPX/SPX

   d. AppleTalk

13. Which of the following network services automatically assigns IP addresses and configuration information to client computers?

   a. NAT

   b. WINS

   c. DHCP

   d. PPTP

14. Which of the following are VPN protocols? (Choose all that apply.)

   a. NAT

   b. PPTP

   c. L2TP/IPSec

   d. DNS

15. Which of the following network services is used for remote authentication?

   a. IAS

   b. DNS

   c. ICF

   d. ICS

16. Which of the following services allows an office of computers to connect to the Internet using a single IP address? (Choose all that apply.)

   a. DNS

   b. DHCP

   c. NAT

   d. ICS

   e. ICF

17. Routing and Remote Access Service controls VPN connections. True or False?

18. WINS is used by a client to convert host names to IP addresses. True or False?

19. Which of the following is a feature of NDIS? (Choose all that apply.)

    a. acts as an intermediary for communications between protocols and network card drivers

    b. allows multiple protocols to be bound to a single adapter

    c. provides clients and services with access to network resources

    d. is the language clients and services use to communicate

20. When should training for users be done during a project implementation?

    a. well before the roll out

    b. just before the roll out

    c. at the same time as the roll out

    d. after the roll out

21. Which of the following are associated with scope creep? (Choose all that apply.)

    a. The project never completes because the goals keep expanding.

    b. The project is completed on time and under budget.

    c. The original goals may not be completed properly because scarce resources are allocated to meeting new goals.

    d. You get a promotion.

22. Which of the following services are added when a server is promoted to a domain controller? (Choose all that apply.)

    a. Terminal Services

    b. File Replication Service

    c. Distributed File System

    d. Net Logon

    e. Kerberos Key Distribution Center

    f. Windows Time

23. Which of the following client operating systems can log on to Windows Server 2003 without applying any patches or installing the Active Directory client? (Choose all that apply.)

    a. Windows 95

    b. Windows 98

    c. Windows NT

    d. Windows 2000

    e. Windows XP

24. Which of the following operating systems can be upgraded to Windows Server 2003?

a. Windows 98

b. Windows Me

c. Windows NT Server 3.51

d. Windows NT Server 4.0 with Service Pack 6

e. Windows 2000 Professional

25. The operating system should reside on a separate partition from applications and data. True or False?

CASE PROJECTS

Case Project 1-1: Choosing a Network Operating System

As the person in charge of implementing network services for Arctic University, you are responsible for ordering Windows Server 2003 for the faculties. To decide which software needs to be ordered, you are meeting with the head of each faculty. Create a document describing the benefits and drawbacks to each edition of Windows Server 2003 and when each is appropriate. You can distribute this document to each faculty head before the meetings.

Case Project 1-2: Choosing Network Services

As part of the planning process, you are meeting with the rest of the IT Department to brainstorm on which services may be required on the network. Make a list of the network services that you think may be required and describe why.

Case Project 1-3: Choosing Network Drivers

A colleague is concerned that some network card drivers will not function after the existing Windows NT and Windows 2000 servers are upgraded to Windows Server 2003. What can you tell your colleague about network driver compatibility with previous versions of Windows and the role that NDIS plays in this?

Case Project 1-4: Creating a Project Plan

The Accounting Department has been complaining for some time that the current account-ing system does not meet their needs. Your supervisor has asked you to look into the problem. He thinks that funding may soon be available to implement a new accounting system, but he needs to make the case to the university governors.

Make a project plan to help your supervisor make his case to the university governors. Be sure to include who would be a member of your project team and why, a list of likely goals for the project, how the project would be tested, and how the project would be rolled out.

2

TCP/IP ARCHITECTURE

After reading this chapter, you will be able to:

♦ Understand TCP/IP addressing

♦ Describe the overall architecture of TCP/IP

♦ Describe Application layer protocols

♦ Discuss Transport layer protocols

♦ Understand the role of various Internet layer protocols, including IP, ICMP, and ARP

♦ Understand Network Interface layer protocols

The most popular protocol in use on LANs and WANs is TCP/IP. It is widely supported and provides access to the Internet. Understanding the fundamentals of TCP/IP is essential to planning, managing, and troubleshooting a Windows Server 2003 network.

Windows Server 2003 requires the TCP/IP protocol. It is automatically installed and cannot be removed.

This chapter covers the entire TCP/IP protocol suite, including TCP, UDP, IP, ICMP, HTTP, FTP, and SMTP.

Introduction to **TCP/IP**

Transmission Control Protocol/Internet Protocol (TCP/IP) is the most commonly used network protocol suite in use today. There are several reasons why TCP/IP is so prevalent:

- *It has wide vendor support*—Vendors understand that their products will be more popular if their products can integrate with products from other vendors. Most vendors support TCP/IP, and, therefore, all new products are developed with TCP/IP support to make them interoperable.

- *It is an open protocol*—An open protocol is not controlled by any single company or individual; it is controlled by a standards process. This means that companies choosing to use TCP/IP do not need to be concerned that the owner of the protocol will charge expensive royalties or make changes that will affect their products.

- *It provides access to Internet services*—Access to Internet services is required in business today and TCP/IP is the protocol that is used on the Internet. Common Internet service protocols such as Hypertext Transfer Protocol (HTTP), File Transfer Protocol (FTP), and Simple Mail Transfer Protocol (SMTP) are part of the TCP/IP protocol suite, and the Domain Name System (DNS), which you learn about later in this chapter, functions only with TCP/IP.

NOTE

The protocol TCP/IP is actually a combination of several protocols that are always installed together.

TIP

The term TCP/IP is used to refer specifically to protocols that perform Network layer and Transport layer functionality. The term TCP/IP protocol suite refers to a wide range of protocols related to TCP/IP that perform tasks from the Network layer to the Application layer.

Although Windows Server 2003 has the ability to use several protocols, it has been designed so that many of its main features require the use of TCP/IP. For example, only TCP/IP can enable **Active Directory** to integrate with DNS for service location. Active Directory is the central database of resource information for a domain. In addition, only TCP/IP can enable Windows XP Professional computers to use DNS to locate domain controllers for logging onto the network.

Occasionally, when the TCP/IP protocol was installed on older versions of Windows, it would become corrupt in some way. The solution to this problem was to uninstall TCP/IP and reinstall it. This is no longer possible in Windows Server 2003 because TCP/IP is automatically installed and cannot be removed. If the configuration of TCP/IP becomes corrupt, you must repair the network connection, which is found in Network Connections in Control Panel.

Activity 2-1: Repairing a Network Connection

Time Required: 5 minutes

Objective: Repair a connection that has a corrupt TCP/IP configuration.

Description: One of the servers you have installed in your test lab has mysteriously stopped communicating with the other servers at irregular intervals. You have recently been installing and removing a number of services and you suspect that, as part of the process, the TCP/IP protocol may be corrupt. Even though your server is functional right now, to rule out the possibility of a corrupt TCP/IP protocol you, repair the network connection.

1. If necessary, start your server and log on as **Administrator**.

2. Click **Start**, point to **Control Panel**, point to **Network Connections**, right-click **Classroom**, and click **Repair**.

3. Click **OK** to close the Repair Connection dialog box.

IP Addresses

An IP address is just like the mailing address for a house, in that it must be unique. If any two computers have the same IP address, it is impossible for information to be correctly delivered to them.

The most common format for IP addresses is four numbers, each called an **octet**, that are separated by periods. An example of an IP address is 192.168.5.66. Each octet can range in value between 0 and 255. These numbers are normally displayed in dotted decimal notation because that is what most people are used to and find the easiest to use. However, you occasionally find some applications that allow the octets to be entered as hexadecimal numbers ranging between 0 and FF.

Each **octet** in an IP address represents eight bits of information. The prefix "oct" in "octet" means eight. If each octet is eight bits, then a full IP address of four octets is 32 bits long. When a computer works with an IP address, it is treated as a lump of 32 bits rather than four octets. The division into octets just makes it easier for people to use the addresses.

When the computer looks at an IP address, the numbers are converted to binary. It is only in binary that some of the more complex features of TCP/IP, such as subnetting and supernetting, are fully understandable.

An IP address is composed of two parts: the network ID and the host ID. The **network ID** represents the network on which the computer is located. All movement of packets between **routers** is based on networks, and, therefore, movement of packets on the Internet is also based on networks. No two networks can have the same network ID or else routers cannot determine where to deliver packets that are addressed to that network ID. The **host ID** represents the individual computer on a network. No two computers on the same network can have the same host ID; however, two computers on different networks can have the same host ID.

NOTE You can compare the network ID and the host ID to a postal mailing address within a city. A postal mailing address is composed of two portions: the street name and the house number. The street name is similar to a network ID. No two streets can have the same name, just as no two networks can have the same network ID. The host ID is like the house number. Two houses can have the same house number as long as they are on different streets, just as two computers can have the same host ID as long as they are on different networks.

The IP addresses that can be used on the Internet are assigned by an **Internet service provider (ISP)**. An ISP sells access to the Internet. When an organization signs up with an ISP, it is given at least one IP address. Generally, if the organization wants more than one or two IP addresses, it has to pay a monthly fee for them. Normally, each computer that is accessing the Internet requires its own IP address from the ISP. However, if **Network Address Translation (NAT)** or a **proxy server** is used, then a single IP address can be shared by multiple computers. These two topics are explored in Chapter 4.

The organization with overall authority for IP address assignments on the Internet is the Internet Corporation for Assigned Names and Numbers (ICANN). ICANN then works with regional authorities to manage addresses within a given region. Your ISP obtains IP addresses from these organizations. There are three regional authorities:

- American Registry for Internet Numbers (ARIN) is responsible for North America, Central America, South America, and sub-Saharan Africa.

- Asia Pacific Network Information Center (APNIC) is responsible for the Asia and Pacific region.

- Réseaux IP Européens (RIPE) is responsible for Europe and surrounding regions.

Subnet Masks

Each computer is configured with a **subnet mask** that defines which part of its IP address is the network ID and which part is the host ID. Subnet masks are composed of four octets just like an IP address. The simplest subnet masks use only the two values of 0 and 255. Wherever there is a 255 in the subnet mask, that octet is part of the network ID. Wherever there is a 0 in the subnet mask, that octet is part of the host ID.

Table 2-1 shows two examples of how the network ID and host ID of an IP address can be calculated using the subnet mask. In the first example, the IP address 192.168.100.33 and subnet mask of 255.255.255.0 are paired. Each octet in the subnet mask that has a value of 255 signifies that the corresponding octet in the IP address is the network ID. In this instance, the value of the first, second, and third octets are 255. Therefore, the first, second, and third octets of the IP address represent the network ID. When writing the network ID, the final octet is 0 to fill in the remaining octet. Each octet in the subnet mask that has a value of 0 signifies that the corresponding octet in the IP address is the host ID. The fourth octet in the subnet mask is 0. Therefore, the fourth octet in the IP address is the host ID. When writing the host ID, the first, second, and third octets are given a value of 0 to fill in the remaining octets. The second example follows this same pattern.

NOTE If you add the octets from the network address to the octets from the host address, the total will be the IP address. This is true even for more complex examples that you will see in Chapter 3.

Table 2-1   Examples of using a subnet mask to calculate network and host IDs

Description	Address Information
IP address	192.168.100.33
Subnet mask	255.255.255.0
Network ID	192.168.100.0
Host ID	0.0.0.33
IP address	172.16.43.207
Subnet mask	255.255.0.0
Network ID	172.16.0.0
Host ID	0.0.43.207

No matter how many octets are included in the network ID, they are always contiguous and start on the left. If the first and third octets are part of the network ID, then the second must be as well.

Table 2-2 shows examples of valid and invalid subnet masks. The first invalid subnet mask is invalid because the leftmost octet is 0, and the 255s must begin with the leftmost octet. The second and third invalid subnet masks are invalid because the 255s are not contiguous.

Table 2-2   Examples of valid and invalid subnet masks

Valid Subnet Masks	Invalid Subnet Masks
255.0.0.0	0.255.255.255
255.255.0.0	255.0.255.0
255.255.255.0	255.255.0.255

A computer uses its subnet mask to determine which network it is on and whether other computers with which it is communicating are on the same network or a different network. If two computers on the same network are communicating, then they can deliver packets directly to each other. If two computers are on different networks, they must use a router to communicate. An example of two computers that are on the same network is shown in Figure 2-1.

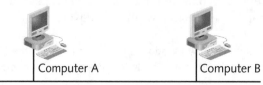

IP Address: 192.168.23.77   IP Address: 192.168.23.228
Subnet Mask: 255.255.255.0   Subnet Mask: 255.255.255.0

Computer A   Computer B

Network ID: 192.168.23.0

Figure 2-1   Two computers communicating on the same network

In Figure 2-1, there are two computers. Computer A has an IP address of 192.168.23.77 and a subnet mask of 255.255.255.0. Computer B has an IP address of 192.168.23.228.

Whereas you can look at the IP addresses of Computer A and Computer B and guess (by looking at the similarity of the IP addresses) that they are on the same network, a computer cannot. Computers follow rules, and if Computer A is sending a message to Computer B, then Computer A must use its subnet mask to find out whether the two computers are on the same network or a different network.

Following are the steps that Computer A must follow to send a message to Computer B:

1. Computer A compares its subnet mask and IP address to find its own network ID. Table 2-3 shows the IP address, subnet mask, and network ID for Computer A.

Table 2-3   Network ID calculation for Computer A

Description	Address Information
IP address of Computer A	192.168.23.77
Subnet mask of Computer A	255.255.255.0
Network ID of Computer A	192.168.23.0

2. Computer A compares its subnet mask and the IP address of Computer B to find out whether they are on the same network. Table 2-4 shows the network ID for the IP address of Computer B calculated by using the subnet mask of Computer A.

Table 2-4   Network ID calculation for Computer B

Description	Address Information
IP address of Computer B	192.168.23.228
Subnet mask of Computer A	255.255.255.0
Network ID of Computer B	192.168.23.0

3. Both network IDs are the same, so Computer A delivers the packet directly to Computer B.

Default Gateway

In TCP/IP parlance, **default gateway** is another term for router. If a computer does not know how to deliver a packet, it gives the packet to the default gateway to deliver. This happens every time a computer needs to deliver a packet to a computer on a network other than its own.

A **router** is often a dedicated hardware device from a vendor such as Cisco, D-link, or Linksys. Other times, a router is actually a computer with multiple network cards. Operating systems such as Windows Server 2003, **Linux**, and **NetWare** have the ability to perform as routers.

The one consistent feature of routers, regardless of the manufacturer, is that they can distinguish multiple networks and how to move packets between them. Routers can also figure out the best path to use to move a packet between different networks.

It is important to note that routers keep track of networks, not computers.

NOTE

A router has an IP address on every network to which it is attached. When a computer sends a packet to the router (default gateway) for further delivery, the address of the router must be on the same network as the computer, because computers can talk directly only to devices on their own network. An example of a computer using a default gateway to communicate with another computer on a different network is shown in Figure 2-2.

In Figure 2-2, Computer A is sending a packet to Computer C. Computer A uses its subnet mask to determine whether the default gateway is required. The steps in the process are as follows:

1. Computer A compares its subnet mask and IP address to find its own network ID. Table 2-5 shows the network ID for Computer A based on its IP address and subnet mask.

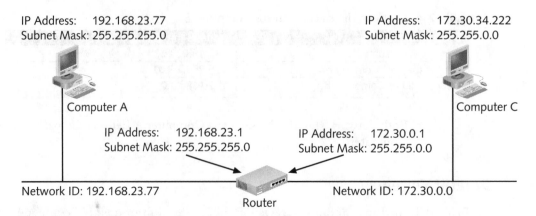

Figure 2-2   Two computers on different networks communicating

Table 2-5   Network ID calculation for Computer A

Description	Address Information
IP address of Computer A	192.168.23.77
Subnet mask of Computer A	255.255.255.0
Network ID of Computer A	192.168.23.0

2. Computer A compares its subnet mask and the IP address of Computer C to see if it is on the same network. This step does not calculate the network ID for Computer C. It only tests whether it is the same as Computer A. Computer A is not configured with the subnet mask of Computer C. So, it is impossible for Computer A *to find* the network ID for Computer C. It can only *make a comparison* of available information. Table 2-6 shows testing the network ID for the IP address of Computer C using the subnet mask of Computer A.

Table 2-6   Network ID calculation for Computer C

Description	Address Information
IP address of Computer C	172.30.34.222
Subnet mask of Computer A	255.255.255.0
Network ID of Computer C	172.30.34.0

3. The two network IDs are different, so Computer A sends the packet to the router for delivery.

4. The router looks in its routing table to see if it knows where the network 172.30.0.0 is located.

5. Because the router is attached to network 172.30.0.0, it delivers the packet to Computer C. If the router were not attached to network 172.30.0.0, then it would forward it to another router.

Activity 2-2: Viewing IP Address Configuration

Time Required: 10 minutes

Objective: View the current IP address settings on a server.

Description: The test lab in your office is also being used by other technical staff at Arctic University. You allow them access because you feel it is important for all staff to be familiar with Windows Server 2003 before you roll it out to the various faculties. To ensure that the test server is properly configured later, you are documenting its IP address configuration now. This makes it easy to reset when any given test is complete.

1. If necessary, start your server and log on as Administrator.
2. Click **Start**, point to **Control Panel**, point to **Network Connections**, right-click **Classroom**, and click **Properties**.
3. Click the **Internet Protocol (TCP/IP)** option, and click the **Properties** button.
4. Click the **Advanced** button.
5. Document the IP address, subnet mask, and default gateway on a sheet of paper.
6. Click the **DNS** tab.
7. Document the DNS servers and any additional DNS suffixes on a sheet of paper.
8. Click the **WINS** tab.
9. Document the WINS addresses and NetBIOS setting on your sheet of paper. There will most likely not be any listed.
10. Click the **Options** tab, and then click the **Properties** button.
11. Document the TCP/IP filtering settings on your sheet of paper.
12. Click the **Cancel** button in all windows to exit without saving any changes.

IP Address Classes

IP addresses are divided into classes. The class of an IP address defines the default subnet mask of the device using that address.

All of the IP address classes can be identified by the first octet of the address, as shown in Table 2-7. The value listed for the first octet is a range of valid values. For example, the first octet of a Class A address can have a value from 1 to 127.

Table 2-7   IP address classes

Class	Address Range	Subnet Mask
A	1-127.x.x.x	255.0.0.0
B	128-191.x.x.x	255.255.0.0
C	192-223.x.x.x	255.255.255.0
D	224-239.x.x.x	n/a

Table 2-7 IP address classes (continued)

Class	Address Range	Subnet Mask
E	240-255.x.x.x	n/a

Class A addresses use eight bits for the network ID and 24 bits for the host ID. You can identify this from the subnet mask of 255.0.0.0. The value of the first octet is always in a range from 1 to 127. This means there are only 127 potential Class A networks available for the entire Internet, and even this small number of Class A networks is reduced by reserved address ranges. Class A networks are only assigned to very large companies and Internet providers.

The number of hosts available on a Class A network is 16,777,214, as shown in Table 2-8; however, it is not reasonable to have this many hosts on a single unmanaged network. In the rare cases in which a Class A network is in use, it is subnetted. **Subnetting** is the process in which a single large network is subdivided into smaller networks to control traffic flow. Chapter 4 covers subnetting, as well as the process of finding the number of available host IDs on a given network.

Table 2-8 Hosts and networks for IP address classes

Class	Subnet Mask	Number of Networks	Number of Hosts
A	255.0.0.0	127	16,777,214
B	255.255.0.0	16,384	65,534
C	255.255.255.0	2,097,152	254

Class B addresses use 16 bits for the network ID and 16 bits for the host ID. The number of bits in the network ID and host ID are defined by the subnet mask of 255.255.0.0. The value of the first octet ranges from 128 to 191. There are 16,384 Class B networks with 65,534 hosts on each network.

The number of Class B networks is reduced slightly by reserved address ranges, but there are many more Class B networks than Class A networks. Class B networks are assigned to many larger organizations, such as governments, universities, and companies with several thousand users.

Class C addresses use 24 bits for the network ID and eight bits for the host ID. The number of bits in the network ID and host ID are defined by the subnet mask 255.255.255.0. The value of the first octet ranges from 192 to 223. There are 2,097,152 Class C networks with 254 hosts on each network. Although there are very many Class C networks, they have a relatively small number of hosts, and, thus, are suited only to smaller organizations.

Class D addresses are not divided into networks and they cannot be assigned to computers as IP addresses. Class D addresses are used for multicasting. The value of the first octet ranges from 224 to 239.

Multicast addresses are used by groups of computers. A packet addressed to a multicast address is delivered to each computer in the multicast group. This is better than a **broadcast**

message because routers can be configured to allow multicast traffic to move from one network to another. In addition, all computers on the network process broadcasts, whereas only computers that are part of that multicast group process multicasts.

Class E addresses are considered experimental and are not used. The first octet of Class E addresses ranges from 240 to 255.

Classless Inter-domain Routing

At one time, routers on the Internet used IP address classes to move packets. Specifically, the routers used the network address and default subnet mask. Such use was called **classful routing**.

With classful routing, each Internet backbone router potentially needs to keep 2,097,152 entries in its routing table for Class C networks alone. As the number of Class C networks assigned grew, this became unsustainable. Classful routing also wasted many IP addresses. If an organization needed 20 IP addresses, it required an entire Class C address. Out of the 254 hosts on a Class C network, 234 would be unused.

To make Internet routing and the assignment of IP addresses more efficient, **classless inter–domain routing (CIDR)** was introduced. CIDR does not use the default subnet masks for routing. Instead, the subnet mask must be defined for each network. A definable subnet mask is more flexible and efficient because a single network can be subnetted and organizations assigned only a small part of a Class C network. For example, a company that needs 20 IP addresses can be assigned a block of addresses as small as 32. This wastes only 12 addresses instead of 234 from the previous example. CIDR also reduces the number of routing table entries that Internet backbone routers must hold. A single routing table entry can replace hundreds or thousands of entries for Class C networks.

CIDR notation is a common mechanism to indicate the number of bits in the network ID of an IP address. After the IP address, /xx is added, with xx being the number of bits in the host ID, as shown in Table 2-9.

Table 2-9   CIDR notation

CIDR Notation	Subnet Mask
192.168.1.0/24	255.255.255.0
172.16.0.0/16	255.255.0.0
10.0.0.0/8	255.0.0.0

Reserved Addresses

There are a number of IP addresses and IP networks that are reserved for special purposes and either cannot be assigned to hosts or cannot be used on the Internet.

When packets need to be delivered to all computers on a network, they are addressed to a broadcast IP address. There are two different types of broadcast IP addresses: local and directed.

A packet addressed to a local broadcast address is delivered to all computers on a local network and is discarded by routers. The IP address 255.255.255.255 is a local broadcast; all bits in the address are set to 1.

A packet addressed to a directed broadcast address is a broadcast on a specific network. These packets can be routed to get to the network to which it is aimed. The IP address for a directed broadcast is composed of the network ID to which it is directed and then all host bits are set to 1. Routers can be configured to block directed broadcasts, but forwards them by default. Table 2-10 shows some examples of IP networks and directed broadcasts for those networks.

Table 2-10   Directed broadcasts on specific network

Network	Directed Broadcast
192.168.1.0/24	192.168.1.255
172.16.0.0/16	172.16.255.255
10.0.0.0/8	10.255.255.255

Any IP address with all host bits set to 0 refers to the network itself and cannot be assigned to a host. Table 2-11 shows some examples of IP addresses with all host bits set to 0.

Table 2-11   Host bits in IP addresses

IP Address	Network ID	Host ID
192.168.1.0/24	192.168.1.0	0.0.0.0
172.16.0.0/16	172.16.0.0	0.0.0.0
10.0.0.0/8	10.0.0.0	0.0.0.0

Any IP address with 127 as the first octet cannot be assigned to a host. These are referred to as **loopback** addresses. The most commonly used loopback address is 127.0.0.1. However, all of these addresses starting with 127 are actually the local host. If you **ping** 127.0.0.1, you are actually pinging the machine you are on. These addresses are used to test IP stack software because this function works even if the network card is not functioning.

Several networks are reserved for internal use and packets using IP addresses on these networks are always discarded by Internet routers. However, packets using internal IP addresses can be routed internally within a corporate network. To provide Internet access to computers using these addresses, a proxy server or Network Address Translation is required. It is very common to use these addresses in a corporate environment. Table 2-12 shows the network addresses that are reserved for internal networks.

Table 2-12 Addresses for internal networks

CIDR Notation	IP Address Range
192.168.0.0/16	192.168.0.0-192.168.255.255
172.16.0.0/12	172.16.0.0-172.31.255.255
10.0.0.0/8	10.0.0.0-10.255.255.255

The network 169.254.0.0/16 is reserved for **Automatic Private IP Addressing (APIPA)**. Windows 2000/XP workstations automatically generate an address in this range if they are configured to lease an address from a Dynamic Host Configuration Protocol (DHCP) server and are unable to contact one. These addresses are not routable on the Internet. Windows Server 2003 also uses APIPA addresses if the server is configured to obtain a DHCP address and a DHCP server cannot be reached. However, most servers have static IP addresses.

DNS

Domain Name System (DNS) is essential to a Windows Server 2003 network. It is used to resolve host names to IP addresses, find domain controllers, and find e-mail servers. DNS is essential for Active Directory to work properly.

The most common use for DNS is resolving host names to IP addresses. When you access a Web site, you access a location such as *www.microsoft.com*. This is a **fully qualified domain name (FQDN)**, which is a combination of **host name** and **domain name**. A host name is the name of your computer. A domain name is part of DNS namespace that is registered and controlled by an organization to hold information about their network. Workstations cannot connect to a service on the Internet directly using a host name. Instead, they convert the host name to an IP address and then access the service via an IP address. Because it performs this critical service, DNS is essential for Internet connectivity.

Windows XP clients use DNS when finding a Windows Server 2003 domain controller to log onto Active Directory. During logon, a Windows XP client sends a query to the DNS server asking for a list of domain controllers. The DNS server responds with the IP address of a domain controller. Then, the Windows XP client contacts the domain controller to log on.

E-mail servers on the Internet use DNS to deliver mail messages. When you send a message to *someone@nowhere.com*, a DNS server holds the record that indicates the name of the server responsible for e-mail addressed to the domain *nowhere.com*. Table 2-13 shows several DNS record types, including MX records, that are used to find e-mail servers.

Table 2-13   DNS record types

DNS Record Type	Description
A (host)	An A record is used to convert host names to IP addresses.
SRV (service)	Service records are used to hold information about services; Active Directory uses these to store the addresses of domain controllers.
MX (mail exchange)	Mail exchange records are used to indicate which server is responsible for handling the e-mail for a DNS domain.

WINS

Windows Internet Naming Service (WINS) is used to resolve NetBIOS names to IP addresses. In addition, it stores information about services such as domain controllers.

WINS is used primarily for backward compatibility with Windows NT and Windows 9x. Windows NT and Windows 9x both use NetBIOS names as the primary mechanism for accessing network services. Joining a domain and browsing Network Neighborhood are just two examples of when NetBIOS names are required.

If WINS is configured, Windows Server 2003 registers its IP address and services with the WINS server during startup. When Windows Server 2003 is shut down, it contacts the WINS server and tells it to release the registration of its IP address and services.

DHCP

All IP configuration information can be manually entered on each workstation, but this method is not very efficient. With each manual entry, there is a risk of a typographical error. In addition, if the IP configuration changes, it is a very large task to visit each workstation to modify the IP configuration information.

Dynamic Host Configuration Protocol (DHCP) is an automated mechanism to assign IP addresses to clients. Automating this process avoids the problem of records being entered incorrectly. If a change needs to be made for the IP addressing information, you can simply change the information in the DHCP server.

Take, for example, a 200-workstation network. If you were to change manually the IP addressing information on all of these workstations, it might take several days. With DHCP, the server can be updated and, when the workstations are rebooted they receive the new information.

Windows Server 2003 can obtain its IP addressing information from DHCP, but it is not common to do so. Normally, network administrators prefer that servers have a consistent IP address so that it is easier to troubleshoot network connectivity problems. Newer clients, such as Windows XP, that attempt to contact a DHCP server and are unable to do so, generate an APIPA address in the 169.254.0.0/16 network.

As an alternative to APIPA addresses, Windows Server 2003 can be configured to use an alternative IP configuration. If a DHCP server cannot be contacted, then the alternative static IP settings are used.

Activity 2-3: Using IPCONFIG to View IP Configuration

Time Required: 5 minutes

Objective: View the current IP settings using the IPCONFIG utility.

Description: As part of documenting the configuration of a test server, you need to get the IP configuration from it. You are not sure whether the server is using DHCP or is configured with a static IP address. If the server is using DHCP, you cannot view the current IP configuration in the properties of the network connection. The IPCONFIG utility can be used to view IP configuration information whether the IP address is assigned through DHCP or statically.

1. If necessary, start your server and log on as **Administrator**.
2. Click **Start**, and then click **Run**.
3. Type **cmd.exe** in the Open text box.
4. Click **OK**.
5. Type **ipconfig /all** and press **Enter** to view your IP configuration settings.
6. Close the Command Prompt window.

Activity 2-4: Configuring an Alternative IP Configuration

Time Required: 10 minutes

Objective: Configure alternative IP address information to be used when a DHCP server is unavailable.

Description: Arctic University has a portable, computer-based testing system that moves from location to location. Normally, the server for the testing system gets an address from a DHCP server at the remote site. However, the Iqaluit branch of the Arctic University campus does not use DHCP. You need to configure the server to use an IP address from the Iqaluit location when a DHCP-based address is not available.

Before beginning this activity, confirm that no DHCP servers are running on your network.

1. If necessary, start your server and log on as **Administrator**.
2. Click **Start**, point to **Control Panel**, point to **Network Connections**, right-click **Classroom**, and click **Properties**.
3. Click the **Internet Protocol (TCP/IP)** option, and click the **Properties** button.
4. Click the **Obtain an IP address automatically** option.
5. Click the **Alternate Configuration** tab.

6. Click **User configured**.

7. Enter the following IP configuration information:
   - IP address: **172.30.0.x**, where x is your student number
   - Subnet mask: **255.255.0.0**
   - Default gateway: **172.30.0.254**
   - Preferred DNS server: **172.30.0.253**

8. Click **OK** to save the IP configuration changes, and click Close to exit the Classroom Properties window.

9. Click **Start**, click **Run**, type **cmd.exe**, and press **Enter**.

10. Type **ipconfig** and press **Enter**.

11. If you do not see the address on the 172.30.0.x network, then wait a few minutes and repeat Step 10.

12. Close the Command Prompt window.

13. Click **Start**, point to **Control Panel**, point to **Network Connections**, right-click **Classroom**, and click **Properties**.

14. Click the **Internet Protocol (TCP/IP)** option, and click the **Properties** button.

15. Click the **Use the following IP address** option; type your IP address, subnet mask, and default gateway; and then click **OK**.

16. Click **Close** to exit the Classroom Properties window.

TCP/IP ARCHITECTURE OVERVIEW

Each component of the TCP/IP protocol stack has its own tasks and responsibilities as part of the communication process. It is important to understand the overall architecture of TCP/IP and the roles of each component so that you have a starting point in troubleshooting connectivity issues. In this chapter, you learn about the architecture of the TCP/IP protocol stack and the roles of each layer.

The TCP/IP model can be broken down into four layers: Application, Transport, Internet, and Network Interface. Figure 2-3 shows the protocols that exist in each of the four layers of the TCP/IP model and how they relate to the OSI model. The **Open Systems Interconnection (OSI) reference model** is an industry standard that is used as a reference point to compare different networking technologies and protocols. Table 2-14 describes the layers of the OSI model.

Table 2-14 The OSI model

Layer Number	Layer	Description
7	Application	This layer is responsible for accepting requests for network services from applications. Application Program Interfaces exist here.
6	Presentation	This layer is responsible for data formatting. If compression or encryption are performed, the Presentation layer is responsible for it.
5	Session	This layer is responsible for starting and stopping conversations. In addition, it places checkpoints in the conversation to help recover if communication is interrupted.
4	Transport	This layer prepares data for transport on the network. It breaks large messages into smaller packets and labels them so that they can be reassembled at the receiving end.
3	Network	This layer is responsible for routing and logical addressing. It is the only layer that understands the concept of multiple networks. IP addresses are an example of logical addresses.
2	Data Link	This layer is responsible for physical addressing and proper data transmission. MAC addresses are the physical addresses added by this layer. Proper data transmission is ensured by adding a Cyclical Redundancy Check (CRC) that is used as a checksum by the receiving computer.
1	Physical	This layer is responsible for converting the data passed down from the Data Link layer into electrical signals that can be placed on the cabling.

The **Application layer** provides access to network resources. It defines the rules, commands, and procedures that client software uses to talk to a service running on a server. As an example, the HTTP protocol is an Application layer protocol that defines how Web browsers and Web servers communicate.

The **Transport layer** is responsible for preparing data to be transported across the network. This layer breaks large messages into smaller **packets** of information and tracks whether they arrived at their final destination.

The **Internet layer** is responsible for logical addressing and routing. IP addresses are logical addresses. Any protocol that is network-aware exists in this layer.

The **Network Interface layer** consists of the network card driver and the circuitry on the network card itself.

These layers are discussed in detail in the following sections.

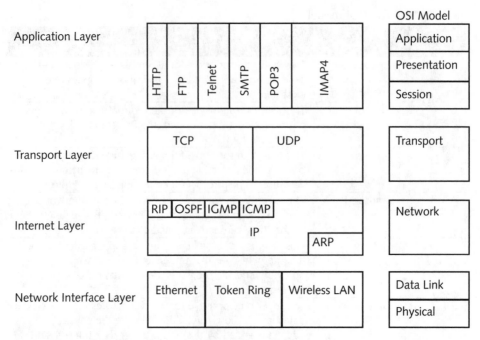

Figure 2-3   TCP/IP compared to the OSI model

APPLICATION LAYER PROTOCOLS

There are many Application layer protocols, each of which is associated with a client application and service. For example, FTP clients use the FTP protocol and telnet clients use the **Telnet** protocol.

In the following sections, each of the Application layer protocols is discussed.

HTTP

Hypertext Transfer Protocol (HTTP) is the most common protocol used on the Internet today. This is the protocol used by Web browsers and Web servers. HTTP defines the commands that Web browsers can send and how Web servers are capable of responding. For example, when requesting a Web page, a Web browser sends a GET command. The server then responds by sending the requested Web page. Many commands are defined as part of the protocol.

Information can also be uploaded using the HTTP protocol. A survey form on a Web page is an example of information moving from a Web browser to a Web server. The capabilities of Web servers can also be extended using a variety of mechanisms that allow Web servers to pass data from forms to applications or scripts for processing. Some of the common methods for passing data from a Web server to an application are as follows:

- Common Gateway Interface (CGI)
- Internet Server Application Program Interface (ISAPI)
- Netscape Server Application Program Interface (NSAPI)

 NOTE The World Wide Web Consortium (W3C) is the standards body responsible for defining the commands that are part of HTTP.

FTP

File Transfer Protocol (FTP) is a simple file-sharing protocol. It includes commands for uploading and downloading files, as well as requesting directory listings from remote servers. This protocol has been around the Internet for a long time and was originally implemented on UNIX during the 1980s. The first **Request for Comment (RFC)** describing FTP was created in 1985.

 NOTE TCP/IP is an open protocol that is developed based on RFCs that are contributed by the Internet community. Anyone can contribute. For more information about RFCs, visit the Internet Engineering Task Force Web site at *www.ietf.org/rfc.html*.

 NOTE Although there are still FTP servers running on the Internet, they number fewer than in previous years. This is because HTTP is capable of uploading and downloading files, which is slowly making FTP obsolete.

FTP is implemented in stand-alone FTP clients as well as in Web browsers. It is safe to say that most FTP users today are using Web browsers.

 ACTIVITY

Activity 2-5: Using FTP to Download a File

Time Required: 10 minutes

Objective: Use FTP to download a utility.

Description: There is a utility that you want to download from the Microsoft FTP server. Normally, you would use Internet Explorer to download this file, but Internet Explorer is not functioning properly on your workstation. As a result, you need to use the command-line FTP client to download the index of available files.

1. If necessary, start your server and log on as **Administrator** of the Artic domain.

NOTE   For all activities, log on as the domain Administrator.

2. Click the **Start** button, and then click **Run**.

3. Type **FTP** and press **Enter**.

4. Type **open ftp.microsoft.com** and press **Enter**.

5. Type **anonymous** and press **Enter**.

6. Type your e-mail address, and then press **Enter**.

7. Type **ls** and press **Enter**.

8. Type **cd softlib** and press **Enter**.

9. Type **dir** and press **Enter**.

10. Type **get index.txt** and press **Enter**. This command retrieves the file index.txt from the remote server. All retrieved files are placed in the current directory on the local machine. In this instance, the current directory is C:\Documents and Settings\ Administrator.ARCTIC.

11. Type **bye** and press **Enter**.

Telnet

Telnet is a terminal emulation protocol that is primarily used to connect remotely to UNIX and Linux Systems. The Telnet protocol specifies how a telnet server and telnet client communicate.

The most common reason to connect to a server via Telnet is to manage remotely UNIX or Linux systems. All of the administration for these systems can be done through a character-based interface. This is important because Telnet does not support a **graphical user interface (GUI)**, only text.

Telnet is similar to the concept of a mainframe and dumb terminal. The telnet server controls the entire user environment, processes the keyboard input, and sends display commands back to the client. A telnet client is responsible only for displaying information on the screen and passing input to the server. There can be many telnet clients connected to a single server at one time. Each client that is connected receives its own operating environment; however, these clients are not aware that other users are logged onto the system.

SMTP

Simple Mail Transfer Protocol (SMTP) is used to send and receive e-mail messages between e-mail servers that are communicating. It is also used by e-mail client software, such as Outlook Express, to send messages to the server. SMTP is never used to retrieve e-mail from a server when you are reading it. Other protocols control the reading of e-mail messages.

Activity 2-6: Using Telnet to Verify SMTP

Time Required: 10 minutes

Objective: Use Telnet to verify the functionality of an SMTP server.

Description: A client is having a problem sending e-mail to a person at Microsoft. You want to verify that Microsoft's SMTP server is responding on the Internet. If you can Telnet to the mail server on port 25, it indicates that the server is operational and accepting connections.

1. If necessary, start your server and log on as **Administrator**.

2. Click the **Start** button, and then click **Run**.

3. Type **cmd** and click **OK**.

4. Type **telnet** and press **Enter**.

5. Type **set localecho** and press **Enter**. This displays the commands that you type in the Telnet window.

6. Type **open maila.microsoft.com 25** and press **Enter**.

7. Type **help** and press **Enter**. What commands does the mail server support?

8. Type **helo** and press **Enter**. What is the FQDN of the mail server?

9. Type **quit** and press **Enter**.

10. If you are prompted to press any key to continue, press **Enter** twice.

11. Type **quit** and press **Enter** to close the Telnet utility.

12. Close the Command Prompt window.

POP3

Post Office Protocol version 3 (POP3) is the most common protocol used for reading e-mail messages. This protocol has commands to download messages and delete messages from the mail server. POP3 does not support sending messages. By default, most e-mail client software using POP3 copies all messages onto the local hard drive and erases them from the server. However, you can change the configuration so that messages can be left on the server. POP3 supports only a single inbox and does not support multiple folders for storage on the server.

IMAP4

Internet Message Access Protocol version 4 (IMAP4) is another common protocol used to read e-mail messages. The abilities of IMAP4 are beyond those of POP3. For example, IMAP can download message headers only, then allow you to choose which messages to download. In addition, IMAP4 allows for multiple folders on the server side to store messages.

TRANSPORT LAYER PROTOCOLS

Transport layer protocols are responsible for getting data ready to move across the network. The most common task performed by Transport layer protocols is breaking entire messages down into packets. For instance, if an entire file is being moved from one computer to another, then a Transport layer protocol breaks the file down into smaller pieces that can be transmitted more easily on the network.

One of the defining characteristics of Transport layer protocols is the use of **port** numbers. Each service running on a server listens at a port number. Each Transport layer protocol has its own set of ports. When a packet is addressed to a particular port, the Transport layer protocol knows to which service to deliver the packet. The combination of an IP address and port number is referred to as a socket.

A port number is like an apartment number for the delivery of mail. The network ID of the IP address ensures that the packet is delivered to the correct street (network); the host ID ensures that the packet is delivered to the correct building (host); the Transport layer protocol and port number ensure that the packet is delivered to the proper apartment (service).

The two Transport layer protocols in the TCP/IP protocol suite are Transmission Control Protocol (TCP) and User Datagram Protocol (UDP). Table 2-15 shows well-known services and the ports they use.

Table 2-15   Common services and ports

Internet Services	Port	Windows Services	Port
FTP	TCP 21, 20	Kerberos	TCP 88, UDP 88
Telnet	TCP 23	RPC Endpoint Mapper	TCP 135, UDP 135
SMTP	TCP 25	NetBIOS Name Service	TCP 137, UDP 137
HTTP	TCP 80	NetBIOS Datagram Service	UDP 138
DNS	TCP 53, UDP 53	NetBIOS Session Service	TCP 139
Trivial FTP (TFTP)	UDP 69	LDAP	TCP 389
POP3	TCP 110	SMB over IP	TCP 445, UDP 445
NNTP	TCP 119	MS SQL Server	TCP 1433

Table 2-15 Common services and ports (continued)

Internet Services	Port	Windows Services	Port
Network Time Protocol	UDP 123	IAS (RADIUS)	TCP 1812, UDP 1812
IMAP	TCP 143	Global Catalog LDAP	TCP 3268
Secure HTTP (HTTPS)	TCP 443	Terminal Services	TCP 3389

Activity 2-7: Using Port Numbers

Time Required: 5 minutes

Objective: Connect to resources using TCP and UDP port numbers.

Description: You have been explaining the concept of port numbers to a colleague. He is still unsure that he understands how they are used. You have explained that a Web browser automatically uses the default port for a protocol. In this activity, you demonstrate for your colleague what happens when an incorrect port number is used.

1. If necessary, start your server and log on as **Administrator**.

2. Open Internet Explorer.

3. Type **http://www.microsoft.com** in the Address Bar, and press **Enter**. The Web browser automatically connects you to port 80 on this server.

4. Type **http://www.microsoft.com:21** in the Address Bar, and press **Enter**. The Web browser cannot connect because port 21 is not used for HTTP.

5. Type **http://www.microsoft.com:80** in the Address Bar, and press **Enter**. The Web browser connects and gives you the same Web page as in Step 3.

6. Type **ftp://ftp.microsoft.com** in the Address Bar, and press **Enter**. The Web browser automatically connects you to port 21 when using FTP.

7. Type **ftp://ftp.microsoft.com:80** in the Address Bar, and press **Enter**. The Web browser cannot connect because port 80 is not used for FTP.

8. Click **OK** to clear the error message window.

9. Type **ftp://ftp.microsoft.com:21** in the Address Bar, and press **Enter**. The Web browser connects and gives you the same information as in Step 6.

10. Close Internet Explorer.

TCP

Transmission Control Protocol (TCP) is the most commonly used Transport layer protocol. TCP is connection-oriented and reliable. **Connection-oriented** means that

TCP creates and verifies a connection with a remote host before sending information. This verifies that the remote host exists and is willing to communicate before starting the conversation.

The establishment of a connection is a three-packet process between the source and destination host. It is often called a three-way handshake. Figure 2-4 shows the packets involved in the three-way handshake performed when a connection is established between Computer A and Computer B.

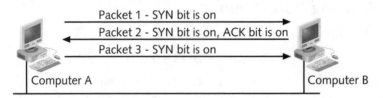

Figure 2-4   Establishing a TCP connection

In Figure 2-4, you can see that the connection is initiated by Computer A. An option in the packet called the SYN bit is turned on. The **SYN bit** indicates that this packet is a request to negotiate a connection. This request includes parameters for the conversation such as the maximum packet size.

The response packet from Computer B to Computer A has the ACK and SYN bits turned on. The **ACK bit** is an option in a packet that indicates this packet is a response to the first packet. The SYN bit is on because this packet contains the parameters that Computer B wants to use when communicating with Computer A. If Computer B is able to use the parameters received in the first packet, then those are the parameters sent in this packet. If Computer B cannot use a parameter from the first packet, then it replaces that parameter with one that it can use in this packet.

The third packet is the final agreement from Computer A indicating that it has accepted the terms of Computer B. This packet has the ACK bit turned on to indicate it is a response to the second packet.

TCP is considered reliable because it tracks each packet and makes sure that it arrives at its destination. If a packet is lost or damaged as part of the communication process, then the packet is transmitted again. The overall process is called a **sliding window**.

If a thousand packets are waiting to be sent as part of the communication process, not all of the packets are sent at once because it would be too difficult to track. Only a few packets are sent at a time. The number of packets is negotiated as part of the process of establishing the connection and is considered as being the size of the sliding window. For example, if the sliding window size is set to 10 packets, only 10 packets are sent at a time. When the destination computer acknowledges receipt of the first 10 packets, then the window slides forward and another 10 packets are sent.

The sliding window cannot be moved past a packet that has not been received and acknowledged by the destination. If a packet goes missing, it must be retransmitted and acknowledged before the sliding window can move past that point. A common reason why there is a pause in the middle of large downloads from the Internet is that a packet has been lost and must be retransmitted before the conversation can continue.

Being reliable and connection-oriented are generally desirable qualities. Consequently, TCP is the Transport layer protocol used for most Internet services. HTTP, FTP, SMTP, POP3, and IMAP4 all use TCP.

Activity 2-8: Installing Network Monitor

Time Required: 5 minutes

Objective: Install Network Monitor to enable packet capturing.

Description: You want to see exactly how some of the data packets on your network are addressed. To see packet details, you install the application Network Monitor, which is included with Windows Server 2003.

1. If necessary, start your server and log on as **Administrator**.

2. Click the **Start** button, point to **Control Panel**, and then click **Add or Remove Programs**.

3. Click **Add/Remove Windows Components**.

4. Scroll down in the Components section, and then double-click **Management and Monitoring Tools**.

5. Check the **Network Monitor Tools** check box, and click **OK**.

6. Click the **Next** button. If necessary, click **OK** in the Insert Disk dialog box, browse to the C:\I386 folder, and click **OK** in the Files Needed dialog box.

7. Click the **Finish** button and close the Add or Remove Programs window.

Activity 2-9: Viewing a TCP Connection in Network Monitor

Time Required: 30 minutes

Objective: Capture and view TCP connection packets in Network Monitor.

Description: You are going to be configuring the Arctic University firewall in the next few weeks and want to be familiar with the detailed packet information that is used when creating a TCP connection. In this activity, you capture and view the packets used when a TCP connection is created with HTTP.

1. If necessary, start your server and log on as **Administrator**.

2. Open Internet Explorer.

3. Click the **Start** button, point to **Administrative Tools**, and click **Network Monitor**.

4. The first time you start Network Monitor, you must select the network interface on which Network Monitor will look for packets. If necessary, click OK to close the dialog box.

5. If this is the first time Network Monitor is run, click the **+** (plus sign) beside **Local Computer**, click **Classroom**, and click **OK** to select a network interface.

6. Press **F10** to start capturing packets.

7. In Internet Explorer, type **www.google.com** in the Address Bar, and press **Enter**.

8. In Network Monitor, press **F11** to stop capturing packets.

9. Press **F12** to view the captured packets.

10. It's now time to filter the display to show only packets with a TCP source port or a TCP destination port of 80. This shows all packets addressed to the Web server or coming from the Web server:

    a. Click the **Display** menu, and click **Filter**.

    b. Double-click the green **AND** to change it to **OR**.

    c. Double-click **Protocol==Any**.

    d. Click the **Property** tab.

    e. Double-click **TCP** in the Protocol:Property box; then, underneath TCP, click **Destination Port**, click the **Decimal** radio button, type **80** in the Value box, and click **OK**.

    f. In the Add box, click **Expression**.

    g. Under TCP, click **Source Port** and click **OK**.

    h. Click **ANY<--> ANY** and then click **Line** in the Delete box.

    i. Click **OK**.

11. View the first packet in a TCP handshake:

    a. Double-click the first packet in the Capture:1(Summary) window.

    b. Expand the **IP** section of the middle window to view the source and destination IP addresses. The source IP address is your computer. The destination IP address is the Web server.

    c. Expand the **TCP** section of the middle window to view the source and destination TCP ports. The source port varies, but the destination port is World Wide Web HTTP. Network Monitor substitutes the phrase World Wide Web HTTP for the number 80 to make it easier to read and understand.

    d. Expand the **TCP: Flags** section of the middle window to view the acknowledgment (ACK) and synchronize (SYN) flags. In this packet, the ACK flag is set to 0 and the SYN flag is set to 1.

e. Expand the **TCP: Options** and **TCP: Maximum Segment Size Option** to view the packet size that is being requested.

12. View the second packet in a TCP handshake:

   a. Click the second packet in the top window.

   b. In the IP section of the middle window, view the source and destination IP addresses. The source IP address is the Web server. The destination IP address is your server.

   c. In the TCP section of the middle window, view the source and destination TCP ports. The destination port is the same as the source port in the first packet. The source port is World Wide Web HTTP.

   d. In the TCP: Flags section of the middle window, view the acknowledgment (ACK) and synchronize (SYN) flags. In this packet, the ACK flag is set to 1 and the SYN flag is set to 1.

   e. In the TCP: Options and TCP: Maximum Segment Size Option, view the packet size that is being requested. This is the same as the first packet or smaller.

13. View the third packet in a TCP handshake:

   a. Click the third packet in the top window.

   b. In the IP section of the middle window, view the source and destination IP addresses. The source IP address is your server. The destination IP address is the Web server.

   c. In the TCP section of the middle window, view the source and destination TCP ports. The source port is the same as the first packet and the destination port is World Wide Web HTTP.

   d. In the TCP: Flags section of the middle window, view the acknowledgment (ACK) and synchronize (SYN) flags. In this packet, the ACK flag is set to 1 and the SYN flag is set to 0.

   e. Notice that **TCP: Options** does not exist in this packet because the negotiation of the Maximum Segment Size is already complete.

14. Click the fourth packet in the top window to view an HTTP GET request. This packet is the request for the Web page.

15. Click the fifth packet in the top window to view the response to the GET request. This is the information returned from the Web server based on the GET request.

16. Close Network Monitor (click No if prompted to save the capture) and Internet Explorer.

UDP

User Datagram Protocol (UDP) is not as commonly used as TCP and is used for different services. UDP is **connectionless** and unreliable. **Connectionless** means that UDP does not attempt to negotiate terms with a remote host before sending information.

UDP simply sends the information. If any terms need to be negotiated, the Application layer protocol has to do it. There is no handshake for UDP. Unreliable means that UDP does not track or guarantee delivery of packets between the source and destination. UDP just sends a stream of packets without waiting for acknowledgment. There is no sliding window for UDP.

UDP is the appropriate Transport layer protocol to use when you are unconcerned about missing packets or want to implement reliability in a special way. Streaming audio and video are in this category. If streaming audio were to pause and wait for missing packets to be sent again, then there could be long pauses in the sound. Most people prefer a small amount of static or silence to be inserted for the missing packet and for the rest of the audio track to continue to play. UDP does this because it does not keep track of packets that are missing or needing to be sent again. In the case of streaming audio, re-sent packets are handled by the Application layer protocol.

Connectionless communication also makes sense when the amount of data being exchanged is very small. Using three packets to set up a connection for a two-packet conversation is very inefficient. The resolution of a DNS name is a two-packet communication process and is done via UDP.

ACTIVITY

Activity 2-10: Capturing UDP Packets in Network Monitor

Time Required: 15 minutes

Objective: Capture and view UDP packets in Network Monitor.

Description: As preparation for configuring the Arctic University firewall in the next few weeks, you want to be familiar with the detailed packet information that is used in UDP packets. In this activity, you view DNS packets.

1. If necessary, start your server and log on as **Administrator**.

2. Open Internet Explorer.

3. Click the **Start** button, point to **Administrative Tools**, and click **Network Monitor**.

4. Click the **Start** button, and then click **Run**.

5. Type **ipconfig /flushdns** and press **Enter**. This removes any cached DNS lookup information. This ensures that, later in the activity, a DNS lookup will be required rather than getting DNS information from cache.

6. In Network Monitor, press **F10** to start capturing packets.

7. In Internet Explorer, type **www.google.com** in the Address Bar, and press **Enter**.

8. In Network Monitor, press **F11** to stop capturing packets.

9. Press **F12** to view the captured packets.

10. Filter the display to only show packets with a TCP source port or a TCP destination port of 53. This shows all packets addressed to the DNS server or coming from the DNS server:

    a. Click the **Display** menu, and click **Filter**.

    b. Double-click the green **AND** to change it to **OR**.

    c. Double-click **Protocol==Any**.

    d. Click the **Property** tab.

    e. Double-click **UDP** in the Protocol: Property box, and then, underneath UDP, click **Destination Port**, click the **Decimal** radio button, type **53** in the Value box, and click **OK**.

    f. In the Add box, click **Expression**.

    g. Under UDP, click **Source Port** and click **OK**.

    h. Click **ANY<--> ANY** and then click **Line** in the Delete box.

    i. Click **OK**.

11. View the first UDP DNS packet:

    a. Double-click the packet with the description **Std Qry for www.google.com**.

    b. Expand the **IP** section of the middle window to view the source and destination IP addresses. The source IP address is your computer. The destination IP address is the DNS server.

    c. Expand the **UDP** section of the middle window to view the source and destination UDP ports. The source UDP port varies. The destination UDP port is Domain Name Server.

    d. Expand the **DNS** section of the middle window to view the DNS-specific information.

12. View the second UDP DNS packet:

    a. Click the packet with the description **Std Qry Resp. for www.google.com**.

    b. In the IP section of the middle window, view the source and destination IP addresses. The source IP address is the DNS server. The destination IP address is your server.

    c. In the UDP section of the middle window, view the source and destination UDP ports. The source UDP is the Domain Name Server. The destination UDP port is the same as the source UDP port in the previous packet.

    d. In the DNS section of the middle window, view the DNS-specific information.

13. Close Network Monitor (click **No** if prompted to save capture) and Internet Explorer.

TCP Versus UDP

TCP is connection-oriented and reliable. This is similar to delivering a letter by registered mail. Inside the letter, each page is numbered so that it can be read in the proper order. When the message is received, the sender receives notice that it arrived properly at its destination.

UDP is connectionless and unreliable. If you were to take the same message as in the preceding example and place it on several postcards, take all of the postcards and dump them in the mail box separately, then the likelihood is that the recipient would be able to put them in the proper order and understand the message. However, if one postcard was missing, it would be very difficult for the recipient to understand the complete message.

INTERNET LAYER PROTOCOLS

Internet layer protocols are responsible for all tasks related to logical addressing. An IP address is a logical address. Any protocol that is aware of other networks, as in how to find them and how to reach them, exists at this layer. Each Internet layer protocol is very specialized. They include: IP, RIP and OSPF, ICMP, IGMP, and ARP.

IP

Internet Protocol (IP) is responsible for the logical addressing of each packet created by the Transport layer. As each packet is built, IP adds the source and destination IP address to the packet.

When a packet is received from the network, IP verifies that it is addressed to this computer. IP looks at the destination IP address of the packet to verify that it is the same as the IP address of the receiving computer, or a broadcast address of which this computer is a part. For example, if a computer has an IP address of 192.168.1.50/24, then IP would accept packets addressed to 192.168.1.50, 192.168.1.255, and 255.255.255.255.

RIP and OSPF

Routing Information Protocol (RIP) and **Open Shortest Path First (OSPF)** are both routing protocols. They are responsible for defining how paths are chosen through the internetwork from one computer to another. They also define how routers can share information about the networks of which they are aware.

RIP and OSPF are covered in more detail in Chapter 4.

ICMP

Internet Control Messaging Protocol (ICMP) is used to send IP error and control messages between routers and hosts. The most common use of ICMP is the ping utility.

The **ping** utility uses ICMP packets to test connectivity between hosts. When you use ping to communicate with a host, your computer sends an ICMP Echo Request packet. The host that you are pinging sends an ICMP Echo Response packet back. If there is a response, you can be sure that the host you have pinged is up and functional. However, if a host does not respond, that does not guarantee it is nonfunctional. Many firewalls are configured to block ICMP packets.

NOTE

The Internet Assigned Numbers Authority (IANA) maintains a complete list of ICMP packet types, which can be found at *www.iana.org/assignments/icmp-parameters*. Table 2-16 lists the most common ICMP packet types.

Table 2-16   Common ICMP packet types

Packet Type	Packet Name	Description
0	Echo Reply	Used in response to an Echo packet from a host
3	Destination Unreachable	Used by routers to indicate that the intended destination IP address cannot be reached
4	Source Quench	Used by routers to indicate that packets are being sent too fast and should be slowed down; this is seldom used
8	Echo	Used to generate an Echo Reply packet from a host
11	Time Exceeded	Used by routers to indicate that the Time to Live (TTL) of a packet has expired

The Time Exceeded ICMP packet type indicates that a packet could not reach its destination because delivery took too long. The **Time to Live (TTL)** of a packet is a combination of router hops and seconds. Each router that forwards a packet reduces the TTL of the packet by one. If it takes longer than 1 second to forward the packet, then the TTL is also reduced by one for each second that it is delayed.

The default TTL of Windows Server 2003 is 128. The default TTL used by other operating systems varies widely, but 64 is recommended by IANA.

ACTIVITY

Activity 2-11: Testing Host Functionality

Time Required: 5 minutes

Objective: Test the functionality of a host using the ping command.

Description: One of your users has called with a problem. He is unable to connect to *www.microsoft.com* with his Web browser. In this activity, you use the ping utility to test Internet connectivity by connecting to *www.microsoft.com*.

1. If necessary, start your server and log on as **Administrator**.

2. Click **Start**, click **Run**, type **cmd.exe**, and press **Enter**.

3. Type **ping www.microsoft.com** and press **Enter**. This server responds. This confirms that the server is definitely functional and Internet connectivity is working.

4. Close the Command Prompt window.

5. Open Internet Explorer.

6. Type **www.microsoft.com** in the Address Bar, and press **Enter**. The Microsoft Web site appears. This confirms that the Web site is functional.

7. Close Internet Explorer.

Activity 2-12: Viewing TTL

Time Required: 5 minutes

Objective: View the TTL of a ping packet.

Description: One of your users is complaining of slow Internet connectivity. To test the distance from Arctic University to the site, you use the ping utility. The ping utility shows the TTL of the packet, giving an approximation of how fast the connection is. Because the TTL is reduced by one for each router that is crossed, a smaller TTL means that there are more routers between you and the remote host.

1. If necessary, start your server and log on as **Administrator**.

2. Click **Start**, click **Run**, type **cmd.exe**, and press **Enter**.

3. Type **ping 192.168.1.10** and press **Enter**. The TTL in the response is the TTL when no routers are passed through.

4. Type **ping www.google.com** and press **Enter**. You can determine the number of routers between you and www.google.com by calculating the TTL from pinging the default gateway minus the TTL from pinging www.google.com. For example, if you received a TTL of 128 when pinging your default gateway and a TTL of 113 when pinging www.google.com, then the number of routers between your computer and www.google.com is 15 (128-113=15).

5. Type **ping –i 1 www.google.com** and press **Enter**. This forces a TTL of 1. This results in an ICMP error message indicating that the TTL expired in transit.

6. Close the Command Prompt window.

IGMP

Internet Group Management Protocol (IGMP) is used for the management of multicast groups. Hosts use IGMP to inform routers of their membership in multicast groups. Routers use IGMP to announce that their networks have members in particular multicast groups. The use of IGMP allows multicast packets to be distributed only to routers that have interested hosts connected.

ARP

Address Resolution Protocol (ARP) is used to convert logical IP addresses to physical MAC addresses. This is an essential part of the packet delivery process.

Network cards use a MAC address to filter irrelevant packets. When a packet is received, the network card verifies that the destination MAC address matches the MAC address of the network card or is a broadcast MAC address. For example, if the receiving computer has a MAC address of A1:B2:C3:D4:E5:F6, then the network card of the receiving computer passes the packet up to IP if the destination MAC address of the packet is A1:B2:C3:D4:E5:F6 or FF:FF:FF:FF:FF:FF (broadcast MAC address). This process off-loads the responsibility for analyzing all the network packets from IP to the network card. This reduces CPU utilization on the computer.

Data packets have four addresses: source IP address, destination IP address, source MAC address, and destination MAC address. When a packet is created, the source computer must find the MAC address of the destination computer based on the destination IP address.

There are many terms that can be used to describe packets of information as they are being processed for transmission on a network. The term "frame" is used to describe a fully formed Ethernet packet on the network. "Datagram" is used to describe packets that exist at the Network layer before MAC addresses have been placed in the header. In this discussion, the term "packet" is equivalent to "frame."

ARP uses a two-packet process to find the MAC address of the destination computer. The first packet is an ARP Request that is broadcast to all computers on the local network asking for the MAC address of the computer with the destination IP address. The destination computer sees this packet and sends an ARP Reply containing its MAC address. The sending computer can then create data packets using the destination MAC address. Figure 2-5 page shows an example of a small computer network. Computer A needs to find the MAC address of Computer B before data packets can be delivered.

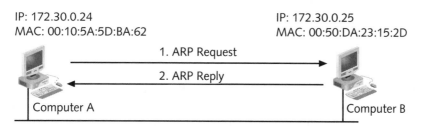

Figure 2-5   The ARP process

Figure 2-6 shows the structure of an ARP Request packet sent as the first step of the resolution process. The ETHERNET section of the packet contains the MAC address information used by network cards when analyzing whether the packet should be passed up to IP. In this packet, the source MAC address is the MAC address of Computer A, and the destination MAC address is the broadcast MAC address of FF:FF:FF:FF:FF:FF. All computers on the local segment process this packet and pass it up to ARP because the broadcast MAC address is the destination MAC address.

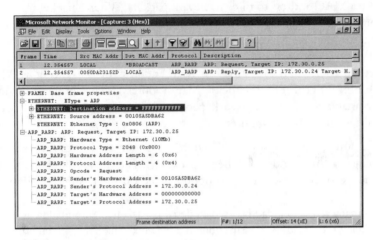

Figure 2-6   ARP Request packet

The ARP_RARP section of the packet shown in Figure 2-6 is the ARP information that is processed by ARP on the receiving computer. The most important information in this part of the packet is the Target's Protocol Address. This is the IP address of the destination computer. If the Target's Protocol Address matches the IP address of Computer B, then an ARP Reply packet is created. If the Target's Protocol Address does not match the IP address of Computer B, then the packet is discarded.

Figure 2-7 shows the structure of an ARP Reply packet sent as the second step of the resolution process. The ETHERNET section of the packet contains the MAC address information used by network cards when analyzing whether the packet should be passed up to IP. In this packet, the source MAC address is the MAC address of Computer B and the destination MAC address is the MAC address of Computer A. The ARP_RARP section of the packet has the ARP information required by Computer A to create proper data packets. The Sender's Hardware Address is the MAC address that is required by Computer A.

If routers are forwarding packets, then the ARP process is modified. The first ARP Request is for the default gateway, then the ARP Response includes the MAC address of the router. The data packet is then built and sent to the router. The router removes and then replaces the source MAC address with its own and uses ARP to find the MAC address of the next router, if required, or the final destination host.

In Figure 2-8, Computer A is sending a data packet to Computer B. The data packet is addressed to Computer B at the IP layer, but must be given to the router for delivery. The MAC address is used to deliver the packet to the router.

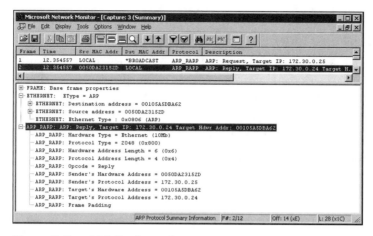

Figure 2-7   ARP Reply packet

IP: 172.30.0.24
MAC: 00:10:5A:5D:BA:62

IP: 192.168.1.10
MAC: 00:50:DA:23:15:2D

IP: 172.30.0.1
MAC: A1:B2:C3:D4:E5:F6

IP: 192.168.1.1
MAC: A1:B2:C3:D4:E5:F7

Computer A

Computer B

Router

Source IP: 172.30.0.24
Source MAC: 00:10:5A:5D:BA:62
Destination IP: 192.168.1.10
Destination MAC: A1:B2:C3:D4:E5:F6

Source IP: 172.30.0.24
Source MAC: A1:B2:C3:D4:E5:F7
Destination IP: 192.168.1.10
Destination MAC: 00:50:DA:23:15:2D

Figure 2-8   Computer A communicates with Computer B across a router

The router removes the MAC address information from the data packet and replaces it with the MAC addresses required to deliver it to Computer B. The source and destination IP addresses of the packet do not change.

Activity 2-13: Viewing the ARP Cache

Time Required: 5 minutes

Objective: View the contents of the ARP cache.

Description: You are concerned that a user connectivity issue is being caused by incorrect MAC address information in the ARP. In this activity, you view the contents of the ARP cache and clear the cache to force the rebuilding of the cache information. In this activity, your instructor assigns you a partner.

1. If necessary, start your server and log on as **Administrator**.

2. Click **Start**, click **Run**, type **cmd.exe**, and press **Enter**.

3. Type **arp -d** and press **Enter**. This clears the contents of the ARP cache.

4. Type **ping partnercomputer** and press **Enter** (where partnercomputer is the IP address of your partner's computer). Be sure that your partner's computer is on the same network as your computer.

5. Type **arp -g** and press **Enter**. This shows the contents of the ARP cache. Right now, it shows the IP address and MAC address of your partner's computer.

6. Type **ping www.google.com** and press **Enter**.

7. Type **arp -g** and press **Enter**. Notice that the cache does not have an entry for www.google.com. The cache has a new entry for your default gateway.

8. Close the Command Prompt window.

NETWORK INTERFACE LAYER PROTOCOLS

Most of the common Network Interface layer protocols are defined by the **Institute of Electrical and Electronics Engineers (IEEE)**. The IEEE has a system of numbered committees that each defines a different Network Interface layer protocol. Table 2-17 lists some of the IEEE Network Interface layer protocols for which they are responsible.

Table 2-17   IEEE protocols

Protocol	Description
802.3	Ethernet
802.5	Token Ring
802.11	Wireless LAN
802.15	Wireless personal area network

Ethernet is the most common Network Interface layer protocol used in corporate networks today. There are many different varieties of Ethernet, all of which use Carrier Sense Multiple Access/Collision Detection (CSMA/CD) for access control. The most common version of Ethernet is implemented with twisted-pair cabling at 100 Mbps. Table 2-18 shows the different speeds of Ethernet for different cabling types.

Table 2-18   Ethernet cabling types and speeds

Cabling	Speed
Coaxial	10 Mbps
Twisted-pair (Cat 5e)	10 Mbps to 1 Gbps
Fiber-optic	10 Mbps to 10 Gbps

Token Ring is an older technology created by IBM that was implemented in the late 1980s and early 1990s. It was commonly implemented with mainframe computers. This standard uses twisted-pair cabling and operates at 4 Mbps or 16 Mbps. The access method used is token passing.

Wireless LAN is one of the fastest growing network types. The 802.11b standard defines the most common wireless standard. It uses radio signals to send data at 11 Mbps. The maximum distance of 802.11b is approximately 300 feet indoors and up to 1000 feet outdoors. The 802.11g standard transfers data at 54 Mbps and is backward compatible with 802.11b.

NOTE Microsoft has added a number of features for wireless networks to Windows Server 2003. A wireless snap-in allows you to monitor and manage wireless access points and wireless clients. Group Policy has been extended to allow the management of wireless clients, including encryption settings. Some wireless functionality for network cards is also available in the operating system to make driver development easier for hardware developers and more reliable for users.

The IEEE standard 802.15 defines the Physical layer portion of the **Bluetooth** standard. **Bluetooth** is a short-range wireless communication system with a maximum distance of approximately 30 feet and a maximum speed of 720 Kbps. This is a much shorter range and much slower data transfer rate than 802.11b. The IEEE 802.15 committee intends to increase this speed. Support for Bluetooth is built into many smaller devices that need to minimize energy consumption, such as Palm and Windows CE devices.

Infrared communication is built into many devices for wireless connectivity. It is very common on laptops, Palm devices, and Windows CE devices. The official protocol implementation for infrared communication is Infrared Data Association (IrDA). This is also the name of the group responsible for defining the protocol implementation. IrDA has a maximum range of three feet and maximum speed of 4 Mbps. The use of IrDA is being reduced as Bluetooth becomes more popular.

Chapter Summary

- ❏ Windows Server 2003 uses TCP/IP as its primary networking protocol. An IP address is composed of both a network ID and a host ID. A subnet mask is used to define which part of the IP address is the network ID and which part is the host ID. A default gateway is required to deliver packets of information from one network to another.

- ❏ There are several IP address networks reserved for internal use that are not routable on the Internet. These networks are 10.0.0.0/8, 172.16.0.0/12, and 192.168.0.0/16.

- ❏ DHCP is used to allocate IP addresses and other IP configuration information to clients automatically.

- ❏ If a DHCP server cannot be contacted, then clients use APIPA, which randomly generates an IP address in the range 169.254.X.X.

- The TCP/IP model is composed of four layers: the Application layer, the Transport layer, the Internet layer, and the Network Interface layer.

- There are many Application layer protocols, each of which is associated with a client application and service.

- HTTP is the most common protocol used on the Internet today.

- FTP is used for transferring files across the Internet.

- Telnet is used to connect remotely to UNIX and Linux systems.

- SMTP is used to send and receive e-mail messages between e-mail servers.

- POP3 is the most common protocol used for reading e-mail messages. IMAP4 is another protocol used for reading e-mail messages.

- The two Transport layer protocols are TCP and UDP.

- TCP is connection-oriented and reliable.

- UDP is connectionless and unreliable.

- Internet layer protocols are responsible for all tasks related to logical addressing and are all very specialized.

- Internet layer protocols include IP, RIP, OSPF, ICMP, IGMP, and ARP.

- Ethernet is the most common Network Interface layer protocol used in corporate networks today.

- Wireless LANs are one of the fastest growing network types.

KEY TERMS

ACK bit — A bit used in TCP communication to indicate that a packet is an acknowledgment of a previous packet.

Active Directory — A directory service for Windows 2000/2003 servers that stores information about network resources.

Address Resolution Protocol (ARP) — A protocol used by hosts to find the physical MAC address of another host with a particular IP address.

Application layer — The layer of the TCP/IP architecture that provides access to network resources.

Automatic Private IP Addressing (APIPA) — A feature of newer Windows operating systems that automatically generates an IP address on the 169.254.X.X network when a DHCP server cannot be contacted.

Bluetooth — A short-range wireless communication protocol.

broadcast — A packet that is addressed to all computers on a network. A broadcast for the local network is addressed to 255.255.255.255.

classful routing — An older style of routing in which routing table entries would be based on Class A, B, and C networks with default subnet masks.

2

classless inter-domain routing (CIDR) — An addressing scheme that uses a defined number of bits for the subnet mask rather than relying on default lengths based on address classes. The number of bits in the network ID is defined as /XX after the IP address. XX is the number of bits.

Common Gateway Interface (CGI) — A vendor-neutral mechanism used to pass information from a Web page to an application running on a Web server.

connectionless — A term used to describe a protocol that does not establish a communication channel before sending data.

connection-oriented — A term used to describe a protocol that verifies the existence of a host and agrees on terms of communication before sending data.

default gateway — A dedicated hardware device or computer on a network that is responsible for moving packets from one IP network to another. This is another term for IP router.

domain name — The portion of a DNS namespace that can be registered and controlled by an organization or individual.

Domain Name System (DNS) — A service used by clients running TCP/IP to resolve host names to IP addresses. Active Directory uses DNS to store service location information.

Dynamic Host Configuration Protocol (DHCP) — A protocol used to assign IP addressing information automatically to clients.

File Transfer Protocol (FTP) — The protocol used by FTP clients and servers to move files. By default, it uses TCP port 21 for control information and TCP port 20 for data transfer.

fully qualified domain name (FQDN) — The combination of a host name and domain name that completely describes the name of a computer within the global DNS system.

graphical user interface (GUI) — A user interface for an operating system that supports graphics in addition to characters.

host ID — The portion of an IP address that uniquely identifies a computer on an IP network.

host name — The name of a computer using the TCP/IP protocol.

Hypertext Transfer Protocol (HTTP) — The protocol used by Web browsers and Web servers. By default, it uses TCP port 80.

Institute of Electrical and Electronics Engineers (IEEE) — The organization responsible for maintaining many Physical layer protocols used in networks, including Ethernet and Token Ring.

Internet Control Messaging Protocol (ICMP) — The protocol used by routers and hosts to send Internet protocol error messages.

Internet Group Management Protocol (IGMP) — The protocol used by routers to track the membership in multicast groups.

Internet layer — The layer of the TCP/IP architecture that is responsible for logical addressing and routing.

Internet Message Access Protocol version 4 (IMAP4) — A protocol used to retrieve e-mail messages from an e-mail server. It is more flexible than POP3 for managing message storage.

Internet Server Application Program Interface (ISAPI) — A programmer interface defined by Microsoft for passing information from Web pages to programs running on a Web server.

Internet service provider (ISP) — A company that sells Internet access.

Linux — An open source operating system that is very similar to UNIX.

loopback — Any IP address that begins with 127.X.X.X. These addresses represent the local host.

multicast — A packet that is addressed to a specific group of computers rather than a single computer. Multicast addresses range from 224.0.0.0 to 239.255.255.255.

Netscape Server Application Program Interface (NSAPI) — A programmer interface defined by Netscape to pass information from Web pages to applications running on a Web server.

NetWare — A network operating system from Novell that traditionally uses the IPX/SPX protocol.

Network Address Translation (NAT) — A service that allows multiple computers to access the Internet by sharing a single IP address.

network ID — The portion of an IP address that designates the network on which a computer resides. This is defined by the subnet mask.

Network Interface layer — The layer of the TCP/IP architecture that controls placing packets on the physical network media.

octet — A group of eight bits. An IP address is composed of four octets, with each expressed as a decimal number.

Open Shortest Path First (OSPF) — A protocol that is used by routers to share information about known networks and calculate the best path through an internetwork. OSPF calculates routes based on user-definable cost values.

Open Systems Interconnection (OSI) reference model — An industry standard that is used as a reference point to compare different networking technologies and protocols.

packets — A packet is a single unit of data sent from one computer to another. It contains a source address, destination address, data, and error-checking information.

ping — A utility used to test connectivity by sending an ICMP Echo packet.

port — A TCP port or UDP port is used by Transport layer protocols to direct network information to the proper service.

Post Office Protocol version 3 (POP3) — A protocol that is used to retrieve e-mail messages from an e-mail server.

proxy server — A server that can be used to control and speed up access to the Internet. It also allows multiple computers to access the Internet through a single IP address.

Request for Comment (RFC) — A submission to the Internet Engineering Task Force that is evaluated for use as part of the TCP/IP protocol suite.

router — A network device that moves packets from one network to another. TCP/IP, IPX/SPX, and AppleTalk can be routed.

Routing Information Protocol (RIP) — A protocol used by routers to exchange routing table information and determine the best path through an internetwork based on the number of hops.

Simple Mail Transfer Protocol (SMTP) — A protocol used by e-mail clients to send messages to e-mail servers. It uses TCP port 25.

sliding window — A process used in the TCP protocol to track which packets have been received by the destination host.

subnet mask — A string of 32 bits that is used to define which portion of an IP address is the host ID and which part is the network ID.

subnetting — A process by which a single large network is subdivided into smaller networks to control traffic flow.

SYN bit — A bit used in TCP communication to indicate a request to start a communication session.

Telnet — A protocol used to access remotely a command-line interface on UNIX and Linux servers.

Time to Live (TTL) — A parameter of IP packets used to ensure that if a packet becomes trapped in a router loop, it will expire. Each hop through a router reduces TTL by one.

Transmission Control Protocol (TCP) — A connection-oriented and reliable Transport layer protocol that is part of the TCP/IP protocol suite.

Transmission Control Protocol/Internet Protocol (TCP/IP) — A suite of protocols that allows interconnected networks to communicate with one another. It is the most common protocol in Windows networking and must be used to access the Internet.

Transport layer — The layer of the TCP/IP architecture that breaks messages into smaller packets and tracks their delivery.

User Datagram Protocol (UDP) — A connectionless, unreliable Transport layer protocol used in the TCP/IP protocol suite.

Windows Internet Naming Service (WINS) — A Windows service used to resolve NetBIOS names to IP addresses as well as store NetBIOS service information.

REVIEW QUESTIONS

1. For what type of protocol is the development process controlled by a standards committee rather than any single company or individual?

    a. open

   b. standard

   c. dynamic

   d. legacy

2. Which of the following protocols is required for Active Directory?

   a. IPX/SPX

   b. NetBEUI

   c. IPv4

   d. IPv6

3. Which of the following network services is used by Active Directory for service location?

   a. DHCP

   b. DNS

   c. WINS

   d. TCP/IP

4. What is the total number of octets in an IP address?

   a. 2

   b. 4

   c. 8

   d. 16

5. What is the total number of bits in an octet?

   a. 2

   b. 4

   c. 8

   d. 16

6. Which of the following defines the part of an IP address that is the host ID and the part that is the network ID?

   a. default gateway

   b. DNS server

   c. WINS server

   d. subnet mask

7. What is the default subnet mask for a Class C IP address?

   a. 255.0.0.0

   b. 255.255.0.0

   c. 255.255.255.0

   d. 0.255.255.255

8. A computer uses a default gateway if the destination IP address is on a different network. True or False?

9. Which of the following is another name for default gateway?
   a. router
   b. switch
   c. hub
   d. host

10. IP address 227.43.76.109 is an example of which of the following classes of IP addresses?
    a. Class A
    b. Class B
    c. Class C
    d. Class D
    e. Class E

11. Which of the following was introduced to make Internet routing and the assignment of IP addresses more efficient?
    a. subnet masks
    b. switches
    c. DHCP
    d. CIDR

12. What is the total number of octets that are part of the host ID for the IP address 176.167.98.3/24?
    a. 1
    b. 2
    c. 3
    d. 4

13. What type of server does a Windows client use to resolve NetBIOS names to IP addresses?
    a. DNS
    b. DHCP
    c. WINS
    d. Remote Access

14. Which transport protocol establishes a connection with the remote host before sending data?
    a. UDP
    b. TCP
    c. ARP
    d. FTP

15. Which protocol supports the use of multicast groups?

    a. UDP

    b. TCP

    c. ARP

    d. ICMP

    e. IGMP

16. Which of the following is not an Application layer protocol?

    a. FTP

    b. HTTP

    c. IP

    d. Telnet

    e. SMTP

17. Which Network layer protocol is responsible for routing packets on the network?

    a. TCP

    b. UDP

    c. IP

    d. ICMP

    e. IGMP

18. ARP is used to resolve IP addresses to what?

    a. NetBIOS names

    b. MAC addresses

    c. fully qualified domain names

    d. Internet addresses

19. When a packet crosses a router, what happens to the packet's TTL?

    a. nothing

    b. It is decremented by one.

    c. It is incremented by one.

    d. It is reset to the default TTL.

20. You ping a host that is on a remote subnet. When you view your ARP cache, which MAC address do you see for the remote host?

    a. your own MAC address

    b. the MAC address of the remote host

    c. the MAC address of the router

    d. all of the above

21. A network card operates at which layer of the IP stack?

    a. Application

    b. Transport

    c. Internet

    d. Network Interface

22. Which of the following statements regarding TCP are false?

    a. TCP is a connection-oriented protocol.

    b. TCP uses a three-way handshake to establish a connection to the remote host.

    c. Packets lost during transit are re-sent.

    d. HTTP and POP3 use TCP.

    e. none of the above

23. Which of the following statements regarding e-mail protocols are true? (Choose all that apply.)

    a. SMTP is only used by clients to send e-mail.

    b. POP3 allows the user to view multiple folders.

    c. IMAP4 can be configured to download only mail headers.

    d. POP3 stores all e-mail messages on the server.

24. Which port is used by HTTP?

    a. 21

    b. 23

    c. 25

    d. 53

    e. 80

    f. 110

25. Which Transport layer protocol is most likely to be used for streaming media?

    a. TCP

    b. DNS

    c. UDP

    d. HTTP

    e. ARP

CASE PROJECTS

Case Project 2-1: IP Troubleshooting

One of your colleagues, Jeff, at Arctic University has just installed a new server in a student lab. The network ID for the lab is 172.20.10.0/24. The address for the lab router is 172.20.1.1.

Standard policies dictate that you must patch the server up to current levels before allowing students to use the server. Jeff has attempted to access patches that are stored on the server utilities.arctic.local and was unable to connect. He has also attempted to ping utilities.arctic.local and was unsuccessful.

What are the potential IP configuration issues that could be causing this problem?

Case Project 2-2: Planning Application Layer Protocols

Because Arctic University is in a remote part of the north, Internet access has not been available. Now, thanks to a new satellite system, you will be able to receive high-speed Internet access from ZAP Internet Services, despite your location.

One firewall that you are evaluating has the ability to control network traffic at the Application layer. As part of your own planning process, list the Application layer protocols that you would allow through the firewall, those you would block, and your reasons for doing so.

Case Project 2-3: Slow Internet Access

Bob Jones, an Arts professor, has written an e-mail message to you complaining about the speed of his Internet connection. He regularly downloads large files from a particular Web site. Downloads from this Web site regularly pause for 10 to 15 seconds, then resume. This does not happen when he downloads information from other Web sites. Write an e-mail response to Bob explaining the likely cause of the problem and what you can do to correct it.

Case Project 2-4: Planning Physical Layer Protocols

Your supervisor has been approached by the head of the Arts faculty about redesigning the physical infrastructure for the network. Most of the Arts professors have laptop computers but are unable to use them in the classrooms because there are no LAN hookups. The offices of the Arts professors are wired with twisted-pair (Cat 5e) cabling. Write a short report with your recommendations for the Network Interface layer protocols that should be implemented to support the professors.

3

PLANNING NETWORK DATA FLOW

After reading this chapter, you will be able to:

- ♦ Describe the three types of network traffic
- ♦ Understand unique characteristics of Ethernet
- ♦ Use physical components of a network to control data flow
- ♦ Monitor network performance
- ♦ Optimize network settings
- ♦ Use network troubleshooting utilities

To consistently plan reliable networks, you must understand how data moves on the network and how your choice of different network components affects data flow. Understanding data flow allows you to identify and eliminate potential bottlenecks in a network architecture before it is deployed.

After the network plan has been implemented, it must be monitored to ensure that performance continues to be consistent. In addition, if necessary, you can restore performance levels by optimizing the network settings.

This chapter guides you through the process of planning, monitoring, and optimizing a physical network with different types of media and various network devices. In addition, it teaches you how to troubleshoot network connectivity.

TYPES OF NETWORK TRAFFIC

Network traffic is defined as packets of data that are sent on the network. Different types of network traffic are moved and controlled in different ways on an IPv4-based network. You need to understand how the different types of traffic move on the network to ensure appropriate network performance.

There are three types of IPv4 packets:

- Unicast
- Broadcast
- Multicast

Unicast Packets

Most network traffic is composed of unicast packets. A **unicast** packet is one that has been addressed to a single computer. The destination IP address in a unicast packet is a Class A, B, or C IP address that has been assigned to a single host. This type of traffic is used to communicate on the Internet and perform file and printer sharing in the network.

Network devices allow unicast packets to move from the source host to the destination host without intermediaries. Unicast packets are not blocked by hubs, switches, or routers. Because the packets have a defined destination, all these network devices move the unicast packets as directly as possible to that destination.

Switches and routers control the movement of unicast packets. Hubs allow unicast packets to propagate on the network, but do not control them. How these devices do this and why is covered in more detail in the "Physical Components" section of this chapter.

Broadcast Packets

As discussed in Chapter 2, **broadcast** packets are addressed to all computers on the local network or to all computers on a particular network. When a packet is addressed to the IP address 255.255.255.255, this is a **local broadcast**. A local broadcast is blocked by routers, but is propagated by hubs and switches.

Local broadcasts are used by many applications to announce status and ensure that all interested hosts are informed of that status. Routers use broadcasts to inform other routers about information in their routing table. In addition, ARP Request packets are addressed to the local broadcast address.

A **directed broadcast** is an IP address with all the host bits set to 1. Computers use directed broadcasts to deliver a packet to all computers on a particular subnet. This is by Wake On LAN technology to remotely start computers. An example of a directed broadcast is 192.168.10.255/24. The first three octets represent the network number; the last octet is the host portion of the address.

3

NOTE

Routers on the Internet are configured to block directed broadcasts to stop smurf attacks. A **smurf attack** involves sending a ping packet with a falsified source IP address to a directed broadcast address. The computers receiving directed broadcast respond with a ping response packet to the falsified source IP address. Effectively, this allows a hacker to send one packet and have many packets sent to the falsified source IP address. The intent is to overwhelm the computer that is using the falsified IP address.

Routers within a company can be configured to forward or block directed broadcasts. If there is no known need for directed broadcasts, then they should be blocked. However, some network management tools use directed broadcasts. If you are using one of these tools, you should configure your routers to allow directed broadcasts.

Broadcast packets are inefficient because they are processed by all hosts on a subnet. When a broadcast packet is received, it is processed by the Network Interface layer, passed up to the Internet layer, processed at the Internet layer by IP, passed up to the Application layer, and processed at the Application layer. It is only at the Application layer that a host can determine whether this packet is relevant to it. This forces many hosts that are not interested in the packet contents to process the entire packet. On a busy host, this may reduce performance levels.

NOTE

If it is not specified, the term broadcast usually refers to a local broadcast that is blocked by routers.

ACTIVITY

Activity 3-1: Analyzing a Broadcast

Time Required: 10 minutes

Objective: View the contents of a broadcast packet.

Description: In this activity, you ping a local broadcast address. You then view the contents of the packet to understand how it is delivered.

1. If necessary, start your server and log on as **Administrator**.

2. Click **Start**, point to **Administrative Tools**, and click **Network Monitor**.

3. Press **F10** to start capturing packets.

4. Click **Start**, click **Run**, type **cmd**, and then press **Enter**.

5. Type **ping 192.168.1.255** and press **Enter**. None of the hosts respond. This is normal.

6. Close the Command Prompt window.

7. In the Network Monitor window, press **F11** to stop capturing packets.

8. Press **F12** to view the captured packets.

9. Filter the display to show only ICMP packets with your IP address as the source:

   a. Click the **Display** menu, and then click **Filter**.

   b. Double-click **Protocol==Any**.

   c. Click the **Disable All** button.

   d. In the Disabled Protocols box, scroll down and double-click **ICMP:** to make it appear in the Enabled Protocols box, and then click **OK**.

   e. Double-click **ANY<-->ANY**.

   f. In the Station1 box, click your server and the IP address on the classroom network. The IP address is 192.168.1.1xx, where xx is your student number.

   g. In the Direction box, click **-->**.

   h. In the Station2 box, click **ANY**, if necessary, and then click **OK**.

   i. Click **OK**.

10. Read the captured packets that are listed in the window. Notice that four ICMP packets are listed with the description "Echo: from192.168.01.1xx to 192.168.01.255," where xx is your student number. These are the four ICMP Echo packets generated by the ping command.

11. Double-click the first packet in the list.

12. In the middle frame, double-click **Ethernet**.

13. Read the contents inside the Ethernet section of the packet. Notice that the destination MAC address is FFFFFFFFFFFF. This is the MAC address used by all broadcast packets. When a network card receives a packet with a destination MAC address of FFFFFFFFFFFF, it passes it up to IP for further evaluation.

14. Close Network Monitor. Click **No** when asked to save the capture.

Multicast Packets

Multicast packets are addressed to a group of computers using a Class D IP address. All computers that are part of a multicast group use the same multicast address. Any packets addressed to the multicast address are delivered to all computers in the multicast group.

When a computer joins a multicast group, it informs the local router by sending an IGMP Join Group Request packet via multicast. The router tracks which subnets it has multicast clients on and ensures that multicast packets are forwarded to the proper subnets.

Multicast packets are an improvement compared with broadcast packets because multicast packets are processed by all hosts up to only the Internet layer rather than up to the Application layer. This reduces the processing load on busy hosts. Many newer applications have the option to use multicasts rather than broadcasts to announce status.

A popular application that uses multicasts to reduce network traffic is Ghost. Ghost is used to copy operating systems and application software onto workstations using image files. Each

3

image file can be several GB. If five workstations are imaged with unicast packets using Ghost with a 2 GB image file, then 10 GB of network traffic is generated because each packet needs to be sent once to each workstation. However, if five workstations are imaged with multicast packets using Ghost with a 2 GB image file, then only 2 GB of network traffic is generated because all five workstations receive each packet.

Multicast packets have a TTL field that limits how far packets are delivered through the network. Most applications use a TTL of 32, which limits propagation of multicast packets to a maximum of 32 hops.

Border routers between different sections of the network can be configured to block multicast packets with a TTL less than a specified amount. This can be useful to limit multicast traffic and service discovery across wide area links.

Hubs and switches propagate multicast packets, but do not control them. Routers do control multicast traffic. How these devices do this and why is covered in more detail in the "Physical Components" section of this chapter.

ETHERNET

By far the most common network technology used for LAN connectivity is IEEE 802.3, commonly known as Ethernet. The 802.3 standard is actually a group of standards describing how Ethernet functions on different media types and at different speeds.

The popularity of Ethernet is due to its high performance and low price. The highest speed of Ethernet available in 2003 is 10 Gbps, although the most common implementations currently in use are 100 Mbps and 1 Gbps. The price of an Ethernet network card capable of 100 Mbps is as low as $15 depending on the vendor. Network cards from a competing technology called Token Ring are over $100 and operate at only 16 Mbps.

To design an Ethernet network properly, you must understand how it works. Three of the most important concepts are collisions, collision domains, and transmission modes.

Collisions

One of the defining characteristics of Ethernet is the access method used to determine which computer is allowed to send data on the network and when. Ethernet uses **Carrier Sense Multiple Access/Collision Detection (CSMA/CD)** as its access method.

In the name, "Carrier Sense" indicates that a network card listens for traffic on the network to ensure that no other computers are currently transmitting. "Multiple Access" in the name indicates that there is no defined order for the computers to transmit data. Any computer can transmit as long as no other computer is transmitting.

"Collision Detection" comes into play because there is no control over when computers transmit on an Ethernet network. Eventually, two computers will attempt to transmit at the same time. If two computers happen to transmit information on the network at the same time, then a **collision** results. When a collision occurs, the two computers that are transmitting data stop and wait for a random period of time before resending.

On a busy Ethernet network using hubs, collisions are very common and can significantly reduce the potential **throughput** of the network, which is the actual amount of data that can be transmitted on a network rather than the theoretical data-carrying capacity. For instance, a busy 10-Mbps Ethernet network may experience real throughput of only 3 to 4 Mbps due to the time spent recovering from collisions.

Collision Domains

The area of a network in which a collision can occur in is called a **collision domain**. The more computers that exist in a collision domain, the greater the likelihood of a collision occurring. One way to reduce the number of collisions on an Ethernet network is to divide it into multiple collision domains. Reducing the number of collisions results in higher throughput.

If a network uses only hubs, instead of switches and routers, then all computers are in the same collision domain. However, switches and routers have the capability to buffer and retransmit packets. Thus, each port on a switch or router is always a separate collision domain.

The actual throughput of a fully switched network approaches the full speed of the media. For instance, a busy 10-Mbps Ethernet network that is fully switched has a real throughput very close to 10 Mbps.

Transmission Modes

A transmission mode is how data is sent on the network. Ethernet networks are capable of transmitting at either half-duplex mode or full-duplex mode. A computer that is connected at **half-duplex** can send data or receive data, but cannot do both at the same time. That is, it cannot send a packet of data at the same time it is receiving another packet of data.

Full-duplex connections can transmit and receive information at the same time. This effectively doubles the throughput of the network. For instance, a server with a 100-Mbps full-duplex connection can transmit 100 Mbps and receive 100 Mbps at the same time, for a total throughput of 200 Mbps.

The average user on a network does not send and receive packets at the same time very often. Most of the time, he or she is opening only a single file from the network or saving a single file to the network. Thus, providing full-duplex connections to user desktops provides minimal benefits.

On the other hand, several users can be opening files on a network server while several other users are saving files on that same network server. A full-duplex connection to the server keeps the network traffic caused by the saving of files from interfering with the network traffic caused by opening files.

The major points on a network that can be bottlenecks are the **backbone** (a central communication point on a network that handles most of the data traffic) and network servers because many users generate traffic on them at the same time. If a half-duplex connection to a server is a bottleneck, replacing it with a full-duplex connection can up to double the amount of traffic that the server can handle. The same principle applies to a network backbone.

NOTE   A common reason for slow network connections is the failure of network cards to negotiate properly the speed and transmission mode of the network due to poor cabling or incompatibilities between equipment from different vendors. This can be fixed by manually setting the speed and transmission mode of the network card.

Activity 3-2: Viewing Ethernet Settings

ACTIVITY

Time Required: 5 minutes

Objective: View various Ethernet settings.

Description: One of your colleagues has been complaining that one of the servers he is responsible for is very slow when users access it across the network. You want to see whether his system is connecting at 10 Mbps or 100 Mbps. You also suspect that the connection may be having trouble detecting the correct transmission mode, so you force the connection to half-duplex. Doing so helps the situation because the network card stops changing modes, which interrupts data transmission.

1. If necessary, start your server and log on as **Administrator**.

2. Press **Ctrl+Alt+Del** and click the **Task Manager** button.

3. Click the **Networking** tab. At the bottom of the window, there is a list of the network cards installed in this computer and the speed at which they have connected.

4. Close Task Manager.

5. Click **Start**, point to **Control Panel**, point to **Network Connections**, right-click **Classroom**, and click **Status**.

6. The General tab in the Classroom status window also shows the current connection speed. Click the **Properties** button.

7. Click the **Configure** button to view the settings of your network adapter.

8. Click the **Advanced** tab.

9. If it is not already selected, click the item that represents your network speed in the Property box. This item may be named Connection Type, Media Type, or another similar name. The name of this item varies depending on the manufacturer of the network card.

10. Click the **Value** box to view a list of available options. The most common options available are as follows: Auto Detect, 10 Mbps Half Duplex, 10 Mbps Full Duplex, 100 Mbps Half Duplex, and 100 Mbps Full Duplex. These options vary depending on the manufacturer of the network card, and the capabilities of the network card.

11. Click the **100 Mbps Half Duplex** option in the Value box.

12. In a real-life troubleshooting situation, you would click OK. However, you do not want to save the changes. Click the **Cancel** button.

13. Click the **Close** button.

Physical Components

Data flow on a network is influenced and controlled by the physical components (or parts) that make up the network. Depending on the traffic patterns that are desired, different components need to be used.

Media

One of the most visible parts of a network is the media, which is the physical component that connects all of the devices together. Each type of media has varying benefits and limitations. The most common media types used in computer networks are twisted-pair, fiber-optic, and coaxial. Wireless connectivity has also recently become very popular.

Twisted-pair cabling is the most common type of cabling used in computer networks. When used on an Ethernet network, it can carry data at up to 1 Gbps at a maximum distance of 100 meters over a single segment. This type of cabling is inexpensive and many qualified installers are available.

Fiber-optic cabling is commonly used for network backbones in which twisted-pair cabling cannot transmit the distance that is required. When used with an Ethernet network, it can carry data at up to 10 Gbps at a maximum distance of 2 kilometers. This type of cabling is more expensive than twisted-pair and fewer qualified installers are available. Two fibers are required for each connection. One fiber is used for sending data, and the other for receiving.

Coaxial cabling was common on older Ethernet networks, but has been removed from most networks. Newer fast standards were never developed for coaxial cable and the maximum speed available is 10 Mbps. Other disadvantages of this type of cabling include the inability to transmit in full-duplex mode, and in common implementations, all computers are on a bus topology with only one collision domain. Coaxial cabling is now relatively expensive compared to twisted-pair cabling.

Wireless connectivity is not part of the Ethernet standard. However, many switches are available that have Ethernet connections and wireless capability to facilitate communication between Ethernet and wireless networks. The network cards for wireless networks are more expensive than twisted-pair, but less than the price of fiber-optic network cards. A major cost savings in wireless implementations is the lack of cabling installation. However, security is a concern.

Hubs

A **hub** acts as a central connection point on a network that allows multiple computers to communicate with each other. A hub can also be used to extend the network for greater distance. Figure 3-1 shows a hub being used in a star **topology**. A topology is the physical layout of the network.

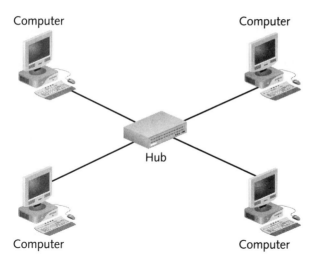

Figure 3-1 Star topology

When a computer transmits a packet on the network in Figure 3-1, the packet is received by the hub. When a hub receives the packet, it regenerates it, and sends it out to every port except the one on which it was received. Each computer receives the packet and looks at the destination MAC address. If the destination MAC address does not match the MAC address of the receiving network card, the packet is ignored. If the destination MAC address does match the MAC address of the network card, the packet is passed up to the protocol stack, usually to the IP protocol.

A hub operates at the Physical layer of the OSI model. The Physical layer of the OSI model is responsible for media characteristics and electrical signaling. A hub looks at each electrical signal as it is received and regenerates it. Regenerating each signal allows it to travel the full distance allowed by the media type. For instance, twisted-pair cabling is capable of carrying an electrical signal 100 m before the signal attenuates so much that it cannot be understood by the receiving computer. If a hub is used at 100 m, then the signal can travel another 100 m before becoming unreadable.

Because a hub deals only with electrical signals, it cannot perform tasks that require an understanding of an entire packet of information. Consequently, it cannot direct packets to a particular location because it does not understand MAC addresses or IP addresses.

All of the computers connected to a hub, or a series of hubs, belong to the same collision domain. In a large network, this results in a significant degradation of network throughput due to many collisions.

Latency

When a signal passes through a hub, it takes a small amount of time for the signal to be regenerated. The time lag, or delay, between receiving the signal and sending it out again is called **latency**. When many hubs are linked, a high level of latency is introduced for packets traveling from one end of the collision domain to the other, and the carrier sense portion of CSMA/CD becomes unreliable. When the latency is too high, the number of collisions increases because a computer at one end of the collision domain can begin sending a packet while another computer at the other end is sending a packet at the same time. A collision is the result.

On 10-Mbps Ethernet, the rule of thumb is that no more than four hubs can be daisy-chained together. (Daisy-chaining means linking components one after the other.) Daisy-chaining is shown in Figure 3-2.

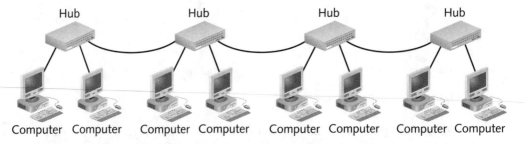

Figure 3-2   Daisy-chained 10-Mbps hubs

On 100-Mbps Ethernet, the number of hubs that can be daisy-chained depends on the type of hub. If the hubs are Class II, two of them can be linked together. If the hubs are Class I, they cannot be linked together at all. On 100-Mbps networks, switches are used to link hubs.

NOTE

Most hubs are not capable of full-duplex communication, only half-duplex.

Switches

A **switch** has several benefits over a hub:

- Each port on a switch is a separate collision domain allowing the division of large networks and a reduction in the number of collisions.

- In addition, a switch is capable of directing traffic only to the port to which the destination computer is attached, which reduces overall levels of network traffic.

- Switches are also capable of connecting dissimilar network architectures, such as Ethernet and wireless.

Switches operate at the Data Link layer of the OSI model. This means that they are capable of performing tasks that deal with full packets of data and MAC addresses. These are sometimes referred to as layer 2 switches.

A switch divides network traffic based on MAC addresses. When a switch is first turned on, it is not configured with any information about which computers are connected to which ports. When a switch does not know where to deliver a packet, it is delivered to all ports. Therefore, in the first few moments of operation, it functions very much like a hub, in that it forwards each packet received to every port except the one from which the packet came. Broadcast packets are always forwarded to all ports.

As each packet is processed by the switch, the switch tracks the source MAC address of the packet and the port on which it was received. In this way, the switch eventually builds a list that contains the location of each computer on the network. Based on this list, the switch forwards packets only to the relevant port. This enhances network throughput by reducing traffic on the overall network.

A major limitation of hubs is their lack of scalability at higher speeds. When only one or two hubs can be linked together, the network must remain quite small. Switches expand the network by creating separate collision domains on each port. When a switch receives a packet, it is buffered in the memory of the switch. This allows the switch to resend the packet if there is a collision. Many switches can be linked, or many hubs can be linked to a single switch, as shown in Figure 3-3.

Switches are capable of operating at full-duplex. This can be a major enhancement for network backbones and servers.

The internal speed of a switch is much faster than the individual ports. For instance, a switch with twenty-four 100-Mbps ports has a **backplane** speed (the internal data processing area of a switch) of 2 Gbps or faster. This allows multiple computers to communicate through the switch at their full link speed.

Many Switches Linked Together

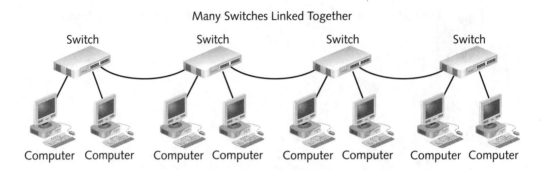

Many Hubs Linked to a Switch

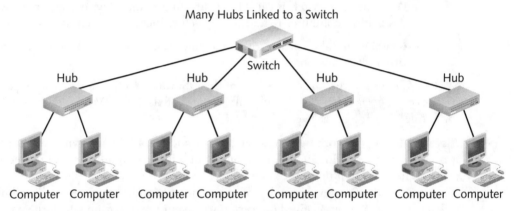

Figure 3-3   Configurations for switched networks

When you link multiple switches, ensure that there are not any segments that act as bottlenecks. To do this, make sure that all segments of your backbone run at a faster speed than links to the individual workstations or servers. Figure 3-4 shows a switched network with bottlenecks. Figure 3-5 shows a switched network without bottlenecks.

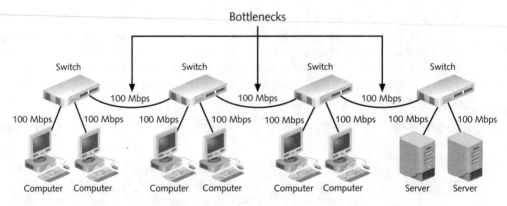

Figure 3-4   Switched network with bottlenecks

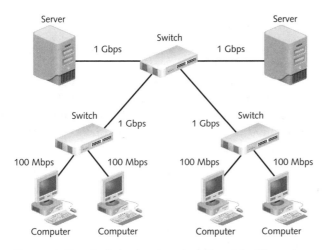

Figure 3-5   Switched network without bottlenecks

Routers

Routers are used to move traffic between networks. A router operates at the Network layer of the OSI model. This allows the control of network traffic based on logical IP addresses rather than physical characteristics such as cabling or MAC addresses.

Routers maintain a list of IP networks called a **routing table**. Note that the routing table does not contain the addresses of individual computers. This makes routers much more scalable than switches, which track each computer based on MAC addresses. Routers can control traffic for hundreds of thousands of computers, whereas switches normally can track thousands of computers.

NOTE

Routers are the only network devices that block broadcast packets. Each port on a router is also a collision domain.

Planning network routing is covered in Chapter 4. Subnetting and supernetting are also part of that chapter.

MONITORING AND OPTIMIZING NETWORK PERFORMANCE

Network performance is limited by bottlenecks. A **bottleneck** is any point in the communication process that cannot perform at the same level as other components. These bottlenecks can occur in the physical network or in server components. This part of the chapter discusses network performance problems and the tools that you can use to monitor network performance.

Network Performance Problems and Solutions

On the physical network, the most likely cause of a bottleneck is a slow segment on the backbone acting as a choke point. This slow segment may be due to a poorly designed network that includes a 10-Mbps segment in the backbone of a mixed-speed network, or a switch port may begin to fail and corrupt packets, resulting in packets being resent many times. In addition, a bad patch cable can result in ports negotiating speed at 10 Mbps instead of 100 Mbps. Solutions may include replacing broken components or redesigning the network to eliminate slow segments in the backbone.

On a server, bottlenecks can be caused by lack of capacity in the processor, RAM, storage subsystem, or network card. Which of these is likely to be a bottleneck is influenced by the role each server performs.

The processor is a bottleneck if it rises to 100% utilization and stays there for extended periods of time. If it only briefly hits 100% utilization, then it is not having a significant performance impact. If the CPU is at any level below 100%, it is not a bottleneck. To monitor CPU utilization effectively, the utilization should be logged and reviewed over time. The processor will be stressed more on an application server than on a file and print server.

To fix an overloaded processor, you can add new hardware or move some tasks to another server. An overloaded Web server can be load-balanced with an additional Web server. If an application server needs extra processing power, a second CPU or more can be added if the hardware supports it. If a server is running multiple tasks, such as SQL Server and Exchange, processor utilization can be reduced by moving SQL Server to another server.

The RAM in a server can be a bottleneck if all of the physical memory in a server is used by applications and the swap file is being used frequently. Memory use is fairly static in most situations and can be monitored on a periodic basis. Memory is stressed more on an application server than on a file and print server.

To fix a system that is low on RAM, you can simply add more RAM. Windows Server 2003 Standard Edition supports up to 4 GB of RAM, and Enterprise Edition supports up to 8 GB of RAM. Server hardware is designed only to support certain levels of RAM chosen based on the amount of RAM you require. Most single-processor and dual-processor servers support 4 GB of RAM.

The storage subsystem can be a bottleneck if there is frequent disk activity. Frequent disk activity is seen on busy file and print servers and on application servers running many queries against a database. Queued disk operations are a good indicator of a bottleneck in the storage subsystem.

The storage subsystem in most servers can be upgraded to a higher performance level. If the server is currently running IDE-based disks, they can be upgraded to SCSI. If the server is running stand-alone SCSI disks, they can be upgraded to a **RAID5** array (a disk storage system that spreads data across multiple hard drives and adds parity information) or a **stripe set** (a storage system in which data is evenly spread among hard drives with no parity information).

The network card in a server can be a bottleneck if there is too much data that needs to be transferred to the network and the card is not fast enough, or if it is a low-quality card. The average hard drive can transfer data at approximately 30 Mbps. However, a 100-Mbps network card can transfer data at only approximately 12 Mbps. This can easily result in the network card being the bottleneck on file servers. In addition, a low-quality network card cannot sustain a transfer rate of 100 Mbps. It is only able to deliver bursts of network traffic at that speed.

The network card can be upgraded in any server. A higher quality card can be added or a 100-Mbps card can be replaced with a 1-Gbps card.

The tools used to monitor network performance include:

- Protocol analyzers
- Cable testers
- Task Manager
- Performance snap-in

Protocol Analyzers

Protocol analyzers can capture network traffic and monitor network performance. Network Monitor is a limited protocol analyzer included with Windows Server 2003. Ethereal is an alternative packet analyzer that is very popular and free. Figure 3-6 shows the general information that can be gathered from Network Monitor during a capture.

When a protocol analyzer is used to capture network traffic, an administrator can look at each packet in the communication process to see where the problem is. Most administrators do not have the exact structure of IP communication memorized, but can look at the packets in the communication process and have a good guess as to what might be wrong. For instance, by reading the contents of a packet, an administrator may see an error message that an application did not display on the screen. In addition, by watching packet flow, an administrator can see which computer did not respond to the other.

Protocol analyzers run on standard workstations or laptops. To capture all of the traffic on the network, a protocol analyzer puts the network card into promiscuous mode. A network card in **promiscuous mode** allows all packets to travel up the protocol stack regardless of the destination MAC address. Otherwise, the protocol analyzer is only able to capture traffic that is addressed to the computer it is installed on.

NOTE The version of Network Monitor that is included with Windows Server 2003 does not use promiscuous mode. The version of Network Monitor that supports promiscuous mode is included in Microsoft Systems Management Server (SMS). Ethereal supports promiscuous mode.

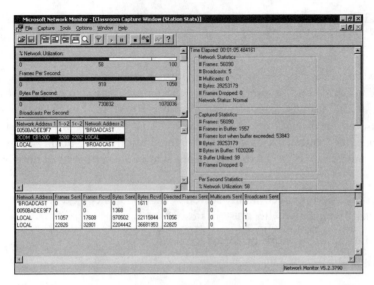

Figure 3-6   General information in Network Monitor

With the proper network card, a packet analyzer can be used to see overall network utilization and errors. Errors may give an indication of a bad network card that has started to jabber, a loose network connection, or a bad switch port.

Network card drivers that adhere to the NDIS standard filter out errors that happen on network cabling. Under normal circumstances, this is good because it stops useless information from being passed up the protocol stack. However, when using a protocol analyzer, this stops you from being able to see the errors happening on the network. To work around this problem, various vendors of protocol analyzers have developed special drivers for a few brands of network cards. Be sure to check the documentation that came with your protocol analyzer to find network cards that work best with it.

In switched networks, protocol analyzers are limited in their effectiveness. A switched network controls packet movement based on MAC addresses. Packets are sent only to the switch port to which the destination host is connected. This means that a protocol analyzer may not be able to see the packets, even in promiscuous mode. Higher quality, and more expensive, switches allow you to enable port mirroring so you can copy network traffic from one switch port to another. This allows you to use a protocol analyzer to view traffic anywhere on a switched network.

Cable Testers

A number of vendors have created physical devices that can be used to test network cabling. One of the most popular companies that produces this type of device is Fluke (*www.fluke.com*).

A cable tester checks the ability of a cable to carry the electrical signals properly that are sent by the computers. Each cable tester can verify the proper installation of only certain types of cabling. For instance, most cable testers that test twisted-pair cabling for Ethernet are not capable of testing fiber-optic cabling.

Task Manager

Task Manager is a simple tool that can be used to check memory, processor, and network utilization quickly. This is not a tool that supports long-term monitoring, but it can be used to see a point in time.

Figure 3-7 shows the Performance tab in Task Manager, which can be used to monitor memory utilization and overall processor usage. The memory statistic that is of the most concern is the Available in Physical Memory (K). When the available physical memory is low (close to zero), the swap file is used extensively. Such use is bad because a swap file is much slower than physical memory and it increases disk utilization.

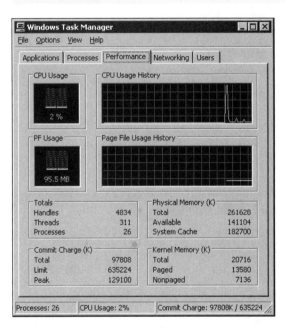

Figure 3-7   Performance tab in Task Manager

Processor utilization is a problem when it stays at 100%. To find the individual process that is causing high utilization, you can view the list of running processes on the Processes tab, as shown in Figure 3-8. On the Processes tab, you can view the percentage of processor time that each process is consuming. This guides you in deciding which applications need to be moved to a different server.

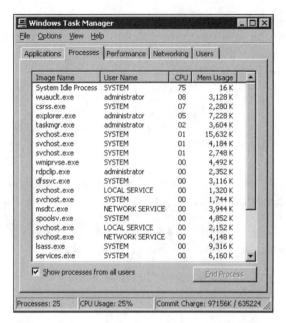

Figure 3-8   Processes tab in Task Manager

The Networking tab in Task Manager shows the percentage of network utilization for each network connection. If this percentage is consistently high, it is likely that the network speed is becoming a bottleneck.

Performance Snap-in

The Performance snap-in located in Administrative Tools can be used to generate graphs and log many Windows Server 2003 performance indicators.

Various areas of system performance that can be monitored are called objects and include Processor, Network Interface, Memory, and PhysicalDisk. Within each object are a variety of counters that can be monitored. Table 3-1 shows some of the counters you are likely to monitor.

Table 3-1   Performance snap-in counters

Object	Counter	Description
Memory	Pages/sec	The number of 4 KB pages of memory transferred to the swap file per second
PhysicalDisk	Avg. Disk Queue Length	The number of disk commands waiting to be executed
Processor	% Processor Time	The percentage utilization of the processor
Network Interface	Bytes Received/sec	The number of bytes received per second

Table 3-1 Performance snap-in counters (continued)

Object	Counter	Description
Network Interface	Bytes Sent/sec	The number of bytes sent per second
LogicalDisk	% Free Space	The percentage of free disk space on a partition or volume

The graphs generated by the Performance snap-in can capture short- and medium-term information.

For long-term monitoring, counter logs or trace logs should be used instead. Counter logs query and log the value of a counter at a defined interval. This gives a good idea of trends and long-term performance. Trace logs place information in a log file based on an event such as a page fault occurring. The information in trace logs requires a parsing tool to interpret the results. Microsoft provides Tracerpt to interpret trace logs and generate reports based on them.

To be notified when a counter hits a certain value, use alerts. These are valuable for monitoring memory usage and disk space availability. When an alert threshold has been passed, an event can be written to the event log, a network message can be set to a user, a performance log can be started, or a program can be run. By running a program, you can even send an e-mail message or page to an administrator to alert him of the problem.

ACTIVITY

Activity 3-3: Monitoring Network Performance

Time Required: 15 minutes

Objective: View network utilization using Network Monitor, Task Manager, and the Performance snap-in.

Description: You want to see how the various tools for monitoring network performance will show you a network under high utilization. To simulate a high network load, you copy the C:\I386 folder from the instructor server to your server.

1. If necessary, start your server and log on as **Administrator**.

2. Click **Start**, click **Run**, type **cmd**, and press **Enter**.

3. Type **copy \\instructor\c$\i386*.* c:\i386** and press **Enter**. If you are asked to overwrite a file, type **a** for all and press **Enter** so that you will not be asked again. This file copy should last several minutes, giving you enough time to complete the exercise. However, if the file copy finishes before the exercise is complete, perform this step again.

4. Press **Ctrl+Alt+Del** and click **Task Manager**.

5. Click the **Networking** tab. The utilization level for the Classroom interface should be 50% or higher.

6. Close Task Manager.

7. Click **Start**, point to **Administrative Tools**, and click **Network Monitor**.

8. Press **F10** to begin capturing data. The capture screen shows overall network utilization on the network card being monitored, as well as the frames per second and bytes per second.

9. Press **F11** to stop the capture.

10. Close Network Monitor. Click **No** when asked to save the capture.

11. Click **Start**, point to **Administrative Tools**, and click **Performance**.

12. Right-click the graph and click **Properties**.

13. Click the **Remove** button three times to remove the existing counters.

14. Click the **Add** button.

15. Click the **Performance object** drop-down arrow, and click **Network Interface**.

16. Click the **Select counters from** drop-down arrow, and then click **Bytes Received/sec**.

17. In the Select instances from list box, select the network interface that is your Classroom connection. If necessary, view the properties of the Classroom connection to confirm.

18. To view more information about this performance counter, click **Explain**. To see a list of all the perfomance counters available for Windows Server 2003 and their explanations, see *http://www.microsoft.com/technet/prodtechnol/windowsserver 2003/proddocs/deployguide/counters_overview.asp*.

19. Click the **Add** button, and click **Close**.

20. Click **OK** to view the graph. Remember, if the file copy is completed, redo Step 3.

21. When you are finished watching the graph, close the Performance snap-in.

22. Close the Command Prompt window to stop the file copy.

OPTIMIZING NETWORK SETTINGS

Implementing a new network architecture with higher bandwidth is often the most obvious solution to increasing network throughput. However, the cost of implementing a new network architecture is often quite high once the costs of new cabling, hubs, switches, and routers are included. In certain situations, gains can be made by modifying the network configuration of the servers, at no cost. This part of the chapter concentrates on explaining those network configuration options.

Utilizing the Binding Process

Binding is the process in which a network protocol is configured to use a network adapter. When a protocol is added to a network connection, it is bound to the network adapter and the services that are part of that connection.

Windows Server 2003 allows you to optimize your network connectivity by adjusting the order in which protocols are used and defining the priority of network services. These settings are found in the Advanced Settings dialog box, as shown in Figure 3-9.

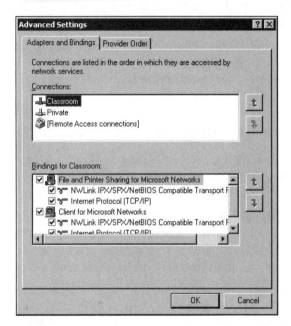

Figure 3-9   Adapters and Bindings tab

The Adapters and Bindings tab allows you to adjust the bindings for your adapters. For each adapter, you can choose which clients and services are bound and which network protocols are bound to each client or service. You can also choose the order of the bindings.

When multiple protocols are bound to a single service, the service attempts to use each protocol in order until it is successful. The first protocol listed is the first used. The protocols used most often should be at the top of the list.

As an example of binding optimization, you could remove the NWLink protocol from File and Printer Sharing for Microsoft Networks if you decided that it was not required. This would mean that clients could access shared folders and printers on this server only if they were using TCP/IP. However, this server would still be able to access other NWLink-based resources on Microsoft networks because NWLink would still be bound to the Client for Microsoft Networks.

Minimizing Network Protocols

If a busy server is configured to use many protocols, such as TCP/IP, IPX/SPX, and AppleTalk, server performance suffers. The server requires processing power to determine which protocol should be used each time it communicates. If there are more protocols configured on the server, more processing power is required.

Some services advertise their availability on the network. If these services are installed on a server with multiple protocols, the service advertises availability using all of the protocols that are bound on the server. This means that a server with three protocols generates three times as much service advertisement traffic as a server with one protocol.

Carefully analyze your protocol requirements. If a protocol is required to support older clients, explore centralizing all services using that protocol on a single server. This reduces the service advertisements produced by other servers and reduces the processing required on other servers.

Implementing the Maximum Transmission Unit (MTU) Setting

The **Maximum Transmission Unit (MTU)** setting is used by Windows Server 2003 to set the maximum packet size that TCP/IP will try to negotiate when creating a TCP connection. The default MTU setting is 1,500 bytes on an Ethernet network.

When a TCP connection is created, only the two endpoints in the conversation negotiate the MTU. It is possible that network segments between the two endpoints will have a smaller MTU. In this situation, TCP/IP is designed to fragment the original large packet into smaller packets that will be able to travel across the network segment with a smaller MTU.

Unfortunately, fragmentation generates a major decline in network performance. To avoid this, most servers perform a process called **Path MTU Discovery (P-MTU-D)** as defined in RFC 1191. Servers performing P-MTU-D set the Don't Fragment bit on in all of their packets. When a packet that has Don't Fragment turned on reaches a router and the packet is too large for the next network segment, the router responds back with an ICMP Can't Fragment error. The ICMP Can't Fragment error contains the MTU that is allowed. The server will then start using this as the new MTU.

NOTE   Windows Server 2003 performs P-MTU-D by default, but it can be disabled by setting the registry key HKEY_LOCAL_MACHINE\SYSTEM\CurrentControlSet\ Services\Tcpip\ Parameters\EnablePMTUDiscovery to a value of 0.

The P-MTU-D process can be broken by misconfigured firewalls and routers that block ICMP Can't Fragment errors. This results in any packets larger than the remote router MTU being discarded and no error message returning to the server. When the server does not receive an error, it eventually assumes that the connection is lost, and it will be unable to communicate across the segment with the smaller MTU.

To work around this problem, you can reduce the size of the MTU on the server or enable Black Hole router detection. The MTU is set in the registry key HKEY_LOCAL_MACHINE\ SYSTEM\CurrentControlSet\Services\Tcpip\Parameters\Interfaces*AdapterID*\MTU. Black Hole router detection is enabled by setting the registry key HKEY_LOCAL _MACHINE\ SYSTEM\CurrentControlSet\Services\Tcpip\Parameters\EnablePMTUBHDetect to a value of 1. Black Hole router detection is disabled by default.

NOTE   The oversized MTU error is most often seen when using Internet sharing routers that use PPPoE. They take a 1,500 byte packet and add a PPPoE header to it. This makes the packet too large to be handled by the ISP. When PPPoE software is installed directly on Windows, the PPPoE software drops the MTU to allow for the PPPoE header.

TROUBLESHOOTING UTILITIES

Windows Server 2003 has a wide variety of utilities that can be used to troubleshoot network problems. It is important to understand not only what each tool does, but also when it is appropriate to use. This part of the chapter covers these utilities in detail.

Ping

Ping is one of the most common troubleshooting tools. It sends an ICMP Echo packet to a host. That host then responds with an ICMP Echo Reply packet. This process confirms that a host is active at an IP address. However, it does not confirm that any particular service is functioning properly on a remote host. Ping is not a reliable indicator of whether Internet hosts are functioning because many firewalls filter out ping packets.

Ping can also be used to test for DNS resolution problems. When you ping a DNS name, it is resolved to an IP address. If you can ping the IP address of a host, but not the DNS name, you are experiencing DNS resolution problems. This may be due to incorrect DNS server configuration or incorrectly configured IP settings on the host.

Network congestion can cause erratic network problems. Ping can be used as a crude tool to measure network congestion. When you ping a host, the Ping utility indicates how long it took for the remote host to respond. If the response time is significantly longer than normal, network congestion may be the culprit.

Table 3-2 shows some of the more useful options for the ping command.

Table 3-2 Ping utility options

Option	Description
-a	Performs a reverse lookup on an IP address
-i *TTL*	Sets the TTL to a specific number of hops
-n *count*	Sets the number of ICMP Echo packets to send
-t	Continues pinging the remote host until stopped with Ctrl+C

Tracert

The Tracert utility is used to view the routers that a packet passes through between the local host and a remote host. Tracert begins by sending an ICMP Echo packet with a TTL of 1 to the remote host. After 1 hop, an ICMP Time Exceeded packet is returned to the local host. Tracert uses the source IP address of the ICMP Time Exceeded packet as the first router hop. Tracert then sends additional packets incrementing the TTL by one until the remote host is reached.

When using the Tracert utility to troubleshoot Internet connectivity, the key is to look for the router that stops responding. This is the router that is preventing you or your users from accessing a particular server. You then are in the position to identify who is responsible for the problem router: you, your ISP, or someone else. If the router is not controlled by you or your ISP, there is not much you can do about it other than wait until it is fixed.

Tracert provides the response time for each router in the path. This can be used as a tool to identify where a network is congested. The router that shows a significantly increased response time is suffering performance problems. The problems may be due to too much traffic, a bad cable connection, or a denial of service attack.

Pathping

The Pathping utility provides basically the same functionality as the Tracert utility. It can be used to view the routers used to move a packet from the local host to a remote host. However, the Pathping utility sends 100 packets to each router in the path to provide a more accurate measure of response times. In addition, it indicates the percentage of packets to which a router responded. A low response rate for a router may be an indicator of network congestion.

TIP The Pathping utility can take up to 10 minutes to complete testing because of the large number of packets generated. For a quick overview of the same information, use the Tracert utility instead.

ACTIVITY

Activity 3-4: Testing for Network Congestion with Pathping

Time Required: 10 minutes

Objective: Using the pathping command, test to see if the network is congested.

Description: One of the professors has indicated that the Web site *www.yahoo.com* seems to be very slow today. He has asked you if there is anything you can do about it. To test the problem, you use the pathping command.

1. If necessary, start your server and log on as **Administrator**.

2. Click **Start**, click **Run**, type **cmd**, and press **Enter**.

3. Type **pathping www.yahoo.com** and press **Enter**. First, pathping performs a tracert to *www.yahoo.com* to identify the routers. Then, it pings each router in the path 100 times to compile statistics. It is likely that this process will take about 5 minutes.

4. After pathping is complete, read the results on the screen. The first column of information is the hop number. Hop number 1 is the first router on the path to *www.yahoo.com*. The second column is the amount of time that it took for the remote server to respond to ICMP Echo packets. If a one router has a significantly higher time than the other, it is likely congested. The third column is the percentage of packets that were lost in transit anywhere in the path. Ideally, this should be 0. The fourth column is the percentage of packets that were lost by this router. Ideally, this should be 0. The fifth column is the IP address and DNS name (if available) of the router.

5. Close the Command Prompt window.

Nbtstat

Nbtstat is used to view NetBIOS over TCP/IP statistics. It can view the list of NetBIOS services available on the local host or remote hosts, and it can view the local NetBIOS name cache. Viewing the local NetBIOS name cache is useful to find the IP address of a host that you have been accessing via its NetBIOS name.

If the IP address of a computer has been recently changed, incorrect information may be held in the NetBIOS name cache. In this case, the nbtstat command can be used to clear the NetBIOS name cache. It can also be used to reload an lmhosts file that contains entries that are loaded into cache. This is useful for changing the contents of an lmhosts file without rebooting.

Table 3-3 shows some useful options for the nbtstat command.

Table 3-3   Nbtstat utility options

Option	Description
-A *IPAddress*	Lists the NetBIOS services of a remote computer defined by its IP address
-n	Lists the NetBIOS services of the local computer
-c	Lists the contents of the local NetBIOS name cache
-R	Empties and reloads the NetBIOS name cache, which reloads entries in lmhosts with the PRE tab
-RR	Releases and refreshes the names registered with a WINS server

Netstat

Netstat is used to display TCP connection information as well as various IP statistics, such as the number of UDP and TCP packets and the IP routing table. The ability to view TCP connections is useful for finding **rogue services** (the unauthorized services that may have been installed by an administrator or a hacker) that have been installed on your server and viewing the remote hosts that are connected to the services on your server.

Figure 3-10 shows the results of the netstat –a command. The output shows all TCP connections and listening services. Without the -a option, it would have shown only active TCP connections.

The connection state listening indicates that a service is using the port and listening for connections. The connection state established indicates that a connection is active and being used for communication. The connection state close_wait indicates that the connection is in the process of closing. The connection state time_wait indicates that the connection is closed and will expire in 240 seconds. All listening UDP ports are listed but do not show status because UDP ports are connectionless.

Figure 3-10   Results of netstat -a

Network Diagnostics

Network Diagnostics can be used to view a variety of settings on your server. It builds a list of information about your server and tests services such as DNS and WINS to ensure that they are available. Figure 3-11 shows the results of Network Diagnostics.

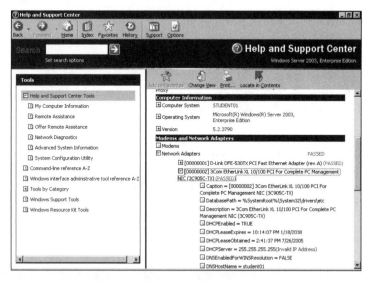

Figure 3-11   Network Diagnostics results

Activity 3-5: Viewing TCP Connections with Netstat

Time Required: 5 minutes

Objective: View open connections and running services with the Netstat utility and view the current network configuration with Network Diagnostics.

Description: You are not sure which services are running on your server and are using the netstat command to view the TCP connections that are currently active as well as those listening for connections. You also use Network Diagnostics to view your current network configuration.

1. If necessary, start your server and log on as **Administrator**.

2. Click **Start**, click **Run**, type **cmd**, and press **Enter**.

3. Type **netstat** and press **Enter**. This shows all of the TCP connections that are currently active. However, it does not show all of the services that are waiting for connections.

4. Type **netstat –a** and press **Enter**. This shows all of the TCP connections that are currently active as well as the services that are waiting for connections.

5. Close the Command Prompt window.

6. To start Network Diagnostics, click **Start**, click **Help and Support**, click **Tools**, click **Help and Support Center Tools**, and click **Network Diagnostics**.

7. Click **Scan your system**.

8. Read the results in the right pane. Notice the wide range of information that is returned.

9. Close the Help and Support Center window.

Ipconfig

Most of the time, the ipconfig command is used to view IP configuration information. However, it can also be used to release and renew IP addresses that are obtained from a DHCP server.

A less known function of the ipconfig command is flushing the DNS cache. Windows Server 2003 caches all DNS lookups. If you are making changes to DNS, you may need to remove these entries from the cache before the TTL expires. The TTL of each entry varies depending on the DNS server configuration.

Table 3-4 shows useful options for the Ipconfig utility.

Table 3-4   Ipconfig utility options

Option	Description
/all	Shows all IP configuration information
/release	Releases an IP address leased from a DHCP server
/renew	Renews an IP address leased from a DHCP server
/dnsflush	Deletes the contents of the DNS client cache
/displaydns	Displays the contents of the DNS client cache
/registerdns	Reregisters DNS information via dynamic DNS

NOTE The /registerdns option registers only the host record in DNS. To force registration of the service records required for domain controllers, you restart the netlogon service.

Netsh

Netsh is a command-line utility that can be used to modify and view IP configuration information. It is useful for remotely managing IP configuration when Terminal Services is unavailable and via scripts.

TIP

When in netsh, you can use ? to view a list of available commands.

3

Nslookup

Nslookup is used to query DNS servers. When you need to confirm that a DNS server is functioning properly, this utility is indispensable. It can be configured to query any DNS server you want, making it easy to confirm the configuration of a particular DNS server that you think may be having problems.

CHAPTER SUMMARY

❑ There are three types of network traffic: unicast, broadcast, and multicast. Unicast packets are addressed to a single host. Broadcast packets are addressed to all hosts on a network. Multicast packets are addressed to a group of computers.

❑ Ethernet is the most common network architecture. One of the defining Ethernet characteristics is CSMA/CD.

❑ A collision domain is an area of a network where a collision can happen. More computers in a collision domain results in a higher number of collisions and lower throughput.

❑ The two transmission modes are half-duplex and full-duplex. Full-duplex is normally not possible when using hubs; switches or routers are required instead.

❑ Hubs operate at the Physical layer of the OSI model and send received data to all ports except the one from which it was received. All computers connected to a hub are part of the same collision domain.

❑ Switches operate at the Data Link layer of the OSI model and control data flow based on MAC addresses. Each port of a switch is a collision domain.

❑ Routers operate at the Network layer of the OSI model and control data flow based on IP addresses.

❑ The areas likely to be network performance bottlenecks are server processor utilization, server RAM, server storage subsystems, and network speed. Tools used to find bottlenecks include protocol analyzers, cable testers, Task Manager, and the Performance snap-in.

❑ You can optimize network settings by adjusting bindings, minimizing the number of protocols, and adjusting the MTU.

❑ IP troubleshooting utilities included in Windows Server 2003 are as follows: Ping, Tracert, Pathping, Nbtstat, Netstat, Network Diagnostics, Ipconfig, Netsh, and Nslookup.

KEY TERMS

backbone — A central communication point on a network that handles most of the data traffic.

backplane — The internal data processing area of a switch. This operates at a much faster speed than the individual ports to allow multiple conversations to pass through the switch at once.

binding — The process of configuring a network adapter to use a protocol. In Windows Server 2003, bindings are controlled by NDIS.

bottleneck — A point in the communication process that is slower than the others. Eliminating a bottleneck speeds up a process.

broadcast — A packet that is addressed to all computers on a network. A broadcast for the local network is addressed to 255.255.255.255.

Carrier Sense Multiple Access/Collision Detection (CSMA/CD) — The access method used by Ethernet networks to decide which computer can communicate on the network and when.

coaxial — An older type of cabling that used a single conducting core to transmit data. The cabling for cable TV is a type of coaxial cable.

collision — The result of two computers transmitting data on a CSMA/CD network at the same time.

collision domain — The area of a network in which a collision can occur when two computers communicate. Each port of a switch or router is a separate collision domain.

directed broadcast — A broadcast packet that can be routed to a particular network. The address is composed on the network address with all of the host bits set to 1.

fiber-optic — A type of cabling that uses glass fiber for a conducting core. This type of cabling is very difficult to tap into.

full-duplex — A transmission mode in which a computer can send and receive data at the same time.

half-duplex — A transmission mode in which a computer can transmit or receive data, but not both at the same time.

hubs — A device that propagates all packets that receive it. Hubs operate at the Physical layer of the OSI model and forward packets to all ports except the one on which they received the packets.

latency — The time lag between a network device receiving a signal and sending it out again.

local broadcast — A broadcast packet addressed to the IP address 255.255.255.255. This is received by all computers on the local network.

Maximum Transmission Unit (MTU) — The largest size of packet that Windows Server 2003 will create. By default, this is defined by the network architecture being used. The default MTU for Ethernet is 1,500 bytes.

multicast — A packet that is addressed to a specific group of computers rather than a single computer. Multicast addresses range from 224.0.0.0 to 239.255.255.255.

Path MTU Discovery (P-MTU-D) — A process used by servers to determine the largest MTU supported by all networks between the server and a remote host. This is done to eliminate packet fragmentation.

promiscuous mode — A network card mode in which all packets are passed up the protocol stack regardless of the destination MAC address.

RAID5 — A disk storage system that spreads data across multiple hard drives and adds parity information. A single disk in a RAID5 set can fail with no loss of data.

rogue services — The unauthorized services that may have been installed by an administrator or a hacker.

routers — The network devices that operate at the Network layer of the OSI model and control packet movement based on IP addresses. Routers maintain a list of IP networks, not individual hosts.

routing table — A list of IP networks maintained by a router. Routers use this table to look up where packets should be forwarded.

smurf attack — An attack in which ping request packets with a false source IP address are sent to a directed broadcast address. All hosts that receive the directed broadcast respond by sending a ping reply to the false source IP address, resulting in a denial of service attack on the false source IP address.

stripe set — A storage system in which data is evenly spread among hard drives with no parity information. If any disk in a stripe set fails, all data is lost.

switches — A network device that operates at the Data Link layer of the OSI model and control the movement of packets based on MAC addresses. Switches propagate broadcasts, but control unicast packets.

throughput — The actual amount of data that can be transmitted on a network rather than the theoretical data-carrying capacity.

topology — The physical layout of the network and how signals travel on the network.

twisted-pair — A type of cable that is composed of pairs of wires, with each pair twisted together. The most common variety of twisted pair cabling is Category 5 Enhanced, which has four twisted pairs.

unicast — A packet addressed to a single IP host.

REVIEW QUESTIONS

1. Which type of packet is addressed to all of the computers on a network?

   a. unicast

   b. broadcast

   c. multicast

   d. netcast

2. Which type of packet is addressed to a group of computers that can exist on multiple networks?

   a. unicast

   b. broadcast

   c. multicast

   d. netcast

3. The IP address 192.168.30.255 is an example of which type of packet?

   a. unicast

   b. broadcast

   c. multicast

   d. netcast

4. The IP address 55.109.255.255 is an example of which type of packet?

   a. unicast

   b. broadcast

   c. multicast

   d. netcast

5. Which access method is used by Ethernet?

   a. token passing

   b. directed broadcast

   c. CSMA/CD

   d. CSMA/CA

6. The fewer computers that exist in a collision domain, the slower the network. True or False?

7. Which of the following options is the least likely to impact network performance?

   a. upgrading the network backbone to full-duplex

   b. upgrading user desktop connections to full-duplex

   c. replacing all switches with hubs

   d. upgrading the network architecture from 10 Mbps to 100 Mbps

8. Which type of media has the most severe security concerns?

   a. twisted-pair

   b. fiber-optic

   c. coaxial

   d. wireless

9. Which type of media can carry Ethernet signals up to 2 kilometers?

    a. twisted-pair

    b. fiber-optic

    c. coaxial

    d. wireless

3

10. Hubs are used with which topology?

    a. ring

    b. bus

    c. star

    d. mesh

11. What factor limits the number of hubs that can be daisy-chained together?

    a. latency

    b. number of ports

    c. MAC address uniqueness

    d. duplex level

12. Which type of device creates separate collision domains on each port? (Choose all that apply.)

    a. hub

    b. switch

    c. router

    d. server

13. Which type of device controls data flow based on MAC addresses?

    a. hub

    b. switch

    c. router

    d. server

14. How can you upgrade the performance of a server storage subsystem? (Choose all that apply.)

    a. Upgrade IDE disks to SCSI disks.

    b. Eliminate unnecessary protocols.

    c. Upgrade SCSI disks to RAID5.

    d. Upgrade SCSI disks to IDE disks.

15. At what percentage of utilization does the processor become a bottleneck?

   a. 25%

   b. 50%

   c. 75%

   d. 100%

16. Which performance monitoring tool can be used to capture network packets and view their contents?

   a. protocol analyzer

   b. cable tester

   c. Task Manager

   d. Performance snap-in

17. Which performance monitoring tools can be used to view processor utilization? (Choose all that apply.)

   a. protocol analyzer

   b. cable tester

   c. Task Manager

   d. Performance snap-in

18. Which process is used by servers to discover the largest MTU that is supported across all network segments?

   a. ICMP

   b. Path MTU Discovery

   c. Quality of Service (QoS)

   d. PPPoE

19. Which troubleshooting utility can be used to view the routers between the local host and a remote host? (Choose all that apply.)

   a. Ping

   b. Tracert

   c. Pathping

   d. Netstat

   e. Network Diagnostics

   f. Ipconfig

20. Which troubleshooting utility can be used to view the services that are listening for TCP connections?

a. Ping

b. Tracert

c. Pathping

d. Netstat

e. Network Diagnostics

f. Ipconfig

3

Case Projects

CASE PROJECTS

Case Project 3-1: Planning an Ethernet Network

Arctic University is opening a new satellite location and it has been decided that it will use a combination of Ethernet and wireless networks. The location will be composed of 4 computer labs, 20 classrooms, and 50 offices for administrative staff.

1. What type of media would be most appropriate for the network backbone? At what speed would it operate?

2. What type of media would be most appropriate for the 50 administrative offices? At what speed would it operate? How does this relate to the speed of the backbone?

3. Where would you most likely use wireless connectivity?

4. What types of devices would you use in this network? What benefits would you gain from using switches in the labs rather than hubs? When might these be important?

CASE PROJECTS

Case Project 3-2: Enhancing Network Speed

The Arts college at Arctic University is configured with an Ethernet network on twisted-pair cabling. Over the last few years, two new computer labs with 50 computers each have been added to the network. In addition, all professors now have computers in their offices. The only network devices currently being used are hubs.

In past years, you have had some complaints that the network is slow, but this year there have been many complaints. What can you do to improve network throughput and why will this improve performance?

CASE PROJECTS

Case Project 3-3: Network Troubleshooting

One professor has just brought his personal laptop into the office and is unable to access any of the network resources. He indicates that he has tried everything and still cannot access the network servers or the Internet. You let him know that you will be right over to his office. What troubleshooting tools will you use? For what purpose will you use each of them?

Case Project 3-4: Monitoring Network Performance

You have recently implemented a new Windows Server 2003, Enterprise Edition file server. Accessing data on this server seems to be slower than accessing data off the other servers running Windows Server 2003. What are the potential sources of slow data transfer? How would you confirm the problem and how would you solve it?

4

PLANNING AND CONFIGURING ROUTING AND SWITCHING

After reading this chapter, you will be able to:

♦ Build IP networks

♦ Configure Windows Server 2003 as a router

♦ Create and configure demand-dial connections

♦ Understand the purpose of virtual LANs

♦ Implement Network Address Translation

♦ Work with Internet Connection Sharing

♦ Configure Internet Connection Firewall

♦ Plan Internet connectivity

An understanding of IP routing concepts is essential for all network administrators today. Whether you are troubleshooting a wide area network or planning Internet connectivity, knowing how routing, NAT, and firewalls are configured will help you perform your job.

This chapter explores subnetting and supernetting IP networks, as well as configuring Windows Server 2003 as a router. In addition, Internet connectivity concepts such as Network Address Translation, firewalls, and proxies are covered.

BUILDING A SUBNETTED IP NETWORK

A single network is appropriate for many small and midsized companies. However, larger companies with multiple physical locations or a very large single location usually need to use multiple smaller networks. The process of breaking a single large IP network into smaller networks is called subnetting. The main benefit of subnetting is network traffic control.

When planning subnets, you must be sure to create the subnets with the proper number of hosts and networks. To calculate these, you must be familiar with the binary numbering system.

Supernetting is the opposite process of subnetting. It is used to combine multiple small networks into one large network. This process is used when one large network cannot be obtained from an ISP.

Binary Numbering and TCP/IP

IP addresses are expressed in dotted decimal notation. An example of such notation is 192.168.1.10. Most utilities and other software use IP addresses in this format as well. Internally, however, a computer looks at an IP address as a single group of 32 **binary** digits. The subnet mask—which is another 32-bit number—determines which **bits** (single binary digits) are part of the network ID and which bits are part of the host ID.

Decimal Numbering

Decimal is the numbering system you use on a daily basis. It is a base-ten numbering system, which means that each digit can be one of 10 different values. The decimal system uses the values from 0 to 9 for each digit.

NOTE In this section, decimal numbering is explained in detail. You may think that you've got this whole counting thing down and don't need a review, but this review is included because most people don't remember the patterns that are involved. I've found that without such a review, students tend to have difficulty understanding the binary numbering system.

When counting in decimal, you start with a single digit. Starting with 0, you increment that digit by 1 until it reaches the maximum value of 9. To further increase the value, you must add a digit to the left one column (or space) with a value of 1 and set the original digit to 0. This gives a value of 10. This pattern repeats as the rightmost digit reaches 9 again. To further increase 19, you increment the left digit by 1 and set the right digit to 0. This gives a value of 20. Similarly, when the value has reached 99, to further increase it you add a digit to the left with a value of 1, and set the other two digits to 0. This gives a value of 100. Table 4-1 shows counting examples in decimal.

Table 4-1   Counting in decimal

Example 1	Example 2	Example 3	Example 4
7	17	97	197
8	18	98	198
9	19	99	199
10	20	100	200
11	21	101	201

4

The base of the numbering system determines the overall value of each digit. In the example shown in Table 4-2, each column has a particular value. The value of each column in a numbering system is the base of the numbering system (10 in decimal) to the power of the column number. The numbering of the columns starts with 0. Therefore, the value of the first column in the decimal numbering system is ten to the zero power ($10^0=1$), the value of the second column in the decimal numbering system is ten to the first power ($10^1=10$), and the value of the third column in the decimal numbering system is ten to the second power ($10^2=100$). Table 4-2 shows the values of each column in the decimal numbering system.

Table 4-2   Decimal column values

Column Number	4	3	2	1	0
Value	10^4	10^3	10^2	10^1	10^0
Expanded value	10000	1000	100	10	1

Any number to the power of zero has a value of 1.

NOTE

Binary Numbering

You don't normally use binary when configuring and working with computers. Values expressed in binary are very long compared with values expressed in decimal and are difficult to work with. However, subnetting is based on binary. To understand subnetting, you must understand binary.

Binary is a base-two numbering system, which means that there are only two potential values for each digit, 0 and 1. Binary counting works on the same principle as counting in decimal. As each column reaches its maximum value, the digit to the left is incremented and the digits to the right are set to 0. However, in binary, the maximum value is reached much faster. Table 4-3 shows an example of binary counting and the equivalent numbers in decimal notation.

Table 4-3 Binary counting

Binary	Decimal Equivalent
0000	0
0001	1
0010	2
0011	3
0100	4
0101	5
0110	6
0111	7
1000	8

In binary, the value of each digit is still determined by the base of the numbering system. As in the previous example, the value of each column is the base of the numbering system to the power of the column number. Table 4-4 shows the values of each column in the binary numbering system.

Table 4-4 Binary column values

Column Number	7	6	5	4	3	2	1	0
Value	2^7	2^6	2^5	2^4	2^3	2^2	2^1	2^0
Value in decimal	128	64	32	16	8	4	2	1

Conversion Between Binary and Decimal

Because most IP address configuration is done with dotted decimal notation, you need to convert any subnetting work you do from binary back to decimal. Fortunately, the largest number of bits you need to work with at any given time is eight. These are the octets in dotted decimal notation.

To convert a binary octet to a decimal value, you must multiply the digit in each column by the value of each column and then determine the sum of those products. Binary digits are always either 1 or 0, so you multiply the value of each column by 1 or 0. Table 4-5 shows the conversion of the binary number 10011011 to decimal.

Table 4-5   Binary to decimal conversion

Column Number	7	6	5	4	3	2	1	0	
Value	2^7	2^6	2^5	2^4	2^3	2^2	2^1	2^0	
Value in decimal	128	64	32	16	8	4	2	1	
Binary number	1	0	0	1	1	0	1	1	
Value of column	128	0	0	16	8	0	2	1	Total value of all columns (in decimal notation)=155

Although you can convert binary to decimal and decimal to binary using charts such as Table 4-5, most people use Windows Calculator to perform the conversion. Figure 4-1 shows Windows Calculator in Scientific mode, which is the mode that is required to perform binary to decimal and decimal to binary conversions.

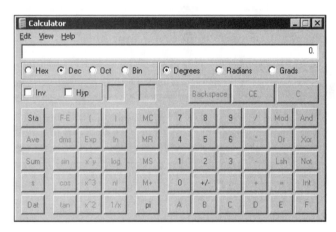

Figure 4-1   Windows Calculator

Activity 4-1: Converting Binary Numbers to Decimal Using Windows Calculator

Time Required: 5 minutes

Objective: Convert numbers between binary and decimal numbering systems.

Description: You will be working on subnetting plans for Arctic University later this week and want to be sure that you understand how to covert binary numbers to decimal and decimal numbers to binary.

1. If necessary, start your server, and log on as **Administrator**.

2. Click **Start**, point to **All Programs**, point to **Accessories**, and click **Calculator**.

3. Click the **View** menu, and then click **Scientific**.

4. Convert the decimal number 177 to binary. To do this, type **177** in the Calculator window, and click the **Bin** option button. The answer should be 10110001. If there are fewer than eight digits, the leading zeros are not shown.

5. Convert the binary number 11001100 to decimal. To do this, type **11001100** in the calculator, and click the **Dec** option button. The answer should be 204.

6. For more practice, convert the numbers in Table 4-6 from decimal to binary.

Table 4-6   Converting decimal to binary worksheet

Decimal	Binary
43	
19	
255	
240	
192	

7. For more practice, convert the numbers in Table 4-7 from binary to decimal.

Table 4-7   Converting binary to decimal worksheet

Binary	Decimal
00110011	
11001010	
11111100	
00000011	
01010101	

Binary Subnet Masks

Again, a subnet mask is a 32-bit number that is used to define which part of an IP address is network ID and which part is host ID. An example of a subnet mask is 255.255.255.0. It is written in dotted decimal notation. However, when your computer calculates the network ID and host ID of an IP address, it is working in binary. Where there is a 1 in the subnet mask, the computer uses that bit as part of the network ID. Where there is a 0 in the subnet mask, the computer uses that bit as part of the host ID.

The binary process used by your computer to find the network ID is called ANDing. This is a mathematical operation that compares two binary digits and gives a result of 1 or 0. If both binary digits being compared have a value of 1, then the result is 1. If one digit is 0 and the other is 1, or if both digits are zero, then the result is 0. Table 4-8 shows an example of calculating the host ID and network ID of an IP address using binary.

Table 4-8   Calculating host ID and network ID

	Dotted Decimal	Binary
IP address	192.168.5.20	11000000 . 10101000 . 00000101 . 00010100
Subnet mask	255.255.255.0	11111111 . 11111111 . 11111111 . 00000000
Network ID	192.168.5.0	11000000 . 10101000 . 00000101 . 00000000
Host ID	0.0.0.20	00000000 . 00000000 . 00000000 . 00010100

4

When an IP address is ANDed with a subnet mask, the result is the network ID. Each bit in the IP address is ANDed with the corresponding bit in the subnet mask. For example, in Table 4-8, the rightmost bit of the IP address is 0, and the far right bit of the subnet mask is 0. When 0 is ANDed with 0, the result is 0, and this is shown in the network ID. The far left bit of the IP address is 1, and the far left bit of the subnet mask is 1. When 1 is ANDed with 1, the result is 1, and this is shown in the network ID.

The host ID is the part of the IP address that is not the network ID.

NOTE

All of the 1s in a subnet mask must be contiguous. There must be no 0s interspersed with the 1s. Table 4-9 shows several examples of invalid subnet masks.

Table 4-9   Invalid subnet masks

Decimal	Binary
255.255.15.0	11111111 . 11111111 . 00001111 . 00000000
255.254.255.0	11111111 . 11111110 . 11111111 . 00000000
254.255.0.0	11111110 . 11111111 . 00000000 . 00000000
255.192.240.0	11111111 . 10101010 . 11110000 . 00000000

Activity 4-2: ANDing

Time Required: 20 minutes

ACTIVITY

Objective: Find the network ID of several IP addresses based on the given subnet mask.

Description: When you are troubleshooting IP address configuration problems, you may need to find the network ID on which an IP address is located. To practice, complete Table 4-10. First, convert the decimal numbers to binary, and then calculate the network ID by ANDing the IP address and the subnet mask.

Table 4-10   Finding network IDs worksheet

	Decimal	Binary
IP address	130.179.16.67	
Subnet maskNetwork ID	255.255.255.0	
IP address	192.168.32.183	
Subnet maskNetwork ID	255.255.255.240	
IP address	10.155.244.2	
Subnet mask	255.224.0.0	
Network ID		

The Benefits of Subnets

As mentioned, **subnetting** refers to the process of separating a network into smaller networks—or subnets—to improve performance.

Subnetting provides these benefits:

- Reduces collisions
- Limits broadcasts
- Controls traffic

NOTE

After a network has been subnetted, a router is required to move packets from one subnet to another.

Reducing Collisions

When two computers on an Ethernet network using CSMA/CD as an access method attempt to transmit packets at the same time, a **collision** occurs. All of the computers involved in the collision wait a random period of time after the collision occurs before attempting to send data again.

On a very busy Ethernet network, the actual throughput may be only 30% to 40% of capacity because of lost efficiency due to collisions. A busy 10-Mbps network may only actually carry 3 to 4 Mbps and a busy 100-Mbps network may actually carry only 30 to 40 Mbps. Subnetting reduces the number of hosts on each network and, therefore, reduces the amount of traffic on the network. With less traffic on each network, the number of collisions is reduced, and the actual throughput is improved. In a routed network, each network is a separate collision domain. Collisions that occur on one network do not affect another network. In a subnetted network, collisions that do occur affect a lower number of hosts. This increases actual throughput.

4

Limiting Broadcasts

Broadcast messages are generated by a variety of network services. For example, NetBIOS name resolution, router communication, service advertisements, and other services send broadcast messages when the destination address of hosts is unknown.

A packet addressed to a broadcast address is read and processed by every computer on the network. This is not a problem when there are only a few broadcast packets on the network, but as more computers are added, broadcasts not only can become a drain on the processing resources of workstations and servers, but can also increase network traffic significantly. Subnetting a network creates multiple networks with fewer hosts on each network. The presence of fewer hosts on each network results in fewer broadcast messages, which reduces the processing load on each host.

Routers do not forward packets addressed to the IP address 255.255.255.255. This address is a broadcast on the local network and is processed by every computer on the local network. Depending on configuration, most routers forward directed broadcasts such as 192.168.4. 255. Packets addressed to this address are routed to the appropriate network and are then processed by all computers on that network.

Controlling Traffic

Introducing routers into a network allows a greater degree of control over network traffic. Most routers have the ability to implement rules about which packets they forward. This lets you control which hosts can talk to each other, as well as which protocols they can use to communicate. On a nonrouted network, the hosts can use any protocol they want and can communicate with any other host on the local network.

When a company has multiple physical locations, routers are used to control the traffic that moves between them. Each location has its own subnet.

Subnetting a Network

To subnet a network, you take some bits from the host ID and give them to the network ID. As the manager and designer of a network, you have the freedom to do this.

A Class B address is very large and generally needs to be subnetted to handle routing between different physical locations. To keep subnetting simple, bits are often taken from the host ID in a group of eight. This keeps the entire octet intact. Table 4-11 shows an example of subnetting a Class B address by taking eight bits from the host ID and giving them to the network ID. Originally, the third octet was part of the host ID, but it is now part of the network ID. Using an entire octet for subnetting gives you 256 possible subnets. Traditionally, the subnets with all 1s and all 0s are discarded, leaving 254 usable subnets.

Table 4-11 Simple subnetting

Description	Decimal	Binary
Original network	172.16.0.0	10101100 . 00010000 . 00000000 . 00000000
Original subnet mask	255.255.0.0	11111111 . 11111111 . 00000000 . 00000000
New subnet mask	255.255.255.0	11111111 . 11111111 . *11111111* . 00000000
Subnet 1	172.16.0.0	10101100 . 00010000 . *00000000* . 00000000
Subnet 2	172.16.1.0	10101100 . 00010000 . *00000001* . 00000000
Subnet 3	172.16.2.0	10101100 . 00010000 . *00000010* . 00000000
Subnet 4	172.16.3.0	10101100 . 00010000 . *00000011* . 00000000
Subnet 5	172.16.4.0	10101100 . 00010000 . *00000101* . 00000000
Subnet 6	172.16.5.0	10101100 . 00010000 . *00000110* . 00000000
Subnet 7	172.16.6.0	10101100 . 00010000 . *00000111* . 00000000
Subnet 256	172.16.255.0	10101100 . 00010000 . *11111111* . 00000000

When simple subnetting is used, it is still very easy to find the network ID and host ID of an IP address, because each octet is still whole. However, sometimes you need to subdivide an octet to get the number of subnets or hosts that you desire.

Complex subnetting takes less than a full octet from the host ID. Table 4-12 shows an example of subnetting a Class B network by taking three bits from the host ID. Traditionally, subnet 1 and subnet 8 are not used because all the subnet bits are set to 0 and 1, respectively. However, today, with classless routing, both subnet 1 and subnet 8 can be used.

Table 4-12 Complex subnetting

Description	Decimal	Binary
Original network	172.16.0.0	10101100 . 00010000 . 00000000 . 00000000
Original subnet mask	255.255.0.0	11111111 . 11111111 . 00000000 . 00000000
New subnet mask	255.255.224.0	11111111 . 11111111 . *111*00000 . 00000000
Subnet 1	172.16.0.0	10101100 . 00010000 . *000*00000 . 00000000
Subnet 2	172.16.32.0	10101100 . 00010000 . *001*00000 . 00000000
Subnet 3	172.16.64.0	10101100 . 00010000 . *010*00000 . 00000000
Subnet 4	172.16.96.0	10101100 . 00010000 . *011*00000 . 00000000
Subnet 5	172.16.128.0	10101100 . 00010000 . *100*00000 . 00000000
Subnet 6	172.16.160.0	10101100 . 00010000 . *101*00000 . 00000000
Subnet 7	172.16.192.0	10101100 . 00010000 . *110*00000 . 00000000
Subnet 8	172.16.224.0	10101100 . 00010000 . *111*00000 . 00000000

The number of subnets can be calculated using the formula 2^n-2. In this formula, n is the number of bits taken from the host ID and used for subnetting. The minus 2 is only used for traditional subnetting in which the subnets of all 1s and all 0s are removed.

Activity 4-3: Complex Subnetting

4

Time Required: 30 minutes

Objective: Subnet a single large network into 10 smaller networks.

Description: A large, internal network address such as 172.20.0.0 is too large to be used without subnetting. To practice subnetting, divide the 172.20.0.0 network into 10 subnets using as few bits from the host as possible. List the new subnet mask and 10 subnets in Table 4-13.

Table 4-13 Complex subnetting worksheet

Description	Decimal	Binary
Original network	172.20.0.0	10101100 . 00010100 . 00000000 . 00000000
Original subnet mask	255.255.0.0	11111111 . 11111111 . 00000000 . 00000000
New subnet mask		
Subnet 1		
Subnet 2		
Subnet 3		
Subnet 4		
Subnet 5		
Subnet 6		
Subnet 7		
Subnet 8		
Subnet 9		
Subnet 10		

Subnet Hosts

The number of hosts available on a subnetted network follows the same pattern as the classful IP networks you have already seen. When the host bits are all set to 0, that address represents the subnet. When the bits are all set to 1, that address is a broadcast on that subnet. Table 4-14 shows the usable hosts for several subnetted networks.

Table 4-14   Usable hosts

Description	Decimal	Binary
Original network	172.16.0.0	10101100 . 00010000 . 00000000 . 00000000
Original subnet mask	255.255.0.0	11111111 . 11111111 . 00000000 . 00000000
New subnet mask	255.255.224.0	11111111 . 11111111 . *111*00000 . 00000000
Subnet 1	172.16.0.0	10101100 . 00010000 . *000*00000 . 00000000
First host on subnet 1	172.16.0.1	10101100 . 00010000 . *000*00000 . 00000001
Last host on subnet 1	172.16.31.254	10101100 . 00010000 . *000*11111 . 11111110
Broadcast on subnet 1	172.16.31.255	10101100 . 00010000 . *000*11111 . 11111111
Subnet 2	172.16.32.0	10101100 . 00010000 . *001*00000 . 00000000
First host on subnet 2	172.16.32.1	10101100 . 00010000 . *001*00000 . 00000001
Last host on subnet 2	172.16.63.254	10101100 . 00010000 . *001*11111 . 11111110
Broadcast on subnet 2	172.16.63.255	10101100 . 00010000 . *001*11111 . 11111111
Subnet 3	172.16.64.0	10101100 . 00010000 . *010*00000 . 00000000
First host on subnet 3	172.16.64.1	10101100 . 00010000 . *010*00000 . 00000001
Last host on subnet 3	172.16.95.254	10101100 . 00010000 . *010*11111 . 11111110
Broadcast on subnet 3	172.16.95.255	10101100 . 00010000 . *010*11111 . 11111111

The formula 2^n-2, which is used to calculate the number of subnets that can be created from a certain number of bits, is also used to calculate the number of usable hosts on a subnet. In both situations, the formula finds the total number of combinations that can be created from n bits. However, when used to calculate the number of usable hosts on a subnet, n is the number of bits in the host ID, and two combinations are removed for the broadcast on the subnet and the subnet itself. Table 4-15 shows the number of usable hosts available for certain numbers of bits.

Table 4-15   Usable hosts formula

Host Bits	Formula	Usable Hosts
6	2^6-2	64-2=62
8	2^8-2	256-2=254
10	$2^{10}-2$	1024-2=1022
12	$2^{12}-2$	4096-2=4094

Activity 4-4: Finding Valid Hosts

Time Required: 30 minutes

Objective: Calculate the number of valid hosts on a subnet.

Description: After you have calculated the network ID for your subnets, you must find out the number of valid hosts on each subnet. These are the IP addresses you can assign to the hosts on your network. Using three subnets from Activity 4-3, find the first host, last host, and broadcast address for each subnet and fill out Table 4-16 with your answers.

Table 4-16   Valid hosts worksheet

Description	Decimal	Binary
Subnet mask	255.255.240.0	11111111 . 11111111 . 11110000 . 00000000
Subnet 1		
First host on subnet 1		
Last host on subnet 1		
Broadcast on subnet 1		
Subnet 2		
First host on subnet 2		
Last host on subnet 2		
Broadcast on subnet 2		
Subnet 3		
First host on subnet 3		
Last host on subnet 3		
Broadcast on subnet 3		

Supernetting

Supernetting is used when a range of IP addresses larger than a Class C network is required, but a full Class B network is not required. For example, a midsized company with 300 computers requires IP addresses from their ISP that are usable on the Internet. It would be wasteful to assign an entire Class B address to the company because thousands of IP addresses would go unused. Instead, the ISP can supernet two Class C addresses. This allows the company to have 510 Internet-usable IP addresses.

Supernetting may also be done to reduce routing complexity. For example, an older network running at 10 Mbps may have been configured with multiple Class C networks to reduce packet collisions. With current technology, the routers could be replaced with switches running at 100 Mbps. The switches still reduce packet collisions, and the complexity of the network is reduced. When the routers are removed, the computers on the network need to be reconfigured with supernetted addresses. If DHCP is being used, then this change is very easy to implement.

Supernetting is the opposite of subnetting. Subnetting is used to create several smaller networks from a large network, whereas **supernetting** is used to create one large network from several smaller ones. Subnetting takes bits from the host ID and moves them to the network ID. Supernetting takes bits from the network ID and gives them to the host ID. All of the networks being combined for supernetting must be contiguous. The IP addresses from the first network to the last must be one single range with no breaks. In the first network being supernetted, the bits being taken from the network ID must be zero. In the final network being supernetted, the bits being taken must be one.

Table 4-17 shows an example of supernetting two Class C networks into one larger network.

Table 4-17   Supernetting two Class C networks

Description	Decimal	Binary
Original network 1	192.168.10.0	11000000 . 10101000 . 00001010 . 00000000
Original network 2	192.168.11.0	11000000 . 10101000 . 00001011 . 00000000
Original subnet mask	255.255.255.0	11111111 . 11111111 . 11111111 . 00000000
Supernetted network	192.168.10.0	11000000 . 10101000 . 00001010 . 00000000
New subnet mask	255.255.254.0	11111111 . 11111111 . 11111110 . 00000000
First host	192.168.10.1	11000000 . 10101000 . 00001010 . 00000001
Last host	192.168.11. 254	11000000 . 10101000 . 00001011 . 11111110
Broadcast	192.168.11. 255	11000000 . 10101000 . 00001011 . 11111111

Table 4-18 shows an example of supernetting four Class C networks into one larger network.

Table 4-18 Supernetting four Class C networks

Description	Decimal	Binary
Original network 1	192.168.76.0	11000000 . 10101000 . 01001100 . 00000000
Original network 2	192.168.77.0	11000000 . 10101000 . 01001101 . 00000000
Original network 3	192.168.78.0	11000000 . 10101000 . 01001110 . 00000000
Original network 4	192.168.79.0	11000000 . 10101000 . 01001111 . 00000000
Original subnet mask	255.255.255.0	11111111 . 11111111 . 11111111 . 00000000
Supernetted network	192.168.76.0	11000000 . 10101000 . 01001100 . 00000000
New subnet mask	255.255.253.0	11111111 . 11111111 . 11111100 . 00000000
First host	192.168.76.1	11000000 . 10101000 . 01001100 . 00000000
Last host	192.168.79.254	11000000 . 10101000 . 01001111 . 11111110
Broadcast	192.168.79.255	11000000 . 10101000 . 01001111 . 11111111

4

ROUTER INSTALLATION AND CONFIGURATION

Windows Server 2003 can be used as a router for many small and midsized organizations. It can perform routing for TCP/IP and AppleTalk. IPX/SPX is not supported for routing.

The main benefit of implementing Windows Server 2003 as a router within a small or midsized organization is cost. If you already have a server, to make it a router, you only need to add a network card, and then configure Windows. This is useful if the routing requirements for your organization are simple, and a server has unused capacity.

To be a router, the server must be connected to at least two networks. A network interface in the server is connected to each network and has an IP address on that network.

Routing is part of **Routing and Remote Access Service (RRAS)** and can be configured using the same wizard that is used to configure dial-up and VPN servers. If RRAS is already configured on a server, such as a VPN server, then routing can be configured as an additional service without losing the existing configuration.

To add routing as an additional service using the Routing and Remote Access snap-in, open the properties of the server, as shown in Figure 4-2. To enable general routing, check the Router check box. When this option is checked, this server becomes a router. However, to act as an IP router, you must also check the Enable IP routing check box on the IP tab, as shown in Figure 4-3.

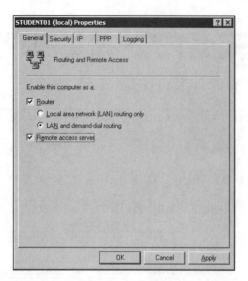

Figure 4-2   Enabling RRAS as a router

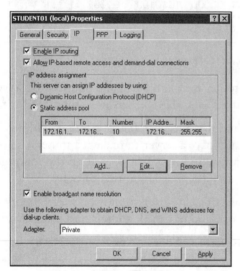

Figure 4-3   Enabling IP routing

Activity 4-5: Configuring RRAS as a Router

Time Required: 10 minutes

Objective: Configure Windows Server 2003 as a router.

Description: You have decided to use Windows Server 2003 as a router in several smaller campus locations for which the cost of a specialized hardware router cannot be justified. You confirm that both network cards in your computer are configured with an appropriate IP address, and then enable routing using the Routing and Remote Access Server Setup Wizard.

1. If necessary, start your server and log on as **Administrator** of the Arctic.local domain.

2. Configure your Private network card with an IP address:

   a. Click **Start**, point to **Control Panel**, point to **Network Connections**, right-click **Private**, and click **Properties**.

   b. Click **Internet Protocol (TCP/IP)**, and click **Properties**.

   c. Click **Use the following IP address**, if necessary.

   d. In the IP address text box, type **172.16.*x*.*yy***, where *x* is your group number and *yy* is your student number.

   e. In the Subnet mask text box, type **255.255.255.0**.

   f. In the Preferred DNS server text box, type **192.168.1.10** and then click **OK**.

   g. Click **Close**.

3. Click **Start**, point to **Administrative Tools**, and then click **Routing and Remote Access**.

4. Right-click your server, and click **Configure and Enable Routing and Remote Access**.

5. Click **Next** to begin the Routing and Remote Access Server Setup Wizard.

6. Click **Custom configuration** and then click **Next**. You want to configure a LAN router, and that is not a standard wizard option.

7. Check the **LAN routing** check box, and click **Next**.

8. Click **Finish**.

9. Click **Yes** to start the Routing and Remote Access Service.

10. View the configuration that has been enabled by the Routing and Remote Access Server Setup Wizard:

    a. Right-click your server, and click **Properties**.

    b. On the General tab, the options Router and Local area network (LAN) routing only are selected. Click the **IP** tab.

    c. The Enable IP routing option is selected. Click **Cancel**.

11. Close the Routing and Remote Access snap-in.

Routing Tables

Routers are responsible for making intelligent decisions about how to move packets from one network to another in the fastest way possible. To keep track of the different networks that are available, a routing table is used.

The **routing table** is a list of the networks that are known to the router. Each entry in an IP routing table contains the IP address of the network, the subnet mask of the network, the gateway that is used to reach the network, the router interface that is used to reach the gateway, and the metric that measures how far away the network is.

NOTE   The meaning of the metric value in a routing table varies depending on which routing protocol is being used.

To view the routing table on a server, you can use the **ROUTE PRINT** command, as shown in Figure 4-4. This figure shows the routing table for a router with two network cards, configured with the IP addresses 192.168.101/24 and 172.16.1.1/24, where /24 represents the number of bits in the network ID. The network 0.0.0.0 listed in the routing table is the default gateway. The subnet mask 255.255.255.255 is used to refer to an individual IP address.

```
C:\WINDOWS\system32\cmd.exe                                              _□×

C:\Documents and Settings\administrator.ARCTIC>route print

IPv4 Route Table
===========================================================================
Interface List
0x1 ........................... MS TCP Loopback interface
0x2 ...00 04 75 85 45 7c ...... 3Com EtherLink XL 10/100 PCI For Complete PC Man
agement NIC (3C905C-TX)
0x3 ...00 50 ba 68 f0 a5 ...... D-Link DFE-530TX PCI Fast Ethernet Adapter (rev.
A)
===========================================================================
===========================================================================
Active Routes:
Network Destination        Netmask          Gateway       Interface  Metric
        0.0.0.0          0.0.0.0      192.168.1.10   192.168.1.101     30
      127.0.0.0        255.0.0.0        127.0.0.1       127.0.0.1      1
    192.168.1.0    255.255.255.0    192.168.1.101   192.168.1.101     30
  192.168.1.101  255.255.255.255        127.0.0.1       127.0.0.1     30
  192.168.1.255  255.255.255.255    192.168.1.101   192.168.1.101     30
      224.0.0.0        240.0.0.0    192.168.1.101   192.168.1.101     30
255.255.255.255  255.255.255.255    192.168.1.101               2      1
255.255.255.255  255.255.255.255    192.168.1.101   192.168.1.101      1
Default Gateway:       192.168.1.10
===========================================================================
Persistent Routes:
  None
```

Figure 4-4   The ROUTE PRINT command

By default, the only networks of which a router is aware are the ones to which it is attached with a network card. Any other entries in the routing table must be added. If entries are added manually, it is referred to as **static routing**. If entries are added automatically, based on a routing protocol, it is referred to as **dynamic routing**.

Static routing is generally used when security is required. With static routing tables, you know exactly what is in each routing table and can exactly control how packets move between networks. For example, in a campus environment, to reduce the chances of a packet sniffer being able to capture traffic, you may configure only one backbone path on which all network traffic travels.

The maintenance of a static routing table on each router can become cumbersome. Each time a new network is added, the routing table of each server must be changed. Each time a change is made, there is also a chance of an error being made in the entry and functionality being lost, even if only for a short period of time.

Dynamic routing is used in most environments. In this system, the routers talk to each other to build their routing tables. By setting the metric on network interfaces, you can still control how packets move through the network without the hassle of configuring each router separately.

Routing Protocols

Routing protocols are responsible for calculating the best path from one network to another and advertising routes for dynamic routing. When calculating the path, each routing protocol uses a different routing algorithm. When advertising routing, each routing protocol advertises different amounts of information and with a different frequency.

The two routing protocols used in Windows Server 2003 for IP routing are:

- Routing Information Protocol (RIP)
- Open Shortest Path First (OSPF)

RIP

Routing Information Protocol (RIP) is the simpler of the two routing protocols and consequently the most popular. No configuration is necessary under most circumstances.

The distance between networks is measured by the number of routers through which the data must pass, or **hops**. For example, if one router must be passed through to reach a network, it is one hop away. The best path from one network to another is the path with the least number of hops. This is known as **distance-vector routing**.

NOTE

The maximum number of hops used by RIP is 15. A network is considered unreachable at 16 hops.

RIP does not differentiate between different link speeds. One hop across an ISDN line is treated the same as one hop across a T-1 line. In larger environments, this is unacceptable and leads to inefficient routing.

Each RIP router sends a broadcast packet every 30 seconds. A complete copy of the routing table is contained in this packet. RIP version 2 is capable of using multicasts instead of broadcast packets for these announcements.

Activity 4-6: Installing and Using RIP

Time Required: 10 minutes

Objective: Configure your server as an RIP router.

Description: The default configuration of the routers you have configured is static routing. You are tired of making manual changes to these routers every time there is a routing change. To implement automatic updating of the routing tables in your routers, you configure RIP on your server.

1. If necessary, start your server and log on as **Administrator**.

2. View the existing routing table on your server:

    a. Click **Start**, click **Run**, type **cmd**, and press **Enter**.

    b. Type **route print** and press **Enter**.

    c. There are only two networks in the routing table with the netmask of 255.255. 255.0. These are the two networks you are connected to on the Private and Classroom interfaces. Also notice that for each of these two entries, the metric is either 20 or 30. Close the Command Prompt window.

3. Click **Start**, point to **Administrative Tools**, and click **Routing and Remote Access**.

4. If necessary, double-click your server to expand it.

5. If necessary, double-click **IP Routing** to expand it.

6. Right-click **General**, and click **New Routing Protocol**.

7. In the New Routing Protocol window, click **RIP Version 2 for Internet Protocol**, and click **OK**. Notice that RIP is added as an option underneath IP Routing.

8. Click **RIP**. Interfaces using RIP are listed here. By default, there are none.

9. Right-click **RIP**, and click **New Interface**.

10. If necessary, click **Classroom**, and click **OK**.

11. Click **OK** to accept the default configuration.

12. Right-click **RIP**, click **New Interface**, click **Private** if necessary, and then click **OK**.

13. Click **OK** to accept the default configuration.

14. As your router communicates with other routers in the classroom that have enabled RIP, the routing table grows.

15. View the new routing table:

    a. Right-click **Static Routes**, and click **Show IP Routing Table**.

    b. Expand the window so you can view all of the columns.

c. Note that the routing table entries with RIP listed in the protocol column are learned through RIP. Close the IP Routing Table window.

16. Close the Routing and Remote Access snap-in.

OSPF

4

Open Shortest Path First (OSPF) is a routing algorithm that determines the best path from one network to another based on a configurable value called **cost**. This makes OSPF more flexible than RIP and better suited to complex routing environments. Because complex routing environments normally use hardware routers, OSPF is not normally implemented on Windows routers.

Each interface on a router using OSPF is assigned a cost. The total cost of a route is calculated by adding the cost value of each router interface that it traveled through. The best path from one network to another is the one with the lowest cost.

Administrators can use the variable cost of router interfaces to differentiate between slower and faster WAN links. For example, a T-1 line may be configured with a cost of 10, while a backup ISDN line can be configured with a cost of 30. Only if the T-1 goes down is the ISDN line used.

When the routing table is built, each router builds a picture of the entire network. This is referred to as **link-state routing**.

When communicating with other routers, an OSPF router sends only changes in its routing table, not the entire routing table. In addition, the changes are sent only when they occur, not every 30 seconds.

OSPF is not available in the 64-bit versions of Windows Server 2003.

NOTE

Configuring RIP

Despite the relative simplicity of RIP compared to OSPF, there are still many options that can be configured, if required. A few RIP options can be configured globally for the entire server in the properties of RIP, but most are configured separately for each interface.

In the properties of RIP, you can configure the type of events to be logged. In addition, you can configure from which IP addresses this router accepts updates, as shown in Figure 4-5. The default setting is the Accept announcements from all routers option. This is a security risk, and should be changed to the Accept announcements from listed routers only option.

In the properties of the interfaces listed in RIP, you can configure settings for each interface. The General tab is shown in Figure 4-6. The Operation mode is set to Periodic update

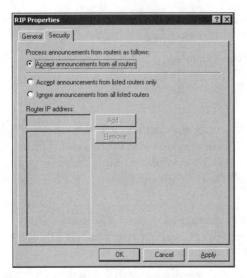

Figure 4-5 RIP security

mode, which removes entries from the routing table if the router that originally advertised them is disabled or unreachable. You can also choose Auto-static update mode, which adds RIP learned routes to the routing table as static entries, which are never removed. This is useful for routing with dial-up connections to maintain a consistent routing table.

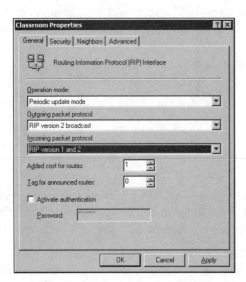

Figure 4-6 Setting RIP interface properties

The Outgoing packet protocol can be configured as RIP version 1 broadcast, RIP version 2 broadcast, RIP version 2 multicast, and Silent RIP. The default setting is RIP version 2 broadcast. Silent RIP disables outgoing RIP announcements.

The Incoming packet protocol can be configured as Ignore incoming packets, RIP version 1 and 2, RIP version 1 only, and RIP version 2 only. The default is RIP version 1 and 2.

RIP routers advertise the routes they learn from other routers. This allows each router to build a large routing table that lists all networks possible. When a router advertises a route learned from another router, the number of hops is incremented by 1. However, you can change this default by modifying the value in the Added cost for routes field.

You can also select the Activate authentication check box to force authentication between routers when announcements are sent. For this to function properly, the feature must be enabled on all routers. The password is sent in plain text and is not an effective form of security.

The Security tab, as shown in Figure 4-7, allows you to configure which incoming and outgoing routes are accepted on this interface. In addition to accepting all routes, you can choose to accept or ignore a range of addresses. If you use only a defined range of network numbers, then it is a good idea to configure the interface to use the Accept all routes in the ranges listed option. The options are the same for announcing outgoing routes as for accepting incoming routes.

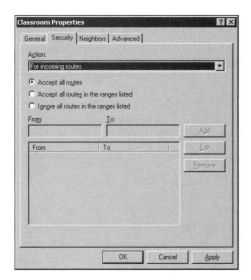

Figure 4-7   Security tab

The Neighbors tab, as shown in Figure 4-8, is used only if broadcasts and multicasts are limited on the network. You can configure unicast IP addresses that are neighbors. This interface then communicates with the neighbors instead of, or in addition to, broadcast and multicast announcements.

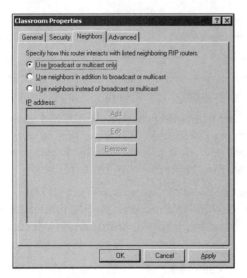

Figure 4-8   Neighbors tab

The Advanced tab, as shown in Figure 4-9, allows you to configure a wide variety of settings. You can adjust how often routing table announcements are sent, how long entries in the routing table last before they expire, and how long after they expire before they are removed from the routing table.

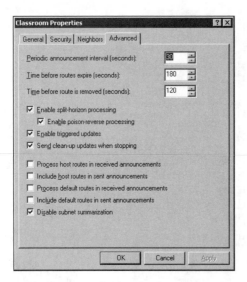

Figure 4-9   Advanced tab

Split-horizon processing and **poison-reverse processing** are used to prevent routing loops in the case of a router failure. Triggered updates are sent when a change is made to the routing table, if this feature is enabled. If the Send clean-up updates when stopping feature is enabled, then a router announcement that expires all of the routes it has been advertising is sent when the router is shut down.

Other options disable the processing or sending of host routes and default routes in router announcements. The Disable subnet summarization option stops the router from aggregating multiple subnets as a single router entry.

4

DEMAND-DIAL CONNECTIONS

A **demand-dial** connection is used to establish a connection between two routers only when there is data to send. When a router with a demand-dial interface receives packets destined for a remote network, a connection is created so the packets can be sent. The connection can also be configured so that if there are no packets for the remote network, it is disconnected.

Traditionally, demand-dial connections are used to minimize the amount of phone time used on a dial-up connection between routers. In this case, the connection is configured to disconnect after a certain period of time if no traffic has crossed the network. In addition, you can configure the connection to be operational only during a time period when phone rates are minimized.

Demand-dial can also be used to initiate VPN connections between Windows routers. In this situation, the purpose of demand-dial is not to minimize connection time, but to automate the establishment of a connection. This is required when the router is rebooted or when a connection is lost because of a network interruption.

Demand-dial connections can also be created for **Point-to-Point Protocol over Ethernet (PPPoE)** connections. PPPoE is used by many high-speed Internet providers to control access to their network. Just like a dial-up or VPN connection, PPPoE requires a user name and password to authenticate the connection. Only after the connection is authenticated does the ISP configure the server with an IP address and allow it on the Internet. Configuring PPPoE for a demand-dial connection ensures the automatic establishment of Internet connectivity when the router is rebooted or connectivity is interrupted.

Creating Demand-Dial Connections

For a demand-dial connection to function properly, you must enable the server to perform demand-dial routing, configure a port to allow demand-dial routing, and then create a demand-dial interface. These tasks are completed using the Routing and Remote Access snap-in.

Enabling the server to allow demand-dial connections is done in the Properties of the server, as shown in Figure 4-10. Check the LAN and demand-dial routing check box to allow demand-dial connections.

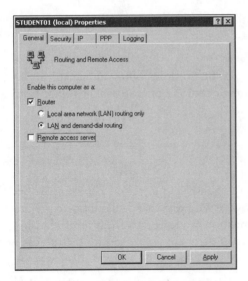

Figure 4-10   Enabling demand-dial routing

After demand–dial routing has been enabled, a Ports option appears under the server in the Routing and Remote Access snap-in. In the Ports properties, you can configure whether particular port types can be used for demand–dial connections. Port types include modems, PPPoE, PPTP, and L2TP.

Configuring the PPTP port type is shown in Figure 4-11. To enable demand–dial connections, you must check the Demand-dial routing connections (inbound and outbound) check box or the Demand-dial routing connections (outbound only) check box.

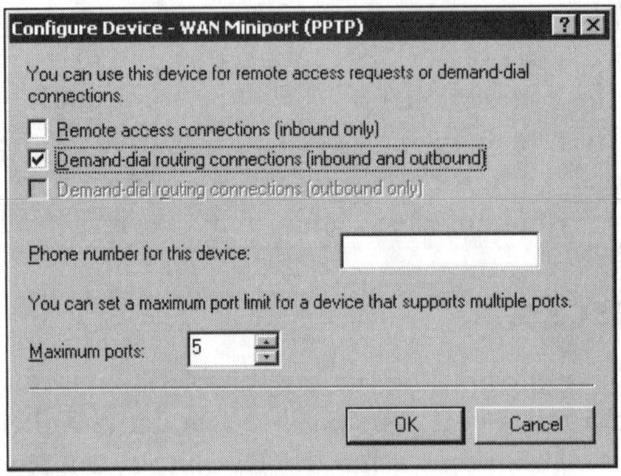

Figure 4-11   Configuring a port for demand-dial routing

Demand-Dial Interface Wizard

New demand-dial connections are created using the Demand-Dial Interface Wizard. To start this wizard in the Routing and Remote Access snap-in, right-click Network Interfaces, and click New Demand-dial Interface. The first option you are asked to configure is the name for the demand-dial interface.

The next screen in the wizard asks you what type of demand-dial connection you want to create, as shown in Figure 4-12. The three options are dial-up, VPN, or PPPoE. Dial-up and VPN are used for connectivity between a remote office and a central office. PPPoE is used to connect to the Internet.

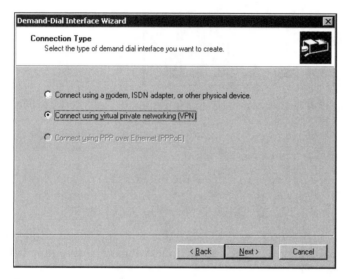

Figure 4-12   Connection Type window of the Demand-Dial Interface Wizard

If you choose to create a VPN connection, then the next step asks you what type of VPN connection to create. Choosing the Automatic selection option negotiates with the remote VPN server to choose PPTP or L2TP. Otherwise, you can force it to be PPTP only or L2TP only. After the type of VPN is chosen, you must also configure the IP address of the remote server.

The next window asks you about protocol and security options, as shown in Figure 4-13. If the Route IP packets on this interface check box is checked, this server routes packets between the networks to which it is connected and the remote network. If it is not selected, then only the server running Routing and Remote Access is able to access the remote network. This may be desired if the connection is only used for remote maintenance or data synchronization.

A user account with remote access permission is required to establish a demand-dial connection. If the Add a user account so a remote router can dial in check box is checked,

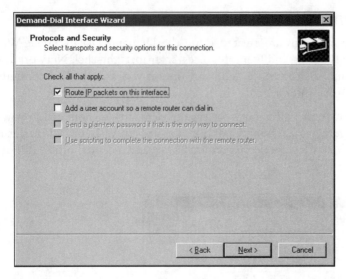

Figure 4-13   Protocols and Security window of the Demand-Dial Interface Wizard

a user account is automatically created for inbound, demand-dial connections. On a member server, the account created is a local user account.

Checking the Send a plain-text password if that is the only way to connect check box should be avoided if possible. If this option is selected, ensure that the user account is only used for connection establishment and has no rights to the remainder of the system.

Checking the Use scripting to complete the connection with the remote router check box allows you to run a script that modifies the connection settings or adds routing table entries. This is not normally required.

The next window, shown in Figure 4-14, asks you to configure **static routes**. At least one static route is required to trigger the demand-dial interface. Static routes must be added for each network on the other side of the demand-dial connection. The demand-dial connection is activated when a packet addressed to a host on one of the static routes needs to be forwarded.

When a packet arrives at the demand-dial router, the router looks in its routing table to see where it should be sent. The static route for the remote network specifies the demand-dial interface to reach the remote network. If a packet is addressed to the remote network, then the demand-dial connection is activated. After the demand-dial connection is activated, the packet is forwarded across the demand-dial connection to the remote network.

If you selected the Add a user account so a remote router can dial in check box in the preceding window, then the next window asks for dial-in credentials. This information is used to create the user account that is used by the remote router to connect to this router. The user name is the same as the name for the demand-dial connection.

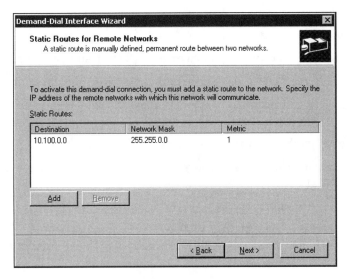

Figure 4-14   Static Routes for Remote Networks window of the Demand-Dial Interface Wizard

Next, you are prompted for dial-out credentials. This is the user name, domain, and password that are used by the demand-dial connection to log on on the remote system. If this information is not correct, the demand-dial connection is unable to connect.

Activity 4-7: Creating a Demand-Dial Connection

Time Required: 15 minutes

Objective: Create a demand-dial VPN connection.

Description: You have configured Windows Server 2003 as a router between sites. To enhance security, you want to configure a dial-up VPN between the locations. In this activity, you configure a demand-dial VPN interface on your server, and test it by connecting to a VPN server on your partner's server.

1. If necessary, start your server and log on as **Administrator**.

2. Click **Start**, point to **Administrative Tools**, and then click **Routing and Remote Access**.

3. Right-click your server, and click **Properties**.

4. Click **LAN and demand-dial routing**, and click **OK**.

5. Click **Yes** to continue and restart RRAS.

6. Right-click **Network Interfaces**, and then click **New Demand-dial Interface**.

7. Click **Next** to begin the Demand-Dial Interface Wizard.

8. In the Interface name text box, type **ArcticDemandx**, where *x* is your partner's student number, and click **Next**.

9. Click **Connect using virtual private networking (VPN)**, and click **Next**.

10. Confirm that the VPN type selected is **Automatic selection**, and click **Next**.

11. In the Host name or IP address text box, type **192.168.1.1xx**, where *xx* is your partner's student number, and click **Next**. This is the IP address of your partner's server.

12. Check the **Route IP packets on this interface** check box, if necessary.

13. Click the **Add a user account so a remote router can dial in** check box to select it, and click **Next**.

14. Click **Add** to add a static route.

15. In the Destination text box, type **10.100.xx.0**, where *xx* is your partner's student number. This network does not really exist in the classroom, but is used to trigger the demand-dial interface.

16. In the Network Mask text box, type **255.255.255.0**, and click **OK**.

17. Click **Next**.

18. In the Password text box of the Dial In Credentials window, type **Password!**. In the Confirm password text box, type **Password!**, and click **Next**. This window gathers the password for the user that is created by the wizard for remote routers to log on.

19. In the User name text box of the Dial Out Credentials window, type **ArcticDemandy**, where *y* is your student number. This account is created by your partner during the creation of the demand-dial interface.

20. In the Domain text box, type **STUDENTxx**, where *xx* is your partner's student number. The account that was automatically created by your partner is a local account. This specifies that the user account is in the local SAM database of your partner's server.

21. In the Password text box, type **Password!**. In the Confirm password text box, type **Password!**, and click Next.

22. Click **Finish**.

23. Configure your server as a VPN server:

    a. Right-click your server, and click **Properties**.

    b. Check the **Remote access server** check box, and click **OK**. Even when configured as a router, RRAS creates five PPTP and five L2TP ports automatically. This enables them to be used.

    c. Click **Yes** to restart the router.

24. View the connection state of your demand-dial connection in Network Interfaces. It should be Disconnected.

25. Wait until your partner has completed Step 19, then test your demand-dial interface:

    a. Click **Start**, click **Run**, type **cmd**, and press **Enter**.

    b. Type **ping 10.100.*xx*.5**, where *xx* is your partner's student number and press **Enter**. This IP address does not exist on the network, but triggers the demand-dial connection based on the static route you configured in the Demand-Dial Interface Wizard.

    c. You receive error messages. This is normal. If you receive the error Destination host unreachable, then the interface is not connected yet. It takes a few moments for the demand-dial connection to complete. If you receive only this error, then repeat Step b. If after two attempts you are still receiving this error, then verify your configuration is correct. To verify the authentication credentials, right-click your demand-dial connection, and click **Set Credentials**.

    d. After the demand-dial connection is connected, the error message will change. If the error changes to Request timed out, it indicates that the demand-dial connection connected, but the host is not responding. This is normal because the host does exist on our network. If the host really existed on the remote network, then you would get a positive response. If the error changes to TTL expired in transit, the demand-dial connection is connected and a routing loop has been created.

    e. Close the Command Prompt window.

26. View the connection state of your demand-dial connection in Network Interfaces. It should be Connected. If the state is not Connected, press **F5** to refresh the screen.

27. Right-click **ArcticDemand*xx***, where *xx* is your partner's student number, and click **Disconnect**. This manually disconnects the demand-dial interface.

28. Close the Routing and Remote Access snap-in.

Demand-dial Interface Properties

Most options for a demand-dial interface can be configured with the Demand-Dial Interface Wizard during creation, but some can only be configured after the interface has been created.

The properties of the demand-dial interface can be used to configure security settings and the idle timeout. The idle timeout is on the Options tab, as shown in Figure 4-15. If the Connection type chosen is the Persistent connection option, then the servers are connected whenever RRAS is functional. This is the normal configuration for a VPN demand-dial connection with a permanent Internet connection.

If the Connection type chosen is Demand dial, then you can set an idle timeout. The default setting for the Idle time before hanging up option is five minutes. If you are using a dial-up connection, you want to set the idle timeout to be 5 or 10 minutes. Then, when there is no traffic to be transmitted, the connection is disconnected to reduce phone charges.

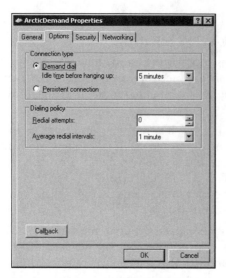

Figure 4-15   Options tab

The Security tab provides the standard security options available on a VPN connection. You can configure the types of authentication allowed and whether data encryption is used.

Dial-out Hours

A demand-dial connection can be configured with a set of **dial-out hours** that control when it can be active. This is very useful to control dial-up connections that might otherwise result in large long-distance charges.

Typically, when dial-out hours are configured, they allow a connection every few hours. This results in data being moved from one network to another in batches every few hours. This is useful for Active Directory replication and data synchronization.

If users are expected to access resources using the demand-dial connection at all times, then the dial-out hours should be left at the default of 24 hours per day, seven days per week. To set the dial-out hours, right-click the demand-dial interface and click Dial-out hours.

Demand-Dial Filters

With the default configuration, a demand-dial connection is triggered by any IP traffic that needs to be routed. This includes relatively unimportant traffic such as ICMP packets.

To reduce the amount of time a demand-dial connection is active, you can configure demand-dial filters. **Demand-dial filters** control which types of network traffic trigger a demand-dial connection. This reduces the number of connections activated and reduces the amount of long-distance charges.

The demand-dial filters are configured the same as a firewall rule. You can set the default option to initiate a demand-dial connection for only specific traffic or for all traffic except that specified by a rule, as shown in Figure 4-16. For each rule, you can specify a source and destination network as well as a protocol type, which includes TCP and UDP port numbers.

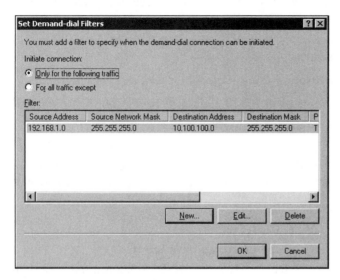

Figure 4-16   Demand-dial filters

Demand-dial filters can be used with a dial-up Internet connection to ensure the connection is not dialed unless it is for allowed traffic. For example, you could configure rules that limit connection establishment to packets that have a source IP address on your internal network and have a destination TCP port of either 80 or 25. Then, only communication with Web servers and e-mail servers can cause the Internet connection to be activated. An attempt to ping an Internet server would not activate the Internet connection.

Activity 4-8: Configuring Demand-Dial Filters

Time required: 5 minutes

Objective: Configure demand-dial filters to control the activation of demand-dial connections.

Description: Arctic University is charged a fee for bandwidth usage on their Internet connection. You want to reduce the amount of the fee by stopping ICMP packets from triggering the demand-dial connection.

1. If necessary, start your server and log on as **Administrator**.

2. Click **Start**, point to **Administrative Tools**, and click **Routing and Remote Access**.

3. Right-click **ArcticDemand*xx***, where *xx* is your partner's student number, and click **Set IP Demand-dial Filters**.

4. Click **New** to create a new demand-dial filter.

5. Confirm that Source network is not selected. This acts as a wildcard to match any source address.

6. Confirm that Destination network is not selected. This acts as a wildcard to match any destination address.

7. Click the drop-down arrow for the Protocol list box, and click **ICMP**.

8. Leave the ICMP type field and ICMP code field empty. This setting acts as a wildcard to match any ICMP type and code.

9. Click **OK**.

10. Confirm that **For all traffic except** is selected. This means that any traffic can initiate the demand-dial connection except the listed filters, in this case ICMP traffic.

11. Click **OK**.

12. Test the new filter:

    a. Click **Start**, click **Run**, type **cmd**, and press **Enter**.

    b. Type **ping 10.100.*x*.5**, where *x* is your partner's student number, and press **Enter**. This IP address does not exist on the network, but can trigger the demand-dial connection based on the static route you configured in the Demand-Dial Interface Wizard.

    c. You receive an error message. This is normal. The only error is Destination host unreachable. This means that the path to the IP address you are pinging is not available because the demand-dial interface is disconnected. This error message does not change because the filter does not allow ICMP packets to trigger the connection. Close the Command Prompt window.

    d. Click **Start**, point to **All Programs**, and click **Internet Explorer**.

    e. In the Address bar, type **http://10.100.*xx*.5**, where *xx* is your partner's student number, and press **Enter**. Internet Explorer cannot connect to a Web site because there is no Web server at this address, but it triggers the demand-dial interface.

    f. After 5 to 10 seconds, close Internet Explorer.

13. View the connection state of your demand-dial connection in Network Interfaces. It should be Connected. If the state is not Connected, press **F5** to refresh the screen.

14. Right-click **ArcticDemand*x***, where *x* is your partner's student number, and click **Disconnect**. This manually disconnects the demand-dial interface.

15. Close the Routing and Remote Access snap-in.

Virtual LANs

The traditional definition of a switch defines them as operating at the Data Link layer of the OSI model. If this is the case, then they operate based on MAC addresses only and cannot understand IP addresses or IP networks. However, some switches are capable of working with IP address information. These are called layer 3 switches. This name is based on layer 3 of the OSI model, the Network layer.

One of the capabilities of layer 3 switches is creating a virtual LAN (VLANs), which segments a large network into smaller networks the same way subnetting with routers does. After VLANs are created, broadcasts do not propagate between them. Each VLAN is a broadcast domain. The switch controls broadcasts between VLANs just like a router.

Layer 3 switches are more flexible than routers for defining broadcast domains. A VLAN can be defined based on IP subnets like a router, but in addition they can be defined based on MAC addresses, protocols, and switch ports.

When a VLAN is created based on MAC addresses, a list of MAC addresses must be provided to define the VLAN. When a computer that is part of the list sends a broadcast, then the broadcast is sent to all of the other computers in the list. This ensures that the broadcast is sent only to the location of a few specific computers in the list. However, it is tedious to create a list of MAC addresses.

When a VLAN is created based on protocols, then different protocols are propagated to different parts of the network. For example, IPX traffic is sent only to computers that are using IPX and does not use bandwidth on sections of the network with IP only hosts.

The most common method used to define VLANs is switch ports. A number of ports are defined as being part of a VLAN and broadcasts are propagated only to ports that are part of the same VLAN. For example, a location in Arctic University may have two departments using applications that rely on broadcasts to announce status. Each department must be able to receive the broadcasts from its own application, but for security reasons they do not want the broadcasts available outside of their own department. If the switch at this location has 8 ports, then ports 1 to 4 could be part of the VLAN for department 1, and ports 5 to 8 could be part of the VLAN for department 2. The switch would then prevent broadcasts from propagating from department 1 to department 2 just the way a router would.

NOTE   The scope of a VLAN is not limited to a single switch. Multiple switches can communicate to build larger VLANs. Using this capability, it is possible to have broadcasts propagated from a port on one switch to ports on other switches if they are defined as part of the same VLAN.

NETWORK ADDRESS TRANSLATION

Most organizations use private internal IP addresses that are not registered for use on the Internet. The address ranges reserved for internal use are:

- 10.0.0.0 through 10.255.255.255
- 172.16.0.0 through 172.31.255.255
- 192.168.0.0 through 192.168.255.255

An organization using these addresses internally must have a mechanism in place to allow client computers to access the Internet. The two most common ways to do this are a proxy server and **Network Address Translation (NAT)**. Both of these allow an organization to use a single Internet IP address to provide Internet access to all client computers.

If a proxy server is implemented, then clients must be configured to use the proxy server. This is a significant administrative drawback. In addition, a proxy server is usually a product that costs extra money. In many cases, a proxy server also provides caching to speed up Internet connectivity.

NAT is included with Windows Server 2003 and is very effective if you are already using your Windows server as a router. Client computers do not need any change in configuration, because all traffic is translated as it is routed through the NAT server.

Some applications do not work properly through NAT. Any application that passes IP address and port information in the data portion of the packet is not properly translated. This includes most remote control software, many authentication algorithms, and FTP. However, most implementations of NAT, including the one on Windows Server 2003, are FTP aware and translate FTP packets properly.

How NAT Works

NAT modifies the IP headers of packets that are forwarded through a router. When a packet is forwarded through the router, NAT removes the original source IP address and source port number. The source IP address is changed to be the IP address of the router. The source port number is changed to a randomly generated port number.

To keep track of the translations that are being performed, NAT builds a table. This table lists the original source IP address, the original source port number, and the new source port number. The new source IP address is always the external interface on the router and does not need to be included in the table.

When a response packet is returned from the Internet, it is addressed to the IP address on the external interface of the router. The destination port in the packet is the randomly generated port number that was used when the original packet was translated. The router looks in its NAT table to find the entry that matches the destination port number.

When the table entry is found, the destination IP address in the packet is changed to be the original source IP address, and the destination port is changed to the original source port. The translated packet is then forwarded to the original host. Using this mechanism allows thousands of computers to access the Internet using a single IP address from an ISP.

Figure 4-17 shows an example of Network Address Translation being performed on a request from a client to a Web server. The IP header is modified when the request reaches the NAT router. The original source IP address (192.168.1.10) is replaced with the IP address of the router's external interface (5.5.5.5). The original source port (2032) is replaced with a randomly generated port number (52333) on the router's external interface. Information about this translation is stored in the NAT table.

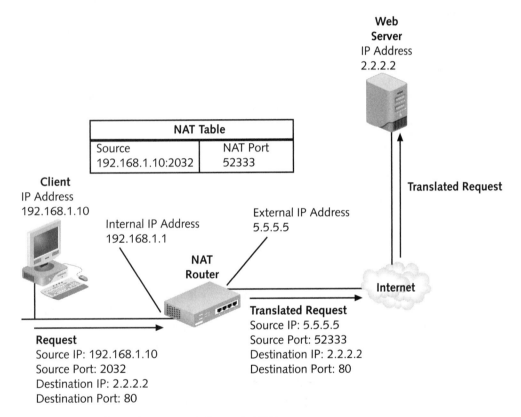

Figure 4-17   Outgoing request through NAT

Figure 4-18 shows an example of a response from a Web server to a client behind a NAT router. The original response packet is addressed to the external interface on the router (5.5.5.5/52333). The response packet is received by the router. The router looks up the port number (52333) in its NAT table. The destination IP address is replaced with the IP address of the client (192.168.1.10), and the destination port is replaced with the port on the client (2032). The packet is then forwarded on to the client.

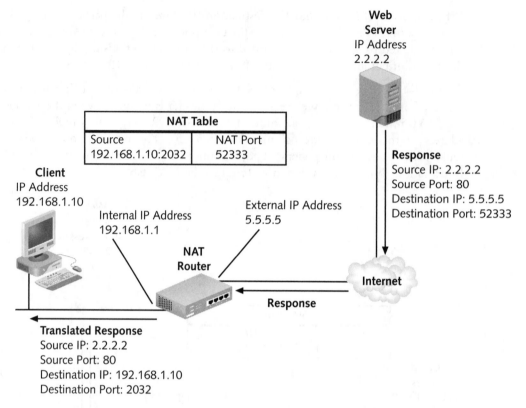

Figure 4-18   Incoming response through NAT

Installing NAT

The NAT protocol is automatically installed when RRAS is configured to be a router. However, you must add interfaces to it before it is actually used. To add an interface to NAT, right-click NAT/Basic Firewall, and click New Interface.

After adding an interface to NAT, the properties are displayed. The NAT/Basic Firewall tab, as shown in Figure 4-19, allows you to configure whether this interface is a private interface, public interface, or basic firewall. The definition of public and private interfaces is important for proper NAT functionality. Outgoing packets to the Internet use the IP address of the public interface for a source address.

For proper NAT functionality, one interface must be configured as a public interface, and at least one interface must be configured as a private interface. Addresses from the private network are translated when they are routed onto the public network.

A basic firewall allows you to configure static packet filters. When static packet filters are used, a rule must be created to allow network traffic out, and another rule must be created to allow response network traffic in. Custom rules can be added.

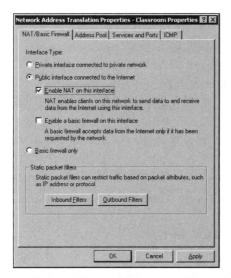

Figure 4-19   NAT/Basic Firewall tab

Normally, connections through a NAT router must be initiated by a client on the private network. However, the Services and Ports tab allows you to configure special NAT mappings that allow you to host services behind NAT, but still allow access to them from the Internet. For example, if you were hosting an e-mail server behind a NAT router, you could configure a rule that takes all packets addressed to port 25 on the external interface and forwards them to port 25 on an internal SMTP server.

The ICMP tab dictates to which types of ICMP packets the interface responds. Disabling response to ping packets (ICMP Echo Request) is a standard security precaution.

The Address Pool tab defines a range of IP addresses that are handed out to client computers. If this is configured, then the NAT router is a DHCP server. This option is not normally implemented.

Activity 4-9: Installing and Testing NAT

Time Required: 15 minutes

Objective: Install NAT and confirm it is functioning using a Web page on your instructor's computer.

Description: You are configuring a new server to perform NAT. To be sure it is working, you use it as a router to access a Web page that echoes back the source IP address and port number. The source IP address and port number will be from the NAT router instead of the client. You will work with a partner. Partner A will be the client computer. Partner B will be the NAT router.

1. If necessary, start your server and log on as **Administrator**.

2. Both partners view IP connection information:

   a. Click **Start**, point to **All Programs**, and click **Internet Explorer**.

   b. In the Address bar, type **http://192.168.1.10** and press **Enter**.

   c. A Web page appears in Internet Explorer indicating the source IP address, source TCP port, server IP address, and server port number. Notice that the source IP address is the IP address of the Classroom interface on your server. Close Internet Explorer.

3. Partner A reconfigures the default gateway and disables the Classroom interface:

   a. Click **Start**, point to **Control Panel**, point to **Network Connections**, right-click **Classroom**, and click **Properties**.

   b. Double-click **Internet Protocol (TCP/IP)**.

   c. Clear the contents of the Default gateway text box, click **OK**, and click **OK**.

   d. Click **Start**, point to **Control Panel**, point to **Network Connections**, right-click **Private**, and click **Properties**.

   e. Double-click **Internet Protocol (TCP/IP)**.

   f. In the Default gateway text box, type **172.16.x.yy**, where x is your group number and yy is your partner's student number. This is the IP address of your partner's server on the private interface. For this activity, you are using your partner's server as a router with NAT enabled.

   g. Click **OK**, and click **OK**.

   h. Click **Start**, point to **Control Panel**, point to **Network Connections**, right-click **Classroom**, and click **Disable**.

4. Partner B configures the Classroom interface for NAT:

   a. Click **Start**, point to **Administrative Tools**, and click **Routing and Remote Access**.

   b. If necessary, expand your server, and double-click **IP Routing** to expand it.

   c. Right-click **NAT/Basic Firewall**, and click **New Interface**.

   d. Click **Classroom**, and click **OK**.

   e. Click **Public interface connected to the Internet**. This indicates that the IP address of this interface will be the source IP address when NAT is performed.

   f. Click the **Enable NAT on this interface** check box. This tells the system to start performing NAT on this interface.

   g. Click **OK**.

5. Partner B configures the Private interface for NAT:

   a. Right-click **NAT/Basic Firewall**, and click **New Interface**.

   b. Click **Private**, and click **OK**.

   c. Confirm that Private interface connected to private network is selected and click **OK**.

6. Partner A tests NAT by accessing the Web page on the Instructor server:

   a. Click **Start**, point to **All Programs**, and click **Internet Explorer**.

   b. In the Address bar, type **http://192.168.1.10** and press **Enter**.

   c. A Web page appears in Internet Explorer indicating the source IP address, source TCP port, server IP address, and server port number. Notice that the source IP address is the IP address of the Classroom interface on the server of partner B. Close Internet Explorer.

7. Partner B disables NAT:

   a. In the NAT/Basic Firewall interfaces, right-click **Classroom**, and click **Delete**.

   b. Click **Yes** to confirm the removal.

   c. Right-click **Private**, and click **Delete**.

   d. Click **Yes** to confirm the removal.

   e. Close the Routing and Remote Access snap-in.

8. Partner A reconfigures the default gateway and enables the Classroom interface:

   a. Click **Start**, point to **Control Panel**, point to **Network Connections**, right-click **Private**, and click **Properties**.

   b. Double-click **Internet Protocol (TCP/IP)**.

   c. Clear the contents of the Default gateway text box, click **OK**, and click **OK**.

   d. Click **Start**, point to **Control Panel**, point to **Network Connections**, right-click **Classroom**, and click **Properties**.

   e. Double-click **Internet Protocol (TCP/IP)**.

   f. In the Default gateway text box, type **192.168.1.10**.

   g. Click **OK**, and click **OK**.

   h. Click **Start**, point to **Control Panel**, point to **Network Connections**, right-click **Classroom**, and click **Enable**.

9. If time permits, reverse roles and repeat the activity.

Configuring NAT

The NAT protocol is configured by right-clicking NAT/Basic Firewall, and clicking Properties. The General tab controls the level of logging that is performed. The default logging setting is to log errors only.

The Translation tab allows you to configure how long **mappings** are kept in the NAT table. A mapping is the listing of an external port number that is linked to an internal IP address and port number. By default, mappings for TCP connections are kept for 1440 minutes, and mappings for UDP are kept for one minute. The Reset Defaults button returns to these defaults.

On the Address Assignment tab, you can configure NAT to act as a DHCP server. To do this, you must configure a static range of IP addresses. Exclusions can be configured within the ranges.

The Name Resolution tab, as shown in Figure 4-20, configures the NAT router to act as a **DNS proxy**. A DNS proxy relays DNS requests on behalf of DNS clients. Client computers can then query the NAT router as a DNS server. The NAT router then forwards the requests on to the DNS server configured in its own network settings. To enable the DNS proxy, select the Clients using Domain Name System (DNS) check box. To enable the activation of a demand-dial connection when name resolution requests are received, select the Connect to the public network when a name needs to be resolved check box. None of the settings on this tab need to be enabled if internal DNS servers exist.

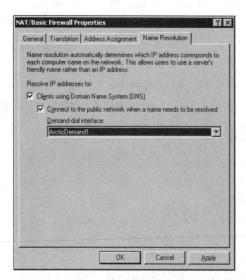

Figure 4-20   Name Resolution tab

You can view statistics related to the **DHCP allocator** and DNS proxy to confirm that they are functioning properly. The DHCP allocator is a simplified DHCP server. To view DHCP allocator statistics, right-click NAT/Basic Firewall, and click Show DHCP Allocator Information. To view DNS proxy statistics, right-click NAT/Basic Firewall, and click Show DNS Proxy Information.

INTERNET CONNECTION SHARING

Internet Connection Sharing (ICS) is a Windows Server 2003 service that provides an automated way for a small office using Windows Server 2003 as a router to connect to the Internet. It automatically performs NAT and configures network connections. Because NAT is used, the server must have at least two network cards. The configuration used by ICS cannot be changed.

ICS makes the following changes:

- The internal network connection is configured with the IP address 192.168.0.1 and the subnet mask 255.255.255.0.

- Autodial is enabled for dial-up/VPN/PPPoE connections.

- A static route for the default gateway is enabled when the dial-up/VPN/PPPoE connection is activated.

- The ICS service is started.

- The DHCP allocator is configured to distribute IP addresses from 192.168.0.2 to 192.168.0.254.

- The DNS proxy is enabled.

ICS is enabled in the properties of the public network interface on the Advanced tab. To enable it, check the Allow other network users to connect through this computer's Internet connection check box, as shown in Figure 4-21.

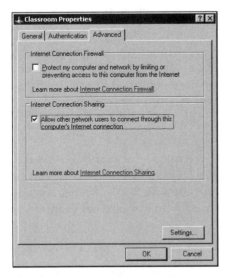

Figure 4-21   Enabling ICS

An ICS server can only have one internal IP address. If an ICS server has multiple internal interfaces, they must be configured to use **network bridging** so that the interfaces can share a single IP address.

 Network bridging is a new feature in Windows Server 2003. It is available only in the 32-bit versions. Network bridging is available in Windows clients starting with Windows XP.

NOTE

A bridge controls network traffic based on MAC addresses. It also allows computers on two different physical network segments to be on the same IP network. This is very useful for small networks with multiple media types for wiring. The two media types can be connected into a single, logical network without the complexity of routing. When network bridging is enabled, you choose multiple network cards in a server to act as a single IP network.

To enable network bridging, open Network Connections, Ctrl-click at least two connections to select them, right-click the selected connections, and click Bridge Connections.

INTERNET CONNECTION FIREWALL

Internet Connection Firewall (ICF) is a stateful packet filter (which is a filter that automatically creates reverse rules for response traffic) that can be used to protect any server running Windows Server 2003. In most situations, ICF is required only if the server is connected directly to the Internet. However, you may choose to implement it internally as well to protect systems from internal hackers.

A standard packet filter, such as a basic firewall, requires you to make two rules to allow Internet connectivity. For instance, if you want to allow internal clients access to Web sites on the Internet, you must create one rule that allows traffic addressed to TCP port 80 out, and another that allows return traffic for any TCP port above 1023. Not only is it an administrative hassle to configure the second rule, but it is also a large security hole. Ports above 1023 are used by many viruses to transmit information and replicate.

A **stateful firewall**, such as ICF, requires only one rule for the outbound traffic. The firewall keeps track of TCP connections that are created by internal clients and automatically allows response packets to return. This reduces administrative hassle. Security is also increased because no rules allow connections to be created from the Internet to internal clients.

Enabling ICF

ICF is configured per connection. Normally, the only connection that needs to be configured is the one that connects to the Internet. ICF is enabled in the properties of a connection. On the Advanced tab, click the Protect my computer and network by limiting or preventing access to this computer from the Internet check box.

If ICF is enabled on a server that is not a router, only that server is protected. If ICF is enabled on a router, then all computers on the internal network are protected.

Configuring ICF

When ICF is enabled, all packets from the network that are addressed to the server are dropped. If this server is running a service, such as a Web server, clients will be unable to communicate with it. However, if the server initiates a request, then the response is allowed to return.

To allow requests from the network to access services on the server running ICF, you need to configure services. The services defined are the firewall rules for ICF. The list of defined services is accessed through the Settings button in the properties of the connection, where ICF is enabled.

The Services tab, as shown in Figure 4-22, has a predefined list of services that you can choose to allow. By default, none are selected. You can also define your own services based on IP addresses and port numbers. These services are also used by ICS for static NAT mappings to access services behind the NAT router.

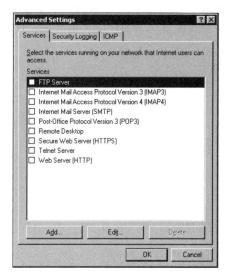

Figure 4-22   Services defined for ICF and ICS

After ICF is enabled, the server does not respond to any ICMP packets on the configured connection. Using the ICMP tab, shown in Figure 4-23, you can allow certain ICMP traffic. For example, to confirm remotely that your server is functional, you may check the Allow incoming echo request check box so that the server responds to the ping utility.

The Security Logging tab, as shown in Figure 4-24, is used to configure the type of information that is logged, the location of the log, and the maximum size of the log. ICF is

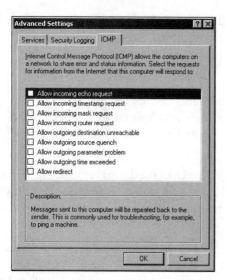

Figure 4-23 ICMP options for ICF

capable of logging both dropped packets and successful connections. The default location of the log file is C:\WINDOWS\pfirewall.log, and it has a maximum size of 4 MB.

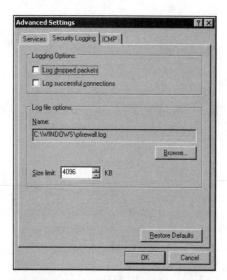

Figure 4-24 Logging options for ICF

NOTE

When the ICF log reaches its maximum size, it is saved as pfirewall.log.old and a new pfirewall.log file is created. If an older pfirewall.log.old already exists, it is overwritten.

In a low-security environment, you may choose not to do any logging at all. In a medium-security environment, you may track dropped packets, although you may be astonished at how many dropped packets there are on an Internet connection. Successful connections are normally logged only in very high-security environments.

ACTIVITY

Activity 4-10: Installing ICF

4

Time Required: 10 minutes

Objective: Install and configure ICF on your server.

Description: To enhance security on all of the Arctic University Web servers, you have chosen to implement ICF. In this activity, you work with a partner to test the functionality of ICF.

1. If necessary, start your server and log on as **Administrator**.

2. Install Internet Information Server 6.0:

   a. Click **Start**, point to **Control Panel**, and click **Add or Remove Programs**.

   b. Click **Add/Remove Windows Components**.

   c. In the Windows Components window, double-click **Application Server**, and if necessary, check the **Internet Information Services (IIS)** check box. The check box will turn gray with a check mark. This indicates that not all components have been installed. The Web server is the only component you require for this activity, and it is installed. Click **OK**.

   d. Click **Next**. If prompted for the Windows Server 2003 CD-ROM, click **OK**. Then click **Browse**, and select the **C:\I386** folder. Click **Open**, and then click **OK** in the Files Needed dialog box.

   e. Click **Finish** to complete the installation.

   f. Close the Add or Remove Programs window.

3. Configure a Web page on your server:

   a. Click **Start**, click **Run**, type **cmd**, and press **Enter**.

   b. Type **copy \\instructor\c$\inetpub\wwwroot\default.asp   c:\inetpub\ wwwroot** and press **Enter**. This file is now the default page on your Web site.

   c. Close the Command Prompt window.

4. Enable ASP scripts on your Web server:

   a. Click **Start**, point to **Administrative Tools**, and click **Internet Information Services (IIS) Manager**.

   b. If necessary, double-click your server to expand it, and click **Web Service Extensions**. This is where you can control the type of scripts that are allowed to run on the Web server.

  c. In the right pane, click **Active Server Pages**, and click **Allow**. This is required to view the default Web page properly you copied onto your Web server.

  d. Close the Internet Information Services (IIS) Manager snap-in.

 5. Test the Web page on your partner's server. Complete this step only if your partner has finished Step 4:

  a. Click **Start**, point to **All Programs**, and click **Internet Explorer**.

  b. In the Address bar, type **http://192.168.1.1xx**, where *xx* is your partner's student number, and press **Enter**. This accesses the Web site on your partner's server.

  c. You should see a Web page that echoes back the source IP address and port number your computer used to request the Web page. This confirms that your partner's Web server is functioning properly and is accessible. Close Internet Explorer.

 6. Disable Routing and Remote Access on your server. ICF and RRAS cannot run on the same server:

  a. Click **Start**, point to **Administrative Tools**, and click **Routing and Remote Access**.

  b. Right-click your server, and click **Disable Routing and Remote Access**.

  c. Click **Yes** to continue.

  d. Close the Routing and Remote Access snap-in.

 7. Configure ICF with default packet filtering options on your server:

  a. Click **Start**, point to **Control Panel**, point to **Network Connections**, right-click **Classroom**, and click **Properties**.

  b. Click the **Advanced** tab.

  c. Check the **Protect my computer and network by limiting or preventing access to this computer from the Internet** check box to select it.

  d. Click **OK**.

 8. Test your connectivity with Internet Explorer. Do not perform this step until your partner has completed Step 7:

  a. Click **Start**, point to **All Programs**, and click **Internet Explorer**.

  b. In the Address bar, type **http://192.168.1.10**, and press **Enter**. This accesses the Web site on the instructor's server.

  c. You should see a Web page that echoes back the source IP address and port number your computer used to request the Web page. This confirms that your server can create Web connections with other hosts after ICF is enabled.

  d. In the Address bar, type **http://192.168.1.1xx**, where *xx* is your partner's student number, and press **Enter**. This accesses the Web site on your partner's server.

  e. You get an error message indicating the server could not be contacted. This is because ICF on your partner's server is blocking your requests. Close Internet Explorer.

9. Configure ICF to allow traffic addressed to port 80 on your server. Do not perform this step until your partner has completed Step 8:

   a. Click **Start**, point to **Control Panel**, point to **Network Connections**, right-click **Classroom**, and click **Properties**.

   b. Click the **Advanced** tab, and click **Settings**.

   c. On the Services tab, double-click **Web Server (HTTP)**.

   d. In the Name or IP address of the computer hosting this service on your network text box, type **192.168.1.1yy**, where yy is your student number. This is the IP address of your server, and allows remote clients to access port 80 on your server.

   e. Click **OK** to save the service settings.

   f. Confirm that the check box beside **Web Server (HTTP)** is selected. If it is not, then click the check box beside **Web Server (HTTP)**.

   g. Click **OK** to close the Advanced Settings window.

   h. Click **OK** to close the Classroom Properties window.

10. Test connectivity to your partner's server with Internet Explorer. Do not perform this step until your partner has completed Step 9:

    a. Click **Start**, point to **All Programs**, and click Internet Explorer.

    b. In the Address bar, type **http://192.168.1.1xx**, where xx is your partner's student number, and press **Enter**. This accesses the Web site on your partner's server.

    c. You should see a Web page that echoes back the source IP address and port number your computer used to request the Web page. This confirms that your server can create a Web connection with your partner's server after the service is configured. Close Internet Explorer.

11. Disable ICF:

    a. Click **Start**, point to **Control Panel**, point to **Network Connections**, right-click **Classroom**, and click **Properties**.

    b. Click the **Advanced** tab.

    c. Check the **Protect my computer and network by limiting or preventing access to this computer from the Internet** check box to deselect it.

    d. Click **OK**.

    e. Click **Yes** to confirm.

PLANNING INTERNET CONNECTIVITY

As use of the Internet has become more common, providing Internet access for users has become a critical business issue. Access to the Internet must be secure and reliable.

The first decision that must be made for Internet connectivity is whether to use internal private addresses or Internet accessible IP addresses for each computer. Using Internet accessible IP addresses is more expensive because each ISP has a limited number of them and they charge for each address. Using internal private IP addresses is more secure because either NAT or a proxy server controls access to the Internet. Most organizations use internal private IP addresses.

When internal private IP addresses are used, you must implement NAT or a proxy server to provide access to the Internet. The main benefit of NAT is that applications are unaware it is happening. NAT is performed by the router and no client configuration is required. NAT does not limit Internet access based on rules.

NAT provides a limited level of security because connections must be initiated from the internal network to the Internet before a mapping is placed in the NAT table of the router. After the connection has been created, it could theoretically be exploited by a hacker. However, port numbers used by NAT are random, and the port mappings are transient, making it difficult to exploit.

Static NAT mappings can be used to provide Internet users with access to internal resources, such as Web servers and e-mail servers.

Using a proxy server is more secure than NAT. A proxy server functions up to the Application layer. This means that the proxy understands all of the information in a data packet, not just addressing information. Therefore, a proxy server can block and allow packets based on very specific information, such as which HTTP commands are being used in the conversation. This prevents a wide range of exploits involving invalid protocol commands.

A proxy server can also control access based on the user. Rules can be configured that allow certain users access to different resources and block certain users from accessing other resources. This can also be used to deny Internet access completely to some users.

If Internet access speed is a problem, a proxy server can perform caching for the most common protocols, such as HTTP and FTP. When a user accesses a Web site, the proxy server keeps a copy of the Web page on its hard drive. Then, when another user requests the same page, the proxy server retrieves the Web page from the cache on the hard drive rather than downloading it from the Internet. This can reduce overall Internet traffic by up to 50% in many organizations.

The major limitation when using a proxy server is that applications need to understand how to use the proxy server. Web browsers, FTP clients, and other common Internet software are designed to work with proxy servers. Many customized applications are not. To work around this limitation, some organizations proxy some protocols and perform NAT for others.

Firewalls should be in place to control user access to the Internet. You should only allow known protocols to be accessed on the Internet. This prevents Trojan horse programs from accessing outside services and potentially creating a security hole. For instance, if internal computers are allowed to access all resources on the Internet, a Trojan horse program can infect a workstation and advertise its availability on an Internet Relay Chat (IRC) server. If the Trojan keeps the connection alive, then an entry in the NAT table is preserved, thus providing an opening for hackers.

CHAPTER SUMMARY

4

- Subnetting is used to divide a single large network into multiple smaller networks. This reduces packet collisions, limits broadcast propagation, and allows you to control network traffic. Each physical location in a network has its own subnet.

- The formula 2^n-2 is used to calculate the number of subnets that can be created from n bits. The -2 is not required when using classless routing. This same formula can be used to calculate the number of hosts on a subnet.

- Supernetting is used to combine multiple smaller networks into one large network. This simplifies routing tables.

- Windows Server 2003 can be configured as a low-cost router for TCP/IP and AppleTalk. IPX/SPX is not supported.

- RIP is a distance-vector routing algorithm that calculates paths based on hops. If a route is 16 hops away, it is considered unreachable. RIP advertises its entire routing table every 30 seconds.

- OSPF is a link-state routing algorithm that calculates paths based on a configurable metric called cost. Each interface in a router can be assigned a cost. OSPF only advertises changes to a routing table when they happen. The 64-bit versions of Windows Server 2003 do not support OSPF.

- Demand-dial connections are activated only when network traffic requires them. They can also be configured to disconnect after a period of time if there is no more traffic to cross the link. Static routes are required for demand-dial connections.

- Demand-dial connections can be configured with dial-out hours to limit the times they are active. They can also be configured with demand-dial filters to limit the types of traffic that can trigger the connection.

- NAT allows many computers to access the Internet using a single Internet-addressable IP address. It functions by modifying the IP headers of packets that are routed through the NAT router. The IP address on the external interface of the NAT router is substituted for the original source IP address.

- ICS is an automated way to configure a router for NAT. However, the default settings, such as IP address, cannot be changed.

- Network bridging is required with ICS if there is more than one internal interface.

- ICF is a stateful packet filter. Rules for ICF are configured using services.

KEY TERMS

binary — A base-two numbering system. There are only two valid values for each digit: 0 and 1.

bit — A single binary digit.

collision — The result when two computers attempt to send a packet on the network at the same time—the signals collide and become unreadable.

cost — In routing, a configurable value assigned to a packet being forwarded through a router interface.

demand-dial — A dial-up/VPN/PPPoE connection that is only activated when required to move network traffic.

demand-dial filters — The rules that limit the types of traffic that can trigger the activation of a demand-dial connection.

DHCP allocator — A simplified DHCP service that can be used by NAT and ICS.

dial-out hours — A limit for demand-dial connections that allows connections only during certain time periods.

distance-vector routing — Any routing algorithm based on simple hop calculation. RIP is the most common example.

DNS proxy — A service that accepts DNS requests from clients and forwards them on to a DNS server.

dynamic routing — The process by which routing tables are automatically generated by routers based on communication with other routers.

hops — In routing, a packet being forwarded by a single router.

Internet Connection Firewall (ICF) — A stateful packet filter that can be used to protect servers connected to the Internet.

Internet Connection Sharing (ICS) — An automated way to implement NAT for a small network.

link-state routing — A routing algorithm in which routers use a configurable cost metric to build a picture of the entire network. OSPF is the most common example.

mappings — An entry in the NAT table maintained by the NAT router that provides correlation between the original source IP address and port number and the port number used on the external interface of the NAT router.

Network Address Translation (NAT) — A protocol used by routers to allow multiple clients to share a single Internet-addressable IP address. IP headers are modified to make the packet look as though it came from the NAT router.

network bridging — A feature that combines two network cards in a server as a single, logical network. This can be used to combine two different media types, such as UTP and coaxial cabling.

Open Shortest Path First (OSPF) — A link-state routing protocol that calculates paths based on a configurable metric called cost. Changes to the routing table are advertised only when they occur.

Point-to-Point Protocol over Ethernet (PPPoE) — A protocol used for authentication and traffic control on high-speed Internet connections such as DSL.

poison-reverse processing — An option for RIP routing in which a router advertises a route as unreachable on the interface from which it was learned.

ROUTE PRINT — A command-line utility used to view the contents of a routing table.

Routing and Remote Access Service (RRAS) — The Windows Server 2003 service that is responsible for controlling routing, dial-up, and VPN connections.

Routing Information Protocol (RIP) — A distance-vector routing protocol that calculates paths based on hops. Complete routing tables are advertised every 30 seconds.

routing table — The list of networks and how to reach them that is maintained by a router.

split-horizon processing — An option for RIP routing in which a router is not advertised back on the same interface from which it was learned to prevent routing loops.

stateful firewall — A firewall that tracks TCP connections to allow response packets to return automatically without configuring a rule.

static routes — An entry in a routing table that is permanently added by an administrator.

static routing — The process by which routing tables are maintained manually by an administrator. Windows 2003 also has the ability to build static routes with an automated process called auto-static updates.

subnetting — The process of dividing a single IP network into several smaller IP networks. Bits are taken from the host ID and made part of the network ID by adjusting the subnet mask.

supernetting — The process of combining several smaller networks into a single large network by taking bits from the network ID and making them part of the host ID.

virtual LAN (VLAN) — A broadcast domain created by a switch based on subnets, protocols, MAC addresses, or switch ports.

REVIEW QUESTIONS

1. Which of the following is not a reason to subnet a network?

   a. to reduce collisions on the network

   b. to limit the number of collisions on the subnet

   c. to combine smaller networks into a larger network

   d. to control the amount of traffic on the network

   e. to reduce the number of IP addresses in use on the network

2. Your computer has an IP address of 172.18.56.17 with a subnet mask of 255.255.248.0. Which of the following IP addresses is on your local subnet? (Choose all that apply.)

   a. 172.18.47.200

   b. 172.18.60.100

   c. 172.18.89.157

   d. 172.18.54.3

   e. 172.18.65.117

   f. 172.18.57.42

3. What is the maximum number of workstations the subnet mask 255.255.240.0 can support on the local subnet?

   a. 2048

   b. 2046

   c. 4096

   d. 4094

   e. 8190

4. You have been assigned the network address 172.32.0.0 to use on your LAN. You need to divide the network into seven subnets. Which subnet mask do you use?

   a. 255.240.0.0

   b. 255.224.0.0

   c. 255.255.248.0

   d. 255.255.240.0

5. You need to connect to a computer on your local subnet. Your computer's IP address is 172.28.17.5, and the other computer's IP address is 172.28.30.252. Which subnet mask can you use? (Choose all that apply.)

   a. 255.0.0.0

   b. 255.255.0.0

   c. 255.255.252.0

   d. 255.255.240.0

   e. 255.255.248.0

6. You are using the network ID 10.0.0.0. You need to divide the network into smaller subnets that can support 6,000 workstations on each subnet. Which of the following subnets supports 6,000 workstations? (Choose all that apply.)

   a. 255.192.0.0.0

   b. 255.255.192.0

   c. 255.255.224.0

   d. 255.255.240.0

   e. 255.255.248.0

7. How many bits are required to supernet seven Class C addresses?

   a. 1

   b. 2

   c. 3

   d. 4

   e. 5

8. Which type of routing allows routers to build their routing tables automatically?

    a. static routing

    b. manual routing

    c. automatic routing

    d. dynamic routing

9. What number of hops is considered unreachable for RIP routing?

    a. 8

    b. 16

    c. 32

    d. 64

    e. 128

10. Why would you enable auto-static update mode for RIP?

    a. to keep permanently routes learned from a demand-dial connection

    b. for higher security

    c. to limit the packets that can trigger a demand-dial connection

    d. to limit a demand-dial connection only to certain users

11. Which type of connection can demand-dial be used to activate? (Choose all that apply.)

    a. VPN

    b. dial-up

    c. IPX/SPX

    d. PPPoE

    e. FTP

12. Which of the following criteria can be used to limit how demand-dial connections are activated? (Choose all that apply.)

    a. time of day

    b. month

    c. type of traffic

    d. user

13. After an outgoing packet has been translated by a NAT router and sent to the Internet, what is the source IP address?

    a. the IP address of the client that generated the request

    b. the IP address of the internal interface of the NAT router

    c. the IP address of the external interface of the NAT router

    d. the IP address of the destination host

14. When an incoming packet is received by the NAT router, which part of the packet determines where it is sent?

    a. source IP address

    b. source port

    c. destination IP address

    d. destination port

15. Services hosted by servers behind a NAT router can never be accessed by hosts on the Internet. True or False?

16. Which service can combine two physical segments using different media types into a single logical network?

    a. NAT

    b. ICS

    c. network bridging

    d. ICF

    e. AppleTalk

17. Which service forces the internal interface of the router to use the IP address 192. 168.0.1?

    a. RRAS

    b. NAT

    c. ICS

    d. network bridging

    e. ICF

18. Which routing protocol announces its entire routing table every 30 seconds?

    a. RIP

    b. SAP

    c. OSPF

    d. AppleTalk

19. Which two additional services can be configured as part of NAT?

    a. DHCP allocator

    b. WINS proxy

    c. DNS proxy

    d. remote access

20. When using classless routing, the formula used to calculate the number of bits required for subnetting is 2^n because the subnets of all 0s and all 1s are allowed. True or False?

CASE PROJECTS

Case Project 4-1: Choosing Subnets for Each Location

There are six different physical locations used by Arctic University to deliver classes. Each of these locations has a minimum of 50 computers and a maximum of 1,000 computers. The IP addressing plan needs to be presented at the IT staff meeting this week. Write a short report indicating the range of addresses that should be used for each location and the reasons you chose those address ranges.

Case Project 4-2: Supernetting to Reduce Routing

A router connecting two small test labs has failed and needs to be replaced. The first lab has 10 computers and is assigned the network ID 192.168.21.0 with a subnet mask of 255.255.255.0. The second lab has 25 computers with the network ID of 192.168.23.0 and a subnet mask of 255.255.255.0. Instead of replacing the failed router, you recommend that the two subnets be combined into a single supernet. Which subnet mask would you use? Which IP addresses are valid for the new supernet?

Case Project 4-3: Hardware Routers Versus Software Routers

As a cost-cutting measure for smaller locations, you have decided to use Windows Server 2003 as a router rather than buying hardware routers. This decision has just been announced to the rest of the IT Department. Some of your colleagues with certifications from hardware router vendors are quite upset and have complained to your supervisor.

Write a report justifying your decision. As part of the report, include a list of routing services provided with Windows Server 2003 and where they can be used in Arctic University.

Case Project 4-4: Internet Connectivity

You have been approached by one of the professors at Arctic University to help his small business connect to the Internet. He already has Windows Server 2003. Evaluate whether it would be more appropriate to implement ICS, NAT, or a proxy server in this situation.

CHAPTER

5

PLANNING, CONFIGURING, AND TROUBLESHOOTING DHCP

After reading this chapter, you will be able to:

- ◆ Understand the DHCP lease and renewal process
- ◆ Plan DHCP for small or large networks
- ◆ Install DHCP
- ◆ Authorize a DHCP server
- ◆ Configure a DHCP server with scopes, superscopes, and more
- ◆ Manage and monitor a DHCP server
- ◆ Troubleshoot DHCP

Manually going to each workstation in an organization to configure IP addresses is a time-consuming task. Fortunately, you can use DHCP (Dynamic Host Configuration Protocol) to reduce the amount of time spent configuring workstations. DHCP automatically configures workstations with an IP address, subnet mask, default gateway, and many other options.

In this chapter, you look at the DHCP lease and renewal process to understand how DHCP works. Then, you plan DHCP for large and small networks. Finally, you learn how to install, authorize, configure, monitor, and troubleshoot a DHCP server.

THE DHCP PROCESS

DHCP is used to deliver IP addressing information automatically to client computers on a network. It can also deliver IP address information to servers and other devices such as printers, although most network administrators prefer to use static IP addresses for network resources such as servers and printers.

Using DHCP reduces the amount of time you spend configuring computers on your network. Imagine that a company with 500 client computers changes the IP address of their router as part of the implementation of a new firewall. If this company is not using DHCP, the network administrator has to visit each client computer and change the default gateway, which might take days. However, if this company is using DHCP, then the new default gateway can be delivered when all the users log on the next morning. In this case, the network administrator does not have to visit any client computers.

Client computers use DHCP by default unless you specify a static IP address during the installation. To confirm that a computer is using DHCP, you can view the properties of TCP/IP in the Internet Protocol (TCP/IP) Properties dialog box. Figure 5-1 shows the TCP/IP properties of a Windows XP client computer. If the Obtain an IP address automatically option is selected, then the computer is using DHCP. Windows XP is shown because it is more likely to be a DHCP client than Windows Server 2003.

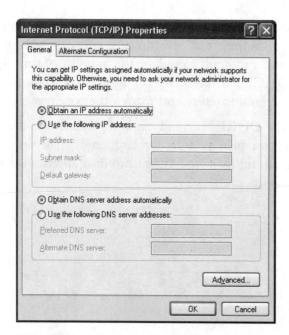

Figure 5-1   Windows XP TCP/IP properties

Leasing an IP Address

A client computer that is configured to use DHCP **obtains a lease for** an IP address during the boot process when the network connection is initialized. A leased address can be used for an Administrator defined period of time and then must be renewed, or released. The overall process to lease an address is composed of four packets:

- DHCPDISCOVER
- DHCPOFFER
- DHCPREQUEST
- DHCPACK

Figure 5-2 shows the four packets transmitted as part of the DHCP process.

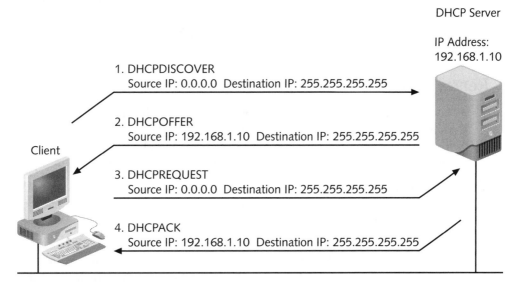

Figure 5-2   The four packets in the DHCP lease process

The **DHCPDISCOVER** packet is sent from the client computer to the broadcast IP address 255.255.255.255. A broadcast IP address must be used because the DHCP clients are not configured with the IP address of a DHCP server. The source IP address in the packet is 0.0.0.0 because the client does not yet have an IP address. The MAC address of the client is included in the packet as an identifier.

Any DHCP server that receives the DHCPDISCOVER packet responds with a DHCPOF-FER packet. The **DHCPOFFER** packet contains DHCP lease information, such as an IP address, subnet mask, default gateway, and length of the lease. The destination IP address for the packet is the broadcast address 255.255.255.255. This destination IP address ensures that the client can receive the packet even though it does not yet have an IP address assigned. The MAC address of the client is included in the data portion of the packet as an identifier.

The DHCP client responds to the DHCPOFFER packet it receives with a DHCPRE-QUEST packet. If there are multiple DHCP servers that send DHCPOFFER packets, the client responds only to the first one that it receives. The **DHCPREQUEST** packet contains the lease information that has been chosen by the client. The first server that responded is the chosen server, and uses this information to identify that it was chosen. Other DHCP servers that were not chosen see this packet and recognize that their lease was not chosen.

The DHCPREQUEST packet is addressed to the broadcast IP address 255.255.255.255. This allows all of the DHCP servers to see the DHCPREQUEST. The servers that were not chosen see this packet and place their offered addresses back into their pool of available addresses.

The chosen DHCP server sends back a **DHCPACK** packet indicating its confirmation that the lease has been chosen and that the client is now allowed to use the lease. This packet is still being sent to the broadcast IP address 255.255.255.255 because the client has not yet initialized IP with the new address. After DHCPACK is received by the client, the client starts using the IP address and options that were in the lease.

Renewing an IP Address

When an IP address is leased using DHCP, it can be either permanent or timed. When a permanent address is given to a client, the DHCP server never reuses that address for another client. A permanent address is a way to distribute IP address and configuration options to clients if there will never be any changes to the information.

Note that it is very rare to find a computer network that never changes its IP addressing configuration. It is quite common to add additional DNS servers or change the default gateway if a new router is installed. To allow for these changes, timed leases are used.

A **timed lease** allows clients to use an IP address for a specified period of time. Windows clients attempt to renew their lease after 50% of the lease time has expired by sending a DHCPREQUEST message directly to the DHCP server from which it obtained the lease. If a DHCP client cannot renew its lease with the original DHCP server, the client broadcasts a DHCPREQUEST to contact any available DHCP server when 87.5% of the lease period has expired, and again at 100% of the lease time.

Figure 5-3 shows the two packets that are used as part of a successful DHCP lease renewal process and an unsuccessful lease renewal process.

The first packet in the renewal process is a DHCPREQUEST packet from the client to the DHCP server. This packet uses the IP address of the client as the source address and the IP address of the DHCP server as the destination address. Broadcast addresses are not required for renewing a DHCP lease because the client already has an IP address and because the client is already aware of the DHCP server's IP address.

The response from the DHCP server is either a DHCPACK packet or a DHCPNAK packet. A DHCPACK packet is used to confirm the renewal of the client lease, whereas a

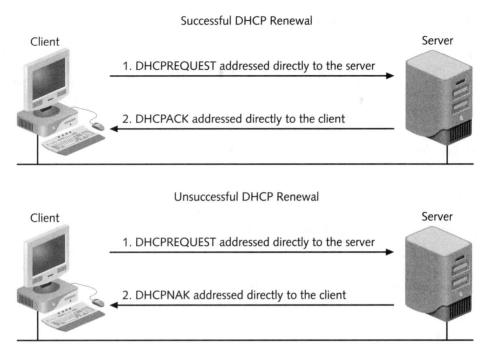

Figure 5-3   The DHCP lease renewal processes

DHCPNAK packet is used to deny the renewal of the client lease. If the renewal is denied, the client can continue to use the current address information until the lease expires.

A client can initiate the release of an IP address before the lease time has expired. When using Windows 98/Me/NT/2000/XP, the command ipconfig/release forces the release of a DHCP address. In this process, the client sends a **DHCPRELEASE** packet to the DHCP server. The DHCP server then makes the released address available to other clients if required.

For more information on the packets sent as part of the DHCP process in various situations, view RFC 2131. It can be found at *www.ietf.org/rfc/rfc2131.txt*.

NOTE

PLANNING DHCP

In most networks, DHCP is used to assign addresses automatically to workstations. Servers and printers are normally assigned static IP addresses. When planning how to implement DHCP, you must first consider whether it is a small or large network. Then, you can make additional choices based on your need for fault tolerance.

When You Have a Small Network

A small network with only a single subnet is very easy to plan. This type of network does not use a router, only hubs and switches. Both hubs and switches forward the broadcast packets used by DHCP. Therefore, a single DHCP server can service all clients with no special configuration. The DHCP server is configured with a single scope that contains all of the IP addresses that are handed out to the workstations.

When You Have a Large Network

Large networks have more than one subnet and use routers to move packets between the subnets. Routers do not forward broadcast packets by default. This keeps DHCP packets from crossing routers, which is not what you want. To overcome this problem, you must configure DHCP relays or multiple DHCP servers.

If you decide to use multiple DHCP servers, you must place a DHCP server on each subnet. Depending on the size of the network, this may result in tens or hundreds of DHCP servers. This makes management very complex because each server is managed separately. Figure 5-4 shows a network with two subnets using multiple DHCP servers.

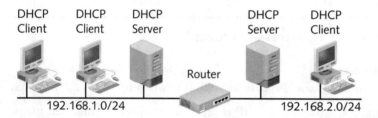

Figure 5-4   Two subnets with multiple DHCP servers

DHCP Relay

A DHCP relay is a device that allows DHCP communication across routers. Using DHCP relays can drastically simplify the implementation of DHCP because it reduces or eliminates the need for multiple DHCP servers. A DHCP relay receives broadcast DHCP packets from clients and forwards them as unicast packets to a DHCP server. The DHCP relay must be configured with the IP address of the DHCP server to deliver the unicast packets.

When the DHCP server receives unicast packets from the DHCP relay, it looks at the source IP address of the DHCP relay and offers a lease from that same subnet. The offer is sent as a unicast packet to the DHCP relay, which broadcasts it on the local subnet. The client receives the broadcast and continues the DHCP leasing process.

A DHCP relay can be implemented on Windows Server 2003 or a router. The RFC that describes a DHCP relay is RFC 1542. Routers that can act as a DHCP relay are referred to as RFC-1542 compliant. Using routers as DHCP relays is advantageous because they are attached to multiple subnets. This reduces the number of devices that need to be configured because one router can service several subnets. Figure 5-5 shows a network using both Windows Server 2003 and a router for DHCP relay.

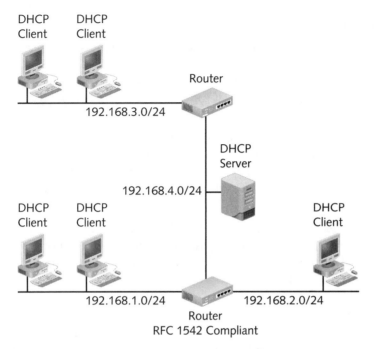

Figure 5-5   A network using DHCP relays

 The DHCP Relay Agent cannot be installed on the same server as the DHCP Service. Both services listen at the same port numbers. If both are installed, the performance is erratic.

Fault Tolerance

DHCP servers are not designed to communicate with each other. As such, they cannot coordinate the servicing of a single IP address range. However, you can design a fault-tolerant DHCP system using multiple DHCP servers, if you ensure that no two servers are handing out the same range of addresses at the same time.

When creating a fault-tolerant DHCP infrastructure, you can implement a hot spare DHCP server, multiple DHCP servers, or clustering. Each is discussed in the subsequent sections.

Hot Spare DHCP Server

One form of fault tolerance for DHCP servers is to have a hot spare, which is a spare server preconfigured and ready to use. In a system that utilizes the hot spare DHCP server, two

DHCP servers are configured, but only one is running. If the first DHCP server fails, the second can be brought online quickly.

The main advantage of a hot spare DHCP server is simplicity. Each server has the same configuration. There is no complex planning.

IP address conflicts may still occur when a hot spare DHCP server is used because the hot spare DHCP server is not aware of which IP addresses have already been leased out. However, this can be avoided by configuring the hot spare DHCP server to ping all IP addresses before leasing them out. If any host responds to the ping, the DHCP server does not lease out the address associated with the ping.

Another significant disadvantage to a hot spare DHCP server is the effort involved to synchronize the information between the two servers. You must do this manually because there is no automated mechanism for synchronizing the information. Over time, many administrators forget to do this, resulting in the hot spare DHCP server having incorrect IP addresses or options leased out to clients.

Yet another disadvantage of using a hot spare DHCP server is that starting the hot spare DHCP server is a manual process. Consequently, the lag time until the hot spare is started may be considerable depending on how long it takes the administrator to notice that the original DHCP server has failed.

Multiple DHCP Servers

Multiple DHCP servers can be configured to service the same subnet as long as they are not configured to lease the same range of IP addresses. For example, on the network 192.168.1.0/24, the first DHCP server could be configured to lease the range 192.168.1.50–149, and the second DHCP server could be configured to lease the range 192.168.1.150–249. In this situation, duplicate IP addresses are not a problem because each DHCP server cannot lease an address leased by the other DHCP server.

Using multiple DHCP servers is particularly effective when a DHCP relay is used. Figure 5-6 shows a router configured as a DHCP relay connecting two subnets. Each subnet has a DHCP server configured on it. When a workstation from the 192.168.1.0/24 subnet broadcasts a DHCPREQUEST packet, it receives an offer from both the local DHCP server and the DHCP server on the remote subnet via the DHCP relay. However, a DHCP client accepts a lease from the first DHCP server to respond. In this case, it is almost always the local DHCP server. The lease offer from the remote DHCP server is accepted only if the lease offer from the local DHCP server fails.

If two DHCP servers are configured on a single subnet, they need to have IP address ranges of equal size. If two DHCP servers have ranges of unequal size, one DHCP server could run out of addresses to lease out. If the server with available addresses fails, leaving the remaining functional DHCP server with no IP addresses to lease out, then no IP addresses are available to lease out. To ensure that the subnet can function properly when either server is unavailable, each DHCP server needs to have an IP address range equal to the number of

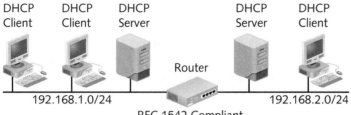

Figure 5-6   Multiple DHCP servers with a DHCP relay

DHCP clients on the subnet. This means twice as many leases need to be available (when both servers are available) as are required.

If a DHCP relay is used between two DHCP servers, the address range needs to be split with 75% to 80% of the addresses on the local DHCP server and 20% to 25% of the addresses on the remote DHCP server. The remote DHCP requires fewer addresses because it is used only if the local DHCP server fails.

Clustering

When clustering is used for DHCP, multiple servers on the same subnet have DHCP installed, but it is active on only one server at a time. When DHCP fails on the first server, it is automatically started on the second server. If it should fail on the second server, it is automatically started on the third server, and so on.

Servers configured in a cluster have the ability to share disk space on an external storage system. This allows them to share configuration information for services. When the DHCP service **fails over** from one server to another, the new DHCP server is automatically configured with the leases that were previously handed out. In addition, you do not need to synchronize information manually between the servers. It happens automatically when the service fails over.

The main disadvantage of clustering is the complexity involved in setting it up. Depending on the chosen configuration, clustering can require shared external storage devices and the addition of extra network cards to servers.

NOTE   Clustering is included only with Windows Server 2003 Enterprise Edition and Windows Server 2003 Datacenter Edition. Chapter 12 covers clustering in more detail.

INSTALLING DHCP

DHCP is a standard service that is included with Windows Server 2003. Note, however, that it is not installed as part of the installation. Instead, you must add it later through Add or Remove Programs. Figure 5-7 shows the Add or Remove Programs option in Control Panel being used to install DHCP.

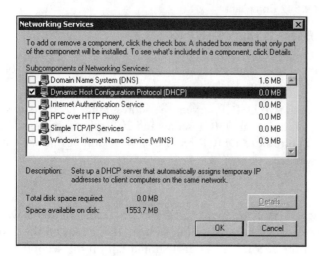

Figure 5-7   Installing DHCP

Activity 5-1: Installing DHCP

Time Required: 5 minutes

Objective: Install DHCP on Windows Server 2003.

Description: Most locations in the Arctic University network use static IP addresses for workstations. To make maintenance of the workstations easier, you configure them to use DHCP. Note that the DHCP server will always have a static IP address. In this activity, you configure your server with a static IP address on the Private connection and install DHCP.

1. If necessary, start your server, and log on as **Administrator** of the Arctic.local domain.

2. Click **Start**, point to **Control Panel**, point to **Network Connections**, right-click **Private**, and click **Properties**.

3. Click **Internet Protocol (TCP/IP)** and click **Properties**.

4. If not already selected, click **Use the following IP address**.

5. In the IP address text box, type **192.168.20$x.y$**, where x is the group number assigned by your instructor and y is your student number.

6. Press **Tab** to fill in the subnet mask as **255.255.255.0**, click **OK**, and click **Close**.

7. Click **Start**, point to **Control Panel**, and then click **Add or Remove Programs**.

8. Click **Add/Remove Windows Components**.

9. Scroll down in the Components section, click **Networking Services** to highlight it, and then click **Details**.

10. Check the **Dynamic Host Configuration Protocol (DHCP)** check box, and then click **OK**.

11. Click **Next**.

12. Click **Finish**.

13. Close the Add or Remove Programs window.

5

DHCP SERVER AUTHORIZATION

Within a corporation's IT Department, control over network resources is always important. In particular, control over DHCP is very important because an unauthorized DHCP server can hand out incorrect IP addressing information to hundreds of client computers very quickly. These computers are then unable to access network resources; such lack of access is as serious as a server crashing.

To exercise control over DHCP, Windows Server 2003 must be authorized to start the DHCP Service. When the DHCP Service is starting, it checks to see that the server is authorized. If the server is authorized, DHCP continues the process of starting. If the server is not authorized, the DHCP Service shuts itself down. Figure 5-8 shows the error message that appears in Event Viewer when an unauthorized DHCP server attempts to start.

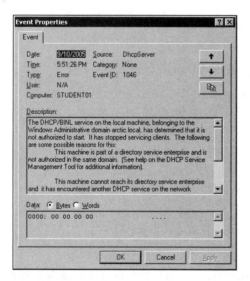

Figure 5-8   Unauthorized DHCP server error in Event Viewer

The authorization of a DHCP server takes place in Active Directory using the DHCP Management snap-in. To authorize a DHCP server, you must be a member of the **Enterprise Admins** group, or a member of the Enterprise Admins group must delegate permissions to you using the Active Directory Sites and Services snap-in. The Enterprise Admins group has administrative permissions for all domains in an Active Directory forest.

Figure 5-9 shows the information message in Event Viewer after the DHCP server is authorized and has started.

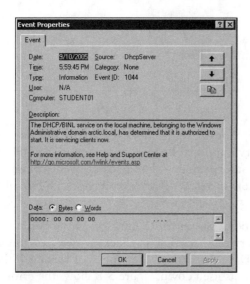

Figure 5-9   Authorized DHCP server information in Event Viewer

Activity 5-2: Starting an Unauthorized DHCP Server

Time Required: 10 minutes

Objective: View the results of starting an unauthorized DHCP server.

Description: You have just installed a new DHCP server on one of your networks. In this activity, you attempt to start the DHCP Service before the server is authorized. You also view the results in the event log.

1. If necessary, start your server, and log on as **Administrator** of the Arctic.local domain.

2. Click **Start**, point to **Administrative Tools**, and then click **Services**.

3. Scroll to the **DHCP Server** service, and view the status. Notice that the status is listed as started even though the service is not authorized.

4. Close the Services window.

5. Click **Start**, point to **Administrative Tools**, and then click **Event Viewer**.

6. In the left pane, click the **System** log if it is not already open.

7. Find the error event generated by the DHCP Service. The type is error, the source is DHCPServer, and the event is 1046. Double-click the error event.

8. Read the contents of the error message, and click **OK**.

9. Close Event Viewer.

Activity 5-3: Authorizing a DHCP Server

Time Required: 10 minutes

Objective: Authorize a DHCP server in Active Directory.

Description: You have just installed a new DHCP server in one of your networks. In this activity, you use the DHCP Management snap-in to authorize your server as a DHCP server.

1. If necessary, start your server, and log on as **Administrator**.

2. Click **Start**, point to **Administrative Tools**, and click **DHCP**.

3. In the DHCP snap-in window, right-click **DHCP** and then click **Manage authorized servers**.

4. Click **Authorize**.

5. Type the IP address of your server's private connection, and click **OK**.

6. Click **OK** again to confirm the authorization.

7. Click **Close** to close the Manage Authorized Servers window.

8. Close the DHCP Management snap-in.

9. Click **Start**, point to **Administrative Tools**, and click **Event Viewer**.

10. Click the **System** log if it is not already open.

11. Find the information event generated by the DHCP Service. The type is Information, the source is DHCPServer, and the event is 1044. Double-click the information event.

12. Read the contents of the information event, and click **OK**.

13. Close Event Viewer.

CONFIGURING DHCP

After DHCP has been installed and authorized, you must configure it with the IP address information that is to be handed out to client computers. All configuration of DHCP is normally done with the DHCP Management snap-in. However, you need to make changes programmatically using batch files, or you can use the NETSH command to configure the

DHCP Service. Most of the time, only larger organizations use batch files to manage DHCP because of the large amount of development time involved in testing them.

The DHCP elements that can be configured include:

- Scopes
- Superscopes
- Multicast scopes
- Reservations
- Additional options
- Vendor and User classes

Scopes

You use a **scope** to define a range of IP addresses for the DHCP server to hand out to client computers. Each scope is configured with a name, starting IP address, ending IP address, subnet mask, lease duration, and description, as shown in Figure 5-10. You can also configure exclusions for the scope.

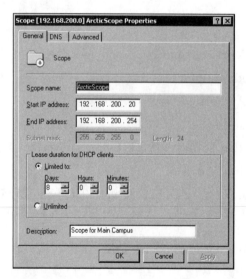

Figure 5-10   Scope settings

The name and description of a scope are what appears in the DHCP Management snap-in. These are for your use as an administrator to make it as easy as possible to manage the system. The DHCP Service does not vary its functionality based on scope names or descriptions.

The starting and ending IP addresses define the range of IP addresses that can be handed out by the DHCP server with this scope. These addresses correspond with the different subnets in your network. Each range of addresses must be within a single subnet. You can use two different strategies when defining the starting and ending IP addresses. First, you can configure the scope to use all available addresses on a subnet, and then exclude the static IP addresses being used by hosts such as printers. This strategy is very flexible because additional exclusions can always be added as required. An **exclusion** is an IP address, or range of IP addresses, within a scope that are not handed out by the DHCP server. Second, you can configure the scope to use only addresses that are not already in use. This strategy is used when statically configured hosts use a range of addresses at the beginning or end of a subnet. For example, many administrators place all statically configured hosts in the first few IP addresses on a subnet, and then allocate the remaining IP addresses to DHCP.

The subnet mask for a scope is the subnet mask that is required for hosts on that subnet.

NOTE

You can use exclusions to prevent some IP addresses in a scope from being handed out dynamically. Choose to use exclusions when any statically configured hosts, such as servers and network printers, have IP addresses that fall between the starting and ending IP address of a scope. If exclusions are not used for statically configured devices, IP address conflicts can occur if the DHCP server leases out those addresses.

The lease duration for a scope defines how long client computers are allowed to use an IP address. The default lease duration used by Windows Server 2003 is eight days. Windows clients attempt to renew their lease after 50% (or four days, using the default setting) of the lease time has passed, again at 87.5% (or seven days) if the first attempt fails, and again at the end of the lease time if the second attempt fails. If a lease expires, the client can no longer use the IP address and cannot communicate on the network.

A DHCP server does not begin using a scope immediately after creation. A scope must be activated before the DHCP Service can begin using the scope. Being forced to activate the service is useful because it means you get a chance to confirm that the configuration of a scope is correct before addresses are handed out.

Activity 5-4: Creating a Scope

ACTIVITY

Time Required: 5 minutes

Objective: Create a scope to distribute IP addresses to client computers.

Description: You must create a scope on your newly installed DHCP server so that it can hand out IP addresses to client computers. After the scope is created, you activate the scope. Your instructor assigns you a group number to complete this exercise.

1. If necessary, start your server, and log on as **Administrator**.

2. Click **Start**, point to **Administrative Tools**, and click **DHCP**.

3. Click your server to select it, right-click the server and click **New Scope**.

4. Click **Next** to begin configuring the new scope.

5. Type *yourname*Scope as the name of the scope, and click **Next**.

6. Type **192.168.20x.100** as the Start IP address, where *x* is the group number assigned by your instructor.

7. Type **192.168.20x.200** as the End IP address, where *x* is the group number assigned by your instructor.

8. Confirm that the length of the subnet mask is 24 bits (255.255.255.0), and click **Next**. If the subnet mask is not 24 bits (255.255.255.0), change it to 24 bits.

9. Exclusions are not required, so there is nothing to change on this page. Click **Next**.

10. Change the lease duration to **1 hour**, and click **Next**.

11. Click **No, I will configure these options later**, and click **Next**.

12. Click **Finish**.

13. Close the DHCP snap-in.

ACTIVITY

Activity 5-5: Activating and Testing a Scope

Time Required: 20 minutes

Objective: Activate a DHCP scope, and then test it with a partner.

Description: In Activity 5-4, you created a scope. In this activity, you allow the DHCP Service to use the information by activating the scope. You work with a partner. When your scope is activated, your partner acts as the client computer. When your partner's scope is activated, you act as the client.

1. If necessary, start your server, and log on as **Administrator**.

2. Partner A: Activate the scope on your server:

   a. Click **Start**, point to **Administrative Tools**, and click **DHCP**.

   b. Click your server to select it, click your scope to select it, right-click your scope, and click **Activate**.

   c. Close the DHCP snap-in.

3. Partner B: Change your private connection to be a dynamic address:

   a. Click **Start**, point to **Control Panel**, point to **Network Connections**, right-click **Private**, and click **Properties**.

   b. Click **Internet Protocol (TCP/IP)** and click **Properties**.

   c. Click **Obtain an IP address automatically**, and click **OK**.

   d. Click **Close** to save the changes.

4. Partner B: View the dynamic IP address on the private connection:

   a. Click **Start** and click **Run**.

   b. Type **cmd** and press **Enter**.

   c. Type **ipconfig /all** and press **Enter**.

   d. If the Private connection is still using an APIPA address, type **ipconfig /renew** and press **Enter**. Then repeat Step c to view the new configuration information.

   e. Close the Command Prompt window.

5. Partner B: Change the Private connection back to a static IP address:

   a. Click **Start**, point to **Control Panel**, point to **Network Connections**, right-click **Private**, and then click **Properties**.

   b. Click **Internet Protocol (TCP/IP)** and click **Properties**.

   c. Click **Use the following IP address**.

   d. In the IP address text box, type **192.168.20x.y**, where *x* is the group number assigned by your instructor and *y* is your student number.

   e. Press **Tab** to fill in the subnet mask as **255.255.255.0**, click **OK**, and click **Close**.

6. Partner A: Deactivate the scope:

   a. Click **Start**, point to **Administrative Tools**, and click **DHCP**.

   b. Click your server to select it, click your scope to select it, right-click your scope, and click **Deactivate**.

   c. Click **Yes** to confirm the deactivation.

   d. Close the DHCP snap-in.

7. Redo this exercise and reverse your roles. If you were Partner A, this time become Partner B.

Superscopes

You use a **superscope** to combine multiple scopes into a single logical scope. You can do this when a single physical part of the network has two subnets on it. Often, a network is organized like this because the number of hosts grew too large for a single subnet.

To conceptualize a superscope, consider the following example. A midsized company that starts out with 200 workstations has a single Class C network. No routers are required because the entire network is switched at 100 Mbps. The DHCP server is distributing addresses to the workstations using a single scope.

Over time, the network grows to the point at which a single Class C network is not large enough. To increase the number of addresses, you add another Class C network to the same segment of the network. You attach computers with addresses from both networks to the same segment and add a router to move packets from one logical network to the other. You then add a second scope to the DHCP server.

When a client broadcasts a DHCPREQUEST packet, the DHCP server sees it. However, the DHCP server does not know which logical network the client is from and offers leases from both scopes. Combining two scopes in a superscope indicates to the DHCP Service that both scopes are on the same network segment and should be treated as a single scope. If the superscope strategy is in use, the DHCP server offers only one lease out to computers on a segment with two logical networks.

Figure 5-11 shows a superscope that contains two scopes. The DHCP server treats the superscope as a single unit. Scopes inside a superscope cannot be activated individually. The superscope must be activated and this, in turn, activates all scopes that are part of the superscope.

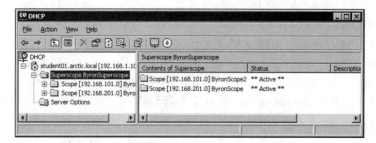

Figure 5-11   A superscope containing two scopes

Activity 5-6: Configuring a Superscope

Time Required: 5 minutes

Objective: Combine two scopes into a single logical unit using a superscope.

Description: One of the sites on your network has grown too large to use a single Class C address. It is already configured with one scope. You add a second scope, and then configure a superscope that combines the two scopes.

1. If necessary, start your server, and log on as **Administrator**.

2. Click **Start**, point to **Administrative Tools**, and click **DHCP**.

3. Create a second scope:

   a. Click your server to select it, right-click your server and click **New Scope**.

   b. Click **Next** to begin configuring the new scope.

   c. Type *yourname***Scope2** as the name of the scope, and click **Next**.

   d. Type **192.168.10x.100** as the Start IP address, where x is the group number assigned by your instructor.

   e. Type **192.168.10x.200** as the End IP address, where x is the group number assigned by your instructor.

   f. Confirm that the length of the subnet mask is 24 bits (255.255.255.0), and click **Next**. If the subnet mask is not 24 bits (255.255.255.0), change it to 24 bits.

   g. Exclusions are not required. Click **Next**.

   h. Change the lease duration to **1 hour**, and click **Next**.

   i. Click **No, I will configure these options later**, and click **Next**.

   j. Click **Finish**.

4. Create a superscope:

   a. Right-click your server and click **New Superscope**.

   b. Click **Next** to begin configuring the superscope.

   c. Type *yourname***Superscope** in the Name text box, and click **Next**.

   d. Press and hold the **Ctrl** key, click *yourname***Scope** and *yourname***Scope2** to select them, and click **Next**.

   e. Click **Finish** to complete the superscope.

5. Click the **+** (plus symbol) beside Superscope *yourname*Superscope to see the scopes inside the superscope.

6. Close the DHCP snap-in.

ACTIVITY

Activity 5-7: Deleting a Superscope

Time Required: 5 minutes

Objective: Delete a superscope and one of the scopes inside it.

Description: A location with a superscope enabled has retired some workstations. You no longer need the second scope and the superscope. You remove the superscope and delete the second scope.

1. If necessary, start your server, and log on as **Administrator**.

2. Click **Start**, point to **Administrative Tools**, and click **DHCP**.

3. Click your server to select it, right-click **Superscope** *yourname***Superscope**, and click **Delete**.

4. Click **Yes** to delete the superscope without deleting any child scopes.

5. Right-click **Scope [192.168.10x.0]** *yourname***Scope2**, where *x* is your group number, and click **Delete**.

6. Click **Yes** to delete the scope.

7. Close the DHCP snap-in.

Multicast Scopes

You use a **multicast scope** to deliver multicast addresses to applications that require it. Applications use a multicast address to deliver packets to groups of computers rather than to a single computer. Most applications that use multicast addresses are hard-coded with a single address that is used for that application rather than using DHCP to find a multicast address. Thus, using a multicast scope on a DHCP server is rare. However, it is desirable to have dynamic multicast addresses for applications because you can ensure there are no conflicts between applications. If there are conflicts, only one application can be used.

When you create a multicast scope, you configure start and end IP addresses, TTL (Time to Live), exclusions, a lease duration, and activation. The start and end IP addresses define the range of multicast addresses that the DHCP server can hand out when this multicast scope is activated. The allowable range of addresses is from 224.0.0.0 to 239.255.255.255.

The TTL of the multicast scope defines the number of routers through which a multicast packet can move. If the TTL is set to 5, the packet is discarded by routers after five hops. You can use this system to control the movement of multicast packets across wide area networks. The default value for the TTL is 32.

Exclusions define addresses between the start and end IP addresses that are not handed out. You use exclusions if there are applications using hard-coded multicast addresses within the range of the scope.

The lease duration is the length of time that an application can use a multicast address. The default lease length is 30 days.

ACTIVITY

Activity 5-8: Creating a Multicast Scope

Time Required: 5 minutes

Objective: Create a multicast scope to deliver multicast addresses to applications.

Description: You have installed a new application that requires a multicast address delivered through DHCP. You must create and activate the multicast scope on your DHCP server.

1. If necessary, start your server, and log on as **Administrator**.

2. Click **Start**, point to **Administrative Tools**, and click **DHCP**.

3. Click your server to select it, right-click your server and click **New Multicast Scope**.

4. Click **Next** to begin creating the multicast scope.

5. Type *yourname*MulticastScope in the Name text box, and then click **Next**.

6. In the Start IP address text box, type **224.0.0.0**.

7. In the End IP address text box, type **224.0.0.255**.

8. In the TTL text box, type **1**, and then click **Next**. Setting the TTL to 1 ensures that your server does not start to distribute to other networks.

9. Click **Next**. There are no exclusions that need to be configured.

10. Click **Next** to confirm the default lease time of 30 days.

11. Click **Next** to activate the scope now.

12. Click **Finish** to complete the creation of the multicast scope.

13. Close the DHCP Management snap-in.

Reservations

You use a **reservation** to hand out a specific IP address to a particular client computer or device on the network. This can be useful when delivering IP addresses to devices that normally use static addresses, such as printers and servers. If the IP addresses of these devices ever need to be changed, it is easier to manage the process centrally through DHCP reservations rather than visiting each device that needs to be reconfigured.

Reservations can also be beneficial when firewalls are in place. Some companies use firewalls internally to limit which client computers can communicate with sensitive resources, such as accounting and human resources information. Normally, DHCP-delivered addresses have the potential to change, which means that firewall rules based on IP addresses are not effective. With reservations for secure clients, the firewall rules can be configured to allow packets from the IP address specified in the reservations.

Reservations are created based on the MAC address of the network card on the client workstation. The MAC address is used as the identifier for the client workstation that is matched to a reservation. If the MAC address of the client matches the MAC address defined in the reservation, the IP address of the reservation is leased to the client. Figure 5-12 shows the creation of a reservation.

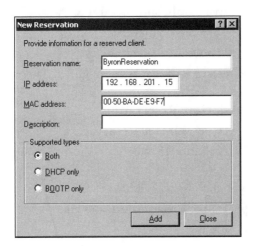

Figure 5-12   Creating a reservation

 Software utilities exist that override the MAC address built into the network card. This makes it possible to falsify the MAC address in a data packet and obtain an improper reservation. Consequently, using DHCP reservations with a firewall offers limited security.

NOTE

Activity 5-9: Creating and Testing a Reservation

Time Required: 15 minutes

Objective: Create a DHCP reservation and test it with a client.

Description: In an effort to control access to the Internet, you have configured a firewall to restrict the use of the Telnet protocol. However, internal technical staff need to use Telnet on occasion to manage Linux servers. To allow this, you have created rules on the firewall that allow Telnet traffic from a few internal addresses. You now configure the DHCP server to hand out those addresses to a few specific computers using reservations. You work with a partner to complete this exercise. Partner A is the DHCP client and Partner B is the DHCP server.

1. If necessary, start your server, and log on as **Administrator**.

2. Partner A: Get the MAC address of the network card on your private connection:
   a. Click **Start** and click **Run**.
   b. Type **cmd** and press **Enter**.
   c. Type **ipconfig /all** and press **Enter**.
   d. Write down the physical address of the network card listed under Ethernet adapter Private. This address is a 12-character hexadecimal number.
   e. Close the Command Prompt window.

3. Partner B: Create a reservation for Partner A:
   a. Click **Start**, point to **Administrative Tools**, and click **DHCP**.
   b. Click your server to see the scopes that are configured.
   c. Click your scope to expand the contents.
   d. Click **Reservations** to view the reservations that are configured. There should be none at this time.
   e. Right-click **Reservations** and click **New Reservation**.
   f. In the Reservation name text box, type *yourname***Reservation**.
   g. In the IP address text box, type **192.168.20x.15**, where *x* is the group number given to you by your instructor.
   h. In the MAC address text box, type the physical address of Partner A.
   i. In the Description text box, type **Telnet Reservation**, and click **Add**.
   j. Click **Close** to stop adding reservations.

4. Partner B: Right-click your scope and then click **Activate**.

5. Partner A: Test the client reservation:
   a. Click **Start**, point to **Control Panel**, point to **Network Connections**, right-click **Private**, and click **Properties**.
   b. Click **Internet Protocol (TCP/IP)** and click **Properties**.

c. Take note of the IP address configuration because this information is required again at the end of the exercise.

d. Click **Obtain an IP address automatically**, and click **OK**.

e. Click **Close** to save the changes.

f. Click **Start** and click **Run**.

g. Type **cmd** and press **Enter**.

h. Type **ipconfig /all** and press **Enter**.

i. The IP address of the Private connection should be 192.168.20x.15. If it is not, verify that the MAC address was entered correctly in the reservation.

j. Close the Command Prompt window.

6. Partner A: Change the private connection back to a static IP address:

a. Click **Start**, point to **Control Panel**, point to **Network Connections**, right-click **Private**, and click **Properties**.

b. Click **Internet Protocol (TCP/IP)** and click **Properties**.

c. Click **Use the following IP address**.

d. Type in the IP address and subnet mask that were configured before you changed the address to DHCP, and click **OK**.

e. Click **Close**.

7. Partner B: Right-click your scope, click **Deactivate**, and click **Yes** to confirm.

8. Partner B: Close the DHCP snap-in.

9. If time permits, reverse roles and repeat the activity.

Additional Options

In addition to handing out IP addresses and subnet masks, DHCP can hand out a variety of other IP configuration options, such as default gateway, DNS server, WINS server, and many more. These options can be configured for the entire server, a scope, or a single reservation.

It is quite common that all workstations within an entire organization use the same DNS servers. Therefore, DNS is often configured at the server level so that it applies to all scopes on that server. The same is true for WINS servers. Figure 5-13 shows the setting of server options.

The default gateway is different for every subnet and is set in the options for a scope. Figure 5-14 shows the setting of scope options.

It is unusual to set options in a reservation, but this may be necessary for some users with a special configuration. For example, accounting staff may use a different default gateway than other staff to allow them access to the accounting systems.

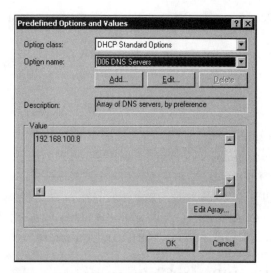

Figure 5-13   Setting server options

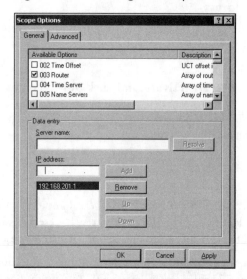

Figure 5-14   Setting scope options

Activity 5-10: Setting Server Options

Time Required: 5 minutes

Objective: Set the DNS server option for a DHCP server.

Description: All of the computers serviced by this DHCP server are using the same DNS server. Rather than configuring each scope with a DNS server option, you have decided to configure the DHCP server with the DNS server option.

1. If necessary, start your server, and log on as **Administrator**.

2. Click **Start**, point to **Administrative Tools**, and click **DHCP**.

3. Click your server to select it, right-click your server and click **Set Predefined Options**.

4. Click the **Option name** drop-down arrow, and then click **006 DNS Servers**.

5. Click **Edit Array**.

6. In the IP address text box, type **192.168.100.8**, and then click **Add**.

7. Click **OK** to save the changes to the DNS server list.

8. Click **OK** to save the changes to the server level options.

9. Close the DHCP snap-in.

Activity 5-11: Setting Scope Options

Time Required: 5 minutes

Objective: Set the default gateway in the scope options.

Description: You have configured a new scope to lease IP addresses to clients. The server is already configured to include the DNS server option as part of the lease. However, for the clients to access resources outside of their own network, you must configure the default gateway option in the scope.

1. If necessary, start your server, and log on as **Administrator**.

2. Click **Start**, point to **Administrative Tools**, and click **DHCP**.

3. Click your server to expand it and see the scopes inside.

4. Click your scope to see the options inside the scope.

5. Click **Scope Options** to select it, right-click **Scope Options** and click **Configure Options**.

6. Check the **003 Router** check box.

7. In the IP address text box, type **192.168.20*x*.1**, where *x* is the group number given to you by your instructor, and then click **Add**.

8. Click **OK** to save the option.

9. Close the DHCP snap-in.

Vendor and User Classes

You can use Vendor and User classes to differentiate between clients within a scope. You can configure each different **Vendor class** and **User class** with its own set of options.

Vendor classes are client categories based on the operating system being used. The Vendor classes predefined within the DHCP server of Windows Server 2003 are:

- *DHCP Standard Options*—Used by all DHCP clients that are not running either Windows 98 or Windows 2000 or identified as members of another Vendor class
- *Microsoft Options*—Used by Windows 2000/XP/2003 and Windows 98 clients
- *Microsoft Windows 2000 Options*—Used only by Windows 2000/XP/2003 clients
- *Microsoft Windows 98 Options*—Used only by Windows 98 clients

Figure 5-15 shows the setting of options for Vendor classes.

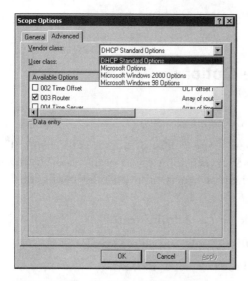

Figure 5-15   Setting Vendor class options

User classes are client categories defined based on how a client is connected to the network or by the network administrator. You can use the ipconfig /setclassid command to set the DHCP User class ID. Figure 5-16 shows the setting of a User class ID on a client.

The DHCP server included with Windows Server 2003 has three predefined User classes:

- *Default User Class*—All clients can use this class, including those that do not specify a User class or if the User class is unknown to the server.
- *Default Routing and Remote Access Class*—Clients that are assigned an IP address through DHCP when remotely accessing the network through a dial-up or VPN connection use this class. The client computer can be running any operating system because Routing and Remote Access obtains the IP address and options on behalf of the client computer.
- *Default BOOTP Class*—Clients using the older BOOTP protocol rather than DHCP use this class.

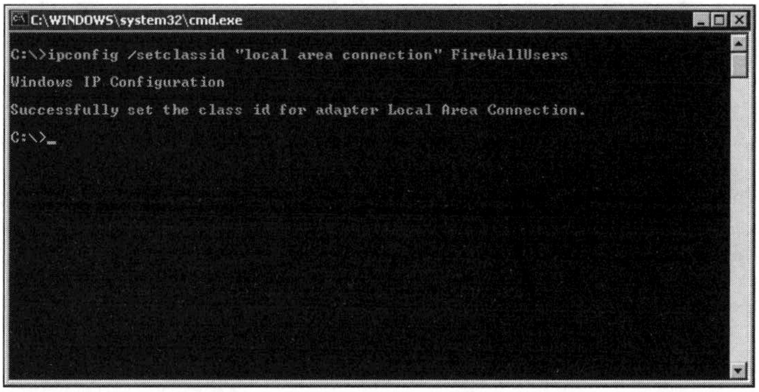

```
C:\WINDOWS\system32\cmd.exe

C:\>ipconfig /setclassid "local area connection" FireWallUsers

Windows IP Configuration

Successfully set the class id for adapter Local Area Connection.

C:\>_
```

Figure 5-16   Setting a class ID

MANAGING AND MONITORING DHCP

To manage and monitor your DHCP server effectively, you can perform a variety of tasks and configure various features, including the following:

- Backing up and restoring DHCP databases
- Reconciling scopes
- Viewing statistics
- Enabling DHCP audit logging
- Enabling conflict detection
- Modifying file paths
- Changing bindings
- Viewing DHCP events in Event Viewer
- Viewing DHCP statistics in the Performance snap-in

Backing Up and Restoring DHCP Databases

The DHCP Service has several files that are stored in C:\WINDOWS\System32\dhcp. The file dhcp.mdb is the database holding the addressing information that has been assigned to client computers. The file dhcp.tmp is a temporary database file only present during maintenance operations. The files j50.log and j50#####.log (where ##### is a five-digit code for uniqueness) are transaction logs of changes to the DHCP database. The file j50.chk is a checkpoint file that keeps track of which entries in the log files have been applied to the database. Backing up the database backs up all of these files, as well as DHCP registry entries.

By default, the DHCP database is backed up every 60 minutes. You can back up the DHCP database manually by right-clicking the server in the DHCP snap-in and clicking Backup. You can also modify the automatic backup time by editing the registry key

HKEY_LOCAL_MACHINE\SYSTEM\CurrentControlSet\Services\DHCPServer\
Parameters\BackupInterval.

To restore the DHCP database, right-click the server in the DHCP Management snap-in, and click Restore. Then select the folder containing the backup, and click OK. Figure 5-17 shows how to access the option to back up or restore the DHCP database.

Figure 5-17   DHCP backup option

Reconciling Scopes

The DHCP database holds a summary version and a detailed version of the IP address lease information for a server. If there is a discrepancy between the two versions of information, you must reconcile the scope to synchronize the information. If information regarding leased addresses is not appearing properly in the DHCP Management snap-in, you may need to reconcile the scope. You may also need to reconcile the scope to show leased addresses properly after restoring the DHCP database. To reconcile a scope, right-click it and click Reconcile.

Viewing Statistics

The Windows Server 2003 DHCP Service automatically tracks statistics that you can view. To view these statistics, right-click the server or scope, and click Display Statistics. By default, to update these statistics, you must manually click the Refresh button while the Statistics window is open. You can configure these statistics to update automatically by selecting the Automatically update statistics every option and specifying how often they are updated.

Enabling DHCP Audit Logging

DHCP audit logs keep detailed information about DHCP server activity. This logging is enabled by default and keeps up to seven audit logs. The audit logs are named dhcpSrvLog-*xxx*.log, where *xxx* is the day of the week. You can use these logs to troubleshoot why a DHCP server is not functioning as you would expect.

To enable DHCP audit logging, select the option Enable DHCP audit logging in the properties of the DHCP server in the DHCP Management snap-in. Audit logs are enabled by default. Figure 5-18 shows the option to turn audit logs off and on.

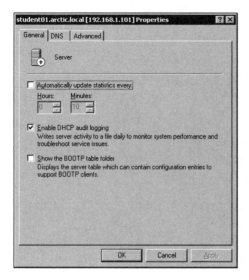

Figure 5-18   Enable audit logs

Enabling Conflict Detection

Conflict detection prevents a DHCP server from creating IP address conflicts. When conflict detection is enabled, a DHCP server pings an IP address before it is leased to a client computer. This ensures that even if another device is statically configured with that IP address, it is not leased.

You can configure how many ping attempts are made before an IP address is leased. The default is zero ping attempts. Each ping attempt adds approximately one second to the overall length of the leasing process. The number of pings for conflict detection is configured in the DHCP server properties in the DHCP Management snap-in.

Modifying File Paths

You can control the location of the audit log file, the DHCP database, and the automatic backup directory. By default, the audit log file and DHCP database are located in C:\WINDOWS\System32\dhcp. The path used for automatic backups of the DHCP database is C:\WINDOWS\System32\dhcp\backup. Generally, you should leave these files in their default locations.

To modify the paths to where these files are stored, access the properties of the DHCP server in the DHCP Management snap-in. Figure 5-19 shows the configuration of the file paths.

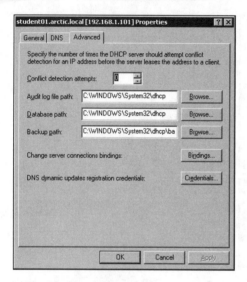

Figure 5-19   File paths

Changing Bindings

If a DHCP server has multiple network cards, you can choose to which network cards the DHCP Service is bound. The DHCP server hands out IP addresses only through a network card to which the DHCP Service is bound. The bindings are controlled in the Advanced tab of the server Properties in the DHCP Management snap-in. Figure 5-20 shows the configuration of DHCP bindings.

Viewing DHCP Events in Event Viewer

In addition to audit logging, some summary information generated by the DHCP Service is placed in the system event log. You can view these events using Event Viewer.

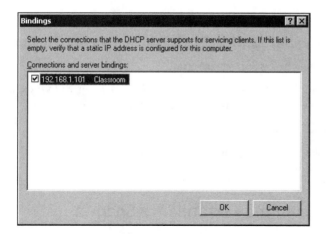

Figure 5-20   DHCP Bindings

Activity 5-12: Viewing DHCP Events in Event Viewer

Time Required: 5 minutes

Objective: See the events placed into the system log by the DHCP Service.

Description: Some of the users on the network have been complaining that they occasionally cannot get an IP address from the DHCP server. As a starting point, you view the system event log to see if the service has been stopped and restarted recently.

1. If necessary, start your server, and log on as **Administrator**.
2. Click **Start**, point to **Administrative Tools**, and click **Event Viewer**.
3. Click **System** to view the system log.
4. Click **View** and click **Filter**.
5. Click the down arrow in the Event source list box, and click **DHCPServer**.
6. Click **OK** to filter the system log.
7. View the DHCPServer events.
8. Click the **View** menu and click **All Records** to remove the filter.
9. Close Event Viewer.

Activity 5-13: Removing DHCP

Time Required: 5 minutes

Objective: Remove the DHCP Server service from your server.

Description: Remove the DHCP Server service to ensure that it does not interfere with activities later in this book.

1. If necessary, start your server, and log on as **Administrator**.

2. Click **Start**, point to **Control Panel**, and click **Add or Remove Programs**.

3. Click **Add/Remove Windows Components**.

4. Scroll down in the Components box, double-click **Networking Services**, and deselect the **Dynamic Host Configuration Protocol (DHCP)** check box.

5. Click **OK** and then click **Next**.

6. Click **Finish** to complete removing the DHCP Server service, and close the Add or Remove Programs window.

Viewing DHCP Statistics in the Performance Snap-in

When DHCP is installed on Windows Server 2003, new objects and counters are added to the Performance snap-in. You can monitor these counters to track the performance of DHCP over time. If you establish an initial benchmark of DHCP performance under average conditions, then you can tell if something is functioning abnormally later.

Figure 5-21 shows some of the DHCP performance counters that can be monitored. The number of Discovers/sec indicates how many new clients are being added to the network. If this number is higher than normal, it may indicate that the lease length is too short and that computers are not able to renew their lease before it expires. Any number of Declines/sec indicates that some computers are using dynamic IP addresses not assigned by this DHCP server. This may be an indication that someone has installed an unauthorized DHCP server on an operating system such as Linux.

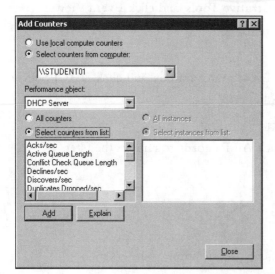

Figure 5-21   DHCP performance counters

DHCP Troubleshooting

DHCP is a fairly simple broadcast-based protocol that seldom has problems. However, some problems that you may encounter include:

- *All computers are unable to lease addresses*—Your solution is to confirm that the DHCP Service is running and authorized. If the DHCP Service is authorized, confirm that the proper scope has been activated and that the DHCP Service is bound to the proper adapter.

- *A single computer is unable to lease an address*—Your solution is to confirm that the cabling is correct and that the proper network driver is loaded. If the TCP/IP configuration is corrupt, repairing the network connection may also fix the problem.

- *Some computers have incorrect address information*—If the computers have addresses in the range 169.254.*x*.*x*, they were unable to contact the DHCP server. Your solution is to confirm that the DHCP server is functional. Be aware that Windows XP can also be configured with alternative addresses to use when DHCP is unavailable.

- *A single computer has incorrect address information*—If this computer has a reservation, your solution is to check the configuration of the reservation. Options set in a reservation override options set in a scope or at the server level.

- *A rogue DHCP server is leasing addresses*—Windows 2000 and Windows Server 2003 must be authorized to function as DHCP servers. Your solution is to check for this authorization. However, other operating systems such as Linux, UNIX, and NetWare are not aware of authorization information.

- *Two DHCP servers configured to be redundant on a network segment are leasing the same range of IP addresses and causing conflicts*—DHCP servers are not designed to be redundant. A better solution is to cluster your DHCP Service. However, if you cannot cluster the service and still require redundancy, you should configure the servers to each handle only a portion of the entire subnet.

- *IP address conflicts are created when the DHCP server hands out addresses already used by hosts with static IP addresses*—Your ideal solution to this problem is to create exclusions in the scope for the IP addresses used by hosts that are statically configured. However, if this information is not documented, turning on conflict detection ensures that a DHCP server does not hand out an IP address that is already in use.

- *A client is using an APIPA address*—If a DHCP was down briefly, some clients may be using APIPA addresses. If you want a client to reattempt leasing an IP address, use the command ipconfig /renew.

CHAPTER SUMMARY

- You use DHCP to assign IP address information dynamically to clients on a network. You can also use DHCP to assign multicast IP addresses to applications that request them.

- The DHCP lease process is composed of four packets: DHCPDISCOVER, DHCPOFFER, DHCPREQUEST, and DHCPACK. DHCP servers use DHCPNAK packets to decline the renewal of a lease. Clients use DHCPRELEASE packets to inform a DHCP server that their lease is no longer required.

- A DHCP client attempts to renew its lease at 50%, 87.5%, and 100% of the lease time. If it is unsuccessful in renewing the lease before it expires, it loses the ability to access network resources.

- Enterprise implementations of DHCP use DHCP relay agents or RFC-1542 compliant routers to simplify the management of DHCP. For fault tolerance, you can use a hot spare DHCP server, multiple DHCP servers, or clustering.

- You can use the commands ipconfig /release and ipconfig /renew release and renew DHCP leases.

- A DHCP server must be authorized in Active Directory to lease addresses to clients. To authorize a DHCP in Active Directory, you must be a member of Enterprise Admins.

- A scope defines a range of IP addresses that are leased to clients. A scope must be activated before the DHCP server leases addresses in the scope.

- A superscope combines two scopes into a single logical unit to service network segments with two subnets.

- An exclusion in a scope stops a DHCP server from handing out specific addresses or a range of addresses within a scope.

- A reservation allows you to give a specific workstation a defined IP address by tying the DHCP lease to the MAC address of the client.

- You can use vendor and User classes to configure some client computers with different options depending on the class to which they belong.

- When managing and monitoring DHCP, you can perform a number of tasks, including backing up and restoring DHCP databases, reconciling scopes, viewing statistics, enabling DHCP audit logging, enabling conflict detection, modifying file paths, changing bindings, viewing DHCP events in Event Viewer, and viewing DHCP statistics in the Performance snap-in.

- You may encounter a variety of different problems with DHCP server, including computers not able to obtain IP addresses, computers obtaining duplicate IP addresses, and computers obtaining incorrect IP addresses. Conflict detection sends a ping packet before leasing an IP address to ensure that it is not in use.

Key Terms

DHCPACK — A packet sent from a DHCP server to a client when a renewal attempt or DHCP lease is successful.

DHCPDISCOVER — The first packet in the DHCP lease process. This packet is broadcast on the local network to find a DHCP server.

DHCPNAK — A packet sent from a DHCP server to a client when it denies a renewal attempt.

DHCPOFFER — The second packet in the DHCP lease process. This packet is a broadcast from the DHCP server to the client with an offered lease.

DHCPRELEASE — A packet sent from a DHCP client to a DHCP server to indicate it is no longer using a leased IP address.

DHCPREQUEST — The third packet in the DHCP lease process. This packet is a broadcast from the DHCP client indicating which DHCPOFFER has been chosen.

Enterprise Admins — A default group in Active Directory with administrative rights for the entire forest.

exclusion — An IP address or range of IP addresses within a scope that are not leased to clients.

fails over — The process of a service stopping on one member of a cluster and starting on another.

lease — The length of time a DHCP client computer is allowed to use IP address information from the DHCP server.

multicast scope — A range of multicast IP addresses that are handed out to applications that request them.

reservation — A DHCP IP address that is leased only to a computer with a specific MAC address.

scope — A range of addresses that are leased by a DHCP server.

superscope — A logical grouping of scopes that is used to service network segments with more than one subnet in use.

timed lease — An IP address and set of configuration options given to a client computer from a DHCP server for a limited period of time.

User class — An identifier from the DHCP client that is sent as part of the DHCP lease process. This can be set manually by the administrator on workstations.

Vendor class — An identifier from the DHCP client that is sent as part of the DHCP lease process. This is based on the operating system in use.

REVIEW QUESTIONS

1. After installing the DHCP Service, you must _____ before the DHCP Service can begin delivering leased IP addresses.

   a. authorize it in Active Directory

   b. reboot the server

   c. activate the DHCP Service

   d. modify the firewall rules

2. After creating a scope, you must _____ before the DHCP Service begins servicing the scope.

   a. authorize the scope

   b. reboot the server

   c. activate the scope

   d. modify the firewall rules

3. Which of the following types of packets is used during the DHCP leasing process?

   a. unicast

   b. multicast

   c. broadcast

   d. None—it is all performed internally on the client.

4. How many packets are transmitted as part of the DHCP renewal process?

   a. only 1

   b. only 2

   c. only 3

   d. only 4

5. Which type of packet is sent if a request to renew a lease is denied?

   a. DHCPDISCOVER

   b. DHCPACK

   c. DHCPOFFER

   d. DHCPNAK

6. Which command can be used on Windows XP and Windows Server 2003 clients to force the renewal of a DHCP lease?

   a. ipconfig /release

   b. ipconfig /renew

   c. dhcpcon /renew

   d. winipcfg /release

   e. winipcfg /renew

7. Which type of packet is first in the DHCP lease process?
   a. DHCPACK
   b. DHCPOFFER
   c. DHCPDISCOVER
   d. DHCPREQUEST

8. Which utility is used to configure DHCP?
   a. DHCP Management snap-in
   b. Active Directory Users and Computers
   c. Active Directory Sites and Services
   d. ipconfig

9. At what levels can you apply different options for leased IP addresses? (Choose all that apply.)
   a. server
   b. scope
   c. exclusion
   d. reservation

10. You can use exclusions to allow certain computers to use a predefined IP address. True or False?

11. Which of the following allows DHCP packets to cross over a router? (Choose all that apply.)
    a. DHCP relay
    b. switch
    c. RFC-1542 compliant router
    d. IPSec

12. Which of the following is used to logically combine multiple scopes into a single unit?
    a. megascope
    b. superscope
    c. metascope
    d. It is not possible.

13. What is the default lease length used by a scope created in the Windows Server 2003 DHCP Service?
    a. three hours
    b. three days
    c. seven days
    d. eight days
    e. 30 days

14. Which characteristic of a multicast scope controls how many routers a multicast packet travels through?

   a. lease duration

   b. Time to Live

   c. hop count

   d. half life

15. Which of the following DHCP features allows you to distribute a chosen IP address to a particular computer?

   a. exclusion

   b. scope

   c. reservation

   d. User class

   e. Vendor class

16. Which characteristic of a client computer is used to match a client computer with a reservation?

   a. Vendor class

   b. User class

   c. operating system

   d. computer name

   e. MAC address

17. Which file stores the list of IP addresses leased through DHCP?

   a. dhcp.mdb

   b. dhcp.tmp

   c. j50.log

   d. j50.chk

   e. j50#####.log

18. Which utility can you use to create a baseline of DHCP functionality?

   a. Active Directory Sites and Services

   b. Event Viewer

   c. Performance

   d. Task Manager

19. Which feature do you enable to ensure that a DHCP server does not hand out IP addresses that are already in use on the network?

   a. audit logging

   b. conflict detection

   c. dynamic DNS

   d. bindings

20. Which of the following are client options that can be set at the scope level? (Choose all that apply.)

   a. DNS

   b. WINS

   c. ROUTER

   d. MAC address

5

CASE PROJECTS

Case Project 5-1: Multiple Subnets

You are planning how DHCP will be used to deliver IP addresses to clients on one of your larger campuses with five different subnets. Write a short memo describing the advantages and disadvantages of using a single DHCP server versus multiple DHCP servers.

Case Project 5-2: Avoiding IP Address Conflicts

One of your newly configured sites is having a problem with IP address conflicts. Some of the addresses being leased by the DHCP server are already configured on servers, printers, and workstations. The DHCP servers are using 192.168.1.10 through 192.168.1.19. The printers are using 192.168.1.20 through 192.168.1.29. What are your options for eliminating these conflicts?

Case Project 5-3: DHCP and Firewalls

As a security measure, you have stopped all of the faculty and students from using instant messaging clients by blocking the ports used by the software at the firewall. However, some of the faculty use an application based on instant messaging. How can you use DHCP to help you allow just these clients access to instant messaging ports?

Case Project 5-4: Planning DHCP

The main campus of Arctic University has 7 subnets, and each subnet has approximately 100 client computers. How would you configure DHCP to service the client computers?

6

PLANNING, CONFIGURING, AND TROUBLESHOOTING WINS

After reading this chapter, you will be able to:

- ◆ Describe the NetBIOS name resolution process
- ◆ Choose a NetBIOS name resolution method
- ◆ Describe the tasks performed by WINS
- ◆ Install WINS
- ◆ Choose WINS fault-tolerance options
- ◆ Configure WINS replication
- ◆ Manage WINS
- ◆ Describe NetBIOS security issues

WINS (Windows Internet Naming Service) is required to support NetBIOS name resolution for pre-Windows 2000 clients. These clients use WINS to find domain controllers, which are required for the clients to log on to the network. WINS is also used to resolve NetBIOS names to IP addresses. This is critical in an environment with pre-Windows 2000 clients. Windows 9x/NT clients access network resources such as shares and printers using NetBIOS names. The NetBIOS name resolution methods covered in this chapter are required only when using NetBIOS over TCP/IP. If IPX/SPX is used, the resolution of NetBIOS names is handled automatically, even across routers.

NetBIOS Name Resolution

As you may recall, WinSock (Windows Sockets) and NetBIOS are the two standard methods Windows-based applications can use to access network resources. When NetBIOS is used, the NetBIOS name of the remote resource must be resolved to an IP address.

All of the networking functions in pre-Windows 2000 operating systems, such as UNC paths, use NetBIOS names. In addition, many older applications that access database application servers, such as Microsoft SQL Server, use NetBIOS names. An example of using a NetBIOS name is a Windows NT computer attempting to access a share using the UNC path \\server5\datashare. The name "server5" is a NetBIOS name, and must be resolved to an IP address before the Windows NT client can contact the server. After the name is resolved to an IP address, the share named "datashare" can be accessed.

Microsoft clients use four methods to resolve NetBIOS names. If the first one is not successful, the client proceeds to the next method. The methods in the default order of precedence are as follows:

1. NetBIOS name cache

2. Windows Internet Naming Service (WINS)

3. Broadcast

4. LMHOSTS

You can change the order in which the NetBIOS name resolution methods are used, and you can even disable some of them. However, it is unusual to do so. You can modify NetBIOS name resolution order by defining your server as a node type. You can configure this by editing the registry key HKEY_LOCAL_MACHINE\SYSTEM\CurrentControl Set\Services\Netbt\Parameters\NodeType or as an option in a DHCP lease. Table 6-1 lists the node types.

Table 6-1   NetBIOS node types

Registry Value	Node Type	Description
1	B-node	When configured as a broadcast node, a computer uses only the NetBIOS name cache, broadcasts, and LMHOSTS to resolve NetBIOS names. WINS is not used. This is also referred to as Microsoft enhanced b-node because of the inclusion of LMHOSTS. RFC 1001, which defines concepts and methods for NetBIOS over TCP/IP, does not include LMHOSTS files. This is the default configuration when a WINS server is not configured.
2	P-node	When configured as a peer-to-peer node, a computer uses NetBIOS name cache, WINS, and LMHOSTS to resolve NetBIOS names. Broadcasts are not used.

Table 6-1 NetBIOS node types (continued)

Registry Value	Node Type	Description
4	M-node	When configured as a mixed node, a computer attempts to use broadcasts before using a WINS server.
8	H-node	When configured as a hybrid node, a computer attempts to use a WINS server before broadcasts. This is the default configuration when a WINS server is configured.

6

NetBIOS Name Cache

Client computers use the NetBIOS name cache to speed up the name resolution process. It is implemented automatically.

When a Windows client resolves a NetBIOS name, it keeps a record of the results in the **NetBIOS name cache**. Entries are kept in the NetBIOS name cache for 10 minutes.

When a NetBIOS name is resolved several times in rapid succession, it can result in a significant reduction in network traffic. This reduction occurs because if the current NetBIOS name being resolved has a record in the cache, the corresponding IP address in the cache is used and no further resolution is performed.

To view the contents of the NetBIOS name cache, use the command nbtstat –c. The results of this command are shown in Figure 6-1.

Figure 6-1   Results from nbtstat -c

WINS

The second method you can use to resolve NetBIOS names is a WINS server. A WINS server is a central repository of NetBIOS name information on the network. All computers on the network register their NetBIOS name information with the WINS server when they boot up. This makes the information available for other computers.

All computers need to use the WINS server. If they do not, the database will be incomplete and name resolution will not be possible for some hosts. Even the server running the WINS service must be configured to use itself.

WINS has an advantage over other NetBIOS name resolution methods because it:

- *Functions across routers*—WINS communication is performed with unicast packets because all of the clients are configured with the IP address of the WINS server. WINS is required in routed networks because unicast packets are routable.

- *Can be dynamically updated*—The WINS database is dynamically updated as computers are added or removed from the network. Each client computer registers its name during the boot process.

- *Can be automated*—The maintenance of the WINS database contents is automatic. After the client computers have been configured with the IP address of the WINS servers, the process requires no manual updates.

- *Offers client configuration through DHCP*—WINS clients can be configured with the IP address of the WINS server using DHCP. Because this is the only client configuration required, WINS can be implemented without ever visiting the client computers on your network.

- *Offers integration with DNS*—WINS can be integrated with DNS to resolve host names. If a DNS server does not have the IP address for a host name, the DNS server submits the host name to WINS in an attempt to resolve it. This can be useful if there are older Windows clients on your network that use WINS, but that do not support dynamic DNS.

Broadcast

If WINS has not been installed on the network or the client has been incorrectly configured, WINS cannot resolve the NetBIOS name. In such a case, a **broadcast** is sent on the network. The computer using the NetBIOS name being resolved receives the request and then responds with its IP address.

For example, if a workstation is resolving the name server5, the workstation sends a broadcast out asking server5 to identify its IP address. The computer named server5 receives the name resolution broadcast and responds by broadcasting back its IP address.

Broadcast name resolution is completely automatic and requires no configuration. However, this method of name resolution is not scalable to large networks because broadcasts do not cross routers.

LMHOSTS

If no other method is successful, Windows clients parse an LMHOSTS file to find the NetBIOS name. The **LMHOSTS** file is a static text file located on the workstation. The file contains a list of NetBIOS names and their associated IP addresses, as shown in Figure 6-2. On

Windows 95/98/Me computers, the LMHOSTS file is found in C:\WINDOWS. On Windows NT/2000/XP/2003 computers, the LMHOSTS file is found in %SYSTEMROOT%\system32\drivers\etc, where %SYSTEMROOT% is C:\WINDOWS on Windows XP/2003 and C:\WINNT on Windows NT/2000.

```
lmhosts - Notepad                                                    _ □ ×
File  Edit  Format  View  Help
#
# The following example illustrates all of these extensions:
#
# 102.54.94.97     rhino         #PRE #DOM:networking #net group's DC
# 102.54.94.102    "appname  \0x14"                   #special app server
# 102.54.94.123    popular       #PRE                 #source server
# 102.54.94.117    localsrv      #PRE                 #needed for the include
#
# #BEGIN_ALTERNATE
# #INCLUDE \\localsrv\public\lmhosts
# #INCLUDE \\rhino\public\lmhosts
# #END_ALTERNATE
#
# In the above example, the "appname" server contains a special
# character in its name, the "popular" and "localsrv" server names are
# preloaded, and the "rhino" server name is specified so it can be used
# to later #INCLUDE a centrally maintained lmhosts file if the "localsrv"
# system is unavailable.
#
# Note that the whole file is parsed including comments on each lookup,
# so keeping the number of comments to a minimum will improve performance.
# Therefore it is not advisable to simply add lmhosts file entries onto the
# end of this file.

192.168.1.249 SQLSERVER
```

Figure 6-2   LMHOSTS file

LMHOSTS files are found only on Microsoft operating systems and are not commonly used. They are difficult to maintain because they must be copied to every client.

The most common use of LMHOSTS files is to test NetBIOS name resolution. When you suspect that an application is not functioning because of a NetBIOS name resolution problem, you can add an entry to the LMHOSTS file of the workstation running the application. If the application begins to function properly, you know that NetBIOS name resolution is the problem.

Activity 6-1: Creating an LMHOSTS File

Time Required: 10 minutes

Objective: Create an LMHOSTS file for NetBIOS name resolution.

Description: You are installing a new accounting application for some of the finance staff. The application uses a NetBIOS name to contact the SQL database server. When you start the application, errors indicate that the server cannot be contacted. To ensure that NetBIOS name resolution is not a problem, you create an LMHOSTS file to resolve the server name, SQLSERVER, to the IP address 192.168.1.249.

1. If necessary, start your server and log on as **Administrator**.

2. Click **Start**, right-click **My Computer**, and click **Explore**.

3. In the right pane, double-click **Local Disk (C:)**, double-click **WINDOWS**, double-click **system32**, double-click **drivers**, and then double-click **etc**.

4. If LMHOSTS exists, then skip to Step 5. If there is not already an LMHOSTS file, you must create one based on the lmhosts.sam file.

   a. Right-click **lmhosts.sam** and click **Copy**.

   b. Right-click the **etc** folder and click **Paste**.

   c. Right-click **Copy of lmhosts.sam** and click **Rename**.

   d. Type **lmhosts** and press **Enter**.

5. Right-click **lmhosts**, click **Open**, click **Notepad**, and click **OK**.

6. On a blank line at the end of the file, type **192.168.1.249 SQLSERVER**.

7. Click **File** and click **Save**.

8. Close Notepad and Windows Explorer.

CHOOSING NETBIOS NAME RESOLUTION METHODS

The methods you choose to implement NetBIOS name resolution will vary depending on the size and capacity of your network. Certain resolution methods are better suited to small networks, whereas others are suited to large networks. In addition, some non-Windows clients are not capable of using WINS.

Single Subnet Networks

A network with only a single subnet can use broadcast name resolution. This is easy to implement because no client configuration is required.

The only potential drawback to broadcast name resolution on a single subnet is the number of broadcast packets that will be sent on the network. On a network with many computers or limited bandwidth, this can affect network performance. If a reduction in broadcast traffic is desired, WINS should be implemented.

An LMHOSTS file can be used on a single subnet network; however, this is not required. Broadcast name resolution is easier to implement and LMHOSTS files are difficult to manage because they must be configured on each computer.

Large Multisubnet Networks

When a network has more than one subnet, broadcast name resolution cannot be used because broadcasts do not cross routers. The only possible name resolution methods for large networks with multiple subnets are LMHOSTS or WINS.

LMHOSTS files are not practical for large networks because it is too difficult to maintain the file on each computer.

On large networks, WINS is used for name resolution. All the clients can be configured dynamically by using DHCP, making implementation and maintenance very easy.

Small Multisubnet Networks

Most small networks with multiple subnets use a WINS server for NetBIOS name resolution. Like large networks, the clients can easily be configured using DHCP, making the implementation very easy. However, sometimes network administrators use LMHOSTS files.

It is reasonable to use an LMHOSTS file on smaller multisubnet networks because there are a limited number of client computers to configure. To make the implementation of LMHOSTS files easier, they can be copied out to client computers as part of the logon process.

If you want to limit cross-subnet traffic to only a few computers, LMHOSTS can be configured on only a few Windows clients.

Non-WINS Clients

You can use a **WINS proxy** for computers that need to participate in NetBIOS name resolution but that cannot be configured to use WINS. These computers are often UNIX or Linux clients that need to access NetBIOS resources. Using a WINS proxy allows these clients to resolve NetBIOS names to IP addresses using records in a WINS database.

NOTE Windows Server 2003 can be used as a WINS proxy. You can enable this by setting the registry key HKEY_LOCAL_MACHINE\SYSTEM\CurrentControlSet\ Services\NetBT\Parameters\EnableProxy to a value of 1.

All NetBIOS clients are capable of using broadcasts for name resolution. A **WINS proxy** receives the NetBIOS broadcasts on a local segment and forwards them to a WINS server. This allows any NetBIOS client to participate in WINS. The WINS proxy must be configured with the IP address of a WINS server.

Take the example of a UNIX client, which is unable to use WINS, accessing NetBIOS-based services on a Windows Server 2003 system. To use these services, it must resolve the name of the Windows Server 2003 system. The UNIX client sends a broadcast-based name resolution request. A WINS proxy on the local subnet sees the broadcast and forwards it to the WINS server as a properly formed WINS name query. The WINS server resolves the request and sends the response back to the WINS proxy. The WINS proxy broadcasts the response back to the UNIX client. Figure 6-3 shows the name query process when using a WINS proxy.

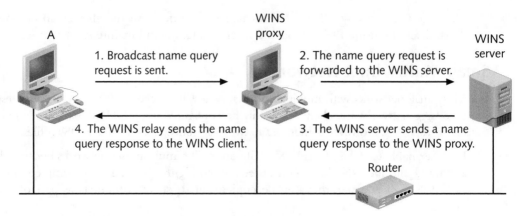

Figure 6-3   Name query process with a WINS proxy

WINS FUNCTIONS

Each NetBIOS name is tied to a service such as file sharing or Windows Messenger. A WINS server is a central repository for NetBIOS name and service information. To configure a client or server to use WINS, you must edit the properties of the TCP/IP protocol. Figure 6-4 shows the configuration of a WINS server on a Windows XP client. The same tab can be used to import a file as LMHOSTS.

WINS can perform four common tasks:

- Name registration
- Name renewal
- Name release
- Name query

Name Registration

When a WINS client boots up, it performs a name registration. The name registration places NetBIOS information about the client into the WINS database. This makes the information available to other clients performing name queries. Name registration is a two-packet process.

The first packet is generated by the client and sent directly to the WINS server using a unicast packet. This packet is a **name registration request** and contains the NetBIOS name that the client computer is attempting to register.

If the NetBIOS name is not already registered by another client, then a successful **name registration response** packet is sent from the WINS server to the client computer. This packet contains the NetBIOS name that has been registered and a TTL (Time to Live). Figure 6-5 shows the communication process for a successful name registration.

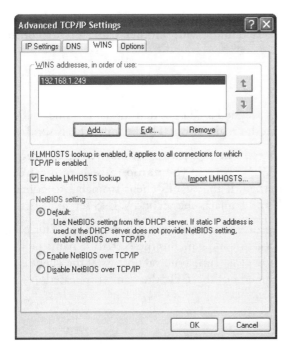

Figure 6-4 WINS configuration in Windows XP

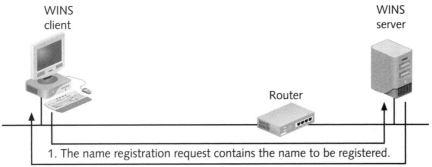

1. The name registration request contains the name to be registered.
2. The name registration response contains the TTL.

Figure 6-5 Name registration

If the NetBIOS name is already registered by another client, the WINS server sends a challenge to that host. If the original owner of the name does not respond, the NetBIOS name is registered to the new client and a successful name registration response packet is sent back to the new client. If the original owner of the name responds to the challenge, the new client is sent a negative name registration response.

WINS clients can be configured with multiple WINS servers. If a WINS client cannot contact the first WINS server in the list after three attempts, the second server is contacted. This process continues to the end of the list. However, the second WINS server is not contacted if a negative name registration response is received from the first WINS server. In such a case, the client must be reconfigured with another name or it is unable to use NetBIOS-based services.

Name Renewal

Each NetBIOS name registration is assigned a TTL. When the TTL is one-half completed, the WINS client attempts to refresh the registration. The default TTL is six days.

Name renewal is a two-packet process. The first packet is a **name refresh request** and is sent from the WINS client to the WINS server. The **name refresh request** contains the NetBIOS name that is being refreshed. If the WINS client is unable to contact the first WINS server for one hour, it fails and contacts the second WINS server.

The second packet in the renewal process is a **name refresh response**. This packet is sent from the WINS server to the WINS client and contains the NetBIOS name being renewed, as well as a new TTL. Figure 6-6 shows the name renewal process. If the client is not able to renew its NetBIOS name before the end of the TTL, the name is released.

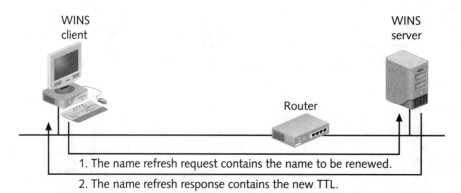

Figure 6-6   Name renewal

Name Release

When a computer is properly shut down, it contacts the WINS server and releases its NetBIOS name. The first packet in this process is a **name release request** sent from the WINS client to the WINS server. This request includes the NetBIOS name being released and the IP address of the WINS client.

The WINS server sends a name release response to the WINS client. The **name release response** contains the NetBIOS name being released and a TTL of zero. Another computer can now register the released name. Figure 6-7 shows the name release process.

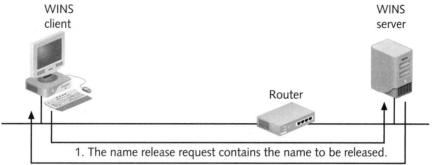

1. The name release request contains the name to be released.

2. The name release response contains the name to be released and a TTL of zero.

Figure 6-7   Name release

Name Query

A name query is used to resolve a NetBIOS name to an IP address. This is done by a client computer that is accessing resources on a server. A WINS client queries a WINS server if the NetBIOS name being resolved has not been recently resolved and stored in the NetBIOS name cache.

The first packet in the name query process is a **name query request** from the WINS client to the WINS server. This packet contains the NetBIOS name to be resolved. The second packet is a **name query response** from the WINS server to the WINS client. If the WINS server is able to resolve the query, this packet contains the IP address registered in the WINS database for the NetBIOS name being resolved. If the WINS server is not able to resolve the query, the packet contains a message indicating the name could not be resolved. Figure 6-8 shows the name query process.

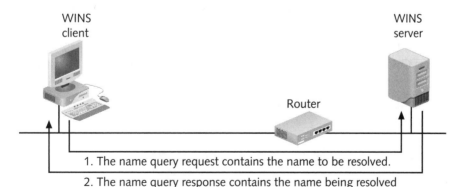

1. The name query request contains the name to be resolved.

2. The name query response contains the name being resolved and the corresponding IP address.

Figure 6-8   Name query

Each WINS client can have a list of multiple WINS servers. If the first WINS server in the list cannot be contacted, the WINS client queries the second WINS server in the list.

Installing WINS

Windows Server 2003 has the ability to act as a WINS server. WINS is the Microsoft implementation of a NetBIOS name server. A **NetBIOS name server** is responsible for accepting NetBIOS name registrations and queries. Although it is possible for a NetBIOS name server to run on operating systems other than Windows servers, it is very unusual.

In larger organizations with expansive WANs, there are several WINS servers. If this is the case, then WINS must be installed individually on each server. WINS is never installed automatically.

Activity 6-2: Installing WINS

Time Required: 10 minutes

Objective: Install WINS on your server.

Description: To ensure that all of the client computers on your network can resolve the NetBIOS names in a routed network, you have decided to implement WINS. In this activity, you install WINS on your server.

1. If necessary, start your server and log on as **Administrator**.

2. Click **Start**, point to **Control Panel**, and click **Add or Remove Programs**.

3. Click **Add/Remove Windows Components**.

4. Scroll down in the Components window, and double-click **Networking Services**.

5. Check the **Windows Internet Name Service (WINS)** check box, and then click **OK**.

6. Click **Next** to install WINS. If prompted for the Windows Server 2003 CD-ROM, click **OK**. Click the **Browse** button, select the **C:\I386** folder, and then click **Open**. Click **OK** in the Files Needed dialog box.

7. When the installation is complete, click **Finish**, and close the Add or Remove Programs window.

Activity 6-3: Configuring a WINS Client

Time Required: 5 minutes

Objective: Configure your server to be a WINS client.

Description: Servers must also be configured as WINS clients. If they are not, the NetBIOS names and IP addresses of the servers are not listed in the WINS database, and client computers cannot use NetBIOS resources on the servers. For these reasons, you configure your server as a WINS client.

1. If necessary, start your server and log on as **Administrator**.

2. Click **Start**, point to **Control Panel**, point to **Network Connections**, right-click **Classroom**, and then click **Properties**.

3. Click **Internet Protocol (TCP/IP)** and then click **Properties**.

4. Click **Advanced** and then click the **WINS** tab.

5. Click **Add**.

6. Type the IP address of your Classroom connection, and then click **Add**.

7. Click **OK**, click **OK** again, and then click **Close**.

WINS FAULT TOLERANCE

To configure fault tolerance for WINS, you must have multiple WINS servers or configure clustering.

Clustering is the best mechanism to provide WINS fault tolerance because it provides almost instant failover. WINS clients are configured with the IP address of the WINS service. When the original WINS server fails, the WINS service falls over to another server in the cluster and continues using the same IP address. The performance of WINS clients is not affected.

It is much more common to use multiple WINS servers for fault tolerance. This is much easier to implement, particularly if you have already configured multiple WINS servers on your network to reduce WAN traffic.

To use multiple WINS servers for fault tolerance, the WINS clients must be configured with the IP address of both WINS servers. A WINS client uses only the first WINS server in the list (**primary WINS server**) until it is unavailable. It then uses the second WINS server in the list (**secondary WINS server**). Windows 2000, and newer, WINS clients can be configured with up to 12 WINS servers. However, it is unusual to configure WINS clients with more than two or three.

 The process of using a secondary WINS server is relatively slow when compared to clustering. It takes 4.5 seconds (3 attempts x 1.5 seconds each) for the WINS client to realize that the primary WINS server is not responding.

NOTE

WINS REPLICATION

A single WINS server can handle at least 10,000 WINS clients. However, you may choose to implement multiple WINS servers in much smaller environments to control network traffic or to provide fault tolerance.

In a large network with multiple physical locations, you can reduce network traffic across WAN links by using multiple WINS servers. If a WINS server is located at each physical location, WINS clients do all of their registrations and queries with the local server. This creates no WAN traffic. Smaller networks may also benefit from having multiple WINS servers. When two WINS servers are implemented, WINS clients are still able to resolve NetBIOS names if one WINS server fails.

In most circumstances, the replication topology for WINS matches the physical WAN structure. The **topology** that provides the fastest synchronization of information between WINS servers is a **star topology**. A topology is the physical layout of the network. In a star topology all nodes connect through a central point. When a star topology is used, complete synchronization takes only two hops. Most WANs use this topology. Figure 6-9 shows a star replication topology.

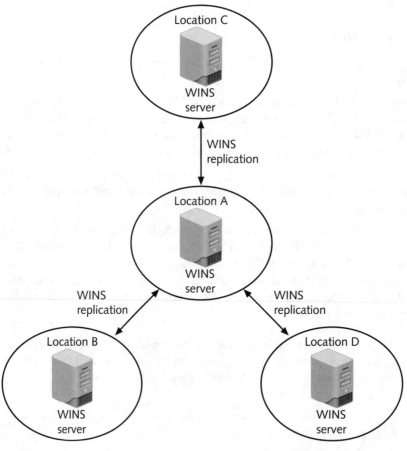

Figure 6-9   Star topology

When more than one WINS server is implemented, you must configure the WINS servers as **replication partners**. Replication partners synchronize information between each other. Replication can be configured in three ways:

- Push
- Pull
- Push/Pull

Default replication properties can be configured in the properties of the Replication Partners folder. You can also set the replication properties for a particular partner. To configure replication, right-click the replication partner, and then click Properties. Figure 6-10 shows the replication properties of a replication partner.

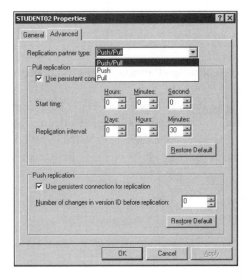

Figure 6-10   Advanced tab of the Properties dialog box

Push replication is initiated by the sending WINS server and occurs based on a certain number of changes occurring in the WINS database. When a defined number of changes occur, the replication partner is notified. The replication partner then requests a copy of the changes. Only changes are replicated between replication partners. Figure 6-11 shows the Push Replication tab.

In a network with few changes, push replication may not be sufficient. If the value is set too high in the Number of changes in version ID before replication field, an extended period of time may pass before changes are replicated. Until the changes are replicated, WINS clients resolving queries on the out-of-date server cannot resolve the unreplicated records.

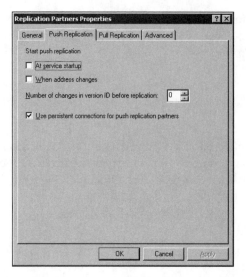

Figure 6-11 Push Replication tab of the Replication Partners Properties dialog box

Pull replication is initiated by the receiving WINS server and occurs based on a set time schedule. You can set a start time and the interval for replication to occur. This type of replication ensures that all changes are replicated between two WINS servers regularly. Figure 6-12 shows the Pull Replication tab.

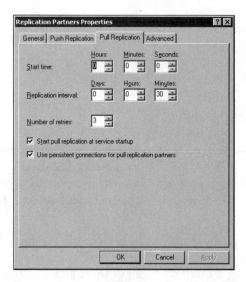

Figure 6-12 Pull Replication tab of the Replication Partners Properties dialog box

Normally, a combination of push and pull replication is used. This is configured by enabling both push and pull replications separately. Push replication ensures that, during periods of high change, records are replicated regularly. Pull replication ensures that, during periods of low change, records are replicated even if the criterion for push replication is not met.

You can configure both push and pull replication to use **persistent connections**. Persistent connections result in faster replication because a new connection does not need to be created for each replication. However, this causes a small amount of additional network traffic that may not be appropriate for slow WAN links.

NOTE   You can force replication by right-clicking the Replication Partners folder and clicking Replicate Now.

You can control several replication settings on the General tab of the Replication Partners Properties dialog box. The Replication only with partners option forces a server to only replicate its records to servers configured as replication partners. This ensures that replication is two-way. The Overwrite unique static mappings at this server (migrate on) option allows dynamic WINS registrations from other servers to overwrite static mappings created on this server.

You can enable WINS servers to find automatically replication partners. To do this, a WINS server uses multicast packets to find other replication partners. You can control how often the multicast is sent and the TTL of the packet. A multicast TTL controls the number of routers it can pass through.

A WINS server may hold records for registrations that were not taken by itself or its direct replication partners. In the case of three WINS servers, Server1 replicates to Server2, and Server2 replicates to Server3. You can restrict the records being accepted by a server based on the owner. The owner is the server that originally accepted the registration.

You can configure both the automatic partner configuration and restricting record replication based on the owner on the Advanced tab of the Replication Partners Properties dialog box, as shown in Figure 6-13.

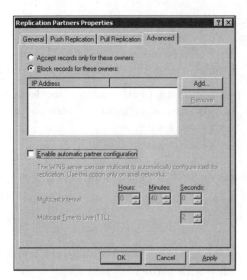

Figure 6-13   Advanced tab of the Replication Partners Properties dialog box

Activity 6-4: Configuring Replication Partners

Time Required: 10 minutes

Objective: Configure your server to replicate WINS information with a partner.

Description: A WINS server has been installed at each physical location on your network to reduce the WAN traffic generated by NetBIOS name resolution. Replication must now be configured so each WINS server can resolve names from other locations. You configure WINS replication with your partner. For this activity to be completed, you and your partner must have successfully completed Activities 6-2 and 6-3.

1. If necessary, start your server and log on as **Administrator**.

2. Click **Start**, point to **Administrative Tools**, and click **WINS**.

3. If necessary, double-click your server to expand it.

4. Right-click the **Replication Partners** folder, and click **New Replication Partner**.

5. Type the IP address of your partner's Classroom connection, and click **OK**.

6. Click **Replication Partners** in the left pane to see the configured partner in the right pane of the window. Note that, by default, this replication partner uses both push and pull replication.

7. Right-click **Replication Partners** and click **Replicate Now**. Click **Yes** to start replication, and click **OK** to close the information dialog box. The event log contains messages regarding the success or failure of replication.

8. Close the WINS snap-in.

Managing WINS

In general, the default settings for a WINS server provide adequate service. However, you can modify some settings, if required, to optimize perfomance.

The General tab of the WINS server Properties dialog box allows you to configure how often statistics are updated for the server, the path for backing up the WINS database, and whether the WINS database should be backed up each time the server is shut down. Figure 6-14 shows the General tab of the STUDENT01 Properties dialog box.

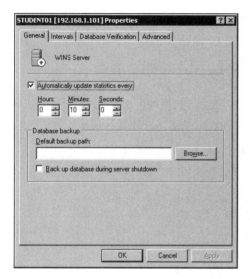

Figure 6-14   General tab of the STUDENT01 Properties dialog box

The Intervals tab allows you to configure how names are expired and deleted from the WINS database. The **renewal interval** refers to the TTL that is given to WINS clients when a name is registered with the WINS server. The **extinction interval** refers to how long an unused record exists in the WINS database before being marked as extinct. The **extinction timeout** refers to how long an extinct record is kept in the database. When an extinct record has existed in the database for the length of the extinction timeout, it is removed. The **verification interval** refers to how long a WINS server waits before validating a record that is replicated from another WINS server. Figure 6-15 shows the default values on the Intervals tab.

The Database Verification tab allows you to automate database verification. When database verification occurs, other WINS servers are contacted to confirm that they hold the same WINS information. You can choose whether the records are verified with the original server that took the registration or randomly. Figure 6-16 shows the database verification settings.

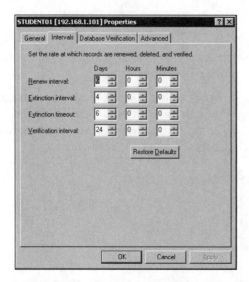

Figure 6-15   Intervals tab of the STUDENT01 Properties dialog box

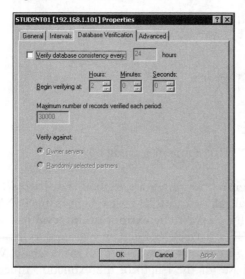

Figure 6-16   Database Verification tab of the STUDENT01 Properties dialog box

The Advanced tab allows you to set several options, as shown in Figure 6-17.

You can enhance the logging of events by checking the Log detailed events to Windows event log check box. This should only be used for troubleshooting because the number of events logged can adversely affect server performance.

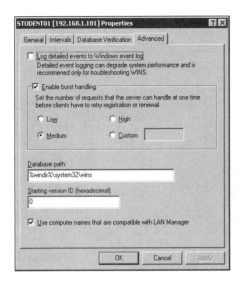

Figure 6-17   Advanced tab of the STUDENT01 Properties dialog box

Burst handling allows a WINS server to handle large volumes of name registration requests in a very short time period. If the number of name registration requests becomes too large to verify in the WINS database, the WINS server begins to send successful name registration responses without verifying whether the name is already registered. Later, the WINS server registers the name in the WINS database.

The database path indicates where the WINS database is stored. The default path is %windir%\system32\wins.

NOTE

The Starting version ID (hexadecimal) field is used to force WINS replication. Incrementing this number indicates to replication partners that there is a new version of the WINS database.

The Use computer names that are compatible with LAN Manager check box restricts registered names to 15 characters. Some non–Microsoft operating systems can use NetBIOS names that are 16 characters long. This option is enabled by default.

Viewing Database Records

To verify that a client is registered in the WINS database, you may want to view the contents of the WINS database. To view the records that exist in the WINS database, right-click Active Registrations, and click Display Records. This opens a dialog box that allows you to search the WINS database. You can search for records based on name, IP address, owner, or record type. Figure 6-18 shows the Display Records dialog box used for searching the WINS database.

Figure 6-18   The Display Records dialog box

When viewing records, you also have the option to delete them. To delete a record, right-click the record, and select Delete. When a record is deleted, you must choose whether to delete it from just the local server or from all databases. If you choose to delete the record from all servers, then the record is **tombstoned**. The tombstoned status replicates to all servers.

Activity 6-5: Viewing WINS Records

Time Required: 5 minutes

Objective: View WINS records on your server.

Description: A client computer on your network is having problems resolving the NetBIOS name APPSERVER. You have confirmed that the client computer is correctly configured to use the WINS server. You now verify that the record exists in the WINS database on your server.

1. If necessary, start your server and log on as **Administrator**.

2. Click **Start**, point to **Administrative Tools**, and click **WINS**.

3. If necessary, expand your server, click **Active Registrations**, right-click **Active Registrations**, and then click **Display Records**.

4. Leave the fields blank to view all records, and click **Find Now**.

5. You should see WINS records for the ARCTIC workgroup, your server, and your partner's server. There is no record for APPSERVER.

6. Close the WINS snap-in.

Adding Static Records

If non-Microsoft servers provide NetBIOS resources on the network, they may not be able to use a WINS server. If the non-Microsoft server cannot use WINS, then WINS clients cannot resolve their NetBIOS names. To eliminate this problem, you can create a static record in WINS.

For each **static mapping**, you enter the computer name, record type, and IP address. Figure 6-19 shows the creation of a static mapping.

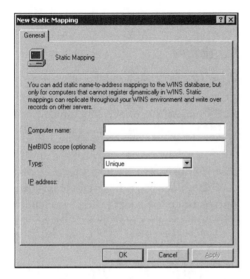

Figure 6-19   Creating a static mapping

Activity 6-6: Creating a Static Mapping

Time Required: 5 minutes

Objective: Add a static mapping to the WINS database.

Description: A UNIX server named APPSERVER runs a database required by an accounting application used by the finance staff. This application uses NetBIOS names, but APPSERVER cannot be configured to use WINS. In this activity, you create a static mapping for APPSERVER so that client computers can use WINS to resolve the name APPSERVER to an IP address.

1. If necessary, start your server and log on as **Administrator**.

2. Click **Start**, point to **Administrative Tools**, and click **WINS**.

3. If necessary, expand your server, then right-click **Active Registrations**, and click **New Static Mapping**.

4. In the Computer name text box, type **APPSERVER**.

5. In the Type drop-down list, leave the default of **Unique**. "Unique" is used to identify the name of a single computer and adds records for the Workstation Service, Messenger Service, and File Server Service. Other available options here include Group, Domain name, Internet group, and Multihomed.

6. In the IP address text box, type **192.168.1.202**, and then click **OK**.

7. To view the new records, click **Active Registrations**, right-click **Active Registrations**, click **Display Records**, and then click **Find Now**. Notice that the expiration of the records for APPSERVER is infinite.

8. Close the WINS snap-in.

Backing Up and Restoring the Database

On a network using NetBIOS-based services, WINS is essential. As a critical resource, the WINS database needs to be backed up in the same way that data needs to be backed up. If the WINS database becomes corrupt, the WINS server stops servicing clients. This results in client computers being unable to access NetBIOS-based resources because NetBIOS names cannot be resolved to IP addresses.

You can easily fix a corrupt WINS database if you have a backup of the WINS database. Simply stop the WINS service and restore the database. After the database has been restored, the WINS server receives changes that occurred since the backup from replication partners. The WINS servers determine the changes to replicated partners based on the version ID of the database records.

ACTIVITY

Activity 6-7: Backing Up and Restoring the WINS Database

Time Required: 10 minutes

Objective: Back up and restore the WINS database on your server.

Description: To ensure that you can quickly recover your server from a corrupt WINS database, you configure your server to back up automatically the WINS database. Then, you perform a manual backup and restore to test the process and ensure that it is working properly.

1. If necessary, start your server and log on as **Administrator**.

2. Create a new folder named C:\winsbak:
   a. Click **Start**, click **Run**, type **cmd**, and press **Enter**.
   b. Type **cd ** and press **Enter**.
   c. Type **md winsbak** and press **Enter**.
   d. Type **exit** and press **Enter**.

3. Click **Start**, point to **Administrative Tools**, and click **WINS**.

4. Right-click your server and click **Properties**.

5. On the General tab, in the Default backup path text box, type **C:\winsbak**. After a default backup path has been specified, the database is backed up every three hours. The statistics update interval that is also shown on this tab is not related to the backup.

6. Check the **Back up database during server shutdown** check box. This ensures that your server creates a current backup every time it is rebooted.

7. Click **OK**.

8. Right-click your server and click **Back Up Database**.

9. A dialog box opens with the folder C:\winsbak selected. Click **OK** to confirm that this folder is to be used.

10. Click **OK** to close the Backup Confirmation window.

11. Right-click your server, point to **All Tasks**, and then click **Stop**.

12. Delete the WINS database:

    a. Click **Start**, click **Run**, type **cmd**, and press **Enter**.

    b. Type **cd \windows\system32\wins** and press **Enter**.

    c. Type **del *.*** and press **Enter**.

    d. Type **Y** and press **Enter** to confirm the deletion.

    e. Type **exit** and press **Enter**.

13. Right-click your server and click **Restore Database**.

14. Click **OK** to use the default restore path of C:\winsbak.

15. Click **OK** to close the WINS restore confirmation.

16. View the active registrations:

    a. Right-click **Active Registrations** and click **Display Records**.

    b. Click **Find Now** to accept the default filter and view all records. You may need to click Active Registrations to view the records.

    c. The records should be as they were when you backed up the database.

17. Close the WINS snap-in.

Migrating the WINS to a New Server

Eventually, one of the WINS servers on your network will be taken out of service simply because the hardware needs to be replaced. When an old server is retired, you must have a plan to move the WINS database to a new server and potentially reconfigure the client computers. Reconfiguring clients is much easier if DHCP is used.

The overall process for client configuration is as follows:

1. Configure clients with the new WINS server as a secondary WINS server.

2. Install the new WINS server.

3. Configure clients to use the new WINS server as the primary WINS server.

4. Remove the old WINS server.

If this process is used, the WINS clients do not experience downtime. They are always configured to use the current WINS server.

The easiest way to migrate the contents of the WINS database from the old WINS server to a new WINS server is through replication. They can be configured as replication partners, and when the old server is no longer needed, replication can be removed.

If the WINS database is very large, or migration needs to be very fast, you can copy the WINS database directly from the old server to the new server. The steps are as follows:

1. Install WINS on the new WINS server.

2. Stop the WINS service on the old and new WINS server.

3. Copy the WINS files in %SYSTEMROOT%\system32\wins from the old WINS server to the new WINS server.

4. Start the WINS service on the new WINS server.

You can also use this process when migrating the WINS database from Windows NT. However, when you attempt to start WINS the first time, you receive an error that the database cannot start. The database is then converted to the new format. The conversion of the database can take up to half an hour for large databases with thousands of records.

Compacting the WINS Database

Over time, as records are added to and deleted from the WINS database, it becomes larger than the actual amount of data stored in the database. Unused space left from deleted records is left behind. Compaction reclaims this unused space.

Windows Server 2003 performs dynamic compaction of the database during idle times. Dynamic compaction occurs while the database is in use. Therefore, dynamic compaction is not as good as manual compaction.

Manual compaction of the WINS database is performed when the WINS service is stopped. On a busy WINS database of 1,000 computers or more, you should perform manual compaction about once per month.

To compact the WINS database manually:

1. Open a command prompt window and change to the C:\WINDOWS\system32\wins folder.

2. To stop the WINS service, type **net stop wins** and press **Enter**.

3. Type **jetpack wins.mdb temp.mdb** and press **Enter**. Any file name can be substituted for temp.mdb. Jetpack creates a compacted copy of wins.mdb with the file name temp.mdb, then deletes the original wins.mdb, and renames temp.mdb to wins.mdb.

4. To start the WINS service, type **net start wins** and press **Enter**.

5. Close the command prompt window.

NETBIOS SECURITY

6

NetBIOS over TCP/IP must be enabled for Windows Server 2003 to perform file and print sharing with pre-Windows 2000 clients such as Windows 9x and Windows NT. It is also required by all Windows operating systems to browse Windows networks and available shares in My Network Places. Browsing in My Network Places is still desired by many network administrators. Therefore, even though it is possible to disable NetBIOS over TCP/IP in the properties of the TCP/IP protocol, it is seldom done.

To facilitate browsing of resources in My Network Places, Windows NT allowed null sessions to be used when querying available shares from a server. A null session is an anonymous NetBIOS session in which no authentication credentials have been given to the server.

A number of security risks are associated with using NetBIOS over TCP/IP when null sessions are allowed. First, null sessions allow unauthenticated users to scan the network for available resources.

Null sessions allow unauthenticated users to query domain controllers for a list of users and groups, including their Security Identifiers (SIDs) and description. For this reason, you should never place the password for service account users in the description of the user. Write the password down on a piece of paper or store it in a separate secure file instead. Also, be aware that the Administrator account always has an identifiable SID number. Hackers can use a null session to identify the Administrator account even if it has been renamed. Hackers can then perform a brute force password attack on the Administrator account because it can never be locked out.

A user connected with a null session is also part of the Everyone group. If any resources are available to the Everyone group, they are available via a null session. Windows Server 2003 removes much of this risk by using the Authenticates Users group instead of the Everyone group for most tasks.

By default, Windows 2000 and Windows Server 2003 do not allow null sessions. This restricts unauthenticated users from browsing available shares, querying lists of users and groups, and accessing resources available to the Everyone group. If all of your users log onto the domain, there is no need to enable null sessions. If you want users who are not part of the domain to browse available shares, then you must enable null sessions.

Windows Server 2003 has a number of group policy settings in Security Options that you can use to control access via null sessions. Figure 6-20 shows the default settings on a domain controller.

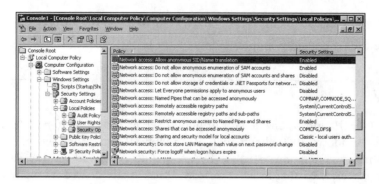

Figure 6-20   Default Security Options on a domain controller

Activity 6-8: Removing WINS

Time Required: 5 minutes

Objective: Remove WINS from your server.

Description: You have upgraded all the client computers and services on your network so that NetBIOS is no longer required. In this activity, you remove the WINS service from your server and configure your server to no longer be a WINS client.

1. If necessary, start your server and log on as **Administrator**.

2. Click **Start**, point to **Control Panel**, and click **Add or Remove Programs**.

3. Click **Add/Remove Windows Components**.

4. Scroll down in the Windows Components window, and double-click **Networking Services**.

5. Deselect the **Windows Internet Name Service (WINS)** check box, and click **OK**.

6. Click **Next** to remove WINS.

7. When the removal is complete, click **Finish**, and then close the Add or Remove Programs window.

8. Click **Start**, point to **Control Panel**, point to **Network Connections**, right-click **Classroom**, and then click **Properties**.

9. Click **Internet Protocol (TCP/IP)** and then click **Properties**.

10. Click **Advanced** and then click the **WINS** tab.

11. If necessary, click the IP address of your server, and click **Remove**.

12. Click **OK**, click **OK** again, and then click **Close**.

CHAPTER SUMMARY

- The resolution of NetBIOS names to IP addresses is critical for pre-Windows 2000 clients. Pre-Windows 2000 clients use NetBIOS to find domain controllers and use network resources.

- A NetBIOS name can be resolved using four different methods: NetBIOS name cache, WINS, broadcast, and the LMHOSTS file.

- Broadcast name resolution is not suitable for large networks because it does not work across routers. This method is most often used on small single-subnet networks.

- An LMHOSTS file is not suitable for large networks because the file needs to be copied to every server and workstation.

- A WINS server is a central repository for resolving NetBIOS names and offers several benefits over other NetBIOS name resolution methods. A WINS server functions across routers, can be dynamically updated, can be automated, offers client configuration through DHCP, and offers integration with DNS.

- A WINS proxy lets non-WINS clients use the WINS service and verify the validity of NetBIOS names over the network. The WINS proxy forwards broadcasts from the local segment to the WINS server.

- A WINS server performs four common tasks: name registration, name renewal, name release, and name query.

- When a name is registered with a WINS server, the client is assigned a TTL. If the name is not renewed by the end of the TTL, the client stops using the name.

- To configure WINS for fault tolerance, you must use clustering or implement multiple WINS servers. Clustering is faster to fail over but more difficult to implement.

- When two or more WINS servers exist on a network, replication must be configured between them to synchronize their contents. Only changes to the WINS database are replicated between servers.

- Two types of WINS replication exist: push and pull. Push replication is based on a certain number of changes triggering replication. Pull replication is based on a certain period of time passing. Most WINS servers use both push and pull replication.

- You can configure a static mapping for resources that are unable to register themselves with WINS.

- You can view and delete the records in a WINS database.

- You should back up the WINS database just like any other critical resource on a network.

KEY TERMS

broadcast — A packet that is addressed to all computers on a network. A broadcast for the local IP network is addressed to 255.255.255.255.

burst handling — A process used by a WINS server that cannot write name registrations to the WINS database fast enough to keep pace with the number of registrations. The WINS server ceases verifying that the names are not in use before sending out successful name registration requests with a short TTL.

extinction interval — The period of time that unused records exist in the WINS database before being marked as extinct.

extinction timeout — The period of time that extinct records exist in the WINS database before being removed.

LMHOSTS — A static text file located on the hard drive of NetBIOS clients that is used to resolve NetBIOS names to IP addresses.

name query request — A packet from a WINS client to a WINS server requesting the resolution of a NetBIOS name to an IP address.

name query response — A packet from a WINS server to a WINS client in response to a name query request. If the request is successful, this contains the IP address for the NetBIOS name in the original request.

name refresh request — A packet from a WINS client to a WINS server requesting that the registration for a NetBIOS name be renewed.

name refresh response — A packet from a WINS server to a WINS client in response to a name refresh request. If the response is successful, the TTL of the client lease is extended.

name registration request — A packet generated by a WINS client and sent to a WINS server requesting to register the NetBIOS name and IP address.

name registration response — A packet generated by a WINS server in response to a name registration request from a WINS client. The response can be successful or negative.

name release request — A packet sent from a WINS client to a WINS server when the WINS client shuts down.

name release response — A packet from a WINS server to a WINS client in response to a name release request. This packet contains the NetBIOS name being released and a TTL of zero.

NetBIOS name cache — The location in which the results of Windows client NetBIOS name resolutions are stored for 10 minutes. The storage of these resolutions increases network performance by reducing the number of name resolutions on the network.

NetBIOS name server — A server that holds a centralized repository of NetBIOS name information. The Microsoft implementation of a NetBIOS name server is WINS.

persistent connections — A connection that is created once and maintained over time for data transfer. This reduces communication overhead by reducing the number of packets used to establish connections over time.

primary WINS server — The first WINS server that a WINS client is configured to use.

pull replication — The replication between two WINS servers triggered by a defined amount of time passing.

push replication — The replication between two WINS servers triggered by a defined number of changes in the WINS database.

renewal interval — The TTL handed out to WINS clients when they register NetBIOS names.

replication partners — Two WINS servers that synchronize information in their databases.

secondary WINS server — A WINS server that is used by a WINS client when it is unable to contact the primary WINS server.

star topology — A physical network layout in which one central location is connected to several satellite locations.

static mapping — An entry manually placed in the WINS database. These are normally created for servers providing NetBIOS services that are unable to use WINS.

tombstoned — The term used to describe a WINS record that has been marked for deletion from all WINS servers. The tombstoned status is replicated among all WINS servers.

topology — The physical layout of a network.

verification interval — The period of time a WINS server waits before validating a record that has been replicated from another WINS server.

Windows Internet Naming Service (WINS) — The service in Windows that resolves NetBIOS names to IP addresses as well as stores NetBIOS service information.

WINS proxy — A service that forwards local broadcast NetBIOS requests to a WINS server. This is implemented for NetBIOS clients that are unable to use WINS.

REVIEW QUESTIONS

1. Which of the following client operating systems require WINS to function properly in a routed network? (Choose all that apply.)

   a. Windows 95

   b. Windows 98

   c. Windows NT

   d. Windows 2000

   e. Windows XP

2. WINS is designed to be used with NetBIOS and which protocol?

   a. TCP/IP

   b. IPX/SPX

   c. NetBEUI

   d. AppleTalk

3. Which of the following situations use NetBIOS names? (Choose all that apply.)

    a. resolving a UNC path

    b. accessing the Web page *www.microsoft.com*

    c. opening My Network Places

    d. a Windows NT workstation logging onto the domain

4. Which NetBIOS name resolution method is used to resolve a name if it has recently been resolved?

    a. NetBIOS name cache

    b. WINS

    c. broadcast

    d. LMHOSTS

5. Which NetBIOS name resolution method can be used by all NetBIOS clients, including UNIX clients?

    a. NetBIOS name cache

    b. WINS

    c. broadcast

    d. LMHOSTS

6. Which NetBIOS name resolution method dynamically updates a central database?

    a. NetBIOS name cache

    b. WINS

    c. broadcast

    d. LMHOSTS

7. Which NetBIOS name resolution method uses a static text configuration file on the client computers?

    a. NetBIOS name cache

    b. WINS

    c. broadcast

    d. LMHOSTS

8. Which file extension is used with an LMHOSTS file?

    a. .txt

    b. .sam

    c. .dat

    d. .nbt

    e. No file extension is used.

9. Which of the following describe WINS? (Choose all that apply.)

   a. functions across routers

   b. uses a static text configuration file

   c. clients are configured via DHCP

   d. integrates with DNS

   e. uses broadcast packets

10. Which methods can be used to configure a Windows XP computer with the IP address of a WINS server? (Choose all that apply.)

   a. DNS distributes the address

   b. DHCP distributes the address

   c. broadcasts distribute the address

   d. edit the properties of TCP/IP to assign the address

   e. multicasts distribute the address

11. Which WINS process is performed as the WINS client boots up?

   a. name registration

   b. name renewal

   c. name release

   d. name query

12. Which WINS process is used by WINS clients to resolve NetBIOS names to IP addresses?

   a. name registration

   b. name renewal

   c. name release

   d. name query

13. Which WINS process is initiated by WINS clients when one-half of the TTL is complete?

   a. name registration

   b. name renewal

   c. name release

   d. name query

14. Which WINS process is initiated by WINS clients during shutdown?

   a. name registration

   b. name renewal

   c. name release

   d. name query

15. Which process is implemented between two WINS servers to synchronize the contents of their databases?

    a. synchronization

    b. zone transfer

    c. database transfer

    d. replication

16. Which type of replication is triggered by a defined period of time passing?

    a. push replication

    b. pull replication

    c. time replication

    d. pulse replication

17. Records are deleted from the WINS database when the _____ is complete.

    a. renewal interval

    b. extinction interval

    c. extinction timeout

    d. verification interval

18. WINS clients send a name refresh request when one-half of the _____ is complete.

    a. renewal interval

    b. extinction interval

    c. extinction timeout

    d. verification interval

19. What status is assigned to a WINS record that is being deleted from all WINS databases, not just a single server?

    a. extinct

    b. expired

    c. dead

    d. tombstoned

    e. defunct

20. What can be done to accommodate NetBIOS servers that are unable to participate in a WINS environment? (Choose all that apply.)

    a. Create a HOSTS file on each client.

    b. Configure a WINS proxy.

    c. Create static mappings in the WINS database for each server.

    d. Configure replication between WINS servers.

CASE PROJECTS

Case Project 6-1: Choosing a Name Resolution Method

The Arctic University network is composed of hundreds of client and server computers. All of them need to be able to resolve NetBIOS names. As part of the network design process, create a document that analyzes the benefits and drawbacks of each name resolution method and decide which you think is most appropriate.

Case Project 6-2: Configuring Replication

Arctic University has eight physical locations connected by WAN links. Each of these WAN links is slow, so you have decided to install a WINS server at each location. Occasionally, clients at each location need to access NetBIOS resources in other locations. To accommodate this, you must configure replication. What things need to be taken into consideration when designing the replication topology? What does the replication topology look like?

Case Project 6-3: Accommodating Non-Windows Operating Systems

The main campus of Arctic University is routed and has a variety of operating systems in use as both clients and servers. Many of the clients and servers are non-Windows operating systems such as Macintosh OS, Linux, and UNIX. Some of the non-Windows operating systems are not able to participate in WINS. How do you accommodate these operating systems?

Case Project 6-4: Migrating a WINS Server

Arctic University has finally given you budget approval to replace your aging Windows NT WINS server. This server is used by all of your Windows 9x/NT clients and cannot be unavailable during regular work hours. Describe the process you use to implement the new server.

7

PLANNING A DNS STRATEGY

After reading this chapter, you will be able to:

♦ Describe the functions of the Domain Name System

♦ Choose a DNS namespace strategy

♦ Install DNS

♦ Explain the function of DNS zones

♦ Integrate Active Directory and DNS, including Dynamic DNS

♦ Integrate DNS with WINS

DNS is a critical service for networks that are using Active Directory and for access to Internet resources. In this chapter, you learn how DNS functions, see the benefits of different DNS namespace strategies, install DNS, and work with different DNS zone types. To help with Active Directory implementation, you also learn how DNS integrates with Active Directory and WINS.

FUNCTIONS OF THE DOMAIN NAME SYSTEM

DNS (Domain Name System) is an essential service for a network that uses Active Directory. DNS is used to resolve host names to IP addresses and find services. Active Directory is a central store of information about users and other resources in a Windows network. Windows 2000/XP client computers use DNS to find domain controllers, which the clients require to log on to Active Directory. DNS is also required if you want resources such as Web servers available on the Internet. Often for Internet resources, your ISP handles the DNS hosting and configuration.

The DNS Services on Windows Server 2003 and Windows 2000 Server are unique because they can store DNS information in Active Directory. After the information is stored in Active Directory, it is automatically replicated to all domain controllers, providing an easy backup mechanism.

DNS is used primarily to resolve host names to IP addresses. This is referred to as a forward lookup. To integrate in with the global DNS system, so that forward lookups function properly on the Internet, you must register your DNS domain name. DNS is also used to resolve IP addresses to host names. This is referred to as a reverse lookup. In addition, DNS stores service location information. Finally, DNS is available as a service on many different operating systems. However, the most common operating system it is implemented on is UNIX/Linux, and this can be integrated with the Windows version of DNS.

Host Name Resolution

WinSock (Windows Sockets) and NetBIOS are the two standard methods Windows applications can use to access network resources. Both mechanisms can be used to access IP-based resources. When a name is used to access a resource through WinSock, it is referred to as a **host name**. Host names are used because they are easier to remember than IP addresses.

When a program such as a Web browser or e-mail client uses a host name, the host name must be converted to an IP address before the resource can be contacted. The steps followed by Windows Server 2003 to resolve host names are as follows:

1. *Host name is checked*—Windows Server 2003 first checks to see if the host name being resolved is the same as its own host name. If it is, it uses its own IP address and the resolution process stops. If the host name being resolved is not the host name of this server, Step 2 is performed.

2. *Hosts file is loaded into cache*—Windows Server 2003 loads the hosts file into its cache so that it can be evaluated in Step 3. A **hosts** file is a simple text file that lists host names and IP addresses for resolution. This hosts file is a static text file located on the workstation. The contents of the hosts file are placed in the DNS cache.

3. *DNS cache is searched*—After the hosts file is loaded into the DNS cache, Windows Server 2003 evaluates the contents of the DNS cache. If the host name being resolved is in the DNS cache, the IP address in the cache is used and no further resolution is performed. The DNS cache also contains the results of previous DNS resolution attempts.

4. *DNS server is queried*—If the required host name is not the host name of this server and has not been found in DNS cache, Windows Server 2003 submits a request to a DNS server for resolution. Using DNS as the final host name resolution method limits the amount of network traffic and speeds the resolution process.

A hosts file was the original method to convert host names to IP addresses. For the hosts file to work in Windows Server 2003, it must be located in C:\WINDOWS\system32\drivers\etc.

A hosts file does not have a file extension.

NOTE

The contents of a hosts file are a list of IP addresses and host names. Each host name entry in the file has the IP address on the left and the host name on the right. In addition, comments can be added to the file using the # symbol. Any information after the # symbol is ignored.

Figure 7-1 shows an example of a hosts file. Two hosts are defined in the figure. The host name localhost resolves to the IP address 127.0.0.1. The host name myserver.mydomain.local resolves to the IP address 10.0.0.5.

ACTIVITY

Activity 7-1: Configuring a Hosts File

Time Required: 5 minutes

Objective: Configure and test a hosts file.

Description: You are testing the configuration of a new application. This application is hard-coded to access the host name applicationserver.arctic.local. For testing purposes, you use a hosts file to provide name resolution. Of course, when the application is rolled out live, you will put this entry in DNS to save time and effort.

1. If necessary, start your server and log on as **Administrator** of the Arctic.local domain.

2. Click **Start**, click **Run**, type **cmd.exe**, and press **Enter**.

3. In the command prompt window, type **ping applicationserver.arctic.local**, and then press **Enter**. The ping is not successful because host name resolution has not been configured.

7

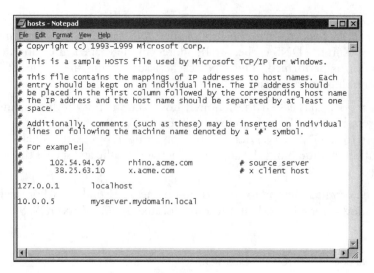

Figure 7-1   Hosts file

4. Close the command prompt window.

5. Right-click **Start** and click **Explore**.

6. In Windows Explorer, go to the **C:\WINDOWS\system32\drivers\etc** directory, and double-click **hosts**.

7. At the Open With dialog box, click **Notepad**, and then click **OK**.

8. Place your cursor at the end of the very last line in the hosts file, and press **Enter**.

9. Type the IP address of the classroom connection on your server, press **Tab**, and then type **applicationserver.arctic.local**.

10. Exit **Notepad**, click **Yes** when asked if you want to save changes, and then close Windows Explorer.

11. Click **Start**, click **Run**, type **cmd.exe**, and press **Enter**.

12. In the command prompt window, type **ping applicationserver.arctic.local**, and then press **Enter**.

13. The ping should be successful. The hosts file entry you created in this activity is used to resolve the name applicationserver.arctic.local to the IP address of your server.

14. Close the command prompt window.

Forward Lookup

The most common task a DNS server performs is resolving a host name to an IP address. This is called a **forward lookup**.

Resolving host names within an organization is a two-packet process. The first packet is a request from the DNS client to the DNS server containing the host name to be resolved. The second packet is the response from the server to the client containing the IP address of the requested host name. The DNS Service listens for host name resolution requests on UDP port 53.

When host names are resolved on the Internet, the process is more complex. There are 13 **root servers** that control the overall DNS lookup process for the entire Internet. These servers are located around the world and are maintained by various organizations under the direction of the ICANN DNS Root Server System Advisory Committee. The root servers are responsible for directing requests to DNS servers responsible for top-level domain names, such as .com and .net. If these 13 servers were to become unavailable, much of the Internet would be inaccessible. Resources would have to be accessed via IP address, not by host name.

NOTE

On October 21, 2002, hackers attempted to perform a denial-of-service attack on the 13 DNS root servers. This attack resulted in degraded performance on 11 of 13 servers. However, because other DNS servers cache much of the root server information, and thus provide redundancy, Internet users did not even notice.

Figure 7-2 shows the DNS lookup process that is used when the local DNS server does not hold the requested information. The local DNS server attempts to resolve the query by contacting other DNS servers. This is called a **recursive lookup** and is a type of forward lookup. An iterative lookup is another type of forward lookup in which the DNS server does not contact other DNS servers to resolve the query.

The recursive lookup process in Figure 7-2 uses the following steps:

1. The client computer is attempting to resolve the host name *www.microsoft.com*. The request is sent from the client computer to the local DNS server. (In a corporate environment, the local DNS server is installed and managed by the internal technical staff. In a home or small office environment, the local DNS server is likely to be the DNS server of the ISP.)

   When the local DNS server receives the request, it looks to see if it has the information that is being requested. Information could be on this server because it is authoritative for the domain or because it has previously looked up the information and has cached it. If the local DNS server does have the information, it responds to the client with the IP address of the host name. If the local DNS server does not have information about the host name, it starts resolving the name by first sending a request to a root server on the Internet.

2. The request from the local DNS server to the root server asks for the location of a DNS server that can help further resolve the host name. In this case, the name being resolved is *www.microsoft.com*, and the first step to resolve it is to find a server

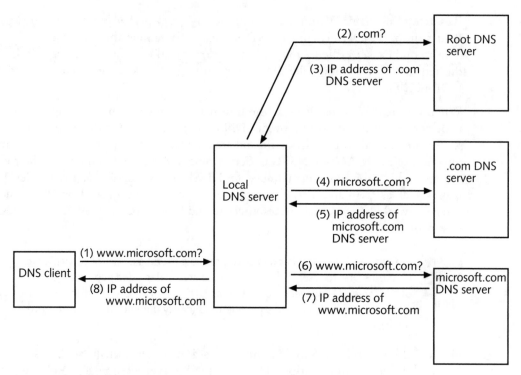

Figure 7-2   DNS lookup process

that knows about the .com domain. The local DNS server asks the root server for the IP address of a DNS server that has information about .com DNS servers.

3. The root server responds with the IP address of a DNS server responsible for the .com domain.

4. The local DNS server then contacts the .com DNS server and requests the IP address of a DNS server responsible for the microsoft.com domain.

5. The .com DNS server responds with the IP address of the DNS server responsible for the microsoft.com domain.

6. The local DNS server then contacts the microsoft.com DNS server and requests the IP address of *www.microsoft.com*.

7. The microsoft.com DNS server responds with the IP address of the host name *www.microsoft.com*.

8. Finally, the local DNS server responds back to the original DNS client with the IP address of the host name *www.microsoft.com*.

Registering a Domain Name

A **top-level domain (TLD)** name is the highest level of domain in the DNS system. TLDs used by DNS on the Internet are organized by either country or category. The country codes are standard two-character abbreviations for country names. ICANN (Internet Corporation for Assigned Names and Numbers) defines the category names. Table 7-1 shows some of the top-level domains that are used on the Internet.

Table 7-1   Top-level domains

Category	Description	Country	Description
.com	Commercial	.us	United States
.edu	Educational	.ca	Canada
.org	Nonprofit organization	.uk	United Kingdom
.net	Networking	.de	Germany
.biz	Business	.au	Australia
.name	Personal use	.tw	Taiwan
.pro	Professionals	.ru	Russia

To participate in the worldwide DNS lookup system, you must register your domain name with a **registrar**. A **registrar** is an organization that has the ability to put domain information into the top-level domain DNS servers so that your domain will be integrated with the worldwide DNS system. For instance, if you register the domain arctic.edu, the registrar would put records into the .edu DNS server that points to the DNS servers for your arctic.edu domain. You would then be responsible for creating and maintaining the records in the arctic.edu domain.

To verify that a domain name you want to register is available, you can use WHOIS. This is a service provided by domain name registrars. You can also find a Web-based WHOIS tool at *www.uwhois.com*.

Reverse Lookup

In addition to resolving host names to IP addresses, DNS can also be used to resolve IP addresses to host names. This is called a reverse lookup. A **reverse lookup** allows you to specify an IP address and the DNS server returns the host name that is defined for it.

Reverse lookups are often performed for the system logs of Internet services. A Web server can be configured to perform a reverse lookup of all clients accessing a Web site. This makes it easier to read the log files because the log files list the host names instead of IP addresses.

Mail servers also use reverse DNS lookups to verify the authenticity of e-mail messages. When an e-mail message is received, the receiving mail server uses a reverse lookup to resolve the domain name of the sending e-mail server. The receiving e-mail server then verifies that the sending e-mail server is in the same domain as the "from" e-mail address. This helps prevent spam.

7

Reverse lookup DNS information is maintained by the organization that has been assigned an entire class of addresses. Normally this is your ISP. To ensure that the addressing information is correct, you must contact your ISP.

DNS Record Types

DNS records are created on a DNS server to resolve queries. Each type of record holds different information about a service, host name, IP address, or domain. Different queries request information contained in specific DNS record types. For example, to find the server responsible for e-mail in a domain, an MX record is required. An MX record contains the name of an e-mail server for a domain.

DNS can hold many different record types. However, there are only a few record types that you use on a regular basis. Table 7-2 shows some of the DNS record types and their purposes.

Table 7-2   DNS record types

Record Type	Purpose
A	*Host*—Resolves host names to IP addresses
MX	*Mail exchanger*—Points to the mail server for a domain
CNAME	*Canonical name*—Resolves one host name to another host name; an alias
NS	*Name server*—Holds the IP address of a DNS server with information about this domain
SOA	*Start of authority*—Contains configuration information for the domain on this DNS server
SRV	*Service*—Stores the location of domain controllers; used by Active Directory
AAAA	*IPv6 host*—Resolves host names to IPv6 addresses
PTR	*Pointer*—Resolves IP addresses to host names

RFC 1123 defines requirements for IP-based hosts. One of the requirements addressed is the format of DNS names. DNS names may contain uppercase letters, lowercase letters, numbers, and the hyphen.

 NOTE Windows Server 2003 DNS servers are able to use the underscore ("_") character. However, it is preferable to avoid using this character because it may not be compatible with some applications or other implementations of DNS.

DNS and BIND

Berkeley Internet Name Domain (BIND) is a version of DNS that runs on UNIX/Linux. It is the de facto standard for DNS implementation and many other implementations of DNS reference BIND version numbers for feature compatibility. Table 7-3 lists several important BIND versions and the features that make them important. All of these features are discussed later in the chapter.

Table 7-3 BIND versions and features

BIND Version	Feature
4.9.6	SRV records
8.1.2	Dynamic DNS
8.2.1	Incremental zone transfers

NOTE   The Internet Software Consortium is responsible for the maintenance and development of BIND. If you want more information about BIND, visit *www.isc.org/products/BIND*.

DNS NAMESPACE STRATEGIES

The DNS namespace can be broken into external and internal DNS. The **DNS namespace** is the part of DNS that your organization is responsible for that holds DNS records for your organization. **External DNS** is used to hold records for Internet resources, such as company Web servers and e-mail servers. **Internal DNS** is used to hold records for internal resources, such as Active Directory and internal Web applications.

To maintain security, the servers holding internal and external DNS records must remain separate. If internal DNS records are made available on the Internet, hackers can use the information to target internal servers.

The three options for utilizing DNS namespaces in Windows Server 2003 are as follows:

- Use the existing external namespace.
- Use a delegated subdomain of the external namespace.
- Use a separate unique namespace.

Using the Existing External Namespace

When the existing external namespace is also used for the internal namespace, it is relatively difficult for administrators but easier for users. Users are less likely to be confused accessing resources when both namespaces are the same. Using this strategy, Arctic University would use a DNS domain name, such as arctic.edu, that is registered on the Internet for both internal and external resources.

Using the existing external namespace does have its disadvantages:

- It is awkward to synchronize DNS records between the internal and external DNS servers because no automated mechanism can be used. Therefore, this option is not recommended.

- The automated synchronization mechanisms, such as zone transfers and Active Directory replication, synchronize all DNS records between two DNS servers, not just the appropriate records. This results in internal DNS records being available on the external DNS servers, which is a security risk.

- The records for external resources must be manually added to the internal DNS servers. If the records for external resources are not added to the internal DNS servers, users cannot resolve the names of external resources properly. For example, if an internal user attempts to resolve *www.arctic.edu*, he or she communicates with the internal DNS server responsible for the arctic.edu domain. If the internal arctic.edu DNS server does not have the www record, the user receives an error.

NOTE To function properly, the www record from the external DNS server must be copied to the internal DNS server. However, this does not affect the ability to resolve DNS records for other domains on the Internet such as Microsoft.com.

Using a Delegated Subdomain of the External Namespace

If you want to avoid the complexity of multiple namespaces to limit user confusion, but want to avoid the synchronization issues experienced when using the existing external namespace, then using a delegated subdomain of the external namespace is a good choice. A **delegated subdomain** is a subdomain that has been configured as its own zone so that it can be placed on DNS servers independently of the parent domain. A delegated subdomain allows you to keep separate DNS servers for internal and external resources with no need to synchronize records.

If Arctic University were using the domain name arctic.edu for Internet resources, a delegated subdomain for Active Directory might be ad.arctic.edu. The external DNS server continues to be responsible for the arctic.edu domain, but the internal DNS server would be responsible for the ad.arctic.edu domain. The only potential drawback to using a delegated subdomain of the external namespace is the length of the domain name, which can be awkward to use. A longer name is always more awkward to type in than a shorter one. The maximum allowable length for a DNS name is 254 characters, but this is unlikely to be an issue.

Using a delegated subdomain of the external namespace is also a good solution for situations in which UNIX servers are used to manage the external namespace and you prefer to use Windows-based DNS servers for the internal namespace. Retaining (or trying to retain) UNIX DNS servers is often a political power struggle within large organizations implementing Active Directory, as the people responsible for DNS management under UNIX fear becoming less relevant to the organization.

Using a Separate Unique Namespace

Using a completely unique namespace internally is easy for network administrators to implement, although this can be confusing to some users because they do not understand why the company Web site uses one naming convention whereas internal resources use another. Administrators like the system because the internal and external domain names are completely separate; thus, there are no record synchronization issues between the internal and external DNS servers. In addition, no delegation needs to be performed in the external namespace.

You should not use a domain name for your internal namespace if it has already been registered for use on the Internet. For example, Arctic University should not use arctic.com internally if another organization is already using it on the Internet. If it is used already on the Internet, the users at Arctic University cannot access Internet resources provided by arctic.com.

You should register the internal namespace you choose, if it is possible to do so. This ensures that no other organization will register the domain name at a later time causing problems when you need that name to function both internally in your organization and externally on the Internet.

You can also choose a domain name that is not even possible to use on the Internet. This ensures that there will be no conflict with Internet resources. For example, Arctic University could use arctic.local internally. The "local" top-level domain has not been officially reserved for internal use; it is, however, commonly used for internal purposes because there is no chance of it conflicting with Internet resources or other organizations using it as an internal domain name.

INSTALLING DNS

Windows Server 2003 can act as a DNS server. A DNS server provides host name resolution services for clients. Most organizations using Active Directory use Windows for their DNS server.

During the installation of Active Directory, if no DNS server has been configured for the domain, the Dcpromo wizard asks whether it should install DNS during the installation of Active Directory. This is a very easy way to implement DNS in a small organization with a single server. The Dcpromo wizard is used to promote a Windows Server 2003 member server to a domain controller.

In larger organizations, you often install DNS on multiple servers. If this is the case, you must add DNS individually to each of these servers. It is not automatically added when member servers are promoted to domain controllers. When deciding which of your servers will be DNS servers, you must consider server capacity and network traffic.

The DNS Service does not use a significant amount of memory or processing capacity on a server. The service itself uses about 4 MB of RAM and each record uses an additional 100 bytes of RAM. This has very little impact on average servers with 512 MB to 1 GB of RAM.

In a large organization, a single DNS server can be overwhelmed by the volume of DNS requests. The network card may not be able to handle the number of requests, particularly if the server is already performing other duties, such as domain logons, file services, and print services. In addition, WAN links can be overwhelmed by DNS lookups that are all directed to a central server. In addition, WAN links can be overwhelmed by DNS lookups that are all directed to a central server.

To reduce WAN traffic, DNS servers can be placed in each physical location. However, you must take into account the amount of synchronization traffic this generates between DNS servers. For small locations, it may generate less WAN traffic if DNS clients use a central server rather than having DNS servers synchronize DNS information across WAN links.

To decide the best placement of DNS servers during the planning process, you must estimate the amount of traffic that will be generated by DNS. This is best done by measuring an existing implementation and extrapolating this information to your plan. For example, if your test environment has 10 client computers, but your live network has 100 client computers, multiply your test results by a factor of 10 to find the estimated traffic. After the plan is implemented, you must measure the actual traffic amounts. Depending on the results, you may need to adjust the original plan by adding or removing DNS servers.

Activity 7-2: Installing DNS

Time Required: 10 minutes

Objective: Install DNS on your server and confirm it is running.

Description: You have already installed the main DNS server for Arctic University. To reduce network traffic, you have decided to place a DNS server at each physical campus location. In this activity, you install DNS on your server. In later activities, you configure it to communicate with the instructor's server.

1. If necessary, start your server and log on as **Administrator**.

2. Click **Start**, point to **Control Panel**, and click **Add or Remove Programs**.

3. Click **Add/Remove Windows Components**.

4. Scroll down in the Components box, click **Networking Services** in the Windows Components window, and click **Details**.

5. Check the **Domain Name System (DNS)** check box, and click **OK**.

6. Click **Next** to start the installation. If prompted for the Windows Server 2003 CD-ROM, click **OK**. Click the **Browse** button, select the **C:\I386** folder, and click **Open**. Click **OK** in the Files Needed dialog box.

7. Click **Finish**.

8. Close the **Add or Remove Programs** window.

9. To verify the installation, click **Start**, point to **Administrative Tools**, and click **Services**.

10. Double-click **DNS Server**.

11. Verify that the Startup type is set to **Automatic** and that the Service status is started.

12. Click **OK** to close the DNS Server Properties window.

13. Close the Services window.

7

DNS Zones

A **DNS zone** (commonly referred to as a zone) is the part of the DNS namespace for which a DNS server is responsible. For instance, Arctic University is using the domain arctic.local to store all of the Active Directory information. To store the records for this domain on a DNS server, you first create a zone on the DNS server. Once inside the zone, you can create DNS records and subdomains.

When a zone is created, you designate whether it will hold records for forward lookups or reverse lookups. A zone that holds records for forward lookups is called a **forward lookup zone**. A zone that holds records for reverse lookups is called a **reverse lookup zone**.

Primary and Secondary Zones

For fault tolerance and to reduce network traffic, it is often useful to keep copies of DNS domain information on more than one server. For instance, you might keep a copy of DNS information at each physical location in an organization to limit WAN traffic.

If you store DNS information on multiple servers, it is essential that these servers automatically synchronize information between them. If the information between multiple DNS servers gets out of synchronization, replication of Active Directory may be affected and clients may be prevented from logging on to the network. From an administrative point of view, it is convenient to automate this process to save time and effort.

Primary and secondary zones are traditionally used to synchronize DNS information automatically between DNS servers. A **primary zone** is the first to be created, and all of the DNS records are created in the primary zone. A **secondary zone** takes copies of primary zone information. You cannot directly edit the records in a secondary zone because they are copied from the primary zone.

The process of moving information from the primary zone to the secondary zone is called a **zone transfer**. Older DNS servers copied the entire zone database every time the secondary zone synchronized with the primary zone. However, new implementations of DNS, including the DNS server included with Windows Server 2003, are capable of performing incremental zone transfers. An **incremental zone transfer** copies only information that has changed from the primary zone.

There can be only one primary zone in control of a domain. Secondary zones can be created as required for fault tolerance or to reduce WAN traffic.

NOTE

When primary and secondary zones are created on Windows Server 2003, the contents of each zone are held in a file on the hard drive. The name of the file is the name of the zone with a .dns extension. For example, the zone file for the domain arctic.local is arctic.local.dns, whether it is a primary zone or a secondary zone. This file is stored in C:\WINDOWS\system32\dns.

Activity 7-3: Creating a Primary Zone

ACTIVITY

Time Required: 10 minutes

Objective: Create a primary zone to hold resource records.

Description: Arctic University is creating DNS domains for each campus location. Because these servers will communicate with some non-Windows DNS servers, it has been decided that you will create a primary zone that can communicate with non-Windows secondary zones. You create the required records for the mail servers in each domain.

1. If necessary, start your server and log on as **Administrator**.

2. Click **Start**, point to **Administrative Tools**, and click **DNS**.

3. Double-click your server to expand it.

4. Click **Forward Lookup Zones** to view the existing zones. No zones are created by default when DNS is installed.

5. Right-click **Forward Lookup Zones** and click **New Zone**.

6. Click **Next**.

7. Confirm that **Primary zone** is selected, and click **Next**.

8. In the Zone name text box, type **locationxx.arctic.local**, where *xx* is your student number, and click **Next**.

9. Leave the default name for the zone file of **locationxx.arctic.local.dns**, and click **Next**.

10. Leave the default of **Do not allow dynamic updates**, and click **Next**.

11. Click **Finish**.

12. Double-click **locationxx.arctic.local**. Notice that only the NS and SOA records are created by default.

13. Right-click **locationxx.arctic.local** and click **New Host (A)**.

14. In the Name (uses parent domain name if blank) text box, type **mail**. The fully qualified domain name is modified to be mail.locationxx.arctic.local.

15. In the IP address text box, type **172.30.0.24**. In the classroom environment, no mail server actually exists. This would be the IP address of the mail server if one existed.

16. Click **Add Host**.

17. Click **OK** to confirm the creation of the A record, and click **Done**.

18. Right-click **locationxx.arctic.local** and click **New Mail Exchanger (MX)**.

19. Leave the Host or child domain text box blank. By leaving this blank, you are indicating that this is for the current domain. In the Fully qualified domain name (FQDN) of mail server text box, type **mail.locationxx.arctic.local**, and click **OK**.

20. Close the DNS snap-in window.

Activity 7-4: Creating a Secondary Zone

Time Required: 10 minutes

Objective: Create a local copy of DNS information using a secondary zone.

Description: You have found that users at some locations often need to resolve host names in other locations. To reduce the amount of WAN traffic, you have decided to create secondary zones in some of the locations.

For this activity, you require a partner that has completed Activity 7-3. You modify your zone to allow zone transfers and create a secondary zone of your partner's primary zone.

1. If necessary, start your server and log on as **Administrator**.

2. Click **Start**, point to **Administrative Tools**, and click **DNS**.

3. Double-click **locationxx.arctic.local**, where xx is your student number.

4. Right-click **locationxx.arctic.local**, where xx is your student number, and click **Properties**.

5. Click the **Zone Transfers** tab.

6. Confirm that **Allow zone transfers** is selected, click **To any server**, and click **OK**. This ensures that your DNS server will allow your partner to create a secondary zone for this subdomain.

7. Right-click **Forward Lookup Zones** and click **New Zone**.

8. Click **Next**.

9. Click **Secondary zone** and click **Next**.

10. In the Zone name text box, type **locationyy.arctic.local**, where yy is the student number of your partner, and click **Next**.

11. In the IP address text box, type the IP address of the classroom connection on your partner's server, click **Add**, and click **Next**.

12. Click **Finish**.

13. Double-click **locationyy.arctic.local**, where *yy* is the student number of your partner. The records from your partner's domain are now stored on your server. You may receive the error Zone not loaded by DNS server. If you receive this error, right-click locationY.arctic.local, and click **Transfer from Master**. This forces the secondary zone to update from the primary zone. You may also need to press **F5** to refresh the view.

14. Close the DNS snap-in.

ACTIVE DIRECTORY INTEGRATED ZONES

An **Active Directory integrated zone** stores information in Active Directory rather than in a file on the local hard drive. To store DNS information in an Active Directory integrated zone, the DNS server must also be a domain controller.

Storing DNS information in Active Directory offers the following advantages over traditional primary and secondary zones:

- *Automatic backup of zone information*—When zone information is stored in Active Directory, it is automatically replicated to all domain controllers that have been configured to hold the zone information. This means that if a DNS server fails, the zone information is not lost because a copy of the zone information exists in Active Directory on other domain controllers.

- *Multimaster replication*—Active Directory integrated zones offer the advantage of multimaster replication. Multimaster replication allows any server to initiate changes. In traditional DNS zones, changes are made to the primary zone and replicated to the secondary zone. With Active Directory integrated zones, changes can be made on any DNS server servicing the zone. The changes are then replicated through Active Directory to other DNS servers. This is a benefit because when DNS servers are widely dispersed, administrators can more easily make changes to zone information via a local server. In addition, using Active Directory replication reduces complexity because only the Active Directory replication system is maintained.

- *Increased security*—Security is increased when zone information is stored in Active Directory. Traditional primary zones have no security mechanism to control which users are allowed to update DNS records. Active Directory integrated zones use the security mechanisms built into Active Directory to control which users or computers can update DNS records. After a DNS record is created, only the user or computer that created it can modify it.

DNS Zone Storage in Active Directory

Two areas in Active Directory can be used to store DNS zones:

- The domain directory partition
- The application directory partition

The **domain directory partition** of Active Directory holds information about the objects specific to a particular Active Directory domain, such as users and computers. This partition is replicated to all domain controllers in an Active Directory domain. The information in this partition cannot be replicated to domain controllers in other Active Directory domains.

One drawback to this method of storing a DNS zone is that if a DNS zone is stored in the domain directory partition, all domain controllers in the same domain receive copies of the zone even if they are not configured as DNS servers. This may result in unnecessary network traffic from additional Active Directory synchronization.

If one of the servers holding the Active Directory integrated zone is a Windows 2000 server, the zone must be stored in the domain directory partition of Active Directory. Figure 7-3 shows a zone being created in the domain directory partition of Active Directory.

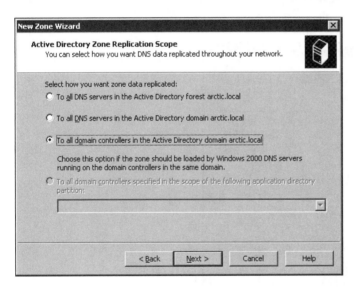

Figure 7-3   Storing a zone in the domain directory partition

Application directory partitions are a new feature of Active Directory in Windows Server 2003. They allow information to be stored in Active Directory but be replicated only among a defined set of domain controllers. The domain controllers that hold an application directory partition must be in the same Active Directory forest but can be in different Active Directory domains.

Using an application directory partition to store a DNS zone in Active Directory offers much more flexibility than storing a DNS zone in a domain directory partition. With a zone stored in a domain directory partition, the zone cannot be replicated to domain controllers outside the Active Directory domain. A zone stored in an application directory partition can be replicated to any domain controller you choose within the same Active Directory forest.

There are three options for where you can store DNS zones in an application directory partition:

- In all DNS servers in the Active Directory forest
- In all DNS servers in the Active Directory domain
- In all servers specified in the scope of an application directory partition

If you choose to store a DNS zone on all DNS servers in the Active Directory forest, an application directory partition is created to hold this information. This new application directory partition and the zone in it are automatically replicated to all domain controllers in the forest that are configured as DNS servers. In a very large organization with many DNS servers, this may not be acceptable because of the synchronization traffic that would be generated. Figure 7-4 shows the properties of a zone stored on all DNS servers in the Active Directory forest.

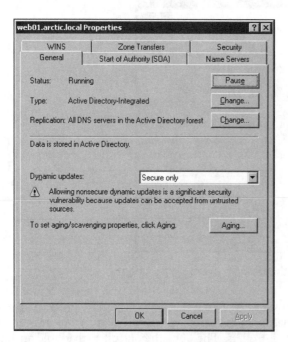

Figure 7-4   The properties of a zone stored on all servers in an Active Directory forest

Alternatively, if you choose to store a DNS zone on all DNS servers in the Active Directory domain, an application directory partition is created to hold this information. The new application directory partition and the zone in it are automatically replicated to all domain controllers in the domain that are configured as DNS servers. This is more efficient than storing the zone in the domain directory partition because synchronization happens only between servers using the DNS information.

If you want to be more precise with the replication of zones between domain controllers, you can create your own application directory partition. As part of creating the application directory partition, you must define the domain controllers that will hold a copy of the application directory partition you are creating. Using this option, you can replicate zone information to only a few servers throughout an Active Directory forest or domain rather than to all DNS servers.

ACTIVITY

Activity 7-5: Promoting a Member Server to a Domain Controller

Time Required: 30 minutes

Objective: Promote a member server to a domain controller.

Description: To reduce WAN traffic, you have decided to keep a copy of the Arctic.local DNS domain in each location. You have also decided that you want the zones to be Active Directory integrated. To store an Active Directory integrated zone, you must promote your server to a domain controller using the utility Dcpromo.

1. If necessary, start your server and log on as **Administrator**.

2. Click **Start**, click **Run**, type **dcpromo**, and press **Enter**.

3. Click **Next** to begin the wizard, and then click **Next** again after reading the Operating System compatibility information.

4. Click **Additional domain controller for an existing domain**, and click **Next**.

5. In the User name text box, type **Administrator**, and in the Password text box, type **Password!**. Confirm that the domain is **Arctic.local**, and click **Next**.

6. Confirm that **Arctic.local** appears in the Domain name text box, and click **Next**.

7. Click **Next** to accept the default Active Directory file locations.

8. Click **Next** to accept the default SYSVOL folder location.

9. In the **Restore Mode Password** text box, type **Password!**, and in the Confirm password text box, type **Password!**, and then click **Next**.

10. Click **Next** to continue, and wait for the Active Directory Installation wizard to complete.

11. Click **Finish** to complete the wizard, and click **Restart Now**.

12. Log on to your server as **Administrator**.

13. Click **Start**, point to **Administrative Tools**, and click **DNS**.

14. Double-click your server, if necessary.

15. Double-click **Forward Lookup Zones**.

16. The zone Arctic.local is an Active Directory integrated zone that is configured to replicate to all domain controllers within the Arctic.local Active Directory domain. As a result, the DNS Service on your server automatically begins servicing the Arctic.local zone when it is replicated to your server in Active Directory. This process may take some time.

ACTIVITY

Activity 7-6: Creating an Active Directory Integrated Zone

Time Required: 5 minutes

Objective: Create an Active Directory integrated zone.

Description: To reduce network traffic, you have decided to place a copy of the web.arctic. local domain at each location. You add an Active Directory integrated zone to your server. This zone is used for Internet services.

1. If necessary, start your server and log on as **Administrator**.

2. Click **Start**, point to **Administrative Tools**, and click **DNS**.

3. Right-click **Forward Lookup Zones** and click **New Zone**.

4. Click **Next** to begin creating the zone.

5. Confirm that the options **Primary zone** and Store the zone in Active Directory (available only if DNS server is a domain controller) are selected, and click **Next**.

6. Click **Next** to accept the default replication option To all domain controllers in the Active Directory domain Arctic.local.

7. In the Zone name text box, type **webxx.arctic.local**, where *xx* is your student number, and click **Next**.

8. Click **Next** to accept the default dynamic update option of Allow only secure dynamic updates (recommended for Active Directory).

9. Click **Finish**.

10. Close the DNS snap-in.

Integrating Active Directory Integrated Zones with Traditional DNS

Active Directory integrated zones replicate information in a fundamentally different way than traditional DNS zones. Consequently, they are limited in how they interact with traditional DNS zones. Active Directory integrated zones interact with traditional zones by acting as a primary zone to traditional secondary zones. This is useful when not all DNS servers are capable of participating in an Active Directory integrated zone.

A DNS server cannot participate in an Active Directory integrated zone in certain situations:

- The DNS server is pre-Windows 2000.

- The DNS server is Windows 2000 and the Active Directory integrated zone is stored in an application directory partition.

- The DNS server is a non-Windows server.

- The DNS server is a member server, but not a domain controller.

- The DNS server is in a different forest.

Active Directory integrated zones can act only as primary zones when integrating with traditional DNS zones. They cannot act as secondary zones.

Stub Zones

On the Internet, when a DNS server does not have the information to resolve a host name, it contacts a root server on the Internet to continue the resolution process and find the DNS server that is authoritative for the domain with the requested information. However, this process works only if the domain name is registered on the Internet.

When Active Directory is implemented, many organizations choose to use a domain name that is not registered on the Internet. If a domain name is not registered on the Internet, an alternative to using root servers must be implemented to ensure the lookup process is functional. In this case, DNS servers can be configured with a stub zone to help them resolve DNS requests. A **stub zone** is a DNS zone that holds only NS records for a domain. NS records define the name servers that are responsible for a domain. When a client submits a DNS request to a server with a stub zone, the DNS server continues the lookup process by sending a request to a DNS server specified in the NS records of the stub zone.

For example, in Figure 7-5, Arctic University has a subdomain for student resources called students.arctic.local. This subdomain is created as a separate zone on the server STUDENTDNS. The STUDENTDNS server also has a stub zone for the domain arctic.local. This stub zone has a NS record that points to the server ARCTICDNS, which holds the arctic.local zone. When student computers submit DNS requests to STU-DENTDNS for arctic.local records, STUDENTDNS reads the NS record from the arctic.local stub zone. Based on the NS record in the arctic.local stub zone, STUDENTDNS then submits a query to ARCTICDNS. ARCTICDNS responds to STUDENTDNS and STUDENTDNS then responds back to the student client computer.

7

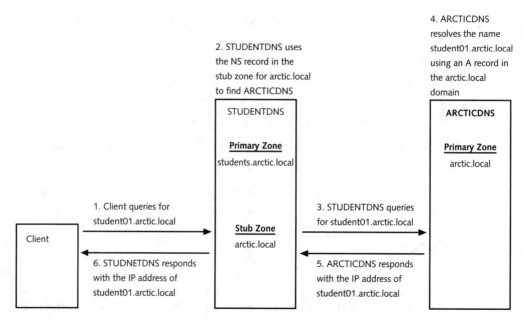

2. STUDENTDNS uses
the NS record in the
stub zone for arctic.local
to find ARCTICDNS

4. ARCTICDNS
resolves the name
student01.arctic.local
using an A record in
the arctic.local
domain

STUDENTDNS

Primary Zone
students.arctic.local

ARCTICDNS

Primary Zone
arctic.local

1. Client queries for
student01.arctic.local

Client

Stub Zone
arctic.local

3. STUDENTDNS queries
for student01.arctic.local

6. STUDNETDNS responds
with the IP address of
student01.arctic.local

5. ARCTICDNS responds
with the IP address of
student01.arctic.local

Figure 7-5   DNS lookup using a stub zone

Activity 7-7: Removing Active Directory Integrated Zones

Time Required: 30 minutes

Objective: Remove an Active Directory integrated zone.

Description: After measuring the network traffic caused by Active Directory integrated zones, you have decided to remove them from your network because most DNS lookups were local and the replication of zones to all domain controllers was excessive. In this activity, you remove Active Directory from your server, which also removes Active Directory integrated zones.

If more than one server in a domain removes Active Directory at the same time, errors may result. Your instructor will closely coordinate this activity. Do not start until given permission to do so. Your instructor will allow a second student to begin removing Active Directory after all services are stopped and the securing process has begun on the first student's server.

Under normal circumstances, only one domain controller should be demoted in a domain at one time. However, in a classroom environment, it is necessary to compress this task as much as possible. As a result, the final status window may indicate that errors have occurred because some final updates were not possible, but the demotion will be successful.

1. If necessary, start your server and log on as **Administrator**.

2. Do not begin until allowed by your instructor. Click **Start**, click **Run**, type **dcpromo**, and press **Enter**.

3. Click **Next** to begin the wizard.

4. Ensure that the option **This server is the last domain controller in the domain** is not selected, and click **Next**.

5. In the New Administrator Password text box, type **Password!**, and in the Confirm password text box, type **Password!**, and then click **Next**.

6. Click **Next** to confirm the removal of Active Directory from your server. Your server is no longer required to be a domain controller because Active Directory integrated zones are no longer required on your server. The instructor's server is still configured as a domain controller for the domain to handle logon requests.

7. Click **Finish** and click **Restart Now**.

Activity 7-8: Creating a Stub Zone

Time Required: 5 minutes

Objective: Create a stub zone to direct recursive queries.

Description: Your DNS server is configured so that it performs a recursive query with root servers on the Internet if it does not have the appropriate information. However, the root servers on the Internet have no information about the Arctic.local domain. To help your server resolve domain names in the Arctic.local domain, you create a stub zone.

The previous activity removed Active Directory integrated zones from your server. However, it takes a significant period of time for the NS record to be removed from the arctic.local zone. The instructor will manually remove the NS record created by your server to avoid errors in the following activity.

1. If necessary, start your server and log on as **Administrator**.

2. Click **Start**, point to **Administrative Tools**, and click **DNS**.

3. Right-click **Forward Lookup Zones** and click **New Zone**.

4. Click **Next** to begin creating the stub zone.

5. Click **Stub zone** and click **Next**.

6. In the Zone name text box, type **Arctic.local** and then click **Next**.

7. Accept the default file name by clicking **Next**.

8. In the IP address text box, type **192.168.1.10**, click **Add**, and then click **Next**.

9. Click **Finish** to complete creating the stub zone.

10. Double-click **Arctic.local**. The name server records for the Arctic.local domain have been copied to your server. When a DNS query for a record in the Arctic.local domain is submitted to your server, it now submits that query directly to the proper name servers rather than the root servers on the Internet.

11. Close the DNS snap-in.

ACTIVE DIRECTORY AND DNS

Active Directory requires DNS to function properly. The most important function that DNS performs for Active Directory is locating services, such as domain controllers. The naming structure for Active Directory domains is exactly the same as DNS domains so that service information about an Active Directory domain can be stored in the corresponding DNS domain. The service information that is stored in DNS helps client computers find domain controllers to log onto, and it also helps domain controllers find each other for replication of Active Directory information.

For example, Arctic University has an Active Directory domain named Arctic.local. Domain controllers for Arctic.local hold a copy of the Active Directory database for the domain. DNS servers are configured to hold a copy of the Arctic.local zone information. In this zone, there are SRV records that describe where to find services such as Kerberos and **Lightweight Directory Access Protocol (LDAP)**. **Kerberos** is the authentication system used by Windows 2000 and newer clients when logging on to an Active Directory domain. LDAP is a protocol that is used to query directories such as Active Directory. Client computers use SRV records to find the domain controllers that provide these services.

Figure 7-6 shows some of the DNS records created to support the Active Directory domain Arctic.local.

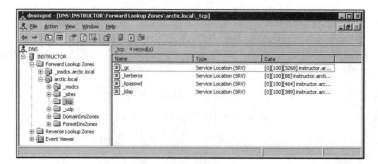

Figure 7-6   DNS records for Active Directory

In addition to the SRV records required by Active Directory, it is preferable to have A records for the names and IP addresses of all the servers and client workstations in DNS. Many utilities such as the Microsoft Management Console (MMC) rely on host name resolution. MMC uses snap-ins to allow you to manage various network services. For example, if you right-click a client workstation in Active Directory Users and Computers and click Manage, this opens the Computer Management snap-in for that computer. To do this, the MMC must be able to resolve the host name for the computer to an IP address. If DNS is not configured properly, the attempt to manage the client computer fails.

It is possible to add manually all of the required SRV and A records that an Active Directory domain requires, but this is very difficult to manage. To simplify management of DNS records for Active Directory, you can implement Dynamic DNS.

Dynamic DNS

Dynamic DNS is a system in which records can be updated on a DNS server automatically rather than forcing an administrator to create records manually. It is defined by RFC 2136. Windows 2000/XP/2003 operating systems are compliant with RFC 2136 and have the ability to perform Dynamic DNS updates themselves. Windows 9x/NT are not compliant with RFC 2136 and rely on a DHCP server to perform Dynamic DNS updates for them.

The service records for domain controllers are placed in a DNS zone using Dynamic DNS. The **netlogon** service is required to handle logon authentication requests. When the netlogon service of the domain controller starts, the DNS zone is updated by Windows Server 2003. If the service records for a domain controller become corrupt or are accidentally deleted, you can re-create them by stopping and starting the netlogon service on the domain controller.

Windows 2000/XP clients perform their own Dynamic DNS updates. During the boot process, the clients contact their DNS server to perform a dynamic update, and then they create an A record for their host name and IP address. Using this mechanism, DNS records for client computers are correct even when using DHCP because the A record is created after the IP address is leased from the DHCP server.

To force manually Windows 2000/XP clients to update their Dynamic DNS information, use the command ipconfig /registerdns.

NOTE

ACTIVITY

Activity 7-9: Testing Dynamic DNS

Time Required: 10 minutes

Objective: Verify that a computer is registering a host name using Dynamic DNS.

Description: You are not sure that a member server is properly registering its IP address and host name using Dynamic DNS. To confirm that it is working properly, you delete the existing A record from the instructor server and force the reregistration in DNS.

1. If necessary, start your server and log on as **Administrator**.
2. Click **Start**, point to **Administrative Tools**, and click **DNS**.
3. Right-click **DNS** and click **Connect to DNS Server**.
4. Click **The following computer**, type **instructor** in the text box, and click **OK**.
5. Double-click **instructor**.

6. Double-click **Forward Lookup Zones**.

7. Double-click **Arctic.local**.

8. Right-click **studentxx**, where *xx* is your student number, click **Delete**, and click **Yes** to confirm.

9. Click **Start**, click **Run**, type **ipconfig /registerdns**, and press **Enter**.

10. In the DNS snap-in, click **Arctic.local**. If you do not see a new host record for your server, press **F5** to refresh the view.

11. Close the DNS snap-in.

Dynamic DNS and DHCP

The Dynamic DNS information updated by Windows 2000/XP is negotiated with the DHCP server during the lease process. A Windows 2000/XP client requests that the DHCP server update the PTR record for reverse lookups and that the client update its own A record. If the DHCP server does not support Dynamic DNS, Windows 2000/XP clients can also update the PTR record. Figure 7-7 shows the options that can be configured on the scope of a Windows Server 2003 DHCP server.

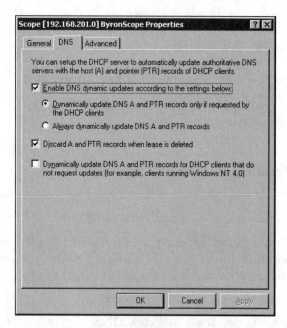

Figure 7-7   Dynamic DNS configuration of a DHCP scope

By default, a DHCP server running on Windows Server 2003 updates DNS records only for Windows 2000/XP clients and only if requested to do so. If you want the DHCP server to always update the A and PTR records for Windows 2000/XP clients, select the Always dynamically update DNS A and PTR records option button. It is unusual to configure this option. It can be used anytime you would prefer this traffic to originate from the DHCP server rather than from the clients. For instance, if DNS and DHCP are running on the same server, this setting reduces network traffic. It may also make firewall configuration simpler.

If you want the DHCP server to update A and PTR records for clients that are not compliant with RFC 2136, enable the "Dynamically update DNS A and PTR records for DHCP clients that do not request updates (for example, clients running Windows NT 4.0)" check box. This is an excellent way to create automatically DNS records for pre-Windows 2000 clients when required. For example, it is easier to use DNS names when connecting to client computers via a remote control application than it is to use IP addresses.

To specify that the DHCP server delete DNS records it has created when a lease expires, select the Discard A and PTR records when lease is deleted check box. If this option is not enabled, A and PTR records created by the DHCP server are never deleted by the DHCP server and out-of-date information may be left in DNS.

WINS Integration

Before Dynamic DNS was developed as a standard, Windows-based DNS servers used integration with WINS to provide a similar level of functionality. WINS was a requirement for early Windows networks that were routed, and it made sense to utilize this existing infrastructure.

To integrate with WINS, a DNS zone can be configured with a WINS server that is used to help resolve names. If a DNS zone receives a query for a host name for which it has no A record, it forwards the request to a WINS server. For example, if a DNS server with the zone arctic.local receives a host name resolution request for workstation85.arctic.local and does not have a matching A record, the DNS server forwards a WINS lookup request for the name workstation85 to the WINS server. In this situation, each time a record is resolved in WINS, both the DNS server and the WINS server must process the request. This results in slower response times and increased processor utilization. If DNS and WINS are running on separate servers, it also results in increased network traffic and even slower response times. For these reasons, Dynamic DNS is preferred to WINS integration.

 Integrating a WINS server with a DNS forward lookup zone creates a WINS record in the zone. However, you do not need to be aware of the details for this record because it is created automatically when you configure WINS integration settings in the properties of the zone.

Figure 7-8 shows the WINS tab in the properties of a zone. You can specify that records resolved via WINS are not replicated to other DNS servers by selecting the Do not replicate this record check box. This can be useful if you are integrating with non-Windows DNS servers that may not expire the records in a timely manner.

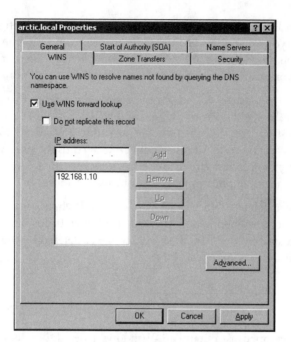

Figure 7-8   Zone properties WINS tab

By using the Advanced button on the WINS tab in the properties of a zone, you can configure timeout intervals. The **Cache time-out** controls how long DNS servers and DNS clients cache this record after it is resolved. If your WINS records are relatively static, this value can be raised above the default value of 15 minutes. This reduces network traffic by reducing the number of queries from clients and remote DNS servers. However, this creates the risk of outdated information being cached.

The **Lookup time-out** controls how long the DNS server waits for a response from WINS before sending an error to the requesting client. The default value for this is 2 seconds. If the network or WINS server is very busy, you may experience many lookup errors because the WINS server is not able to respond quickly enough. In this case, raising the Lookup time-out value may be a temporary solution until you can increase the performance of the local network or the WINS server.

CHAPTER SUMMARY

- Host name resolution is performed in four steps. The first step is to check if the host name being resolved matches the host name of the local computer. The second step is to load the hosts file into DNS cache. The third step is to check the DNS cache. The final step is to use DNS, if required.

- A forward lookup resolves host names to IP addresses. A reverse lookup resolves an IP address to a host name.

- A recursive lookup is performed when a local DNS server queries the root servers on the Internet on behalf of a DNS client.

- Common DNS record types include: A, MX, CNAME, NS, SOA, SRV, AAAA, and PTR.

- A DNS zone holds records for a portion of the DNS namespace. You must register your portion of the DNS namespace with a registrar to integrate into the worldwide DNS system on the Internet.

- Traditional primary and secondary zones are stored in a zone file on the hard drive of the DNS server.

- Active Directory integrated zones are stored in Active Directory. As a result, Active Directory integrated zones can use the security permissions in Active Directory to control updates.

- Active Directory integrated zones can be stored on all domain controllers in a single domain, all DNS servers in a domain, or all DNS servers in the forest.

- Active Directory integrated zones can act as primary zones to secondary zones.

- A stub zone contains name server records that are used for recursive lookups.

- Dynamic DNS allows records to be automatically updated on a DNS server. Client computers create A and PTR records using Dynamic DNS. Older Windows clients are not able to use Dynamic DNS directly, and a DHCP server must perform the updates on their behalf. Domain controllers create SRV records using Dynamic DNS.

- A WINS server can be used to help resolve host names if a DNS server does not have an A record that matches a query. This is useful when clients are not able to perform dynamic DNS but can register with a WINS server.

KEY TERMS

Active Directory integrated zone — A DNS zone in which DNS information is stored in Active Directory and supports multimaster updates and increased security.

application directory partitions — The partitions that store information about objects that is replicated to a set of defined domain controllers within the same forest.

Berkeley Internet Name Domain (BIND) — A UNIX-based implementation of the Domain Name System created by the University of California at Berkeley.

Cache time-out — The interval that defines how long other DNS servers and DNS clients cache records resolved through WINS. This is independent of the cache value used for other DNS records.

delegated subdomain — A subdomain for which the authority for management has been assigned to a different DNS server than the one that is authoritative for the main domain. For example, a UNIX server may be authoritative for the external domain used by a company, but a Windows DNS server is responsible for handling the internal subdomain that holds the records for Active Directory.

DNS namespace — The portion of DNS for which a server or organization is responsible. For example, a domain name that can be registered is a DNS namespace.

DNS zone — The part of the domain namespace for which a DNS server is authoritative. Commonly referred to as a "zone."

domain directory partition — A partition that stores information about objects in a specific domain that is replicated to all domain controllers in the domain.

Domain Name System (DNS) — The method used to resolve Internet domain names to IP addresses.

Dynamic DNS — A system in which DNS records are automatically updated by the client or a DHCP server.

external DNS — The DNS namespace that is used to hold records for Internet accessible resources.

forward lookup — The process of resolving a domain name to an IP address.

forward lookup zone — A zone that holds records used for forward lookups. The primary record types contained in these zones are A records, MX records, and SRV records.

host name — The unique name that identifies the computer on the network.

hosts — A local text file used to resolve fully qualified domain names to IP addresses.

incremental zone transfer — The process of updating only modified DNS records from a primary DNS server to a secondary DNS server.

internal DNS — The DNS namespace that is used to hold records for internal resources that are not accessible from the Internet.

Kerberos — An authentication protocol designed to authenticate both the client and server using secret-key cryptography.

Lightweight Directory Access Protocol (LDAP) — A protocol used to look up directory information from a server.

Lookup time-out — The time a DNS server waits for a WINS server to respond before returning an error to the requesting client.

netlogon — A service that controls user authentication, Active Directory replication, and Dynamic DNS updates for domain controllers.

primary zone — A zone that is authoritative for the specific DNS zone. Updates can only be made in the primary zone. There is only one primary zone per domain name.

recursive lookup — A DNS query that is resolved through other DNS servers until the requested information is located.

registrar — A company accredited by ICANN who has the right to distribute and register domain names.

reverse lookup — The process of resolving an IP address to a domain name.

reverse lookup zone — A zone that contains records used for reverse lookups. The primary record type in these zones is PTR records.

root servers — A group of 13 DNS servers on the Internet that are authoritative for the top-level domain names, such as .com, .edu, and .org.

secondary zone — A DNS zone that stores a read-only copy of the DNS information from a primary zone. There can be multiple secondary zones.

stub zone — A DNS zone that stores only the NS records for a particular zone. When a client requests a DNS lookup, the request is then forwarded to the DNS server specified by the NS records.

top-level domain (TLD) — The broadest category of names in the DNS hierarchy under which all domain names fit. Some top-level domains include .com, .edu, and .gov.

zone transfer — The process of updating DNS records from a primary DNS server to a secondary DNS server.

7

REVIEW QUESTIONS

1. Which port and transport protocol does the DNS Service use to listen for host name resolution requests?

   a. TCP port 53

   b. TCP port 25

   c. UDP port 53

   d. UDP port 51

   e. UDP port 389

2. Which DNS record is used to point to a mail server for a specific domain?

   a. MX

   b. A

   c. CNAME

   d. SOA

   e. SRV

3. Resolving an IP address to a host name is which type of lookup?

   a. forward

   b. cache

   c. reverse

   d. primary

4. Which of the following is not a type of DNS zone in Windows Server 2003? (Choose all that apply.)

   a. Active Directory integrated

   b. primary

   c. secondary

   d. stand-alone

   e. root

5. A stub DNS zone stores only which type of domain record?

   a. NS

   b. A

   c. CNAME

   d. SOA

   e. MX

6. Which DNS records do clients use to locate domain controllers?

   a. CNAME

   b. MX

   c. SOA

   d. NS

   e. SRV

7. A DHCP server running under Windows Server 2003 updates DNS records for which operating systems by default? (Choose all that apply.)

   a. Windows XP Professional

   b. Windows 2000 Professional

   c. Windows NT 4 Professional

   d. Windows 98

   e. Linux

8. Which of the following statements regarding Active Directory integrated zones is false?

   a. Active Directory integrated zones are automatically replicated to all domain controllers.

   b. Active Directory integrated zones support multimaster replication.

   c. Only Active Directory integrated zones support dynamic updates.

   d. Only Active Directory integrated zones support secure dynamic updates.

9. Which of the text files can be used to resolve domain names to IP addresses?

   a. LMHOSTS

   b. HOST

   c. HOSTS

   d. HOSTS.SAM

   e. PROTOCOL.INI

10. Which version of BIND supports incremental zone updates?

    a. BIND 4.9.6

    b. BIND 8.1.2

   c. BIND 8.2.1

   d. all of the above

11. Which of the following zones stores a read-only copy of another zone?

   a. primary

   b. Active Directory integrated

   c. root

   d. secondary

12. What type of zone resolves host names to IP addresses?

   a. forward lookup zone

   b. reverse lookup zone

   c. primary zone

   d. secondary zone

13. Which of the following servers can participate in Active Directory integrated zones? (Choose all that apply.)

   a. Windows 2000 Advanced Server domain controller

   b. Windows NT 4 Server

   c. BIND version 8.2.1 DNS server

   d. Windows Server 2003 member server

   e. all of the above

14. A backup network administrator accidentally deleted all the service records in DNS. What is the quickest method to recover the information?

   a. Reinstall DNS server.

   b. Reboot the server.

   c. Restore from backup tape.

   d. Stop and start the netlogon service.

   e. Manually create the deleted records.

15. Which of the following DNS records defines information about the primary zone, such as the serial number?

   a. A

   b. MX

   c. NS

   d. SRV

   e. SOA

7

16. The process of updating information from the primary zone to a secondary zone is called?

    a. replication

    b. zone transfer

    c. forwarding

    d. scavenging

17. Your company has a remote site containing five workstations connected by a very slow link. Users are complaining of slow DNS lookups. What type of DNS server can you configure in the remote site to speed up DNS resolution without creating more WAN traffic?

    a. Active Directory integrated

    b. primary

    c. secondary

    d. caching-only

18. Which command can be used to force manually a supported client's Dynamic DNS information?

    a. ipconfig /refresh

    b. ipconfig /registerdns

    c. ipconfig /flushdns

    d. ipconfig /displaydns

19. Which of the following are characteristics of using a separate unique namespace for internal DNS records? (Choose all that apply.)

    a. Users are less likely to become confused.

    b. Synchronization of records between the internal and external namespace does not need to be performed.

    c. It is difficult to synchronize records between the internal and external namespaces.

    d. A Windows-based DNS can be used internally while a UNIX-based DNS server is used externally.

20. Which of the following are mechanisms that can be used to provide dynamically updated records through DNS automatically? (Choose all that apply.)

    a. Windows 2000/XP clients update DNS records directly using Dynamic DNS.

    b. Windows 95/98 clients update DNS records directly using Dynamic DNS.

    c. DHCP can update Dynamic DNS records on behalf of clients that do not support Dynamic DNS.

    d. WINS can be integrated with DNS to provide functionality similar to Dynamic DNS.

CASE PROJECTS

Case Project 7-1: Integrating Windows Server 2003 DNS with BIND

The university currently has seven UNIX servers providing DNS Services for the whole campus. They are all running BIND version 8.1.2. Another administrator has recommended that the UNIX DNS servers be upgraded to Windows Server 2003 to support the new Windows Server 2003 domain controllers. What options does the university have for DNS? What are the advantages and disadvantages of each option? Which do you recommend?

Case Project 7-2: Creating DNS Zones

It has been decided that the university will not replace the UNIX DNS servers with Windows Server 2003. It has also been discovered that a few small departments also have Windows NT 4 servers running DNS. To reduce replication traffic, not all Windows Server 2003 domain controllers will run as DNS servers. In addition, some Windows Server 2003 member servers will run DNS. The head of the Computer Services Department recommends that only Active Directory integrated zones be created to reduce administrative and management overhead. What are the implications of such a decision? How can all DNS servers be integrated without upgrading the servers to Windows Server 2003?

Case Project 7-3: Choosing a Namespace Strategy

Arctic University has already registered the domain name arctic.edu for providing Internet services. However, now that Active Directory is being implemented, you need a namespace strategy for the internal network. What are the benefits and drawbacks for each of the three internal namespace strategies? Which would you recommend for Arctic University?

Case Project 7-4: Integrating DNS and WINS

There are still a large number of Windows 98 and Windows NT workstations in use at Arctic University. Due to budget constraints, it is unlikely that you will be able to update these workstations anytime soon.

You have been able to purchase new remote control software to help you manage the workstations on the network. However, right now the remote control software is only functioning properly for Windows 2000 and Windows XP because it requires DNS to convert host names to IP addresses, and the Windows 98 and Windows NT workstations are not in your DNS system.

How can you use WINS to help integrate the Windows 98 and Windows NT machines into the DNS system?

8

MANAGING AND
TROUBLESHOOTING DNS

After reading this chapter, you will be able to:

♦ Optimize DNS performance

♦ Secure DNS replication and Dynamic DNS

♦ Manage DNS servers

♦ Manage DNS zones

♦ Troubleshoot DNS issues using various tools

The default configuration options for DNS servers and DNS zones are sufficient in many situations. However, if you have slow WAN links, or are concerned about security, then you need to optimize your DNS configuration.

In this chapter, you learn to optimize DNS performance by configuring a DNS server for different roles, such as caching-only, nonrecursive, forwarding-only, and conditional forwarder. You also learn to secure DNS replication traffic and Dynamic DNS. You manage DNS servers and zones by configuring bindings and root hints as well as aging and scavenging of old DNS records. Finally, you troubleshoot DNS using tools such as Nslookup and DNSLint.

Optimizing DNS Performance

Performance degradation can come from a variety of sources. For instance, DNS lookup and replication traffic has the potential to affect adversely WAN performance. In addition, the design of your DNS namespace can affect performance.

In this part of the chapter, you learn that giving separate physical locations their own portion of namespace often reduces DNS synchronization traffic and that by assigning parts of the DNS namespace to various DNS servers, you delegate authority. You then learn that DNS servers can be configured to perform different roles depending on what is required for your network design. Each role has an effect on WAN traffic and performance levels in larger networks. The four roles are caching-only, nonrecursive, forwarding-only, and conditional forwarder.

Delegating Authority

When a zone is created on a DNS server, that server is responsible for all of the DNS namespace below that DNS name. For example, if the zone arctic.local is created on a DNS server, that server is also responsible for the subdomains location01.arctic.local and location02.arctic.local.

When an organization has multiple physical locations, dividing the DNS namespace and storing it only on local servers may reduce network traffic. For example, Arctic University has a main campus and three satellite locations. Each location has its own domain, as shown in Figure 8-1. If the DNS namespace is not subdivided, the zone contains information for the domain arctic.local, location01.arctic.local, location02.arctic.local, and location03.arctic.local. If a DNS server at each location holds a copy of the zone, the network traffic generated by synchronization of the DNS zone might overwhelm slow WAN links. By dividing the zone arctic.local into four separate zones, you can store only the local DNS information on the DNS server at each location. This eliminates network traffic generated by synchronization.

NOTE   In most cases, it is not realistic for large companies to keep DNS information in a single location. For fault tolerance, at least one copy is kept somewhere else on the network. This minimizes the network traffic caused by DNS synchronization, but does not eliminate it.

To divide the DNS namespace, you must **delegate authority** for a subdomain. When authority for a subdomain is delegated, a name server record is created for the subdomain. The name server record points to the server that contains the DNS information for the subdomain. In the preceding example, the Administrator of arctic.local would delegate authority for the subdomain location01.arctic.local to a DNS server in location01. If the DNS server responsible for arctic.local is queried for records in the location01.arctic.local subdomain, the requesting client is redirected to the DNS server in location01.

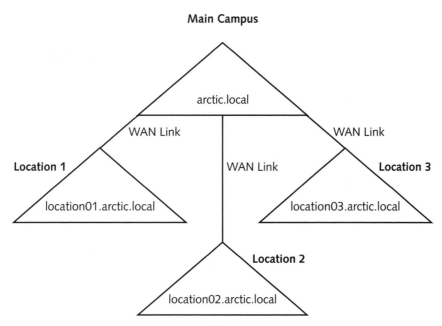

Figure 8-1   Arctic University DNS domains

Activity 8-1: Delegating Authority for a Subdomain

Time Required: 5 minutes

Objective: Delegate authority for a subdomain to another DNS server.

Description: To reduce DNS replication traffic, Arctic University has decided that each remote location will hold its own DNS records. The primary zone for each location has already been created and is stored on the servers. Now, you must delegate authority for the location subdomain.

1. If necessary, start your server and log on as **Administrator**.

2. Click **Start**, point to **Administrative Tools**, and click **DNS**.

3. In the left pane, right-click **DNS**, and click **Connect to DNS Server**. Click **The following computer:**, type **Instructor**, and click **OK**.

4. Double-click **Instructor**, double-click **Forward Lookup Zones**, and double-click **arctic.local**.

5. In the left pane, right-click **arctic.local**, and click **New Delegation**.

6. Click **Next** to begin delegating authority for the subdomain location*xx*.arctic.local, where *xx* is your student number.

7. In the Delegated domain box, type **location*xx***, where *xx* is your student number, and click **Next**.

8. To add your server as authoritative, click **Add**.

9. In the Server fully qualified domain name (FQDN) text box, type **Studentxx.arctic.local**, where *xx* is your student number, click **Resolve**, and click **OK**.

10. Click **Next** to continue and click **Finish**. The delegation is now complete. Your server is now responsible for the subdomain location*xx*.arctic.local.

11. Close the DNS snap-in.

Caching-only DNS Servers

A **caching-only DNS server** does not permanently store any DNS namespace information. DNS information is stored on a caching-only server only after a client has requested the information. For example, if there is a caching-only DNS server named DNS1, it contains no DNS records when it is started for the first time. When a DNS client sends a lookup request for *www.microsoft.com* to DNS1, then DNS1 looks up that record on behalf of the client, and returns the results to the client. DNS1 also retains a copy of the *www.microsoft.com* record.

NOTE   All DNS servers perform caching by default to reduce the number of DNS lookups on the network. A caching-only DNS server is unique because it is used only for caching. It is not responsible for any DNS zones.

Caching-only DNS servers reduce DNS lookup traffic across an Internet connection or on a WAN. In the preceding example, when other DNS clients resolve *www.microsoft.com* using the server DNS1, DNS1 resolves the name again by going out to the Internet. DNS1 retrieves the information by looking at the copy of the record it stored after performing the lookup the first time. This reduces DNS lookup traffic across the Internet connection.

On a WAN, caching-only DNS servers can reduce DNS lookup traffic and reduce DNS synchronization traffic. In a company with six locations and a single domain, a DNS server is often placed in each location. If each DNS server has a copy of the DNS zone that holds Active Directory information, there may be a large amount of DNS synchronization traffic when workstations use Dynamic DNS to add their records to the zone. These DNS records for workstations are not required in the other locations most of the time. If the DNS zone were kept in only one central location and caching-only DNS servers were placed at the remote locations, this synchronization traffic would be eliminated.

A certain level of fault tolerance is achieved when caching-only DNS servers are used. After a DNS lookup has been cached on a local DNS server, the DNS record can be resolved even if the original source DNS server is unavailable. The original DNS server may be unavailable because the server is being rebooted, the server is under attack by hackers, or a network link is down.

The major disadvantage of caching-only DNS servers is the potential for caching out-of-date information. Each zone, and potentially each DNS record, is configured with a period of time that it is allowed to be cached. A caching-only server respects this information and caches the DNS record for the time period allowed. When a DNS record is changed, a cached copy of that DNS record may be incorrect for up to the length of time caching is allowed. For example, if a DNS record that is allowed to be cached for 1 day is changed, cached copies of that record may be incorrect for up to 1 day.

Nonrecursive DNS Servers

When the DNS service is installed on Windows Server 2003, it performs recursive DNS lookups by default. In most situations, this is desired because you want the local DNS server to resolve requests on behalf of clients. However, if you want a DNS server to resolve only the zones for which it is responsible, you can disable recursion, as shown in Figure 8-2.

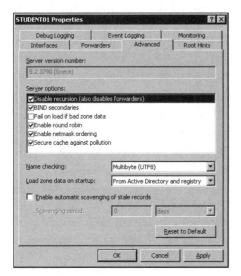

Figure 8-2   Disabling recursion

When a DNS server looks only at its own records, the action is referred to as an iterative lookup. If the DNS server has a copy of the requested record, it resolves the query and returns the record to the client. If the DNS server has a stub zone that references the domain of the requested record, it returns the name server responsible for that domain. If the DNS server has no information about the requested record, it returns an error. When a recursive lookup is performed, the DNS server contacts other DNS servers in an attempt to resolve the query for the client.

When you do not want your client computers to resolve Internet DNS names directly, configuring your DNS server as a **nonrecursive DNS server** stops them. You may do this when a proxy server is being used to provide Internet access because the proxy server performs any DNS resolution that is required.

When a DNS server is placed on the Internet, it accepts DNS lookup requests from any client. This could result in your Internet DNS server being overwhelmed by unauthorized DNS lookup requests from anonymous users on the Internet. Disabling recursion prevents this from happening. If you disable recursion on your Internet DNS server, it still resolves DNS lookup requests for the zones you have placed on it. Therefore, any records you want Internet users to resolve related to Internet services that you provide, such as Web servers and e-mail servers, still function properly.

Forwarding-only DNS Servers

The default process used by a DNS server when resolving recursive DNS lookups is to first look for the DNS record locally; if the DNS record is not found locally, it then queries the root servers on the Internet. If you have delegated subdomains, this is not the best process to use. For example, the server DNS1 at corporate head office is responsible for arctic.local and the server DNS2 at location1 is responsible for the subdomain location01.arctic.local. If a DNS lookup request for server1.arctic.local is sent to DNS2, DNS2 queries the root servers on the Internet to find the servers that are responsible for the domain arctic.local.

Forwarding is used to modify the DNS lookup process used by DNS servers for recursive queries. When a DNS server is configured to use forwarders, it first looks for the DNS record locally. Then, if the DNS record is not found locally, the DNS server queries its forwarders. If the forwarders are not able to provide the required DNS record, only then does the DNS server query the root servers on the Internet.

If the authority for subdomains has been delegated, configuring forwarders is more efficient than the default recursive lookup process. In the example of Arctic University, if the server DNS2 is configured with DNS1 as a forwarder, DNS lookup requests for records in the Arctic.local domain do not result in Internet traffic. When DNS2 receives requests for records in the Arctic.local domain, it queries DNS1 before querying the root servers on the Internet.

A **forwarding-only DNS server** is a DNS server that is configured to look only at local DNS zones and forwarders. It never queries the root servers on the Internet. This can be useful if your WAN is configured with only a single Internet connection. For example, if DNS2 at location1 of Arctic University is configured as a forwarding-only DNS server and uses DNS1 as a forwarder, all DNS lookups for the Internet are performed by DNS1. This is more efficient because DNS1 caches all of the DNS lookups performed, making them available locally to all of the users at the corporate head office.

ACTIVITY

Activity 8-2: Configuring a Forwarding-only DNS Server

Time Required: 10 minutes

Objective: Configure your DNS server to use forwarders, but not additional recursive lookups using root servers.

Description: The WAN for Arctic University is configured with each location connecting to the main campus and the main campus connecting to the Internet. To take advantage of DNS caching, it has been decided that for DNS, servers in the remote locations will use the main campus DNS server as a forwarder. After this is in place, the stub zone for arctic.local is not required and you remove it. In addition, you disable recursion on your DNS server so that it does not attempt to contact the root servers directly on the Internet.

1. If necessary, start your server and log on as **Administrator**.

2. Click **Start**, point to **Administrative Tools**, and click **DNS**.

3. If necessary, in the left pane, click your server.

4. Right-click your server and click **Properties**.

5. Click the **Forwarders** tab.

6. Confirm that **All other DNS domains** is selected, type **192.168.1.10** in the Selected domain's forwarder IP address list box, and then click **Add**.

7. Click **Do not use recursion for this domain** to enable this option, and click **OK**.

8. In the right pane, double-click **Forward Lookup Zones**.

9. Right-click the **Arctic.local** stub zone, and click **Delete**.

10. Click **Yes** to confirm deleting the stub zone.

11. Close the DNS snap-in.

Conditional Forwarders

A DNS server that is configured as a **conditional forwarder** uses a forwarder for requests only if they are for records in certain domains. This is useful for reducing WAN traffic when the authority for subdomains is delegated and each location has its own Internet connection.

If each location of Arctic University has its own Internet connection, then the WAN would carry unnecessary DNS lookup traffic if all requests were forwarded to DNS1 at the corporate head office. It reduces WAN traffic if the DNS servers in each location perform their own DNS lookups on the Internet and only use DNS1 as a forwarder when requests are made for records in the Arctic.local domain.

8

NOTE   Stub zones can also be used to redirect DNS lookup requests for a specific domain.

Figure 8-3 shows the configuration of conditional forwarding. In this figure, the server STUDENT01 is configured to forward all requests for the domain arctic.local to the DNS server 192.168.1.10.

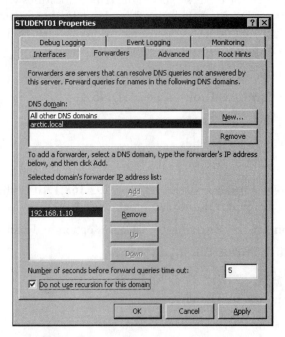

Figure 8-3   Conditional forwarding

DNS SECURITY

DNS security is very important in a network using Active Directory because DNS is critical for the proper functioning of Active Directory. Incorrect DNS records can prevent workstations from logging onto the network and stop the proper replication of Active Directory.

Security concerns for DNS are related to zone replication or Dynamic DNS. Each is discussed next. In addition, the text covers Dynamic DNS and DHCP servers.

Zone Replication Security

Active Directory-integrated zones use Active Directory replication to synchronize zone information between servers. This means that all of the security used by Active Directory replication is applied to the synchronization of Active Directory-integrated zones. This security includes authentication of computer accounts and encryption of all replication traffic. Using Active Directory-integrated zones is the easiest way to secure zone synchronization.

When traditional primary and secondary zones are used, the traffic from zone transfers is not encrypted. A hacker could use a packet sniffer to view zone transfer packets and use the information to learn about your internal network. If you want to encrypt zone transfers, you must use an additional mechanism, such as IPSec or a VPN.

A much easier exploit for hackers to use is requesting **unauthorized zone transfers**. An unauthorized zone transfer occurs when any person not specifically authorized takes a copy of your zone information. The default configuration for DNS servers is to allow zone transfer requests from any IP address. This is true for traditional primary zones and for Active Directory-integrated zones. Hackers can simply make the request and receive a copy of all your DNS records.

8

The best method to prevent hackers from learning about internal resources is to ensure that DNS records for internal resources are never made available on the Internet. However, resources such as Web server and e-mail servers must have their DNS records available on the Internet.

To prevent hackers from easily learning all of your external DNS records, you need to restrict zone transfers to specific IP addresses. This is configured in the properties of the primary zone, as shown in Figure 8-4.

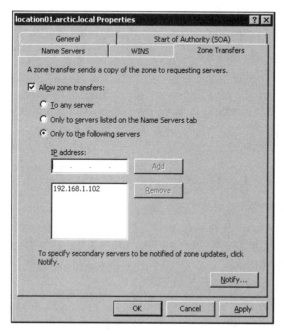

Figure 8-4   Securing zone transfers

ACTIVITY

Activity 8-3: Securing Zone Transfers

Time Required: 5 minutes

Objective: Configure traditional primary zones to limit zone transfers to approved secondary zones.

Description: Originally, when the DNS servers for remote Arctic University locations were configured, any server could act as a secondary zone. This made troubleshooting easy in the beginning. However, when this is allowed, the Nslookup command can be used to request a complete list of records in the domain. This gives potential hackers a starting point to begin probing your network for vulnerabilities. To eliminate this problem, you secure zone transfers from primary zones to only approved secondary zones.

After the zone configuration is complete, you use Nslookup to verify that zone transfers are allowed.

1. If necessary, start your server and log on as **Administrator**.

2. Click **Start**, point to **Administrative Tools**, and click **DNS**.

3. If necessary, in the left pane, select your server.

4. In the right pane, double-click **Forward Lookup Zones**, and double-click your primary zone **locationxx.arctic.local**, where *xx* is your student number.

5. In the left pane, right-click **locationxx.arctic.local**, and click **Properties**.

6. Click the **Zone Transfers** tab.

7. Confirm that the **Allow zone transfers** check box is checked.

8. Click **Only to the following servers** to limit zone transfers to a list of IP addresses.

9. In the IP address text box, enter the IP address of your partner's classroom connection. This is 192.168.1.1*yy*, where *yy* is your partner's student number.

10. Click **Add** and then click **OK**.

11. Close the DNS snap-in.

12. Click **Start**, click **Run**, type **cmd**, and press **Enter**.

13. Type **Nslookup** and press **Enter**.

14. Type **server 192.168.1.1*yy***, where *yy* is your partner's student number, and press **Enter**. This configures Nslookup to use your partner's server for queries.

15. Type **ls locationyy.arctic.local**, where *yy* is your partner's student number, and press **Enter**. This performs a zone transfer and lists all of the records in the location*yy*.arctic.local zone.

16. Close the command prompt window.

Dynamic DNS Security

Active Directory relies on SRV records to find domain controllers. Windows 2000 and newer clients also use SRV records to find domain controllers for authentication. Most Windows networks use Dynamic DNS to create SRV records. If these are incorrect, the resources may become unavailable to users.

When traditional primary zones are used, there is no way to secure them for Dynamic DNS. Any client can place DNS records into the zone and even overwrite existing DNS records. Hackers can use this to place incorrect IP addresses into A records or to create incorrect SRV records. This is a type of denial of service attack.

Active Directory-integrated zones can be secured for Dynamic DNS. You do this by allowing only **secure dynamic updates** in the properties of the zone, as shown in Figure 8-5.

8

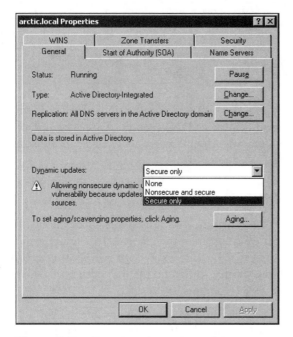

Figure 8-5   Securing dynamic updates

When secure dynamic updates are enabled, the permissions in Active Directory control who is able to update DNS records. Table 8-1 lists the default permissions for a DNS zone. The Authenticated Users group is allowed to Create All Child objects, which allows computers to create their own DNS records. This does not give computers the ability to modify each others' DNS records.

Table 8-1 Default zone permissions

Security Principle	Permissions
Administrators	Allow: Read, Write, Create All Child objects, Special Permissions
Authenticated Users	Allow: Create All Child objects
Creator Owner	Special Permissions
DnsAdmins	Allow: Full Control, Read, Write, Create All Child objects, Delete Child objects, Special Permissions
Domain Admins	Allow: Full Control, Read, Write, Create All Child objects, Delete Child objects
Enterprise Admins	Allow: Full Control, Read, Write, Create All Child objects, Delete Child objects
Enterprise Domain Controllers	Allow: Full Control, Read, Write, Create All Child objects, Delete Child objects, Special Permissions
Everyone	Allow: Read, Special Permissions
Pre-Windows 2000 Compatible Access	Allow: Special Permissions
System	Allow: Full Control, Read, Write, Create All Child objects, Delete Child objects

Computers can modify the records that they have created because Creator Owner is given special permissions that allow the modification of DNS records. This ensures that computers can automatically update their DNS records when they are assigned a new IP address. When DHCP is used, this ability is particularly important.

Dynamic DNS and DHCP Servers

When DHCP servers perform secure dynamic updates on behalf of clients, the DHCP server is the owner of the DNS record rather than the client computer. After that DHCP server is the owner of the record, only that DHCP server may modify the record. When a roaming client receives an IP address from a different DHCP server, that DHCP server cannot update the record with the new IP address.

A group named **DnsUpdateProxy** is provided to solve this problem. Any DNS records created by members of this group have no security. If all DHCP servers are made members of this group, they can update DNS records created by each other.

Records created by members of the DnsUpdateProxy group are vulnerable to compromise. Most servers providing resources use static IP addresses and should not be configured to use a DHCP server for secure dynamic updates. For example, if a DHCP server that is a member of DnsUpdateProxy creates an A record for server1.arctic.local, any other computer or user can update this record. If a hacker renames a workstation to server1.arctic.local and configures it with a static IP address, the workstation can perform a secure dynamic update, configure the record with an incorrect IP address, and become owner of the record. After the workstation is the owner of the record, the DHCP server is not able to modify it. An Administrator must manually delete the DNS record.

Domain controllers should never be members of the DnsUpdateProxy group. If they are, the SRV records that are created by the netlogon service are vulnerable to hackers, just as if they were created by the DHCP Service. For this reason, the DHCP Service should not be installed on a domain controller if the DnsUpdateProxy group is being used.

Managing DNS Servers

8

You can configure many DNS options at the server level, including the following:

- Configure aging and scavenging
- Update server data files
- Clear cache
- Configure bindings
- Edit the root hints
- Set advanced options
- Configure security
- Modify EDNSO

Configuring Aging and Scavenging

With **aging and scavenging**, DNS records created by Dynamic DNS can be removed after a certain period of time if they have not been updated. This prevents out-of-date information from being stored in a zone.

For scavenging to occur, it must be enabled on the Advanced tab of the DNS server properties. Figure 8-6 shows the aging and scavenging option being enabled. Scavenging is disabled by default. The Scavenging period option specifies how often scavenging is to be performed. By default, the scavenging is performed every seven days.

After scavenging has been enabled at the server level, you can configure the aging of DNS records for each zone. To configure the aging/scavenging properties for all zones on a server, right-click the server and select Set Aging/Scavenging for All Zones. Figure 8-7 shows the options available when you right-click the server.

Updating Server Data Files

The Update Server Data Files option is available when you right-click the server. If a zone is Active Directory-integrated, this has no effect. If a primary zone is not Active Directory-integrated, it forces all of the DNS changes in memory to be written to the zone file on disk.

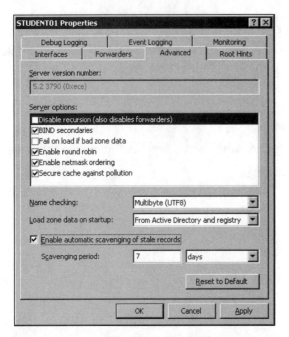

Figure 8-6   Enabling aging and scavenging

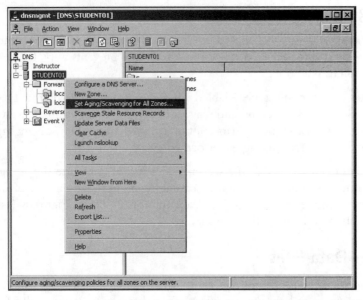

Figure 8-7   Configuring the aging/scavenging properties for all zones on a server

Clearing Cache

A DNS server automatically caches all lookups that it performs. Occasionally, you may have outdated information in the cache. To force a DNS server to perform a new lookup before the record in cache times out, you must clear the cache. To clear the cache, right-click the server and select Clear Cache.

Configuring Bindings

By default, the DNS Service listens on all IP addresses that are bound to the server on which it is running. However, you can also configure DNS to respond only to those certain IP addresses that are bound to the server. This may be useful if you have bound extra addresses to the server for specific purposes such as Web hosting.

The Interfaces tab of the server properties allows you to configure the IP addresses to which the DNS Service listens. Figure 8-8 shows the Interfaces tab of the server properties.

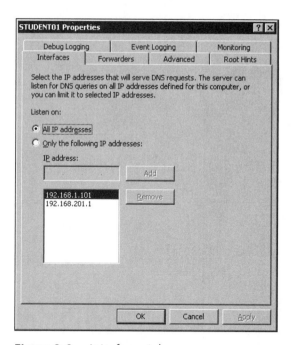

Figure 8-8 Interfaces tab

Editing the Root Hints

Root hints are servers that are used to perform recursive lookups. The Root Hints tab of the server properties is automatically populated with the names and IP addresses of the DNS root servers on the Internet. The list of root servers is loaded into the root hints from the file cache.dns stored in C:\WINDOWS\system32\dns. The contents of cache.dns are shown in

Figure 8-9. Figure 8-10 shows the Internet root DNS servers listed in the Root Hints tab of the server properties.

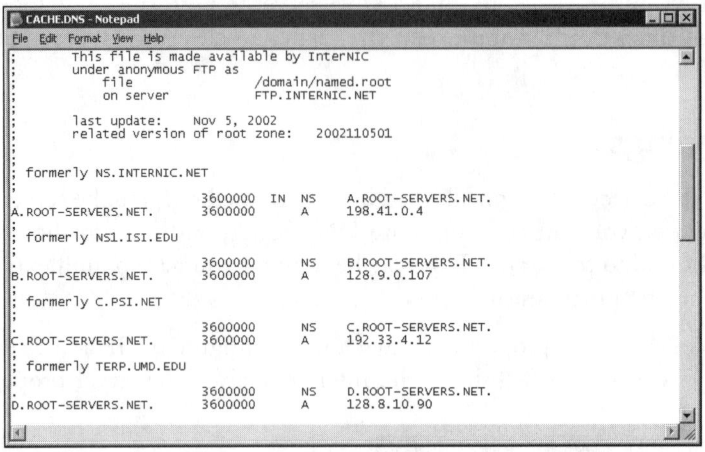

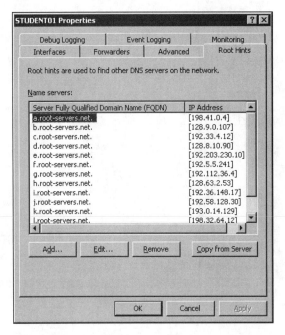

Figure 8-9 Contents of CACHE.DNS

Figure 8-10 Root Hints tab

If your DNS system is completely self-contained and does not need to access the root servers on the Internet, you can configure one of your internal DNS servers to act as a root server. You can do this by creating a forward lookup zone named "." (a period). If a DNS server holds a zone named ".", it is considered to be a root server and does not load the list of Internet root DNS servers from cache.dns. You can then edit the list of root hints for other DNS servers to point only at the new root server you have configured.

When a server holds a root zone, it does not use any forwarders that you may have configured.

NOTE

Activity 8-4: Creating a Root Server

ACTIVITY

Time Required: 10 minutes

Objective: Configure your server as a root DNS server.

Description: Some locations on the Arctic University network are not allowed access to the Internet. To keep DNS servers in these locations from performing DNS lookups, you configure your server as a DNS root server.

1. If necessary, start your server and log on as **Administrator**.

2. Click **Start**, point to **Administrative Tools**, and click **DNS**.

3. If necessary, in the left pane, click your server.

4. In the right-pane, double-click **Forward Lookup Zones**.

5. Right-click **Forward Lookup Zones** and then click **New Zone**.

6. Click **Next**.

7. Ensure that **Primary zone** is selected, and click **Next**.

8. In the Zone name text box, type **.** (a single period), and click **Next**. This indicates that this is to be a root zone.

9. Click **Next** to accept the default file name root.dns.

10. Click **Next** to accept the default of not allowing dynamic updates.

11. Click **Finish**. Your server now performs DNS lookups only for zones for which it has configuration information.

12. Right-click your server and then click **Properties**.

13. Click **Root Hints**. This tab is empty because your server is configured as a root server. This tab shows the Internet root servers when not configured as a root server.

14. Click **Cancel**.

15. Close the DNS snap-in.

Setting Advanced Options

You can configure several options on the Advanced tab of the server properties, including:

- Disable recursion (also disables forwarders)
- BIND secondaries
- Fail on load if bad zone data
- Enable round robin
- Enable netmask ordering
- Secure cache against pollution

Figure 8-11 shows the options you can configure on the Advanced tab of the server properties.

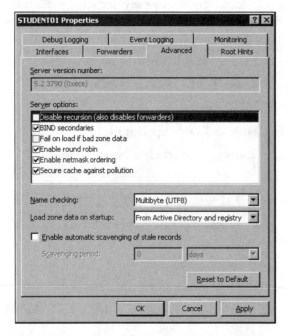

Figure 8-11   Advanced tab in DNS server Properties

The Disable recursion (also disables forwarders) option stops this DNS server from contacting any other DNS servers in an attempt to find DNS records. This DNS server recognizes DNS records configured only on this server. This option is selected when you want the server to be a nonrecursive DNS server.

NOTE The BIND secondaries option disables fast transfers between primary and secondary zones. This is necessary only if the DNS server holding the secondary zone is a non-Windows DNS server and supports a BIND version less than 4.9.4. BIND version 4.9.4 is very old (released in 1996) and this option is unlikely to be required. BIND is used by UNIX/Linux DNS servers and you may need to integrate with UNIX/Linux DNS servers when working with an ISP. When fast transfers are enabled, zone transfer traffic is compressed and multiple records are sent in each message.

By default, if errors are found in a zone file, the DNS server logs the errors and ignores the affected records. You can configure the server to disable the zone when any errors are found by selecting the Fail on load if bad zone data option. You may enable this if you want to ensure that all of the zone data is available. However, under most circumstances, it is more desirable to have a partially functional DNS server than one that is disabled.

Round robin DNS occurs when more than one record exists for a DNS query. The answer returned for the query alternates between the records. If there are two records, each is returned 50% of the time. For example, there may be two A records configured for a single host name, which allows a single host name to be tied to multiple IP addresses. This is sometimes done with Internet resources such as a Web server, and it is a simple way to implement "poor man's" load balancing. To enable round robin DNS, select the Enable round robin option. This option is enabled by default.

When a DNS query has multiple matches, a DNS server configured on Windows Server 2003 responds with the IP address that most closely matches the IP address of the client making the request. For instance, if a client with the IP address 192.168.5.100 makes a DNS query with valid responses 10.0.10.98 and 192.168.5.20, then the DNS server responds with IP address 192.168.5.20 because it most closely matches the IP address of the client. In most cases, this results in a response with an IP address that is physically closest to the client. If your routing environment is not composed of large networks subnetted to smaller networks, this may result in situations in which netmask ordering does not properly find the record that represents the IP address physically closest to the client. This feature can be disabled by deselecting the Enable netmask ordering option.

The Secure cache against pollution option controls how the DNS server caches lookups. With this option enabled, the DNS server does not cache lookup responses from nonauthoritative DNS servers. A nonauthoritative DNS server is any server that does not have a copy of the zone data. This prevents hackers from placing false information about other domains in your DNS cache. For example, if a DNS server queries an authoritative DNS server for microsoft.com, any information about records not within the microsoft.com domain are not cached. This option is enabled by default and should not be disabled on DNS servers connected to the Internet. If you use DNS forwarding internally on your network, this option needs to be disabled. Otherwise, lookups that are resolved by forwarders may not be cached.

8

The Name checking list box allows you to specify what characters are allowed in the zones. The default setting is "Multibyte UTF8," which allows non-ASCII characters. The setting "Strict RFC (ANSI)" allows only those characters that are defined in RFC 1123 ("a–z", "0–9", "-", and "."). The setting "Non-RFC (ANSI)" allows only ASCII characters to be part of DNS names, but they do not have to conform to RFC 1123. The setting "All names" permits any naming convention.

The Load zone data on startup list box allows you to select from where the DNS Service reads its configuration information. This option is server specific and not zone specific. Therefore, it is not affected by whether zones are Active Directory-integrated or not. The default option is "From Active Directory and registry." Other options are "From registry" and "From file." If the option to start from file is chosen, a configuration file named boot is used. This option needs to be chosen if configuration information has been copied from a BIND-based server.

Configuring Security

The Security tab of the server properties allows you to view and modify which users and groups can modify the configuration of the DNS server. The Domain Admins group, Enterprise Admins group, and DnsAdmins group are allowed to manage DNS.

Modifying EDNS0

The Windows Server 2003 DNS Service supports a relatively new protocol called **Extension Mechanisms for DNS (EDNS0)**. This protocol is defined by RFC 2671 and allows DNS servers to send UDP packets with more than 512 bytes of information.

DNS uses both UDP port 53 and TCP port 53. Zone transfers are performed using TCP port 53 because they are a relatively large amount of information and the reliability of TCP is desired. Most lookup requests are very small, and the overhead of establishing and tearing down a TCP connection is not worthwhile. Therefore, most lookup requests use UDP port 53.

Occasionally, a DNS lookup request has a result of more than 512 bytes. RFC 1035 defines the largest DNS message size over UDP as 512 bytes. When the results are more than 512 bytes, the DNS server sends a request to the DNS client to repeat the request using TCP instead of UDP so that the response can be delivered. Unfortunately, this process results in slower responses and increased network traffic. In addition, many organizations and ISPs are not aware that TCP port 53 should be open on their firewall, resulting in failed lookup requests. EDNS0 solves both of these problems by allowing messages over 512 bytes to be sent using UDP packets.

Servers that support EDNS0 send an OPT record before their DNS lookup requests. This OPT record gives the maximum size of DNS message that is supported over UDP. After the OPT record is received, the receiving server caches the information. Windows Server 2003 caches this information for one week (25,200 seconds) by default.

NOTE You can modify the amount of time OPT records are cached by editing the registry key HKEY_LOCAL_MACHINE\SYSTEM\CurrentControlSet\Services\Dns\Parameters\EDNSCacheTimeout. The value entered in this key is the number of seconds and the valid range is 3,600 (1 hour) to 15,724,800 (182 days).

When a DNS server receives a DNS lookup request from a server for which it has cached an OPT record, it supports the maximum UDP packet size allowed by the OPT record. When a DNS server receives a DNS lookup request from a server for which it does not have a cached OPT record, the DNS server assumes the requesting DNS server does not support EDNS0.

MANAGING DNS ZONES

You can configure a variety of options for a zone. These include:

- Reload zone information
- Change the type of zone and replication
- Configure aging and scavenging
- Modify the SOA (start of authority) record
- Modify the list of name servers
- Enable WINS resolution
- Enable zone transfers
- Configure security

The following sections discuss each in turn.

Reloading Zone Information

To perform mass editing of DNS information stored in a non-Active Directory-integrated zone, you may find it easier to edit the zone file stored in C:\WINDOWS\system32\dns rather than using the DNS snap-in. To get the DNS server to use the newly edited zone file, you must restart the DNS Service or tell it to reload the zone file. To reload the zone file, right-click the zone, and click Reload.

Changing the Type of Zone and Replication

When a zone is created, you must select whether it is a primary zone, secondary zone, or stub zone. If it is a primary zone, you must also choose whether it is stored in Active Directory. If the zone is stored in Active Directory, you also must choose how it is replicated. All of these options can be changed after the zone is created.

The zone type and replication for an existing zone can be modified on the General tab of the zone properties, as shown in Figure 8-12.

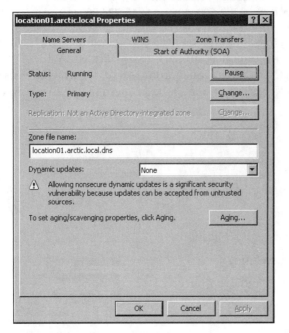

Figure 8-12   General tab

Configuring Aging and Scavenging

The button to change the replication for a zone is available only for Active Directory-integrated zones. If the button is grayed out, the zone is not stored in Active Directory.

NOTE

After scavenging has been enabled at the server level, the aging/scavenging properties must be configured at the zone level. To configure the aging/scavenging properties of a zone, click the Aging button on the General tab of the zone properties. Figure 8-13 shows the aging/scavenging properties of a zone.

To enable the deletion of old DNS records, select the Scavenge stale resource records check box. After scavenging is enabled, the No-refresh interval option lets you specify how often a DNS record can be refreshed. By default, there is a no-refresh interval of seven days. This means that Dynamic DNS clients cannot refresh their DNS record more than once every seven days. A refresh is a reregistration of existing DNS information with no changes. DNS updates in which there are changes to the DNS record are always allowed regardless of the no-refresh interval. If a DNS record is updated, the time stamp on the record is updated and the no-refresh interval begins again for that record.

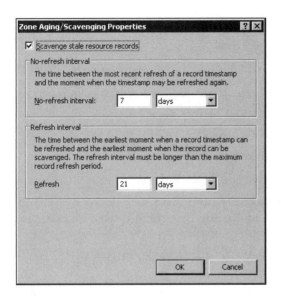

Figure 8-13   Aging/scavenging properties of a zone

The Refresh interval option is the period of time that must pass after the no-refresh interval has expired before DNS records are deleted. During the refresh interval, DNS records can be refreshed by Dynamic DNS clients. If a record is refreshed, a new time stamp is created and the no-refresh interval begins again for that record. If the record is not refreshed during the refresh interval, then the DNS server deletes the record during its next scavenging.

Manually created DNS records are never scavenged. Dynamic DNS records are scavenged only if they have not been updated or refreshed and both the no-refresh interval and refresh interval have expired.

ACTIVITY

Activity 8-5: Configuring Aging and Scavenging

Time Required: 10 minutes

Objective: Configure a zone to remove old records automatically.

Description: Dynamic DNS is used to create host records in your zone location*xx*.arctic.local. To ensure that outdated information is not left in the zone, you configure it to remove Dynamic DNS records automatically that have not been updated or refreshed for four weeks.

1. If necessary, start your server and log on as **Administrator**.

2. Click **Start**, point to **Administrative Tools**, and click **DNS**.

3. Right-click your server and click **Properties**.

4. Click **Advanced**, check the **Enable automatic scavenging of stale records** check box, and click **OK**. This configures the server to look for old records to delete every seven days.

5. Expand your server, if necessary.

6. Double-click **Forward Lookup Zones**.

7. Click **location*xx*.arctic.local**, where *xx* is your student number.

8. Right-click **location*xx*.arctic.local**, where *xx* is your student number, and click **Properties**.

9. Click **Aging** on the General tab.

10. Check the **Scavenge stale resource records** check box.

11. Confirm that the No-refresh interval is set to **7 days**.

12. In the Refresh field, enter **21 days**. Dynamic DNS records are now eligible to be scavenged after the total of 28 days has passed without the record being updated or refreshed.

13. Click **OK**, click **Yes** to confirm the change, and click **OK**.

14. Close the DNS snap-in.

Modifying the Start of Authority Record

The **start of authority (SOA)** record for a domain defines a number of characteristics for a zone, including serial number and caching instructions. The SOA record is configured in the Start of Authority (SOA) tab of the zone properties, as shown in Figure 8-14.

The serial number of a zone is automatically updated when a change is made to the zone. This is used by secondary zones to request changes to the zone. A secondary zone requests a zone transfer if the serial number of the primary zone is higher than the serial number of the secondary zone. You can force all secondary zones to request a zone transfer by manually incrementing the serial number by one.

The Refresh interval option specifies how often secondary zones can attempt to update from the primary zone. The Retry interval option specifies how long a secondary zone waits before reattempting to contact the primary zone if an initial attempt fails. The Expires after option specifies how long a secondary zone can go without contacting the primary zone before it stops functioning because its data is considered unreliable.

The Minimum (default) TTL option is used by remote DNS servers that are caching records from this zone. A record that is cached from this zone is not resolved again for the time period specified. If this value is too high, it is difficult to make DNS changes because old DNS information is cached for a long period of time. Consider reducing this value several days before DNS changes are scheduled to occur. This time is also used as the maximum time that a DNS error can be cached.

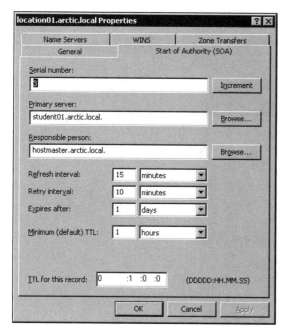

Figure 8-14   Start of Authority (SOA) tab

Modifying the List of Name Servers

The name servers configured for a zone are the authoritative DNS servers for the zone. They are used in the recursive lookup process to resolve requests for the domain. In addition, they are used by Dynamic DNS clients for dynamic updates.

NOTE   Dynamic DNS cannot be performed on secondary zones. A DNS server holding a secondary zone should never be added as a name server for a zone if Dynamic DNS is being used.

Figure 8-15 shows the Name Servers tab in the properties of a zone.

Enabling WINS Resolution

A DNS zone can be configured with a WINS server that is used to help resolve names. If a DNS zone receives a query for a host name for which it has no A record, it forwards the request to a WINS server. For example, if a DNS server with the zone arctic.local receives a host name resolution request for workstation85.arctic.local and does not have a matching A record, then the DNS server forwards a WINS lookup request for the name workstation85 to the WINS server.

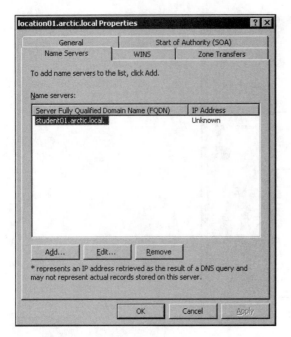

Figure 8-15   Name Servers tab

Figure 8-16 shows the WINS tab in the properties of a zone. You can specify that records resolved via WINS are not replicated to other domain controllers by selecting the Do not replicate this record check box.

Enabling Zone Transfers

Zone transfers are used to copy zone information from a primary zone to a secondary zone. You can configure which IP addresses can request zone transfers. Figure 8-17 shows the Zone Transfers tab of the zone properties.

By default, zone transfers are allowed. To disable zone transfers, deselect the Allow zone transfers check box. If zone transfers are enabled, you can choose whether they are enabled to any server, to only servers listed in the Name Servers tab for the zone, or to specific IP addresses.

You can also specify a list of secondary zones to notify of zone changes by clicking the Notify button. When a secondary zone is notified of a zone change, it immediately requests a zone transfer. This significantly speeds up the synchronization between primary and secondary zones. Without notification, a secondary zone checks for updates every 15 minutes.

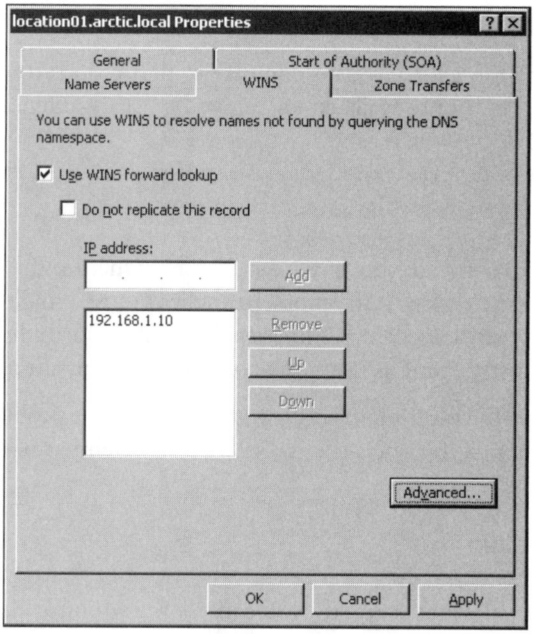

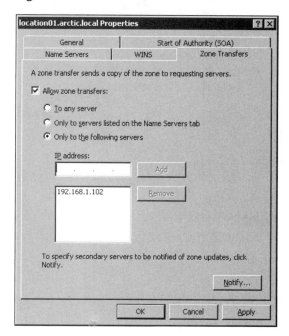

Figure 8-16   WINS tab

Figure 8-17   Zone Transfers tab

Configuring Security

The Security tab in the zone properties allows you to control the permissions to modify the records for this zone. The Security tab is only available for Active Directory–integrated zones.

TROUBLESHOOTING DNS

When DNS problems are being experienced, you must first discover whether the problem is limited to one client or applies to many clients. If the problem applies to just a single client, it is likely a configuration problem with only that client. To fix a single client, confirm that the client is configured with the correct DNS server and is using the correct DNS domain name.

If a DNS resolution problem exists for multiple clients, it is likely a server problem. Server level problems may include incorrect records, the DNS Service being unavailable, or improper firewall configuration.

Server Functionality

To test whether a DNS server is functioning correctly, you can use the Monitoring tab of the DNS server properties, as shown in Figure 8-18.

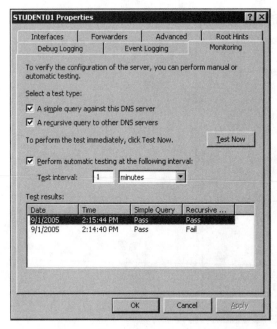

Figure 8-18   Monitoring tab

If a simple query is requested, test the server for iterative query functionality. An iterative query is a query in which the DNS server looks only in the zones for which it is responsible.

If a recursive query is requested, submit a NS query for the root domain ".". If this query is unsuccessful, it may be due to incorrectly configured Internet connectivity or root hints.

You can choose to perform a simple query or recursive query manually or at a scheduled interval. To perform a test manually, select the type of test you want to perform (simple, recursive, or both), and then click Test Now. To perform tests at a scheduled interval, select the type of test you want to perform, and then select Perform automatic testing at the following interval. After automatic testing has been enabled, you can choose the interval at which it is repeated.

The results of automatic and manual tests appear only in the Test results box.

Nslookup

The utility **Nslookup** queries DNS records. It is an indispensable tool when troubleshooting DNS problems. With Nslookup, you can query any DNS record from a DNS server. This allows you to confirm that each DNS server is configured with the correct information.

Nslookup can be used from a command prompt to resolve host names, but is most powerful in interactive mode. To run Nslookup in interactive mode, open a command prompt, type Nslookup, and press Enter. Inside Nslookup, you can use the help command to get a list of available commands, as shown in Figure 8-19.

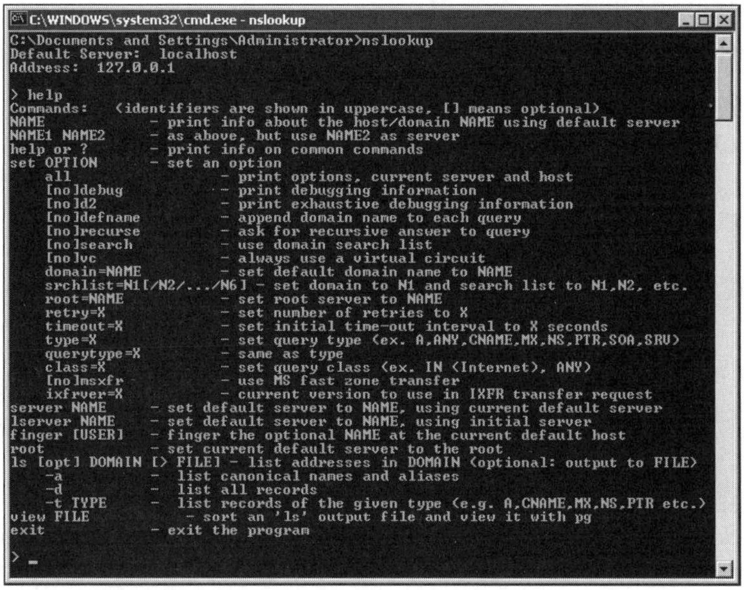

Figure 8-19   Nslookup help

In interactive mode, you can use Nslookup to view any DNS records available for a zone. Figure 8-20 shows Nslookup being used to find the MX records for the domain hotmail. com. MX records list the mail servers for a domain.

```
C:\WINDOWS\system32\cmd.exe - nslookup

C:\Documents and Settings\Administrator>nslookup
Default Server:  localhost
Address:  127.0.0.1

> set type=mx
> hotmail.com
Server:  localhost
Address:  127.0.0.1

Non-authoritative answer:
hotmail.com      MX preference = 5, mail exchanger = mx1.hotmail.com
hotmail.com      MX preference = 5, mail exchanger = mx2.hotmail.com
hotmail.com      MX preference = 5, mail exchanger = mx3.hotmail.com
hotmail.com      MX preference = 5, mail exchanger = mx4.hotmail.com

mx1.hotmail.com internet address = 65.54.254.129
mx1.hotmail.com internet address = 65.54.252.99
mx2.hotmail.com internet address = 65.54.254.145
mx2.hotmail.com internet address = 65.54.252.230
mx3.hotmail.com internet address = 65.54.254.140
mx3.hotmail.com internet address = 65.54.253.99
mx4.hotmail.com internet address = 65.54.254.151
mx4.hotmail.com internet address = 65.54.253.230
>
```

Figure 8-20   Using Nslookup to find MX records

Activity 8-6: Verifying DNS Records with Nslookup

Time Required: 10 minutes

Objective: Verify proper DNS lookups using the utility Nslookup.

Description: You have configured a stub zone on your server and delegated authority for a domain on the instructor server. To confirm that both of these actions are working properly, you use Nslookup.

1. If necessary, start your server and log on as **Administrator**.

2. Click **Start**, click **Run**, type **cmd**, and press **Enter**.

3. Type **nslookup** and press **Enter**.

4. If necessary, to change the server that Nslookup queries, type **server 192.168.1.10**, and press **Enter**. Now, all the queries Nslookup performs are completed by contacting the instructor server.

5. To view MX records, type **set type=mx**, and press **Enter**.

6. To view the MX records for your location zone, type **location*xx*.arctic.local**, where *xx* is your student number, and press **Enter**. This verifies that the delegation from the instructor server to your server is working properly.

7. To view A records, type **set type=a**, and press **Enter**.

8. To have Nslookup query your server, type **server *yourIPaddress***, where *yourIPaddress* is the IP address of the classroom connection on your server, and press **Enter**.

9. Type **studentxx.arctic.local**, where *xx* is your student number, and press Enter. Your server does not hold a copy of the Arctic.local domain. This query verifies that the forwarder configured on your server is functioning and recursive queries are directed to the instructor server.

10. To close Nslookup, type **exit** and press **Enter**.

11. Close the Command Prompt window.

DNSLint

DNSLint is a command-line utility that allows you to verify correct DNS configuration. It has commands that help you confirm that a zone is correctly configured or verify records for Active Directory.

NOTE

You must download the DNSLint utility from Microsoft at *http://support.microsoft.com/?kbid=321045*. It comes with a documentation file describing how the utility can be used.

This utility uses command-line switches to control functionality. Some of the more common switches are listed in Table 8-2.

Table 8-2 DNSLint switches

Switch	Description
/d	Domain name tests—Tests general DNS functionality
/ad	Active Directory tests—Tests the DNS records used by Active Directory
/ql	Query list—Tests a list of DNS records and servers specified in a text file
/c	E-mail connectivity—Tests e-mail server functionality by connecting to POP, IMAP, and SMTP ports
/r	Report file—Specifies the name of a report file that is generated in HTML
/s	Server—Specifies the DNS server to query when performing the test
/t	Text file—Dumps output from DNSLint as a text file in addition to the standard HTML file
/test_tcp	TCP test—Tests the functionality of TCP port 53; only UDP port 53 is tested by default
/v	Verbose—Displays additional information to the screen
/y	Overwrite report file—Automatically overwrites the existing report file without being prompted

ACTIVITY

Activity 8-7: Using DNSLint to Verify Active Directory DNS Records

Time Required: 10 minutes

Objective: Use the DNSLint utility to confirm that the proper DNS records exist for Active Directory.

Description: Some faculty members have been complaining that they are occasionally unable to log on to the network. To rule out DNS configuration as a possible cause, you are using the DNSLint utility to verify the DNS records used by Active Directory.

1. If necessary, start your server and log on as **Administrator**.

2. Click **Start**, point to **All Programs**, and click **Internet Explorer**.

3. In the Address bar, type **http://support.microsoft.com/?kbid=321045** and press **Enter**.

4. Click the link **Download the Dnslint.exe package now**.

5. In the warning window, click **Add**.

6. Click **Add** to add the site *download.microsoft.com* to the list of approved sites, and click **Close**.

7. Click the link **Download the Dnslint.exe package now** again to download the file.

8. Click the **Save** button.

9. If necessary, click the **Desktop** button on the left side of the window, and click **Save**.

10. When the download is complete, click **Close**, and close **Internet Explorer**.

11. On the desktop, double-click **dnslint.exe**.

12. In the Unzip to folder box, type **c:\temp**, click **Unzip**, click **OK**, and click **Close**.

13. Click **Start**, click **Run**, type **cmd.exe**, and press **Enter**.

14. Type **cd \temp** and press **Enter**.

15. Type **dir** and press **Enter**. You should see two files: DNSLint Documentation.doc and dnslint.exe. If you do not see these two files, repeat Steps 11–15, as you likely unzipped them to the wrong location.

16. Type **dnslint /ad 192.168.1.10 /s 192.168.1.10** and press **Enter**. The /ad switch specifies the domain controller to be queried, and the /s switch specifies the DNS server to query records from. The results of this command are shown in a Web page that Internet Explorer automatically opens to view.

17. View the report that is generated by DNSLint, then close Internet Explorer, and close the command prompt window.

DNSCmd

DNSCmd is a command-line utility that can be used to view DNS server status and to configure DNS servers, DNS zones, and DNS records. This utility can be used in a script that is useful when you want to make changes on many servers.

DNSCmd is available in the \SUPPORT\TOOLS directory on the Windows Server 2003 CD-ROM. It can be installed using SUPTOOLS.MSI or copied directly out of SUPPORT.CAB.

Resetting Default Settings

When you are attempting to optimize DNS, you may render DNS inoperable or impair functionality. When making system changes, you should always fully document the existing configuration before making changes. However, many administrators forget to perform this step. Then, when a configuration mistake is made, they are unable to reconfigure their system easily to be functional again.

If you find yourself in this situation, Windows Server 2003 allows you to reset the configuration of a DNS server back to the defaults. Default settings should restore functionality. Table 8-3 lists the default settings for a DNS server.

Table 8-3   Default DNS server settings

Setting	Value
Disable recursion	Off
Bind secondaries	On
Fail on load if bad zone data	Off
Enable round robin	On
Enable netmask ordering	On
Secure cache against pollution	On
Name checking	Multibyte (UTF8)
Load zone data on startup	From Active Directory and registry
Enable automatic scavenging of stale records	Off

Activity 8-8: Resetting a DNS Server to the Defaults

Time Required: 5 minutes

Objective: Reset the settings on a DNS server back to installation defaults.

Description: One of the DNS servers in your test lab has been used extensively by other technical staff. To ensure that your DNS tests begin with the default settings, you reset the server settings to the defaults.

1. If necessary, start your server and log on as **Administrator**.

2. Click **Start**, point to **Administrative Tools**, and click **DNS**.

3. In the left pane, select your server.

4. Right-click your server and click **Properties**.

5. Click the **Advanced** tab.

6. Click **Reset to Default** and click **OK**.

7. Close the DNS snap-in.

Resetting Default Security

When attempting to optimize security settings for DNS, you may render your server inoperable or impair its operation. If you did not properly document the default security permissions, you can reset them in the Advanced Security Settings of the zone properties, as shown in Figure 8-21.

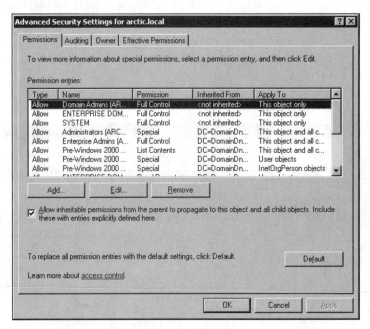

Figure 8-21   Reset default security for a zone

DNS Server Logging

DNS servers are capable of event logging and debug logging. **Event logging** records errors, warnings, and information to the event log. Debug logging records much more detailed information.

The Event Logging tab of the DNS server properties gives you the option to record:

- No events
- Errors only
- Errors and warnings
- All events

Debug logging records packet-by-packet information about the queries that the DNS server is receiving. This type of logging is enabled only for troubleshooting because it records a large volume of information. To reduce the amount of information recorded, you can specify what type of information should be logged, including:

- Packet direction
- Transport protocol
- Packet contents
- Packet type

Figure 8-22 shows the configuration of debug logging in the DNS server properties.

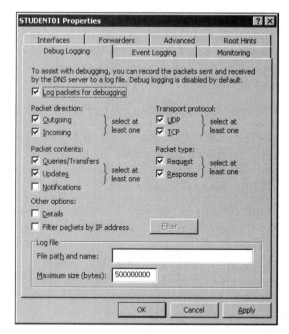

Figure 8-22   Debug Logging tab

Chapter Summary

- To optimize DNS, you can delegate authority for subdomains to different servers. This allows you to place DNS records closest to the users and services that require them.

- A caching-only server is not authoritative for any DNS records. It is used to speed up DNS name resolution.

- Nonrecursive DNS servers look only at DNS records they are authoritative when attempting to resolve queries. A nonrecursive DNS server does not communicate with other DNS servers when resolving queries. This may be used if you do not want users accessing resources on the Internet.

- Forwarding-only DNS servers use forwarders (other specified DNS servers) to resolve recursive queries rather than root servers on the Internet. This is useful when a large WAN only has one access point to the Internet.

- Conditional forwarders use forwarders only for certain specified DNS domains. This is useful as a replacement for stub zones.

- To secure the replication between primary and secondary zones, you can restrict which hosts are allowed to request zone transfers. This can be restricted to the listed name servers for the zone or a list of IP addresses.

- Dynamic updates for Active Directory-integrated zones can be secured by enabling secure dynamic updates that restrict updates to DNS records based on security permissions in Active Directory. When multiple DHCP servers are updating records, they should be made members of the DnsUpdateProxy group.

- You can perform several DNS Server management tasks. Aging and scavenging is used to remove outdated DNS records created by Dynamic DNS. Updating server data files forces DNS changes in memory to be written to disk. If the zone is Active Directory-integrated, it has no effect. Clearing the cache deletes information from the DNS server cache. The DNS server can be bound to any or all IP addresses a server is using. Root hints can be modified to adjust the process used for recursive lookups.

- Most DNS servers send packets larger then 512 bytes as TCP packets. By using EDNSO, Windows Server 2003 is able to send UDP packets larger than 512 bytes. This works around firewall configuration problems.

- You can perform a variety of zone management tasks, including reloading zone information from file, changing the type of zone and replication, configuring aging and scavenging, modifying the SOA record, modifying the list of name servers, enabling WINS resolution, enabling and securing zone transfers, and configuring permissions for Active Directory-integrated zones.

- The Monitoring tab of a DNS server can be used to verify that the DNS server is performing recursive and iterative queries properly. The Logging tab can be used to configure event logging and diagnostic logging.

◻ Nslookup and DNSLint are used to verify that certain DNS records exist and are configured properly. DNSCmd is a command-line utility that is used to manage DNS servers, zones, and records.

◻ The Advanced Security Settings for a zone can be used to reset zone security back to defaults for an Active Directory-integrated zone.

KEY TERMS

aging and scavenging — A feature of the Windows Server 2003 DNS server that deletes Dynamic DNS records after they have not been refreshed for a period of time.

caching-only DNS server — A DNS server that is not responsible for any zones. It is used only to cache lookups as they occur to increase the speed of lookup times.

conditional forwarder — A DNS server that uses forwarders based on the domain name being resolved. It uses forwarders for some domains, but not others.

debug logging — The process of logging additional DNS-related events or messages for troubleshooting purposes.

delegate authority — The process of specifying a different DNS server as authoritative for a subdomain. This is done by dividing the DNS namespace among multiple DNS servers.

DNSCmd — A command-line utility for viewing and managing DNS information on Windows Server 2003.

DNSLint — An advanced utility for DNS troubleshooting that generates reports in HTML format.

DnsUpdateProxy — A group used when multiple DHCP servers will be performing secure Dynamic DNS updates. Updates performed by members of this group have no security permissions assigned.

event logging — The logging of status messages in an event log. This logging is less detailed than debug logging.

Extension Mechanisms for DNS (EDNSO) — A new protocol for DNS that allows DNS servers to send query responses in UDP packets larger than 512 bytes.

forwarding-only DNS server — A DNS server that uses forwarders when attempting to resolve DNS queries, but does not use the root servers on the Internet.

nonrecursive DNS server — A DNS server that looks only at zones stored locally when attempting to resolve DNS queries.

Nslookup — A command prompt-based utility for troubleshooting DNS.

root hints — The list of root servers that is used by DNS servers to perform forward lookups on the Internet.

round robin DNS — The process of creating multiple IP addresses for a specific host name for fault tolerance and load balancing.

secure dynamic updates — The process of controlling Dynamic DNS updates based on Active Directory permissions. These are available only for Active Directory-integrated zones.

start of authority (SOA) — A DNS record that defines which DNS server is authoritative for that particular domain and defines the characteristics for the zone.

unauthorized zone transfers — A zone transfer requested and obtained by an unauthorized server or person.

REVIEW QUESTIONS

1. When the responsibility for maintaining a subdomain is given to a different DNS server, this is referred to as _____ .

   a. forwarding authority

   b. assigning authority

   c. delegating authority

   d. authorizing

2. Which type of DNS server can be placed at remote locations to speed up name resolution and is not authoritative for any zones?

   a. caching-only DNS server

   b. nonrecursive DNS server

   c. forwarding-only DNS server

   d. conditional forwarder

3. Which types of DNS servers do not query root servers on the Internet? (Choose all that apply.)

   a. caching-only DNS server

   b. nonrecursive DNS server

   c. forwarding-only DNS server

   d. conditional forwarder

4. Which type of DNS server modifies the process used for recursive lookups based on the domain name being resolved?

   a. caching-only DNS server

   b. nonrecursive DNS server

   c. forwarding-only DNS server

   d. conditional forwarder

5. Which type of DNS server does not communicate with other DNS servers when resolving DNS queries?

   a. caching-only DNS server

   b. nonrecursive DNS server

   c. forwarding-only DNS server

   d. conditional forwarder

6. What are the three options for controlling zone transfers from primary zones?

    a. Allow zone transfers to anywhere

    b. Restrict zone transfers to servers in a list of IP networks

    c. Restrict zone transfers to servers listed in the Name Servers tab

    d. Restrict zone transfers to servers in a list of IP addresses

7. Which group should the DHCP servers be made members of when secure dynamic updates are enabled?

    a. SecureUpdaters

    b. DnsUpdateProxy

    c. DnsSecurityProxy

    d. SecureUpdateProxy

8. When secure dynamic updates are enabled, who is allowed to modify DNS records created by a workstation? (Choose all that apply.)

    a. everyone

    b. the workstation that created the record

    c. Administrators

    d. DnsAdmins

    e. DHCP servers

9. When secure dynamic updates are enabled, who is allowed to view DNS records created by a workstation? (Choose all that apply.)

    a. everyone

    b. the workstation that created the record

    c. Administrators

    d. DnsAdmins

    e. DHCP servers

10. Which DNS server option automatically deletes old, unused DNS records created by Dynamic DNS?

    a. Root hints

    b. EDNSO

    c. Aging and scavenging

    d. Update server data files

    e. Clear cache

11. Which DNS server option allows Windows Server 2003 DNS servers to respond with UDP packets larger than 512 bytes?

    a. Root hints

    b. EDNSO

    c. Aging and scavenging

    d. Update server data files

    e. Clear cache

12. The DNS server at the head office was misconfigured for a short period of time, but has now been fixed. However, when your users attempt to resolve DNS named at the head office, they are still receiving incorrect information. What should you do to solve this problem?

    a. Delete the root hints on the server.

    b. Enable EDNSO.

    c. Configure aging and scavenging.

    d. Update server data files on the local DNS server.

    e. Clear the cache on the local DNS server.

13. A new root server has been created on the Internet for handling recursive DNS lookups. What file do you modify on your server to add the new root server?

    a. C:\WINDOWS\system32\dns\hints.dns

    b. C:\WINDOWS\system32\dns\cache.dns

    c. C:\WINDOWS\system32\dns\root.dns

    d. C:\WINDOWS\system32\drivers\etc\HOSTS

    e. C:\WINDOWS\system32\drivers\etc\LMHOSTS

14. When creating a root zone on a DNS server, what name do you give it?

    a. ?

    b. *

    c. root

    d. .

    e. #

15. Which DNS feature can be used for load balancing?

    a. secure dynamic updates

    b. round-robin DNS

    c. netmask ordering

    d. disable recursion

16. Which DNS troubleshooting utility generates an HTML report to display testing results?

   a. Nslookup

   b. DNSCmd

   c. DNSLint

   d. the Monitoring tab in DNS server properties

   e. audit logging

17. Which DNS troubleshooting utility can be configured to perform tests of recursive and iterative DNS lookups on a server at a defined interval?

   a. Nslookup

   b. DNSCmd

   c. DNSLint

   d. the Monitoring tab in DNS server properties

   e. audit logging

18. If DHCP servers are required to be members of the DnsUpdateProxy group, it is a security risk to run the DHCP Service on domain controllers. True or False?

19. Which advanced DNS server option is used to disable fast zone transfers?

   a. Disable recursion

   b. BIND secondaries

   c. Enable round robin

   d. Enable netmask ordering

   e. Secure cache against pollution

20. Which type of logging writes detailed information about DNS queries to a log file?

   a. audit logging

   b. query logging

   c. lookup logs

   d. event logging

CASE PROJECTS

Case Project 8-1: Choosing Server Roles

Arctic University has four physical locations: the main campus and three satellite campuses. The main campus is the only location with Internet connectivity. WAN links operating at 128 Kbps connect the three satellite campuses to the main campus.

The zone arctic.local is hosted on a DNS server. It includes subdomains for each of the satellite campuses. The computers in the satellite campuses are using the DNS server on the main campus for DNS lookups.

Based on what you know about server roles, how would you configure DNS to minimize traffic across the WAN?

Case Project 8-2: Planning Security for Dynamic DNS

As part of the Windows Server 2003 roll out, Active Directory has been implemented at Arctic University. All of the Windows 2000 and Windows XP workstations are using Dynamic DNS to place A records into DNS with the host name and IP address.

Arctic University did not have a large enough capital budget to replace all of the workstations when Active Directory was implemented. How can Windows 95/98/NT computers participate in Dynamic DNS? What security issues are involved?

Case Project 8-3: DNS Troubleshooting

One of the professors at the main campus has an e-mail account with a local Internet service provider. Today, when he attempts to access the account using a POP3-based e-mail client, he receives the error "DNS Error." You attempt to find some additional information about the error, but the application does not have any log files.

The professor is using the Arctic University DNS server. How can you use DNS trouble-shooting tools to solve this problem?

Case Project 8-4: Planning Security for DNS Replication

Now that DNS is being implemented at the satellite locations as well as the main campus, security for DNS replication is a concern. What are your options for securing replication traffic between the DNS server at the main campus and the DNS servers at the satellite campuses?

PLANNING AND MANAGING CERTIFICATE SERVICES

After reading this chapter, you will be able to:

- Describe the types of cryptography
- Understand how cryptography is used for encryption and digital signatures
- Understand the components of Certificate Services
- Install and manage Certificate Services
- Manage certificates
- Implement smart card authentication

Certificates are used to encrypt and decrypt data such as e-mail and files. In addition, certificates are used as part of the encrypting file system (EFS) built into Windows 2000 and newer versions of Windows. In this chapter, you learn about the different types of cryptography used with Windows Server 2003 and how these types of cryptography are applied. You also learn how to install, configure, and manage Certificate Services. Finally, you learn to use smart cards for authentication.

Cryptography and certificates are only one part of creating and maintaining a secure network. Other security topics are covered in Chapter 13.

CRYPTOGRAPHY

Cryptography is the process of encrypting and decrypting messages and files to ensure that they are read only by the intended recipient or recipients. When a message uses **encryption**, it is converted to a format that is unreadable. **Decryption** is the reverse of encryption, and this process makes the data readable again. The term **ciphertext** is used to refer to encrypted information.

To encrypt information, an algorithm is used. In computerized cryptography, an **algorithm** is a mathematical formula that is used to modify the data. Also required for encryption and decryption are keys. A **key** is a large number, which is often represented as a series of numbers, letters, and symbols. The key is large so that it is difficult to guess. It is used in combination with an algorithm to encrypt and decrypt data.

There are four main objectives for cryptography. Depending on the method of cryptography used, some or all of these objectives can be achieved. The four objectives of cryptography are defined in the following list:

- *Confidentiality* — Ensures that the data cannot be read by an unauthorized person
- *Integrity* — Ensures that the data has not been modified
- *Nonrepudiation* — Guarantees that the sender or creator cannot deny that the process happened
- *Authentication* — Ensures that the identity of the sender or creator can be verified

Depending on the goals that need to be accomplished, one or several types of encryption may be used. The three generic types of encryption are:

- Symmetrical
- Asymmetrical
- Hash

Symmetric Encryption

Symmetric encryption uses a single key to encrypt and decrypt data. For example, if User A sends a file to User B using symmetric encryption to encrypt the file, then User B decrypts the file using the same key that is used to encrypt the file.

This type of encryption is relatively simple from a mathematical perspective. A computer can symmetrically encrypt large amounts of data quickly. Consequently, this type of encryption is used when encrypting files and large amounts of data across network transmissions.

Asymmetric Encryption

Asymmetric encryption uses two separate keys, called the public key and the private key, to encrypt and decrypt data. Anything encrypted by the public key can be decrypted with the private key, and anything encrypted by the private key is decrypted with the public key.

When asymmetric encryption is used, the **public key** is made available to anyone who wants it. The **private key** is held only by the individual, or computer, to which it is assigned. This provides enhanced security when two people or computers need to encrypt communication data because the private key is never transmitted on the network. There is a security risk with symmetric encryption if the key is moved across the network.

This type of encryption is more mathematically complex than symmetric encryption. As a result, asymmetric encryption requires more processing power than symmetric encryption. Thus, it is not practical or efficient to use asymmetric encryption for large amounts of data.

9

Hash Encryption

Hash encryption is unique because it is one-way encryption. A hash algorithm uses a single key to convert data to a hash value. The **hash value** is a summary of the data. For example, a 128-bit hash value might be generated for a 100 KB file. Even if the algorithm is publicly known, the hash value cannot be decrypted because the hash value does not contain enough information. The purpose of a hash value is to be a unique identifier, not to secure data.

This type of encryption is often used to store passwords. This ensures that the database storing the hash values for the passwords can be publicly available, but the actual passwords are unknown. To verify a password, the system applies the hash algorithm to a submitted password and compares the newly generated hash value with the hash value in the password database. If the two hash values match, the password is correct. If the two hash values do not match, the password is incorrect.

Uses for Cryptography

Cryptography is commonly used for a number of computing tasks in which confidentiality is required, integrity of data must be ensured, or the identity of the sender must be verified. Nonrepudiation can also be attained if a randomized sequence number or time stamp is included in the encrypted data. Depending on the task being performed, more than one of these goals may be achieved.

Three common tasks that use different types of encryption are:

- Encrypting e-mail
- Ensuring data integrity with digital signatures
- Securing data communication with Secure Sockets Layer (SSL)

The following sections discuss each in turn.

Encrypting E-Mail

Encrypting e-mail ensures that a message in transit cannot be read by unauthorized people. Sending an encrypted e-mail message between two clients using asymmetric encryption requires each user to have a public key and a private key. The private key is known only to the person to which it is assigned. The public key is known to all clients, and, thus, is not inherently secure.

The process for encrypting e-mail uses the public and private keys of the recipient. First, the sender creates an e-mail message. Then, the e-mail software used by the sender encrypts the message using the public key of the recipient. The public key of the recipient may be published in a directory or given to the sender via e-mail before the encryption process is performed. The encrypted message is then sent to the recipient. The intended recipient receives the encrypted message and his e-mail software decrypts the message using the recipient's private key. This process is shown in Figure 9-1.

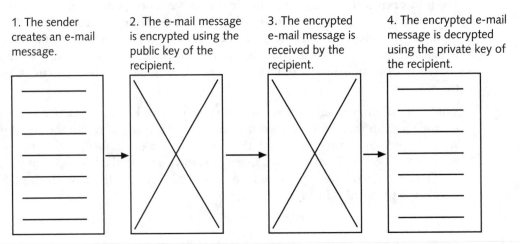

1. The sender creates an e-mail message.

2. The e-mail message is encrypted using the public key of the recipient.

3. The encrypted e-mail message is received by the recipient.

4. The encrypted e-mail message is decrypted using the private key of the recipient.

Figure 9-1   Encrypting mail

Using this type of encryption, no one is able to read the message while it travels from the sender to the recipient. The message has been encrypted with the recipient's public key and can be decrypted only by using the recipient's private key. The recipient's private key is known only to the recipient.

Digital Signatures

A **digital signature** is a hash value that is encrypted and attached to a message. It is used to ensure that a message has not been modified while in transit and that it truly came from the named sender. This is important when electronically delivering information such as contracts and agreements.

NOTE   A digital signature does not encrypt the contents of a message.

The public and private keys of the sender are used for a digital signature. First, the sender creates the document that is to be signed. Then, a hash algorithm is used to create a hash value of the document, and the hash value is encrypted with the sender's private key. Then, the sender transmits the original document and the encrypted hash value. This process is shown in Figure 9-2.

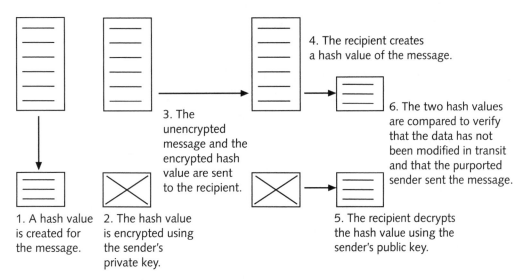

Figure 9-2   Digital signature

The recipient takes the original document and creates a hash value using the same hash algorithm as the sender. The recipient then decrypts the encrypted hash value from the sender using the sender's public key. If the two hash values match, the document was not modified in transit. This also verifies the message came from the named sender, as only that sender has access to the private key that matches the public key used.

Secure Sockets Layer

Secure Sockets Layer (SSL) is a Transport Layer protocol that can be used with any application protocol that is designed to communicate with it. SSL is used to secure communication between Web servers and Web browsers, e-mail clients and e-mail servers, and other service combinations.

Servers are the only participants in SSL that are required to be configured with a public key and a private key. The public key and private key are used to encrypt a symmetrical key and make it secure during transit. The symmetrical key is used to encrypt data transferred between the client and server.

When a Web browser is connecting to a secure Web server, it uses HTTPS (Secure Hypertext Transport Protocol). When the browser connects to the server, the server sends the client the server's public key. The browser then generates a key to be used for symmetric encryption, encrypts it using the server's public key, and sends the encrypted symmetrical key to the server. This process is shown in Figure 9-3.

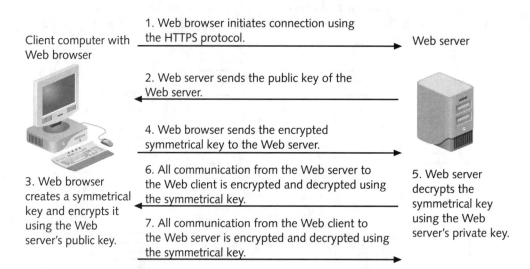

Figure 9-3   Secure Sockets Layer (SSL)

The server decrypts the symmetrical key using the server's private key. The symmetrical key has been securely transmitted from the browser to the server, and both the browser and the server have a copy of the symmetrical key. The symmetrical key is now used to encrypt and decrypt all data sent between the browser and the server.

CERTIFICATE SERVICES COMPONENTS

Certificate Services is the Microsoft implementation of **PKI (Public Key Infrastructure)**. PKI is a system for creating and managing public keys, private keys, and certificates. A **certificate** contains information about a user or computer and a public key. There is no standard that defines how PKI overall is supposed to work, but there are several standards for PKI components. One of the standards, **X.509**, was created by the International Telecommunication Union–Telecommunication (ITU-T) and defines how a certificate should be structured. The fields required in an X.509 certificate are listed in the "Certificates" section.

NOTE The terms "certificate," "digital certificate," and "public key certificate" are often used interchangeably when reading documentation from different vendors.

PKI using Certificate Services is composed of these components:

- Certificates
- Certification authority (also known as certificate authority)
- A Certificate Revocation List (CRL)
- Certificate-enabled applications

The following subsections discuss each in turn.

Certificates

9

A certificate defined by the X.509 standard has fields such as subject (or user name), serial number, validity period, public key, issuer name, and issuer signature. An X.509 certificate is not private information, and can be used to distribute a public key to validate a digital signature or create encrypted e-mail.

The issuer name and signature are an important part of the certificate because they are used to validate the certificate. The signature of the issuer ensures that the certificate has not been modified; otherwise, anyone could make up a certificate for themselves, and, thus, the certificate would be rendered useless as a means of identifying the certificate holder.

NOTE The certificates created by Certificate Services are X.509 certificates.

Certification Authority

A **certification authority (CA)** is a server that issues certificates to client computers, applications, or users. The certification authority is responsible for taking certificate-signing requests from clients and approving them. As part of the approval process, the identity of the requester is verified.

NOTE When implementing PKI, you can install your own internal certification authority using Certificate Services, or you can buy certificates from a third-party certification authority, such as VeriSign or Thawte.

When a certificate is presented as proof of identity, it must be validated. This is accomplished using the digital signature of the certification authority. For a client application to trust that this information in the certificate is correct, it must trust the certification authority that issued the certificate.

Every Web browser and many other applications include a list of **trusted root certification authorities**, which are certificate authorities that are trusted by the application. When using Internet Explorer, any Web site using a certificate signed by one of the trusted root certification authorities is accepted without any messages appearing on the screen.

However, if a Web site is using a certificate that is not issued by a trusted root certification authority, a warning message appears on the screen, as shown in Figure 9-4. This error indicates that Internet Explorer does not trust the source of the certificate. The error appearing is not acceptable for most applications because it makes users nervous about using the service if there is an error message indicating it is not trusted, even though as a service provider you understand that you can be trusted.

Figure 9-4   Certification authority warning message

Third-party certification authorities are in the list of trusted root certificate authorities used by Internet Explorer. If you implement an internal certification authority using Certificate Services, your certification authority is not automatically included in the list of trusted root certificate authorities. You need to add your internal certification authority to the list of trusted root certificate authorities on each workstation to prevent warning messages from appearing.

In general, internal certification authorities are used only with internal clients because you have control over internal client computers and can add the internal certification authority to the list of trusted root certification authorities. In most cases, you do not have the ability to visit clients outside of your organization to configure them to trust your internal certification authority.

The main benefits of using an internal certification authority are cost and control. With an internal certification authority, you can create as many certificates as you like for no cost other than the time spent managing the certification authority and approving certificate requests. You also have complete control over when and how certificates are issued.

Third-party certification authorities are used when an application or server needs to be trusted by clients outside of your organization where you do not have control over their computers and applications. Because a third-party certification authority is already listed as a trusted root certification authority, there is no need to modify the client. The main disadvantage of a third-party certification authority is cost. You must pay for each certificate provided. Each certificate costs between 10 and 20 dollars.

ACTIVITY

Activity 9-1: Viewing Trusted Root Certification Authorities

Time Required: 5 minutes

Objective: View the trusted root certification authorities installed by default on Windows Server 2003.

Description: You are considering using a third-party certification authority to provide certificates for Web servers using SSL. However, the lowest bid on the contract is so low, you are concerned about the quality. To verify that this company is in the list of trusted root certification authorities installed by default, you view the list of trusted root certification authorities included with Windows Server 2003.

1. If necessary, start your server and log on as **Administrator**.
2. Click **Start**, point to **Control Panel**, and click **Internet Options**.
3. Click the **Content** tab and click **Certificates**.
4. Click the **Trusted Root Certification Authorities** tab, and read the list.
5. Click **Close**.
6. Click **Cancel**.

Certificate Revocation List

The certification authority maintains a **Certificate Revocation List (CRL)**, which is a list of certificates issued by the certification authority that are no longer valid. The administrator adds certificates to this list. It is not created automatically.

You add certificates to the CRL if you think there has been a security breach or something unexpected has happened. If the private key of a user is stolen, or if a user unexpectedly quits, then you would add his or her certificate to the CRL to prevent it from being used fraudulently.

Each certificate issued by the certification authority has an expiration date. If the certificate is presented after this date, then, depending on the application, a warning message appears, or the application fails. Certificates that have expired are not added to the CRL because the certificate has the expiration date embedded in it.

Certificate-enabled Applications

Not all applications can use certificates for encryption and authentication. An application must be designed by its developer to use certificates. Some of the more common applications for certificates include e-mail clients, Web browsers, and smart cards.

Windows client computers have the ability to store certificates in a store that can be used by multiple applications. Many certificate-enabled applications running on Windows use this central windows store, but other applications store certificates in a private database.

Installing and Managing Certificate Services

If you have made the decision to implement an internal certification authority, you need to install Certificate Services on Windows Server 2003. There are two classes of certification authorities available:

- Enterprise
- Stand-alone

An **enterprise certification authority** integrates with Active Directory. As a result, an enterprise certification authority has an expanded feature set when compared with stand-alone certification authorities.

When issuing certificates, an enterprise certification authority is able to use certificate templates, which define how a particular certificate can be used. Access to these templates is based on the permissions of the user requesting the certificate. This allows the certificate creation process to be entirely automated with no action on the part of an administrator.

A **stand-alone certification authority** does not integrate with Active Directory. As a result, it is unable to issue certificates automatically based on a user object in Active Directory. All certificate requests must be manually approved by an administrator. Certificate templates cannot be used by a stand-alone certification authority because access to the certificate templates is based on user permissions that are not understood by a stand-alone certification authority. A stand-alone certification authority also cannot issue certificates used for smart card authentication.

Both enterprise certification authorities and stand-alone certification authorities do publish CRLs in Active Directory. This ensures that, regardless of which certification authority you choose, the CRL is accessible to client computers. In addition, both classes of certification authorities create a CertificationAuthority object in Active Directory to describe themselves.

Only enterprise certification authorities use Active Directory as a publication point for user certificates. A certificate is published as part of the user object. For example, if user Bob is issued a certificate by an enterprise certification authority, then the certificate is added as an attribute of Bob's user object.

If you are issuing certificates internally in an Active Directory-enabled environment, it is wise to use an enterprise certification authority to take advantage of the extra features it affords. If you are issuing certificates externally or in an environment in which Active Directory does not exist, you can use a stand-alone certification authority.

Certificate Hierarchy

A **certificate hierarchy** is a chain of trust through which client computers and applications are assured that a certificate is valid. Within the hierarchy, a certification authority is either a root certification authority or a subordinate certification authority, as shown in Figure 9-5.

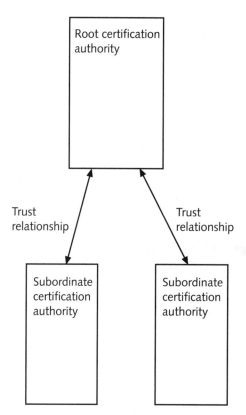

Figure 9-5   Certificate hierarchy

A **root certification authority** is a starting point for a certificate hierarchy. This is the certification authority that must be trusted by client computers. Only if the root certification authority is trusted can certificates issued by the root certification authority be accepted by client computers and applications.

A **subordinate certification authority** is certified by another certification authority, usually a root certification authority. After a subordinate certification authority has been certified, it can issue certificates based on the trusted status of the certification authority that certified it. For example, the server SECURE1 has been installed as a root certification authority, and the server SECURE2 has been certified as a subordinate certification authority. If a client trusts the server SECURE1, then it also trusts certificates issued by SECURE2. The entire hierarchy is trusted based on the root certification authority being trusted.

It is very important that root certificate authorities are kept secure. If the security of a root certification authority is compromised, then all certificates issued by it and all its subordinate certificate authorities are considered compromised and must be revoked and reissued. For example, if the private key of the root certification authority were stolen, all certificates issued by the root certification authority would need to be revoked. This includes the certificates that certify the subordinate certification authorities. The certificates issued by the subordinate certification authorities would also need to be revoked. Then, the root certification authority must be re-created, the subordinate certificate authorities recertified, and new certificates issued to all users.

Installing Certificate Services

When installing a certification authority, the first step in the installation requires you to choose which type of certification authority you are installing: enterprise root CA, stand-alone root CA, enterprise subordinate CA, or stand-alone subordinate CA, as shown in Figure 9-6. You also have the option to configure custom settings for the key pair and CA certificate.

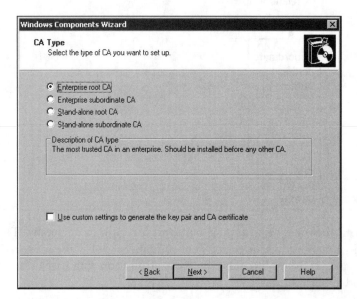

Figure 9-6   Choosing a CA type

The custom settings for the key pair and CA certificate, shown in Figure 9-7, allow you to configure the **cryptographic service provider (CSP)**, hash algorithm, key length, or to use an existing key. The CSP determines the algorithms you can use and the key length that is used. The hash algorithm is the mathematical formula that is used in the creation of the CA certificate. The key length is the number of bits in the key used in the creation of the CA certificate. A longer key is more secure. You are also given the option to use an existing key. An existing key is used when Certificate Services is being reinstalled.

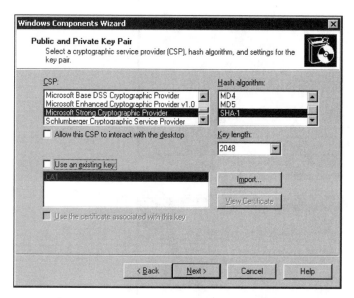

Figure 9-7   Custom settings for the key pair and CA certificate

The second step, shown in Figure 9-8, requires you to assign a name to the certification authority. This is the name of the CertificateAuthority object created in Active Directory. If this is a stand-alone CA that is going to be accessible to Internet clients, the distinguished name suffix should match the DNS name of the server. If this is a root certification authority, you can choose the lifetime of the certificate. If this is a subordinate certification authority, the lifetime is specified by the certification authority that authorizes it.

The third step, shown in Figure 9-9, allows you to set the location of a certificate database and certificate database log. The default location for both locations is C:\WINDOWS\ system32\CertLog. You can also specify a shared folder for storing the CA certificate and information about the certification authority. The information in the shared folder is normally available only through a Web browser. The name of the share created for the folder is CertConfig.

The fourth step, shown in Figure 9-10, is only required when installing a subordinate certification authority. A subordinate certification authority must be certified by another certification authority, and this can be done directly across the network or via a certification

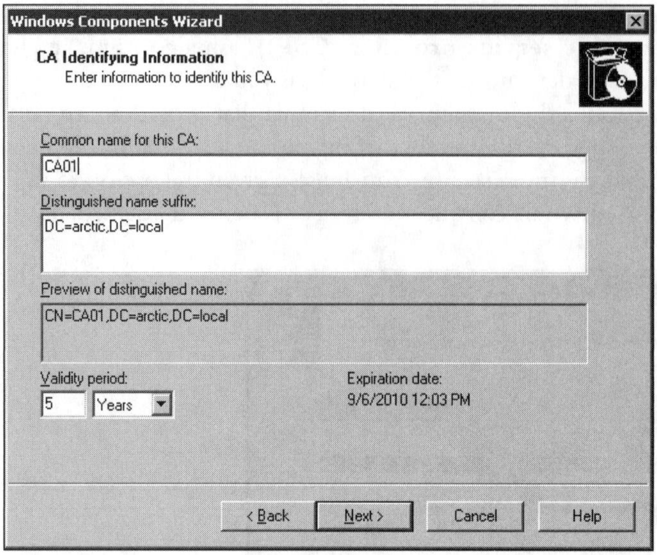

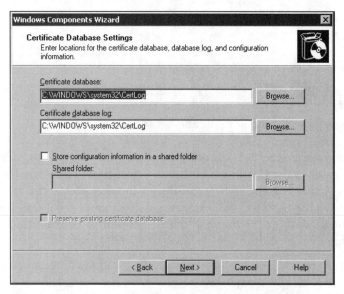

Figure 9-8   CA Identifying Information

Figure 9-9   Choosing database and log locations

request that is saved to file. If the parent certification authority is online, making the request directly across the network is faster. However, if the parent certification authority is a third-party certification authority outside of your network, you are required to save the request to file. After the request is saved to file, it must be sent to the parent certification authority. The process for sending the request varies depending on the parent certification authority.

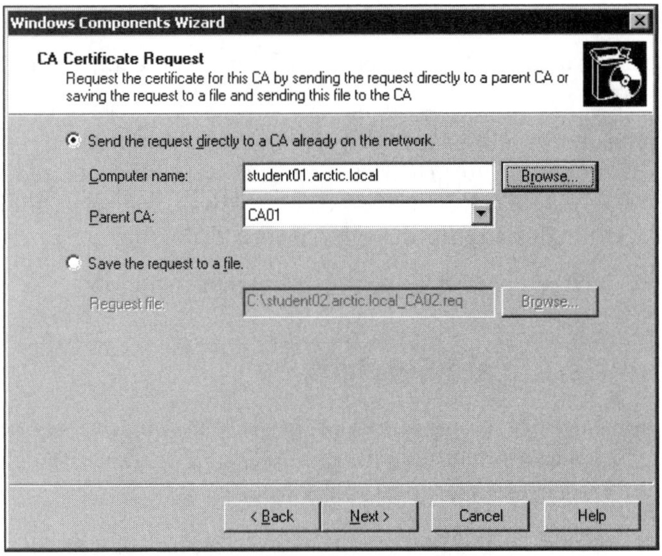

Windows Components Wizard

CA Certificate Request
Request the certificate for this CA by sending the request directly to a parent CA or saving the request to a file and sending this file to the CA

⊙ Send the request directly to a CA already on the network.

Computer name: student01.arctic.local   [Browse...]

Parent CA: CA01 ▾

○ Save the request to a file.

Request file: C:\student02.arctic.local_CA02.req   [Browse...]

[< Back] [Next >] [Cancel] [Help]

Figure 9-10   Certificate request for subordinate CA

When a subordinate certification authority saves a request to file, the installation is not complete. The response to the request is received as a file, and must be imported to certify the subordinate certification authority. To import the response, open the Certification Authority snap-in, right-click the subordinate certification authority, click Install CA certificate, browse to the response file, click the response file, and click Open.

Activity 9-2: Installing Certificate Services

ACTIVITY

Time Required: 10 minutes

Objective: Install Certificate Services and configure your server as an enterprise root certification authority.

Description: Arctic University is interested in enhancing the level of security for the workstations in the Payroll Department. To do this, smart cards will be issued to authorized payroll staff, and the workstations will be configured to accept only smart card authentication. You install Certificate Services to enable your server to create certificates that can be used for smart card authentication.

1. If necessary, start your server and log on as **Administrator**.

2. Click **Start**, point to **Control Panel**, and click **Add or Remove Programs**.

3. Click **Add/Remove Windows Components**.

4. Check the **Certificate Services CA** check box, and then click **Yes**.

5. Click **Next**.

6. Click **Enterprise root CA** if it is not already selected, and click **Next**.

7. In the Common name for this CA text box, type **CA*xx***, where *xx* is your student number, and click **Next**.

8. Click **Next** to accept the default locations for the certificate database and certificate database log. Click **Yes** to stop Internet Information Services. If prompted for the Windows Server 2003 CD-ROM, click **OK**. Click **Browse**, and select the **C:\I386** folder. Click **Open**, then click **OK** in the Files needed dialog box.

9. Click **Finish** and then close the Add or Remove Programs window.

Back Up and Restore Certificate Services

Certificate Services is normally backed up as part of the daily backup process on Windows Server 2003. Certificate Services is included with the backup of system state data, which is the preferred method for backing up Certificate Services.

You also have the option to back up and restore manually just Certificate Services using the Certification Authority snap-in. A manual backup and restore of Certificate Services is necessary if you do not back up the system state data on a server or if you do not want to restore all of the system state data on a server. For example, if you back up the system state data on a server only once per week and have made many registry changes since the last backup, you may prefer to restore just the Certificate Services database.

ACTIVITY

Activity 9-3: Backing Up Certificate Services

Time Required: 5 minutes

Objective: Perform a manual backup of Certificate Services.

Description: You have installed Certificate Services to issue certificates for Arctic University. Soon after installation, you issue certificates for over 200 staff members. You are concerned that the system state data on this server will not be backed up for another 16 hours during the nightly backup. To be sure that you do not need to reissue the certificates, you decide to back up the Certificate Services database manually.

1. If necessary, start your server and log on as **Administrator**.

2. Click **Start**, point to **Administrative Tools**, and click **Certification Authority**.

3. Right-click your server, point to **All Tasks**, and click **Back up CA**.

4. Click **Next** to start the Certification Authority Backup Wizard.

5. Check the **Private key and CA certificate** check box to select them for backup.

6. Check the **Certificate database and certificate database log** check box to select them for backup.

7. In the Back up to this location text box, type **C:\CERTBAK**, and press **Enter**.

8. Click **OK** to create the **C:\CERTBAK** directory.

9. In the Password text box, type **Password!**.

10. In the Confirm password text box, type **Password!**.

11. Click **Next** and click **Finish**.

12. Close the Certification Authority snap-in.

Activity 9-4: Restoring the Certificate Services Database

Time Required: 5 minutes

Objective: Perform a manual restore of Certificate Services.

Description: The Certificate Services database on one of your servers has become corrupt. Fortunately, you performed a manual backup of Certificate Services earlier today. To bring Certificate Services to the most recent state possible, you restore from the manual backup rather than the previous night's backup.

1. If necessary, start your server and log on as **Administrator**.

2. Simulate the loss of the Certificate Services database.
   a. Click **Start**, click **Run**, type **cmd**, and then press **Enter**.
   b. Type **net stop "certificate services"** and press **Enter**.
   c. Type **del c:\windows\system32\certlog*.*** and press **Enter**.
   d. Type **y** and press **Enter** to confirm the deletion.
   e. Close the command prompt window.

3. Click **Start**, point to **Administrative Tools**, and click **Certification Authority**.

4. Right-click your server, point to **All Tasks**, and click **Restore CA**.

5. Click **Next** to start the Certification Authority Restore Wizard.

6. Check the **Private key and CA certificate** check box to select them for restore.

7. Check **Certificate database and certificate database log** check box to select them for restore.

8. In the Restore from this location text box, type **C:\CERTBAK**, and press **Enter**.

9. In the Password text box, type **Password!**, and click **Next**.

10. Click **Finish**.

11. Click **Yes** to restart Certificate Services.

12. Close the Certification Authority snap-in.

MANAGING CERTIFICATES

Implementing Certificate Services first requires you to plan and implement a certification hierarchy. After the hierarchy is implemented by installing Certificate Services and choosing the class and type of each server, certificates must be issued and managed.

The tasks related to issuing and managing certificates are:

- Issuing certificates
- Renewing certificates
- Revoking certificates
- Publishing a Certificate Revocation List
- Importing and exporting certificates
- Mapping accounts to certificates

Most certificate management is done using snap-ins. However, there is a command-line utility, CERTUTIL, that can be used to manage both certificates and Certificate Services. This can be useful for scripting maintenance.

Issuing Certificates

Certificates can be requested using the **Certificate Request Wizard**, the Certificate Services Web pages, and autoenrollment. The Certificate Request Wizard and autoenrollment are available only for enterprise certification authorities, whereas the Certificate Services Web pages can be used by both stand-alone and enterprise certificate authorities.

The Certificate Request Wizard

The Certificate Request Wizard is run by users to create certificates. The types of certificates that can be created are controlled by **certificate templates**. The administrator can create, configure, and control access to these templates. Users are given the option to create certificates based on the templates to which they have either read or enroll permissions. Table 9-1 lists some of the default certificate templates that are enabled on an enterprise certification authority.

Table 9-1   Default certificate templates

Certificate Template	Description
EFS Recovery Agent	Issued to users; it can be used for file recovery for the encrypting file system (EFS)
Basic EFS	Issued to users; it can be used to encrypt files for the EFS
Domain Controller	Issued to computers; it can be used for client authentication and server authentication
Web Server	Issued to computers; it can be used for server authentication

Table 9-1   Default certificate templates (continued)

Certificate Template	Description
Computer	Issued to computers; it can be used for client authentication and server authentication
User	Issued to users; it can be used for the EFS, secure e-mail, and client authentication
Subordinate Certification Authority	Issued to computers; it can be used for any task
Administrator	Issued to users; it can be used for the EFS, secure e-mail, client authentication, and Microsoft trust list signing

The modification and creation of templates is accomplished by using the Certificate Templates snap-in. Access control for templates is also controlled using this snap-in.

The Certificate Request Wizard is initiated with the Certificates snap-in. This snap-in is not part of Administrative Tools. You need to start an empty MMC console and add the Certificates snap-in.

Certificates requested using the Certificate Request Wizard are automatically issued if the default settings are used. This is done because access to the certificate templates used by the Certificate Request Wizard allows you to control access. However, individual templates can be configured such that manual approval is required.

ACTIVITY

Activity 9-5: Requesting a Certificate

Time Required: 10 minutes

Objective: Request a user certificate using the Certificate Request Wizard.

Description: Arctic University has completed the installation of Certificate Services, and users now need to be issued certificates. A colleague is going to help each user request their certificate, but first you must show him how it is done. You request a user certificate using the Certificate Request Wizard.

1. If necessary, start your server and log on as **Administrator** of the Arctic.local domain.

2. Create a new user using Active Directory Users and Computers by performing the following steps:

   a. Click **Start**, click **Run**, type **mmc**, and press **Enter**.

   b. Click **File**, click **Add/Remove Snap-in**, click **Add**, double-click **Active Directory Users and Computers**, click **Close**, and click **OK**.

   c. Double-click **Active Directory Users and Computers**, double-click **arctic.local**, right-click **Users**, point to **New**, and click **User**.

   d. In the First name text box, type **Student*xx***, where *xx* is your student number.

    e. In the User logon name text box, type **Studentxx**, where *xx* is your student number.

    f. Click **Next**.

    g. In the Password text box, type **Password!**.

    h. In the Confirm password text box, type **Password!**.

    i. Click **User must change password at next logon** to deselect this option.

    j. Click **Next** and click **Finish**.

    k. Close the Active Directory Users and Computers snap-in. Click **No** if you are prompted to save the console settings.

3. Log off as Administrator.

4. Log on as **Studentxx**, where *xx* is your student number. Use **Password!** as the password.

5. If necessary, click **Start**, click **Run**, type **mmc**, and press **Enter**.

6. Click **File** and click **Add/Remove Snap-in**.

7. Click **Add** and double-click **Certificates**.

8. Click **Close** and click **OK**.

9. In the left pane, double-click **Certificates – Current User**, and click **Personal**.

10. Right-click **Personal**, point to **All Tasks**, and click **Request New Certificate**.

11. Click **Next** to start the **Certificate Request Wizard**.

12. Click **User**, check the **Advanced** check box, and click **Next**.

13. Click **Next** to accept the default cryptographic service provider information.

14. Ensure that the CA selected is your server. If your server is not selected, click **Browse** and select your server. Click **Next** to continue.

15. In the Friendly name text box, type **MyUserCertificate**, and click **Next**.

16. Click **Finish**.

17. Click **OK** to close the successful completion message.

18. To view your certificate, double-click **Certificates** in the right pane.

19. Close the Certificates snap-in. If you are asked to save the console settings, click **No**.

20. Log off as Studentxx.

Certificate Services Web Pages

The Certificate Services Web pages can be used by users to request certificates from both enterprise certification authorities and stand-alone certification authorities.

When a stand-alone certification authority is used, the certificate request must be manually approved by an administrator. After the certificate is approved, it is retrieved through a Web page as well. When an enterprise certification authority is used, the certificate request is automatically generated. However, the user must still retrieve the certificate from a Web page.

Authentication is an important consideration when using an enterprise certification authority and the Certificate Services Web pages. When a user accesses Web pages through IIS (Internet Information Services), there is no authentication by default. IIS automatically logs on as a user named IUSR_*servername*. Whatever permissions are granted to this user determines the permissions of anonymous Web users. If you do not force Web users to authenticate before requesting a certificate, the subject of the certificate (user) is IUSR_*servername*.

You can force users to authenticate by restricting the file permissions for the folder storing the Certificate Services Web pages. If IUSR_*servername* does not have permission to read the files in C:\WINDOWS\system32\certsrv, IIS asks for authentication information. The users can then authenticate using their user name and password. The user must have permissions for the C:\WINDOWS\system32\certsrv.

 The Certificate Services Web pages are accessed through the URL *http://server/certsrv*.

NOTE

IIS is required for the Certificate Services Web pages. IIS is not installed on Windows Server 2003 during a default installation because of security enhancements. If IIS is installed after the Certificate Services Web pages, the administrator must create a virtual directory called CERTSRV that points to C:\WINDOWS\system32\certsrv. This is done automatically if IIS is installed first.

Autoenrollment

Autoenrollment issues certificates to users automatically without any intervention on the part of the user. If certificates are required for a task in which there is no user intervention, this can be very useful. Users receive their certificates, and the application works without the user being inconvenienced by being asked questions he may not understand.

Autoenrollment is a new feature of Windows Server 2003, and works only when the domain controller is Windows Server 2003 and the client is Windows XP. To enable autoenrollment, you perform the following general steps:

1. Duplicate an existing certificate using the Certificate Templates snap-in. Autoenrollment is automatically enabled.

2. Ensure that the option Publish certificate in Active Directory is selected.

3. On the Security tab of the certificate, add the required users or groups, and assign them the enroll and autoenroll permissions.

4. Enable the new certificate template in the Certification Authority snap-in.

5. Configure a group policy to enable Enroll certificates automatically.

For step-by-step instructions on enabling and configuring autoenrollment, search for "autoenrollment" in Help and Support.

Renewing Certificates

All certificates are issued with an expiration date. This ensures that in the event a certificate becomes compromised, it is not a security risk for an extended period of time. If an employee unexpectedly leaves, this ensures that the employee does not have access to company resources after the certificate has expired.

To avoid an interruption in service, a user must renew a certificate before it expires. The lifetime of a certificate is defined by the administrator when a certificate template is created. A shorter lifetime is more secure than a longer one. However, a shorter lifetime also inconveniences the user by forcing renewal of his certificate more often.

NOTE If autoenrollment is used to issue certificates, it can also be used to renew certificates. In this case, the lifetime of the certificate can be kept very short with no inconvenience to the user. If autoenrollement is not used, certificates are renewed using the Certificates snap-in.

Revoking Certificates

When a certificate has been compromised or a user has left the company, you need to revoke the certificate. This places the certificate on the CRL of the certification authority. Windows 2000 and newer clients automatically download the CRL for Active Directory.

Windows Server 2003 publishes delta CRLs in addition to the entire CRL. The delta CRLs are changes that have occurred since the full CRL was published. A client that downloads the delta CRLs rather than the full CRL helps to reduce network traffic in high-volume environments.

A CRL has a default lifetime of seven days. After a client has downloaded the CRL, it does not download another copy until the local copy expires in seven days. This applies even if a new CRL has been published. The CRL lifetime can be changed in the Certification Authority snap-in by right-clicking Revoked Certificates and clicking Properties. Figure 9-11 shows the Revoked Certificates Properties dialog box.

Activity 9-6: Revoking a Certificate

Time Required: 10 minutes

Objective: Revoke a certificate and publish a new CRL.

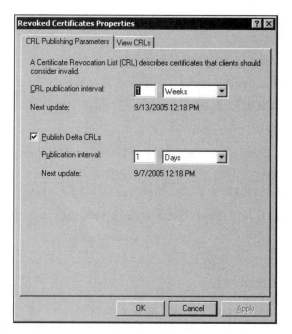

Figure 9-11   Revoked Certificates Properties dialog box

Description: A laptop used by one of the professors has been stolen from an office on campus. The laptop has a user certificate stored on it that was used by the professor for digital signatures. To ensure that other users are informed that this certificate is no longer valid for signatures, you revoke the certificate and publish a new CRL. After the certificate is revoked, you remove it from your server.

1. If necessary, start your server and log on as **Administrator**.

2. Click **Start**, point to **Administrative Tools**, and click **Certification Authority**.

3. Double-click your server.

4. Click **Issued Certificates**.

5. Click the certificate you created in Activity 9-5 on page 20. This certificate has the Requester Name of ARCTIC\Student*xx*, where *xx* is your student number.

6. Click **Action**, point to **All Tasks**, and click **Revoke Certificate**.

7. In the Reason code box, click **Key Compromise**, and click **Yes**.

8. Click **Revoked Certificates**. Notice that the certificate you revoked is now listed here.

9. Click **Action**, point to **All Tasks**, and click **Publish**.

10. Click **OK** to publish a new CRL.

11. Close the Certification Authority snap-in.

12. Log off as Administrator, and log on as Student*xx*, where *xx* is your student number. Use **Password!** as the password.

13. Click **Start**, click **Run**, type **mmc**, and press **Enter**.

14. Click **File** and click **Add/Remove Snap-in**.

15. Click **Add** and double-click **Certificates**.

16. Click **Close** and click **OK**.

17. In the left pane, double-click **Certificates – Current User**, double-click **Personal**, and click **Certificates**.

18. Right-click your **certificate**, click **Delete**, and click **Yes** to confirm the deletion.

19. Close the Certificates snap-in. If prompted to save console settings, click **No**.

20. Log off as Student*xx*.

Importing and Exporting Certificates

At times, you may want to move or copy certificates from one computer to another. For instance, if a user receives a new workstation, you need to move his certificates to the new workstation. In addition, if a user uses more than one workstation, you must create copies of his certificates on each workstation.

When a key is exported, you can choose from these standard formats:

- *DER encoded binary X.509 (.cer)* — This type of file is only available if the private key is not being exported. This is a standard file type used by non-Windows applications and operating systems.

- *Base-64 encoded X.509 (.cer)* — This type of file is only available if the private key is not being exported. This is a standard file type used by non-Windows applications and operating systems.

- *Cryptographic Message Syntax Standard – PKCS #7 Certificates (.p7b)* — This type of file is only available if the private key is not being exported. This is a standard file type used by non-Windows applications and operating systems. The advantage of this file format is the ability to export all of the certificates in the certification path.

- *Personal Information Exchange – PKCS #12 (.pks)* — This is the only option available if the private key is being exported. This type of file uses a password to encrypt the contents of the file. When the file is imported, the password must be entered to decrypt the file.

Activity 9-7: Moving a Certificate

Time Required: 10 minutes

Objective: Move a user certificate from one computer to another.

Description: A professor has received a new laptop computer. He has been using a personal certificate to access a secure Web site. It must be moved to the new laptop. In this activity, you create the personal certificate, export the certificate, and then import it, all on the same computer. Normally, the certificate would be exported on the old computer, and then imported on the new computer.

1. If necessary, start your server and log on as **Studentxx**, where *xx* is your student number. Use **Password!** as the password.

2. Click **Start**, click **Run**, type **mmc**, and press **Enter**.

3. Click **File** and click **Add/Remove Snap-in**.

4. Click **Add** and double-click **Certificates**.

5. Click **Close** and click **OK**.

6. Double-click **Certificates – Current User**, and click **Personal**.

7. Right-click **Personal**, point to **All Tasks**, and click **Request New Certificate**.

8. Click **Next** to start the Certificate Request Wizard.

9. Click **User**, check the **Advanced** check box, and click **Next**.

10. Click **Next** to accept the default cryptographic service provider information.

11. Ensure that the CA selected is your server. If your server is not selected, click **Browse** and select your server. Click **Next** to continue.

12. In the Friendly name text box, type **MyUserCertificate2** and click **Next**.

13. Click **Finish**.

14. Click **OK** to close the successful completion message.

15. To view your certificate, double-click **Certificates** in the right pane.

16. Right-click your certificate, point to **All Tasks**, and click **Export**.

17. Click **Next** to start the Certificate Export Wizard.

18. Click **Yes, export the private key**, and click **Next**.

19. To accept the default settings for file format, click **Next**.

20. In the Password text box, type **Password!**. In the Confirm password text box, type **Password!**, and click **Next**.

21. Click **Browse** and then click **My Documents** to select it if required. In the File name text box, type **MyCertificate**, click **Save**, and click **Next**. To make it easier to transfer this file, you would normally save it to a network drive or a floppy disk.

22. Click **Finish** and click **OK**.

23. Right-click your certificate, click **Delete**, and click **Yes**.

24. Right-click **Certificates**, point to **All Tasks**, and click **Import**.

25. Click **Next** to start the Certificate Import Wizard.

26. Click **Browse** and click **My Documents** to select it, if necessary.

27. Click the **Files of type** drop-down arrow, and click **Personal Information Exchange (*.pfx;*.p12)**.

28. Double-click **MyCertificate.pfx** and click **Next**. If your server is configured to hide known file extensions, the .pfx file extension may not be visible.

29. In the Password text box, type **Password!**, and click **Next**.

30. Confirm that Place all certificates in the following store is selected, and click **Next**.

31. Click **Finish** and click **OK**. The imported certificate can now be used.

32. Close the Certificates snap-in. If prompted to save the console settings, click **No**.

33. Log off as Student*xx*.

SMART CARD AUTHENTICATION

Smart cards are the strongest form of authentication supported by Windows Server 2003. They are the strongest form of authentication because users are required to have a physical device (the smart card) and enter a **personal identification number (PIN)**. When smart cards are implemented, users are issued a physical card that contains a certificate. Each time the card is used, a PIN is required. The PIN is used to decrypt the certificate stored on the smart card.

NOTE

The PIN used by smart cards is not the same as a PIN for a bank card. The PIN used by smart cards can contain alphanumeric letters just like a password used by Active Directory.

Once issued, smart cards can be used to authenticate network logons or VPN connections. However, smart cards cannot be used to authenticate Terminal Server sessions because the smart card reader must be attached to the machine performing the authentication. When Terminal Services is used, the terminal server performs the authentication, but the local workstation would have the smart card reader attached.

The following steps are involved in implementing smart card authentication:

1. Prepare the certification authority to issue smart card certificates.

2. Prepare a smart card certificate enrollment station.

3. Configure a smart card for user logon.

4. Map the smart card certificate to a user account.

5. Attach a smart card reader to the client computer.

Preparing the Certification Authority to Issue Smart Card Certificates

Two types of certificates are required to implement smart card authentication. The first type of certificate is placed on the smart card, and it is used for authentication. The two templates that can be used by enterprise certification authorities to issue certificates for smart card authentication are listed in Table 9-2.

Table 9-2   Certificate templates for smart card authentication certificates

Certificate Template	Description
Smartcard Logon	Allows the holder to authenticate using a smart card
Smartcard User	Allows the holder to authenticate and protect e-mail using a smart card

The second type of certificate required to issue smart cards is an enrollment agent certificate. An **enrollment agent** certificate is required by the user that is creating the smart cards for the users. It authorizes a user or computer to create certificates on behalf of another user. Table 9-3 lists the certificate templates that can be used to issue certificates for an enrollment agent.

Table 9-3   Certificate templates for enrollment agent certificates

Certificate Template	Description
Enrollment Agent	Used by a user to request certificates on behalf of another subject
Enrollment Agent (Computer)	Used by a computer to request certificates on behalf of another computer subject

An enterprise certification authority must be configured to issue certificates based on at least one certificate template that creates smart card authentication certificates, as well one certificate template that creates enrollment agent certificates.

 NOTE   Remember that access to the certificate templates is controlled based on NTFS permissions. Use NTFS permissions to limit the users who can obtain enrollment agent certificates.

Preparing a Smart Card Certificate Enrollment Station

A **smart card certificate enrollment station** is a computer that is used to configure smart cards for users. As such, it must have a **smart card reader** attached and properly configured. A smart card reader is a device that smart cards are inserted into to read their contents.

After the smart card reader is attached, the user performing the smart card configuration must obtain an enrollment agent certificate. This can be done through the Certificate Services Web pages at *http://server/certsrv* or by using the Certificates snap-in. To obtain an enrollment agent certificate from an enterprise certification authority, the user must have Read NTFS permissions to the Enrollment Agent certificate template.

Configuring a Smart Card for User Logon

An enrollment agent configures smart cards for other users through the Certificate Services Web pages on a certification authority. After selecting to perform an advanced certificate request, you must choose the "Request a certificate for a smart card on behalf of another user using the smart card certificate enrollment station" on the Advanced Certificate Request Web page.

On the Smart Card Certificate Enrollment Station Web page, you must select the template that will be used to create the certificate. In addition, you must select the certification authority that will issue the certificate, the cryptographic service provider of the smart card manufacturer, the enrollment agent certificate that will sign the enrollment request, and the user the certificate is for.

To create the smart card, click the Enroll button and place the smart card in the smart card reader when prompted. You are also prompted for the PIN to be used on the smart card. If a certificate already exists on the smart card, you are prompted to overwrite it.

Smart cards used on Windows 2000 workstations must be created using a Windows 2000 enrollment station. Smart cards used on Windows XP and Windows Server 2003 can be created using an enrollment station on Windows 2000, Windows XP, or Windows Server 2003.

Mapping the Smart Card Certificate to a User Account

If certificates are used to authenticate users for Windows Server 2003 services, the certificate must be mapped to a user account. If a certificate is mapped to a user account, whenever that certificate is presented, the person presenting it gets the permissions of the account to which it is mapped. In addition to smart cards, certificate-based authentication can be used to manage access to Web sites.

For example, assume that a certificate is created and mapped to the user account WebUser. This certificate is distributed to several people who remotely access a Web site. The users import the certificate into Internet Explorer. Then, when the users access the Web site, the certificate is presented to the Web server. The Web server allows the user access to all parts of the Web site to which WebUser has been granted access.

Active Directory Users and Computers is used to map certificates to user accounts. To map a certificate to a user, right-click the user and click Name Mappings. This option is only available if you have enabled Advanced Features in the View menu.

You can use three options when mapping certificates to user accounts:

- *One-to-one mapping*—A single certificate is mapped to a single user account.

- *Many-to-one mapping (subject)*—All certificates with the same subject are mapped to a single user account regardless of the issuing CA.

- *Many-to-one mapping (CA)*—All certificates with the same issuing CA are mapped to a single user account regardless of the subject.

Figure 9-12 shows the available options when mapping a certificate to a user account. If the "Use Issuer for alternate security identity" check box is checked alone, it is a many-to-one mapping based on the issuing CA. If the "Use Subject for alternate security identity" check box is checked alone, it is a many-to-one mapping based on the subject. If both options are checked, it is then a one-to-one mapping.

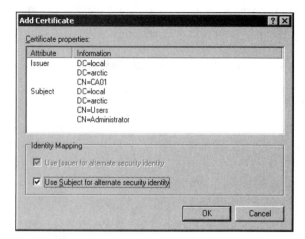

Figure 9-12   Certificate mapping options

When smart cards are used to authenticate network logons and VPN connections, a one-to-one mapping is most common. This allows network access to be controlled on a per user basis.

NOTE   User principal name mapping is a special type of one-to-one mapping. When a certificate is issued by Windows 2000 or Windows Server 2003, it includes the user principal name as a field in the certificate. This can be matched to the user principal name of a user to perform a one-to-one mapping.

Many-to-one mappings are less secure than one-to-one mappings. The auditing in Windows Server 2003 is based on user accounts. If a many-to-one mapping is used, auditing records all smart cards as the same user account. This is appropriate only in low security environments in which auditing is not required and many users require exactly the same level of access.

Attaching a Smart Card Reader to the Client Workstation

Each computer using smart cards must have a smart card reader. Many newer computers have these available as an optional component that appears on the face of the computer. When installed internally, smart card readers are about the size of a floppy disk drive. Smart card readers are also commonly available as USB devices.

The detailed steps for installing a smart card reader vary depending on the manufacturer and how it connects to the system. Read the documentation that comes with your smart card reader for detailed instructions.

CHAPTER SUMMARY

- Cryptography uses algorithms and keys to encrypt and decrypt information. Depending on the process used, cryptography can ensure or perform confidentiality, integrity, nonrepudiation, and authentication.

- Symmetric encryption uses the same key to encrypt and decrypt information.

- Asymmetric encryption uses a pair of keys. Information that is encrypted by one key is decrypted by the other key. These keys are often referred to as the private key and the public key.

- Hash encryption is a form of one-way encryption. Anything encrypted with hash encryption cannot be decrypted.

- A digital signature does not ensure the confidentiality of the information, only its integrity, nonrepudiation, and authentication.

- Certificate Services is the Microsoft implementation of a certification authority for PKI. A certification authority issues certificates to users, computers, and applications.

- Internal certification authorities are used when supporting only internal clients. They are inexpensive, and you have complete control.

- Third-party certification authorities are used when supporting external clients. The main disadvantage is the cost of certificates.

- Certificates issued by Certificate Services are X.509 certificates.

- Only certificate-enabled applications are able to use certificates. They are designed that way by the developer.

- Enterprise certification authorities integrate with Active Directory and can issue certificates without intervention by an administrator. A stand-alone certification authority does not integrate with Active Directory, and can only issue certificates after the request is approved by an administrator.

- Clients trust a certificate because they trust the root certification authority. There is only one root certification authority in a certificate hierarchy. All other certification authorities are subordinate certification authorities.

❑ The Certificate Request Wizard, the Certificate Services Web pages, and autoenrollment can be used to issue certificates. A stand-alone certification authority can only issue certificates using the Certificate Services Web pages. An enterprise certification authority can use any method to issue certificates.

❑ Certificates can be revoked if they are compromised or if an employee leaves the company. Revoked certificates are published in a Certificate Revocation List.

❑ When certificates are used to authenticate services on Windows Server 2003, the certificates must be mapped to a user account.

❑ To use smart cards for authentication, you must prepare the certification authority to issue smart card certificates, prepare a smart card certificate enrollment station, configure a smart card for user logon, map the smart card certificate to a user account, and attach a smart card reader to the client computer.

9

Key Terms

algorithm — A mathematical formula used to process data for encryption or decryption.

asymmetric encryption — An encryption method that uses two different keys. When one key is used to encrypt, the other key must be used to decrypt.

certificate — A part of Public Key Infrastructure that contains a public key and an expiration date. Certificates are presented for authentication and to share public keys.

certificate hierarchy — The structure of trusted certification authorities consisting of a single root CA and possibly subordinate CAs.

Certificate Request Wizard — A wizard used to request certificates from an enterprise certification authority.

Certificate Revocation List (CRL) — A list of certificates that have been revoked before their expiration date.

Certificate Services — A service installed on Windows Server 2003 that allows it to act as a certification authority.

certificate templates — A template used by enterprise certification authorities to issue certificates with certain characteristics.

certification authority (CA) — A server that issues certificates.

ciphertext — The data that has been encrypted.

cryptographic service provider (CSP) — The software or hardware that provides cryptographic services.

cryptography — The process of encrypting and decrypting messages and files using an algorithm.

decryption — The process of making encrypted data readable.

digital signature — A process using a cryptographic algorithm that ensures data integrity and nonrepudiation.

encryption — The process of rendering data unreadable by applying an algorithm.

enrollment agent — A user authorized to request certificates for other users. An enrollment agent loads certificates onto smart cards for users.

enterprise certification authority — A certification authority that integrates with Active Directory, and can issue certificates without administrator intervention.

hash encryption — A type of one-way encryption that cannot be decrypted. It is used to store information such as passwords and to create checksums.

hash value — A summary of the data being encrypted using hash encryption.

key — A number, usually large, to prevent it from being guessed, used in combination with an algorithm to encrypt data.

personal identification number (PIN) — An alphanumeric password that is required to decrypt the contents of a smart card.

private key — The key in asymmetric encryption that is seen only by the user to which it is issued.

public key — The key in asymmetric encryption that is freely distributed to other users.

(PKI) Public Key Infrastructure — The system that supports the issuance and management of certificates, public keys, and private keys.

root certification authority — The first CA in the certificate hierarchy. Clients trusting this CA trust certificates issued by this CA and all subordinate CAs.

Secure Sockets Layer (SSL) — A Transport Layer protocol that encrypts data communication between a client and service. Both the client and service must be written to support SSL.

smart card — A physical device about the size of a credit card that contains a certificate that can be used to identify users. It can also hold additional information about users.

smart card certificate enrollment station — A computer that is used to configure smart cards for users.

smart card reader — A device used to read smart cards. It can be an internal or external device.

stand–alone certification authority — A certification authority that does not integrate with Active Directory, and requires an administrator to approve certificate requests.

subordinate certification authority — A certification authority that has been authorized by a root CA or another subordinate CA.

symmetric encryption — Encryption that uses the same key to encrypt and decrypt data.

trusted root certification authorities — A CA from which a client or application accepts certificates.

X.509 — A standard for certificates that was created by the International Telecommunication Union–Telecommunication (ITU-T).

REVIEW QUESTIONS

1. Verifying that data has not been modified is called _____ .
   a. confidentiality
   b. authentication
   c. repudiation
   d. integrity

2. Which of the following encryption methods uses a single key to encrypt and decrypt data?
   a. symmetrical
   b. asymmetrical
   c. hash
   d. Blowfish

3. Darrin wants to encrypt an e-mail message to Tracey. Which key does Tracey use to open the encrypted e-mail?
   a. Darrin's public key
   b. Darrin's private key
   c. Tracey's public key
   d. Tracey's private key

4. Erin digitally signs an e-mail message to Jennifer. Which key does Jennifer use to verify the digital signature?
   a. Erin's public key
   b. Erin's private key
   c. Jennifer's public key
   d. Jennifer's private key

5. Which of the following statements regarding enterprise certification authorities is false?
   a. Enterprise CAs require Active Directory.
   b. Enterprise CAs can use templates.
   c. Certificate requests to an Enterprise CA must be manually approved by the administrator.
   d. Enterprise CAs should not issue certificates outside the organization.

9

6. Users require a certificate for secure remote mail. An Enterprise CA has been installed on a server named Apollo. What Web site does the user access to request a certificate?

   a. https://apollo/certsrv

   b. http://apollo/certsrv

   c. http:/apollo/certreq

   d. http://apollo/certsvr

7. A third-party CA is normally used in which of the following scenarios? (Choose all that apply.)

   a. The server needs to be trusted by clients outside your organization.

   b. You need full control over how and when certificates are issued.

   c. You need a low-cost solution.

   d. Client computers require no modifications to use the certificate.

8. A list of certificates that are no longer valid is called a(n) _____ .

   a. certification authority

   b. Expired Certificate List

   c. Certificate Revocation List

   d. Certificate Expiration List

9. Certificates created by a stand-alone CA follow which format?

   a. X.400

   b. X.500

   c. X.509

   d. X.501

10. Which of the following components is not part of a certificate hierarchy?

    a. enterprise root CA

    b. stand-alone subordinate CA

    c. stand-alone root CA

    d. enterprise child CA

11. Which of the following use symmetric encryption?

    a. digital signature

    b. EFS

    c. encrypting e-mail

    d. password-protected files

12. A certification authority is a server that issues certificates to which of the following? (Choose all that apply.)

    a. users

    b. computers

    c. applications

    d. routers

13. Web browsers contain a list of certification authorities that are trusted by the application. What are these CAs called?

    a. root certification authorities

    b. trusted certification authorities

    c. enterprise certification authorities

    d. stand-alone certification authorities

14. Certificates that have expired are added to the Certificate Revocation List. True or False?

15. A subordinate certification authority can be certified by which certification authorities?

    a. external CA

    b. enterprise root CA

    c. stand-alone root CA

    d. all of the above

16. Hash encryption is often used for which of the following? (Choose all that apply.)

    a. EFS

    b. e-mail encryption

    c. passwords

    d. digital signatures

17. Certificate Services can be included in the daily backup by selecting which option in the backup application?

    a. Certification Authority

    b. System State

    c. Registry

    d. COM+ Class Registration Database

18. Which of the following certificate templates can be used for EFS, e-mail, and client authentication?

    a. Computer

    b. Basic EFS

    c. Web Server

    d. User

    e. Domain Controller

19. What is the default lifetime of a Certificate Revocation List?

    a. 24 hours

    b. two days

    c. five days

    d. seven days

    e. 14 days

20. Which format must be selected when exporting a private key?

    a. DER encoded binary X.509

    b. Personal Information Exchange

    c. Base-64 encoded X.509

    d. Cryptographic Message Syntax Standard

CASE PROJECTS

CASE PROJECTS

Case Project 9-1: Deciding on a Certificate Strategy

Because of privacy issues and concerns regarding security, the university IT management wants to encrypt all internal e-mail and create a secure Web site for ordering books and paying for courses. You have been asked to create a PKI infrastructure that addresses the following:

1. All internal e-mail must be digitally signed and encrypted.

2. All credit card numbers and ordering information must be encrypted between the client and the Web server when ordering materials on the university's Web site.

3. Certificates must be issued without administrative intervention.

4. Internal users must be able to request certificates using an automated process.

5. Web browsers must not display a warning message about not trusting the certificate.

Explain how you would implement PKI given this set of criteria.

Case Project 9-2: Certificate Server Roles

A backup administrator has asked you to explain the difference between an enterprise root CA and a stand-alone root CA. She wants to implement a certification authority in an NT domain for remote authentication. Which CA would you recommend and why?

Case Project 9-3: Certificate Services Features

The board of directors has approved your plan for implementing a PKI infrastructure. However, they are concerned that staff will be confused about how to renew certificates and how to install them on their local workstations. What additional functionality does Windows Server 2003 have that addresses the board of director's concerns? What additional upgrades must be performed to support the enhanced functionality?

Case Project 9-4: Implementing Smart Cards

One of the professors just bought a new computer with a smart card reader. He thinks that you should be able to get the smart card reader working in an afternoon. As a result, your boss has committed you to implementing the smart cards as an option for all users that ask for it. Document the process that is required to implement smart cards, and explain why it may take longer than an afternoon to implement for all of the users.

9

10

PLANNING AND MANAGING IP SECURITY

After reading this chapter, you will be able to:

♦ Describe IP Security issues and how the IPSec protocol addresses them

♦ Choose the appropriate IPSec mode for a given situation

♦ Implement authentication for IPSec

♦ Enable IPSec

♦ Create IPSec policies

♦ Monitor and troubleshoot IPSec

Although TCP/IP is very popular and used worldwide on the Internet, it is not very secure. Each IP packet that is sent on a local area network or on the Internet can be read by people other than the intended recipients. Even worse, the potential exists for IP packets to contain false information that permits you or anyone to be impersonated by someone else.

IPv6 has new features that allow IP packets to be both digitally signed to prevent impersonation and encrypted to prevent unauthorized people from reading the contents of the packets. Unfortunately, IPv4 has no such features built in. However, IPSec is an enhancement for IPv4 that allows packets to be digitally signed and encrypted.

In this chapter, you learn how to choose the appropriate IPSec mode to use, implement and enable IPSec, create IPSec policies, and perform IPSec monitoring and troubleshooting.

WHY IPSEC IS IMPORTANT

Security is a concern for all networks. IPSec provides security for IP-based networks. Depending on how it is implemented, it authenticates both computers engaged in a conversation, uses digital signatures to verify that data has not been tampered with while in transit, and encrypts data while in transit.

How Hackers Work

IPv4 has no built-in security mechanisms to protect the communication between two hosts. This opens IPv4 to a variety of ways in which hackers can corrupt or eavesdrop on communications:

- *Packet sniffing*—Using special software called a **packet sniffer**, a hacker can view all of the packets traversing your network. Using these sniffed packets, a hacker can view the contents of files that are being stored on network servers, read e-mail, and possibly even view passwords. It may seem unlikely that a hacker can gain access to your premises to run a packet sniffer, but hacked Internet routers can also be used for packet sniffing.

- *Data replay*—Advanced packet sniffers can capture packets and allow the user to resend them at a later time; this is called **data replay**. For example, a hacker could capture the packets involved in transferring money from one bank account to another and, even without understanding the contents of the packets, could replay the packets from one side of the communication to initiate the transaction again and again.

- *Data modification*—Some packet sniffers allow the user to change the contents of packets before replaying them; this is called **data modification**. For example, an e-mail message with a contract attached could be modified while in transit and the recipient would never know.

- *Address spoofing*—The only way IPv4 can control which users can access resources is via a firewall. Most firewall rules control access to resources based on the source IP address. Clever hackers can falsify the source IP address in a packet and gain unauthorized access to resources. Falsifying the source IP address in a packet is called **address spoofing**.

Authentication, Encryption, and Digital Signatures

IPSec (IP Security) is a standards track protocol, supported by the Internet Engineering Task Force (IETF), that is designed to secure IP-based communication. To do this, it uses authentication, encryption, and digital signatures. A standards track protocol is one that the IETF is endorsing as one that is likely to become an Internet standard that will be implemented by all IP hosts.

IPSec authenticates the endpoints of any IP-based conversation using IPSec. This means that each participant must be known and trusted. When the two partners in a conversation using IPSec are authenticated, IP addresses are no longer used to verify the identity of the partners. Authentication stops unauthorized communication that is missed by firewalls, which are vulnerable to spoofed IP addresses. IPSec authentication identifies computers or devices involved in any IP-based communication using IPSec, not individual users.

Encryption can be used by IPSec to hide the contents of data packets. This prevents hackers with a simple packet sniffer from eavesdropping on network communication. Hackers are still able to capture the packets, but the contents are unreadable.

Digital signatures on each packet of information in a conversation ensure that a packet has not been modified while in transit. In addition, time stamps placed in the signatures ensure that the data cannot and is not being replayed.

Advantages of IPSec

IPSec exists at the network layer of the TCP/IP architecture. Because applications communicate with the transport layer of the TCP/IP architecture, and because IPSec operates at the network layer, applications are unaware of the existence of IPSec. Any TCP/IP-based application can use IPSec without being specially written to do so. This is a significant advantage over other data encryption methods such as SSL, which need to be embedded in the client software.

As a standards track protocol sponsored by the IETF, IPSec is widely used by many vendors. Although it is possible that parts of IPSec may be modified in the future, the current specifications ensure at least a minimal level of compatibility between implementations from different vendors. As a result, you should be able to use a Windows Server 2003 router with IPSec to communicate with a Cisco router using IPSec.

IPSec is a valuable addition to a network when data integrity or confidentiality are required. On a LAN, IPSec can be implemented between client computers and specific servers holding confidential data, such as financial records or human resources information. On a WAN, IPSec can be used to create a cost-effective virtual private network that allows a company to securely send private data across the Internet without fear of eavesdropping.

Disadvantages of IPSec

Given the advantages of IPSec, you would think that all IP-based communications would use it. However, it is not practical or desired in all situations. Pre-Windows 2000 operating systems from Microsoft do not support the IPSec protocol. This prevents any network with Windows 9x/NT clients from implementing IPSec for all communications. You can use a mix of IPSec-protected packets and unprotected packets to increase security for those operating systems that do support IPSec.

IPSec can also significantly slow communication on a network. Authenticating, digitally signing each packet, and encrypting the contents of each packet consume processing resources and time. A busy server may not have enough processing power to support using IPSec for all communications. Fortunately, you can buy network cards with devoted processors to speed IPSec calculations.

Another drawback to using IPSec is that the majority of businesses connected to the Internet use some type of NAT (Network Address Translation) to allow an entire office to share one IP address when accessing the Internet. Only the very latest versions of IPSec can be routed through NAT, and this is a very serious limitation for remote users. However, if NAT and IPSec are implemented on the same router, it functions properly. Figure 10-1 shows implementations of NAT and IPSec.

Computer A and Computer B cannot communicate because IPSec packets cannot travel through NAT.

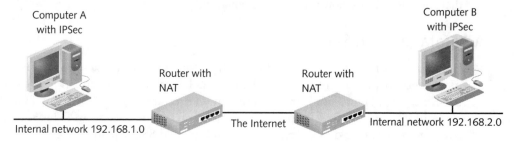

Computer A and Computer B can communicate because NAT and IPSec are configured on the same device.

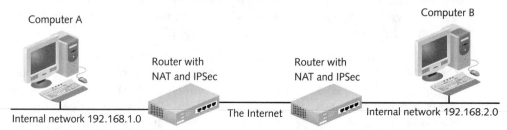

Figure 10-1 Implementing NAT and IPSec

 Windows Server 2003 and Windows XP Service Pack 1 support the IPSec-NAT-T protocol. IPSec-NAT-T allows IPSec packets to be moved through NAT without corrupting them.

NOTE

IPSec adds complexity to a network. Although the Windows Server 2003 implementation of IPSec is reliable, any service added to a network has the potential to break. In real terms, a broken service translates into lost money via user downtime and additional administrative expense. Without a demonstrated need, IPSec should not be implemented.

IPSec Modes

When configuring IPSec, you must choose between different modes of operation. The modes of operation define whether communication is secured between two hosts or two networks, and which IPSec services are used. Attempting to use all modes of operation is not appropriate because the large amount of processing power required on routers and hosts slows down network communications.

Authentication Headers (AH) mode enforces authentication of the two IPSec clients and includes a digital signature on each packet. **Encapsulating Security Payload (ESP) mode** has all the features of AH mode plus encryption of data in the packet. IPSec communication between two networks is called **tunnel mode**. IPSec communication between two hosts is called **transport mode**.

When implementing IPSec, you must choose tunnel mode or transport mode. In addition, you must choose AH mode or ESP mode. For example, you could choose to implement IPSec in tunnel mode and ESP mode if encryption is required. Or, you could choose to implement IPSec in tunnel mode and AH mode if encryption is not required.

The following sections discuss each mode in turn.

AH Mode

The AH mode of IPSec provides authentication of the two endpoints and adds a checksum to the packet. (Authentication guarantees that the two endpoints are known.) The checksum on the packet guarantees that the packet is not modified in transit, including the IP headers. AH mode does not provide data confidentiality, however; the payload of the packet is unencrypted.

It would be appropriate to use AH mode in a situation in which you are concerned about packets being captured with a packet sniffer and replayed later. The checksum feature ensures that packets cannot be modified to create a new connection. AH mode is less processor-intensive than ESP mode because there is no need for encryption calculations.

ESP Mode

The ESP mode of IPSec provides authentication of the two endpoints, adds a checksum to each packet, and encrypts the data in the packet. Authentication performs the same function as in AH mode. The checksum guarantees that the packet was not modified in transit, excluding the IP headers. Encryption ensures that unintended recipients cannot read the data in the packet.

Most implementations of IPSec use ESP mode because data encryption is desired. When implementing IPSec in ESP mode, you must ensure that the devices have enough processing power to encrypt and decrypt all of the packets addressed to, or passing through, them. For example, if two routers are using IPSec in ESP mode to encrypt all of the packets transmitted across the Internet between two locations, the processors in those routers must be able to encrypt and decrypt all the packets moving between the two networks.

Transport Mode

IPSec in transport mode is used between two hosts. Both endpoints in the communication must support IPSec. This limits the implementation of IPSec because many devices, such as printers, rarely offer IPSec support. Figure 10-2 shows IPSec in transport mode. In this example, packets are encrypted on both internal networks as well as on the Internet.

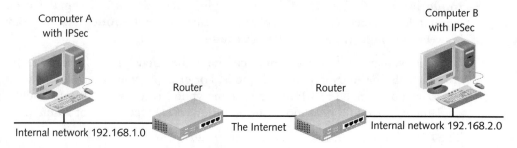

Figure 10-2   IPSec in transport mode

The two endpoints authenticated in this example are the computers communicating when transport mode is used. Therefore, you are guaranteed to be communicating with a known host. This may be required for some secure communications.

The structure of a packet built using ESP in transport mode is shown in Figure 10-3. This packet is built locally on the host and, therefore, includes all of the IPSec information inside the original IP header. There is no need to encapsulate an entire packet.

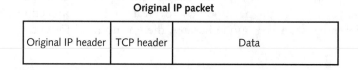

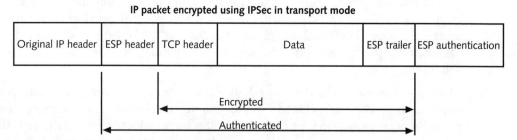

Figure 10-3   Packet structure for ESP in transport mode

Tunnel Mode

IPSec in tunnel mode is used between two routers. The two hosts communicating through the routers do not need to support IPSec; rather, the routers take the original IP packets and encapsulate them. This means that any IP devices can take advantage of routers running IPSec in tunnel mode.

Figure 10-4 shows IPSec in tunnel mode between two routers. All of the communication between computers on both internal networks is encrypted as it crosses the Internet because the routers encapsulate the original IP packets. However, communication within each internal network is not encrypted.

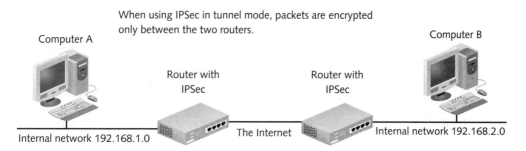

Figure 10-4   IPSec in tunnel mode

Figure 10-5 shows the structure of a packet built using ESP in tunnel mode.

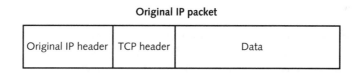

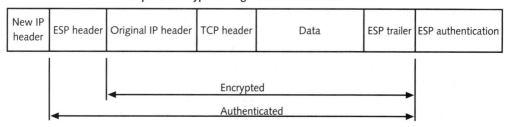

Figure 10-5   Packet structure for ESP in tunnel mode

Authentication takes place between the two routers when using IPSec in tunnel mode. The computers taking part in the conversation are not authenticated. Effectively, this authenticates the two networks instead of the individual computers. This is less secure because a hacker could place an unauthorized computer on a trusted network.

IPSec Authentication

Both endpoints of an IPSec communication are authenticated. When two routers are engaged using IPSec in tunnel mode, both are authenticated to each other (the authentication is not done on the users logged onto the devices, however). When two computers are engaged using IPSec in transport mode, both computers are authenticated to each other.

Internet Key Exchange (IKE) is the process used by two IPSec computers or routers to negotiate their security parameters. The security parameters negotiated include the method of authentication, AH or ESP mode, transport or tunnel mode, encryption and hashing algorithms, and parameters for key exchange. When security parameters have been agreed upon, this is referred to as a **security association (SA)**.

There are three methods Windows Server 2003 can use to authenticate IPSec connections:

- Preshared key
- Certificates
- Kerberos

Preshared Key

A **preshared key** is simply a combination of characters entered at each endpoint of the IPSec connection. Authentication is based on the fact that both endpoints know the same secret, and no one else has been told the secret. Effectively, this is the same as configuring both ends of the IPSec connection with a password. If both ends are using the same password, the connection is established. The major advantage of this authentication method is its simplicity. Authentication occurs as long as the preshared key is typed in correctly on each device.

The major disadvantage of this authentication method is movement of the preshared key when configuring the two devices. For example, if Bob is configuring a device in New York to use IPSec and authenticate using a key he has generated, Bob needs to give that key to Susan in Atlanta so that she can configure her device before they can communicate using IPSec. When Bob gives the key to Susan using e-mail, postal mail, or over the telephone, there is a risk someone might intercept the message.

Certificates

Certificates may be presented for authentication. If the two certificates used are part of the same certificate hierarchy, each IPSec device accepts the certificate of the other device.

This type of authentication is very useful when clients are from outside of your organization. The clients can obtain a certificate from a third-party certificate authority so that you, as network administrator, are not responsible for maintaining the infrastructure that creates and approves certificates.

The main disadvantage of using third-party certificates is cost. Each client needs to buy a certificate. If there are hundreds or thousands of clients, this can be expensive. In addition, many clients may not be technically savvy enough to obtain a certificate.

Kerberos

Kerberos is the authentication system used by Windows 2000, Windows XP, and Windows Server 2003 for access to network resources. The two devices must be in Kerberos realms that trust each other. In Active Directory, a domain is equivalent to a Kerberos realm.

The main benefit of Kerberos as an authentication method for IPSec is its seamless integration with domain security. The client computers do not need to be configured with any extra information if they have a computer account in the Active Directory forest.

Kerberos is not a commonly supported authentication system for IPSec on non-Microsoft products such as routers, and it is not appropriate for Windows computers that are not part of the Active Directory forest.

10

ENABLING IPSEC

IPSec is enabled on Windows Server 2003 using IPSec policies. These policies can be configured manually on each server or distributed through Group Policy. IPSec policies configured on each server can be accessed through the Local Security Policy snap-in found in Administrative Tools, by using the IP Security Policy Management console available in MMC, or by using Netsh commands for IPSec from a command line. IPSec policies distributed through Group Policy can be configured using the Active Directory Users and Computers snap-in or the Group Policy Object Editor snap-in.

IPSec policies define the circumstances under which IP traffic is tunneled using IPSec, permitted without using IPSec, or blocked. In addition, the policies define the type of authentication, which network connections are affected, and whether IPSec is to be used in tunnel mode or transport mode.

The three policies installed by default are as follows:

- Server (Request Security)
- Client (Respond Only)
- Secure Server (Require Security)

The default policies are configured to use Kerberos for authentication. This allows them to be used internally within an Active Directory forest with no configuration.

All ICMP traffic is permitted by the default policies. This means that network traffic generated by utilities such as ping and tracert is not encapsulated using IPSec. It is assumed that this traffic is public and does not need to be kept secure.

All of the default policies respond to requests to use IPSec. However, they differ in whether they request security. The Client (Respond Only) policy never requests IPSec for IP communication, but uses it if requested. The Server (Request Security) policy always requests IPSec for IP communication, but it can communicate without it if a security association cannot be established using IPSec. The Secure Server (Require Security) policy does not respond to any non-IPSec traffic for IP communication.

An IPSec policy must be in place to use IPSec. If there is no IPSec policy established, IPSec cannot be used.

Assigning a Default IPSec Policy

A single server can be configured with many IPSec policies. However, no policy is used until it is assigned. Only one policy can be assigned at a time per machine. The Local Security Policy snap-in can be used to assign an IPSec policy on a single computer. Group Policy can be used to assign an IPSec policy to a group of computers.

After a policy has been assigned, it does not take effect immediately. The IPSec Policy Agent must be restarted for the change to take effect. You can restart the IPSec Policy Agent by rebooting the server. However, the preferred method is by using the Services snap-in. In the Services snap-in, the IPSec Policy Agent is named IPSEC Services.

Activity 10-1: Assigning an IPSec Policy

Time Required: 10 minutes

Objective: Assign an IPSec policy to enable encryption of data packets.

Description: Several of your servers hold confidential student information. You want to enable IPSec on these servers to protect the information from packet sniffers. The client computers accessing your confidential servers are a mix of Windows XP/2000 and Windows 9x/NT. You enable the Server (Request Security) policy to accommodate the older clients that do not support IPSec.

1. If necessary, start your server and log on as **Administrator**.

2. Click **Start**, point to **Administrative Tools**, and click **Local Security Policy**.

3. Under Security Settings, click **IP Security Policies on Local Computer**.

4. In the right pane, right-click **Server (Request Security)**, and click **Assign**. Notice that under the column Policy Assigned, "Yes" now appears next to the description for this policy.

5. Close the Local Security Settings window.

6. Click **Start**, point to **Administrative Tools**, and click **Services**.

7. Scroll down through the list of services, right-click **IPSEC Services**, and click **Restart**.

8. Close the Services window.

ACTIVITY

Activity 10-2: Verifying an IPSec Security Association

Time Required: 10 minutes

Objective: Verify that the IPSec policy you have enabled is working.

Description: To verify that the IPSec policy you created in the preceding exercise is working, you use the IPSec Monitor snap-in. This snap-in shows you the status of IPSec security associations. Working with a partner, the test you perform first creates a file share on your server and then connects to the file share created on your partner's computer.

1. If necessary, start your server and log on as **Administrator**.

2. Create a new folder in the root of your C: drive named **test**, and share it by following these steps:

   a. Click **Start**, point to **Administrative Tools**, and click **Computer Management**.

   b. In the left pane, click **Shared Folders**. In the right pane, right-click **Shares**, and click **New Share**.

   c. In the Share a Folder Wizard dialog box, click **Next**.

   d. In the Folder path text box, type **c:\test**, click **Next**, and click **Yes** to create the specified path.

   e. Click **Next** to accept the default share name of test.

   f. Click **Administrators have full access; other users have read-only access**, and click **Finish**.

   g. Click **Close**.

   h. Close the Computer Management window.

3. Click **Start**, click **Run**, type **mmc**, and then press **Enter**.

4. Click **File**, click **Add/Remove Snap-in**, click **Add**, scroll through the list and double-click **IP Security Monitor**, click **Close**, and then click **OK**.

5. Double-click **IP Security Monitor**.

6. Double-click your server.

7. Click **Active Policy**. Notice the information displayed in the right pane.

8. Double-click **Main Mode** and click **Security Associations**. At the moment, it shows that there are no items to display in this view.

10

9. Next, you and your partner establish a secure connection between your computers. You can view the status of security associations on your computer during the connection. These steps can be performed by both partners at the same time.

   a. Click **Start**, click **Run**, type **\\Student*xx*\test**, where *xx* is your partner's student number, and then press **Enter**.

   b. A window should open showing the test share on your partner's computer. If the policies have been applied properly on each server, a secure connection should be established.

10. In the IP Security Monitor window, click **Action**, and click **Refresh**. Note the details of the security association that has now been established between the two servers.

11. Close all open windows. If asked to save console settings, click **No**.

CREATING YOUR OWN IPSEC POLICY

In many circumstances, the three default IPSec policies are sufficient for your needs. However, you can create your own IPSec policies that are tailored to your environment. For example, the default policies encrypt all IP communication between two hosts. You may only want to encrypt the traffic for one application that handles confidential information.

Each IPSec policy is composed of **IPSec rules**, as shown in Figure 10-6. An IPSec rule controls how IPSec is implemented and each rule is composed of:

- An IP filter list
- An IPSec filter action
- Authentication methods
- A tunnel endpoint
- A connection type

An **IP filter list** is a list of protocols that will be affected by the rule. An **IPSec filter action** is what will be done to the protocols defined in the filter list. Authentication methods are the protocols that can be used for authentication if IPSec is performed based on a rule. The **tunnel endpoint** is the remote host IPSec is being performed with when tunnel mode is used. The connection type defines the type of connections to which this rule applies.

IP filter lists and IPSec filter actions are maintained in a central list by Windows Server 2003. This means that any IP filter list or IPSec filter action created can be reused by other rules within a policy or other policies. IP filter lists and IPSec filter actions can be added to this central list when using the Local Security Policy snap-in to create and edit policies, or by right-clicking IP Security Policies on Local Computer and clicking Manage IP filter lists and filter actions, as shown in Figure 10-7.

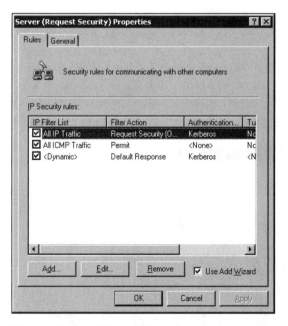

Figure 10-6   IPSec policy rules

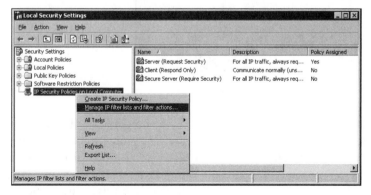

Figure 10-7   Local Security Policy snap-in

To create a new IPSec policy, you use the IP Security Policy Wizard. This wizard helps you create an IPSec policy, but cannot completely define it for you. It asks you for a name, description, whether to activate the default response rule, and authentication type.

The name and description for the policy are shown in IP Security Policies on Local Computer when you are assigning IPSec policies. These should be descriptive so they can be easily picked from the list.

You are given the choice of activating the default response rule, as shown in Figure 10-8. The default response rule specifies that on any port, the local computer will attempt to negotiate an SA if requested. The default response rule is only used if no other IPSec rules apply. For example, an IPSec policy may have one rule that requires security for a Web application on port 80 and the default response rule. The default response rule is used for all incoming packets not addressed to port 80. If the default response rule is not activated and a rule is not defined for a particular port, traffic addressed to that port cannot use IPSec.

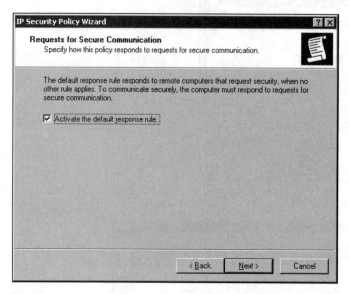

Figure 10-8   Activating the default response rule

If the default response rule is activated, there are three choices for authentication, as shown in Figure 10-9. The Active Directory default (Kerberos V5 protocol) option is generally used for internal client computers and servers. The Use a certificate from this certification authority (CA) option is generally used to support external clients or in an environment in which Certificate Services are already configured. The Use this string to protect the key exchange (preshared key) option requires both devices in an IPSec communication to be configured with the same key.

Activity 10-3: Creating an IPSec Policy

Time Required: 5 minutes

Objective: Create a new IPSec policy that is more flexible than the default policies.

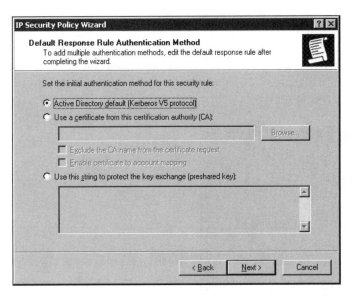

Figure 10-9   Authentication options for the default response rule

Description: All of the faculties have agreed that they will upload final marks for the students using FTP. FTP was chosen because all of the client operating systems throughout Arctic University support it. However, you are concerned that this confidential information may be viewed by unauthorized people using packet sniffers on the network. To secure this traffic, you implement IPSec because FTP has no built-in security.

1. If necessary, start your server and log on as **Administrator**.

2. Click **Start**, point to **Administrative Tools**, and click **Local Security Policy**.

3. Right-click **IP Security Policies on Local Computer**, and click **Create IP Security Policy**.

4. Click **Next** to start the IP Security Policy Wizard.

5. In the Name text box, type **FTP Traffic Policy**. In the description text box, type **Secure FTP Traffic**, and then click **Next**.

6. Confirm that the **Activate the default response rule** check box is selected, and click **Next**. If it is not selected, select it.

7. Confirm that **Active Directory default (Kerberos V5 protocol)** is selected, and then click **Next**. If it is not selected, select it.

8. Click **Edit properties** to deselect it, and click **Finish**. Note that the FTP Traffic Policy now appears in the right pane as an IP Security policy.

9. Close the Local Security Settings window.

10

Adding and Creating Rules

After an IPSec policy is created, you must edit it to add the rules that define how different types of IP traffic are handled. The only rule that can be created automatically is the default response rule, as shown in Figure 10-10. This is present if you choose to add it during the IPSec policy creation process.

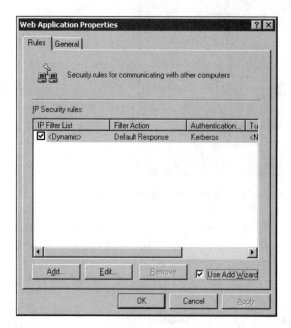

Figure 10-10   Properties of an IPSec policy

When you add a rule, the Create IP Security Rule Wizard is used by default. This wizard allows you to configure the most commonly used options. If you prefer not to use the wizard, deselect the Use Add Wizard check box before clicking the Add button.

The first screen in the Create IP Security Rule Wizard, shown in Figure 10-11, prompts you to choose tunnel mode or transport mode. If you choose the "This rule does not specify a tunnel" option, transport mode is used. If the "The tunnel endpoint is specified by the following IP address" option is chosen, tunnel mode is used between this computer and the IP address specified.

The second screen presented by the Create IP Security Rule Wizard concerns the network type, as shown in Figure 10-12. Here, you can choose whether this rule applies to All network connections, Local area network (LAN) connections, or Remote access connections. If Remote access is chosen, this applies to both dial-up and VPN connections.

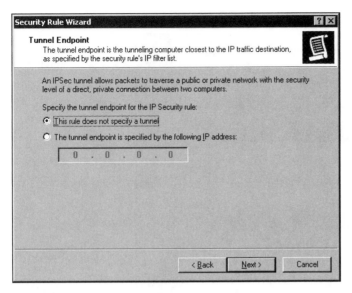

Figure 10-11   Tunnel endpoint for a new rule

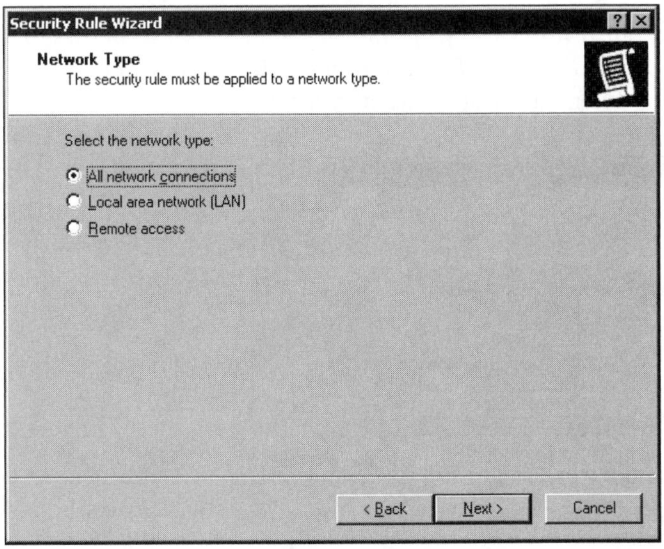

Figure 10-12   Network type for a new rule

Next, you are presented with the IP Filter List window, as shown in Figure 10-13. IP filters define packet types to which actions are applied. The two IP filter lists that exist by default are All IP Traffic and All ICMP Traffic. However, you can create new IP filter lists here that suit your needs. The All IP Traffic IP filter list is normally used to specify that all IP packets be encrypted. The All ICMP Traffic IP filter list is normally used to specify that all ICMP packets not be encrypted.

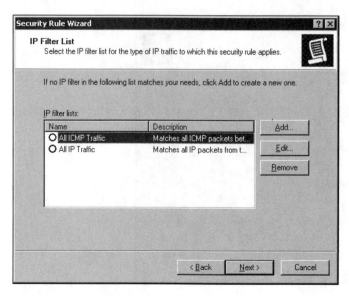

Figure 10-13   IP filter lists

After you have selected an IP filter list, you must select an action to be performed on the packets that match the IP filter list. The Filter Action window, shown in Figure 10-14, allows you to select an existing filter action or create new actions.

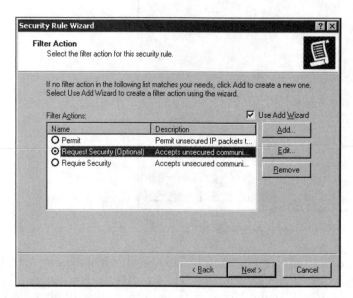

Figure 10-14   Filter actions

The three filter actions that exist by default are:

- *Permit*—Allows packets to pass through the IP filter unmodified

- *Request Security (Optional)*—Attempts to create IPSec connections with all other computers, but uses non-IPSec communication if an SA cannot be established

- *Require Security*—Accepts non-IPSec packets, but responds only using IPSec packets; if Require Security is chosen, this computer is only able to communicate with other computers using IPSec when packets match the IP filter

The Authentication Method window appears next. Here, you can choose to use Active Directory, certificates, or a preshared key for authentication.

Activity 10-4: Creating a New IPSec Filter Rule

Time Required: 10 minutes

Objective: Add a new IPSec filter rule that allows ICMP traffic to pass through unmodified.

10

Description: ICMP traffic is often used for network troubleshooting. As such, you want it to never be encrypted by IPSec. You create a new IPSec filter rule that ensures ICMP packets are not modified by IPSec even if the client computer requests it.

1. If necessary, start your server and log on as **Administrator**.

2. Click **Start**, point to **Administrative Tools**, and click **Local Security Policy**.

3. Click **IP Security Policies on Local Computer** to select it, if necessary. Right-click **IP Security Policies on Local Computer**, and then click **Add**.

4. Click **Next** to start the Create IP Security Rule Wizard.

5. Confirm that **This rule does not specify a tunnel** is selected, and click **Next**.

6. Confirm that **All network connections** is selected, and click **Next**.

7. On the IP Filter List page, click the **All ICMP Traffic** option button, and click **Next**.

8. On the Filter Action page, click the **Permit** option button, if necessary, and then click **Next**.

9. Click **Finish**.

10. Click **OK** to close the FTP Traffic Policy Properties dialog box.

11. Close the Local Security Settings window.

IPSec Filter Lists

The two default IPSec filter lists for all IP traffic and all ICMP traffic do not allow you very much control over which traffic uses IPSec and which does not. If multiple applications are running on a server, it may be unnecessary for all IP traffic to be encrypted. For instance, if a server is running file and print services as well as SQL Server, it may be necessary to protect the SQL Server traffic, but not the file and print services traffic. If this is the case, only network traffic on TCP port 1433 needs to be encrypted, and not all IP traffic.

NOTE Encrypting only the necessary packets reduces the load on the CPU. Performing encryption and decryption can create a significant load on a busy server.

When a new IP filter list is created, you give it a name and have the option of giving it a description. In addition, you must add IP filters that make up the list and specify the traffic to which this list applies. By default, when an IP filter is added, the IP Filter Wizard is used. If you prefer not to use the IP Filter Wizard, deselect the Use Add Wizard check box. Figure 10-15 shows the dialog box used for adding an IP filter list.

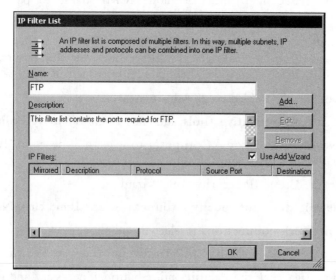

Figure 10-15   Creating an IP filter list

The IP Filter Wizard first requests a description for the new IP filter you are creating, as shown in Figure 10-16. In addition, this same screen has a Mirrored check box. This check box automatically applies this IP filter to the opposite source and selected destination ports specified in the IP filter. For example, if an IP filter is created for a source of any IP address, any port, and a destination of the local server and port 80, the mirrored option automatically applies this IP filter to the return traffic with a source IP address of the local server and port 80 to a destination of any IP address and any port.

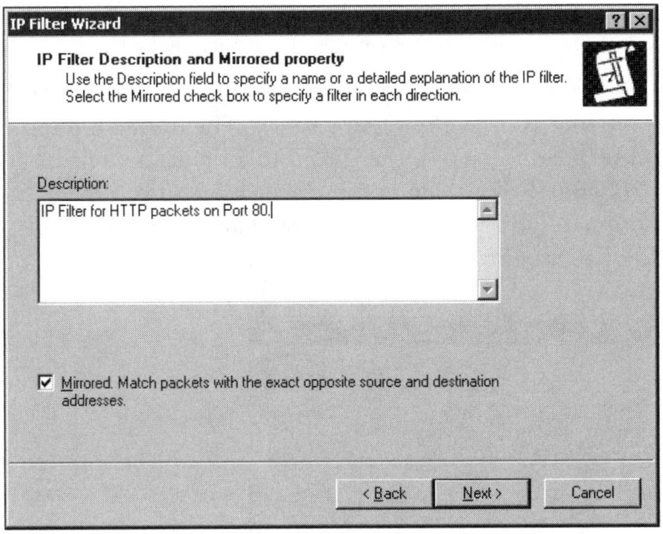

Figure 10-16   The mirrored option for a new IP filter

The second window of the IP Filter Wizard asks for the source IP address in the filter. As shown in Figure 10-17, this can be statically configured as: My IP Address, Any IP Address, A specific DNS Name, A specific IP Address, or A specific IP Subnet. In addition, there are dynamic source IP addresses that can be configured. These are based on the IP configuration of the computer using the filter and are DNS Servers, WINS Servers, DHCP Server, and Default Gateway.

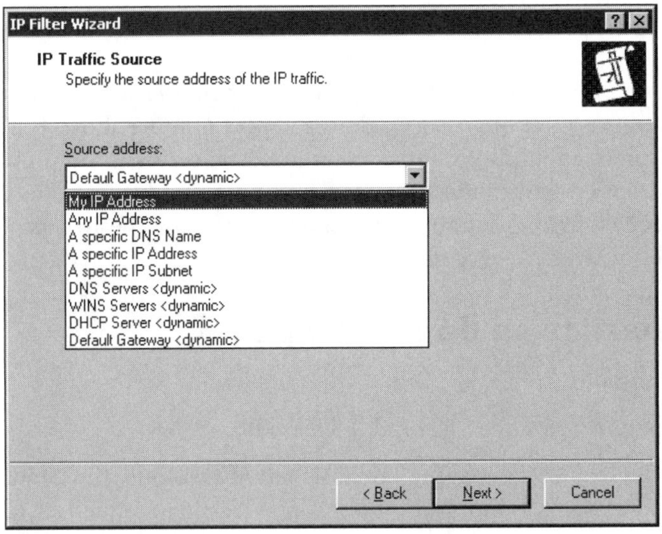

Figure 10-17   Source IP address for a new IP filter

10

The next window in the IP Filter Wizard asks for the destination IP address in the filter. This window provides the same choices as for the source IP address as in the filter.

Within IP packets, there is a field to describe the protocol type. You can set this as part of an IP filter in the next window, as shown in Figure 10-18. The most common IP protocol types used here are TCP, UDP, and ICMP. Other IP protocol types are relatively rare. If the packet type you want to define is not in the drop-down list, you can enter in a protocol number directly by choosing Other. An Internet standard list of protocol numbers is maintained by the IETF (Internet Engineering Task Force).

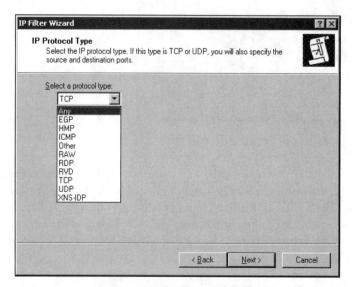

Figure 10-18   Protocol type for a new IP filter

If TCP or UDP is chosen for the packet type, you must define the source and destination port numbers. Most client applications use a randomized port number above 1023. To affect incoming traffic from client applications, filters configured on servers should use the From any port option. Most server applications use a defined port number. To affect incoming traffic to server applications, filters configured on servers should use the To this port option. Figure 10-19 shows the window where this is configured.

ACTIVITY

Activity 10-5: Creating an IPSec Filter List

Time Required: 15 minutes

Objective: Create a new IPSec filter list for all FTP traffic.

Description: The policy you created in the previous activity has only the default response rule enabled. This allows IPSec communication to happen if a client requests it, but does not force the client to use IPSec. You must create a new rule that encrypts all FTP traffic. The TCP port used for control messages is 21, and the TCP port used for data transfer is 20.

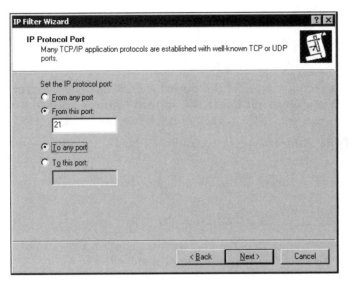

Figure 10-19   TCP or UDP port for a new IP filter

1. If necessary, start your server and log on as **Administrator**.

2. Click **Start**, point to **Administrative Tools**, and click **Local Security Policy**.

3. Right-click **IP Security Policies on Local Computer**, and click **Manage IP filter lists and filter actions**.

4. Click **Add** to create a new IP filter list.

5. In the Name text box, type **FTP**.

6. Click **Add** to create a new IP filter.

7. Click **Next** to start the IP Filter Wizard.

8. In the Description text box, type **FTP Data - TCP Port 20**, confirm that the **Mirrored. Match packets with the exact opposite source and destination addresses** check box is selected, and click **Next**. If it is not selected, select it.

9. Confirm that **My IP Address** is selected, and click **Next**. If it is not selected, select it.

10. Confirm that **Any IP Address** is selected, and click **Next**. If it is not selected, select it.

11. Click the drop-down arrow, click **TCP**, and click **Next**.

12. Click **From this port**, type **20** as the port number, confirm that **To any port** is selected, and click **Next**. If To any port is not selected, select it.

10

13. Click **Finish**.

14. Click **Add** to create a new IP filter.

15. Click **Next** to start the IP Filter Wizard.

16. In the Description text box, type **FTP Control - TCP Port 21**, confirm that the **Mirrored. Match packets with the exact opposite source and destination addresses** check box is selected, and click **Next**. If it is not selected, select it.

17. Confirm that **My IP Address** is selected, and click **Next**. If it is not selected, select it.

18. Confirm that **Any IP Address** is selected, and click **Next**. If it is not selected, select it.

19. Click the drop-down arrow, click **TCP**, and click **Next**.

20. Click **From this port**, type **21** as the port number, confirm that **To any port** is selected, and click **Next**. If To any port is not selected, select it.

21. Click **Finish**.

22. Click **OK** to close the IP Filter List dialog box.

23. Click **Close**.

24. Close the Local Security Settings window.

Filter Actions

Filter actions define what is done to traffic that matches an IP filter list. There are only three default filter actions available: Permit, Request Security (Optional), and Require Security. All the default filter actions define a number of security parameters, including the type of encryption that can be negotiated. In highly secure situations, you may want to modify these or create your own.

To create a new filter action, you can use the IP Security Filter Action Wizard. This is invoked by default when you choose to add a new filter action. To avoid using the wizard, deselect the Use Add Wizard check box, as shown in Figure 10-20.

The first window of the IP Security Filter Action Wizard requests a name and description for the new filter action. The second window, shown in Figure 10-21, asks for an action behavior. Selecting the Permit option allows the traffic to move without being affected by IPSec. The Block option discards traffic that matches the IP filter list. The Negotiate security option lets you define which encryption options are used.

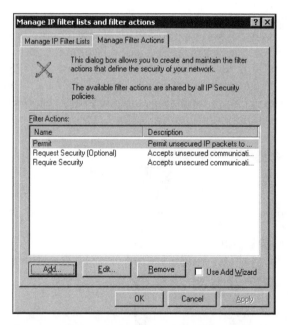

Figure 10-20   Creating an IPSec filter action

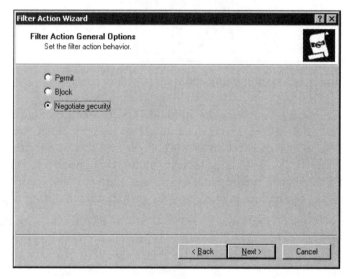

Figure 10-21   Action behavior for a new filter action

In the next window, shown in Figure 10-22, you are asked whether to allow unencrypted communication with computers that do not support IPSec. If you choose the "Do not communicate with computers that do not support IPSec" option, computers using this filter action cannot communicate with Windows clients that do not have an IPSec policy assigned. This is appropriate in high-security situations. If you choose the "Fall back to unsecured communication" option, communication is possible with any client, regardless of whether an IPSec policy is assigned. This is not appropriate for high-security environments.

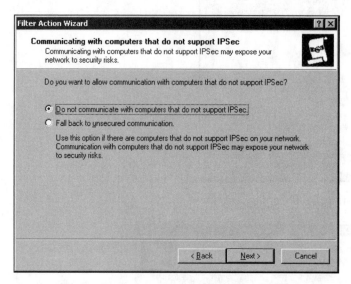

Figure 10-22   Allow unencrypted communication

Each filter action requires at least one security method. The security method defines the algorithms used for encryption and authentication, as well as whether IPSec modes AH or ESP are used. The IP Security Filter Action Wizard allows you to add only one security method, as shown in Figure 10-23. Additional security methods can be added by editing the filter action after creation. Security methods are prioritized with the first security method listed in a filter action being the highest priority and the first attempted during negotiation.

The Integrity and encryption option specifies using IPSec in ESP mode with the SHA1 algorithm for data integrity and the 3DES algorithm for data encryption. The Integrity only option specifies using IPSec in ESP mode with the SHA1 algorithm for data integrity, but no encryption is performed. Performing only data integrity is useful when you want to be certain the data has not been modified in transit, you are not concerned about data confidentiality, and want to conserve processing power by avoiding the CPU time required by encrypting the data portion of the packet.

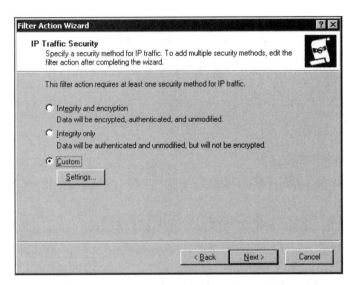

Figure 10-23   Security method for a new filter action

You can also specify custom settings for the security method, as shown in Figure 10-24. In this window, you can specify that IPSec modes AH and ESP are used. ESP mode ensures integrity and performs encryption on the data portion of the packet. AH mode ensures integrity of the data portion of the packets as well as the IP headers in the packet.

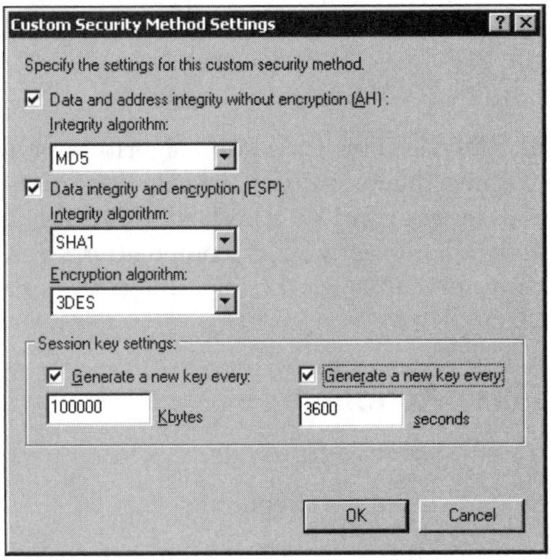

Figure 10-24   Custom security method settings

The custom settings for a security method also allow you to define how often the key used for encryption and integrity is changed. You can define that the key is changed based on the amount of data transmitted, time passed, or both. If you do not define this setting, the default values of 100 MB (100000 KB) and 1 hour (3600 seconds) are used. The first parameter reached triggers a key change. For example, if an IPSec communication sends 100 MB of data in 20 minutes, a key change is triggered. Likewise, if less than 100 MB of data is transmitted in an IPSec communication, a key change is triggered after one hour.

Cryptography Algorithms

IPSec offers both data integrity and encryption. Each type of cryptography uses different algorithms.

The two algorithms that can be used for AH and ESP data integrity are as follows:

- *Secure Hash Algorithm (SHA1)*—A widely used hashing algorithm that produces a 160-bit message digest. Federal Information Processing Standards (FIPS) specifies the **Secure Hash Algorithm (SHA1)** for use in U.S. federal government contracts.

- *Message Digest 5 (MD5)*—The most commonly used hashing algorithm for commercial applications. **Message Digest 5 (MD5)** produces a 128-bit message digest. It is less secure than SHA1, but it is faster.

The two algorithms that can be used for ESP data encryption are as follows:

- *Data encryption standard (DES)*—This is a common encryption algorithm that uses a 56-bit key. **Data encryption standard (DES)**was first designated for U.S. federal government use in 1977. Because of enhancements in computational power, it is now recommended that 3DES be used instead.

- *Triple data encryption standard (3DES)*—This encryption algorithm performs three rounds of encryption using three different 56-bit keys giving an effective key length of 168 bits. **Triple data encryption standard (3DES)**is significantly stronger than DES and requires significantly more computational power to use. Windows 2000 computers must have installed the High Encryption Pack or have Service Pack 2 to use 3DES.

ACTIVITY

Activity 10-6: Creating a Filter Action

Time Required: 10 minutes

Objective: Create a new filter action that enforces encryption.

Description: You must define a filter action needs to be defined to describe what will be done when the security matches the filter list for FTP packets. The university policy dictates that secure transmissions use SHA1 for data integrity and 3DES for data encryption.

1. If necessary, start your server and log on as **Administrator**.

2. Click **Start**, point to **Administrative Tools**, and click **Local Security Policy**.

3. Right-click **IP Security Policies on Local Computer**, and click **Manage IP filter lists and filter actions**.

4. Click the **Manage Filter Actions** tab, and click **Add**.

5. Click **Next** to start the IP Security Filter Action Wizard.

6. In the Name text box, type **FTP Packet Filter Action**, and click **Next**.

7. Confirm that **Negotiate security** is selected, and click **Next**. If it is not selected, select it.

8. Confirm that **Do not communicate with computers that do not support IPSec is selected**, and click **Next**. If it is not selected, select it.

9. Click **Custom** and click **Settings**.

10. Verify that **Data integrity and encryption (ESP)** is selected. Also verify that the integrity algorithm is set to **SHA1** and that the encryption algorithm is set to **3DES**. If these are not correct, then change them. Click **OK** to close the Custom Security Method Settings dialog box.

11. When the IP Security Policy Management message box appears, indicating that the settings you have selected correspond to an encryption and integrity security level and that your security method's type will be changed to reflect this state, click **OK**.

12. Click **Next** and click **Finish**.

13. Click **Close**.

14. Close the Local Security Settings window.

Activity 10-7: Adding a Customized Filter List and Filter Action

Time Required: 10 minutes

Objective: Edit your FTP filter and add a rule using the customized filter list and filter action you have created.

Description: The filter list and action you have created are not yet part of a policy. You must edit your FTP policy and add a new rule using the FTP filter list and filter action you created. Finally, to use the policy, you must assign it.

1. If necessary, start your server and log on as **Administrator**.

2. Click **Start**, point to **Administrative Tools**, and click **Local Security Policy**.

3. Right-click **FTP Traffic Policy** and click **Properties**.

4. Click **Add**.

5. Click **Next** to start the Create IP Security Rule Wizard.

6. Confirm that **This rule does not specify a tunnel** is selected, and click **Next**. If it is not selected, select it.

7. Confirm that **All network connections** is selected, and click **Next**. If it is not selected, select it.

8. Click the **FTP** option button to select it, and click **Next**.

9. Click the **FTP Packet Filter Action** option button to select it, and click **Next**.

10. Confirm that **Active Directory default (Kerberos V5 protocol)** is selected, and click **Next**. If it is not selected, select it.

11. Click **Finish**.

12. Click **OK**.

13. Right-click the **FTP Traffic Policy**, and click **Assign**.

14. Close the Local Security Settings window.

TROUBLESHOOTING IPSEC

IPSec troubleshooting can cover a wide range of possibilities dealing with general network issues, IPSec-specific configuration settings, and group policy settings.

NOTE

Remember that both participants in an SA must be configured to use the same modes, encryption algorithms, and authentication method.

The most common IPSec troubleshooting tools and utilities are:

- Ping
- IPSec Security Monitor
- Event Viewer
- Resultant Set of Policy
- Netsh
- Oakley logs
- Network Monitor

Ping

The ping utility is used to test network connectivity between two hosts. The default IPSec policies permit ICMP packets and do not interfere with the operation of ping. This utility does not test IPSec specifically, but it can be used to confirm that the two hosts can communicate. If they cannot communicate, they are not able to create an IPSec SA.

IPSec Security Monitor

IPSec Security Monitor is an MMC snap-in that allows you to view the status of IPSec SAs. IPSec Security Monitor can be used to confirm that an SA was negotiated between two hosts. In addition, IPSec Security Monitor can be used to view the configuration of the IPSec policy that is applied.

Event Viewer

Event Viewer can be used to view the events that the IPSec Policy Agent writes to the event log. These show the configuration settings that IPSec is using as well as events generated during the creation of SAs. These events are only written to the log if the Audit logon events option has been enabled in the local security policy or Group Policy.

Additional information from the IPSec Policy Agent can be written to the system log. To enable this logging, you must modify the registry. Set the key HKEY_LOCAL_MACHINE\ SYSTEM\CurrentControlSet\Services\IPSec\EnableDiagnostics to a value of 7.

10

Resultant Set of Policy Snap-in

Applying Group Policies can be quite complex. If you are attempting to distribute and apply IPSec policies through Group Policy, and they are not functioning as you expect, you can use the **Resultant Set of Policy (RSoP) snap-in**. The RSoP snap-in allows you to view which policies apply and to simulate the application of new policies to test their results.

Netsh

The Netsh utility allows you to configure a number of network-related settings. This is useful when batch scripts are used to remotely make changes on clients and servers. Configuration categories include bridging, DHCP, diagnostics, IP configuration, remote access, routing, WINS, and remote procedure calls.

IPSec configuration can also be modified using Netsh. Some of the IPSec management tasks that can be performed with Netsh include:

- Viewing policies
- Adding policies
- Deleting policies

Oakley Logs

Oakley logs track the establishment of SAs. This logging is not enabled by default and must be enabled with the command "netsh ipsec dynamic set config ike logging 1". The log file created is C:\WINDOWS\Debug\Oakley.log.

Network Monitor

Network Monitor can be used to view packets that are traveling on the network and to identify IPSec traffic. However, it cannot view encrypted information inside of an IPSec packet.

Network Monitor is useful for determining whether packets are being properly transmitted between computers, but Network Monitor is not useful for troubleshooting application-level problems if the traffic is encrypted. For application troubleshooting purposes, you may need to disable IPSec or encryption within IPSec.

ACTIVITY

Activity 10-8: Disabling IPSec

Time Required: 5 minutes

Objective: Disable IPSec policies that have been applied.

Description: In this activity, you unassign all IPSec policies so that they do not interfere with activities later in the course.

1. If necessary, start your server and log on as **Administrator**.

2. Click **Start**, point to **Administrative Tools**, and click **Local Security Policy**.

3. Right-click **FTP Traffic Policy** and click **Un-assign**.

4. Close the Local Security Settings window.

5. Click **Start**, point to **Administrative Tools**, and click **Services**.

6. Scroll through the list of services until you see IPSEC Services. Right-click **IPSEC Services**, and click **Restart**.

7. Close the Services window.

CHAPTER SUMMARY

□ IPv4 has no built-in security mechanisms and uses IPSec as an add-on protocol to make communication secure from packet sniffing, data replay, data modification, and address spoofing.

□ IPSec operates at the network layer and can be used by any IP application without the application being modified.

□ Pre-Windows 2000 operating systems do not support IPSec.

❏ IPSec cannot be used with NAT.

❏ IPSec AH mode does not perform data encryption, but can authenticate and guarantee data integrity for an entire IP packet, including the IP headers.

❏ IPSec ESP mode has the ability to perform data encryption, authentication, and guarantees data integrity for the data portion of the packet, but not the IP headers.

❏ Transport mode is used between two hosts. Tunnel mode is used between two routers.

❏ The Windows Server 2003 implementation can perform authentication using a preshared key, certificates, or Kerberos. IKE is used to negotiate the security association.

❏ IPSec policies contain rules that control authentication, which traffic is affected, what is done to the affected traffic, the type of connections affected, and whether this computer is a tunnel endpoint.

❏ Filter lists are used in IPSec rules to define the packets affected by a rule. Filter actions are used to define what is done to the traffic that matches the filter list.

❏ The two algorithms used for data integrity are SHA1 and MD5.

❏ The two algorithms used for data encryption are DES and 3DES.

❏ Tools that can be used to troubleshoot IPSec include ping, IPSec Security Monitor snap-in, Event Viewer, Resultant Set of Policy snap-in, Netsh, Oakley logs, and Network Monitor.

10

KEY TERMS

address spoofing — The act of falsifying the source IP address in an IP packet, usually for malicious purposes.

Authentication Headers (AH) mode — The IPSec mode that performs authentication and ensures data integrity on the entire IP packet, including the headers.

data encryption standard (DES) — An algorithm for data encryption defined by the U.S. government in 1977 that uses a 56-bit key.

data modification — The process of modifying the contents of packets that have been captured with a packet sniffer before resending them on the network.

data replay — The process of resending packets that have been previously captured with a packet sniffer.

Encapsulating Security Payload (ESP) mode — The IPSec mode that performs authentication, data integrity, and encryption on the data portion of an IP packet. Integrity of IP headers is not performed.

Internet Key Exchange (IKE) — A protocol used by IPSec to negotiate security parameters, perform authentication, and ensure the secure exchange of encryption keys.

IP filter list — A list of IP protocols that are affected by a rule in an IPSec policy.

IPSec (IP Security) — A protocol that adds security functions to IPv4.

IPSec filter action — The setting that defines what is done to traffic that matches an IP filter list in an IPSec rule.

IPSec policies — The sets of rules that define how packets are treated by IPSec. An IPSec policy must be applied to be in use.

IPSec rules — The combination of an IP filter list and an IPSec filter action.

IPSec Security Monitor — An MMC snap-in that allows the monitoring of IPSec security associations and configurations.

Kerberos — The preferred authentication method used by Active Directory. It is the simplest authentication method to implement for IPSec if all devices are part of the same Active Directory forest.

Message Digest 5 (MD5) — A hashing algorithm that produces a 128-bit message digest.

packet sniffer — The software used to view (capture) all packets that are traveling on a network.

preshared key — An IPSec authentication method in which each device is preconfigured with a string of text.

Resultant Set of Policy (RSoP) snap-in — An MMC snap-in that is used to troubleshoot the implementation of Group Policies.

Secure Hash Algorithm (SHA1) — A hashing algorithm that produces a 160-bit message digest.

security association (SA) — The security terms negotiated between two hosts using IPSec.

transport mode — The IPSec mode used when two hosts create a security association directly between them.

triple data encryption standard (3DES) — A data encryption algorithm that uses three 56-bit keys in three rounds to give an effective key length of 168 bits.

tunnel endpoint — The other end of the tunnel with the local host (in tunnel mode).

tunnel mode — The IPSec mode used when two routers encapsulate all traffic transferred between two or more networks.

REVIEW QUESTIONS

1. Applications must be written in a specific way to take advantage of IPSec. True or False?

2. Which operating systems do not support IPSec? (Choose all that apply.)

   a. Windows 95

   b. Windows 98

   c. Windows NT

   d. Windows 2000 Professional

   e. Windows XP Professional

3. Which of the following statements about IPSec is false?

   a. IPSec adds complexity to the network.

   b. IPSec is a standards track protocol.

   c. IPSec can be routed through NAT.

   d. IPSec requires additional processing power.

4. IPSec between two hosts is called _____ mode.

   a. tunnel

   b. transport

   c. encrypted

   d. VPN

5. You want to implement IPSec to authenticate two computers and encrypt data. Which mode do you select?

   a. AH

   b. ESP

   c. tunnel

   d. transport

6. Which of the following is not encrypted with the default IPSec policy? (Choose all that apply.)

   a. FTP

   b. HTTP

   c. ping

   d. tracert

   e. SMTP

7. After an IPSec policy has been defined, it takes effect immediately. True or False?

8. Which of the following is not an authentication option when creating an IPSec policy?

   a. password

   b. Kerberos

   c. certificate

   d. preshared key

10

9. Which of the following cryptography algorithms is used for U.S. government contracts and generates a 160-bit hash?

    a. MD5

    b. SHA1

    c. DES

    d. 3DES

10. Which of following cryptography algorithms uses three different 56-bit keys for encryption?

    a. MD5

    b. SHA1

    c. DES

    d. 3DES

11. In tunnel mode, which traffic is encrypted?

    a. all workstation-to-router traffic

    b. all workstation-to-workstation traffic

    c. only router-to-router traffic

    d. all traffic

    e. none of the above

12. The default IPSec policies are configured to use which of the following authentication methods?

    a. Kerberos

    b. preshared key

    c. certificates

    d. access token

13. You want to enable IPSec encryption on a Windows Server 2003 server and still allow communication with Windows 98 workstations. Which filter action(s) would you implement?

    a. Permit

    b. Request Security (Optional)

    c. Require Security

    d. all of the above

14. Which of the following cryptography algorithms are used for ESP data encryption? (Choose all that apply.)

    a. SHA1

    b. MD5

    c. DES

    d. 3DES

15. Which troubleshooting utility allows you to simulate the application of new IPSec policies?

    a. IPSec Monitor

    b. Resultant Set of Policy

    c. Network Monitor

    d. Oakley logs

    e. Netsh

16. AH mode performs which of the following functions? (Choose all that apply.)

    a. authenticates two endpoints

    b. generates a checksum to verify a packet was not modified in transit

    c. encrypts data

    d. authenticates applications

10

17. Which of the following situations can use Kerberos for authentication in IPSec? (Choose all that apply.)

    a. any two routers on the Internet

    b. any two workstations in the same Active Directory domain

    c. any two workstations in the same Active Directory forest

    d. any two workstations on the same subnet

18. What is the maximum number of IPSec policies that can be assigned to a workstation at one time?

    a. one

    b. two

    c. five

    d. ten

    e. unlimited

19. A combination of characters entered at both endpoints of an IPSec connection is called a _____ .

    a. password

    b. certificate

    c. preshared key

    d. shared secret

20. By default, Oakley logs are stored in which folder?

    a. \WINDOWS\OAKLEY

    b. \WINDOWS\LOGS

    c. \WINDOWS\SYSTEM32\OAKLEY

    d. \WINDOWS\DEBUG

CASE PROJECTS

Case Project 10-1: Selecting an IPSec Policy

Because of security concerns, an IPSec security policy is being evaluated for the university. The board of directors wants all communication between staff workstations and all servers encrypted. They also want to encrypt all communication between students' computers and the servers. Student computers run various operating systems, including Windows 95, UNIX, Linux, Windows 2000, and Windows XP.

How would you implement IPSec to encrypt as much TCP/IP traffic as possible with minimum overhead?

Case Project 10-2: Encrypting Remote Traffic

Arctic University has three satellite campuses set up in various remote locations. Students can take courses and connect to the university's servers from the remote locations. Each remote campus connects to the main campus using a Cisco router. Your manager wants to encrypt all traffic from the remote sites through the Internet to the main campus. He has recommended implementing IPSec in transport mode using third-party certificates. What are your concerns?

Case Project 10-3: Evaluating IPSec

A junior administrator has commented that implementing IPSec is a waste of time. He used Network Monitor to capture ICMP packets between two systems and was able to view the packet details. He also doesn't believe that IPSec can protect the university computers from hackers. What do you tell him?

Case Project 10-4: IPSec Filters, Rules, and Actions

Your supervisor originally proposed that all traffic possible on your network be encrypted using IPSec. However, after you explain that this could significantly slow down your servers, he decides this is not a good idea. After further discussions, you both decide that it is only necessary to encrypt the network traffic generated by the accounting application.

The client software for the accounting application is installed on the user workstations. The source TCP port number is a randomly generated number above 1023. The SQL server that it connects to for data storage runs on TCP port 1433.

How should IPSec filters, rules, and actions be configured to encrypt only network traffic generated by this application?

10

11

PLANNING NETWORK ACCESS

After reading this chapter, you will be able to:

♦ Describe the purpose and features of Windows Server 2003 remote access methods

♦ Configure a remote access server (RAS)

♦ Allow remote clients access to network resources

♦ Create and configure remote access policies

♦ Understand and describe the purpose of the RADIUS protocol

♦ Troubleshoot remote access

Remote access, used to provide users outside of an office access to resources on the internal network, is a vital component to many networks today. Without remote access, frequent business travelers, such as salespeople, would not have the use of the basic resources necessary to complete their jobs.

In this chapter, you learn about the remote access capabilities of Windows Server 2003. Specifically, you learn how to create and configure dial-up and VPN connections, how to grant users access to network resources, how to create remote access policies, and how to configure RADIUS servers and relay agents. Finally, you learn how to troubleshoot remote access.

INTRODUCING REMOTE ACCESS METHODS

Remote access allows remote and **mobile users** access to network resources on the internal network, including files, printers, databases, and e-mail, among others, from outside the internal network. Traveling salespeople, for instance, often need network access from hotel rooms and client sites to make orders and retrieve updated price lists, and executives often need to access their e-mail from hotels and conferences when they are on the road. Network administrators also need remote access to network resources, as they can save hours of valuable time if they can repair after-hours network problems remotely from home. Windows Server 2003 has the ability to be a remote access server (RAS).

The two types of remote access—dial-up and VPN—are discussed in the following sections.

Dial-up Remote Access

Remote access using dial-up connections over phone lines is the oldest type of remote access. In the past, this type of connection was very slow, and transferring even the smallest files was a tedious process. However, with advances in **modems**, the devices that let computers communicate across phone lines, current speeds are more reasonable when transferring documents less than 1 MB in size.

A **dial-up** connection allows two computers to connect and transfer information using modems and a phone line. The modems convert the digital signals of the computer to analog signals that can be transmitted across the phone line. Both the dial-up server and dial-up client must have a modem. When the analog signals reach the computers on each end of the phone line, the modems then convert the signals back to digital format, which can then be interpreted by the computers.

When a connection is created between a dial-up server and a dial-up client, the client can access resources on the network on which the dial-up server is located. From the perspective of the user, the modem acts like a network card to provide access to network resources. Files can be downloaded, and e-mail can be read.

Current modems can download information at 56 Kbps when using modems that are based on the **v.90** or **v.92** standards from the ITU-T. These standards are asymmetrical standards that allow faster download speeds than upload speeds. The v.90 standard allows uploads at 33.6 Kbps, and the v.92 standard allows uploads at 48 Kbps.

Line noise in the phone system can limit connection speeds. Line noise can be introduced by low-quality phones connected to the circuit, poor-quality lines from the phone system provider, or electrical interference. The existence of line noise can likely cause modem connections to be limited to 50 Kbps or less.

The main benefit of dial-up connections is availability. Roaming users almost always have access to a phone line. Most hotels include a data port for dial-up connectivity as a standard feature in rooms.

The main drawback of dial-up connections is their speed. When compared with connectivity options, such as cable modems and DSL modems, a dial-up connection is very slow. In addition, maintenance of a modem pool at the office for dial-up users can be expensive and time-consuming as new standards are introduced and modems need to be replaced. A **modem pool** is a group of modems maintained to allow remote access.

Enabling and Configuring a Dial-up Server

Windows Server 2003 uses **Routing and Remote Access Service (RRAS)** to act as a dial-up server. This service is always installed, but is not configured by default. Using the Routing and Remote Access Setup Wizard, you can configure RRAS as a dial-up server, a VPN server, or a router.

For your server to act as a dial-up server, it must have a modem installed. Modems are installed using Phone and Modem Options in Control Panel. The first time you open Phone and Modem Options, you are forced to configure a location, as shown in Figure 11-1.

Figure 11-1   Configuring a location

Locations are used to control how Windows Server 2003 creates dial-up connections. For instance, locations allow you to specify whether any special codes need to be dialed from this location. This is useful if the internal phone system in a company requires you to dial "9" to get an outside line.

After a location has been configured, the Phone and Modem Options dialog box appears. To add a modem to your server, click the Modems tab, and click Add. This starts the Add Hardware Wizard, as shown in Figure 11-2. By default, Windows Server 2003 attempts to find the modem through plug and play. However, if the modem is not a plug and play device, or has known plug and play detection problems, you can instead choose to select your modem from a list of known vendors. This can also be used in a test environment when a physical modem is not present, but a modem driver must be configured for other software to be installed or configured.

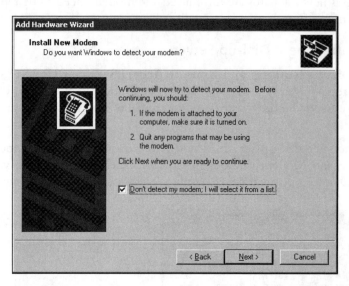

Figure 11-2   Add Hardware Wizard

If plug and play is unable to find a modem, or you have chosen to add your modem manually, then you are prompted to choose a driver from a list, as shown in Figure 11-3. Windows Server 2003 ships with several standard modem drivers, but you can also use drivers from a vendor by clicking the Have Disk button and browsing to the location of the driver.

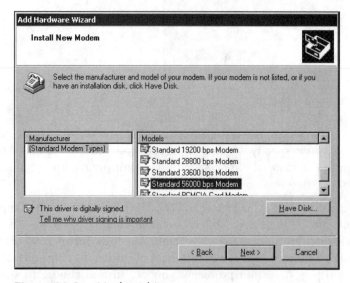

Figure 11-3   Modem drivers

After choosing a driver, you must choose the COM port to which the driver is connected, as shown in Figure 11-4. A **COM port** is a serial port. External modems normally use either COM1 or COM2, as they represent internal serial ports that are built into the computers. Internal modems normally use a COM port numbered from COM3 to COM8 that is chosen by plug and play.

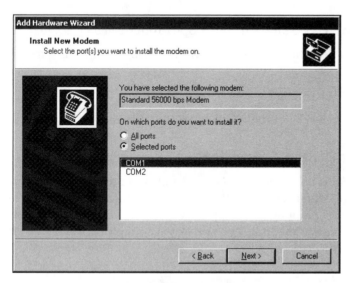

Figure 11-4 Selecting a COM port

Activity 11-1: Installing a Modem

Time Required: 5 minutes

Objective: Install a modem on your server.

Description: You want to configure Windows Server 2003 as a dial-up server. Before configuring RRAS, you must install a modem.

1. If necessary, start your server and log on as **Administrator** of the Arctic.local domain.

2. Click **Start**, point to **Control Panel**, and click **Phone and Modem Options**.

3. In the What area code (or city code) are you in now? text box, type **555**, and click **OK**.

4. Click the **Modems** tab.

5. Click **Add**.

6. Check the **Don't detect my modem; I will select it from a list** check box to select this option. You are selecting this option because your server does not have a modem physically installed. You are installing the software manually to simulate a modem being installed. If a modem were physically installed in this server, then you would allow the wizard to detect the modem.

7. Click **Next**.

8. In the Models box, click **Standard 56000 bps Modem**, and click **Next**.

9. Click **COM1** to select this as the serial port on which the modem is installed, and click **Next**.

10. Click **Finish** to close the Add Hardware Wizard.

11. Click **OK** to close the Phone and Modem Options dialog box.

Enabling RRAS for Dial-up Connections

Management of RRAS is done with the Routing and Remote Access snap-in available in the Administrative Tools menu. When the Routing and Remote Access snap-in is started for the first time, a red arrow pointing down appears beside the name of your server, as shown in Figure 11-5. This indicates that RRAS is not started. In this case, it is because RRAS has not yet been configured.

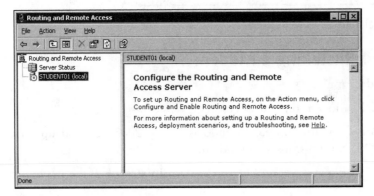

Figure 11-5 RRAS is not configured

The Routing and Remote Access Wizard is used to enable and configure RRAS for the first time. After you have completed the wizard and RRAS is started, the arrow beside your server in the Routing and Remote Access snap-in points up and is green, as shown in Figure 11-6.

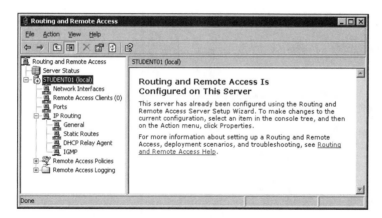

Figure 11-6   RRAS is configured and functional

Activity 11-2: Enabling RRAS as a Dial-up Server

Time Required: 10 minutes

Objective: Configure RRAS on your server to act as a RAS.

Description: Arctic University needs to provide professors with access to the network file system when they are away on conferences. Most professors need to access the RAS using a laptop computer and hotel phone line. To support this, you configure your server as a dial-up server.

1. If necessary, start your server and log on as **Administrator**.

2. Click **Start**, point to **Administrative Tools**, and click **Routing and Remote Access**. Notice that your server has a red arrow pointing down beside it to indicate that RRAS is not functional.

3. Right-click your server and click **Configure and Enable Routing and Remote Access**.

4. Click **Next** to begin the Routing and Remote Access Server Setup Wizard.

5. Confirm that the **Remote access (dial-up or VPN)** option button is selected, as shown in Figure 11-7, and click **Next**.

6. Check the **Dial-up** check box to allow this server to be a dial-up server, as shown in Figure 11-8, and then click **Next**.

11

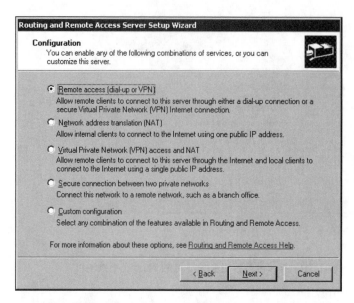

Figure 11-7   Choosing an RRAS configuration

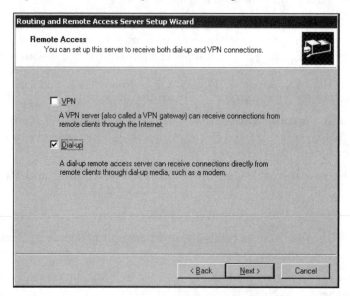

Figure 11-8   Choosing Dial-up as a RAS type

7. If necessary, click **Classroom** in the Network Interfaces box to select it, as shown in Figure 11-9, and click **Next**. This indicates that dial-up clients receive IP addresses on the classroom network.

8. Confirm that **Automatically** is selected as the method of IP address assignment, as shown in Figure 11-10, and click **Next**.

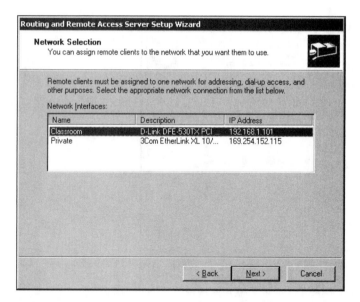

Figure 11-9 Choosing an interface for dial-up clients

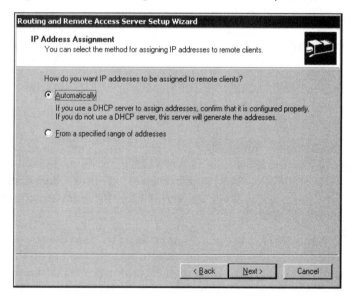

Figure 11-10 Choosing how IP addresses are assigned to dial-up clients

9. Confirm that **No, use Routing and Remote Access to authenticate connection requests** is selected, as shown in Figure 11-11, and click **Next**.

10. Click **Finish** to complete the Routing and Remote Access Server Setup Wizard.

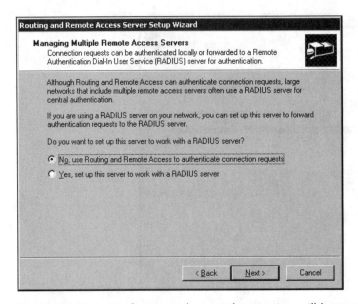

Figure 11-11   Configuring where authentication will happen

11. Click **OK** to close the warning dialog box about DHCP relay. Notice that the arrow next to your server is now green and pointing up to indicate that RRAS is configured and started.

12. Close the Routing and Remote Access snap-in.

Dial-up Protocols

LAN protocols and remote access protocols need to be considered when configuring Windows Server 2003 for dial-up networking. **LAN protocols** supported by RRAS for dial-up networking are TCP/IP, IPX/SPX, and AppleTalk. **Remote access protocols** supported by RRAS for dial-up networking are **Serial Line Internet Protocol (SLIP)** and **Point-to-Point Protocol (PPP)**.

When a dial-up client is connected to the dial-up server, it has access to the resources on the LAN. The same protocols required by client computers to access resources on the LAN are required by dial-up clients to access resources on the LAN through the dial-up server. Most dial-up clients use TCP/IP, but support for IPX/SPX is included to support older applications, and support for AppleTalk is included to support Macintosh clients. These LAN protocols can also be used for VPN connections.

Remote access protocols are used only for dial-up connections, not VPN connections. SLIP is an older, and rarely used, remote access protocol supported only when Windows Server 2003 is acting as a dial-up client. SLIP cannot be used when Windows Server 2003 is a dial-up server. The only time SLIP is used is when dialing up to older UNIX RASs and TCP/IP is the only LAN protocol required.

PPP is a newer remote access protocol that is commonly in use. Windows Server 2003 can use PPP when acting as a dial-up client or server. PPP has a number of advantages over SLIP, including the ability to configure clients automatically with IP configuration information, wide availability, and the ability to use multiple LAN protocols.

Two remote access protocols supported in Windows 2000 Server have been removed in Windows Server 2003. The Microsoft RAS protocol used to support older Microsoft clients using the NetBEUI protocol has been removed. In addition, the AppleTalk Remote Access Protocol used to support older Macintosh clients has been removed.

The selection of a remote access protocol when using Windows Server 2003 as a dial-up client is made on the Networking tab of the dial-up connection Properties dialog box, as shown in Figure 11-12.

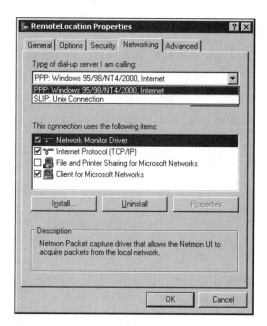

Figure 11-12   Networking tab of the RemoteLocation Properties dialog box

Activity 11-3: Creating a Dial-up Connection

Time required: 5 minutes

Objective: Configure your server with a dial-up connection.

Description: One of the more remote locations for Arctic University is unable to use Internet connectivity to communicate with the other locations. As a short-term solution, you want to dial-up to the server in the remote location to download data on a daily basis. You have configured an old UNIX server in the remote location to act as a dial-up server. You now need to configure your server to be a dial-up client using the SLIP remote access protocol.

1. If necessary, start your server and log on as **Administrator**.

2. Click **Start**, point to **Control Panel**, and double-click **Network Connections**.

3. Double-click **New Connection Wizard** to start the New Connection Wizard.

4. Click **Next** to begin the New Connection Wizard.

5. Click **Connect to the network at my workplace**, and click **Next**.

6. Confirm that **Dial-up connection** is selected, and click **Next**.

7. In the Company Name text box, type **RemoteLocation**, and click **Next**. This is the name you see for the connection after it is created. It is best to use a descriptive name here.

8. In the Phone number text box, type **555-1212**, and click **Next**.

9. In the next window, confirm that the **Anyone's use** option button is selected, and click **Next**. If the My use only option button were selected, only the user account that is creating the dial-up connection could initiate the dial-up connection at a later time.

10. Click **Finish**.

11. In the Connect RemoteLocation dialog box, click **Properties**, and click the **Networking** tab.

12. Click the **Type of dial-up server I am calling** drop-down list box, and click **SLIP: Unix Connection**.

13. Click **OK** to save the new settings.

14. Click **Cancel** because you don't want to connect to the remote server right now.

15. Close the Network Connections window.

PPP has several options that can be enabled to enhance performance. These options are enabled using the Routing and Remote Access snap-in on the PPP tab of the server Properties dialog box, as shown in Figure 11-13.

A **multilink** connection combines multiple dial-up connections into a single logical connection to speed up data transfer. For example, a client computer with two modems can dial-up to the RAS and connect to two modems on the RAS. When data is transferred between the client and the server, the speed of the connection is twice as fast as a single dial-up connection. To use two modems, there must be two phone lines. Multilink is enabled by checking the Multilink connections check box.

If the Dynamic bandwidth control using BAP or BACP check box is checked, it allows the multilink connection to dynamically add and drop modems from a dial-up connection as the amount of data transferred varies. This is very useful for long-term connections between physical locations, particularly if long-distance charges are incurred, because phone line use is minimized. The criteria used for controlling the addition or removal of modems from the

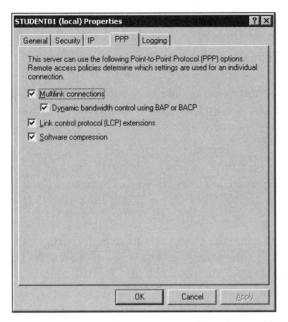

Figure 11-13   PPP tab of the STUDENT01 (local) Properties dialog box

multilink connection are set in remote access policies. Remote access policies are covered later in this chapter.

Checking the Link control protocol (LCP) extensions check box allows the dial-in server to use enhancements to LCP that control callbacks and other options. **Link Control Protocol (LCP)** is a protocol that controls the establishment of PPP sessions. If this option is disabled, using callback is not possible.

If the Software compression check box is checked, data transferred on this connection is compressed using Microsoft Point-to-Point Compression Protocol.

VPN Remote Access

A **virtual private network (VPN)** uses a public network to transmit private information. Encryption is used to keep the private information from being read by unauthorized persons as it traverses the public network. This allows a relatively inexpensive public network to be used in place of a relatively expensive private network.

The public network most commonly used for VPN connections is the Internet. The client computers can be connected to the Internet via dial-up, a company LAN, or broadband, such as cable or DSL modems. VPN remote access started to become popular in the mid-1990s. As the Internet became popular and more available, so did the popularity of VPN remote access.

11

After they are connected to the Internet, client computers initiate a VPN connection with a VPN server. The VPN client is then able to access the network on which the VPN server is located, in the same way that a dial-up client is able to access the network on which the dial-up server is located.

Maintaining a VPN server is much easier than maintaining a dial-up server. A VPN server generally uses a standard network card to communicate with the Internet; thus, no special hardware, such as a modem pool, is required.

The speed of VPN connections is potentially much higher than those of dial-up connections. When high-speed access to the Internet is available through broadband or a company LAN, a VPN connection may be as fast as 10 Mbps. However, if Internet access is provided through a dial-up connection, the VPN connection is limited to the speed of the dial-up connection.

The main advantages of VPN connections are their potentially high speed and the reduced maintenance achieved by eliminating a modem pool. The main drawback to VPN connections is the security risk presented by allowing access to network resources from the Internet.

Enabling and Configuring a VPN Server

Windows Server 2003 also uses RRAS to act as a VPN server. In many ways, VPN connections behave like dial-up connections. However, when a RAS is configured to provide VPN connections, no special equipment is required. All connectivity is accomplished through a regular network card.

Enabling a VPN server is accomplished using the Routing and Remote Access Server Setup Wizard. If RRAS has already been configured, you must disable routing and remote access before you can reconfigure it with the Routing and Remote Access Server Setup Wizard. You can reconfigure the server manually without the wizard, but this often takes longer and is more prone to error.

The first few windows of the Routing and Remote Access Server Setup Wizard are the same when configuring a VPN server and a dial-up server, including choosing to configure the server as a RAS. However, when asked the type of RAS, choose VPN instead of Dial-up, as shown in Figure 11-14.

The next window, shown in Figure 11-15, asks you to select the network interface that is connected to the Internet. This is the network interface to which VPN clients will be connecting. Checking the Enable security on the selected interface by setting up static packet filters check box stops all packets going in and out of the selected interface unless they are part of a VPN connection.

The option to enable packet filters should be chosen only if the server has multiple network cards with the filtered card connected to the Internet and the unfiltered cards connected to the LAN. In this configuration, the interface connected to the Internet responds only to VPN traffic, and the VPN clients can connect to the interface on the Internet. After the VPN

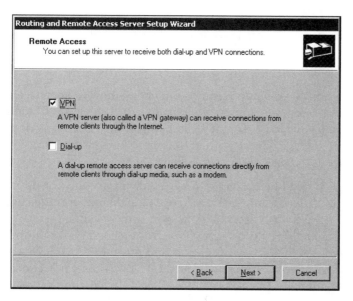

Figure 11-14   Choosing VPN as a RAS type

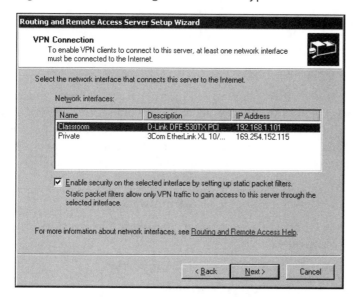

Figure 11-15   Choosing an interface for VPN clients

connection is created, the VPN clients can access any services on the LAN because the internal interface does not restrict traffic. All requests are tunneled inside VPN packets to the VPN server and then unpacked and delivered to the LAN. Responses are tunneled inside VPN packets by the VPN server and sent to the VPN client.

If a VPN server has multiple network interfaces, VPN clients receive an IP address from an interface not connected to the Internet.

NOTE

Just like a dial-up server, the next window asks you to choose how IP addresses are handed out to VPN clients. If you choose the Automatically option, the RAS leases IP addresses from a DHCP server on the network and passes the IP addresses to the VPN clients. If you choose the From a specified range of IP addresses option, you must configure the RAS with a static range of IP addresses for it to hand out to VPN clients.

Finally, you must choose how authentication is performed, just like the dial-up server. Your first choice is the No, use Routing and Remote Access to authenticate connection requests option, and this means that each RAS performs its own authentication by querying Active Directory and using policies that exist on that server. Your second choice is the Yes, set up this server to work with a RADIUS server option, and this means that all authentication requests are forwarded to a RADIUS server, and the RAS allows connections based on results from the RADIUS server. The details of how RADIUS functions are covered in the RADIUS section later in this chapter.

Activity 11-4: Enabling RRAS as a VPN Server

ACTIVITY

Time Required: 5 minutes

Objective: Enable RRAS as a VPN server.

Description: Several professors have high-speed Internet access at home and want to use it for remotely accessing files on campus. You reconfigure your server as a VPN server. The classroom connection simulates the Internet-connected interface, and the private connection simulates the LAN interface. The private interface is configured with a static IP address. For this activity, your instructor will provide you with your student number and group number.

1. If necessary, start your server and log on as **Administrator**.

2. Click **Start**, point to **Control Panel**, point to **Network Connections**, right-click **Private**, and click **Properties**.

3. Click **Internet Protocol (TCP/IP)** and click **Properties**.

4. Click **Use the following IP address**, if necessary.

5. In the IP address text box, type **172.16.*x*.*y***, where *x* is your group number and *y* is your student number.

6. In the Subnet mask text box, type **255.255.255.0**.

7. In the Preferred DNS server text box, type **192.168.1.10** and click **OK**.

8. Close the dialog box.

9. Click **Start**, point to **Administrative Tools**, click **Routing and Remote Access**.

10. Right-click your server and click **Disable Routing and Remote Access**.

11. Click **Yes** to confirm you want to continue. When RRAS is disabled, a red arrow appears beside your server.

12. Right-click your server and click **Configure and Enable Routing and Remote Access**.

13. Click **Next** to begin the Routing and Remote Access Server Setup Wizard.

14. Confirm that **Remote access (dial-up or VPN)** is selected, and click **Next**.

15. Check the **VPN** check box to configure the server as a VPN server, and click **Next**.

16. Click **Classroom** to select it as the interface that is connected to the Internet.

17. Deselect the **Enable security on the selected interface by setting up static packet filters** check box to disable this option, and click **Next**. In a real-life situation, in which this server is connected to the Internet, you would normally leave this option enabled unless the server is providing services other than VPN remote access.

18. Click **From a specified range of addresses**, and click **Next**. In the classroom, you are not using DHCP, so you are selecting to hand out IP addresses from a static range. Most networks use DHCP to assign the addresses automatically.

19. Click **New** to create a new address range.

20. In the Start IP address text box, type **172.16.x.y0**, where x is your group number and y is your student number.

21. In the Number of addresses text box, type **10**, and click **OK**. For the purposes of this activity, you only need one IP address to hand out. When a VPN server is put into production, it is configured to hand out one IP address for each simultaneous client connection. This may be many more than the 10 you have just configured.

22. Click **Next**.

23. Confirm that **No, use Routing and Remote Access to authenticate connection requests** is selected, and click **Next**.

24. Click **Finish**.

25. Click **OK** to close the warning dialog box about DHCP relay. Notice that the arrow next to your server is now green and pointing up to indicate that RRAS is configured and started.

26. Close the Routing and Remote Access snap-in.

Overview of VPN Protocols

Point-to-Point Tunneling Protocol (PPTP) and **Layer Two Tunneling Protocol (L2TP)** are VPN protocols supported by Windows Server 2003 when configured as a VPN server. By default, 128 PPTP ports and 128 L2TP ports are provided, as shown in Figure 11-16.

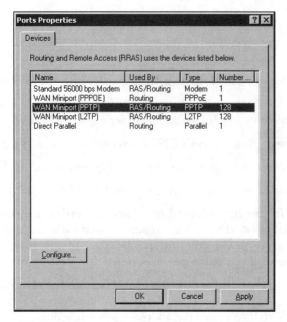

Figure 11-16   PPTP and L2TP port configuration

If your VPN server needs to support more than 128 VPN clients using either protocol, the number of ports must be increased. If you choose not to allow PPTP because it is less secure than L2TP, the number of PPTP ports can be reduced to zero. Conversely, if you only want to support PPTP because of its ease of configuration, the number of L2TP ports can be reduced to zero.

Activity 11-5: Modifying the Default Number of VPN Ports

Time Required: 5 minutes

Objective: Reduce the number of PPTP and L2TP VPN ports to 10 each.

Description: You have a server with RRAS configured to be a VPN server. By default, 128 PPTP ports and 128 L2TP ports have been created. You are concerned that if this number of connections were ever created on the server, your Internet connection would become congested. You have decided to limit the number of PPTP and L2TP connections to 10 each.

1. If necessary, start your server and log on as **Administrator**.

2. Click **Start**, point to **Administrative Tools**, and click **Routing and Remote Access**.

3. If necessary, double-click your server to expand it.

4. Right-click **Ports** and click **Properties** to view the port drivers that are installed.

5. Double-click **WAN Miniport (PPTP)**.

6. In the Maximum ports text box, type **10**, and click **OK**.

7. Click **Yes** to close the warning box and continue.

8. Double-click **WAN Miniport (L2TP)**.

9. In the Maximum ports text box, type **10**, and click **OK**.

10. Click **Yes** to close the warning dialog box and continue.

11. Click **OK** to close the Ports Properties dialog box.

12. Close the Routing and Remote Access snap-in.

PPTP

PPTP was developed in 1996 by Microsoft, 3Com, U.S. Robotics, and several other companies. As one of the oldest VPN protocols, it is also the most popular and widely supported. It is supported by all versions of Windows starting with Windows 95.

One of the main advantages offered by PPTP is the ability to function properly through NAT. This is very important because many times roaming users are not assigned an Internet-addressable IP address, but are behind NAT implemented at a hotel or client site.

Authentication for PPTP is based on a user name and password, and does not authenticate the computers involved in the connection. This means that there is no assurance that the VPN server or VPN client are authorized. For example, a hacker could obtain control of a router and redirect packets destined for a company VPN server to a VPN server controlled by the hacker where passwords are collected. Because the server and client computers are not authenticated, there is no way the client can prevent this or be warned about it.

The encryption used by PPTP is Microsoft Point-to-Point Encryption (MPPE) protocol. This is a part of PPTP, and no extra configuration is required.

L2TP

L2TP alone is not sufficient to provide a VPN connection. It is designed only for tunneling data, not encrypting it. The L2TP implementation used by Microsoft for VPN connections uses IPSec for encryption of data packets. This protocol is supported only by Windows 2000 and newer Microsoft operating systems.

A data packet is first encapsulated in an L2TP packet. This allows non-IP protocols to travel across an IP-based network. Then, the L2TP packet is encapsulated in an IPSec packet using ESP for data encryption. The encrypted IPSec packet travels from VPN client to VPN server, where the L2TP packet is decrypted and removed from the IPSec packet, and the data packet is removed from the L2TP packet. The structure of an L2TP/IPSec packet is shown in Figure 11-17.

11

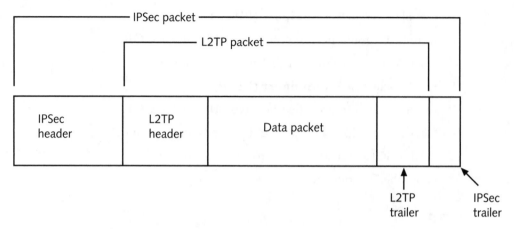

Figure 11-17   Structure of an L2TP/IPSec packet

Until recently, L2TP/IPSec connections could not function properly through NAT. However, if the devices implementing IPSec conform to the specifications laid out in the IPSec Protocol Working Group drafts "Negotiation of NAT-Traversal in the IKE" and "UDP Encapsulation of IPSec Packets," then operation over NAT is possible. Windows Server 2003 supports these drafts. The only Microsoft client operating system that supports these drafts is Windows XP with Service Pack 1.

NOTE   You can find more information about the latest IPSec drafts at *www.ietf.org/html.charters/ipsec-charter.html*.

The authentication used by L2TP is based on a user name and password, just like PPTP. However, the addition of IPSec adds computer-level authentication as well. This means that IPSec authentication needs to be configured on the VPN clients and VPN server. The options for IPSec authentication include PKI certificates and preshared keys. Kerberos authentication is not supported for L2TP/IPSec connections.

The main disadvantage of L2TP/IPSec VPN connections is the relative complexity involved in configuring them when compared to PPTP. The second main disadvantage of L2TP/IPSec VPN connections is the limited support for traversing NAT. However, L2TP/IPSec VPN connections are more secure than PPTP connections because in addition to the user authentication performed by L2TP, IPSec performs tunnel authentication, which confirms the identity of both the VPN server and VPN client.

CONFIGURING REMOTE ACCESS SERVERS

The default configuration options for a RAS are generally sufficient for day-to-day operations, but there may be some situations in which you need to modify these settings to allow particular types of clients to connect or to modify the performance of the system.

The General tab of the server Properties dialog box, as shown in Figure 11-18, allows you to specify whether the server is a RAS. This is normally configured using the Routing and Remote Access Server Setup Wizard, but you can enable it manually if this server is already functioning and you do not want to lose the current configuration.

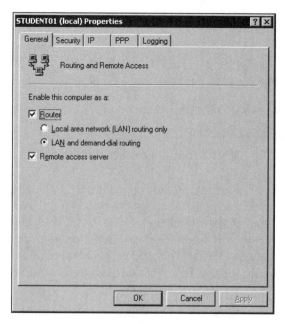

Figure 11-18   General tab of the STUDENT01 (local) Properties dialog box

The Security tab of the server Properties dialog box, as shown in Figure 11-19, allows you to control authentication and logging. The Authentication Methods button allows you to specify which authentication methods this server supports for dial-up, PPTP, and L2TP connections. The Authentication provider drop-down list controls whether authentication is performed by Windows or a RADIUS server. The Accounting provider drop-down list defines whether logging of connections is disabled, stored on the local server, or passed to a RADIUS server.

The Allow custom IPSec policy for L2TP connection check box is used when an IPSec policy is already in place for use on the LAN. When this check box is selected, you can specify a preshared key used by L2TP/IPSec clients when connecting to the VPN server. This reduces the complexity of configuring IPSec policies for a VPN server.

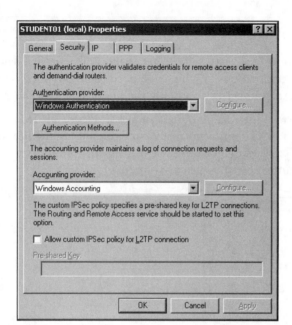

Figure 11-19 Security tab of the STUDENT01 (local) Properties dialog box

The IP tab of the server Properties dialog box, as shown in Figure 11-20, allows you to configure whether this server is a router for IP and if it allows IP-based remote access connections. The IP address assignment for the client can be configured here to allow automatic assignment via DHCP or manual assignment via a static pool of addresses. You can also choose the adapter used to obtain DHCP, DNS, and WINS configuration for clients. All of these are normally configured using the Routing and Remote Access Server Setup Wizard.

The Enable broadcast name resolution check box is a new feature in Windows Server 2003. In the past, because the VPN server acts as a router for VPN clients, NetBIOS name resolution by broadcast for clients was not possible; a WINS server was required. Even with a WINS server, browsing in My Network Places was sometimes unreliable. With this check box enabled, the VPN server acts as a proxy for NetBIOS broadcasts, and the VPN client does not need to be configured with a WINS server if the network being connected to is a single subnet (not routed).

The Logging tab of the server Properties dialog box, as shown in Figure 11-21, allows you to control the events that are written to the event log. In addition, you can check the Log additional Routing and Remote Access information (used for debugging) check box to create C:\WINDOWS\tracing\ppp.log to track detailed information on the establishment of PPP connections.

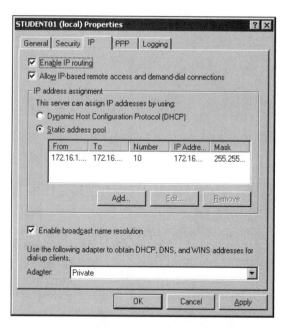

Figure 11-20   IP tab of the STUDENT01 (local) Properties dialog box

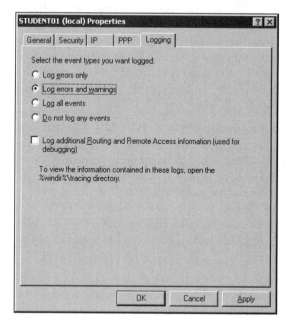

Figure 11-21   Logging tab of the STUDENT01 (local) Properties dialog box

NOTE

The logging configured on the Logging tab is not the same as the accounting information configured on the Security tab.

Authentication Methods

Windows Server 2003 has the ability to use a number of different authentication methods. These authentication methods can be used for authenticating dial-up, PPTP, and L2TP connections:

- *No Authentication*—If you choose to have no authentication, all users are permitted access regardless of their user name and password.

- *Password Authentication Protocol (PAP)*—PAP transmits passwords across the network in plain text. This makes it unsuitable for use except as a last resort for clients that support no other authentication methods. MPPE cannot be used in conjunction with PAP, which means that a PPTP VPN cannot encrypt the data packets when PAP is used. PAP also cannot change the password during the authentication process. This authentication method is disabled by default.

- *Shiva Password Authentication Protocol (SPAP)*—SPAP uses reversible encryption to transmit passwords. This means that the password can be decrypted if captured with a packet sniffer. It is also vulnerable to replay attacks because the password is encrypted exactly the same each time it is transmitted on the network. MPPE cannot be used in conjunction with SPAP, which means that a PPTP VPN connection cannot encrypt the data packets when SPAP is used. SPAP also cannot change the password during the authentication process. This authentication method is disabled by default.

- *Challenge Handshake Authentication Protocol (CHAP)*—CHAP is a significant enhancement over SPAP because it uses the one-way hashing algorithm MD5 to secure passwords in transit. However, it does require passwords stored in Active Directory to be encrypted in a reversible format, which is a security risk. This authentication method is widely supported by many vendors. MPPE cannot be used in conjunction with CHAP, which means that a PPTP VPN connection cannot encrypt the data packets when CHAP is used. CHAP also cannot change the password during the authentication process. This authentication method is disabled by default.

- *Microsoft Challenge Handshake Authentication Protocol (MS-CHAP)*—This is an enhancement to CHAP that allows Active Directory passwords to be stored using nonreversible encryption. MPPE can be used in conjunction with MS-CHAP, which means that a PPTP VPN can encrypt the data packets. In addition, MS-CHAP can be used to change the password during the authentication process if the password has expired. Passwords are limited to 14 characters. This authentication method is enabled by default.

- *Microsoft Challenge Handshake Authentication Protocol version 2 (MS-CHAPv2)*—This enhanced version of MS-CHAP corrects several problems. LAN Manager support for older Windows clients is no longer supported because of their weak encryption algorithms. Authentication is performed for both computers in the communication (not just the client), similar to the mutual authentication provided by IPSec. Encryption keys vary with each connection, unlike MS-CHAP, which reused the same encryption key for each connection.

- *Extensible Authentication Protocol (EAP)*—This is not an authentication method as much as it is an authentication system. EAP allows multiple authentication mechanisms to be configured. The client and server can negotiate which authentication mechanism to use. The authentication mechanism options included with Windows Server 2003 are MD5-Challenge, Protected EAP (PEAP), and Smart Card or other certificate. In Windows 2000, the Smart Card or other certificate option was known as Transport Layer Security (EAP-TLS). Authentication mechanisms are also known as EAP types.

IP Address Management

When dial-up and VPN clients connect to Windows Server 2003 configured as a RAS, they are assigned an IP address. The IP address can be from a static pool configured on the RAS or leased from a DHCP server.

Regardless of which IP allocation method is used, the options for the DNS server and the WINS server assigned to the client are taken from the configuration of a specified interface on the RAS. As you can see in Figure 11-22, the RAS is configured to use DHCP for assigning IP addresses to clients. The internal network interface is chosen to provide the DNS option to clients. WINS is not configured. The RAS leases an IP address from the DHCP server for the client. This is the IP address that is assigned to the remote access client. The DNS option sent to the remote access client is obtained from the internal network interface of the RAS. The options in the DHCP lease are not used.

Windows 2000 and newer clients have the ability to send a **DHCPINFORM** packet after a remote access connection has been established. This packet allows clients to query a DHCP server for configuration options. If the query is successful, the options from the DHCP server override the options from the network interface of the RAS. For this system to work, the DHCP relay agent on the RAS must be configured to pass the DHCPINFORM messages on to a DHCP server. The DHCP relay agent is also known as a DHCP proxy.

In Figure 11-23, a remote access connection has been established between the remote access client and the RAS. The remote access client sends a DHCPINFORM message to the RAS. The DHCP relay agent on the RAS forwards the DHCPINFORM message to the DHCP server. The DHCP server sends the DNS configuration option back to the DHCP relay agent on the RAS. Finally, the RAS passes the DNS configuration option to the remote access client, where the remote access client overwrites the existing DNS server option with the new configuration.

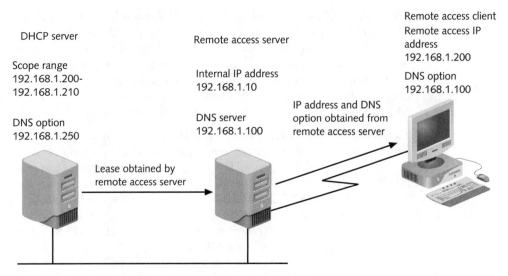

Figure 11-22   IP options configured from interface of a RAS

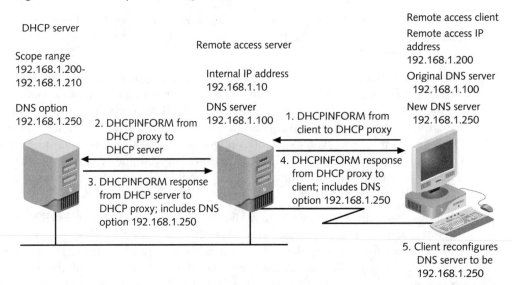

Figure 11-23   IP options configured from the DHCP server through DHCP relay agent

NOTE   If a remote access client attempts to use a DHCPINFORM packet and does not receive a response, the IP options configured by RRAS continue to be used.

ACTIVITY

Activity 11-6: Configuring the DHCP Relay Agent

Time Required: 5 minutes

Objective: Configure the DHCP relay agent on a RAS.

Description: All of the servers on your network are configured to use the DNS server 192.168.1.10. However, you want remote access clients to use a different DNS server that is configured as an option on a DHCP server. You configure the DHCP relay agent on your server to query the DHCP server. Note that there is not a DHCP server actually running on this network. For this activity, you are just simulating it.

1. If necessary, start your server and log on as **Administrator**.

2. Click **Start**, point to **Administrative Tools**, and click **Routing and Remote Access**.

3. If necessary, double-click your server to expand it.

4. Double-click **IP Routing** to expand it.

5. Click **DHCP Relay Agent** to view the interfaces that are connected to this service. The only interface that should be connected is Internal. You must add the interface that is on the same network as the remote access clients.

6. Right-click **DHCP Relay Agent** and click **New Interface**.

7. Click **Private** and click **OK**. Remember that the Classroom interface is the Internet connection in our scenario.

8. Confirm that the **Relay DHCP packets** option is selected, and click **OK**.

9. Right-click **DHCP Relay Agent** and click **Properties**.

10. In the Server address text box, type **172.16.0.1**, click **Add**, and click **OK**. Communication between the DHCP relay agent and the DHCP server uses unicast packets, so this DHCP server can be on any network.

11. Close the Routing and Remote Access snap-in.

11

ALLOWING CLIENT ACCESS

In most organizations, not all users are allowed to access network resources remotely. When remote access is first configured on Windows Server 2003, none of the users are granted remote access permission. Remote access permission allows users to act as dial-up or VPN clients.

In a mixed-mode domain with pre-Windows 2000 domain controllers, the dial-in permission is either allowed or denied. When all domain controllers are Windows 2000 or later and the domain has been switched to at least Windows 2000 native mode, remote access policies can be used to control remote access permission.

Remote access permission for users is controlled by their user object in Active Directory. The settings are configured on the Dial-in tab of the user object Properties dialog box, as shown in Figure 11-24. Some of the options on this tab are not available unless the domain is in Windows 2000 native mode.

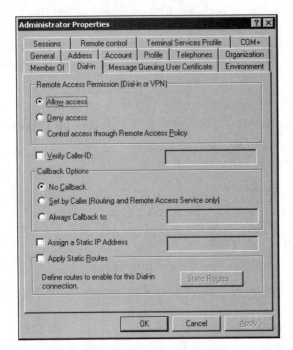

Figure 11-24   Dial-in tab of the Administrator Properties dialog box

The Remote Access Permission option group on the Dial-in tab allows you to control whether a user has access. The Allow access option means that a user is allowed to connect remotely. The Deny access option means that a user is not allowed to connect remotely. The Control access through Remote Access Policy option means that a remote access policy allows or denies the user access. By default, all users are denied access.

Selecting the Verify Caller-ID check box allows the user to connect only if they are calling from a particular phone number. For this option to work, the modems used must be capable of reading caller-ID information, the phone company must provide caller-ID information, and the domain must be in at least Windows 2000 native mode. This option is useful to prevent stolen user accounts and passwords from being used anywhere except from a designated location. Requiring the use of a particular phone line makes remotely hacking into a system much more difficult.

The Callback Options option group has settings that allow you to enable or disable callback. If the No Callback option is selected, the user is allowed to connect immediately and stay connected. If the Set by Caller (Routing and Remote Access Service only) option is selected, first the client computer gives the RAS a phone number as part of the connection establishment process. Both client and server then hang up, and the server calls the client. This is useful to ensure that long-distance charges are borne by the main office and to log where all calls come from. If the Always Callback to option is selected, a phone number must be entered, and when the user dials in, the server always calls the user back at the configured number. This provides the same type of protection for stolen user accounts and passwords as the caller-ID option.

The Assign a Static IP Address check box ensures that a user gets the same IP address each time they dial in. This overrides the settings configured at the server level for DHCP-based addresses or a static pool. This is useful if firewalls are configured to allow a particular IP address access to network resources not accessible to most users. This check box is available only if the domain is in at least Windows 2000 native mode.

The Apply Static Routes check box is designed for use with demand-dial connections configured between routers. The demand-dial connection logs on with the user account; then, static routes are added to the routing table of the RAS. These static routes allow the RAS to route packets back to the network of the demand-dial router. This check box is available only if the domain is in at least Windows 2000 native mode.

11

ACTIVITY

Activity 11-7: Allowing a User Remote Access Permission

Time Required: 10 minutes

Objective: Create a new user and allow him remote access permission.

Description: A new professor who requires VPN access has started working for Arctic University. You must create a new account for him in Active Directory and allow him remote access permission.

1. If necessary, start your server and log on as **Administrator**.

2. Click **Start** and click **Run**.

3. Type **mmc** and press **Enter**.

4. Click the **File** menu and click **Add/Remove Snap-in**.

5. Click **Add**, double-click **Active Directory Users and Computers**, click **Close**, and click **OK**. This adds the snap-in that allows you to manage users in Active Directory.

6. Click the **File** menu and click **Save As**.

7. In the File name text box, type **AD Users**, and press **Enter**. This adds the current console to the Administrative Tools menu.

8. Double-click **Active Directory Users and Computers** to expand it.

9. Click **Arctic.local** to select it.

10. Double-click **Arctic.local** to expand it.

11. Right-click **Users**, point to **New**, and click **User**.

12. In the First name text box, type **Sherman**.

13. In the Last name text box, type **Klump*xx***, where *xx* is your student number.

14. In the User logon name text box, type **SKlump*xx***, where *xx* is your student number, and click **Next**.

15. In the Password text box, type **Password!**, and in the Confirm password text box, type **Password!**.

16. Deselect the **User must change password at next logon** check box to disable this feature, and click **Next**.

17. Click **Finish**.

18. In the left pane, click **Users**.

19. In the right pane, right-click **Sherman Klump*xx***, where *xx* is your student number, and click **Properties**.

20. Click the **Dial-in** tab.

21. Click **Allow access** and click **OK**.

22. Close the MMC. If prompted to save changes, click **No**.

Creating a VPN Client Connection

Most of the time, VPN clients are configured on client operating systems such as Windows XP. However, Windows Server 2003 can also be configured as a VPN client. This can be useful when Windows Server 2003 is configured to act as a router between two locations. VPN connections can be used to encrypt traffic sent between the two routers.

VPN client connections are created using the same New Connection Wizard that is used when configuring dial-up connections. If you have a dial-up connection created, you are asked if an initial connection should be dialed before attempting to create the VPN connection. You can select the Do not dial the initial connection option if it is not required. This is the appropriate setting if you are connecting via a LAN. You can also choose the Automatically dial this initial connection option, and then choose an existing dial-up connection, as shown in Figure 11-25.

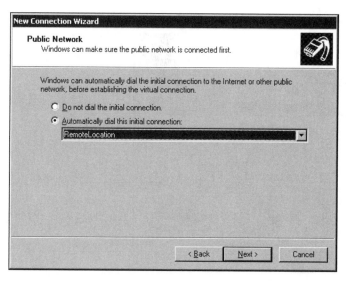

Figure 11-25   Dial initial connection option for a VPN connection

Activity 11-8: Creating a Client VPN Connection

Time Required: 10 minutes

Objective: Create a client VPN connection and then test it.

Description: After installing and configuring a VPN server, you want to test it using one of the servers in your test lab. In this activity, you create a VPN client connection on your server and connect to the VPN server configured on your partner's server.

1. If necessary, start your server and log on as **Administrator**.

2. Click **Start**, point to **Control Panel**, right-click **Network Connections**, and click **Open**.

3. Double-click **New Connection Wizard**.

4. Click **Next** to begin the New Connection Wizard.

5. Click the **Connect to the network at my workplace** option button, and click **Next**.

6. Click the **Virtual Private Network connection** option button, and click **Next**.

7. In the Company Name text box, type **ArcticVPN**, and click **Next**.

8. Click the **Do not dial the initial connection** option button. This feature is not required as you are connecting across the LAN using a network card. Click **Next**.

9. In the Host name or IP address text box, type **studentxx.arctic.local**, where *xx* is your partner's student number, as shown in Figure 11-26.

10. Click **Next**.

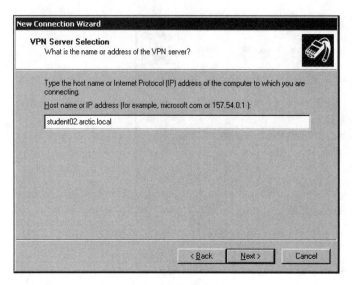

Figure 11-26   Entering the host name or IP address of the VPN server

11. Click the **Anyone's use** option button, so that all users can use this connection, and click **Next**.

12. Click **Finish**.

13. In the User name text box, type **SKlump*xx***, where *xx* is your student number. This is the user you created and allowed remote access permission in Activity 11-7.

14. In the Password text box, type **Password!**.

15. Click **Connect** to enable the connection. After the connection is established, you should see an icon of two computers in the system tray.

16. In the Network Connections window, the status of ArcticVPN should now be connected. Double-click **ArcticVPN**. On the General tab, you can view how long the VPN connection has been active and the amount of data that has traveled through it.

17. Click the **Details** tab. Here, you can view the authentication protocol, encryption protocol, server IP address on the VPN, and the client IP address on the VPN.

18. Click the **General** tab and click **Disconnect**.

19. Close the Network Connections window.

Configuring a VPN Client Connection

Most configuration of a VPN client connection is done with the New Connection Wizard. However, you can configure all of the same options in the Properties dialog box of the VPN connection.

The General tab of the VPN connection Properties dialog box, as shown in Figure 11-27, allows you to configure the IP address of the VPN server to which you are connecting. In addition, you can configure whether an initial connection is created and control whether an icon is placed in the system tray when this connection is active.

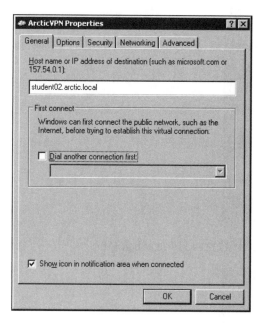

Figure 11-27   General tab of the ArcticVPN Properties dialog box

The Options tab of the VPN connection Properties dialog box, as shown in Figure 11-28, allows you to configure dialing options and redialing options. The redialing options are useful primarily for busy dial-up connections. VPN connections are less likely to be successful with redial attempts.

The Security tab of the VPN connection Properties dialog box, as shown in Figure 11-29, allows you to set whether password encryption and data encryption are required. Based on those settings, only certain authentication methods are allowed. You can also manually choose the authentication methods by clicking Advanced. The IPSec Settings button allows you to configure a preshared key that is used for L2TP/IPSec connections.

The Networking tab of the VPN connection Properties dialog box, as shown in Figure 11-30, allows you to configure the network configuration for the VPN connection. This includes setting a static IP address if required. You can also set the type of VPN connection to PPTP or L2TP. By default, the type of VPN connection is negotiated between the client and server.

The Advanced tab of the VPN connection Properties dialog box allows you to configure Internet Connection Firewall and Internet Connection Sharing for this connection.

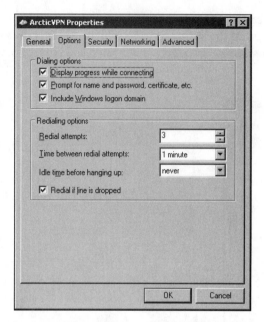

Figure 11-28   Options tab of the ArcticVPN Properties dialog box

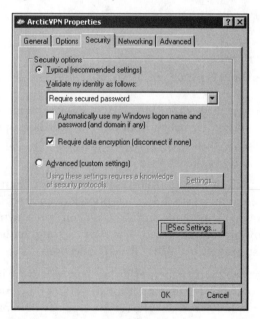

Figure 11-29   Security tab of the ArcticVPN Properties dialog box

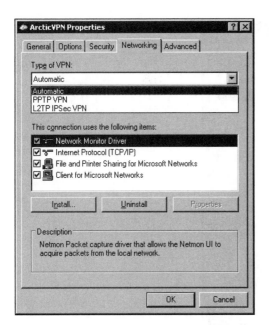

Figure 11-30   Networking tab of the ArcticVPN Properties dialog box

REMOTE ACCESS POLICIES

Remote access policies are configured on RASs to control how remote access connections are created. They are a critical part of controlling and allowing remote access. How remote access policies are applied varies depending on whether the domain is in mixed mode or native mode. Figure 11-31 shows the Properties dialog box of a default remote access policy.

These policies are stored on each individual RAS, not in Active Directory. This means that the policies applied to a user creating a remote access connection vary depending on the RAS to which the user connects. As an administrator, this offers you the extra flexibility to provide RASs that service only certain types of users. For example, you may configure one RAS that services all remote users, and configure another that services only executives. In this way, you can be sure the executives are never denied access to a busy RAS. Or, you may configure one RAS that allows connections for an unlimited period, and configure another that only allows connections for up to 10 minutes. This ensures that all users who need to check e-mail quickly are able to do so, and are not denied access to a busy RAS.

NOTE

Configuring RASs with different policies can be confusing for users. If you do this, be certain to provide documentation for your users describing exactly what is different between the RASs so they understand which one to use for a given situation.

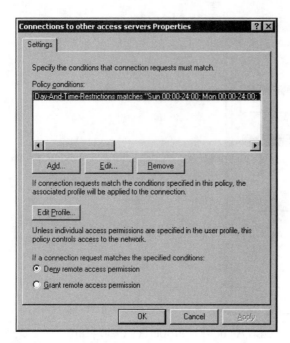

Figure 11-31   Connections to other access servers Properties dialog box

To use remote access policies effectively, you must understand:

- Remote access policy components
- Remote access policy evaluation
- Default remote access policies

Remote Access Policy Components

Remote access policies are composed of conditions, remote access permissions, and a profile. When a domain is in native mode, all three of these components are used. When a domain is in mixed mode, only the conditions and profile are used.

Conditions are criteria that must be met for a remote access policy to apply to a connection. A variety of conditions are available to be set. Some of the more common conditions used are listed in Table 11-1. To view a complete list of available conditions and their descriptions, visit *www.microsoft.com/technet/prodtechnol/windowsserver2003/proddocs/ entserver/sag_rap_elements.asp.*

Table 11-1 Common remote access policy conditions

Condition	Description
Authentication type	Identifies the authentication method being used by the client; these include CHAP, MS-CHAP, and MS-CHAPv2
Called station ID	Identifies the phone number phoned by the user; this information is available only if arranged with the phone company
Calling station ID	Identifies the phone number from which the user is calling; this information is available only if arranged with the phone company
Day and time restrictions	Sets specific days of the week and times of the day; the time is based on the time set on the server providing authorization, which is either the RAS or RADIUS server
NAS fort type	Identifies the media used to make the connection, including phone lines (async), ISDN, VPN (virtual), IEEE 802.11 wireless, and Ethernet switches
Tunnel type	Identifies the VPN protocol being used (either PPTP or L2TP)
Windows group	Identifies group membership for the user attempting the connection; to create a policy with multiple groups, you can add this condition several times with different groups, or use nested groups

11

Several conditions can be combined in a single remote access policy. All of the conditions in a remote access policy must be matched for a remote access policy to apply.

If the conditions of a remote access policy are met, then the remote access permission is verified. The **remote access permission** set in a remote access policy has only two options:

- Deny remote access permission
- Grant remote access permission

The permission setting in a remote access policy can only be used for native mode domains. If the domain is in mixed mode, the permission is always taken from the user object in Active Directory.

The **profile** of a remote policy contains settings that are applied to a remote access connection if the conditions have been matched and permission has been allowed. If the settings in a profile, such as the authentication method, cannot be applied, the connection is denied.

The Dial-in Constraints tab of the profile, as shown in Figure 11-32, allows you to set the number of minutes a connection can be idle before it is disconnected, the maximum number of minutes for a connection, and day and time restrictions. In addition, you can configure caller ID settings and port type settings, such as Wireless—IEEE 802.11, ISDN, or Async (modem).

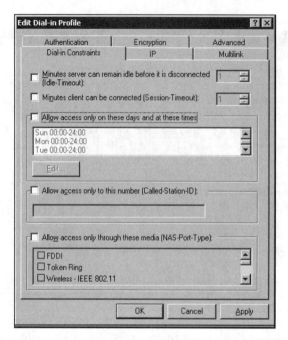

Figure 11-32   Dial-in Constraints tab of a profile

The IP tab of the profile, as shown in Figure 11-33, allows you to not only configure how IP addresses are assigned for a connection, but also to set filters to control traffic across the VPN connection. The IP address assignment setting configured in the policy overrides the settings configured on the server and the client. The IP filters can be used to control traffic based on source and destination IP addresses, source and destination port numbers, and packet type. You can use these to control which services are allowed on a connection. For example, to restrict Web-browsing traffic, you can configure a profile that denies outgoing packets for which the destination TCP port is 80.

The Multilink tab of the profile, as shown in Figure 11-34, allows you to control the maximum number of lines used for a multilink connection—and if multilink is allowed at all. In addition, you can set the capacity percentage at which the multilink connection is reduced by a line and how long it must be at that capacity. If you select the Require BAP for dynamic Multilink requests check box, multilink connections are not allowed unless **Bandwidth Allocation Protocol (BAP)** can be used to control the number of phone lines used. BAP automatically adds and removes phone lines from a multilink connection.

The Authentication tab of the profile allows you to control the types of authentication that are allowed. These authentication methods must be enabled on the client and on the server for them to be used.

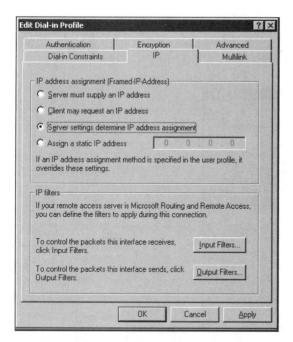

Figure 11-33   IP tab of a profile

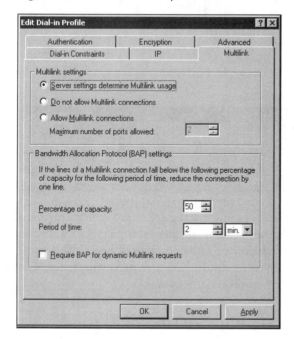

Figure 11-34   Multilink tab of a profile

The Encryption tab of the profile, as shown in Figure 11-35, allows you to control the types of encryption that are allowed. Table 11-2 lists the types of encryption allowed for each option when PPTP and L2TP/IPSec VPN connections are used.

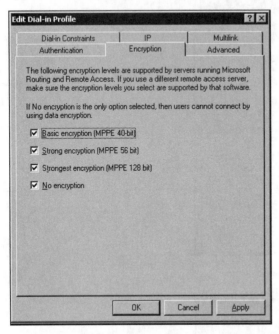

Figure 11-35 Encryption tab of a profile

Table 11-2 Allowed encryption types

Encryption Level	PPTP Encryption	L2TP/IPSec Encryption
Basic encryption	40-bit MPPE	56-bit DES
Strong encryption	56-bit MPPE	56-bit DES
Strongest encryption	128-bit MPPE	Triple DES (3DES)
No encryption	None	None

The Advanced tab of the profile contains settings that are generally intended to be configured when Windows Server 2003 is used as a RADIUS server. The **Ignore-User-Dialin-Properties** attribute can be configured here. If this attribute is false, remote access policies are processed normally. If this attribute is true, the dial-in settings in the properties of a user account are ignored.

Activity 11-9: Creating a Remote Access Policy

Time Required: 10 minutes

Objective: Create a new remote access policy on your server.

Description: Arctic University has a wide variety of users accessing resources through remote access. You want to force all of the department heads to use high levels of data encryption and MS-CHAPv2 for authentication when they connect via VPN. The easiest way to implement this is by creating a new policy with a condition for a Windows group and a profile with the encryption settings.

1. If necessary, start your server and log on as **Administrator**.

2. Click **Start**, point to **All Programs**, point to **Administrative Tools**, and click **AD Users.msc**.

3. Double-click **Active Directory Users and Computers** to expand it.

4. Click **Arctic.local** to select it.

5. Double-click **Arctic.local** to expand it.

6. Right-click **Users**, point to **New**, and then click **Group**.

7. In the Group name text box, type **HighSec*xx***, where *xx* is your student number, and then click **OK**.

8. Click **Users** in the left pane; in the right pane, double-click **HighSec*xx***, where *xx* is your student number.

9. Click the **Members** tab and click **Add**.

10. Type **Sherman Klump*xx***, where *xx* is your student number, and click **OK**.

11. Click **OK** to close the HighSec*xx* Properties dialog box.

12. Close MMC. If prompted to save the console settings, click **No**.

13. Click **Start**, point to **Administrative Tools**, and click **Routing and Remote Access**.

14. In the left pane, click **Remote Access Policies**. Notice that there are two policies already created by default.

15. Right-click **Remote Access Policies** and click **New Remote Access Policy**.

16. Click **Next** to start the New Remote Access Policy Wizard.

17. Confirm that the **Use the wizard to set up a typical policy for a common scenario** check box is checked.

18. In the Policy name text box, type **HighSecurity**, and click **Next**.

19. Confirm that the **VPN** option is selected, and click **Next**.

20. Confirm that the **Group** option is selected, click **Add**, type **ARCTIC\HighSec*xx***, where *xx* is your student number, click **OK**, and click **Next**.

21. Verify that the only check box checked is Microsoft Encrypted Authentication version 2 (MS-CHAPv2), and click **Next**.

11

22. Deselect the **Basic encryption (IPSec 56-bit DES or MPPE 40-bit)** check box to disable it.

23. Deselect the **Strong encryption (IPSec 56-bit DES or MPPE 56-bit)** check box to disable it.

24. Verify that the **Strongest encryption (IPSec Triple DES or MPPE 128-bit)** check box is checked, and click **Next**.

25. Click **Finish**. Notice that your new policy has been placed first in the priority order.

26. If time permits, view the properties of your policy to verify the settings.

27. Close the Routing and Remote Access snap-in.

Remote Access Policy Evaluation

To create remote access policies and understand what their results will be, you need to understand not only the contents of remote access policies, but also how they are evaluated by RRAS. If you do not understand this process, you may find users who should be able to create remote access connections unable to do so. The evaluation process varies depending on whether the domain is in mixed mode or native mode.

Evaluating Conditions

Evaluating conditions follows the same process for mixed-mode domains and native mode domains, and it is shown in Figure 11-36. The first step in the process checks to see if there are any policies at all. If no remote access policies exist, the connection attempt is rejected. If remote access policies exist, their conditions are evaluated.

The second step is to compare the conditions set in the remote access policies with the actual conditions of the connection being attempted. Remote access policies are assigned an order. The attempt to match conditions of the remote access policies starts with the remote access policy that comes first in order, and it continues until a match is found or no remote access policies remain. If no match is found, the connection attempt is rejected.

If multiple remote access policies match the conditions, only the first one evaluated is used. For example, a VPN server has four remote access policies. A user is attempting to create a VPN connection and remote access policy 2 and remote access policy 4 match the conditions of the connection. When the user connects, remote access policy 1 is evaluated to see if it matches the conditions. Because it does not match, remote access policy 2 is evaluated. Because remote access policy 2 matches the conditions, remote access policies 3 and 4 are never evaluated.

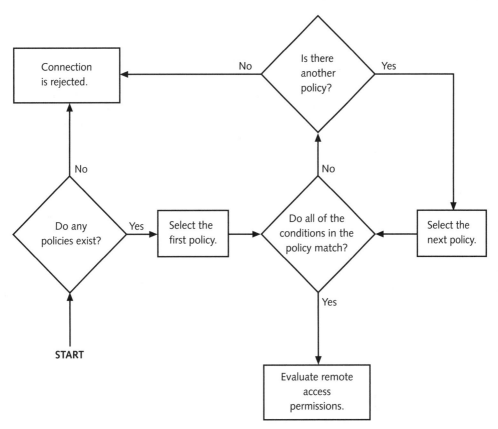

Figure 11-36 Condition evaluation process for remote access policies

Evaluating Permissions

After a condition match has been found, the permissions of the user attempting the connection must be evaluated, as shown in Figure 11-37. The first step is to check for the Ignore-User-Dialin-Properties attribute in the profile of the remote access policy. This is true for mixed-mode and native mode domains.

In a mixed-mode domain, if the Ignore-User-Dialin-Properties attribute is set to False, the remote access permission from the user object is used to determine whether a user is allowed or denied remote access permission. If the Ignore-User-Dialin-Properties attribute is set to True, the permission setting of the remote access policy is used to determine whether a user is granted or denied remote access permission.

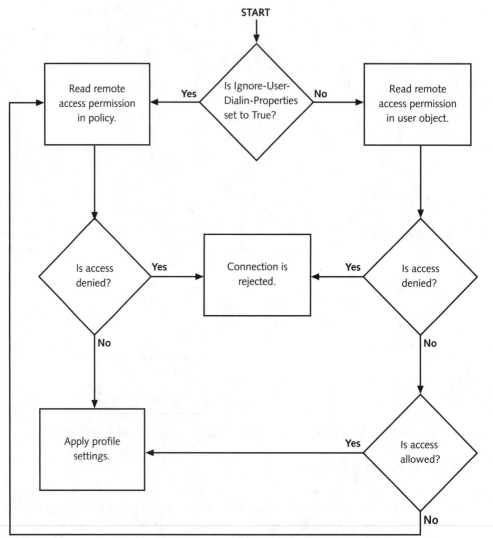

Note: If a domain is in mixed mode, the remote access permission in the user object is
      always Allow access or Deny access.

Figure 11-37   Remote access permission evaluation process

In a native mode domain, if the Ignore-User-Dialin-Properties attribute is set to False, the
remote access permission from the user object is used to determine whether a user is allowed
or denied access, unless the user object is configured with the remote access permission
Control Access Through Remote Access policy. If this option is configured, the remote
access policy defines whether the user is granted or denied remote access permission. If the
Ignore-User-Dialin-Properties attribute is set to True, the remote access policy always
defines whether the user is granted or denied remote access permission.

The Ignore-User-Dialin-Properties attribute is new in Windows Server 2003.

If a Windows NT 4.0 RAS attempts to read the remote access permissions from a native mode Active Directory domain and the setting is Control Access Through Remote Access policy, it is read as "Deny access."

If permission is denied based on this remote access policy, no other policies are evaluated. For example, a VPN server has four remote access policies. A user is attempting to create a VPN connection and remote access policy 2, which denies access, and remote access policy 4, which allows access, match the conditions of the connection. If remote access policy 2, which is evaluated first, denies access, then the user is denied access and the evaluation of policies stops. Remote access policy 4 is never evaluated.

Evaluating Profile Settings

Even if remote access permission is granted, it does not guarantee that a remote access connection will be successful. Some of the profile settings, such as allowed authentication methods and encryption levels, force a connection attempt to be disconnected.

11

Profile settings are applied in the same way for mixed-mode and native mode domains.

Activity 11-10: Testing Remote Policy Evaluation

Time Required: 20 minutes

Objective: Verify the process by which remote access permission is granted.

Description: In this activity, you perform a series of steps to illustrate the process used to evaluate remote access policies and grant remote access permission. These steps are not meant to simulate any real-world situation. You work with a partner on this activity. One partner performs configuration tasks on their server; the other tests the changes by initiating a VPN connection from their server.

1. If necessary, start your server and log on as **Administrator**.

2. Partner A: Verify that the existing VPN is functional by doing the following:

    a. Click **Start**, point to **Control Panel**, point to **Network Connections**, and then click **ArcticVPN**.

    b. If necessary, type **SKlump*xx*** in the User name text box, where *xx* is your partner's student number.

    c. In the Password text box, type **Password!**, and click **Connect**. The VPN connection should now be active and using the settings configured in the HighSecurity policy on the RAS.

    d. Right-click the VPN icon in the system tray, and click **Status**.

      e. Click the **Details** tab and verify that Authentication is MS CHAP V2 and Encryption is MPPE 128. If these are incorrect, review the Steps in Activity 11-9 to ensure that they were completed correctly.

      f. Right-click the VPN icon in the system tray, and click **Disconnect**.

3. Partner B: Create a new low-security policy and place it first in the order by doing the following:

      a. Click **Start**, point to **Administrative Tools**, and click **Routing and Remote Access**.

      b. Right-click **Remote Access Policies** and click **New Remote Access Policy**.

      c. Click **Next** to start the New Remote Access Policy Wizard.

      d. In the Policy name text box, type **LowSecurity**, and click **Next**.

      e. Confirm that **VPN** is selected, and click **Next**.

      f. Click **User** and click **Next**. This policy applies to all users, because "user" was selected.

      g. Check the **Microsoft Encrypted Authentication version 2 (MS-CHAPv2)** check box, if it is not already selected. Click **Next**.

      h. If necessary, check the **Basic encryption (IPSec 56-bit DES or MPPE 40-bit)** check box.

      i. Uncheck the **Strong encryption (IPSec 56-bit DES or MPPE 56-bit)** check box.

      j. Uncheck the **Strongest encryption (IPSec Triple DES or MPPE 128-bit)** check box, and click **Next**.

      k. Click **Finish**. The LowSecurity remote access policy is now listed as the first and will be applied before any other policy.

4. Partner A: Verify the policy application by doing the following:

      a. Click **Start**, point to **Control Panel**, point to **Network Connections**, and click **ArcticVPN**.

      b. In the Password text box, type **Password!**, and click **Connect**. The VPN connection should now be active and using the settings configured in the LowSecurity policy on the RAS.

      c. Right-click the VPN icon in the system tray, and click **Status**.

      d. Click the **Details** tab and verify that Authentication is MS CHAP V2 and Encryption is MPPE 40. These settings are from the new LowSecurity remote access policy created on your partner's server. The settings are taken from this remote access policy because it has higher priority than the HighSecurity remote access policy.

      e. Right-click the **VPN** icon in the system tray, and click **Disconnect**.

5. Partner B: Verify remote access permission by doing the following:

 a. Right-click **LowSecurity** and click **Properties**. By default, the remote access permission setting in this policy is set to Deny remote access permission. However, this setting is not used because the remote access permission for the user SKlump*xx* is set to Allow access. That is why Partner A was able to connect in Step 4.

 b. Click **Cancel**.

6. Partner B: Set the Ignore-User-Dialin-Properties attribute to True by doing the following:

 a. Right-click **LowSecurity** and click **Properties**.

 b. Click **Edit Profile**.

 c. Click the **Advanced** tab.

 d. Click **Add**.

 e. Scroll down the list of attributes, and double-click **Ignore-User-Dialin-Properties**. Microsoft is listed as the vendor.

 f. Click **True** and click **OK**.

 g. Click **Close** to close the Add Attribute window.

 h. Click **OK** to save the profile changes.

 i. If necessary, select the **Deny remote access permission** option, and click **OK** to save the remote access policy changes.

7. Partner A: Verify the policy application by doing the following:

 a. Click **Start**, point to **Control Panel**, point to **Network Connections**, and click **ArcticVPN**.

 b. In the Password text box, type **Password!**, and click **Connect**. You receive this error message: "Error 649: The account does not have permission to dial in." When the attribute Ignore-User-Dialin-Properties is set to True, the remote access permission setting on the user object is ignored, and the remote access permission from the remote access policy is used instead—even in mixed-mode domains.

 c. Click **Close**.

8. Partner B: Delete the LowSecurity remote access policy by doing the following:

 a. Right-click **LowSecurity** and click **Delete**.

 b. Click **Yes** to confirm you want to delete LowSecurity.

 c. Close the Routing and Remote Access snap-in.

9. If sufficient time exists, trade roles and repeat the Activity.

Default Remote Access Policies

The default remote access policies are created to make managing remote access easier. These default settings reduce the amount of configuration required to have a functional RAS.

The first default remote access policy listed is named Connections to Microsoft Routing and Remote Access server. This policy has a condition that states the attribute MS-RAS-Vendor must contain the characters "311". This applies to all Microsoft RASs. The profile for this policy does not allow unencrypted communication.

The second default remote access policy listed is named Connections to other access servers. This policy has a condition that the Day-And-Time-Restrictions attribute matches Sunday to Monday, 24 hours per day. This policy does allow unencrypted communication.

Remote access permission is denied in both of the default policies. For user objects with remote access permission set to Control access through Remote Access policy, this ensures that a new remote access policy must be created that explicitly grants the user remote access permission. This means that users cannot be accidentally granted remote access permission.

For user objects with remote access permission set to Allow access, the Control Access Through Remote Access policy ensures that they do obtain access. If no policy exists, the users with remote access permission set to Allow access are rejected. For example, assume all of the default remote access policies have been deleted from a RAS. When a user attempts to connect, the first part of the remote access policy evaluation process is to find a remote access policy with matching conditions. Because no remote access policy with matching conditions is found, the connection attempt is rejected.

RADIUS

Remote Authentication Dial-In User Service (RADIUS) is a protocol designed to centralize the authentication process for large, distributed networks. Originally intended for dial-up networks, now RADIUS can be used for many other types of devices, including VPN servers, switches, and wireless access points.

When using Windows Server 2003 for remote access, each server performs its own authentication using local remote access policies, and it also keeps a local access log. With RADIUS, both of these tasks can be centralized on a single server. This makes it easier to create remote access policies because they do not have to be synchronized between multiple RASs. Log analysis is also much easier if the logs are centralized on a single server.

The RADIUS process has two mandatory server roles:

- RADIUS client
- RADIUS server

A **RADIUS client** accepts authentication information from users or devices and forwards the authentication information to a RADIUS server. The RADIUS client is an access point to the network. Traditionally, a RADIUS client is a dial-up RAS or VPN RAS. However, in high-security situations, wireless access points and switches can be configured as RADIUS clients to force authentication before allowing network access.

A **RADIUS server** accepts authentication information from a RADIUS client. The RADIUS server then authorizes or denies the request based on the authentication information. The authorization or denial is returned to the RADIUS client, which then allows or denies a connection attempt.

Windows Server 2003 can act as a RADIUS client or a RADIUS server. RRAS can be configured as a RADIUS client when used for remote access. To act as a RADIUS server, **Internet Authentication Service (IAS)** must be installed. IAS is a service that allows Windows Server 2003 to act as a RADIUS server or RADIUS proxy.

A **RADIUS proxy** is an optional component that is used by organizations using multiple RADIUS servers. The job of a RADIUS proxy is to act as an intermediary between RADIUS clients and RADIUS servers.

If a RADIUS proxy is used, it accepts authentication information from RADIUS clients and passes the authentication information on to the appropriate RADIUS server. The RADIUS server passes the authorization or denial back to the RADIUS proxy, which then passes the authorization or denial back to the appropriate RADIUS client.

IAS can be configured as a RADIUS proxy. This feature is new in Windows Server 2003.

11

Outsourcing Dial-up Requirements

You can use IAS to outsource your dial-up requirements and allow your roaming users to continue logging on using their Active Directory user name and password. To do this, you must coordinate configuration with a remote access provider, usually an ISP. Long-distance charges can be avoided if you choose an ISP with wide geographical coverage.

The ISP supplies a RAS that is the RADIUS client. The ISP also supplies a server that acts as the RADIUS proxy. One of your servers with IAS installed is the RADIUS server.

Your users dial in to the ISP, and the dial-up software on the laptop passes the authentication information to the RAS of the ISP. The RAS of the ISP does not hold any user or password information for authenticating users. As a RADIUS client, it forwards all authentication requests to the RADIUS proxy.

The RADIUS proxy is configured with information that allows it to determine to which RADIUS server an authentication request should be forwarded. The authentication requests from your users are forwarded to your RADIUS server.

When your server running IAS receives authentication requests, it passes them on to an Active Directory domain controller. If IAS successfully authenticates users to Active Directory and remote access policies permit the connections, IAS authorizes the connections.

If the connections are authorized, IAS sends the authorizations to the RADIUS proxy. The RADIUS proxy sends the authorizations to the appropriate RASs. The RASs then connect the dial-up users and allow them access to the network.

Configuring IAS as a RADIUS Server

IAS is a standard component in Windows Server 2003 and is installed through Add or Remove Programs. After IAS is installed, it must be configured using the Internet Authentication Service snap-in before it can be used.

An IAS server must be registered before it can read the remote access properties of users. To register an IAS server, right-click Internet Authentication Service, as shown in Figure 11-38, and click Register Server in Active Directory. This places the computer account for the server in a domain local group named RAS and IAS Servers. Membership in this group grants the proper rights to read the remote access properties of users.

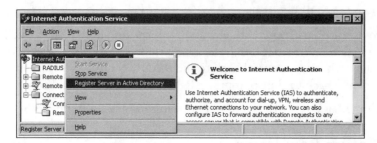

Figure 11-38   Registering an IAS server in Active Directory

IAS servers do not respond to requests from RADIUS clients unless the RADIUS clients are listed in the configuration of IAS. If a RADIUS proxy is used, it is listed here instead of the RADIUS client.

When a RADIUS client is added, you are asked for a friendly name, and an IP address or DNS name, as shown in Figure 11-39. Next, you are also asked for the vendor of the RADIUS client, as shown in Figure 11-40. This screen also allows you to set a shared secret that is used to authenticate connections between the RADIUS client and RADIUS server. In addition, the Request must contain the Message Authenticator attribute option requires that RADIUS clients include an MD5 hash of their request based on the shared secret. The MD5 hash prevents spoofed requests for authentication.

Activity 11-11: Configuring IAS as a RADIUS Server

Time Required: 10 minutes

Objective: Install IAS so your server can act as a RADIUS server.

Description: Many of the professors at Arctic University do not have access to high-speed Internet forVPN remote access at home. Until now, you have been providing a modem pool for them to dial into. However, this is awkward to maintain, and the cost of phone lines is very expensive. To solve this problem, you have struck a deal with a worldwide ISP with 1-800 access. The ISP configures its RADIUS proxy to forward authentication attempts for

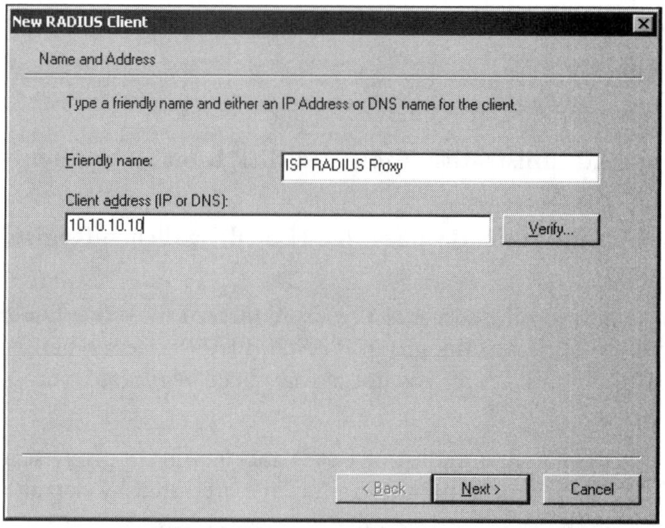

Figure 11-39   Name and address of a new RADIUS client

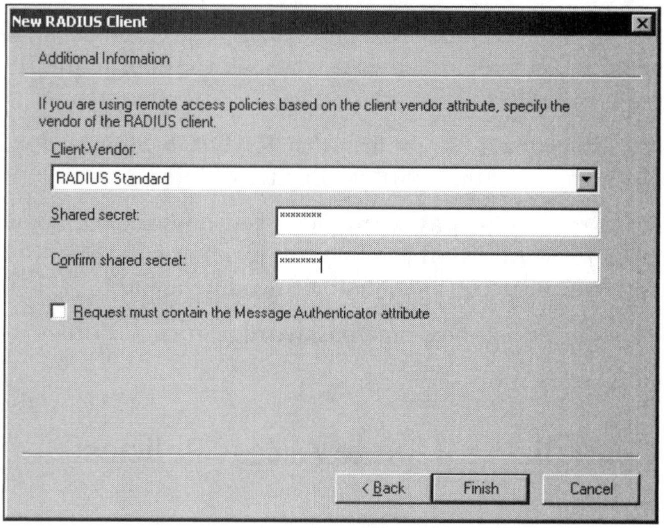

Figure 11-40   Additional information for a new RADIUS client

your professors back to your RADIUS server. You must now install IAS on your server to act as a RADIUS server.

1. If necessary, start your server and log on as **Administrator**.

2. Click **Start**, point to **Control Panel**, and click **Add or Remove Programs**.

3. Click **Add/Remove Windows Components**.

4. Scroll down in the Components box, and double-click **Networking Services**.

5. Select the **Internet Authentication Service** check box, and click **OK**.

6. Click **Next** to install IAS.

7. Click **Finish** and close the Add or Remove Programs window.

8. Click **Start**, point to **Administrative Tools**, and click **Internet Authentication Service**.

9. Right-click **Internet Authentication Service (Local)**, and click **Register Server in Active Directory**.

10. A message appears indicating the server is already registered in Active Directory because your server was added to the group RAS and IAS Servers when RRAS was configured. Click **OK**. If your server has not already been registered, you'll need to click **OK** again.

11. Click **RADIUS Clients** to view the list of RASs and RADIUS proxy servers that can use this RADIUS server for authentication. None are listed by default.

12. Right-click **RADIUS Clients** and click **New RADIUS Client**.

13. In the Friendly name text box, type **ISP RADIUS Proxy**.

14. In the Client address (IP or DNS) text box, type **10.10.10.10**, and click **Next**. This is not a real address on the classroom network. It is used to simulate the IP address of the RADIUS proxy at the ISP.

15. In the Client-Vendor drop-down list, confirm that **RADIUS Standard** is selected. This is the option you choose if the actual vendor is not listed.

16. In the Shared secret text box, type **password**. For a real implementation, you need to pick a more secure password than this. Microsoft recommends that a RADIUS shared secret be at least 22 characters long and changed frequently.

17. In the Confirm shared secret text box, type **password**, and click **Finish**.

18. Close the Internet Authentication Service snap-in.

Activity 11-12: Centralizing Remote Access Policies

Time Required: 10 minutes

Objective: Configure RRAS and IAS to centralize the management of remote access policies on a single server.

Description: You have several VPN servers at different locations. You want all of those VPN servers to read their policies from a central location to minimize maintenance on the servers. To do this, you configure your RAS to use RADIUS for authentication.

1. If necessary, start your server and log on as **Administrator**.

2. Click **Start**, point to **Administrative Tools**, and click **Routing and Remote Access**.

3. Right-click your server and click **Properties**.

4. Click the **Security** tab.

5. Click the **Authentication provider** drop-down list arrow, and click **RADIUS Authentication**.

6. Click **Configure**.

7. Click **Add** to add a new RADIUS server to the list.

8. In the Server name text box, type **studentxx.arctic.local**, where *xx* is your student number. This configures RRAS to pass all authentication requests to IAS on your server.

9. Click **Change** to configure a shared secret for authentication between the RAS and the RADIUS server.

10. In the New secret text box, type **secret**. This shared secret is also configured in IAS.

11. In the Confirm new secret text box, type **secret**, and click **OK**.

12. Click **OK** to close the Add RADIUS Server window.

13. Click **OK** and click **OK**.

14. Read the warning message about restarting RRAS, and click **OK**.

15. Right-click your server, point to **All Tasks**, and click **Restart**.

16. Close the Routing and Remote Access snap-in.

17. Click **Start**, point to **Administrative Tools**, and click **Internet Authentication Service**.

18. Right-click **RADIUS Clients** and click **New RADIUS Client**.

19. In the Friendly name text box, type **MyServer**.

20. In the Client address (IP or DNS) text box, type **studentxx.arctic.local**, where *xx* is your student number, and click **Next**. The RAS running on your server uses RADIUS to communicate with the IAS server also running on your server. Normally, these tasks are performed by separate servers. To centralize authentication and logging, all RASs must be RADIUS clients of a single IAS server.

21. Click the Client-Vendor drop-down list arrow, and click **Microsoft**.

22. In the Shared secret text box, type **secret**.

23. In the Confirm shared secret text box, type **secret**, and click **Finish**.

24. Close the Internet Authentication Service snap-in.

11

Configuring IAS as a RADIUS Proxy

A new feature of IAS in Windows Server 2003 is the ability to act as a RADIUS proxy. The previous version of IAS could only function as a RADIUS server.

IAS has the ability to act as both a RADIUS proxy and a RADIUS server at the same time. As a result, a mechanism is required to determine which RADIUS requests received are authenticated locally and which are forwarded to another RADIUS server. Connection request policies are used to determine how a RADIUS request is handled.

Remote RADIUS Server Groups

Remote RADIUS server groups are required for IAS to act as a RADIUS proxy. RADIUS requests and logging information are forwarded to remote RADIUS server groups, not individual RADIUS servers. However, you can create a remote RADIUS server group with a single RADIUS server in it.

Remote RADIUS server groups allow you to perform load balancing and fault tolerance between RADIUS servers. Each server in a remote RADIUS server group is assigned a priority number and weight, as shown in Figure 11-41. All RADIUS requests are sent to the RADIUS server with the highest priority (1 is the highest possible). If the RADIUS server with the highest priority is unavailable, the request is forwarded to the RADIUS server with the next highest priority. This system allows fault tolerance between RADIUS servers.

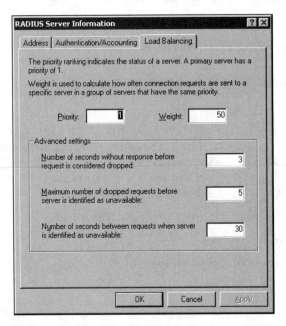

Figure 11-41   Load Balancing tab in the RADIUS Server Information dialog box

To provide load balancing between RADIUS servers, the Weight setting is used. If two RADIUS servers are configured with the same priority, load balancing is performed between them. The weight is used to determine the proportion of requests sent to each RADIUS server. For example, if two RADIUS servers in a remote RADIUS server group are configured with the same priority, but one has a weight of 75 and the other a weight of 25, the RADIUS server configured with a weight of 75 is sent 75% of RADIUS requests by the RADIUS proxy.

ACTIVITY

Activity 11-13: Creating a Remote RADIUS Server Group

Time Required: 5 minutes

Objective: Create a remote RADIUS server group that can be used when IAS is configured as a RADIUS proxy.

Description: The engineering college in Arctic University uses a number of UNIX systems for their day-to-day work. All of their user accounts are held on these machines. You want to configure your remote access system so that engineering users can use your VPN servers to access university resources remotely. To implement this, you configure IAS to act as a RADIUS proxy and forward RADIUS requests for engineering users to the engineering RADIUS servers. The Engineering Department has configured two RADIUS servers to be used for fault tolerance. Load balancing will not be performed.

1. If necessary, start your server and log on as **Administrator**.

2. Click **Start**, point to **Administrative Tools**, and click **Internet Authentication Service**.

3. Double-click **Connection Request Processing**.

4. Right-click **Remote RADIUS Server Groups**, and click **New Remote RADIUS Server Group**.

5. Click **Next** to start the New Remote RADIUS Server Group Wizard.

6. Click the **Typical (one primary server and one backup server)** option button, if necessary.

7. In the Group name text box, type **Engineering**, and click **Next**.

8. In the Primary server text box, type **10.5.5.5**. This is not a real IP address on the classroom network. It is used to simulate one of the engineering RADIUS servers.

9. In the Backup server text box, type **10.5.5.6**. This is not a real IP address on the classroom network. It is used to simulate one of the engineering RADIUS servers.

10. In the Shared secret text box, type **secret**.

11. In the Confirm shared secret text box, type **secret**, and click **Next**.

12. Deselect the **Start the New Connection Request Policy Wizard when this wizard closes** check box, and click Finish.

11

13. If necessary, click **Remote RADIUS Server Groups** to view the remote RADIUS server groups that are created. One named "Engineering" should be here.

14. Double-click **Engineering** to view the properties of it. Two RADIUS servers are listed as part of the group. The first is listed with a priority of 1, the second has a priority of 2. If the first RADIUS server fails, the second one is used.

15. Click **OK** to close the Engineering Properties dialog box.

16. Close the Internet Authentication Service snap-in.

Connection Request Policies

A **connection request policy** is constructed similarly to a remote access policy. Each connection request policy has conditions. If the conditions match the request, a profile is applied. The profile determines whether an authentication request is performed locally or forwarded to another server. It should be noted that there are no permissions in a connection request policy.

The conditions of a connection request policy are a subset of the conditions found in remote access policies. These include Day-And-Time-Restrictions, Client-IP-Address, and Client-Vendor.

The profile in a connection request policy has very different options than a remote access policy. It defines the location for authentication, log settings, rules to modify attributes in requests, and attributes that can be added to requests.

When the location for authentication is defined, as shown in Figure 11-42, you have three choices. The Authenticate requests on this server option means that this server acts as the RADIUS server. The Forward requests to the following remote RADIUS server group for authentication option means that this server acts as a RADIUS proxy and forwards the request to one of a defined group of RADIUS servers. The Accept users without validating credentials option means the users matching the conditions of this policy are authorized regardless of their user name and password.

The Accounting tab of the profile allows you to pick a RADIUS server group to handle logging for this policy.

The Attribute tab of the profile, as shown in Figure 11-43, allows you to create search and replace rules for values of certain attributes. For example, you could configure this connection request policy so that all forwarded RADIUS requests have a single Calling-Station-ID. This could then be used by the RADIUS server to identify requests from this RADIUS proxy and apply special rules.

The Advanced tab of the profile allows you to specify the value of attributes that are added to the RADIUS request. This is similar to the Advanced tab of the profile in a remote access policy.

Only one connection request policy exists by default. It is named Use Windows authentication for all users. This connection request policy is configured so that all RADIUS

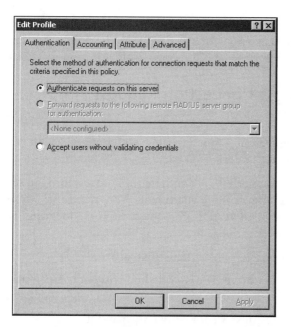

Figure 11-42 Authentication tab in a remote connection policy profile

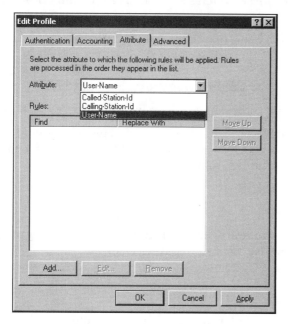

Figure 11-43 Attribute tab in a remote connection policy profile

requests received by this server are authenticated by this server. This means that this server acts as a RADIUS server for all requests it receives.

Connection request policies have an order, just as remote access policies have an order. If you want your server to act as a RADIUS proxy for some requests, the policy that defines those conditions must be a higher priority than Use Windows authentication for all users.

ACTIVITY

Activity 11-14: Creating a Connection Request Policy

Time Required: 5 minutes

Objective: Create a new connection request policy to configure your server as a RADIUS proxy.

Description: In Activity 11-13, you started the configuration process for your server to act as a RADIUS proxy for the Engineering Department. You must now create a new connection request policy that forwards RADIUS requests from engineering users to the engineering remote RADIUS server group.

1. If necessary, start your server and log on as **Administrator**.

2. Click **Start**, point to **Administrative Tools**, and click **Internet Authentication Service**.

3. Double-click **Connection Request Processing** to expand it.

4. Right-click **Connection Request Policies** and click **New Connection Request Policy**.

5. Click **Next** to start the New Connection Request Policy Wizard.

6. Click **A custom policy**.

7. In the Policy name text box, type **EngineeringProxy**, and click **Next**.

8. Click **Add** to add a condition to the connection request policy.

9. Click **User-Name**, click **Add**, type ***-E**, and click **OK**. This connection request policy now applies to all users with "-E" at the end of the user name. All engineering users add this to their regular user names when they remotely log on.

10. Click **Next**.

11. Click **Edit Profile**.

12. Click **Forward requests to the following remote RADIUS server group for authentication**, and confirm that Engineering is selected.

13. Click the **Attribute** tab.

14. Confirm that **User-Name** is selected in the Attribute box.

15. Click **Add** to configure a new rule for the User-Name attribute.

16. In the Find text box, type **–E**, leave the Replace with text box empty, and click **OK**. This removes the "-E" from the user name of engineering users before it is forwarded to the engineering RADIUS server.

17. Click **OK** to finish editing the profile, and click **Next**.

18. Click **Finish** to complete the wizard. Notice that the EngineeringProxy connection request policy has been added as the first in the processing order. This ensures that RADIUS requests for engineering users with "-E" in their user name are forwarded to the Engineering remote RADIUS server group. All other RADIUS requests for users without "-E" in their user name are handled by the default connection request policy.

19. Close the Internet Authentication Service snap-in.

TROUBLESHOOTING REMOTE ACCESS

Providing remote access for users is a very complex process. The more complex a process, the more difficult it is to troubleshoot. Most of the problems with remote access are due to software configuration issues introduced by users and administrators. Occasionally, however, hardware errors may occur.

The following sections explore various software configuration issues, hardware errors, log files that are available for troubleshooting, and troubleshooting tools.

Software Configuration Issues

Users cannot connect remotely if the software on their computers is not configured correctly. The following are some configuration issues to look for:

- *Incorrect phone numbers and IP addresses*—Users cannot connect if they are attempting to connect to a phone number or IP address that does not exist. To reduce client configuration problems, you can use the **Connection Manager Administration Kit (CMAK)**. CMAK allows you to create remote access connections for dial-up and VPN and distribute them to client computers. For more information on CMAK, search for CMAK in Help and Support.

- *Incorrect authentication settings*—Ensure that clients, servers, and remote access policies are configured properly to allow authentication to occur. Authentication errors often result in client errors indicating that the user is not authorized. The error messages do not indicate that an authentication method could not be negotiated.

- *Incorrectly configured remote access policies*—Review your remote access policies to ensure that they really do perform the tasks you think they do. Ensure that the remote access policies are in the proper order. The only remote access policy used is the first one that the conditions match.

- *Name resolution is not configured*—When a remote access client connects to the RAS, name resolution must be configured to access resources on the LAN. Ensure that DNS and WINS are configured properly if resources are not accessible when the connection is made.

11

- *Clients receive incorrect IP options*—A RAS gives remote access clients the WINS and DNS configuration from a designated interface on the RAS. If you want these settings to come from a DHCP server, you must configure the DHCP proxy on the RAS.

- *The RAS leases 10 IP addresses from DHCP at startup*—This is not an error. RRAS is designed to do this if it is configured to hand out IP addresses from a DHCP server. Leasing 10 addresses at a time is faster and more efficient than leasing IP addresses as required.

- *User accounts in Active Directory seem to be locked out at random*—When IAS is used as a RADIUS server, it authenticates accounts in Active Directory. The account lockout in your domain can be triggered by hacking attempts on your RAS when incorrect passwords are attempted.

Hardware Errors

Hardware errors are less common than software configuration errors. If they occur, hardware errors are most common when new hardware is being installed. The following are some considerations for hardware troubleshooting:

- Ideally, new remote access hardware should be on the hardware compatibility list (HCL). Many times, hardware that is not on this list works, but hardware on the list has been tested and approved by Microsoft.

- If a VPN connection cannot find the server, use the ping utility to see if the IP address is reachable. You can ping other servers on the Internet to confirm that your Internet connectivity is functional.

- If you cannot dial in using a new modem, see if you can dial in to a different RAS. This confirms that the hardware is working properly.

- If you have installed a new network card, ensure that you have reconnected the patch cable and there is a link light on the network card. "Is it plugged in?" and "Is it turned on?" are the two most valuable troubleshooting questions there are. Remember the basics.

- Is the type of hardware you are trying to use supported? When configured as a RAS, RRAS supports analog modems, ISDN, X.25, Frame Relay, ATM, cable modems, and DSL modems.

Logging

Logging for remote access can be configured in many places. If RRAS is unable to start or is not performing as expected, one of the first places to check is the event log. You can control the events that are placed in the system log from the Logging tab of the RAS Properties dialog box using the Routing and Remote Access snap-in.

From this same Logging tab, you can configure detailed connection logs. To enable this, select the "Log additional Routing and Remote Access information (used for debugging)" option. This creates a log file named C:\WINDOWS\tracing\ppp.log to track PPP connections. You can also record a log of modem communications. The log file is named C:\WINDOWS\Modemlog_*modemname*.txt, where *modemname* varies depending on your modem.

IAS can log authentication requests to a file or an SQL server. You can control which events are logged, including accounting requests, authentications requests, and periodic status. You can also choose the format of the log and how often a new log file is created. By default, the file location of this log is C:\WINDOWS\system32\LogFiles\IN*yymm*.log, where *yy* is the year, and *mm* is the month. No events are logged by default.

To configure IAS file logging in the Internet Authentication Service snap-in, click Remote Access Logging, and double-click Local File.

Activity 11-15: Modem Logging

Time Required: 5 minutes

Objective: Enable modem logging.

Description: One particular professor has been complaining that he is often unable to connect to the dial-up server. You have checked all of the configuration settings on his laptop and everything seems correct. As a last attempt to troubleshoot the problem, you are enabling modem logging on the server. This way, the next time the professor has problems, you can look at the log to see if there are any clues for further troubleshooting.

1. If necessary, start your server and log on as **Administrator**.
2. Click **Start**, point to **Control Panel**, and click **Phone and Modem Options**.
3. Click the **Modems** tab.
4. Click **Properties**.
5. Click the **Diagnostics** tab.
6. Check the **Record a Log** check box, and click **OK**.
7. Click **OK** to close the Phone and Modem Options window.

Troubleshooting Tools

The ping utility can be used to confirm that a host is reachable. If a host responds to ping attempts, the host is reachable through the network. However, this does not confirm that RRAS is functioning.

The ipconfig utility can be used to confirm that the correct IP settings are being delivered to the remote access client. If incorrect settings are being delivered to the client, the most likely cause is incorrect configuration of the DHCP relay agent on the RAS.

Many of the error messages viewed on the client side of a remote access VPN connection do not give many clues as to the cause of the actual error. Network Monitor can be used to perform packet captures, which may give some further clues as to the cause of the error.

CHAPTER SUMMARY

- RRAS in Windows Server 2003 can be configured as a RAS for dial-up and VPN connections. Dial-up connections are slow, but available from almost anywhere. VPN connections are usually faster, but Internet access is required.

- The LAN protocols supported by RRAS for dial-up networking are TCP/IP, IPX/SPX, and AppleTalk. The remote access protocols supported are PPP and SLIP. SLIP is only supported when acting as a dial-up client.

- A VPN server is easier to maintain than a dial-up server because no specialized hardware such as a modem pool is required.

- VPN connections can use PPTP or L2TP/IPSec. PPTP is more common and works properly through NAT. L2TP/IPSec is more difficult to configure and only works through NAT if the latest options are implemented.

- L2TP does not perform encryption; IPSec is used to perform encryption.

- Many authentication methods are supported by RRAS and include PAP, SPAP, CHAP, MS-CHAP, MS-CHAPv2, and EAP. PPTP VPNs cannot encrypt data if PAP, SPAP, or CHAP is used. Smart cards can only be used with EAP.

- Windows 2000 and newer remote access clients can receive IP configuration options from a DHCP server rather than from the interface of a RAS. To do this, they send a DHCPINFORM packet after the remote access connection is created. The DHCP relay agent must be configured on the RAS for this to work.

- In a mixed-mode domain, remote access permission is controlled using the properties of the user object in Active Directory. In a native mode domain, remote access policies can also be used.

- Remote access policies are composed of conditions, remote access permissions, and a profile. All conditions in a remote access policy must be met for the policy to apply. Remote access permissions grant or deny access. The profile contains settings that apply to the connection.

- RADIUS is composed of the RADIUS clients, RADIUS servers, and RADIUS proxies. RADIUS clients forward authentication requests to RADIUS servers. RADIUS servers then authenticate the requests and authorize the connections. A RADIUS proxy can be used as an intermediary between RADIUS clients and servers in large environments.

- IAS allows Windows Server 2003 to act as a RADIUS server. This allows centralized management of remote access policies and logging. RRAS can act as a RADIUS client when configured as a RAS.

◻ IAS can also be configured as a RADIUS proxy. Connection request policies are used for each request to determine whether IAS acts as a RADIUS server or a RADIUS proxy. Connection request policies are composed of conditions and a profile.

◻ The most common problem with remote access connections is improper software configuration. Hardware configuration problems occur less often, and occur mostly when new hardware is installed.

◻ A variety of logs can be configured to help troubleshoot remote access problems. RRAS logs events to the system log. You can configure PPP logging to obtain detailed information about PPP connections. Logging can be configured for a modem if dial-up remote access is configured. IAS can also log information to a file or SQL server.

◻ The most common troubleshooting tools for remote access are ipconfig, ping, and Network Monitor.

KEY TERMS

Bandwidth Allocation Protocol (BAP) — A protocol used to control dynamically the number of phone lines multilink uses based on bandwidth utilization.

Challenge Handshake Authentication Protocol (CHAP) — An authentication method that encrypts passwords using a one-way hash, but requires that passwords in Active Directory be stored using reversible encryption.

COM port — The Windows term for a serial port in a computer.

conditions — The criteria in a remote access policy, or a connection request policy, that must be met for the policy to be applied.

Connection Manager Administration Kit (CMAK) — A utility that can be used to configure dial-up and VPN connections on client computers.

connection request policy — A policy used by IAS to determine whether a request is authenticated locally or passed on to a RADIUS server. Such policies are composed of conditions and a profile.

DHCPINFORM — A DHCP packet sent by Windows 2000 and newer remote access clients to retrieve IP configuration options from a DHCP server.

dial-up — The connectivity between two computers using modems and a phone line.

Extensible Authentication Protocol (EAP) — An authentication system that uses EAP types as plug-in authentication modules. This is used for smart cards.

Ignore-User-Dialin-Properties — An attribute that can be configured in the profile of a remote access policy that prevents processing of the dial-in properties of a user object in Active Directory.

Internet Authentication Service (IAS) — A service that allows Windows Server 2003 to act as a RADIUS server and a RADIUS proxy.

LAN protocol — A networking protocol required to communicate over a LAN, or over a remote access connection. The same LAN protocol that is used by clients on the LAN must be used by dial-up and VPN clients to access LAN resources remotely.

11

Layer Two Tunneling Protocol (L2TP) — A VPN protocol that works with IPSec to provide secure communication. Only the latest versions traverse NAT properly.

Link Control Protocol (LCP) — An extension to PPP that allows the use of enhancements such as callback.

Microsoft Challenge Handshake Authentication Protocol (MS-CHAP) — An enhancement to CHAP that allows Active Directory passwords to be stored using nonreversible encryption.

Microsoft Challenge Handshake Authentication Protocol version 2 (MS-CHAPv2) — An authentication method that adds computer authentication and several other enhancements to MS-CHAP. This is the preferred authentication protocol for most remote access connections.

mobile users — The users who move from one location to another outside of the local network. They require remote access to use network resources.

modem pool — A group of modems connected to a remote access dial-up server. In high-volume situations, it is implemented as specialized hardware.

modems — The hardware devices that enable computers to communicate over a phone line. They convert digital signals from a computer to analog signals that can travel over a phone line, and then back to digital format.

multilink — A system for dial-up connections that allows multiple phone lines to be treated as a single logical unit to increase connection speeds.

Password Authentication Protocol (PAP) — An authentication method that transmits passwords in clear text.

Point-to-Point Protocol (PPP) — The most common remote access protocol used for dial-up connections. It supports the use of TCP/IP, IPX/SPX, and AppleTalk for remote access.

Point-to-Point Tunneling Protocol (PPTP) — A VPN protocol that can be used with multiple LAN protocols and functions properly through NAT.

profile — The part of a remote access policy, or connection request policy, that contains settings that are applied to the connection.

RADIUS client — A server or device that passes authentication requests to a RADIUS proxy or RADIUS server. Most commonly, these are RASs.

RADIUS proxy — An intelligent server that acts as an intermediary between RADIUS clients and RADIUS servers. This server decides which RADIUS server should be used to authenticate a request.

RADIUS server — A server in the RADIUS process that accepts and authorizes authentication requests from RADIUS clients and RADIUS proxies.

remote access — The ability to access network resources from a location away from the physical network. Connections can be made using dial-up or VPN connections.

remote access permission — The part of a remote access policy that defines whether the policy denies remote access or grants remote access.

remote access policies — The policies configured on RASs to control how remote access connections are created. They are composed of conditions, remote access permissions, and a profile.

remote access protocols — A protocol that is required for dial-up remote access. PPP is the most common remote access protocol.

Remote Authentication Dial-In User Service (RADIUS) — A service that allows RASs (RADIUS clients) to delegate responsibility for authentication to a central server (RADIUS server).

Remote RADIUS server groups — The groupings of RADIUS servers to which IAS forwards connection requests when acting as a RADIUS proxy. Load balancing and fault tolerance can be configured.

Routing and Remote Access Service (RRAS) — A service that allows Windows Server 2003 to act as a router or RAS.

Serial Line Internet Protocol (SLIP) — An older remote access protocol that only supports using TCP/IP as a LAN protocol. It is used by Windows Server 2003 only when acting as a client.

Shiva Password Authentication Protocol (SPAP) — An authentication method that uses reversible encryption when transmitting passwords.

v.90 — A standard for modems that allows downloads at 56 Kbps and uploads at 33.6 Kbps.

v.92 — A standard for modems that allows downloads at 56 Kbps and uploads at 48 Kbps.

virtual private network (VPN) — The encrypted communications across a public network such as the Internet. This is less expensive than implementing private lines for connectivity.

11

REVIEW QUESTIONS

1. Which of the following network resources can be used by remote access clients? (Choose all that apply.)

   a. files

   b. e-mail

   c. applications

   d. databases

2. A VPN connection is often slower than a dial-up connection because of the time required to perform encryption. True or False?

3. How many locations must be configured in Phone and Modem Options?

   a. none

   b. only one

   c. only two

   d. only three

4. What hardware is required for dial-up remote access? (Choose all that apply.)

   a. network card

   b. modem

   c. phone line

   d. cable modem

5. Where do remote access clients obtain IP configuration options from if a RRAS server has just been enabled and no additional configuration has been performed?

   a. the properties of the RAS

   b. a DHCP server

   c. a DHCP relay agent

   d. a defined interface on the RAS

6. How many IP addresses does a RAS lease from a DHCP server at one time?

   a. only 1

   b. only 3

   c. only 5

   d. only 10

   e. only 20

7. Which remote access protocol can be used by Windows Server 2003 only when acting as a dial-up client?

   a. PPP

   b. TCP/IP

   c. AppleTalk

   d. SLIP

   e. IPX/SPX

8. Which of the following options allows multiple phone lines to be configured into a single logical unit to increase the speed of dial-up connections?

   a. multilink

   b. LCP

   c. TurboDial

   d. PPTP

9. Which of the following VPN protocols uses IPSec to provide data encryption?

   a. PPTP

   b. PPP

   c. SLIP

   d. L2TP

   e. TCP/IP

10. Which of the following VPN protocols functions easily through NAT?

   a. PPTP

   b. PPP

   c. SLIP

   d. L2TP

   e. TCP/IP

11. Which of the following authentication methods can be used when PPTP is required to encrypt data? (Choose all that apply.)

   a. PAP

   b. SPAP

   c. CHAP

   d. MS-CHAP

   e. MS-CHAPv2

12. Which of the following configuration options can be used to ensure that users call from a predefined location? (Choose all that apply.)

   a. Packet filters

   b. Verify-Caller-ID

   c. Callback

   d. Assign a static IP address

13. Which of the following options is a component of a remote access policy? (Choose all that apply.)

   a. conditions

   b. profiles

   c. encryption protocols

   d. authentication methods

   e. remote access permissions

14. If you require the strongest encryption in a remote access policy, what level of encryption must be performed for L2TP/IPSec connections?

   a. 56-bit MPPE

   b. 128-bit MPPE

   c. 56-bit DES

   d. Triple DES (3DES)

11

15. If the Ignore-User-Dialin-Properties attribute is set to True when a domain is in mixed mode, there is no effect. True or False?

16. Which RADIUS component authorizes connections?

    a. RADIUS client

    b. RADIUS server

    c. RADIUS proxy

    d. RADIUS gateway

17. Which Windows service functions as a RADIUS server and RADIUS proxy?

    a. RRAS

    b. dial-up networking

    c. IAS

    d. Active Directory

    e. IIS

18. In a remote RADIUS server group with two servers, which of the servers handles the incoming requests?

    a. the server with the highest priority

    b. the server with the highest weight

    c. the server with the lowest weight

    d. neither server; they use load balancing

19. If a connection request policy specifies that authentication happens on the local server, IAS then acts as what type of RADIUS component?

    a. RADIUS client

    b. RADIUS server

    c. RADIUS proxy

    d. RADIUS gateway

20. Which utility can be used to configure connections for client computers?

    a. Connection Manager Administration Kit

    b. Active Directory Users and Computers

    c. ipconfig

    d. Network Monitor

CASE PROJECTS

Case Project 11-1: Traveling Professors

Many of the professors at Arctic University have laptops and are taking them home to finish work on evenings and weekends. However, when they arrive at home, they often find they are missing a file that they need. Write a short proposal indicating how remote access could help solve this problem.

Case Project 11-2: Protocol Problems

You are about to implement remote access for the arts faculty. As part of the planning process, you need to decide which protocols you will implement. Which LAN protocols, remote access protocols, and VPN protocols do you think should be used and why?

Case Project 11-3: RADIUS Configuration

The Engineering Department is using UNIX as its primary operating system. The engineers want to integrate their system with your VPN server. Is this possible? What services do you need to install for this to work properly, and how are they configured? What services does the Engineering Department need to install?

11

Case Project 11-4: Connecting Two Locations

To integrate more closely with the business community, the faculty of law has opened a small office downtown. In the short-term, it has been decided that the cost of a full-time Internet connection or even a dedicated phone line cannot be justified. How can you connect this remote office to campus and minimize the amount of time the phone line is used?

12

PLANNING AND IMPLEMENTING SERVER AVAILABILITY AND SCALABILITY

After reading this chapter, you will be able to:

- Understand availability and scalability
- Differentiate between server clustering and Network Load Balancing
- Implement server clustering
- Describe the concepts involved in server clustering
- Describe the concepts involved in Network Load Balancing
- Implement Network Load Balancing
- Install applications on an NLB cluster

This chapter discusses availability and scalability for applications and services. Two tools used to provide this are server clusters and Network Load Balancing (NLB) clusters.

Server clusters provide high availability by allowing applications and services to fail over from one server to another. A variety of resources must be configured for a server cluster, including shared disks, a quorum resource, cluster communication, resource groups, failover and failback, and virtual servers. Installing a server cluster is covered in this chapter.

NLB clusters provide scalability and high availability. Configuration options include the NLB driver, virtual IP address, application requirements, load balancing options, network communication, and port rules.

The sections in the chapter cover availability and scalability and explain the differences between server clustering and Network Load Balancing. How to implement server clusters and the concepts involved are explored. Finally, the concepts involved in Network Load Balancing are covered along with how to implement Network Load Balancing and how to install applications on an NLB cluster.

AVAILABILITY AND SCALABILITY

As the information systems of an organization change and grow, server availability and scalability are critical. Server **availability** is the percentage of time that servers are providing service on the network. **Scalability** is the ability to expand the number of clients or data that a server can support. How you implement availability and scalability depends on whether your applications are stateful or stateless. Availability, scalability, and stateful and stateless applications are discussed in the following sections.

Server Availability

Each time a server fails and ceases to provide services, there is a cost to your organization. Some of these costs, such as lost staff time, are immediately apparent. Other costs, such as customer loss of confidence, are not easy to quantify. However, to understand what can reasonably be done to prevent outages, you must understand the cost of system failure. For example, if the cost of a one-hour outage is $100,000 and the solution to prevent such an outage is $10,000, it is obvious that the solution is worth the cost.

Some of the things that can cause a server or service to fail are:

- Hardware failure
- Network failure
- Administrator mistakes
- Operating system crashes
- Application crashes

To provide higher server availability, you have a wide variety of options available, including:

- Implement redundant hardware components such as RAID5 for disks and redundant power supplies.
- Implement an uninterruptible power supply (UPS) for temporary power outages.
- Implement a backup power generator for longer power outages.
- Create redundant paths through the network to move data around failed network components.
- Use standardized procedures to perform tasks so that administrators understand how tasks are to be performed.
- Fully document the configuration of your network and servers so that administrators can understand the implications of their actions.
- Regularly patch operating systems and applications to prevent crashes.
- Use Windows Server 2003 clustering to implement server clusters.
- Use Windows Server 2003 clustering to implement Network Load Balancing.

Scalability

As an organization grows, the information systems used by that organization must be able to scale to handle the addition of more users and more data. Scalability can be accomplished by scaling up or scaling out. **Scaling up** is adding capacity to a single server. **Scaling out** is adding capacity by adding additional servers to perform the same task.

Scaling up is the first type of scaling thought of by most network administrators. If a server is unable to handle its exiting load, most network administrators add more RAM, add a faster disk subsystem, or add more processors. This is often an appropriate way to add additional capacity. However, scaling up can be both limiting and expensive.

As systems are scaled up, incremental improvements become more expensive and less effective because the hardware is progressively more specialized. For example, migrating from a single-processor server to a dual-processor server may cost $1,000 or less and adds another 90% of processing capacity to the existing capacity. However, moving from a dual-processor server to a quad-processor server may cost an additional $5,000 and improves processing capacity only an additional 80%. Moving up to eight or more processors is even more expensive for the additional processing capacity received.

Scaling out avoids the problems of scaling up by adding more commonly available hardware rather than using specialized hardware. For instance, if you have a busy Web server hosting multiple Web sites, you can buy an additional Web server and move some Web sites to the new server.

Scaling out works well when many services are running on a single server. You can simply buy a new server and move some services to the new server. However, it becomes more difficult when a single service is running on a server and you want to scale out.

If a single Web site is running on a server and the server is overwhelmed, you can buy an additional server and place another copy of the Web site on the new server. Then, half of the users need to be told to access the Web site on Server1, and half the users told to access the Web site on Server2. This is awkward for both users and the administrator.

Round robin DNS, which allows multiple A records for a single host name, can be used to spread the load between multiple servers hosting the same Web site. However, round robin DNS is unable to account for a failed server. If round robin DNS is spreading the load between two servers and one server fails, then half of the Web site users are directed to the failed server.

Network Load Balancing (NLB) is the best solution for scaling out a single application. Network Load Balancing can distribute the load between multiple servers like round robin DNS, but NLB can also sense a failed server and stop directing clients to the failed server.

Stateful and Stateless Applications

Applications can be broadly separated into stateful and stateless applications. **Stateful applications** require the server to retain knowledge about the client accessing the server.

For instance, a shopping cart application on a Web site may require the server to keep a list of what the user has selected in the shopping cart in a local file, or in memory.

Stateful applications are not well-suited to scaling out because it is difficult for application developers to track client information when client access is spread across multiple servers. It is easier to scale up a stateful application.

It is possible to scale out stateful applications by storing session state information in a database or file available to all servers. In addition, Network Load Balancing attempts to address stateful applications by setting affinity, in which requests from one IP address are always sent to the same server.

A **stateless application** does not require the server to retain knowledge about the client accessing the server. For example, a simple Web site where the same pages are served out to all clients with no dynamic content is stateless.

Stateless applications are well-suited to scaling out because each request from a client is treated independently. Stateless applications can be scaled up, but because it is more cost-effective to scale out, scaling out is the optimal choice.

WINDOWS SERVER 2003 CLUSTERING

Windows Server 2003 provides two clustering mechanisms to provide availability and scalability. **Server clusters** are used to provide highly available services that can fail over from one server to another. NLB is used to scale out applications and provide highly available services. The following sections discuss each in turn and then provide an example of how both can be used.

Server Clusters

A server cluster is used to provide highly available services. A service runs on a single server and if the service fails on that server, it is moved to another server in the cluster. It does not matter whether the application crashed due to poor programming or if the server hardware failed; it is moved automatically to a new server. Moving a service from one server to another is referred to as failover.

When a service is moved from one server to another, clients often notice a brief interruption in service. However, this is a much shorter interruption in service than would be experienced if a service had to be migrated manually to a new server.

Server clusters also provide the ability to upgrade applications with minimal downtime. When an application needs to be upgraded on Server1, it is migrated to Server2, and then the application is upgraded on Server1 and migrated back to Server1. Users see a few moments of interrupted service while it is migrated from one server to another, but much less downtime than if the service were unavailable during the entire migration process.

Server clusters are not available in all versions of Windows Server 2003. Server clusters are available only in Windows Server 2003, Enterprise Edition and Datacenter Edition. Up to eight nodes are supported in each server cluster.

In almost all circumstances, server clusters must have a shared storage. This can be in the form of a shared SCSI bus or a Fibre Channel-based storage area network (SAN). A SAN is a network to which multiple servers and storage devices can attach, where the servers store files and data on the shared storage devices. A SAN can range from $10,000 to millions of dollars.

NOTE The acronym SAN can also stand for system area network, which allows the sharing of resources between multiple computers beyond just storage. However, system area networks are rare, and in most cases when the acronym SAN is used, it refers to a storage area network.

Server clusters are most useful for applications that have been scaled up and need high availability. Remember that to have equivalent performance, the server to which a service fails over must have equivalent hardware to the original server.

To use server clusters for an application, the application must use TCP or UCP packets. Other protocols such as IPX, NetBEUI, or AppleTalk are not supported.

12

Server Cluster Configurations

Windows Server 2003 supports many configurations. Four of the most common are:

- *Active/passive*—An **active/passive server cluster** consists of two nodes, where one is hosting services and the other does not. A node is a server in a cluster. When the active node fails, services fail over to the passive node. If both nodes have the same capacity, you are assured that client performance will not be reduced.

- *N+I failover*—An **N+I failover server cluster** is a variation of an active/passive server cluster. In this configuration, N nodes in the server cluster are active running services, and I nodes are passive in the server cluster ready to accept failed over services. All active nodes in the cluster are configured to fail over to the passive nodes. Other than the overall limit of 32 nodes, there can be any number of active nodes (N) and passive nodes (I).

- *Active/active*—An **active/active server cluster** consists of two or more nodes, all of which are active. In this situation, a service fails over to an active node that is already running other services. Because the remaining node is running a new service in addition to its original services, it may be overloaded and client performance may suffer.

- *Single node virtual server*—A **single node virtual server** does not have failover capability. It consists of only one node. This configuration is often used for server consolidation. When an older server is retired, its resources can be migrated to a virtual server with the same name and IP address. Then, resources continue to be accessible without reconfiguring clients. Because a single node virtual server has only one node, it is used only to virtualize server resources to facilitate management.

Cluster Applications

All applications must have certain characteristics to take advantage of server clusters. These are:

- The application must use an IP-based protocol.
- The application must be able to specify where application data is located so that it can be stored on shared storage.
- Client applications must retry lost connections to reconnect after an application failover.

Some applications are aware of server clusters and are referred to as **cluster-aware applications**. Cluster-aware applications are able to use the clustering API. This allows cluster-aware applications to receive status notifications and manage the cluster. In addition, cluster-aware applications can be taken failed over and taken offline without any data loss.

The following are cluster-aware services and applications:

- Distributed file system (DFS)
- DHCP
- WINS
- Microsoft Exchange Server
- Microsoft SQL Server

Cluster-unaware applications have a risk of data loss when an application is taken offline because the cluster service terminates the process instead of performing a clean shutdown. In addition, the cluster service attempts to monitor registry key changes made by cluster-unaware applications and replicate those changes to the shared storage so they are available to the new node to which an application has failed over.

Network Load Balancing

Network Load Balancing (NLB) spreads application requests from clients among two or more servers. When NLB is configured, an application is installed on multiple servers using a virtual IP address. The virtual IP address is an IP address assigned to represent the application. When clients access the virtual IP address, their requests are redirected to one of the servers hosting the application.

When requests to the virtual IP address are redirected, the load is spread among the servers. NLB can spread network requests evenly among the servers hosting the application or spread network requests based on a weighting that you can assign. Weighting the network requests allows you to place a heavier workload on servers with greater processing power and higher amounts of RAM.

After NLB is configured, you can add a new server at any time. This allows any application that can be supported using NLB to be scaled out up to 32 servers. An NLB cluster is limited to a maximum of 32 servers, and can be implemented on any edition of Windows Server 2003.

If scalability beyond 32 servers is required, multiple NLB clusters can be combined using round robin DNS. Round robin DNS is configured with an A record for each NLB cluster. When the A record is resolved, requests are spread between the different NLB clusters.

Availability is also enhanced by NLB. NLB recognizes when a server has failed and stops distributing client requests to the failed server. This is a significant enhancement over round robin DNS as a load balancing mechanism. However, NLB is not able to recognize a failed service or application, only an entire server failure.

NLB is best suited to applications that are stateless. Then, client requests can be spread among all of the servers without losing information about client sessions. If client sessions are required, the session state data must be stored on the client computers or in a shared location to which all of the application servers have access.

To use NLB for an application, the application must use TCP or UCP packets. Other protocols such as IPX, NetBEUI, or AppleTalk are not supported.

Applications that require data stored on a local drive letter cannot use NLB. NLB does not allow data to be moved from one server to another. Therefore, NLB is not suitable for applications such as Microsoft SQL Server or Microsoft Exchange.

An Example of Windows Server 2003 Clustering

Before you begin working with Windows Server 2003 clustering, you must be certain that you understand how it can be used in different situations. The following example illustrates how both server clusters and NLB can be used for a Web-based application.

Arctic University currently has a cumbersome, manual system for taking student registrations. Each year, students line up for hours in an attempt to get the classes they want. However, the system is reliable and works every year.

The board of governors has talked about computerizing the registration in the past, but it was always dismissed because of concerns about reliability. This year, when the issue is raised again, they have decided to ask the IT Department to explore the possibility of a computerized registration system.

After careful thought, the IT Department has proposed a Web-based application based on Microsoft clustering, as you see in Figure 12-1.

As you can see, the back end of the system is a Microsoft SQL server to store all of the student and course information. To ensure reliability, it will be installed on two Windows Server 2003, Enterprise Edition servers scaled up with quad-processors and 2 GB of RAM configured as a server cluster. The Web portion of the application will run on two low-cost Windows Server 2003, Web Edition servers with one processor and 1 GB of RAM that have

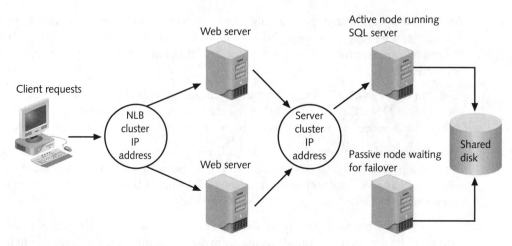

Figure 12-1   Windows Server 2003 clustering example

been load-balanced. If these two Web servers are not sufficient, the solution can be scaled out by adding additional low-cost Web servers.

Activity 12-1: Cluster Concepts

Time Required: 10 minutes

Objective: Learn more about server clusters and NLB.

Description: Arctic University is planning to implement a new Web-based application. You are searching in Help and Support to be certain you understand your options for availability and scalability using server clusters and NLB.

1. If necessary, start your server and log on as **Administrator**.

2. Click **Start** and then click **Help and Support**.

3. In the Search text box, type **cluster overview**, and then press **Enter**.

4. In the left pane under Help Topics, click **Server clusters overview: Server Clusters**.

5. In the right pane, read through the Server clusters overview page.

6. In the left pane under Help Topics, click **Introduction to Network Load Balancing: Network Load Balancing Clusters**.

7. In the right pane, read through the Introduction to Network Load Balancing page.

8. Close Help and Support Center.

Installing and Configuring Server Clusters

The cluster service is installed automatically as part of a Windows Server 2003 installation. You do not need to add it through Add/Remove Programs. To configure a server cluster, you use **Cluster Administrator** (cluadmin.exe), as shown in Figure 12-2. This tool can be used to create new server clusters or add new nodes to an existing server cluster. In addition, the command-line utility **cluster.exe** can be used to configure server clusters.

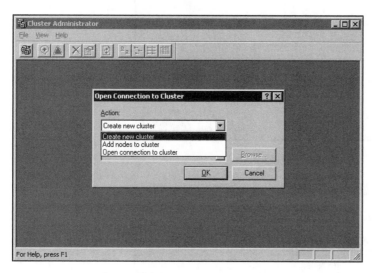

Figure 12-2   Cluster Administrator

When you choose to create a new cluster, the New Server Cluster Wizard is used. First, the wizard asks you for the domain the server cluster is in and a name for the cluster, as shown in Figure 12-3. All cluster nodes must be part of the same domain. The name for the cluster is a virtual server name that is used to manage the cluster.

After configuring the cluster name and domain, you are asked for the name of the server that is hosting in the new server cluster, as shown in Figure 12-4. In addition, the Advanced button allows you to choose a Typical (full) configuration or Advanced (minimum) configuration. Only use the Advanced (minimum) configuration if you require special features that are not available in the Typical (full) configuration.

After you select the server that is hosting the first node in the cluster, the New Server Cluster Administrator analyzes the suitability of your server for hosting a cluster. When the analysis is finished, you are shown the results, as shown in Figure 12-5. In addition, a View Log lets you see a detailed log in text format.

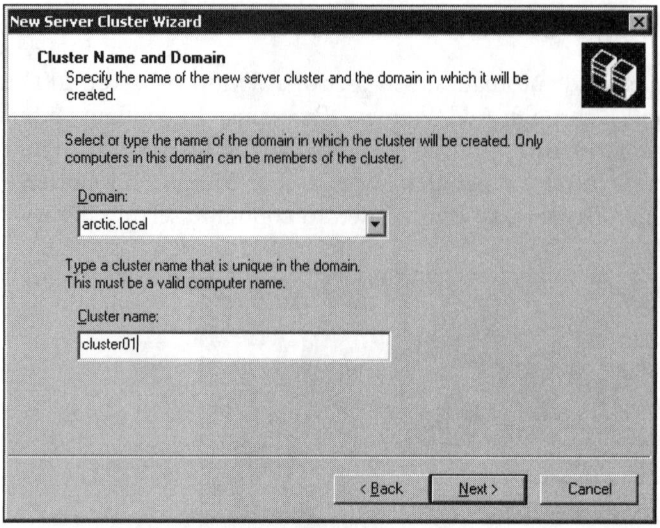

Figure 12-3   Cluster name and domain

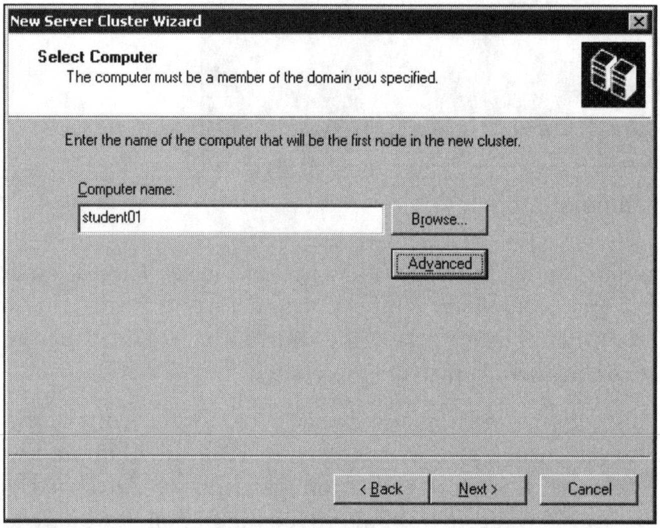

Figure 12-4   Choosing the first node

After the analysis is complete, you are asked for an IP address. This IP address is used for the virtual server. It must be unique from any other IP address in the network. Clients access cluster resources through this IP address, and you can manage the cluster through this IP address.

Next, you are asked for a cluster service account, as shown in Figure 12-6. This account is used by the cluster service to log on. To run properly, it needs to be assigned local administrative rights on all nodes in the server cluster. This is done automatically by the

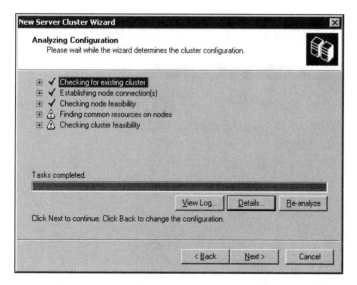

Figure 12-5   Cluster analysis

New Server Cluster Wizard. In most cases, the Administrator account should not be used as the cluster service account because your cluster can fail when the Administrator password is changed. However, this is acceptable for testing purposes.

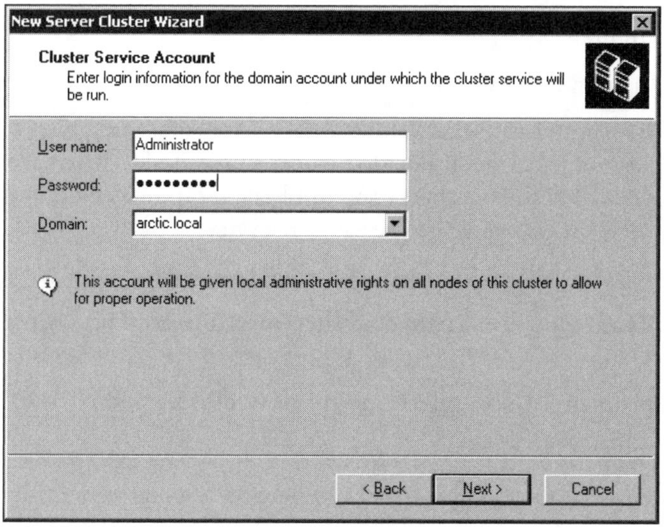

Figure 12-6   Cluster service account

The next screen is a summary of the installation options, as shown in Figure 12-7. You can review these to ensure that you selected the correct options. There is also a Quorum button that you can use to modify the quorum location. After the cluster installation is complete, the current state of your cluster is shown in Cluster Administrator.

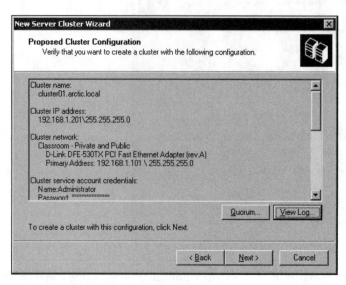

Figure 12-7 Installation summary

Activity 12-2: Installing a Single Node Virtual Server Cluster

Time Required: 10 minutes

Objective: Create a single node virtual server cluster.

Description: Arctic University has several Windows NT servers that are going to be retired soon. To ease the migration, it has been decided that a single node virtual server will be implemented that provides all of the file shares previously held on the Windows NT servers. The first step in the process is to configure the cluster service.

1. If necessary, start your server and log on as **Administrator**.

2. Click **Start**, click **Run**, type **cluadmin**, and then press **Enter**. This starts Cluster Administrator.

3. In the Action drop-down list box, select **Create new cluster** and click **OK**.

4. Click **Next** to begin the New Server Cluster Wizard.

5. In the Cluster name text box, type **clusterxx**, where *xx* is your student number, and click **Next**.

6. If necessary, in the Computer name text box, type **studentxx**, where *xx* is your student number, and then click **Next**. The New Server Cluster Wizard now analyzes whether a cluster is possible.

7. The analysis of your server generates warning messages. To read these messages, expand the sections with error messages. The errors are because you do not have a shared storage system on your server. The error also indicates that a local quorum will be configured. This is normal for a single node virtual server cluster. Click **Next** to continue.

8. In the IP Address text box, type **192.168.1.2xx**, where *xx* is your student number, and then click **Next**.

9. In the User name text box, type **Administrator**, type **Password!** in the Password text box, and then click **Next**.

10. Click **Next** to accept the current configuration. The cluster then begins installation.

11. After the cluster node is installed, a log of the installation process is presented to you. Click **Next** to continue, and then click **Finish**. Notice the Cluster Administrator now shows the status of your new cluster.

12. Click **Groups** to view the resource groups that have been created on this server.

13. Click **Resources** to view the resources that have been created on this server. Notice that three resources have been created: Local Quorum, Cluster IP Address, and Cluster Name.

14. Double-click **Cluster Configuration** to expand it, and click **Networks** to view the networks of which this cluster server is aware.

15. Close Cluster Administrator.

SERVER CLUSTER CONCEPTS

A server cluster is used to provide high availability. To understand the best way to implement a server cluster to protect your applications, you must understand various concepts about server clusters. The concepts include:

- Shared disks
- Quorum resource
- Cluster communication
- Resource groups
- Failover and failback
- Virtual servers

All of these topics are covered in the following sections.

Shared Disks

Shared disks are required for most server clusters. A shared disk is storage that all nodes in a cluster can access. Shared disks are not required when a geographically dispersed server cluster is configured with an alternate data synchronization mechanism, or when a server cluster has a single server for testing purposes. When shared disks are required, you can use either a shared SCSI bus or a Fibre Channel SAN.

NOTE   The shared disks used by a cluster are also referred to as cluster disks.

Shared SCSI Bus

A shared SCSI bus is configured by using an external SCSI storage device and connecting it to the external SCSI connector of both servers, as shown in Figure 12-8. For this configuration to work properly, you must ensure that the SCSI card in each server and the SCSI drives support this configuration. Many SCSI cards and drives do not.

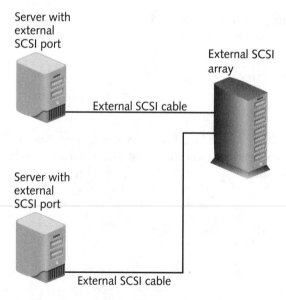

Server with
external
SCSI port

External SCSI
array

External SCSI cable

Server with
external
SCSI port

External SCSI cable

Figure 12-8   Shared SCSI bus

SCSI configuration requirements include:

- An SCSI card that can disable autobus reset.
- All SCSI devices on the SCSI must have unique SCSI IDs. This includes the two SCSI cards.

- Proper termination on the SCSI bus. The most effective mechanism for termination is external Y-cables with terminators.

- SCSI hard drives that are multi-initiator enabled to support multiple SCSI cards on the bus.

A shared SCSI bus is the most inexpensive form of shared storage that can be used by server clusters. It can often be configured for only a few thousand dollars. It is also the most difficult to configure because there are often termination problems.

Fibre Channel

Fibre Channel is designed to be used for storage area networks. Consequently, it is easier to configure and faster than a shared SCSI bus. However, it is also much more expensive. For example, Fibre Channel host bus adapters (HBA) can cost over $1,000, whereas SCSI cards cost approximately $250. Figure 12-9 shows a Fibre Channel SAN.

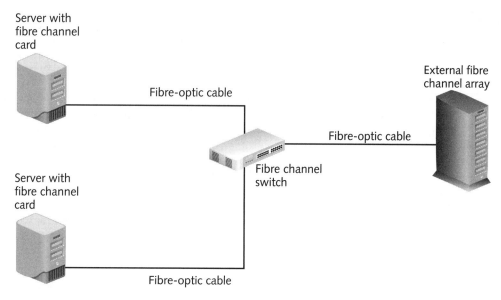

Figure 12-9   Fibre Channel SAN

The requirements for Fibre Channel shared storage are:

- A Fibre Channel card for each node in the server cluster

- An external storage array that supports Fibre Channel

- A Fibre Channel switch to connect the nodes to the external storage array

Quorum Resource

The **quorum resource** is a special disk resource used by the cluster service to store configuration information and to arbitrate which node owns the cluster. The location of the quorum resource is specified when a server cluster is created.

Like other resources, only one node at a time is allowed to own the quorum resource. The first node in the cluster that is available becomes the owner of the quorum. When new nodes come online, they receive configuration updates from active nodes in the server cluster. Only the first node to come online receives updates from the quorum resource.

If there is a failure in network communication, the quorum resource is used to arbitrate which node should keep its resources running. For example, in a two-node cluster, if network communication fails, the node with the quorum brings all resources online, and the node without the quorum takes all resources offline.

Cluster Communication

Nodes in a server cluster are in constant communication with each other using heartbeat packets. **Heartbeat packets** monitor which nodes in the server cluster are still up and available. These packets can be UDP unicast packets or multicast packets.

Each network card in a node is designated as attached to a public, private, or mixed network. Public networks are used only for client-to-node communication and are never used for heartbeat packets. Private networks are used only for node-to-node communication. Mixed networks can be used for client-to-node or node-to-node communication.

It is recommended that all nodes have at least two network cards. One of these network cards should be configured as part of a private network, and the other network card should be configured as part of a mixed network. When configured in this way, if the private network fails, node-to-node communication can still be performed on the mixed network.

Resource Groups

Control of services and applications in a server cluster is based on resource groups. A **resource group** is a logical grouping of all the resources that are required for an application or service to run. Resources can be disk partitions, IP addresses, printers, services, and applications.

You can configure dependencies between resources in a resource group. For example, you can define that an application resource is dependent on the IP address resource and a disk resource. This way, the application cannot be started until the IP address and disk are available.

NOTE Dependencies can only be created between resources in a resource group. They cannot be created between resource groups or between resources in different resource groups.

Resources can be in the following states:

- *Online*—The resource is operational and can be used by clients.
- *Offline*—The resource is not operational and cannot be used by clients.
- *Online pending*—The resource is being put online.
- *Offline pending*—The resource is being taken offline.
- *Failed*—The cluster service was unable to bring the resource online.

Failover and Failback

When a node or resource in a server cluster fails, **failover** occurs. If a server cluster node fails, the resource groups on that node automatically fail over to another node. If a resource fails, the cluster service attempts to restart the service. If the resource cannot be restarted, the resource group it is a part of fails over.

When failover occurs in a server cluster with more than two nodes, a path must be defined for failover. If all nodes in a server cluster are active, you need to configure resource groups to fail over evenly to multiple nodes rather than overloading one node with all of the resource groups from the failed node. You get to choose the nodes to which resource groups fail over.

After failover has occurred, failback is possible. **Failback** occurs when the original node hosting a resource group is available again and the resource group is moved back to the original node. You can define whether a resource group fails back automatically, manually, or not at all. In a server cluster in which all nodes are active, failback is normally configured to be automatic so the load on each node can be reduced. In a server cluster in which passive nodes are available, the load generated on nodes by resources groups that fail over is not a concern and failback is normally a manual process if it is used at all.

Virtual Servers

Resources in server clusters are always accessed through a virtual server. To client computers, this **virtual server** appears to be a normal Windows Server 2003 server. However, it is really a collection of resources in a resource group presented by the cluster service. The node that owns the resource group responds on its behalf. When failover occurs, responsibility for that virtual server is passed to another node.

The virtual servers used by Windows Server 2003 clustering have improved integration with Active Directory over Windows 2000 Server. Virtual servers are now published in Active Directory as a computer object. This allows Kerberos authentication to be used and allows

12

browsing for the computer in a NetBIOS-free environment. Windows 2000 Server clustering requires NetBIOS for browsing and uses NTLM authentication instead of Kerberos authentication.

Activity 12-3: Adding a Printer to a Virtual Server

Time Required: 10 minutes

Objective: Add a printer to a virtual server.

Description: You have already created a virtual server named cluster*xx*, where *xx* is your student number. Now, you are creating a printer so that printing can be available on the virtual server. When performing server consolidation, you add one virtual server for each retiring server and add printers and shares on each one that match the printers and shares available on the original server.

1. If necessary, start your server and log on as **Administrator**.

2. Click **Start**, click **Run**, type **cluadmin**, and press **Enter**.

3. Right-click **Resources**, point to **New**, and click **Resource**.

4. In the Name text box, type **Printers**, select **Print Spooler** in the Resource type drop-down list box, and then click **Next**.

5. In the Possible Owners dialog box, your server is listed in the Possible owners box. Click **Next** to continue.

6. In the Available resources list, double-click **Cluster IP Address**, double-click **Cluster Name**, double-click **Local Quorum**, and click **Next**. This makes all of the Printers resources dependent on all of these resources. It is not brought online if all three are not available. This prevents the cluster from trying to provide resources when it is not possible and ensures proper failover.

7. Accept the default Print Spooler Parameters by clicking **Finish**.

8. Click **OK** to close the dialog box informing you of the successful creation. Notice that your resource named Printers is offline.

9. To start the Printers resource, right-click **Printers**, and click **Bring Online**. The status of the Printers resource is now online. This is the same process you would perform if a resource failed and you wanted to bring it back online.

10. Close Cluster Administrator.

11. Click **Start**, click **Run**, type **\\cluster*xx***, where *xx* is your student number, and press **Enter**.

12. Double-click **Printers and Faxes** and double-click **Add Printer**.

13. Click **Next**, click the **Create a new port** option button, and click **Next**. This triggers the Add Standard TCP/IP Port Wizard. All cluster printers must be IP-based.

14. Click **Next**, type **192.168.1.15** in the Printer name or IP address text box, and then click **Next**. There is no printer with the IP address 192.168.1.15 in the classroom. This IP address is entered to simulate a network printer.

15. Click **Next** to accept the default setting of Generic Network Card. If a real printer were available on the network, you might not see this screen because the type of network device can be auto detected.

16. Click **Finish**.

17. Click **Next** to accept the default printer.

18. If necessary, click the **Keep existing driver (recommended)** option button to select it, and then click **Next**.

19. In the Printer name text box, type **ClusterPrinter**, and click **Next**.

20. If necessary, click the **Share name** option button, and click **Next**.

21. Click **Next** in the Location and Comment dialog box.

22. If necessary, click the **No** option button in the Print Test Page dialog box, click **Next**, and then click **Finish**.

23. Close the Printers and Faxes window.

24. Click **Start**, click **Run**, type **\\clusterxx**, where *xx* is your student number, and press **Enter**. Notice that the shared printer you created on the cluster is now available and shared as ClusterP.

25. Close the \\cluster*xx* window, where *xx* is your student number.

Activity 12-4: Removing a Server Cluster Node

Time Required: 5 minutes

Objective: Remove the final node from a server cluster.

Description: In this activity, you remove the server cluster configuration from your server. This is required before continuing on to perform other activities using Network Load Balancing. NLB should not be configured on the same server as server clustering, or both will be unreliable.

1. If necessary, start your server and log on as Administrator.

2. Click **Start**, click **Run**, type **cluadmin**, and then press **Enter**.

3. Right-click **STUDENT*xx***, where *xx* is your student number, and then click **Evict Node**.

4. Click **Yes** to confirm evicting your server from the cluster. The process of removing your server from the cluster may take several minutes.

5. Close Cluster Administrator.

NETWORK LOAD BALANCING CONCEPTS

An NLB cluster is used to scale out applications and services by making them seamlessly available to clients on multiple servers at the same time. To plan an NLB cluster effectively, you must understand a variety of concepts. These are:

- The NLB driver
- Virtual IP addresses
- Application requirements
- Affinity
- Load balancing options
- Network communication
- Port rules

All of these topics are covered in the following sections.

NLB Driver

The **NLB driver** is the software responsible for performing NLB on each host in an NLB cluster. It must be enabled on each host in an NLB cluster. It is installed and available, but not enabled, on Windows Server 2003 by default, as shown in Figure 12-10.

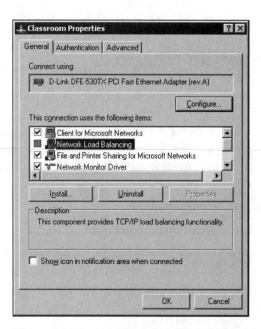

Figure 12-10   Network Load Balancing driver

The NLB driver operates between the network card driver and the IP protocol. This allows it to intercept all incoming IP traffic and filter it as defined by filter rules. It also filters the traffic to ensure that only one host in an NLB cluster responds to a request.

Filtering traffic is required because all hosts in an NLB cluster share a MAC address that is used for the cluster. All network cards using the cluster MAC address pass the packets up to the NLB driver. The NLB driver then discards packets that are not relevant for the local host.

Activity 12-5: Enabling the NLB Driver

ACTIVITY

Time Required: 5 minutes

Objective: Enable the NLB driver.

Description: As a prelude to configuring an NLB cluster, you enable the NLB driver on your server.

1. If necessary, start your server and log on as **Administrator**.

2. Click **Start**, point to **Control Panel**, point to **Network Connections**, right-click **Classroom**, and then click **Properties**.

3. Check the **Network Load Balancing** check box, and then click **OK**.

12

Virtual IP Address

Each NLB cluster has a **virtual IP address**. Unlike a server cluster, which is defined by a virtual server name and IP address, an NLB cluster is defined only by an IP address. The virtual IP address must be unique on the network. In addition, the virtual IP address must be on the same subnet as the hosts in the NLB cluster. The virtual IP address must also be added as a secondary IP address to a network interface on the server.

The virtual IP address cannot be leased from a DHCP server. It must be statically assigned.

NOTE

Application Requirements

Applications that are suitable for NLB must meet certain requirements. These are:

- The application must use TCP or UDP.

- Data modified by the clients must be synchronized between hosts in the NLB cluster or stored in a central location.

- If session state information is used, it must be stored on client computers, stored in a central location, or affinity must be configured.

- The application must not bind to a computer name.
- The applications must not keep files open continually for writing.

Affinity

Affinity is the process whereby responses to requests made originally to one host in an NLB cluster are directed back to the original host. This is required for any applications that keep track of session state information. This is also required if NLB is used for Terminal Services. Each client connecting to Terminal Services must continue to communicate with the same server because their session exists only on one server. SSL for secure Web applications can function without affinity but performance is much faster with affinity enabled.

Affinity can be configured in three ways:

- *None*—Affinity is not performed. This is used when client applications are stateless.
- *Single*—Affinity is performed based on the source IP address of the client. Each request from the same source IP address is directed to the same host in the NLB cluster. This is the most commonly selected option for stateful applications. This option is configured by default.
- *Class C*—Affinity is performed based on the source network of the client. Each request from the same Class C network is directed to the same host in the NLB cluster. This is used when clients are accessing the application through multiple proxy servers with synchronized caching. This occurs through some ISPs such as America Online (AOL).

Load Balancing Options

When hosts are part of an NLB cluster, you can define how the load is balanced between them. There are three options:

- Multiple Host and Equal
- Multiple Host and Load weight
- Single Host

When Multiple Hosts – Equal is chosen, the NLB cluster distributes the load evenly between all hosts in the NLB cluster. This is best suited to situations in which all hosts in the NLB have the same capacity for processing. If one host is less powerful than others in the NLB cluster, the less powerful host acts as a bottleneck for NLB cluster performance.

When Multiple Hosts – Load weight is selected, the NLB cluster distributes requests based on a load weight value that you configure. The load weight value for each host can range from 0 to 100. The number of requests directed to each host is based on its load weight value relative to other hosts. If two hosts have the same load weight value, each one receives the same number of requests. If the load weight value of one host is twice that of another, the number of requests serviced by that host is also twice as high.

The percentage of overall requests serviced by a host is calculated by taking the load weight value assigned to that host and dividing it by the total of the load weight values assigned to all of the hosts in the NLB cluster. Table 12-1 shows an example of the percentage of load assigned to each server in an NLB cluster with three hosts and the percentage of requests serviced by each.

Table 12-1 Load weights for a three-host NLB cluster

Cluster Host	Load Weight Value	Percentage of Requests
NLBHost1	100	100 / (100+50+50) = 50
NLBHost2	50	50 / (100+50+50) = 25
NLBHost3	50	25 / (100+50+50) = 25

Varying the load on each host in an NLB cluster is appropriate when varying levels of hardware are used. In this way, you can give less powerful servers a lower share of client requests.

When Single Host is selected, the load is not spread between multiple servers. All requests to the NLB cluster are directed to a single host. The host that requests are directed to is selected based on the priority setting for the host. Each host in an NLB cluster is assigned a priority setting between 1 and 32, with 1 having the highest priority.

This Single Host setting is used only to provide failover when a host fails. This option is seldom used.

Network Communication

When a client makes a request for a load-balanced application, the request is sent to the virtual IP address of the NLB cluster. Normally, packets contain the MAC address of the network card in the destination computer and that is how the destination computer understands the packet is addressed to it. However, in an NLB cluster, the packet needs to be addressed to all of the hosts in the NLB cluster. So, the MAC addresses of the network cards in the NLB cluster hosts cannot be used.

All hosts in the NLB cluster share a MAC address. All client requests use the MAC address of the NLB cluster as the destination MAC address. This allows all hosts in the NLB cluster to receive packets addressed to the NLB cluster. Then, the NLB driver loaded on each host accepts or discards the packet based on an algorithm that takes into account affinity settings, load weighting, and priority.

12

NLB clusters can be configured to use either unicast MAC addresses or multicast MAC addresses. The following sections discuss when each is appropriate. Both methods send all client requests to all hosts in the NLB cluster.

Unicast

Unicast is the most common method used for distributing client requests. When this method is selected, all hosts in the NLB cluster use the same unicast MAC address. This unicast MAC address is used in place of the MAC address that is embedded in the network card of each host.

If the NLB cluster hosts have only one network card, they are unable to communicate among each other when unicast is selected because they share a single MAC address. If the NLB cluster hosts have two network cards, one network card can be used for receiving client requests and the other can be used for communication between NLB cluster hosts.

The source MAC address used by NLB cluster hosts is different from the MAC address used by the NLB cluster. This is important to prevent a switch from learning the location of an NLB cluster host and mapping it to the MAC address used by the NLB cluster. Switches read the source MAC address in packets; after learning the location of a MAC address, the switches direct all packets with that MAC address to only the port from which the source MAC address was learned. Because packets for the NLB cluster need to be delivered to all ports on the switch, this is unacceptable.

A switch transmits a packet to all ports if it does not know the location of the MAC address. By preventing a switch from learning the NLB cluster MAC address as a source MAC address, all packets addressed to the NLB cluster are always sent to all ports on a switch. However, this does result in an overall increase in network traffic because switches are not able to filter traffic.

Multicast

To prevent the inefficient use of switches and allow NLB cluster hosts with a single network to communicate among themselves, multicast MAC addresses can be used instead of unicast MAC addresses. When multicast MAC addresses are used for the NLB cluster, the network cards still keep their embedded unicast MAC addresses.

The source MAC address used by each host in the NLB cluster is the same multicast MAC address based on the IP address of the NLB cluster. This is acceptable because switches recognize this MAC address as a multicast MAC address that can be assigned to multiple hosts. If the switch supports IGMP (Internet Group Management Protocol) snooping, it learns the locations of the hosts in the NLB cluster and directs packets only to those ports to which an NLB cluster host is attached. If the switch does not support IGMP snooping, it forwards the packets to all ports just as is done with a unicast MAC address.

Port Rules

Port rules are used to control what the NLB driver does with packets. When hosts in the NLB cluster receive packets from clients, port rules define what is done with each packet. Port rules are composed of a cluster IP address, a port address range, a protocol, and a filtering mode that includes load weight and affinity.

If the cluster IP address is varied, different applications can be managed separately and use a different filtering mode. For instance, the NLB cluster may have two Web-based applications, each using a different IP address. The port rule for the first Web application can have one IP address, and the port rule for the other Web-based application can have another IP address. Then, the filtering mode including affinity can be defined separately for each.

The port address range of a port rule can be used to define different filtering modes for applications using the same IP address. For example, Terminal Services and a Web-based application can run on the same IP address in an NLB cluster. The port rule for Terminal Services affects only TCP port 3389, and the port rule for the Web application affects only TCP port 80. Each of these rules can be used to set filtering modes, including affinity.

A default port rule always exists on an NLB cluster and is sufficient in many situations. The default port rule affects all cluster IP addresses, all ports, for TCP and UDP communication, and uses the filtering mode Multiple Hosts, even load distribution, and single affinity. NLB clusters of VPN servers or Terminal Services can use this default port rule if desired.

12

IMPLEMENTING NETWORK LOAD BALANCING

To implement an NLB cluster, the NLB driver must be enabled on all servers that are to be hosts in the NLB cluster. After this has been completed, you can create a new NLB cluster using **Network Load Balancing Manager** (nlbmgr.exe).

When you create a new cluster in Network Load Balancing Manager, you are presented with the Cluster Parameters dialog box, as shown in Figure 12-11. In this dialog box, you can configure the IP address, Subnet mask, Full Internet name (DNS name) of the cluster, Cluster operation mode, and Allow remote control. Allowing remote control means that the cluster can be managed remotely using the command-line utility **nlb.exe**. Allowing remote control is not recommended due to the security risk it presents.

The next dialog box, shown in Figure 12-12, lets you configure additional IP addresses that belong to the NLB cluster. You add additional addresses if you want to bind individual applications to particular IP addresses to manage them separately.

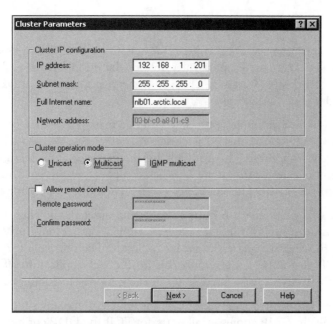

Figure 12-11   Cluster Parameters dialog box

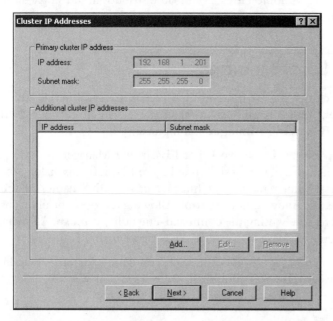

Figure 12-12   Cluster IP Addresses dialog box

After the cluster IP addresses have been configured, you define the port rules. Only the default port rule is defined automatically during the installation process. Any other port rules must be created by you. In this dialog box, you can add new port rules or modify the default port rule. Editing the default port rule is shown in Figure 12-13.

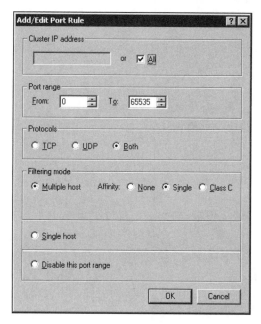

Figure 12-13   Editing the default port rule

Next, you select an NLB cluster host to configure, as shown in Figure 12-14. In this dialog box, you enter the IP address of a cluster host you want to configure, click Connect to get a list of interfaces, and then select the interface you want to configure as part of the NLB cluster.

The host parameters for the selected interface are configured next, as shown in Figure 12-15. In this dialog box, you set the priority for the interface in the cluster. This value must be unique among hosts in the NLB cluster. You can also define the dedicated IP configuration, which is the IP address used for noncluster communication. The dedicated IP configuration should be filled in automatically.

You can also define the initial host state for this host. The default selection is Started, which means that when the server is started, it joins the cluster. If you select Stopped, the host does not join the cluster; you need to start the host manually each time the server is restarted. If you select Suspended, it does not join the cluster immediately after configuration but does join upon reboot.

After the first host has created the NLB cluster, others can join. When a new host is added to the cluster using Network Load Balancing Manager, you first connect to the existing

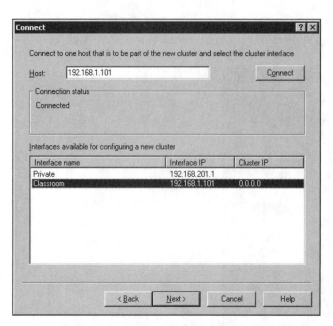

Figure 12-14   Choosing the NLB interface

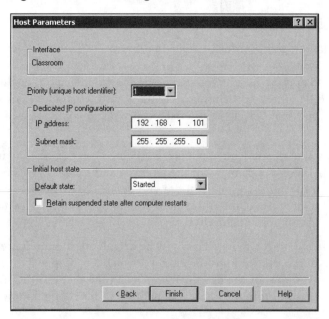

Figure 12-15   Host Parameters dialog box

NLB cluster. Then, you can add a new host from the Cluster menu. When adding the new host, you must supply its IP address and select an interface for the cluster address, as shown in Figure 12-16.

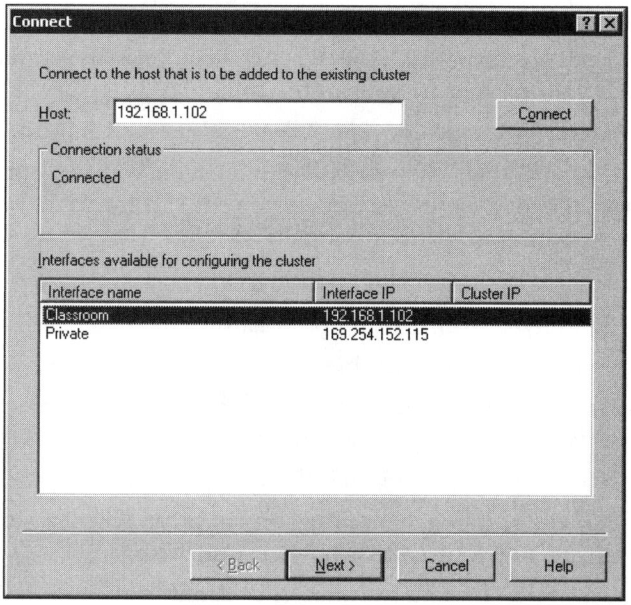

Figure 12-16   Adding a cluster host

After you have selected the host to add, you are asked to configure the host parameters exactly as you were in the original cluster configuration. However, you do not configure port rules because these are taken from the already configured cluster. Now, you can install applications on the NLB cluster.

Activity 12-6: Installing an NLB Cluster

Time Required: 10 minutes

Objective: Install an NLB cluster.

Description: Arctic University has found that their only Web server is overloaded. To scale out the Web site, you create an NLB cluster on which a Web site will be installed. The NLB cluster is composed of two servers. In this activity, you and a partner install an NLB cluster that includes your server and your partner's server. Pay careful attention to which parts of this activity should be completed by each partner.

1. If necessary, start your server and log on as **Administrator**.

2. Both partners: Add a secondary IP address for the cluster to your server by doing the following:

   a. Click **Start**, point to **Control Panel**, point to **Network Connections**, right-click **Classroom**, and then click **Properties**.

   b. Scroll down in the This connection uses the following items box, and double-click **Internet Protocol (TCP/IP)**.

    c. Click **Advanced** and click **Add** in the IP addresses options group.

    d. In the IP address text box, type **192.168.1.2*yy***, where *yy* is the group number assigned to you and your partner by your instructor.

    e. In the Subnet mask text box, type **255.255.255.0**, and then click **Add**.

    f. Click **OK**, click **OK**, and then click **OK**. Depending on your existing network configuration, this step may cause network errors. If errors occur, remove the secondary IP address from both partner computers.

3. Partner 1: Install the new NLB cluster by doing the following:

    a. Click **Start**, click **Run**, type **nlbmgr**, and press **Enter**.

    b. Click the **Cluster** menu and then click **New**.

    c. In the IP address text box, type **192.168.1.2*yy***, where *yy* is the group number assigned to you and your partner by your instructor.

    d. In the Subnet mask text box, type **255.255.255.0**.

    e. In the Full Internet name text box, type **nlb*yy*.arctic.local**, where *yy* is the group number assigned to you and your partner by your instructor.

    f. Select the **Multicast** option button, and then click **Next**.

    g. You do not need to add any additional IP addresses to the cluster at this time. Click **Next** to continue.

    h. In the Port Rules dialog box, click **Edit**. This edits the default port rule. Read the settings here. Notice that it applies to all IP addresses in the cluster, all TCP and UDP ports, and the filtering mode is set to Multiple Host with Single affinity. Click **Cancel** to close the dialog box.

    i. Click **Next**.

    j. In the Host text box, type **192.168.1.1*xx***, where *xx* is your student number, and click **Connect**.

    k. After connecting, both interfaces in your server are listed. Click **Classroom** and then click **Next**.

    l. In the Priority (unique host identifier) drop-down list box, select **1**, if necessary.

    m. Click **Finish**, and then close the Network Load Balancing Manager.

4. Partner 2: Connect to and view the cluster by doing the following:

    a. Click **Start**, click **Run**, type **nlbmgr**, and press **Enter**.

    b. Click the **Cluster** menu and then click **Connect to Existing**.

    c. In the Host text box, type **192.168.1.1*zz***, where *zz* is your partner's student number, and then click **Connect**.

    d. The NLB cluster created by your partner should be shown in the Clusters list. Select it and click **Finish**.

5. Partner 2: Add your server to the cluster by doing the following:

    a. Right-click the cluster and click **Add Host to Cluster**.

b. In the Host text box, type **192.168.1.1xx**, where *xx* is your student number, and then click **Connect**.

c. Click the **Classroom** interface and then click **Next**.

d. Notice that the Priority (unique host identifier) drop-down list box does not allow you to select the value 1 because it is already used by your partner. Click **Finish**.

e. Watch the status of your server in the cluster. When it changes to Converged, your server has finished joining the cluster. Now, all of the network traffic to the NLB cluster IP address of 192.168.1.2*yy*, where *yy* is your group number, is evenly spread between the two hosts in the cluster based on the default port rule. Close the Network Load Balancing Manager.

INSTALLING APPLICATIONS ON AN NLB CLUSTER

There is no special procedure to use when installing applications on an NLB cluster. The application must be installed on all hosts in the cluster. Microsoft strongly recommends that you automate the process of application configuration to ensure that all servers are configured exactly the same. If the application is different on each server, the user experience when communicating with each server will be inconsistent.

ACTIVITY

Activity 12-7: Configuring a Web Application for Load Balancing

Time Required: 10 minutes

Objective: Configure a Web site for load balancing.

Description: Now that load balancing has been configured for your server and your partner's server, you must configure the Web site. In this activity, you and your partner create a Web page and configure a Web site on each server in the NLB cluster.

1. If necessary, start your server and log on as **Administrator**.

2. Click **Start**, click **Run**, type **cmd**, and then press **Enter**.

3. Type **md c:\web** and then press **Enter**.

4. Type **exit** and then press **Enter**.

5. Click **Start**, point to **Administrative Tools**, and then click **Internet Information Services (IIS) Manager**.

6. In the left pane, expand your server, and click **Web Sites**. The only Web site running should be the Default Web Site. For the NLB cluster, you are going to create a new Web site.

7. Right-click **Default Web Site** and then click **Stop**. This ensures that there is no conflict between the Default Web Site and the new Web site you are creating.

8. Right-click **Web Sites**, point to **New**, and then click **Web Site**.

12

9. Click **Next** to begin the Web Site Creation Wizard.

10. In the Description text box, type **NLB Web**, and click **Next**.

11. In the Enter the IP address to use for this Web site drop-down list box, select **192.168.1.2yy**, where *yy* is the group number assigned to you and your partner by the instructor.

12. Click **Next** to continue.

13. In the Path text box, type **c:\web**, and then click **Next**.

14. Click **Next** to accept the default permissions for the Web site, and click **Finish**.

15. Close Internet Information Services (IIS) Manager.

16. Click **Start**, point to **All Programs**, point to **Accessories**, and then click **Notepad**.

17. Type in the information for your Web page, as shown in Figure 12-17.

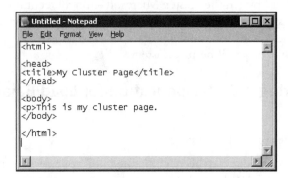

Figure 12-17 Web page content

18. Click the **File** menu, click **Save As**, type **c:\web\default.htm** in the File name text box, and then click **Save**.

19. Close Notepad.

20. Click **Start**, point to **All Programs**, and then click **Internet Explorer**.

21. In the Address bar, type **http://192.168.1.2yy**, where *yy* is the group number assigned to you and your partner by the instructor, and then press **Enter**. You now see your Web page. Be aware that this is not a true test of your NLB cluster because your server accesses this IP address locally. However, this does confirm the Web site is working and now should be available through the NLB cluster.

22. Close Internet Explorer.

23. Optional: To truly test your NLB cluster, perform Steps 20–22 from the Instructor server or have your instructor do it for you.

ACTIVITY

Activity 12-8: Removing an NLB Clustered Application

Time Required: 5 minutes

Objective: Remove an NLB cluster.

Description: When an NLB clustered application is no longer required, both it and the NLB cluster must be removed. In this activity, you and your partner remove the NLB cluster. Unless otherwise specified, both partners perform each step.

1. If necessary, start your server and log on as **Administrator**.

2. Click **Start**, click **Run**, type **nlbmgr**, and then press **Enter**.

3. Click the **Cluster** menu and then click **Connect to Existing**.

4. In the Host text box, type **192.168.1.1xx**, where *xx* is your student number, click **Connect**, and then click **Finish**.

5. Partner 1: Remove your server from the NLB cluster by doing the following:

   a. Right-click your server and then click **Delete Host**.

   b. Click **Yes** to confirm the removal.

6. Partner 2: Remove your server from the NLB cluster by doing the following:

   a. Press **F5** to refresh the screen. You should now see only your server in the cluster. If the first refresh does not work, wait 30 seconds and refresh again. If the second refresh does not work, restart Network Load Balancing Manager.

   b. Right-click your server and then click **Delete Host**.

   c. Click **Yes** to confirm the removal.

7. Both partners: Remove the NLB Web site by doing the following:

   a. Click **Start**, point to **Administrative Tools**, and then click **Internet Information Services (IIS) Manager**.

   b. Expand your server and expand **Web Sites**.

   c. Right-click **NLB Web** and then click **Delete**.

   d. Click **Yes** to confirm the deletion.

   e. Close the Internet Information Services (IIS) Manager window.

8. Close Network Load Balancing Manager.

12

CHAPTER SUMMARY

- Server availability is the percentage of time the server is functional and providing services. Availability is affected by hardware failures, network failures, administrator mistakes, operating system crashes, and application crashes.

❑ Scalability is the ability to expand the capacity of a server or applications. Scaling up is adding additional capacity to a server. Scaling out is adding additional servers to perform the same task.

❑ Stateless applications do not keep information about ongoing client sessions and are the best applications for NLB. Stateful applications track client sessions and can be used with NLB if affinity is configured.

❑ Server clusters are supported on Windows Server 2003, Enterprise Edition and Datacenter Edition. Up to eight nodes are supported.

❑ Server clusters can be configured as active/active, active/passive, N+I failover, and single node virtual server. All of these provide failover capabilities except the single node virtual server, which is used for server consolidation only.

❑ Cluster-aware applications use the clustering API to monitor status of the cluster. Cluster-unaware applications cannot access the clustering API, and may lose some data when they fail over.

❑ NLB is supported by all editions of Windows Server 2003. Up to 32 nodes are supported.

❑ Shared disks for server clusters can be external shared SCSI or Fibre Channel.

❑ The quorum resource is used to store cluster configuration information and arbitrate which node owns the cluster.

❑ Heartbeat packets are used between cluster nodes to test the availability of nodes in the cluster.

❑ Resource groups are logical groups of resources that fail over and fail back as a unit from one node to another.

❑ Failover is the process used to move a resource group from one node to another when the original node fails. Failback is the process of moving a resource group back to its original node after failure.

❑ All server cluster resources are accessed through a virtual server.

❑ Both Cluster Administrator (cluadmin.exe) and cluster.exe can be used to administer server clusters.

❑ The NLB driver must be enabled on servers before NLB can be configured. In addition, the virtual IP address of the NLB cluster must be added as a secondary IP address before the NLB cluster is configured.

❑ To benefit from an NLB cluster, applications must use TCP or UDP, must not bind to a computer name, and must not keep files open continually for writing.

❑ Single affinity assigns client requests from the same IP address to the same server. Class C affinity assigns all of the client requests from the same Class C network to the same server.

❑ Multiple Hosts – Equal spreads the load evenly between all hosts in an NLB cluster. Multiple Hosts – Load weight spreads the load between hosts based on the assigned load weight. Single Host directs all client requests to the server with the lowest priority number.

❑ Network communication for load balancing can use unicast or multicast MAC addresses. When unicast is used, each host must have two network cards or they are unable to communicate with each other. Packets transmitted by the hosts do not use the MAC address in their network cards.

❑ Port rules define how client requests are to be load-balanced.

❑ Network Load Balancing Manager (nlbmgr.exe) and nlb.exe can both be used to manage NLB clusters.

KEY TERMS

active/active server cluster — A cluster configuration in which all nodes provide services.

active/passive server cluster — A server cluster with one active node and one passive node. Services fail over from the active node to the passive node.

affinity — The process for keeping a conversation between a client and server from being load-balanced. All requests from one client are directed to one host in the NLB cluster.

availability — The percentage of time that a server, service, or application is functioning properly.

Cluster Administrator — A GUI utility to manage server clusters.

cluster.exe — A command-line utility to manage server clusters.

cluster-aware applications — The applications that understand clustering and can take advantage of the clustering API.

cluster-unaware applications — The applications that have not been written to use cluster services.

failback — The process whereby a resource group migrates back to its original node after failover has occurred.

failover — The process whereby a resource group migrates from a failed node to a new node.

heartbeat packets — The packets sent between nodes in a cluster to confirm that all nodes are still operational.

N+I failover server cluster — A variation of an active/passive server cluster in which multiple passive nodes wait for services to fail over from multiple active nodes.

Network Load Balancing (NLB) — A service that distributes client requests among multiple servers with the same application installed.

Network Load Balancing Manager — A GUI utility for managing NLB clusters.

NLB driver — The driver that intercepts TCP/IP traffic on an NLB cluster host and applies port rules.

12

nlb.exe — A command-line utility for managing NLB clusters.

port rules — The rules that define how traffic is to be load-balanced among the hosts in an NLB cluster.

quorum resource — A special disk resource used by the server cluster to store configuration information and arbitrate which node owns the cluster.

resource groups — The logical groupings of resources that fail over as a single unit.

scalability — The ability to expand the capacity of a server or application.

scaling out — The process of adding capacity by adding additional servers.

scaling up — The process of adding additional capacity to a single server.

server clusters — The groups of servers that provide highly available services with the ability to fail over from one server in the cluster to another.

shared disks — The storage that is accessible to all nodes in a cluster.

single node virtual server — A type of cluster with only one node that is used to consolidate multiple servers without reconfiguring clients.

stateful applications — An application that tracks ongoing information about a client session.

stateless application — An application that does not track ongoing information about a user session.

virtual IP address — The IP address on which cluster resources are available.

virtual server — The representation of the cluster service on the network.

REVIEW QUESTIONS

1. Which term is used to describe the percentage of time a service is functioning correctly?

    a. uptime

    b. scalability

    c. availability

    d. reliability

2. Which term is used to describe the ability to expand capacity of a server or application?

    a. uptime

    b. scalability

    c. availability

    d. reliability

3. Which of the following can cause a server or service to fail? (Choose all that apply.)

    a. hardware failure

    b. network failure

   c. administrator mistakes

   d. operating system crashes

   e. application crashes

4. Which of the following provides the ability to scale out applications?

   a. RAID5

   b. NLB clusters

   c. stateful applications

   d. server clusters

5. Which of the following enhances application availability? (Choose all that apply.)

   a. RAID5

   b. NLB clusters

   c. stateful applications

   d. server clusters

6. Which type of application is best suited to running on an NLB cluster?

   a. stateless

   b. consecutive

   c. stateful

   d. concurrent

7. Which term describes an application that tracks user information during a session?

   a. stateless

   b. consecutive

   c. stateful

   d. concurrent

8. Which type of server cluster does not provide failover capability?

   a. active/passive server cluster

   b. N+I failover server cluster

   c. active/active server cluster

   d. single node virtual server

9. Which type of server cluster experiences performance degradation if one node fails? (Choose all that apply.)

   a. active/passive server cluster

   b. N+I failover server cluster

   c. active/active server cluster

   d. single node virtual server

10. Which type of application in a server cluster can be migrated with no loss of data?

    a. cluster-unaware applications

    b. cluster-aware applications

    c. stateful applications

    d. concurrent applications

11. Which two ways can a shared disk be configured for a server cluster? (Choose all that apply.)

    a. wireless

    b. SCSI

    c. IDE

    d. Fibre Channel

12. All resources in a resource group fail over together. True or False?

13. When does failback occur? (Choose all that apply.)

    a. automatically when the original node becomes available

    b. when the administrator manually performs it

    c. never

    d. automatically 10 minutes after the original node becomes available

14. Which command-line utility is used to manage server clusters?

    a. cluadmin.exe

    b. cluster.exe

    c. nlbmgr.exe

    d. nlb.exe

15. Which type of affinity is used when you want all requests from one IP address to be sent to the same host in an NLB cluster?

    a. None; this is automatic.

    b. Single

    c. one-to-one

    d. Class C

16. If Server1 in an NLB cluster has a load weight value of 40 and Server2 has a load weight value of 20, what percentage of client requests will be directed to Server 1?

    a. This configuration is not possible because the load weight values must add up to 100.

    b. 40%

    c. 67%

    d. 33%

17. Which GUI utility can be used to manage NLB clusters?

   a. cluadmin.exe

   b. cluster.exe

   c. nlbmgr.exe

   d. nlb.exe

18. Which MAC address appears as the source MAC address when NLB hosts in unicast mode send packets?

   a. the MAC address on the NIC in the host

   b. the MAC address on the NIC in the client

   c. a MAC address that is shared between all NLB hosts

   d. a false MAC address that is unique for all NLB hosts

19. An NLB clustering host must have the NLB virtual IP address added as a secondary IP address before NLB can be configured. True or False?

20. Which characteristics are parts of the default port rule? (Choose all that apply.)

   a. even load distribution

   b. Class C affinity

   c. single affinity

   d. affects all ports 1024 and above

   e. affects only TCP ports

12

Case Projects

Case Project 12-1: Server Clusters

Arctic University is considering investing in three servers that are scaled up to four processors and 4 GB of RAM. All existing Windows NT servers will be consolidated onto these three servers. Because there have been many server outages in the past, some of the Arctic University administration is concerned that this configuration will result in severe outages in the event a server fails. How can server clusters be used to reduce this risk?

Case Project 12-2: NLB Clusters

Arctic University has a single VPN server to handle all of the users who work from home in the evenings. Many users have been complaining that their connections are being dropped or they are unable to connect. How can an NLB cluster fix this problem?

Case Project 12-3: Configuring a Server Cluster

To reduce the cost of implementing a server cluster, Arctic University has decided to use SCSI for the shared disks in a cluster, rather than Fibre Channel. You think that this is a mistake. Explain why Fibre Channel is a better long-term option.

Case Project 12-4: Clustering for a Web Application

Arctic University has bought a new application for managing student records. The application is Web-based, but it requires a lot of processor power on the Web server. There is a lot of concern about the scalability of this application among the university administration.

This application integrates with an entire enterprise suite of applications used to manage many facets of the university. The database is shared by all of the applications and runs on Microsoft SQL Server.

Explain how server clustering and NLB clustering can help in the implementation of this new application.

13

PLANNING SERVER AND NETWORK SECURITY

> ## After reading this chapter, you will be able to:
>
> ◆ Describe three types of security
>
> ◆ Plan security configurations for server roles
>
> ◆ Plan network protocol security
>
> ◆ Plan wireless network security
>
> ◆ Define the default security settings used by Windows Server 2003
>
> ◆ Plan a secure baseline for client computers and servers
>
> ◆ Create a plan for software updates
>
> ◆ Ensure secure administrative access

When computers were configured as stand-alone workstations, security was not a very important concern. However, with the advent of the Internet and computer networks in general, it is much easier for hackers to anonymously attack your systems. Security is now a very important concern.

In this chapter, you learn the three broad types of security, plan security configurations for different server roles, plan network protocol security, and plan wireless network security. In addition, you view the default security settings used by Windows Server 2003, define a secure baseline for client computers and servers, and create a plan for ensuring timely software updates. Finally, you ensure secure administrative access.

Types of Security

As computer systems have progressed from optional to essential within organizations, so has computer system security. Without proper security in place, the potential exists for accidental destruction of data, disgruntled employees stealing data, or even corporate espionage.

Security is a very broad topic. To make it easier to understand, it is helpful to break it down into smaller categories. Three commonly used categories are physical security, network security, and data security. Each of these categories, covered in the following sections, helps you understand the nature of the threats that you face.

Physical Security

Physical security is controlling physical access to the computing devices on your network. It is often overlooked in the planning process because it is not a technical issue. Technical staff like to think about what encryption protocols should be in place or what permissions should be assigned to a resource, but seldom think about who has a key to the server room.

Physical security is very important and should always be included in any security plan. It prevents users and hackers from physically accessing network resources that they have no legitimate need to touch. This is important because after physical security is in place, software-based security is more effective.

Many methods to breach software-based security mechanisms are only possible when a hacker has physical access to a server or workstation. For example, every hacker wants to get Administrative access to systems. Petter Nordahl-Hagen has written a utility (ntpasswd) that can change the password of the local Administrator account on Windows NT/2000/XP/2003 computers. This utility is used from a Linux-based boot floppy or boot CD. Your initial instinct that this utility is very dangerous is correct. However, this utility is effective only if the hacker has physical access to the server or workstation to use the boot floppy or boot CD. Physical security can entirely prevent the risk by stopping a hacker from putting the boot floppy or boot CD into the server or workstation.

All sensitive resources should be kept behind locked doors. Sensitive resources include all servers, some workstations that store data locally, and even printers that are used to print sensitive documents. A locked door need not be a separate room; it can also be a locked cabinet. Access to these resources should be limited to those who need them to perform their jobs.

NOTE

In many office buildings with drop ceilings, the walls do not go up completely to the next floor. Determined hackers can actually crawl over the wall and into a locked room.

Routers, switches, hubs, and network cabling should also be protected behind locked doors or in conduit. A hacker with access to internal network ports can use a packet sniffer to find additional information such as unencrypted passwords, which can be used to further penetrate the network. Physical access to many network devices allows a hacker to reset them to factory defaults and reconfigure them in any way the hacker desires. Finally, physical access to any of these components can result in a denial of service attack, in which the component is disabled or destroyed, preventing legitimate users from accessing network resources.

Network Security

Network security broadly refers to accessing network-based resources through a computer network. After physical security is in place, the only way for most users to access resources is through the network. If network security is implemented well, users have access only to the resources they need to perform their jobs.

Some of the tools available for enforcing network security are:

- Authentication
- IPSec
- Firewalls

Authentication is the first and most important tool in network security. Authentication verifies the identity of users before giving them access to resources. A valid user name and password is the most common way to authenticate users, but other mechanisms such as smart cards are also available. If proper authentication is not performed, it is not possible to control which users get access to which resources.

A number of different protocols can be used as part of the authentication process for a user name and password, including NTLM, NTLMv2, and Kerberos. Kerberos is the most secure of these three, and it is used by default for Windows 2000 and newer Windows operating systems.

IPSec is used to encrypt data packets while they are in transit on the network. This can be used to secure data transfers between two sites across a public network, such as the Internet, or all traffic to a particular server. In addition, IPSec authenticates both computers involved in a conversation to prevent imposters from gathering sensitive information such as passwords.

Firewalls control data movement based on IP addresses as well as UDP and TCP port numbers. Based on these criteria, certain packets are allowed in and out of the network. Firewalls are primarily used to control packet movement between internal networks and the Internet.

The simplest implementation of a firewall when using Windows Server 2003 is Internet Connection Firewall. This can be configured on each server to control which packets are allowed in. The actual packets allowed vary depending on the role of the server. This is effective for protecting a single server, but is awkward to configure for multiple servers because each server must be configured individually.

13

A more common use of a firewall is to protect a group of servers by limiting requests from a location such as the Internet to a group of servers. The default rule on most firewalls filters all packets. This is important for a secure network because you can choose just the packets you want to allow.

Using a single firewall, shown in Figure 13-1, is relatively high risk when providing services on the Internet. The servers that are accessible from the Internet are mixed with servers that are not directly accessible from the Internet. However, if one of the Internet-accessible servers is compromised, or if the firewall is compromised, then hackers can gain access to all of the servers.

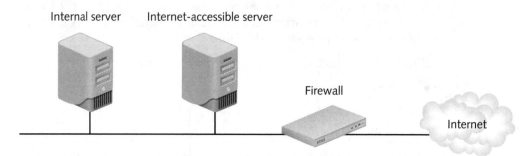

Figure 13-1   A single firewall

To enhance security, most larger organizations that provide services accessible from the Internet use a **demilitarized zone (DMZ)**. A DMZ is an Internet-accessible subnet between the Internet and a private network. Access to the DMZ is controlled by firewalls between the DMZ, the Internet, and the private network, as shown in Figure 13-2. No direct communication is allowed between the private network and the Internet. Even Internet access for clients on the private network is controlled by a proxy server in the DMZ.

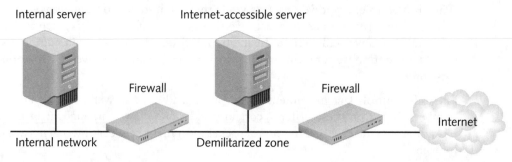

Figure 13-2   A DMZ

Data Security

Data security refers to mechanisms that can be implemented to ensure that only authorized users are able to access sensitive data. Some examples of sensitive data include employee salaries, sales figures and projections, and company trade secrets.

Some of the tools available for enforcing data security include:

- NTFS permissions
- Share permissions
- Auditing
- EFS

NTFS permissions are used to control access to files and folders stored on network servers. Network users are able to access files and folders only if they have been granted proper NTFS permissions. If users do not need to alter data, then only Read and Execute permissions are necessary. If users do need to alter data in files, they are normally granted Modify permissions. Modify does not allow users to take ownership of a file. Administrators should be the only users granted Full Control permissions because they allow modification of NTFS permissions and the ability to take ownership. Taking ownership is important to restrict because the owner of a file or folder can modify its NTFS permissions.

Share permissions are used to control access to a particular network share. Unlike NTFS permissions, which apply when files are accessed locally and remotely, share permissions apply only when accessing network resources across the network through a share. If proper NTFS permissions are in place, share permissions are not required to control access.

To prevent confusion about different access levels between local and remote access, leave the share permissions on a file share as the default of Full Control for the Authenticated Users group. Then, only NTFS permissions are used to control access to files and folders. The one exception to this rule is when files or folders on a FAT or FAT32 partition need to be shared. FAT and FAT32 do not support NTFS permissions and the only way to control access to files on a FAT or FAT32 partition is to use share permissions.

Auditing allows you to track which users have performed, or attempted to perform, certain actions. Although auditing does not prevent users from performing unauthorized tasks, it does inform you when unauthorized tasks are attempted so that the problem can be corrected. For example, if a user repeatedly tries to access payroll information, his supervisor can be informed so that disciplinary action can be taken. Auditing can also inform you that a hacker is attempting to gain access to your system; you can look at attempted logons to the network. Action can then be taken to either track down the hacker or additional security can be implemented if required.

13

Encrypting File System

EFS (encrypting file system) encrypts files that are stored on NTFS partitions. It can be used to encrypt files stored on Windows 2000/XP workstations or on Windows 2000/2003 servers. When files are stored in an encrypted format, only the user who encrypted them, other designated users, or a designated recovery agent can decrypt them and read the contents. The encryption and decryption process is completely transparent to users after it has been configured.

NOTE   The ability of multiple users to use an encrypted file is new in Windows XP and Windows Server 2003. Windows 2000 clients are not able to add multiple users to an encrypted file.

Certificates are used as the basis of EFS. Each time a file is encrypted by a user, a symmetric key is used for encryption. The symmetric key is then encrypted using the public key of the user who encrypted the file and is stored in the header of the file. The symmetric key is also encrypted using the public key of the recovery agent and stored in the header of the file. In addition, the symmetric key is also encrypted using the public key of any additional users who have been assigned to the file. This process is shown in Figure 13-3.

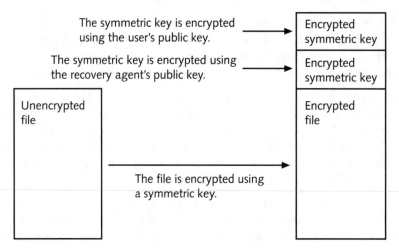

Figure 13-3   Encrypting a file

To open an encrypted file, a user must be able to decrypt the symmetric key. Because a copy of the symmetric key is encrypted using the public key of the user who encrypted it, the recovery agent and the assigned user are the only people who can decrypt the symmetric key and then decrypt the file.

When a user attempts to open an encrypted file, the symmetric key is decrypted using the private key of the user opening the file. The private key of the user opening the file must match the public key that was used to encrypt the symmetric key. In this way, only if a user's public key has encrypted the symmetric key can the user decrypt the symmetric key and thereby decrypt the original file. This process is shown in Figure 13-4.

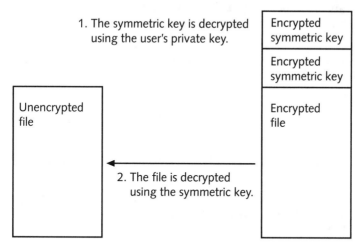

Figure 13-4 Decrypting a file

Certificates used by EFS can be created automatically, through an internal CA or a third-party CA. For the highest levels of manageability, an internal CA should be used. If the EFS certificates are created automatically, you may find it difficult to recover files. If a third-party CA is used, you will encounter significant expense and often a lag time to get new certificates. An internal CA has essentially no cost and you can automate the process of creating certificates for EFS.

ACTIVITY

Activity 13-1: Using EFS to Protect Files

Time Required: 10 minutes

Objective: Use EFS to protect files.

Description: The president of Arctic University uses a laptop to take work home every night and while on business trips. As part of a recent security audit, it was recommended that all laptops use EFS-protected files in the event a laptop is stolen. Before implementing this solution, you test it in your test environment.

1. If necessary, start your server and log on as **Administrator**.

2. Create a new user for testing encryption by doing the following:

   a. Click **Start**, click **Run**, type **mmc**, and then press **Enter**.

   b. Click the **File** menu, click **Add/Remove Snap-in**, click **Add**, double-click **Active Directory Users and Computers**, click **Close**, and then click **OK**.

  c. Double-click **Active Directory Users and Computers**, double-click **Arctic.local**, and then click **Users**.

  d. Right-click **Users**, point to **New**, and then click **User**.

  e. In the First name text box, type **EFS*xx***, where *xx* is your student number. In the User logon name text box, type **EFS*xx***, and then click **Next**.

  f. In the Password text box, type **Password!**, in the Confirm password text box, type **Password!**, deselect the **User must change password at next logon** check box, and then click **Next**.

  g. Click **Finish**.

3. Create an additional new user for testing encryption by doing the following:

  a. Right-click **Users**, point to **New**, and then click **User**.

  b. In the First name text box, type **NoEFS*xx***, where *xx* is your student number. In the User logon name text box, type **NoEFS*xx***, and then click **Next**.

  c. In the Password text box, type **Password!**, in the Confirm password text box, type **Password!**, deselect the **User must change password at next logon** check box, and then click **Next**.

  d. Click **Finish**.

  e. Close MMC. Click **No** if asked to save console settings.

4. Create a new folder for encrypted files and set the security to allow all users access by doing the following:

  a. Click **Start**, click **Run**, type **cmd**, and then press **Enter**.

  b. Type **md c:\encrypt** and press **Enter**.

  c. Close the command prompt window.

  d. Click **Start**, right-click **My Computer**, and then click **Explore**.

  e. In the left pane, click **Local Disk (C:)**, right-click **encrypt**, click **Properties**, and then click the **Security** tab.

  f. In the Group or user names list box, click **Users (STUDENT*xx*\Users)**, where *xx* is your student number.

  g. In the Permissions for Users list box, check the **Allow** check box for the Modify permission, and then click **OK**.

  h. Close Windows Explorer.

5. Log off as Administrator.

6. Log on as **EFS*xx***, where *xx* is your student number.

7. Create and encrypt a file by doing the following:

  a. Click **Start**, right-click **My Computer**, and then click **Explore**.

  b. In the left pane, click **Local Disk (C:)**, right-click **encrypt**, and then click **Properties**.

c. On the General tab, click **Advanced**.

d. Check the **Encrypt contents to secure data** check box, and then click **OK**.

e. Click **OK** to save the changes. Click another folder to change the focus and then notice that the folder name is now green to indicate that it is encrypted.

f. If necessary, in the left pane, click **encrypt** to select it.

g. In the right pane, right-click in an open (white) area, point to **New**, and then click **Text Document**.

h. Type **encrypted file.txt** and press **Enter** to rename the file. Notice that the file is also green to indicate it is encrypted.

i. Double-click **encrypted file.txt** to open it in Notepad, type some text in the file, click the **File** menu, click **Exit**, and then click **Yes** to save the changes.

j. Close Windows Explorer, and log off as EFS*xx*, where *xx* is your student number.

8. Attempt to open the encrypted file as a nonauthorized user by doing the following:

a. Log on as **NoEFS*xx***, where *xx* is your student number.

b. Click **Start**, right-click **My Computer**, and then click **Explore**.

c. In the left pane, click **Local Disk (C:)**, and then click **encrypt**.

d. Double-click **encrypted file.txt** to open it. Notepad opens to edit the file, but you receive an error message indicating that Access is denied. Access is denied because of the encryption. The user you are logged in as is not authorized to view the contents of this file, even though this user has Modify NTFS permission.

e. Click **OK** to close the Access is denied error, close Notepad, and then close Windows Explorer.

f. Log off as NoEFS*xx*, where *xx* is your student number.

Note that by default, Windows Server 2003 does not allow files to be encrypted on a remote computer, just a local computer. If you want to be able to encrypt files on a remote computer, including a network server, you must enable it. In a Windows 2000 mixed-mode or Windows 2000 native mode domain, you must check the Trust computer for delegation check box on the General tab in the properties of the remote computer. In a Windows 2003 native mode domain, you must check the Trust this computer for delegation to any service (Kerberos only) check box on the Delegation tab in the properties of the remote computer. The properties of the remote computer are accessed at the console of the remote computer by clicking Start on the desktop, right-clicking My Computer, and then clicking Properties.

Files that are encrypted on a remote computer are stored in an encrypted state. However, while they are in transit from the local computer to the remote computer, the files are not encrypted. If you want to protect the contents of files while they are in transit, IPSec should be used.

When files are encrypted on a remote computer, users can access them from any workstation. This can create problems because user private keys, which are required to decrypt the files, are stored in the profile of the local workstation. A user may potentially not be able to decrypt files from one workstation when they have been encrypted from another. To prevent this problem, you can implement roaming user profiles. Roaming user profiles follows users from one workstation to another, taking their private key with them.

PLANNING SECURITY CONFIGURATION FOR SERVER ROLES

Many general rules for security apply regardless of the role that a server is playing. Some of these include the following:

- Disable unnecessary services.
- Limit access to the minimum required for users to perform their jobs.
- Use separate administrator accounts for different staff.
- Allow packets to necessary TCP and UDP ports only.

All unnecessary services should be disabled on all servers. Any service is a potential security risk because it may have a flaw that allows unauthorized users to access the system or perform denial of service attacks. There is no way for you to predict which services are flawed. To minimize risk, you must disable all unnecessary services.

All users should be granted only the permissions required to perform their jobs. From an administrator's perspective, sometimes it is easier to give users more access than they require to ensure that they have access to everything they need and reduce requests for enhanced access. However, in the long run, this increases the risk of accidental damage from users because they have access to data they do not require. Creating proper groups to control access to resources significantly reduces the workload involved in managing user permissions.

In many organizations, several administrators use the same Administrator account to manage the system. This is not good; each administrator should use a separate account to perform management tasks. Then, auditing can be performed to track what each administrator has done. If all administrators share the same account, auditing cannot track which person actually performed a task or accessed a file. This is particularly important because administrators have such a high level of system access and can view most, if not all, data on the system.

When a server is configured for a very specific role, you can limit the TCP and UDP ports that are accessible by using a firewall. The firewall can be a separate hardware device, a server running Internet Security and Acceleration Server, or Internet Connection Firewall. By filtering out unnecessary packets, you further reduce the risk that a hacker can gain unauthorized access to a server.

The following sections describe the tasks involved in securing domain controllers, Web servers, database servers, and mail servers.

Securing Domain Controllers

Domain controllers are particularly important to secure in your organization because they contain all of the user accounts for your domain. If a domain controller is compromised, a hacker may potentially get access to all of your network resources.

The first way to secure your domain controller is to ensure that it is not accessible to any users outside of your organization. This means it should be behind a firewall and not visible directly from the Internet.

When authentication services are required for users accessing services from the Internet such as a VPN, the VPN server should be located in a DMZ and communication allowed from the VPN server to the DMZ only.

For even higher levels of security, RADIUS can be used. IAS is installed on a server in the DMZ to configure it as a RADIUS server. The internal firewall is then configured to allow communication between the RADIUS server and the domain controller. The VPN server is configured to use the RADIUS server for authentication. In this situation, a hacker would need to compromise the VPN server to get access to the RADIUS server, and then compromise the RADIUS server to gain access to the domain controller.

NetBIOS ports are the source of many security flaws and vulnerabilities in Windows. If your server is available from the Internet, the NetBIOS ports should be blocked by a firewall. Alternatively, NetBIOS can be disabled on the network connection that is connected to the Internet.

Table 13-1 shows the port numbers that must be open to allow authentication to a domain controller. If a firewall blocks these, authentication is not possible.

Table 13-1   Domain controller authentication ports

Port	Description
88 UDP/TCP	The Kerberos Key Distribution Center (KDC) listens for requests on this port.
135 TCP	RPC (remote procedure call) is required for NTLM authentication.
137 UDP	The NetBIOS name server is part of the NetBIOS over TCP/IP (NetBT) family of protocols and provides a means for host name and address mapping on a NetBIOS-aware network. This is required for NTLM authentication.
138 UDP	The NetBIOS datagram is part of the NetBIOS over TCP/IP (NetBT) family of protocols and is used for network logon and browsing. This is required for NTLM authentication.
139 TCP	NetBIOS session services are part of the NetBIOS over TCP/IP (NetBT) family of protocols and are used for SMB (Server Message Block), file sharing, and printing.
389 UDP	Active Directory is accessed on this port using LDAP.
464 TCP	Password changes through Kerberos are performed using this port.

Table 13-1 Domain controller authentication ports (continued)

Port	Description
636 TCP	Active Directory is accessed on this port using LDAP over SSL. SSL prevents eavesdropping.
3268 TCP	Global catalog servers listen on this port.
3269 TCP	Global catalog servers using SSL listen on this port.

Securing Web Servers

Web servers are normally kept in a DMZ to limit the access of Internet users. For Web sites that do not authenticate users or collect sensitive information, TCP port 80 should be open on the external firewall. Web sites that authenticate users or collect sensitive information should run on TCP port 443 using SSL. SSL prevents hackers from learning passwords and other sensitive information by eavesdropping with a packet sniffer.

To further protect a Web server, install the operating system, IIS, and the Web site data on separate hard drive partitions. Then, if the Web server is compromised, it is more difficult for hackers to find the operating system and other data.

In addition, remove any demonstration scripts that installed by default on the Web server. The scripts are often found to have security issues well after the Web server has been installed and configured. However, most administrators forget to remove them after the flaw is found.

If you do not run scripts on your Web server, disable the ability to run scripts by disabling ASP processing and the processing of all other script types.

ACTIVITY

Activity 13-2: Disabling Script Processing in IIS

Time Required: 5 minutes

Objective: Disable processing of scripts in IIS.

Description: Arctic University has installed a new Web server that will distribute only static Web pages. No dynamic content is required. During testing, script processing was enabled. However, now you want to disable script processing before placing the server in your DMZ.

1. If necessary, start your server and log on as **Administrator**.

2. Click **Start**, point to **Administrative Tools**, and then click **Internet Information Services (IIS) Manager**.

3. Double-click your server to expand it, and then click **Web Service Extensions**.

4. In the right pane, click **Active Server Pages**, and then click **Prohibit**.

5. Click **Yes** to indicate that you want to stop processing of Active Server Pages even though this also disables Certificate Services.

6. If present in the right pane, click **ASP.NET v1.1.4322**, and then click **Prohibit**.

7. Click **Yes** to indicate that you want to stop processing of ASP.NET v1.1.4322.

8. Close Internet Information Services (IIS) Manager.

Securing Database Servers

Database servers are used as the back-end components for both client/server applications and Web applications. Microsoft SQL Server is one of the most common database servers. Microsoft SQL Server uses TCP port 1677 by default, although it can be changed to any port.

When Microsoft SQL Server is used as part of a client/server application, both the clients and the server are on the internal network. When both are on the internal network, a firewall is not commonly used, although you can use Internet Connection Firewall to prevent access to unnecessary server ports. More often, you are concerned with protecting the data while it is in transit on the network between the client and the server. To protect this data, you can use IPSec.

If Microsoft SQL Server is used as part of a Web-based application, it is quite common to place the Web server in the DMZ and the SQL server on the internal, private network. On the internal firewall, only packets to port 1677 of the SQL server are allowed. This prevents hackers on the Internet from directly accessing the database.

A database that holds sensitive information should never be on the same server as the Web site. If the Web server is compromised, the database will likely be compromised as well. If the database runs on a separate server, then the hacker must still find the database. Also, encrypt databases holding sensitive information. Most of the time when you hear about Web sites being hacked and credit card numbers being stolen, it is because the database was on the same server as the Web site and was not encrypted.

Securing Mail Servers

The only protection you can give a mail server is a firewall. A mail server can potentially receive messages from any server on the Internet. Therefore, it is impossible to implement an authentication scheme to prevent unauthorized users. This is one of the reasons that there is so much spam on the Internet.

Mail servers that communicate with the Internet should be placed in the DMZ. The external firewall should allow communication to TCP port 25 on the mail server. If you are supporting POP3 or IMAP access to e-mail from the Internet, you should allow TCP port 110 and 143 respectively, as well.

The best way for clients to access e-mail is from a server on the internal network; this limits the number of ports that must be opened up between the internal network and the DMZ. Configure a second e-mail server on the internal network that forwards all mail to the mail server in the DMZ. This way, the internal e-mail server never communicates directly with the Internet. Configure the mail server in the DMZ to forward all mail it receives from the Internet to the internal mail server.

13

If the mail server in the DMZ is running Exchange 2003 and the clients are using Outlook 2003, RPC over HTTP is supported. Older versions of Outlook, and older versions of Exchange, required many ports to be open to support connectivity (TCP 135, UDP 137, TCP 139, and TCP 445). With RPC over HTTP, the only port that needs to be allowed from the internal network to the DMZ is either TCP port 80 or TCP port 443. TCP port 443 is the port you should choose because this uses SSL to protect the data while in transit. Figure 13-5 shows a firewall configuration in which RPC over HTTP is used.

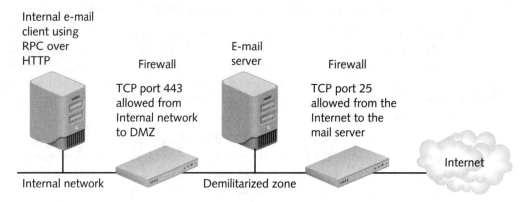

Figure 13-5   Firewall configuration for a mail server

Planning Network Protocol Security

The security methods available to protect network traffic vary depending on the protocol being used. Windows Server 2003 does not have any built-in mechanisms to specifically secure IPX or AppleTalk network traffic. However, a VPN connection can be used to secure IPX, AppleTalk, and TCP/IP network traffic. If TCP/IP is used, traffic can also be secured with IPSec or with SSL.

Using VPNs to Secure Network Traffic

Most of the time, a VPN is used to secure network traffic for remote users. The remote users access the Internet from home or hotel rooms, create a VPN connection from their client computers to the VPN server at the main office, and then are able to access resources on the internal network. All network traffic between the client computer and the VPN server is encrypted. A VPN can be used to ensure that user access to confidential company information is not monitored by an ISP or hackers.

VPNs can also be used internally on the network to protect network traffic to certain areas of the network. For example, the accounting server could be on a private subnet that is accessible only when a VPN connection is made. This ensures that all communication to the accounting server is encrypted so that no one with a packet sniffer can eavesdrop on the communication.

Internal VPNs can be implemented from individual client computers to a VPN server, or from a router to a VPN server. If many users need to access a resource through a VPN, it is often more efficient to use a router with a demand-dial connection to create the VPN connection. This way, individual users are not exposed to the complexity of initiating a VPN connection to access the remote resource.

Using IPSec to Secure Network Traffic

IPSec can be used only with TCP/IP packets. IPSec cannot encapsulate IPX or AppleTalk packets. However, when used in conjunction with L2TP in a VPN, IPX and AppleTalk can be encapsulated.

When IP-based applications are used, IPSec is ideal for securing network traffic. It is very flexible to configure because rules can be configured to protect only certain traffic. In addition to performing encryption, IPSec authenticates both computers in the conversation to prevent imposters. Finally, applications do not have to be aware of IPSec to use it. This means that applications do not have to be developed in a specific way to use IPSec. Any IP-based application can use it.

The major drawback to IPSec is that it does not move through NAT very well. Only the newest implementations of IPSec support IPSec-NAT-T, which allows IPSec packets to properly be transmitted through NAT. Windows Server 2003 supports this natively. Windows XP supports IPSec-NAT-T after Service Pack 1. Service packs are also available for Windows 2000 to support IPSec-NAT-T.

IPSec also supports several authentication mechanisms. Shared secrets can be used but are relatively insecure because the same secret must be entered on both computers in the conversation. Kerberos is the simplest authentication method to use if both computers are part of the same Active Directory forest. Certificates are the preferred method of authentication if the computers are not in the same forest.

Securing Web-based Applications

SSL (Secure Sockets Layer) is often used to secure Web-based applications. SSL requires that a certificate be installed on the server to which it is being connected. No certificate is required on the client computer. After a connection is made using SSL, all data transferred between the client and the server is encrypted.

SSL is a well-recognized, standard protocol. This makes it easy for developers to implement SSL in their programs. Any application that uses SSL must be explicitly written by developers to do so. This is unlike IPSec, of which applications are unaware.

When applications use SSL, they use a different port number than non-SSL communication. For example, regular HTTP uses TCP port 80 and HTTP over SSL uses TCP port 443.

SSL is useful because it is not platform specific in any way. For instance, if Linux clients are connecting to your Web site, SSL can be used. In contrast, there is no guarantee that Linux clients could access your Web site using a VPN.

Microsoft has implemented a newer authentication protocol call Transport Layer Security (TLS). TLS is a broader protocol for authentication that includes SSL. Most of the time, you still hear about SSL being used rather than TLS.

PLANNING WIRELESS NETWORK SECURITY

Wireless networks are quickly becoming commonplace in organizations. Now that wireless networks are relatively inexpensive, with some wireless access points selling for less than $100 and some wireless network cards selling for less than $50, they are starting to pop up everywhere. A wireless **access point (AP)** is a device much like a hub or switch to which wireless clients can connect.

The most common standard for wireless networks is **802.11b**, which operates at up to 11 Mbps. Another common standard is **802.11g**, which operates at up to 54 Mbps and is backward compatible with 802.11b. A less common standard is **802.11a**, which operates at a different frequency range that is less susceptible to interference. However, because 802.11a is not backward compatible with the more popular 802.11b, it has not gained very much market share.

Many wireless networks were not originally installed by IT staff. In many cases, office workers just ran out and bought an AP so they could roam around their office and in the immediate area. From their perspective, there is no harm and no one should care. However, from a security perspective, this is a huge issue.

Most wireless networks installed by end users are not properly configured for security. In fact, many wireless networks installed by IT staff are not properly configured for security. To keep you from falling into the latter category, in the following sections, we cover Wired Equivalent Protocol, authorized MAC addresses, using VPNs to secure wireless access, 802.1X, and Microsoft-specific mechanisms for configuring wireless networks.

Wired Equivalent Protocol

Wired Equivalent Privacy (WEP) is a protocol built into the 802.11 standards for wireless connectivity that governs how data can be encrypted while in transit on the wireless network. For WEP to work, a key is configured on both the AP and the client computer. This key is used to encrypt the data transmitted between the client and the AP. There are no standards for how the WEP key is to be placed on the clients and the AP. Most implementations require you to type in the key manually on each of the clients and the AP.

Although WEP is an easy way to prevent casual hackers from viewing the traffic transmitted on your wireless LAN, it is seriously flawed when dealing with motivated hackers. WEP has known design flaws that make it relatively easy to crack regardless of whether you are using 40-bit WEP or 128-bit WEP.

> For more information about the flaws in WEP, visit *www.isaac.cs.berkeley. edu/isaac/wep-faq.html.*

Even though the implementation of WEP is relatively easy, in many cases, this is not done either because the IT staff does not know about the wireless network, or the IT staff simply never got around to it. This leaves you vulnerable to hackers who are war driving. War driving is simply driving around in a car with a laptop using a wireless network card and seeing which networks you can connect to. Hackers then map out locations of unprotected wireless networks and distribute them online. In some cases, the location of unprotected wireless networks is marked on the sidewalk.

> For more information about war driving, visit *http://www.wardriving.com.*

A new protocol, called WiFi Protected Access (WPA), is replacing WEP and fixes most of its flaws. This will be a standard in all newly certified wireless equipment as of January 2004.

Authorized MAC Addresses

Most APs can be configured with a list of MAC addresses that are allowed to communicate with the AP. If you try to communicate with the AP using a wireless card with a MAC address that is not on the list, the AP ignores you.

This prevents access to resources on your network, but is very awkward to implement because each AP must be configured with the MAC address of each wireless network card. It is also not satisfactory because your data is still vulnerable to being read with a packet sniffer. In addition, someone with a packet sniffer could view your MAC address, and then configure their own computer to use the same MAC address after you turn off your computer, effectively impersonating you on the network.

Using VPNs to Secure Wireless Access

One easy way to secure a wireless network is to require VPN authentication before allowing access to the main network. All Windows 2000 and XP clients can log on to the network via a VPN connection; then, after the VPN connection is made, clients can access resources on the main network. All packets that can be viewed by hackers with wireless connections are encrypted by the VPN.

To implement this system for wireless security, you must have a VPN server that is connected to both the secure internal network and the insecure wireless network. Client computers that connect to the wireless network are given an insecure IP address via DHCP (static can be used if preferred) when they boot. Then during logon, they connect to the VPN server. The VPN server authenticates the client to the secure network and gives the client an IP address on the internal, secure network. At this point, all communication from the client to the internal network is secured by the VPN.

The 802.1X Protocol

The protocol **802.1X** is an authentication protocol defined by the IEEE. This protocol is a mechanism to authenticate wireless users. When properly configured, users are authenticated to the wireless port seamlessly. The basic process used by 802.1X is shown in Figure 13-6.

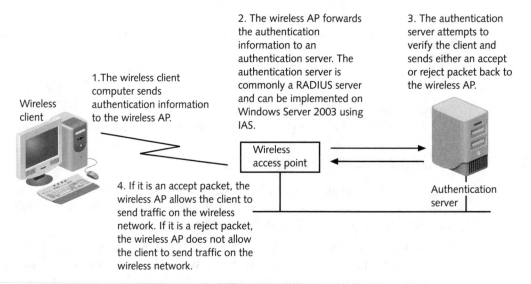

Figure 13-6   The 802.1X process

The 802.1X standard does not include information on WEP keys, but most vendors implement dynamically changing WEP keys as part of their 802.1X implementation. The authentication server can include keys as part of the accept message that is sent back to the AP. In addition, clients are usually able to request a key change. This ensures that keys are changed regularly to limit the ability of hackers to view information on the wireless network that is protected with WEP.

Windows Server 2003 supports 802.1X, but this is not very useful because most servers are not connected directly to wireless networks. They normally provide services to wireless clients through an AP that is connected to the wired network.

Windows XP clients with Service Pack 1 support 802.1X. In addition, the Windows XP clients must be configured to use infrastructure mode and WEP for 802.1X to be used.

Configuring Wireless Networks

Starting with Windows XP clients, many wireless network settings are centralized in the operating system rather than each vendor implementing their version. This is a benefit to vendors because it frees each vendor from the chore of implementing code in their drivers that performs the same task. It is also a benefit for users because a feature implemented in the operating system is often more stable than one implemented by individual vendors. It is also a benefit for Microsoft because new features for management can be added at the operating system level without worrying about many different vendors with slightly different implementations.

Because many of the wireless configuration settings are now managed by the operating system, they can be defined and managed using Group Policy. This makes it easy to centrally deploy configurations to many computers simultaneously.

In a group policy, you can define Wireless Network (802.11) Policies. These policies allow you to define many different characteristics about wireless connections, including the type of wireless networks to access, whether Windows should be used to configure the wireless networks for a client, and whether to connect to nonpreferred networks, as shown in Figure 13-7.

13

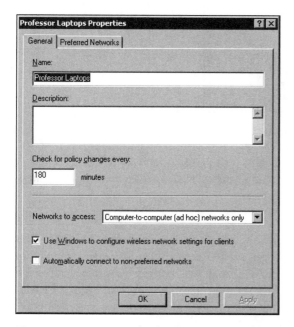

Figure 13-7   General tab of a wireless network policy

When selecting the type of network, you can select Access point (infrastructure) networks only, Computer-to-computer (ad hoc) networks only, or Any available network (access point preferred). Most wireless networks are configured to use APs. If your network is configured to use APs, you should select Access point (infrastructure) networks only to prevent clients from connecting to unauthorized computer-to-computer networks.

You can also define preferred wireless networks, as shown in Figure 13-8. There are a variety of settings, but the most important are the Network Name (SSID), whether 802.1X is used, and whether WEP is used. Each wireless network is configured with a Network Name. This is used by wireless clients to distinguish between multiple wireless networks.

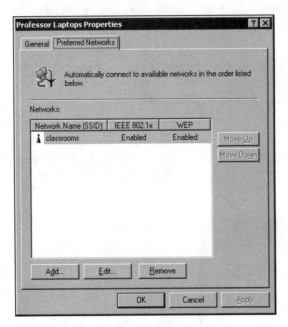

Figure 13-8   Preferred Networks tab

 When multiple APs are configured with the same Network Name (SSID), they are part of the same network and a wireless client can roam from one to another without losing connectivity.

EAP (Extensible Authentication Protocol) is always used with 802.1X. EAP-TLS is used for certificate-based authentication. This is useful for smart-card-based authentication or simply using certificates as an identifier. PEAP (Protected Extensible Authentication Protocol) is a method to enhance other EAP authentication methods using TLS. When PEAP is used, you can select EAP-CHAP-MSv2, which uses the logged on user name and password to connect to the wireless network.

ACTIVITY

Activity 13-3: Creating a Policy for Wireless Workstations

Time Required: 10 minutes

Objective: Create a policy to configure wireless workstations.

Description: Many of the professors at Arctic University are starting to use 802.11b wireless connections in the classrooms while teaching class. This allows them to demonstrate Web sites and access files on the network servers. However, it is becoming an administrative burden to configure them all individually, so you have decided to create a group policy for all of the wireless workstations.

1. If necessary, start your server and log on as **Administrator**.

2. Click **Start**, click **Run**, type **mmc**, and then press **Enter**.

3. Click the **File** menu, click **Add/Remove Snap-in**, click **Add**, double-click **Active Directory Users and Computers**, click **Close**, and then click **OK**.

4. Double-click **Active Directory Users and Computers**, and then click **Arctic.local**.

5. Right-click **Arctic.local**, point to **New**, and then click **Organizational Unit**.

6. In the **Name** text box, type **wirelessxx**, where *xx* is your student number, and click **OK**.

7. Right-click **wirelessxx**, where *xx* is your student number, and click **Properties**.

8. Click the **Group Policy** tab.

9. Click the **New** button, type **wirelessGPOxx**, where *xx* is your student number, and press **Enter**. This policy applies to all computers in the wireless*xx* OU.

10. Click the **Edit** button.

11. Under Computer Configuration, expand **Windows Settings**, expand **Security Settings**, and click **Wireless Network (IEEE 802.11) Policies**. Notice that no wireless policies exist by default.

12. Right-click **Wireless Network (IEEE 802.11) Policies**, and click **Create Wireless Network Policy**.

13. Click **Next** to continue.

14. In the Name text box, type **Professor Laptops**, and then click **Next**.

15. If necessary, check the **Edit properties** check box, and then click **Finish**.

16. In the Networks to access drop-down list box, select **Access point (infrastructure) networks only**. This prevents the professors' laptops from accidentally getting connected to any computer-to-computer (ad hoc) networks configured by students.

17. If necessary, check the **Use Windows to configure wireless network settings for clients** check box; this should be left unchecked only if you have third-party software to configure wireless settings centrally.

13

18. If necessary, deselect the **Automatically connect to non–preferred networks** check box. Having this unchecked prevents the professors' laptops from accidentally connecting to unauthorized access points.

19. Click the **Preferred Networks** tab, and then click the **Add** button.

20. In the Network name (SSID) text box, type **classrooms**.

21. In the Description text box, type **Wireless network for classrooms**.

22. If necessary, select both the **Data encryption (WEP enabled)** and **The key is provided automatically** check boxes. These enable WEP and automatically distribute the WEP key, respectively.

23. Click **OK** to close the New Preferred Setting Properties dialog box.

24. Click **OK** to close the Professor Laptops Properties dialog box.

25. Close the Group Policy Object Editor window.

26. Click **Close**, and close MMC. Click **No** if prompted to save the console settings.

DEFAULT SECURITY SETTINGS

The default security settings used by Windows Server 2003 are significantly more secure than Windows 2000. In Windows 2000, the Everyone group was granted Full Control to the root of the file system for all NTFS partitions. In addition, unnecessary services such as IIS were installed by default. Many of the most severe security flaws in Windows 2000 were in IIS.

In Windows Server 2003, only the Administrators group is given Full Control to the file system. In addition, a minimum of services are installed. In particular, IIS is not installed by default. And even if IIS is installed after the server installation is complete, script processing must be specifically enabled.

The default security settings for Windows 2003 are configured during installation by applying a security template. A **security template** is a group of security settings that can be applied to server or client computers. The template used during installation is Setup security.inf, and it is located in C:\WINDOWS\security\templates. You can view the settings in this security template by using the Security Templates snap-in.

Because domain controllers have additional services and folders that need to be secured, there is a separate template for them. The template defltdc.inf located in C:\WINDOWS\inf is used to apply security settings to domain controllers.

Activity 13-4: Viewing Default Security Settings

Time Required: 10 minutes

Objective: View the default security settings in Setup security.inf.

Description: To be sure you understand the default security settings that are applied during the installation of Windows Server 2003, you view them in the security template Setup security.inf.

1. If necessary, start your server and log on as **Administrator**.

2. Click **Start**, click **Run**, type **mmc**, and press **Enter**.

3. Click the **File** menu, click **Add/Remove Snap-in**, click **Add**, double-click **Security Templates**, click **Close**, and then click **OK**.

4. Double-click **Security Templates**, double-click **C:\WINDOWS\security\templates**, and then click **setup security**.

5. In the right pane, double-click **Local Policies**, and then double-click **User Rights Assignment**.

6. Read the list of user rights in the right pane. Scroll down through the list. These are the default user rights for a new server. Notice that the user right Deny log on locally specifically does not have any users or groups listed. If this security template is assigned to a computer, it removes any existing users or groups from that right. Also notice that the user right Log on locally is not listed. If this security template is assigned, the users assigned that right will not be modified.

7. In the left pane, click **File System**. In the right pane is a list of all the files and folders for which this security template controls NTFS permissions.

8. In the right pane, scroll down and double-click **c:\windows**. You are now in the dialog box that indicates what is done to the NTFS permissions on this folder.

9. Click **Edit Security**. This dialog box lists the NTFS permissions that are applied to the c:\windows folder when this security template is assigned. Notice that Administrators are assigned Full Control, whereas Users are only able to Read and Execute files.

10. Click **Cancel**, and then click **Cancel**.

11. In the left pane, click **Registry** to view a list of registry keys that have security permissions applied when this template is applied. Scroll through the list to view them all.

12. In the left pane, click **System Services** to view the list of services for which this template defines security permissions and startup settings.

13. In the left pane, click **Restricted Groups** to view the lists of groups whose membership is restricted by this security template.

14. Close MMC. Click **No** if requested to save console settings.

13

PLANNING A SECURE BASELINE

Security templates are the key to ensuring a standardized security configuration for workstations and servers throughout your network. Each security template contains settings that can be used to analyze existing security configurations or to enforce new settings.

Although you can create your own security templates, several are included with Windows Server 2003 for specific situations. Table 13-2 shows the default security templates that are available and describes their purpose.

Table 13-2 Default security templates

Name	Description
Setup security.inf	Is a security setting applied during the installation of Windows Server 2003. This can be used to set security settings back to the default.
securews.inf	Applies enhanced security settings for workstations and member servers. This can be applied to Windows XP workstations, Windows 2000 workstations and member servers, and Windows Server 2003 member servers. Specifically, it limits the use of LAN Manager authentication, enables server-side SMB signing, and provides further restrictions on anonymous users.
securedc.inf	Applies enhanced security settings for domain controllers. This can be applied to Windows 2000 or Windows Server 2003 domain controllers. Specifically, it provides enhanced domain account policies, limits the use of LAN Manager authentication, and provides further restrictions on anonymous users. If a DC is configured with securedc, a user with an account in that domain cannot connect to any member server from a LAN Manager only client, such as Windows 3.1 or Windows 95.
rootsec.inf	Resets the file permissions on the OS partition to the default permissions and propagates them to files and subfolders.
iesacls.inf	Configures security and auditing for Internet Explorer registry keys.
hisecws.inf	Provides further restrictions on LAN Manager authentication and further requirements for the encryption and signing of secure channel and SMB data.
hisecdc.inf	Provides further restrictions on LAN Manager authentication and further requirements for the encryption and signing of secure channel and SMB data. To apply hisecdc to a DC, all the DCs in all trusted or trusting domains must be running Windows 2000 or later.
compatws.inf	Is used for Windows 2000 and Windows XP workstations to allow older applications to run properly for members of the Users group. It relaxes the default file and registry permissions for the Users group in a manner that is consistent with the requirements of most noncertified applications. Making users a member of the Power Users group is an alternative to applying this template.

Configuring Client Computers

The most important step in configuring a secure baseline for client computers is categorizing them appropriately. In most organizations, client computers fall into only a few categories because there is little variation between them. Some of the questions you should ask yourself while categorizing client computers include the following:

- Is a password policy required for local accounts?

- Is an account lockout policy required for local accounts?

- Should all users be able to log on to this computer?

- Does auditing need to be performed on this computer?

- Is this workstation in a public access area?

- What services need to be running on this computer?

- Do any special permissions need to be assigned for the file system or registry?

After you have divided your client computers into categories, you define the exact requirements for configuring them and configure a security template that matches the requirements. When defining a security template, it is a good practice to start by copying one of the predefined templates and use it as a starting point. Do not modify the original templates in case you want to refer back to them as known good configurations for troubleshooting.

Some common user rights that may be useful for client computers include the following:

- *Access this computer from the network*—If network workstations are not meant to share data or printers on the network, this can be modified to only allow administrators remote access.

- *Allow log on locally*—By default, all users are able to log on locally to any workstation. However, in sensitive areas, you may want to allow only authorized users to log on to certain workstations, particularly if some resources are only available from certain workstations.

Some common security options that may be useful for client computers include the following:

- The Devices: Unsigned driver installation behavior option allows you to specify whether unsigned device drivers can be installed or whether a warning is displayed.

- The Interactive logon: Do not display last user name option prevents hackers from easily obtaining user names. Hackers require two pieces of information to log on to your systems, a user name and a password.

- With the Interactive logon: Message text for users attempting to log on option, you can define a text message that appears when users attempt to log on. Many companies use this to display a warning message about unauthorized use to protect themselves from a legal perspective.

- The default setting for the Interactive logon: Number of previous logons to cache (in case domain controller is not available) option is 10 logons. This allows users to log on locally using their domain account when a domain controller is not available. There are known security risks associated with this and it should be disabled in high-security situations.

- In high-security situations in which smart cards are used for authentication, the Interactive logon: Require smart card option should be enabled to prevent users from logging on using only a user name and password.

- The Microsoft network client: Digitally sign communications (always) option forces client computers to always use SMB signing when they access files and printers.

- The Network Security: Force logoff when logon hours expire option forces users to log off when the logon hours specified in their account properties expire. This is useful to prevent users accidentally being logged on all night and causing backups to fail because of open files.

With a defined security template, you can evaluate existing security compared to the template and, if required, apply the template to the client computers to change settings. The **Security Configuration and Analysis snap-in** can be used to analyze and configure client computers from a GUI. The command-line utility **Secedit** can be used to perform the same tasks in scripts.

In addition, security templates can be applied using Group Policy. This is the most common way to apply security templates because it is the easiest to perform. Simply, organize the computer accounts into OUs that match the categories you have defined for them, and then apply a group policy with the appropriate security settings to the OU.

Configuring Servers

Like client computers, servers should be categorized and grouped to assist in applying security settings. Because servers are more likely to hold sensitive data than workstations, their settings are likely to be more restrictive for password policies, account lockout policy, users performing local logons, auditing, limiting services, and restricting file and registry permissions.

Some common user rights that may be useful for controlling member servers and domain controllers include the following:

- The Access this computer from the network right can be used to control who is allowed to access files on this server across the network regardless of NTFS permissions. This can be used as an extra level of security to protect against improperly assigned NTFS permissions.

- The Allow log on locally right gives users the right to log on at the server console. By default, all users are allowed to log on locally to member servers, but only administrators are allowed to log on locally to domain controllers. There is no need for average users on the network to log on locally to member servers and this can be restricted. This right is required to log on to a terminal server or a Web server.

- The Deny log on locally right overrides the Allow log on locally right. This is used when a group is allowed to log on locally, but you want to restrict some members of the group. This can be useful when controlling access for Terminal Services or for Web authentication.

- The Deny log on through Terminal Services right overrides the Allow log on locally right when connecting through Terminal Services. This may be required if a server is running Terminal Services and users are authenticating to a Web site through IIS and you do not want some users accessing Terminal Services.

- The Shut down the system right is often used with terminal servers to ensure that users are not allowed to shut down or reboot the terminal server.

Some common security options that may be useful for controlling member servers and domain controllers include the following:

- The Devices: Restrict CD-ROM access to locally logged-on user only option prevents remote users from accessing CD-based software you may have accidentally left in a server.

- The Devices: Restrict floppy access to locally logged-on user only option prevents remote users from accessing floppy-based software you may have accidentally left in a server.

- The Interactive logon: Require smart card option is useful for enforcing a higher level of security for server maintenance. However, it prevents you from using Terminal Services on this server for remote maintenance.

- The Microsoft network server: Digitally sign communications (always) option forces servers to always use SMB signing when they provide access to files and printers.

- The Network access: Restrict anonymous access to Named Pipes and Shares option is on by default. It prevents users who are not authenticated to the domain from browsing the shared resources available on a server.

- The Network security: LAN Manager authentication level option forces Windows Server 2003 to respond with NTLMv2 authentication when LAN Manager authentication is used. This can be set less restrictive to allow for older clients.

The same tools available for analyzing and managing security templates for client computers are also available for analyzing and managing servers. Active Directory automatically places domain controllers in their own OU so that you can manage their security settings manually.

NOTE Password policies, account lockout policies, and Kerberos policies must be enabled at the domain level to apply for domain-level authentication. If password policies and account lockout policies are enabled at any other level, they affect only local user accounts on client computers and member servers. Kerberos policies are not used at any level other than the domain.

Activity 13-5: Analyzing Security

Time Required: 10 minutes

Objective: Compare the default security level of your server to the hisecws.inf template.

Description: Because there are hundreds of settings in a security template, it is very difficult to be sure which settings are different than the current configuration of a workstation or server. The easiest way to find out which changes would be made by applying a template is to use the Security Configuration and Analysis snap-in.

1. If necessary, start your server and log on as **Administrator**.

2. Click **Start**, click **Run**, type **mmc**, and press **Enter**.

3. Click the **File** menu, click **Add/Remove Snap-in**, click **Add**, double-click **Security Configuration and Analysis**, click **Close**, and then click **OK**.

4. In the left pane, click **Security Configuration and Analysis**. This displays the instructions for using the Security Configuration and Analysis snap-in in the right pane.

5. Right-click **Security Configuration and Analysis**, and then click **Open Database**.

6. In the File name text box, type **securetest**, and then press **Enter**. This is a file used to store configuration data during the analysis and any file name can be used.

7. In the Import Template dialog box, double-click **hisecws.inf**.

8. Right-click **Security Configuration and Analysis**, click **Analyze Computer Now**, and then click **OK** to accept the default log file location. The right pane now lists all of the settings in the hisecws.inf security template and how the local computer settings compared to them.

9. In the right pane, double-click **Local Policies**, and double-click **Audit Policy**. Notice that the audit settings on your server are significantly less than what the security template defines. The options marked with a red x indicate that they do not meet the standard defined by the security template.

10. In the left pane, click **Security Options**. Scroll through the list of Security Options. The options marked with a red x indicate that they do not meet the standard defined by the security template.

11. Close MMC. Click **No** if asked to save settings.

Software Updates

Every piece of software, whether it is an application or operating system, is flawed when it is released. In fact, many administrators will not install software until at least one service pack has been released. The flaws in software are often minor, and may never be widely known but they are there. Because Windows is so widely used, most flaws in Windows are very widely publicized.

The patches for Windows operating systems used to be released every few months as a group called a **service pack**. Over the last few years, Microsoft has begun to release **hotfixes**, which are small patches to fix security and stability problems considered too severe to wait for the next full service pack. To many administrators, it seems that there is a new hotfix for Windows released every week.

NOTE Administrators are struggling with trying to keep their systems, both clients and servers, fully patched. It is critical to keep systems fully patched because the majority of viruses take advantage of known flaws in operating systems and applications for which there are patches available.

Microsoft does not announce a flaw in Windows until it has a patch ready for that flaw. Soon after Microsoft announces a flaw and makes a patch available for it, there is at least one if not several viruses that attempt to take advantage of the flaw. Very few viruses exploit unknown flaws. In addition, antivirus software needs one or more days before it can catch new viruses because the signature files need to be updated to recognize new viruses.

To help administrators keep systems patched, Microsoft has released a number of tools:

- Windows Update
- Automatic Updates
- Software Update Services
- Microsoft Baseline Security Analyzer
- Hfnetchk

All of these tools are covered in the following sections.

Windows Update

Windows Update is a Web site that administrators and users can visit to find out which updates are available for their systems. Windows Update is presented as an icon in the Start menu. It is a huge step forward in patching because an administrator does not have to search through many hotfixes and service packs to find out which are applicable to a system. Windows Update automatically checks for the files that are needed, downloads them, and installs them.

The main problem with Windows Update is that it is still a very manual process. Administrators must go to each computer and run Windows Update to ensure that it is done. Most of the time, users on the network do not have sufficient privileges on the workstations to install new patches from Windows Update.

If users are able to apply updates through Windows Update, the risk exists that users apply updates that destabilize the system. It does not happen often, but occasionally a hotfix or service pack causes systems with certain configurations to become unstable. In addition, hotfixes and service packs can cause customized applications to fail. Therefore, all patches should be thoroughly tested before being rolled out to users and servers.

Finally, Windows Update is very inefficient from a network utilization standpoint. Each computer connects to the Windows Update Web site and downloads the patches. This means that if you have 100 client computers and a new 10-MB hotfix for Windows XP is released, the total level of traffic on your Internet connection will be 1000 MB.

Despite these flaws, Windows Update is an excellent solution for small offices with only a few computers. It is simple and easy to implement, just not very scalable. It can also be used for servers and client computers.

Automatic Updates

Automatic Updates is a service that runs on Windows clients and servers that makes the process of downloading and installing hotfixes automatic. Automatic Updates can also be configured to only notify a user when updates are available. This provides flexibility depending on the client computer or server to which the hotfixes are being applied.

Automatic Updates is a significant improvement over Windows Update because it is automatic and configurable. This takes a significant load off of administrators. However, it still is not very efficient because all downloads are from the Internet.

Automatic Updates is installed in several ways:

- With an .msi file available for Windows 2000 and Windows XP
- With Windows 2000 Service Pack 3
- With Windows XP Service Pack 1
- Automatically, as part of Windows Server 2003

ACTIVITY

Activity 13-6: Configuring Automatic Updates

Time Required: 10 minutes

Objective: Configure Automatic Updates to download and install patches automatically.

Description: You have just installed a new server for Arctic University and are very concerned that you may forget to patch it as new hotfixes become available. To ensure that it is patched automatically, you are configuring Automatic Updates. You are also concerned that the download and installation of updates may impact server performance. To address this, you schedule the updates to happen at 4:00 a.m. only.

1. If necessary, start your server and log on as **Administrator**.

2. Click **Start**, right-click **My Computer**, and then click **Properties**.

3. Click the **Automatic Updates** tab.

4. If necessary, check the **Keep my computer up to date. With this setting enabled, Windows Update software may be automatically updated prior to applying any other updates** check box.

5. Select the **Automatically download the updates, and install them on the schedule that I specify** option button.

6. If necessary, in the left drop-down list box, select **Every day**.

7. In the right drop-down list box, select **4:00 AM**.

8. Click **OK**.

Software Update Services (SUS)

Software Update Services (SUS) is a service available for Windows 2000 (with Service Pack 2) and Windows Server 2003 that automatically downloads the latest hotfixes and service packs from the Windows Update Web site. Client computers on your network then can download the hotfixes and service packs from a local server on the network instead of the Internet. You can even configure multiple SUS servers in a hierarchy to create a multitiered solution.

When SUS is used, you must configure the Automatic Updates on the client computers to retrieve updates from your SUS server rather than from the Internet. When this is done, Internet traffic is reduced significantly. For example, in an organization with 1,000 workstations, a hotfix is downloaded once by the SUS server, rather than 1,000 times for each client computer. The easiest way to reconfigure the client computers is through a group policy.

One of the main concerns of any administrator is that service packs and hotfixes are properly tested before they are installed. SUS downloads all service packs and hotfixes automatically, but you have complete control over when they are made available to users. Therefore, you can test a hotfix before it is automatically installed by the client computers.

You can download SUS from *www.microsoft.com/windows2000/windowsupdate/sus/default.asp*.

Microsoft Baseline Security Analyzer

The **Microsoft Baseline Security Analyzer (MBSA)** is a tool that can be used to verify security updates on a wide variety of Microsoft operating systems and applications, including the following:

- Windows NT 4.0
- Windows 2000
- Windows XP
- Windows Server 2003
- IIS versions 4.0 and 5.0

13

- SQL Server 7.0 and SQL Server 2000

- Internet Explorer 5.01 and later

- Exchange 5.5 and Exchange 2000

- Windows Media Player 6.4 and later

In addition, it can check for security related configuration errors on the following products:

- Windows NT 4.0

- Windows 2000

- Windows XP

- Windows Server 2003

- IIS versions 4.0 and 5.0

- SQL Server 7.0 and SQL Server 2000

- Internet Explorer 5.01 and later

- Office 2000 and Office 2002

MBSA can be used to scan a single machine or an entire group of computers on the network. This makes it an ideal security auditing tool to confirm that all client computers and servers are properly obtaining updates through Windows Update, Automatic Updates, or SUS. If desired, MBSA can be configured to compare updates against a SUS server rather than a hotfix list from Microsoft.

MBSA can be obtained from *www.microsoft.com/mbsa*.

Hfnetchk

Hfnetchk is an older command-line utility for verifying patch levels on Windows clients and servers. This utility is no longer offered by Microsoft as a stand-alone utility. The functionality of Hfnetchk is now only available in MBSA.

Securing Administrative Access

Many network administrators spend all of their time ensuring that user access to the network is limited to prevent accidental damage but do not take the same precautions with their own accounts. Administrators should maintain two accounts. One account is used for day-to-day work such as word processing. This account is assigned limited permission just like an average user on the network would have. The second account is assigned elevated privileges and permissions that are required for administration of the network.

This type of system with two accounts has been recommended for many years; however, network administrators found it cumbersome to log on and off of the network as they switched between tasks. Windows Server 2003 eliminates this problem by allowing you to run individual applications as a different user. With this feature, you can log on as a limited user and run Administrative Tools as a user with administrative privileges.

You can run an application as a different user through the Windows GUI or at a command line. To run an application as a different user in the GUI, right-click the executable or shortcut and then click Run as. From a command prompt, you can use the Runas command.

In addition, you should limit the permission of administrators to those required to perform their jobs, just as you do with users. The most effective way to do this for Active Directory is with the Delegation of Authority Wizard in Active Directory Users and Computers. Using this wizard, you can assign the ability to manage just the contents of certain OUs, certain object types, or certain attributes of objects.

CHAPTER SUMMARY

❑ The three broad categories of security are physical, network, and data. Physical security controls physical access to network components and must be in place for software-based security to be effective. Network security includes authentication, IPSec, and firewalls. Data security includes NTFS permissions, share permissions, auditing, and EFS.

❑ EFS is a seamless way for users to encrypt files so that they are secure even if a laptop is stolen.

❑ Broad rules for securing all servers include the following: disable unnecessary services, limit access to the minimum required for users to perform their jobs, use separate administrator accounts for different staff, and allow packets to necessary TCP and UDP ports only.

❑ Domain controllers should not be exposed to traffic from the wider Internet and should not be located in a DMZ. If services that require authentication are located in the DMZ, authentication traffic must be allowed through the firewall. Firewall rules for authentication can be limited by using IAS as a RADIUS server whenever possible, rather than having services communicate with the domain controller directly.

❑ Web servers that are accessible from the Internet should be located in a DMZ where Internet users can only use TCP port 80 and TCP port 443 to communicate with it. Script processing should be disabled if it is not required.

❑ Database servers should be kept on the internal network. If applications in the DMZ need to communicate with a database server, TCP port 1677 should be opened on the firewall to allow communication with Microsoft SQL Server.

❑ Mail servers must be accessible from the Internet and should be located in a DMZ. Only TCP port 25 is required to be accessible on the mail server from the Internet. POP3 uses TCP port 110, and IMAP uses TCP port 143.

❑ A VPN can be used to secure network traffic for IP, IPX, and AppleTalk packets. A VPN can be used internally or across the Internet.

❏ IPSec can only be used to secure IP packets. To pass through NAT properly, IPSec must support IPSec-NAT-T. Services do not need to be aware of IPSec for it to be used.

❏ SSL can be used to secure any IP traffic, but the service and client must be written specifically to use it. It is most commonly used for secure Web sites using HTTPS on TCP port 443.

❏ The two most common standards for wireless networks are 802.11b, which operates at 11 Mbps, and 802.11g, which operates at 54 Mbps. Both of these can use WEP, which encrypts data in transit on the wireless network. You can also use authorized MAC addresses, VPNs, and 802.1X to help secure wireless networks.

❏ Windows Server 2003 and Windows XP support automatic configuration of wireless networks using wireless network policies. These policies can be distributed using Group Policy.

❏ The default security settings for Windows Server 2003 are much more secure than Windows 2000 Server. The default settings are contained in a security template named Setup security.inf.

❏ A number of security templates are included with Windows Server 2003 to help you secure your servers and clients. These should be used as a starting point when configuring a secure baseline for client computers and servers.

❏ Both the Security Configuration and Analysis snap-in and Secedit can be used to analyze and configure security settings for client computers and servers. Security template settings can also be imported into group policies.

❏ Managing software updates is very important. Windows Update is a Web site where patches can be downloaded manually. Automatic Updates is a Windows service that can automatically download and install updates from Windows Update. SUS is a service for Windows 2000 Server and Windows Server 2003 that automatically downloads patches and makes them available on the local network. MBSA is a utility to view patch levels and security configuration problems on Windows clients and servers. Hfnetchk is an older command-line utility that is no longer available.

KEY TERMS

802.11a — A not very common standard for wireless networks that is not backward compatible with 802.11b.

802.11b — A common standard for wireless networks that operates at 11 Mbps.

802.11g — A common standard for wireless networks that operates at 54 Mbps and is backward compatible with 802.11b.

802.1X — An authentication protocol that can be used with 802.11 networks to verify user identity before allowing a connection to the wireless network.

access point (AP) — A device much like a hub or switch to which wireless clients can connect.

Automatic Updates — A Windows service that makes the process of downloading and installing hotfixes automatic.

data security — The process of controlling access to data by ensuring that only authorized users are able to access data.

demilitarized zone (DMZ) — An Internet-accessible subnet between the Internet and a private network that is protected by firewalls.

Hfnetchk — An older command-line utility used to verify patch levels on Windows clients and servers. The functionality of this utility is now in MBSA.

hotfixes — The small patches to fix security and stability problems that are considered too severe to wait for the next service pack.

Microsoft Baseline Security Analyzer (MBSA) — A tool that can be used to verify security updates and security settings on a wide variety of Microsoft operating systems and applications.

network security — The process of controlling access to network resources through a computer network.

physical security — The process of controlling physical access to the computing devices on your network.

Secedit — A command-line utility that can be used to analyze and configure client computers by using security templates.

Security Configuration and Analysis snap-in — A snap-in that can be used to analyze and configure client computers by using security templates.

security template — A group of security settings that can be applied to a server or client computer.

service pack — A collection of patches for the Windows operating system.

Software Update Services (SUS) — A service for Windows 2000 Server and Windows Server 2003 that automatically downloads the latest hotfixes and service packs from Windows Update and makes them available to other computers on the LAN.

Windows Update — A Web site maintained by Microsoft to allow administrators and users to find out which updates are available for their systems and install them.

Wired Equivalent Privacy (WEP) — A protocol that is part of the 802.11 wireless network standards that is responsible for encrypting data transferred on the wireless network.

13

REVIEW QUESTIONS

1. Which type of security would prevent a hacker from using a boot floppy to reset the Administrator password?

   a. physical security

   b. network security

   c. firewall security

   d. data security

2. Which network security mechanism is responsible only for verifying the identity of a user?

    a. IPSec

    b. authentication

    c. firewall

    d. proxy server

3. How many networks must exist for a DMZ to be used?

    a. 1

    b. 2

    c. 3

    d. 4

4. When a DMZ is used, where are Internet-accessible servers hosted?

    a. at an ISP

    b. on the internal network

    c. on the Internet

    d. between the internal network and the Internet

5. Which data security mechanism restricts access to files only when they are accessed across the network?

    a. NTFS permissions

    b. share permissions

    c. auditing

    d. EFS

6. Which data security mechanism logs access or attempted access to resources?

    a. NTFS permissions

    b. share permissions

    c. auditing

    d. EFS

7. Which key does EFS use to encrypt a file?

    a. a symmetric key unique to the file

    b. the public key of the user

    c. the private key of the user

    d. the symmetric key of the user

8. Who can always decrypt a file after it has been encrypted using EFS? (Choose all that apply.)
   a. the user who encrypted it
   b. the domain administrator
   c. the local administrator
   d. the designated recovery agent

9. Which of the following are good security rules? (Choose all that apply.)
   a. Disable unnecessary services.
   b. Grant the Everyone group Full Control to the file system to ensure access.
   c. Limit access to the minimum required for users to perform their jobs.
   d. Have all administrators share one account to enhance auditing capabilities.

10. A domain controller should be placed in a DMZ to support Internet-accessible services. True or False?

11. On what port number does the Kerberos Key Distribution Center listen?
    a. TCP/UDP 88
    b. TCP 135
    c. TCP 389
    d. TCP 3268

12. On what port number does a secure Web server run?
    a. TCP 80
    b. UDP 80
    c. TCP 443
    d. UDP 443

13. When implementing a Web-based application that requires Microsoft SQL Server, where should the SQL server be placed?
    a. directly on the Internet
    b. in the DMZ
    c. at an ISP
    d. on the internal network

14. Which of the following network security mechanisms do not require the application to be aware of the security in place? (Choose all that apply.)
    a. VPN
    b. IPSec
    c. SSL
    d. IPSec-NAT-T

13

15. Which wireless standard operates at up to 11 Mbps and uses WEP?

    a. 802.11a

    b. 802.11b

    c. 802.11g

    d. 802.1X

16. Which wireless protocol is used for authentication?

    a. 802.11a

    b. 802.11b

    c. 802.11g

    d. 802.1X

17. Which security template contains the default NTFS permissions for the file system?

    a. securews.inf

    b. rootsec.inf

    c. iesacls.inf

    d. compatws.inf

18. Which two tools can be used to analyze and apply security settings using a security template?

    a. Security Configuration and Analysis snap-in

    b. Security Templates snap-in

    c. Secedit

    d. SecAlyzr

19. Who can log on locally to a member server by default?

    a. all users

    b. Domain Admins

    c. Local Administrators

    d. Local Administrators and Power Users

20. Which software update method is a manual process that must be initiated by a user or administrator?

    a. Windows Update

    b. Automatic Updates

    c. SUS

    d. MCSA

CASE PROJECTS

Case Project 13-1: Physical Security

Arctic University is undergoing a crisis. A file server has recently been stolen from the office of a department head. Based on this, the head of the IT Department thinks that money should be appropriated in the budget next year to perform upgrades for physical security. He has asked you to create a list of physical security standards for servers, network devices, desktop computers, and laptops.

Compose a list of security recommendations for servers, network devices, desktop computers, and laptops. List each as a separate category.

Case Project 13-2: File Security

Many of the professors at Arctic University carry laptop computers with confidential student information. You are concerned that if a laptop is stolen, this confidential information would be easily accessible to the person who stole it. You think that EFS is ideal for protecting this data, but one of your colleagues is unconvinced. What do you tell him?

Case Project 13-3: Web Application Security

A new Web application is being implemented for student registrations. Students use a Web browser to connect to the Web server running the registration application. All of the data for the application is stored in a Microsoft SQL Server database. Describe how you would configure security for this application.

Case Project 13-4: Software Updates

A virus has recently struck Arctic University and disabled many workstations for several days. The servers were not affected because the IT staff manually patch the servers each time a hotfix is released by Microsoft. How can you implement a system that automatically patches workstations as hotfixes become available, but still gives you the option to approve each hotfix prior to its distribution and installation?

13

14

PROBLEM RECOVERY

After reading this chapter, you will be able to:

- ◆ Back up and restore files
- ◆ Recover corrupted systems
- ◆ Perform remote management
- ◆ Image client computers and servers

Recovering computer systems from problems is an essential part of every network administrator's job, and one of the most visible. You are judged on your ability to respond to high-profile crises such as failed servers because they are very visible to your users.

In this chapter, you learn how to use the Backup utility, to back up and restore files, and to recover corrupted systems using a variety of tools, including safe mode and last known good configuration. You also learn how to perform remote management to increase your effectiveness as an administrator. Finally, you learn how to image clients and servers using Remote Installation Services.

FILE BACKUP AND RECOVERY

File backup and recovery are an essential part of network maintenance. No matter what other fault-tolerance strategies you use, such as RAID5 for your disks or clustering for your servers, file backups are still required.

Windows Server 2003 can mirror volumes and perform RAID5 when dynamic disks are used. In addition, specialized controller cards can be used to perform mirroring and RAID5. Hardware-based disk fault tolerance with specialized controller cards is more popular than software-based disk fault tolerance using the capabilities of Windows Server 2003 because it reduces the load on the server.

Whether hardware or software disk fault tolerance is used, a backup is still required. Disk fault tolerance protects you from a failed hard drive. However, it does not protect you from data that is corrupt. When data is changed on one drive in a mirrored set, it is also changed on the other. When data is backed up, you can recover an uncorrupt version.

Both Backup (ntbackup.exe) and volume shadow copy are part of an effective backup and recovery solution. The following sections cover each in turn.

The Backup Utility

Backup performs traditional file system backups. When backups are performed, they can be stored on tape or in a file.

Backup to tape is the most common method for storing backups. Tapes are small and can easily be stored off-site. Tapes are well-understood and reliable backup media.

NOTE

Backup tapes should be replaced after about one year of weekly use. Otherwise, they start to become unreliable and generate errors.

Backup to file is used when you want to store the backup on nontraditional media, such as a floppy disk, hard drive, or CD-R. The entire backup is stored inside a single file, making it easy to copy and move. If the file is larger than the media you are placing it on, it can be broken into multiple smaller files. For example, if you are backing up 7 MB of data, then the backup software can break it up to fit on multiple floppy disks.

To work effectively with Backup, you need to understand how to back up application data, file backup strategies, system state backup, and automated system recovery. The following sections cover each in turn.

Backing Up Application Data

The Backup utility comes as part of Windows Server 2003. However, third-party backup solutions are also available that are easier to use and have enhanced features. For instance, Backup is not able to back up files when they are open; some third-party software can.

SQL Server databases cannot be backed up while they are running. However, add-ons for third-party software allow you to back up SQL Server databases while they are running. If you do not want the expense of a third-party solution, you can schedule SQL Server to shut down immediately before the backup and then restart after the backup, so that there are no open files. An even better solution is to use the maintenance plans that are available in SQL Server. Using a maintenance plan, you can back up an SQL database to a file on disk while it is running, and then use Backup to back up the file with the SQL database in it. This avoids the need to back up and open files. Note that a maintenance plan can be scheduled on specified days at specified times to automate the backup process and reduce administrator workload.

Exchange Server backups are supported by the Backup utility. The Backup utility can back up and restore the Information Store and individual user mail boxes while the system is live.

File Backup Strategies

You can employ three different file backup strategies for daily file system backups. Note that each time a file is modified, the operating system turns on the archive attribute of that file; each of the following strategies uses and affects the archive attribute of files in a different way:

- Full
- Incremental
- Differential

A **full backup** of data files backs up all of the selected files each time a backup is performed. This is the simplest type of backup to implement because it is the same every day. When files need to be restored, you simply use the backup tape from the previous day to restore the files you require. When a full backup is performed, the archive attribute on each file is turned off.

The primary problem with full backups is the amount of time required to perform them. In large organizations with massive amounts of data, a full backup can take up to 10 or 15 hours depending on the backup technology that is being used. Many of these organizations can arrange for a 10- to 15-hour window during which the system is unused on weekends, but not each night. Therefore, a full backup cannot be performed daily without the risk of open files not being properly backed up. To solve this problem, incremental and differential backups are used.

An **incremental backup** of data files backs up only the files that have changed since the previous backup. The amount of data backed up by an incremental backup is much smaller than a full backup. Usually, an incremental backup is less than 10% the size of a full backup.

Incremental backups are also always used in combination with full backups. Normally, a full backup is performed once per week and incremental backups are performed each day. This way, a full backup can be performed on the weekend, and incremental backups can capture daily changes.

The archive attribute is used to track which files an incremental backup should back up. The incremental backup only backs up files that have the archive attribute turned on. Then, when a file is backed up by an incremental backup, the archive attribute on the file is turned off. For example, on Sunday, a full backup is performed, which turns off the archive attribute on all files. On Monday, the operating system turns on the archive attribute for each file that users modify. Then on Monday night, an incremental backup is performed. The incremental backup backs up all files with the archive attribute turned on and turns off the archive attribute on each file that is backed up. On Tuesday, the operating system turns on the archive attribute for each file that users modify. Then on Tuesday night, an incremental backup is performed that backs up all the files with the archive attribute turned on and turns off the archive attribute for each file that is backed up. An incremental backup is performed each day until another full backup is done on Sunday.

Incremental backups are very fast to perform because they are only capturing daily changes. However, they can be slower to restore. If a full restore is performed, the last full backup must be restored and then each incremental backup since the last full backup must be performed.

A **differential backup** of data files backs up all files that have changed since the previous full backup. Like incremental backups, they are always used in a cycle that begins with a full backup. However, unlike incremental backups, a differential backup does not turn off the archive attribute on files that are backed up. Therefore, a file that is changed on Monday is backed up on Monday and on everyday thereafter until a full backup is completed that turns off the archive attribute on changed files.

Performing differential backups is a compromise between full daily backups and incremental backups. A differential backup is much faster to perform than a full backup, but not quite as fast as an incremental backup. When performing a full restore, differential backups are less complex to work with than incremental backups. Figure 14-1 shows the relative backup times required for backup cycles using full, incremental, and differential backups.

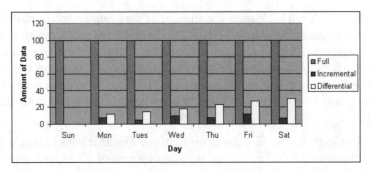

Figure 14-1   Data amounts backed up by full, incremental, and differential backups

In addition to these backup strategies, the Backup utility included with Windows Server 2003 is capable of performing a file copy backup. A file copy backup is a full backup that does not reset the archive attribute, and, therefore, does not interfere with other backup strategies. A file copy backup is commonly used to take an extra copy of backup data to be stored off-site. Storing backups off-site is important to prevent data loss in the event of a fire or other natural disaster that physically destroys equipment and/or backup media.

NOTE   Storing backup tapes in a fire safe box is not effective protection against fire. Backup tapes become unreliable due to heat well before they catch fire. If you have ever seen a cassette tape melt on a car's dashboard, you understand that flames are not required to ruin tape-based data.

Activity 14-1: Performing a Backup

ACTIVITY

Time Required: 10 minutes

Objective: Perform a full and an incremental backup.

Description: Arctic University is performing a full backup every day. However, the amount of data stored on Arctic University servers is becoming too large to perform a full backup each day. To deal with this issue, you have suggested performing a full backup once per week and differential backups each day. You are now performing a test to ensure you understand the ramifications of doing this.

1. If necessary, start your server and log on as **Administrator**.

2. Create a new file in C:\Program Files by doing the following:

   a. Click **Start**, click **Run**, type **cmd**, and then press **Enter**.

   b. Type **cd "c:\program files"** and then press **Enter**.

   c. Type **dir *.* /s > filelist.txt** and then press **Enter**. This performs a dir command and outputs the results to filelist.txt instead of to the screen.

   d. Type **attrib filelist.txt** and then press **Enter**. Notice that an "A" appears beside the file name, indicating that the archive attribute is turned on.

   e. Close the command prompt window.

3. Click **Start**, point to **All Programs**, point to **Accessories**, point to **System Tools**, and then click **Backup**. By default, Backup uses the Backup or Restore Wizard to lead you through the backup process.

4. Click **Advanced Mode** to switch out of the wizard.

5. Click the **Backup** tab.

6. In the left pane, expand **Local Disk (C:)**, and select the **Program Files** check box.

7. In the Backup media or file name text box, type **c:\programfull.bkf**.

8. Click **Tools** and then click **Options**.

14

9. On the Backup Type tab, confirm that Normal is selected in the Default Backup Type drop-down list, and then click **OK**. A Normal backup is a full backup in which the archive attribute is turned off for all files that are backed up.

10. Click **Start Backup**.

11. In the Backup Job Information dialog box, click the **Replace the data on the media with this backup** option button, and then click **Start Backup**.

12. When the backup is complete, click **Close**.

13. Click **Start**, click **Run**, type **cmd**, and then press **Enter**.

14. Type **cd "c:\program files"** and then press **Enter**.

15. Type **attrib filelist.txt** and then press **Enter**. Notice that there is no "A" beside the file name, indicating that the archive attribute is turned off.

16. Type **dir *.* /s > filelist.txt** and then press **Enter**. This re-creates the file and turns the archive attribute on again.

17. Type **attrib filelist.txt** and then press **Enter**. Notice that an "A" appears beside the file name, indicating that the archive attribute is turned on.

18. In the Backup Utility window on the Backup tab, select the **Program Files** check box.

19. In the Backup media or file name text box, type **c:\programdif.bkf**.

20. Click **Start Backup** and then click the **Advanced** button.

21. In the Backup Type drop-down list box, select **Differential**, and then click **OK**.

22. In the Backup Job Information dialog box, click the **Replace the data on the media with this backup** option button, and then click **Start Backup**.

23. Notice the when the backup is complete, only one file has been backed up because only one file has changed since the full backup. Click **Close**.

24. Close the Backup Utility window.

25. In the command prompt window, type **attrib filelist.txt** and then press **Enter**. Notice that the archive attribute is still on because differential backups do not turn off the archive attribute.

26. Close the command prompt window.

Restoring files is just as important as backing them up. In fact, one of the most common mistakes network administrators make is not testing their backups by periodically performing a restore. There are many horror stories out there about network administrators who found only after their systems crashed that their backups had not been functioning properly.

Most of the time, you are restoring files because a user has deleted a file accidentally, or performed a bad modification and saved the file. When you recover files for users, it is a good practice to restore the files to a different location than the original. Then, users can work with both the original and restored files to copy data between them if required.

Activity 14-2: Performing a Restore

Time Required: 5 minutes

Objective: Restore a file from backup.

Description: Part of testing any backup system is ensuring that you can restore files from your backups after they are complete. This is an essential part of any backup system. In this activity, you restore a file from the differential backup created in Activity 14-1.

1. If necessary, start your server and log on as **Administrator**.
2. Click **Start**, click **Run**, type **cmd**, and then press **Enter**.
3. Type **cd "c:\program files"** and then press **Enter**.
4. Type **del filelist.txt** and then press **Enter**.
5. Type **dir *.txt** and then press **Enter**. Notice that filelist.txt is no longer there.
6. Click **Start**, point to **All Programs**, point to **Accessories**, point to **System Tools**, and then click **Backup**.
7. Click **Advanced Mode** to switch out of the wizard.
8. Click the **Restore and Manage Media** tab.
9. In the left pane, expand **File**, expand **programdif.bkf**, click **C:**, expand **C:**, and then click **Program Files**.
10. In the right pane, check the **filelist.txt** check box. This selects only this file to be restored.
11. In the Restore files to drop-down list, ensure that Original location is selected. This is used to place files back in the same location where they were backed up. You can also choose Alternate location if you do not want to overwrite any existing files.
12. Click **Start Restore**.
13. Click **OK** to perform the restore.
14. After the restore is complete, notice that one file was restored. Click **Close**.
15. Close the Backup Utility window.
16. In the command prompt window, type **dir *.txt** and then press **Enter**. Notice that filelist.txt has been restored.
17. Close the command prompt window.

14

System State Backup

In addition to backing up files, the Backup utility is also capable of backing up the system state data. The **system state data** includes the registry, COM+ Class Registration database, boot files, and system files (including the ones covered by Windows File Protection). If Certificate Services is installed, then the Certificate Services Database is included. If it is a domain controller, then the Active Directory database and Sysvol folder are backed up. If IIS is installed, then the IIS metabase is included.

Although files can be backed up across the network via a file share, system state data can be backed up only on the same machine on which Backup is running. However, third-party backup software can back up system state data across the network.

To restore system state data, you must use Directory Services Restore Mode. Directory Services Restore Mode is a startup option similar to safe mode that limits the services that are running so that system state data can be restored properly. To enter Directory Services Restore Mode, press F8 at the beginning of the boot process and select Directory Services Restore Mode.

When system state data is restored on a domain controller, the Active Directory database is also restored on that server. When Active Directory is restored on a domain controller but no special action is taken, it is referred to as a nonauthoritative restore. Any changes to Active Directory that have occurred since the system state backup are replicated back onto the domain controller after Active Directory is restored because the changes have newer time stamps. The replicated changes include the deletion of objects.

A nonauthoritative restore of Active Directory is used when the Active Directory database on a server becomes corrupt and ceases functioning, or if the system disk fails. It is used to place a functioning copy of the Active Directory database back onto the domain controller. It is not used to replace deleted objects.

An authoritative restore of Active Directory is used to replace deleted objects. Ntdsutil is used to make a restore of Active Directory authoritative. Using Ntdsutil, you can select certain objects and mark them as authoritative. This sets the time stamp on those objects to the current time so that changes to them since the system state backup do not overwrite them.

While a domain controller is in Directory Services Restore Mode, it cannot be used to authenticate logons. You must reboot the server normally before Active Directory begins functioning again.

Automated System Recovery

Backup can also be used to perform an **automated system recovery (ASR) backup** that is used to restore the operating system in the event of a disaster such as system disk failure. It is meant as a last resort to recover systems that you have not been able to recover using other more common tools, such as last known good configuration and safe mode. ASR is a new feature in Windows Server 2003.

ASR replaces the Emergency Recovery Disk that could be created in Windows NT and Windows 2000.

When an ASR backup is performed, all of the operating system is backed up. This includes system state data, system service configuration, and all operating system files. In addition, ASR creates a floppy disk that stores information about the backup, disk configuration, and how to perform a restore.

To perform an ASR restore, you must start the installation of the operating system and press F2 when the option appears on the screen. The easiest way to start the installation of the operating system is to boot from the operating system CD-ROM. The drivers required to access the disk subsystem, such as SCSI drivers, must be loaded during the initial boot up. If the disk drivers you require are not included in Windows Server 2003, you must supply them on floppy disk during the startup process.

An ASR restore reads the disk configuration information from the ASR floppy disk and restores the disk configuration. Then, a simple installation of Windows Server 2003 is performed, after which the operating system is restored from the ASR backup.

ASR does not support FAT16 partitions/volumes larger than 2.1 GB, even though Windows Server 2003 supports FAT16 partitions/volumes up to 4 GB.

14

Volume Shadow Copy

Volume shadow copy makes copies of files, including open files, at a particular point in time on NTFS volumes. This can be used to perform open file backups and allow users to restore previous versions of files without administrator involvement.

To perform backups of open files, volume shadow copy can be configured as part of a backup job in the Backup utility. This avoids the need for expensive third-party open file backup software.

You can also configure shadow copies of volumes on your system that hold user data. Then, users are able to recover files that were accidentally deleted and recover previous versions of files that were accidentally overwritten.

A volume shadow copy is unlike a traditional file copy. A volume shadow copy sets aside a specified amount of disk space to store changes to files that have occurred since the volume shadow copy was performed. Only files that have changed take up additional disk space. If you can take a volume shadow copy of a volume with 10 GB of data and only 200 MB of data has changed, then only 200 MB of disk space is used by the volume shadow copy.

Volume shadow copies are not a replacement for regular file system backups because a file can only be recovered from a volume shadow copy if the original source location is also available.

NOTE

Only a certain amount of disk space is allocated for storing the changes to files performed after a volume shadow copy. The minimum size that can be allocated is 100 MB and the default is 10% of the volume size. If the amount of space allocated is not enough to hold all of the changes, older changes are overwritten. Regardless of the amount of disk space allocated, a maximum of 63 previous versions of a file are stored.

Volume shadow copies can be performed manually, but the greatest benefit is obtained when they are scheduled. They can be performed on any schedule you want, but are most commonly performed once or twice per day. Disk performance is reduced during the time a volume shadow copy is performed; therefore, they should be avoided during periods of peak usage.

Operating systems previous to Windows Server 2003 can only use volume shadow copy as a client if additional client software is installed. The Volume Shadow Copy Client software is located in C:\Windows\System32\clients\twclients\x86. In addition, clients can only restore files when accessing them across the network via a UNC path or a mapped drive letter.

Activity 14-3: Configuring and Using Volume Shadow Copy

ACTIVITY

Time Required: 15 minutes

Objective: Configure volume shadow copy to allow users to restore files from the previous day.

Description: A study of the Arctic University help desk found that staff were spending 15% of their time recovering files for users from recent backups. After migrating all of the file servers to Windows Server 2003, you want to configure volume shadow copy so that users can restore their own files from recent versions.

To test volume shadow copy, you must have two servers. In this activity, you work with a partner. All steps are to be completed by both partners simultaneously.

1. If necessary, start your server and log on as **Administrator**.
2. Click **Start** and then click **My Computer**.
3. Right-click **Local Disk (C:)** and then click **Properties**.
4. Click the **Shadow Copies** tab.
5. Click the **Enable** button. This enables shadow copies for all shares on this volume.
6. Read the warning dialog box, check the **Do not show this message again** check box, and then click **Yes**. It may take several minutes to create the first shadow copy.

7. Click the **Settings** button.

8. In the Storage area option group, in the Use limit text box, type **300**. This limits the disk space used by volume shadow copy to 300 MB. If more than 300 MB of changes are made to files, then only the newest changes are retained.

9. Click the **Schedule** button. Notice that the default schedule is to perform a shadow copy each weekday at 7:00 a.m. This allows users to restore files as they were at 7:00 a.m. each day if a file is accidentally deleted or modified.

10. Click **Cancel**, click **OK**, and then click **OK**.

11. Close My Computer.

12. Click **Start**, right-click **My Computer**, and then click **Manage**.

13. In the left pane of the Computer Management window, expand **Shared Folders**, and then click **Shares**.

14. Right-click **Shares** and then click **New Share**.

15. Click **Next** to begin the wizard.

16. In the Folder path text box, type **c:\program files** and then click **Next**.

17. In the Share name text box, type **programs** and then click **Next**.

18. Click the **Administrators have full access; other users have read and write access** option button, and then click **Finish**.

19. Click **Close**. Be certain that you do not proceed to the next step until your partner has completed up to this point in the exercise.

20. Click **Start**, click **Run**, type **\\Student*yy***, where *yy* is your partner's student number, and then press **Enter**. This connects you to your partner's server.

21. Double-click **programs** to view the contents of the programs share on your partner's server.

22. Right-click **filelist.txt**, click **Delete**, and then click **Yes** to confirm. This simulates an accidentally deleted file.

23. Click the **Back** button.

24. Right-click **programs** and then click **Properties**.

25. Click the **Previous Versions** tab.

26. Click the **View** button. This opens a window that shows the contents of programs share when the last volume shadow copy was taken. If multiple shadow copies have been taken, you can choose which one you want to view.

27. Right-click **filelist.txt** and click **Copy**.

28. Close the \\Student*yy*\programs (Today, *date and time of shadow copy*) window, where *yy* is your partner's student number.

29. Click **Cancel**.

30. Double-click **programs**.

31. Right-click in an open area of the right pane, and then click **Paste**. This restores the file you deleted in Step 22.

32. Close the \\Student*yy*\programs window, where *yy* is your partner's student number.

RECOVERY TOOLS

A variety of tools are provided with Windows Server 2003 to help you recover your system when a full operating system restore or system state restore is not desired. These include device driver rollback, safe mode, last known good configuration, and Recovery Console. Each of these is covered in the following sections.

Device Driver Rollback

During the installation of Windows Server 2003, hardware devices are detected and appropriate device drivers are installed from the Windows Server 2003 installation files. All the drivers included in the Windows Server 2003 installation files have been tested by Microsoft and are digitally signed to indicate that they have been approved by Microsoft. All device drivers available on Windows Update are also tested and digitally signed by Microsoft.

Device drivers that are obtained from vendor Web sites may or may not be digitally signed by Microsoft. Some vendors do not submit their driver to Microsoft for testing because of either the cost or the time it takes for Microsoft to test and approve the drivers. When installing drivers that are not digitally signed by Microsoft, you must be certain that you trust the vendor to do adequate testing.

 NOTE Updating an installed driver is always risky—regardless of whether it has been signed by Microsoft. Your specific hardware and software configuration may have problems not encountered in testing by Microsoft or the vendor.

If you install an updated driver that does not function properly, Windows Server 2003 provides an easy mechanism to restore the previous device driver. **Device driver rollback** can be used to revert back to the previous version of the device driver at any time after an update. It is available through Device Manager on the Driver tab of the properties for any device, as shown in Figure 14-2.

Safe Mode

When a server becomes misconfigured or corrupt to the point at which it cannot be booted properly, or when a server is booted but cannot be managed, then safe mode is used. When a computer boots into **safe mode**, a minimal set of drivers is loaded. In most circumstances,

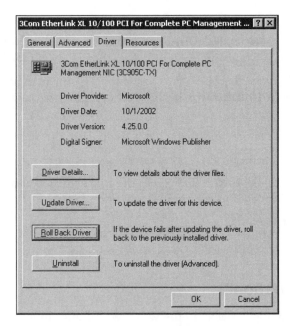

Figure 14-2   Roll Back Driver button

this means that the driver or service that was causing problems is not loaded. Then, when in safe mode, you can repair the system by updating drivers, reinstalling software, or removing corrupt software.

The standard safe mode loads a generic video driver that works with any video hardware that is functioning properly. Safe mode with Networking loads networking components in addition to the standard safe mode components. This lets you access network resources that may be useful for troubleshooting, including downloading drivers from the Internet. Safe Mode Command Prompt starts without a GUI. This is useful if the GUI is corrupt.

Safe mode is available in the Windows Advanced Options menu during startup. To access this menu, press F8 when the boot menu is displayed at the beginning of the startup process.

ACTIVITY

Activity 14-4: Accessing Safe Mode

Time Required: 5 minutes

Objective: Enter into safe mode.

Description: Arctic University has just received a new work experience student from the local computer training school. When talking about recovering systems, you discover that the work experience student has never seen safe mode. Show the student how to enter safe mode and demonstrate that network resources cannot be accessed in safe mode.

1. Restart (or start) your server and press **F8** when the boot menu appears. This brings up the Windows Advanced Options menu.

2. Select **Safe Mode** and press **Enter**.

3. If necessary, select **Windows Server 2003, Enterprise** and press **Enter**. Notice that the boot process lists some of the operating system files as they are being loaded.

4. When Windows has started, notice that the words Safe Mode appear in all four corners of the screen. Log on as **Administrator** of the local computer, because network resources are not available.

5. Read the dialog box about safe mode, and then click **OK** to close the dialog box.

6. Click **Start**, click **Run**, type **cmd**, and then press **Enter**.

7. Type **ping 192.168.1.10** and press **Enter**. This pings the instructor server and is unsuccessful because the network is unavailable in safe mode.

8. Close the command prompt window.

9. Restart your server.

Last Known Good Configuration

Last known good configuration is also available in the Windows Advanced Options menu. However, its use is much more specialized than safe mode. To understand how last known good configuration works, you must understand control sets.

Windows Server 2003 has several registry keys in HKEY_LOCAL_MACHINE\SYSTEM. These keys are called control sets and are shown in Figure 14-3. As you can see, there are three control sets: ControlSet001, ControlSet002, and CurrentControlSet. Each control set has settings that control the startup of services and drivers. CurrentControlSet is the group of settings that are being used by the system at this time. It is created by copying either ControlSet001 or ControlSet002 during the boot process. When configuration changes are made to the CurrentControlSet, a new control set is created.

The registry key HKEY_LOCAL_MACHINE\SYSTEM\Select holds several registry keys used to determine how each control set should be used, as shown in Figure 14-4. The Current key defines which control set is being used as the CurrentControlSet. The Default key defines which control set is used by default to become the CurrentControlSet. The LastKnownGood key specifies which control set was in use when the last successful boot occurred. A successful boot is defined as a boot in which a user was able to log on. The most recent LastKnownGood key is defined when the first user successfully logs on.

Last known good configuration is useful for fixing problems only if no user has logged on since the change was made. For example, if a new device driver for new hardware is installed and the system encounters severe errors, then last known good configuration can be used to restore the registry to before the new device driver was installed. This does not delete the files associated with the driver, but does prevent them from being loaded during startup.

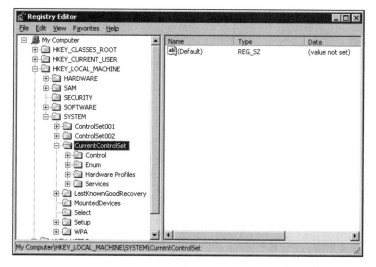

Figure 14-3   Control sets

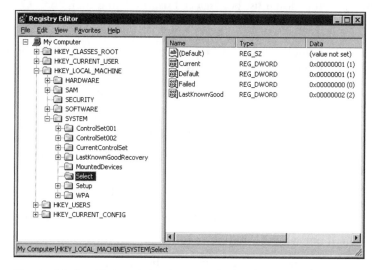

Figure 14-4   Determining how control sets are used

Last known good configuration restores only parts of the registry and does not affect files. Driver updates use new versions of files, but normally do not change registry settings. Because last known good configuration does not affect files, it does not fix problems associated with driver updates.

Activity 14-5: Using Last Known Good Configuration

Time Required: 30 minutes

Objective: Use last known good configuration to restore service and driver settings.

Description: Recently, several servers at Arctic University have been rendered nonfunctional when new hardware and drivers have been added. The servers were able to be restored only by performing a full disaster recovery, which took eight hours per server. You are demonstrating to some of the junior administrators how they can use last known good configuration to solve the problem instead, as long as a successful logon has not been performed since the changes.

1. If necessary, start your server and log on as **Administrator**.

2. Click **Start**, right-click **My Computer**, and then click **Manage**.

3. Expand **Services and Applications** and then click **Services**.

4. Scroll down in the list of services, and double-click **Net Logon**.

5. In the Startup type drop-down list box, select **Disabled**, and then click **OK**.

6. Close the Computer Management window, and restart your server.

7. As your server is restarting, a dialog box appears stating that at least one service or driver failed during system startup. Click **OK** to clear the dialog box.

8. Restart your server by powering it off or pressing the reset button. Do not log on first.

9. When prompted, press **F8** to access the Windows Advanced Options menu.

10. Select the **Last Known Good Configuration (your most recent settings that worked)** menu option, and press **Enter**.

11. Confirm that Windows Server 2003, Enterprise is selected, and then press **Enter**.

12. This time, there are no error messages during the restart. Log on as **Administrator**.

13. Enter a comment about why the computer restarted, and then click **OK**.

14. Repeat Steps 2–6 to re-create the problem with the netlogon service.

15. Click **OK** to clear the error dialog box, and then log on as **Administrator**.

16. Repeat Steps 8–11 to attempt to use last known good configuration to fix the problem again.

17. An error appears indicating that a previous configuration was used. Click **OK** to continue.

18. This time, the error message about services being unable to start is still there during restart because the settings with the netlogon service disabled were saved as last known good configuration when you logged on as Administrator in Step 15. Click **OK** to clear the error message.

19. Log on as **Administrator**.

20. Enter a comment about why the computer restarted, and then click **OK**.

21. Click **Start**, right-click **My Computer**, and then click **Manage**.

22. Expand **Services and Applications** and then click **Services**.

23. Scroll down in the list of services, and double-click **Net Logon**.

24. In the Startup type drop-down list box, select **Automatic**, and then click **OK**.

25. Close the Computer Management window and restart your server.

Recovery Console

Recovery Console is a command-line interface that allows you to access system settings and files when Windows cannot be started properly. This is useful when safe mode and last known good configuration are not effective.

To access Recovery Console, you must boot from the operating system CD-ROM or have previously installed it to the Windows Advanced Options menu that is available during startup.

When Recovery Console starts, you must log on. This allows Recovery Console to control file system access based on NTFS permissions and ensures that not just any user can access files using Recovery Console.

You can access files and folder while in Recovery Console. This makes it useful for retrieving files off of a failed server before reinstalling the server OS. It also allows you to replace corrupt or missing system files, if required.

You can also configure the startup settings for services in Recovery Console. If the startup problem is a particular service that is failing, this allows you to disable that service so that it does not start at startup.

Another task that can be done in Recovery Console is disk management. Recovery Console can re-create the master boot record on the hard drive and the boot sector on the active partition. The master boot record on the hard drive contains a small program that finds the active partition on the hard drive to continue the boot process. If the master boot record is corrupt, the boot process fails. The boot sector on the active partition contains a small program that loads ntldr. Ntldr then starts Windows Server 2003. If the boot sector is corrupt, then the boot process fails.

 When dynamic disks are used, you should not perform disk management operations using Recovery Console, particularly disk partitioning operations. Recovery Console does not manipulate dynamic disks properly.

NOTE

ACTIVITY

Activity 14-6: Installing and Using Recovery Console

Time Required: 15 minutes

Objective: Install and use Recovery Console.

Description: To facilitate disaster recovery on your servers, you have decided to install Recovery Console on all of them. This is a faster way to access Recovery Console than booting off of the Windows Server 2003 CD-ROM. You are also going to test it to ensure that it is functioning properly.

1. If necessary, start your server and log on as **Administrator**.

2. Click **Start**, click **Run**, type **c:\i386\winnt32.exe /cmdcons**, and then press **Enter**. This step assumes that you have copied the \I386 folder from the Windows Server 2003 CD-ROM to your hard drive. If you have not, place the Windows Server 2003 CD-ROM in your CD-ROM drive and substitute the drive letter of your CD-ROM drive for c:.

3. Read the contents of the Windows Setup dialog box. When you have completed reading the contents of the dialog box, click **Yes**.

4. As part of the installation process, Windows attempts to download updates from Microsoft. If the Internet is not available, the process takes 30 seconds or more to timeout and present a dialog box. If necessary, click the **Skip this step and continue installing Windows** option button, and then click **Next**.

5. Click **OK** to close the dialog box indicating that the installation of Recovery Console was successful.

6. Restart your server.

7. When given the option in the boot menu, select **Microsoft Windows Recovery Console**, and then press **Enter**.

8. When prompted for the Windows installation, type **1**, and then press **Enter**.

9. When prompted for the Administrator password, type **Password!**, and then press **Enter**.

10. Type **help** and then press **Enter** to view a list of commands that are available in Recovery Console. Notice that many of these commands are the same as command-line utilities available in a command prompt window. Press **Space** to scroll to the end of the list.

11. Type **dir** and then press **Enter**. Notice that this display is different than the Dir command at a command prompt in Windows. Press **Space** to continue viewing files, or press **Esc** to stop viewing files.

12. Type **bootcfg /list** and then press **Enter** to view the options available in the boot menu. This command can also be used to modify these options.

13. Type **fixboot c:** and then press **Enter** to re-create the boot sector on your C: partition. This is useful if the boot sector becomes corrupt or someone uses the Sys command from a Windows 9x boot disk on your partition.

14. Type **y** to confirm writing a new boot sector, and then press **Enter**.

15. Type **exit** and press **Enter**.

REMOTE MANAGEMENT

Terminal Services is a remote access solution that lets users connect to a remote computer and run applications on the remote computer. The users must have client software installed on their workstations to connect to a terminal server. The client software on the workstations creates a desktop environment based on screen draw commands from the remote computer. In this way, it is very much like remote control. However, Terminal Services can support multiple users connected at the same time, each with their own desktop stored and processed in memory on the server.

Terminal Services is often used for a centralized line of business applications. For example, a firm implementing a new accounting system installs the client software on a terminal server. Then, all clients connect to the terminal server and run the application remotely. This simplifies application management because it is maintained only on the central terminal server. Any updates to the client software only need to be applied once on the terminal server.

Users requiring remote access to applications and data can also use Terminal Services. Terminal Services is much more efficient for remote access than a VPN. A VPN requires users to transfer all of their data across the VPN connection. This is often quite slow, particularly if a dial-up connection is being used. However, if Terminal Services is used for remote access, then all of the applications required by remote users are installed on the terminal server. Then, remote access users connect to the terminal server and are able to run all of their applications remotely through Terminal Services regardless of their connection speed. The screen draw commands sent between the Terminal Services client and server are very small amounts of data, and performance is acceptable even over dial-up links.

When used for remote access and line of business applications, you must buy Terminal Service client access licenses for each user who is connecting. However, for remote management, you can use Terminal Services at no cost. The following two sections show how Terminal Services can be used to remotely administer servers and assist users.

Remote Desktop for Administration

Remote Desktop for Administration allows up to two users at a time to administer a server remotely using Terminal Services. All server features can be accessed just as if you were sitting at the server console. Using Remote Desktop, you can perform all software and operating system maintenance from a centralized location. This is useful when there are multiple offices and you do not want the expense or hassle of traveling to maintain a remote server. It is also useful within a single building because server rooms (closets) are seldom comfortable to work in. Remote Desktop allows you to remain in the comfort of your office while maintaining the server.

When you receive emergency calls on evenings and weekends, Remote Desktop for Administration is indispensable. It allows you to connect and repair your server without leaving the comfort of your home—provided you have properly configured the firewall. Remote Desktop for Administration runs on TCP port 3389 by default. This must be allowed by the firewall. Many companies allow Remote Desktop for Administration connections only if you are connected through a VPN. This provides two layers of authentication to increase security.

By default, Remote Desktop for Administration is disabled. It is enabled on the Remote tab in System Properties, as shown in Figure 14-5. This can be accessed through System in Control Panel, or by right-clicking My Computer and then clicking Properties.

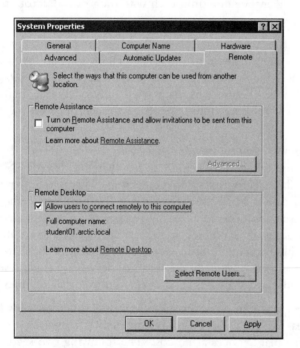

Figure 14-5   Remote tab in System Properties

Only the Administrator account has remote desktop permission by default. Other users can be given remote desktop permission by adding them to the Remote Desktop Users group.

Remote Desktop is also available in Windows XP. However, Windows XP does not allow multiple users to connect at the same time. When a user is at the console in Windows XP and another user connects remotely via Remote Desktop, the console user is disconnected until the remote user logs off.

Remote Desktop for Administration can be accessed using the Remote Desktop Connection utility or the Remote Desktops snap-in. The **Remote Desktop Connection** utility allows you to connect to a single Remote Desktop for Administration server. The **Remote Desktops snap-in** lets you connect to multiple remote servers at once and switch easily between them, as shown in Figure 14-6. The Remote Desktops snap-in also allows you to save the configuration information such as user name and password for each connection.

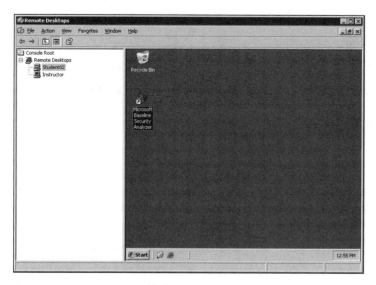

Figure 14-6   Remote Desktops snap-in

You can configure a number of settings for Terminal Services that control when idle connections should time out and if users are allowed to disconnect from a session and leave applications running remotely. You can configure these settings by using the Terminal Services Configuration snap-in available in Administrative Tools.

Sometimes, a terminal server connection becomes hung and you cannot reconnect to it. Because Remote Desktop for Administration allows you to have two connections, this is not an immediate problem. However, if two connections become hung, you will not be able to connect remotely at all. To clear a hung connection without rebooting the server, you use the Terminal Services Manager snap-in available in Administrative Tools.

Activity 14-7: Using Remote Desktop for Administration

Time Required: 5 minutes

Objective: Use Remote Desktop for Administration to remotely connect to a server.

Description: At Arctic University, the administrators spend much of their time traveling between buildings on campus to fix various server issues. In addition, problems at remote sites often must wait for an administrator to fly in on a scheduled visit before they are fixed. To reduce wasted time and enhance server performance, you implement Remote Desktop for Administration on your servers.

This activity requires two servers to complete. You work with a partner. Unless otherwise stated, all steps are performed by both partners simultaneously.

1. If necessary, start your server and log on as **Administrator**.
2. Click **Start**, right-click **My Computer**, and then click **Properties**.
3. Click the **Remote** tab.
4. Check the **Allow users to connect remotely to this computer** check box.
5. Read the warning dialog box that appears, and then click **OK**.
6. Click the **Select Remote Users** button. Notice that no users are listed here by default, but there is a note that ARCTIC\Administrator already has access.
7. Click **Add**.
8. In the Enter the object names to select (examples) text box, type **Studentxx\Administrator**, where *xx* is your student number, and click **OK**. This ensures that the local administrator can perform remote administration rather than just the domain administrator.
9. Click **OK** and click **OK**. Do not go on to the next step until your partner has completed this step.
10. Click **Start**, point to **All Programs**, point to **Accessories**, point to **Communications**, and then click **Remote Desktop Connection**.
11. In the Computer text box, type **192.168.1.1yy**, where *yy* is your partner's student number, and then click **Connect**. This connects you in full screen mode by default. If necessary, in the User name text box, type **Administrator**.
12. In the Password text box, type **Password!**.
13. If necessary, in the Log on to drop-down list box, select **Studentyy (this computer)**, where *yy* is your partner's student number.
14. Click **OK** to log on. Notice that there is a bar at the top of the screen to indicate you are using Terminal Services and listing the IP address of the server to which you are connected. Also notice that you are connected to your partner's server, but the screen on your partner's computer is independent of your display window.
15. Click **Start**, right-click **My Computer**, and then click **Properties**.
16. Click the **Computer Name** tab. Read the computer name to confirm that you are connected to your partner's computer.
17. Click **Cancel**.

18. Click **Start**, click **Log Off**, and then click **Log Off**. Logging off of the remote computer disconnects you from Terminal Services.

Remote Assistance

Remote Assistance is designed as a system for users to ask experts for help. In a corporate setting, the experts are normally the help desk or application support specialists. This feature is not normally enabled on servers because end users do not sit at the server console. The one exception to this rule is a terminal server. You may enable Remote Assistance on a terminal server because users are effectively working at the console when they connect to the terminal server.

NOTE   Windows XP client computers also support Remote Assistance.

Remote Assistance is enabled on the Remote tab of System Properties. Requests for Remote Assistance are performed using Help and Support, as shown in Figure 14-7. Invitations for Remote Assistance can be made through Windows Messenger, through e-mail, or by saving as a file.

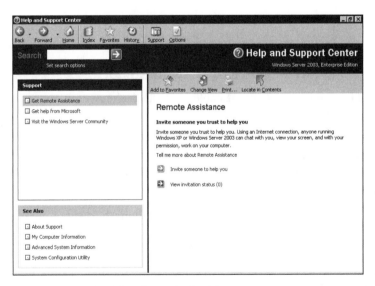

Figure 14-7   Inviting Remote Assistance

If there is a firewall performing NAT between the computer inviting assistance and the computer providing assistance, then, in most cases, Remote Assistance does not function properly. The invitation for Remote Assistance contains the IP address of the computer inviting assistance. If the IP address of the computer inviting assistance is an internal private IP address, the computer providing assistance is not able to connect to it because the internal private IP address is not accessible from outside the firewall performing NAT.

Remote Assistance can be performed through NAT if the machine performing NAT is running Windows Server 2003 or Windows XP running ICS. This is made possible through support for Universal Plug and Play.

The remote control function of Remote Assistance requires TCP port 3389 to be accessible through a firewall.

NOTE

Activity 14-8: Using Remote Assistance

ACTIVITY

Time Required: 15 minutes

Objective: Use Remote Assistance to request help.

Description: Arctic University is considering implementing Remote Assistance for users. To ensure a smooth rollout of this functionality, all of the help desk staff are in the test lab to see how it works. For testing purposes, a file is used to send a request for help. However, the live system uses e-mail and Microsoft Instant Messenger.

Remote Assistance requires two computers. In this activity, you work with a partner. One of you plays the role of the help desk worker and the other plays the role of a user. Unless otherwise specified, both partners complete all steps.

1. If necessary, start your server and log on as **Administrator**.

2. Partner Who Has the Role of User: Enable Remote Assistance on your server by doing the following:

    a. Click **Start**, right-click **My Computer**, and then click **Properties**.

    b. Click the **Remote** tab.

    c. Select the **Turn on Remote Assistance and allow invitations to be sent from this computer**.

3. Partner Who Has the Role of User: Limit invitation length to two hours by doing the following:

    a. Click the **Advanced** button.

    b. In the Invitations option group, set the maximum amount of time invitations can remain open to **2 Hours**.

    c. Click **OK** and then click **OK**.

4. Partner Who Has the Role of User: Send an invitation for help by doing the following:

    a. Click **Start** and then click **Help and Support**.

    b. In the right pane, click **Support**.

    c. In the left pane, click **Get Remote Assistance**.

    d. In the right pane, click **Invite someone to help you**.

    e. Scroll down in the right pane, and then click **Save invitation as a file (Advanced)**.

    f. In the From (the name you want to appear on the invitation) text box, type your name, and then click **Continue**.

    g. In the Type password text box, type **remotepass**; in the Confirm password text box, type **remotepass**, and then click **Save Invitation**.

    h. In the left pane, click **My Computer**, double-click **Local Disk (C:)**, and then click **Save**.

    i. Click **View the status of all my invitations (1)**. This shows the status of outstanding invitations that have been sent for remote assistance.

    j. Close Help and Support Center.

5. Partner Who Has the Role of Help Desk Worker: Accept the invitation for remote assistance by doing the following:

    a. Click **Start**, click **Run**, type **\\Student*yy*\c$**, where *yy* is your partner's student number, and then press **Enter**.

    b. Double-click **RAInvitation.msrcincident**.

    c. In the Password text box, type **remotepass**, and then click **Yes**.

6. Partner Who Has the Role of User: Click **Yes** to accept the offer of remote assistance.

7. Partner Who Has the Role of Help Desk Worker: Read the text below the Chat History heading. Notice that it indicates that the status of this connection is Screen View Only. Click the **Take Control** button in the upper-left corner.

8. Partner Who Has the Role of User: Click **Yes** to allow the Help Desk Worker to take control of your computer.

9. Partner Who Has the Role of Help Desk Worker: Read the Remote Assistance dialog box, and then click **OK** to clear it.

10. Partner Who Has the Role of Help Desk Worker: Start a few applications on the remote computer. Notice that all of the actions you perform appear on the remote console.

11. Partner Who Has the Role of User: In the Remote Assistance window, click **Disconnect** to end the Remote Assistance session, and then close the Remote Assistance window.

12. Partner Who Has the Role of Help Desk Worker: Click **OK**, close the Remote Assistance window, and then close the \\Student*yy*\c$ window, where *yy* is your partner's student number.

14

IMAGING CLIENT COMPUTERS AND SERVERS

Installing each client computer and server from the operating system CD-ROM is a tedious and time-consuming process. Depending on the hardware of each client and server, the installation process may take over an hour for each one. Imaging, which installs an entire operating system in one step, can reduce this process to less than 10 minutes.

Over time, many client computers become unstable when new applications are installed by users. Depending on what has been done to the client computer, it may take hours or days to find out what the problem is and fix it. Imaging can restore the operating system and applications to a computer in 10 minutes or less.

Imaging software takes a copy of an entire hard drive or partition and stores it as a file. Then, instead of installing applications and the operating system, the contents of that file are copied onto a client computer. The time required to perform a file copy is much less than that for full application and operating system installation.

Windows Server 2003 includes a solution for imaging called **RIS (Remote Installation Services)**. A number of third-party imaging solutions, such as Norton Ghost, are also available. Each of these is covered in the following sections.

Remote Installation Services

The version of RIS included with Windows Server 2003 is capable of installing Windows Server 2003, Windows XP, and Windows 2000. Both RIPrep images and flat images are supported for installation.

A **RIPrep image** is a fully installed operating system and applications that are copied to a file. A RIPrep image can be placed on a workstation or server in 10 minutes or less depending on its size. The larger the number of applications that are installed, the longer the imaging process takes.

For a RIPrep image to be used on multiple computers, the computers must have similar hardware. Hardware detection can be used to install basic drivers like network and sound card drivers, but the hardware abstraction layer (HAL) used by machines must be the same. If the HAL is not the same, the systems do not boot properly.

To create a RIPrep image, first install the required operating system on a computer. Then install and configure any required applications. After the computer is configured exactly the way you want it, run RIPrep.exe. This program takes an image of the local computer and copies the image up to the RIS server. The RIS server then stores the image on its local hard drive.

A **flat image** is a scripted installation of the operating system across the network. Because a flat image is the full installation of an operating system, it takes from 45 to 90 minutes depending on the hardware on which it is being installed. Applications are not automatically installed as part of a flat image.

When multiple computers are installed using a flat image, the hardware can be different between the computers. Because it is performing a regular installation, even the HAL can be different because it is detected during the installation.

To create a flat image, the operating system files must be copied to the RIS server. A .sif file is used to set the options during the install. This .sif file is similar to the configuration file used during an unattended install, and is generated by Setup Manager.

To implement RIS effectively, you must understand the RIS server requirements, the RIS client requirements, the required network services, and the RIS process. The following sections discuss each in turn.

RIS Server Requirements

You can install a RIS server on any hardware that meets the minimum requirements for Windows Server 2003, with the following exceptions:

- A single 10/100 Mbps adapter. A RIS server cannot be multihomed.
- A RIS server must have a 4-GB volume, which is not the system or boot volume, to hold RIS images.
- The volume holding RIS must be an NTFS volume.

RIS is installed through Add/Remove Windows Components. However, before it can be used, it must be configured using the Remote Installation Services Setup Wizard (risetup. exe). It is this wizard that asks for the RIS location where images are stored, the location of the installation files for Windows clients to be installed using flat images, and whether the server should begin responding to requests immediately after configuration. Normally, you configure the server to not respond to client requests until you have finished creating images.

NOTE

RIS is not included with Windows Server 2003, Web Edition.

NOTE

RIS must also be authorized before it can function. This prevents unauthorized users from installing RIS servers on the network. To authorize a RIS server, a member of the Enterprise Admins group must run risetup.exe.

RIS servers generate large amounts of network traffic because of the large size of images. For this reason, there should always be fast network links between RIS clients and RIS servers. The recommended speed for the network in RIS servers is at least 100 Mbps. Imaging should never be performed across WAN links because they are far too slow to support it and WAN performance will be severely degraded.

RIS Client Requirements

A RIS client must meet the minimum hardware requirements required by the operating system that is being installed. For instance, if Windows XP is being installed, then the RIS client must meet the minimum hardware requirements for Windows XP.

In addition, the RIS client must have a **Pre-Boot eXecution Environment (PXE) boot ROM** version 1.00 or greater to connect to the RIS server. A PXE boot ROM is embedded in the network card and provides the ability to connect to the network without an operating system installed.

If a computer does not have a PXE boot ROM, a floppy disk can be created that simulates a PXE boot ROM. The boot floppy is generated using the **Remote Boot Floppy Generator (rbfg.exe)**.

RIS clients can be prestaged by creating computer accounts in Active Directory before the client is configured. Prestaging a RIS client allows any user to perform the imaging process even if the user does not have permissions to create computer accounts. Prestaging also allows you to specify a particular RIS server that services a particular RIS client.

To prestage RIS clients, each computer account must be configured with a **globally unique identifier (GUID)**. The GUID is part of the PXE boot ROM. The GUID for your computer can often be found on a sticker on the outside or inside of the RIS client, in the BIOS of the RIS client, or by using a packet sniffer to monitor network traffic generated by the RIS client. RIS clients that are started from a Remote Boot Floppy create a GUID based on the MAC address of the network card.

A GUID is a 128-bit number entered as 32 hexadecimal characters. The following format is used {*dddddddd-dddd-dddd-dddd-dddddddddddd*}, where *d* is a hexadecimal digit. The curly braces are required.

RIS Network Services

The services required by RIS are DHCP, DNS, and Active Directory. DHCP is required to provide an IP address and configuration information to the RIS client. DNS is required to locate a domain controller and authenticate to Active Directory. Active Directory is required to identify prestaged computers, create computer accounts, and authenticate users so that the images to which they have access can be controlled.

The RIS Imaging Process

When a PXE-enabled computer boots, it obtains an IP address and configuration information. It also obtains the IP address of a RIS server from DHCP. To enable this functionality, you must configure the RIS client to boot from the network. This is done in the BIOS of the RIS client. The GUID for the RIS client is included as part of the DHCP request.

After the RIS client receives an IP address, it sends a broadcast request for service. The RIS server then queries Active Directory to find the computer account associated with the

GUID of the client computer. A domain controller is queried first, but if that is unsuccessful, a global catalog is queried. If the GUID is found, it is considered a known client and the computer object is queried for the appropriate RIS server from which to download images for this RIS client. If the GUID is not found, it is considered an unknown client and all RIS servers respond.

After the RIS client gets a reply to its service request, it downloads a bootstrap program from the TFTP (Trivial FTP) service on the RIS server. The file startrom.com is downloaded by default. This file displays a message to press F12 to perform a network installation. If F12 is not pressed after three seconds, the boot process continues to the next device such as a hard drive.

If the user presses F12, then the Client Installation Wizard is downloaded via TFTP from the RIS server. The Client Installation Wizard then gets the user to authenticate. Based on the user that is authenticated, different images are displayed as available to install. If the computer account has not been prestaged, the user performing the imaging must have permission to create computer accounts in Active Directory.

Finally, the user selects an image to install. This downloads the image to the RIS client.

Third-party Imaging Utilities

Despite the fact that RIS is a free part of Windows Server 2003 and Windows 2000 Server, many organizations continue to use third-party imaging software. Some organizations do this to support older Windows clients, such as Windows NT and Windows 9x. Others do it because of their time investment in existing images for the third-party imaging software.

The process for using third-party imaging software is similar to using RIPrep images with RIS. The steps are:

1. The operating system is installed.
2. The applications are installed.
3. Sysprep is run to prepare the computers for imaging.
4. Third-party imaging software is used.

After the operating system and applications are installed, you should configure the default profile. The standard default profile on a Windows computer asks new users for information, such as how to connect to the Internet. You can preconfigure this information so that users are not bothered by this type of request. Create a local user and log on as that user. Then configure the profile as desired, including starting all applications to configure them. After the profile is configured, log off and log on as Administrator. Then copy the user profile you have configured over the existing default profile.

Sysprep is used instead of RIPrep when third-party imaging is performed. Sysprep removes all of the computer-specific information from the operating system. This includes the SIDs, computer name, local users and groups, and domain membership. By default, Sysprep does

14

not redetect hardware but can be configured to do so. The last thing Sysprep does is shut down the computer.

After Sysprep has been run, the third-party imaging software must be used to copy the local disk to an image file. To access the third-party imaging software, a boot floppy, or boot CD-ROM, is normally used to start an operating system with access to a network server where the image file can be copied.

When a Sysprep image is restored, all of the unique information must be re-created. To do this, a mini-setup wizard is run. The mini-setup wizard asks for information such as the computer name and time zone. The mini-setup wizard can be automated using Setup Manager to create an answer file. The answer file must be named winnt.sif and stored on a floppy disk in the computer during startup. The winnt.sif file can also be read from C:\Syspred or C:\I386, but these are more awkward to implement because you must embed the file in your image or copy it there after the image has been placed on the computer but before it has started Windows for the first time.

CHAPTER SUMMARY

- ❑ Backup (ntbackup.exe) can be used to form backup and restore files and perform automated system recovery.

- ❑ Types of file backups that are available include full, incremental, and differential. Full backups turn off the archive attribute on files that are backed up. Incremental backups are used to back up daily changes and also to turn off the archive attribute on files that are backed up. Differential backups are used to back up all files that have changed since the last full backup and do not affect the archive attribute of files that are backed up.

- ❑ A system state backup backs up the system state data, which includes the registry, COM+ Class Registration database, boot files, system files, Certificate Services Database, Active Directory database, Sysvol folder, and the IIS metabase. A system state backup cannot be performed across the network.

- ❑ An automated system recovery (ASR) backup takes a copy of the entire operating system and creates a floppy disk that is used during the disaster recovery process.

- ❑ Volume shadow copy takes a snapshot of files at a given point in time, even if the files are open. Users can then restore files themselves through the properties of the file share.

- ❑ Device driver rollback is used to restore the previous version of a device driver if an updated version is not performing properly.

- ❑ Safe mode starts the operating system with a limited number of services for troubleshooting.

- ❑ Last known good configuration restores the part of the registry responsible for service and driver configuration. The Last Known Good control set is defined when a user logs on.

- Recovery Console is a command-line interface that allows you to access files and systems settings when Windows cannot be started properly.

- Windows Server 2003 includes Remote Desktop for Administration, which allows up to two administrators at a time to connect to a server via Terminal Services. Two client utilities can be used to connect to Terminal Services: Remote Desktop Connection and Remote Desktops snap-in.

- Remote Assistance is a mechanism for users to request help. Help requests can be made via e-mail, Microsoft Instant Messenger, or a file.

- RIS (Remote Installation Services) is used to image and install Windows Server 2003, Windows XP, and Windows 2000. A RIPrep image is a fully installed operating system and applications. A flat image is a scripted installation of an operating system.

- The volume holding RIS must be an NTFS volume and cannot be the system or boot volume.

- RIS clients must have a PXE boot ROM or use a floppy disk created by the Remote Boot Floppy Generator (rbfg.exe).

- If third-party imaging solutions are used instead of RIS, then Sysprep is used to prepare the computers for imaging. Sysprep removes all of the computer-specific information from the operating system.

KEY TERMS

automated system recovery (ASR) backup — A complete system backup that also creates a floppy disk that is used during the disaster recovery process.

backup — A utility included with Windows Server 2003 that can back up and restore files and system state data.

device driver rollback — An option to restore a previously installed device driver.

differential backup — A backup of all files that have changed since a full backup. The archive attribute of backed up files is unaffected.

flat image — An image for RIS that performs a scripted installation of an operating system.

full backup — A backup of all data that turns off the archive attribute on each file that is backed up.

globally unique identifier (GUID) — A unique identifier embedded in a PXE boot ROM.

incremental backup — A backup of files that have changed since the previous incremental backup or previous full backup. The archive attribute is turned off on all files that are backed up.

last known good configuration — A startup option used for troubleshooting that restores the part of the registry responsible for service and device driver configuration.

Pre-Boot eXecution Environment (PXE) boot ROM — A ROM on a network card that allows a computer to boot and run directly from the network without using a local operating system.

Recovery Console — A command-line interface that can be used to access system settings and files when Windows cannot be started properly.

Remote Assistance — A system that allows users to request assistance from support staff via e-mail, Microsoft Instant Messenger, or a file. It allows support staff to view or take remote control of a remote system.

Remote Boot Floppy Generator (rbfg.exe) — A utility that is used to create a bootable floppy disk that emulates a PXE boot ROM.

Remote Desktop Connection — A client utility that connects to a server running Terminal Services.

Remote Desktop for Administration — A remote administration solution for servers that allows two administrators at a time to connect via Terminal Services.

Remote Desktops snap-in — A client utility that connects to multiple terminal servers at the same time.

RIS (Remote Installation Services) — A service included with Windows Server 2003 that can be used to image Windows Server 2003, Windows XP, and Windows 2000 computers.

RIPrep image — An image for RIS that includes a fully installed operating system and applications.

safe mode — A startup option for troubleshooting that loads a minimal set of drivers.

Sysprep — A utility that is used to prepare computers to be imaged with third-party imaging software.

system state data — The set of data that includes the registry, COM+ Class Registration database, boot files, system files, Certificate Services Database, Active Directory Database, Sysvol folder, and the IIS metabase. It cannot be backed up across the network using Backup.

Terminal Services — A remote access solution that lets users connect to and run applications on a remote computer.

volume shadow copy — A service that takes a snapshot of files at a particular point in time, even if they are open.

REVIEW QUESTIONS

1. Volume shadow copy can be used to replace regular file system backups. True or False?

2. Which of the following can the Backup utility back up? (Choose all that apply.)

   a. files

   b. running SQL databases

   c. running Exchange databases

   d. system state data across the network

3. Which type of backup is the fastest to perform?

   a. full

   b. incremental

   c. differential

   d. automated system recovery

4. Which type of backup is the least complex to restore?

   a. full

   b. incremental

   c. differential

   d. automated system recovery

5. Which of the following are included in the system state backup of a member server? (Choose all that apply.)

   a. the registry

   b. boot files

   c. system files

   d. the Active Directory database

   e. the Sysvol folder

6. Which boot option must be selected to perform a restore of Active Directory?

   a. Safe Mode

   b. Safe Mode with Networking

   c. Directory Services Restore Mode

   d. Last known good configuration

7. Which type of restore must be performed to restore a deleted object to Active Directory?

   a. complete

   b. authoritative

   c. nonauthoritative

   d. incremental

8. Volume shadow copy can back up files even when they are open. True or False?

9. Where is volume shadow copy configured?

   a. file properties

   b. folder properties

   c. volume properties

   d. computer properties

14

10. When a volume shadow copy is performed on 10 GB of data, how much disk space is required?

   a. 1 GB

   b. 5 GB

   c. 10 GB

   d. The amount can be configured.

11. Which recovery tool is best suited to recovering from an updated driver that is not functioning properly?

   a. device driver rollback

   b. safe mode

   c. last known good configuration

   d. Recovery Console

12. If you have not yet logged on, which recovery tool is best suited to recovering from a new driver installation that is not functioning properly?

   a. device driver rollback

   b. safe mode

   c. last known good configuration

   d. Recovery Console

13. If you have already logged on, which recovery tool is best suited to recovering from an incorrect video driver installation?

   a. device driver rollback

   b. safe mode

   c. last known good configuration

   d. Recovery Console

14. Which recovery tool is best suited to recovering files from a nonfunctional operating system?

   a. device driver rollback

   b. safe mode

   c. last known good configuration

   d. Recovery Console

15. Which remote management tool allows two administrators to connect at one time via Terminal Services?

   a. Remote Desktop for Administration

   b. Microsoft Instant Messenger

   c. Remote Assistance

   d. NetMeeting

16. Which remote management tool allows users to request help?

    a. Remote Desktop for Administration

    b. Microsoft Instant Messenger

    c. Remote Assistance

    d. NetMeeting

17. Which client utility allows an administrator to connect to multiple terminal servers at the same time?

    a. Remote Desktop Connection

    b. NetMeeting

    c. Remote Assistance

    d. Remote Desktops snap-in

18. Which types of images include an installed operating system and applications? (Choose all that apply.)

    a. RIPrep

    b. flat

    c. full

    d. Sysprep

19. Exactly how many bits long is a GUID used by RIS?

    a. 32

    b. 64

    c. 128

    d. 512

20. Which file system must be used by the volume storing RIS?

    a. FAT

    b. FAT32

    c. NTFS

    d. CDFS

14

CASE PROJECTS

CASE PROJECTS

Case 14-1: Planning Backup and Recovery

Arctic University has four servers at the main campus. In the past, backups on these server has been ad hoc whenever it occurred to one of the administrators. Recently, some files were lost because they could not be restored from backup. Your supervisor has tasked you with planning a backup plan for the servers on the main campus.

Prepare a backup plan for the main campus servers. At minimum, include information about backing up files and system state data.

Case 14-2: Preparing for Server Recovery

Recently, a server that functioned as a domain controller and file server experienced a hardware failure that resulted in a service outage of 12 hours while the server was reinstalled. What are some of the tools that could have made this recovery easier and faster?

Case 14-3: Planning Remote Management

Arctic University has recently completed upgrading all servers to Windows Server 2003 and all clients to Windows XP. You know that both Windows Server 2003 and Windows XP have remote management capabilities and want to start using them. However, your supervisor has asked you to create a plan for how this would be implemented so that it can be discussed among all the administrators first.

Create a remote management plan for servers and workstations. Include the benefits of using remote management.

Case 14-4: Planning Imaging

Your supervisor thinks that you should be imaging computers to speed installation. However, he is not sure whether it is better to use RIS or third-party imaging software. Write a short report comparing the two and making a recommendation.

Exam Objectives Tracking for MCSE Certification Exam #70-293: Planning and Maintaining a Microsoft Windows Server 2003 Network Infrastructure

PLANNING AND IMPLEMENTING SERVER ROLES AND SERVER SECURITY

Objective	Chapter: Section
Configure security for servers that are assigned specific roles.	Chapter 13: Planning Security Configuration for Server Roles
Plan a secure baseline installation. • Plan a strategy to enforce system default security settings on new systems. • Identify client operating system default security settings. • Identify all server operating system default security settings.	Chapter 1: Selecting the Operating System for the Enterprise Chapter 1: Understanding Network Services Chapter 13: Planning a Secure Baseline Chapter 13: Default Security Settings
Plan security for servers that are assigned specific roles. Roles might include domain controllers, Web servers, database servers, and mail servers. • Deploy the security configuration for servers that are assigned specific roles. • Create custom security templates based on server roles.	Chapter 13: Planning Security Configuration for Server Roles Chapter 13: Planning a Secure Baseline
Evaluate and select the operating system to install on computers in an enterprise. • Identify the minimum configuration to satisfy security requirements.	Chapter 1: Selecting the Operating System for the Enterprise

PLANNING, IMPLEMENTING, AND MAINTAINING A NETWORK INFRASTRUCTURE

Objective	Chapter: Section
Plan a TCP/IP network infrastructure strategy. • Analyze IP addressing requirements. • Plan an IP routing solution. • Create an IP subnet scheme.	Chapter 2: Introduction to TCP/IP Chapter 4: Building a Subnetted IP Network
Plan and modify a network topology. • Plan the physical placement of network resources. • Identify network protocols to be used.	Chapter 1: Introducing Windows 2003 Network Architecture Chapter 2: TCP/IP Architecture Overview Chapter 3: Types of Network Traffic Chapter 3: Ethernet Chapter 3: Physical Components Chapter 3: Optimizing Network Settings
Plan an Internet connectivity strategy.	Chapter 4: Demand-dial Connections Chapter 4: Network Address Translation Chapter 4: Internet Connection Sharing Chapter 4: Internet Connection Firewall Chapter 4: Planning Internet Connectivity

A

Objective	Chapter: Section
Plan network traffic monitoring. Tools might include Network Monitor and System Monitor. Troubleshoot connectivity to the Internet. • Diagnose and resolve issues related to Network Address Translation (NAT). • Diagnose and resolve issues related to name resolution cache information. • Diagnose and resolve issues related to client configuration.	Chapter 3: Monitoring and Optimizing Network Performance Chapter 2: Introduction to TCP/IP Chapter 3: Troubleshooting Utilities Chapter 4: Network Address Translation
Troubleshoot TCP/IP addressing. • Diagnose and resolve issues related to client computer configuration. Diagnose and resolve issues related to DHCP server address assignment.	Chapter 2: Introduction to TCP/IP Chapter 2: Internet Layer Protocols Chapter 5: The DHCP process Chapter 5: Configuring DHCP
Plan a host name resolution strategy. • Plan a DNS namespace design. • Plan zone replication requirements. • Plan a forwarding configuration. • Plan for DNS security. • Examine the interoperability of DNS with third party DNS solutions.	Chapter 7: Functions of the Domain Name System Chapter 7: DNS Namespace Strategies Chapter 7: DNS Zones Chapter 8: Optimizing DNS Performance Chapter 8: DNS Security
Plan a NetBIOS name resolution strategy. • Plan a WINS replication strategy. • Plan a NetBIOS name resolution by using the lmhosts file.	Chapter 6: NetBIOS Name Resolution Chapter 6: Choosing NetBIOS Name Resolution Methods Chapter 6: WINS Replication
Troubleshoot host name resolution. Diagnose and resolve issues related to DNS services. Diagnose and resolve issues related to client computer configuration.	Chapter 7: Functions of the Domain Name System Chapter 7: DNS ZONES Chapter 7: Active Directory and DNS Chapter 7: WINS Integration Chapter 8: Managing DNS Servers Chapter 8: Managing DNS Zones Chapter 8: Troubleshooting DNS

PLANNING, IMPLEMENTING, AND MAINTAINING ROUTING AND REMOTE ACCESS

Objective	Chapter: Section
Plan a routing strategy. • Identify routing protocols to use in a specified environment. • Plan routing for IP multicast traffic.	Chapter 4: Router Installation and Configuration Chapter 3: Types of Network Traffic

Objective	Chapter: Section
Plan security for remote access users. • Plan remote access policies. • Analyze protocol security requirements. • Plan authentication methods for remote access clients.	Chapter 11: Introducing Remote Access Methods Chapter 11: Configuring Remote Access Servers Chapter 11: Allowing Client Access Chapter 11: Remote Access Policies Chapter 11: RADIUS Chapter 11: Troubleshooting Remote Access
Implement secure access between private networks. • Create and implement an IPSec policy.	Chapter 10: Creating Your Own IPSec Policy
Troubleshoot TCP/IP routing. Tools might include the route, tracert, ping, pathping, and netsh commands and Network Monitor.	Chapter 3: Troubleshooting Utilities

PLANNING, IMPLEMENTING, AND MAINTAINING SERVER AVAILABILITY

Objective	Chapter: Section
Plan services for high availability. • Plan a high availability solution that uses clustering services. • Plan a high availability solution that uses Network Load Balancing.	Chapter 12: Availability and Scalability Chapter 12: Windows Server 2003 Clustering
Identify system bottlenecks, including memory, processor, disk, and network related bottlenecks. • Identify system bottlenecks by using System Monitor.	Chapter 12: Availability and Scalability Chapter 12: Windows Server 2003 Clustering
Implement a cluster server. • Recover from cluster node failure.	Chapter 12: Installing and Configuring Server Clusters Chapter 12: Server Cluster Concepts
Manage Network Load Balancing. Tools might include the Network Load Balancing Monitor MS Management Console (MMC) snap-in and the WLBS cluster control utility.	Chapter 12: Network Load Balancing Concepts Chapter 12: Implementing Network Load Balancing Chapter 12: Installing Applications on an NLB Cluster
Plan a backup and recovery strategy. • Identify appropriate backup types. Methods include full, incremental, and differential. • Plan a backup strategy that uses volume shadow copy. • Plan system recovery that uses Automated System Recovery (ASR).	Chapter 14: File Backup and Recovery

Planning and Maintaining Network Security

A

Objective	Chapter: Section
Configure network protocol security. • Configure protocol security in a heterogeneous client computer environment. • Configure protocol security by using IPSec policies.	Chapter 10: Enabling IPSec Chapter 13: Planning Network Protocol Security
Configure security for data transmission. • Configure IPSec policy settings.	Chapter 10: Creating Your Own IPSec Policy
Plan for network protocol security. • Specify the required ports and protocols for specified services. • Plan a IPSec policy for secure network communications.	Chapter 2: Application Layer Protocols Chapter 2: Transport Layer Protocols Chapter 10: Creating Your Own IPSec Policy
Plan secure network administration methods. • Create a plan to offer Remote Assistance to client computers. • Plan for remote administration by using Terminal Services.	Chapter 14: Remote Management
Plan security for wireless networks.	Chapter 13: Planning Wireless Network Security
Plan security for data transmission. • Secure data transmission between client computers to meet security requirements. • Secure data transmission by using IPSec.	Chapter 10: Why IPSec Is Important Chapter 10: IPSec Modes Chapter 10: IPSec Authentication Chapter 13: Planning Network Protocol Security
Troubleshoot security for data transmission. Tools might include the IP Security Monitor MMC snap-in and the Resultant Set of Policy (RsoP) MMC snap-in.	Chapter 10: Troubleshooting IPSec

Planning, Implementing, and Maintaining Security Infrastructure

Objective	Chapter: Section
Configure Active Directory directory service for certificate publication.	Chapter 9: Installing and Managing Certificate Services
Plan a public key infrastructure (PKI) that uses Certificate Services. • Identify the appropriate type of certificate authority to support certificate issuance requirements. • Plan the enrollment and distribution of certificates. • Plan for the use of smart cards for authentication.	Chapter 9: Certificate Services Components Chapter 9: Installing and Managing Certificate Services Chapter 9: Managing Certificates Chapter 9: Smart Card Authentication

Objective	Chapter: Section
Plan a framework for planning and implementing security. • Plan for security monitoring. • Plan a change and configuration management framework for security.	Chapter 13: Types of Security Chapter 13: Planning a Secure Baseline Chapter 13: Securing Administrative Access
Plan a security update infrastructure. Tools might include MS Baseline Security Analyzer and MS Update Services.	Chapter 13: Software Updates

B

DETAILED LAB SETUP GUIDE

HARDWARE

Classroom PCs should be configured as follows:

- Pentium 233 MHz processor or faster
- At least 128 MBs of random access memory (RAM)
- At least 1.5 GBs of available hard disk space
- CD-RW or DVD-RW drive
- Keyboard and mouse or some other compatible pointing device
- Video adapter and monitor with Super VGA (800 × 600) or higher resolution
- Sound card for the Instructor PC
- Self-powered/amplified speakers for the Instructor PC
- Internal or external fax/modem
- Two Ethernet network interface controllers per PC
- 3.5" floppy disk drive
- An Ethernet hub or switch with at least as many ports as there are PCs in the classroom
- 1 twisted-pair, Category 5 straight-through cable per PC

Other equipment that may be needed:

- An additional Instructor PC, which will be used as an additional domain controller
- A generic printer
- A crossover cable for each PC

Consumable items that students should bring to class:

- 5 blank CD-R disks
- 5 blank floppy disks

SOFTWARE

The following software is needed:

- Microsoft Windows Server 2003 Enterprise Edition operating system (1 CD media per student)
- Adobe Acrobat Reader (version 4 or greater)
- Microsoft Virtual PC (*www.microsoft.com/windows/virtualpc*) (optional)
- The latest Windows Server 2003 service pack (if available) (optional)

B

SETUP INSTRUCTIONS

To work on the Activities and Case Projects in this book, students need to have administrative privileges over their respective PCs. In a classroom setting, students should have the freedom to make administrative-level configuration errors. Normally such errors can render a PC unbootable or otherwise unusable for participation in the classroom. However, a student's mistakes should never impede completion of lab assignments. In this light, the lab should have a data recovery system and working backups that are both easy to use and reliable.

You should ensure that all hardware used in the classroom is compatible with Windows Server 2003. To do this, it may be necessary to perform a test installation. Once the installation process is complete, use Device Manager to ensure that all devices are functioning correctly and that the appropriate drivers are installed. If a device has a driver that is not functioning, it may be necessary to go to the manufacturer's Web site and see if there is a device for Windows Server 2003.

The instructor computer should be set up as a domain controller for the artic.local domain. The domain administrator password should be set to Password!. The instructor computer should also run Network Address Translation (NAT) to provide student computers with access to the Internet. A good practice would be to label the two network connections as Classroom and External for whichever network they are plugged into. Internet Information Services (IIS) will need to be installed with support for application service provider (ASP) pages for exercises in Chapter 4. After IIS is installed, create the file c:\inetpub\wwwroot\default.asp. The contents of the file should be as follows:

```
<html>
<body>
<p>Source IP address =
<%=Request.ServerVariables("REMOTE_ADDR")%>
<p>Source TCP Port =
<%=Request.ServerVariables("REMOTE_PORT")%>

<p>Server IP address =
<%=Request.ServerVariables("LOCAL_ADDR")%>
<p>Server TCP Port =
<%=Request.ServerVariables("SERVER_PORT")%>

</body>
</html>
```

Because students will have administrative control of their computers, you may need to perform data recovery if a student cannot recover from a configuration change. The most straightforward method of data recovery is the reinstallation of the operating system from the Microsoft factory CDs. However, having to reinstall the operating system from the factory CD every time a student corrupts his or her system can prove to be time consuming and frustrating. There are no activities in the book that go over a Windows Server 2003 install.

This leaves some flexibility for the instructor to decide on how the students should install Windows Server 2003. Therefore, to ensure rapid and reliable data recovery, consider the following guidelines when setting up the lab:

- Microsoft's Virtual PC provides quick access to an operating system from a previous state. The ability to use undoable disks will give students the opportunity to restore their computers to the state before the lab. Students will have to Save State in Virtual PC after each successful lab. Virtual PC is very resource intensive and the student computers should exceed the hardware requirements previously stated if used.

- If using an imaging product, such as Norton Ghost, a single image file that contains all of the data stored on the reference installation is created. This image file even contains the partition table of the hard disk drive, along with the master boot record. Restoring data from such an image will bring the machine back to its original state at the time the backup was created.

- When creating a reference image file, it is important to remember that the image file will be an exact copy of the reference PC's hard disk drive. This means that data such as Network Basic Input/Output System (NetBIOS) computer names and security identifiers (SIDs) will be preserved as they were on the reference PC. This also means that unless further steps are taken, all PCs that are imaged from this reference image will have the *same* NetBIOS computer name, SID, and perhaps even Internet Protocol (IP) address (if the IP addresses are set up statically). However, you do *not* want a classroom where all the PCs have the same NetBIOS name or IP address. You may be able to get away with all the SIDs being the same for a while but this should not be a permanent state. You especially do not want identical SIDs in an environment that employs Active Directory domains.

- In order to make a classroom of uniquely identifiable PCs, utilities such as Microsoft's SysPrep, Norton Ghost Walker, or REMBO Toolkit (the NTChange-Name command) may be executed on each PC. The easiest to use is Ghost Walker; it is an MS-DOS program that not only changes the NetBIOS computer name, but also creates a randomly generated SID in one easy step. If you don't feel the need to change the SID, you can manually change the NetBIOS name by simply right-clicking the My Computer icon, clicking Properties, clicking the Computer Name tab, clicking the Change button, and typing in the desired NetBIOS computer name in the Computer name field. Click OK when finished.

Keep the following in mind if imaging or Virtual PC is not available:

- The instructor needs to decide on the following key points and make them available to all students during their installs:
  - Computer naming convention
  - IP addressing (default gateways, Domain Name System (DNS), and Windows Internet Naming Service (WINS), if necessary)
  - Workgroup/domain names
- Students should install Windows Server 2003 Enterprise Edition from the CD

C

Expanded Chapter Summaries

CHAPTER 1 SUMMARY

Businesses rely more on networks today then ever before. Administrators must be able to build reliable and scalable networks to ensure that business users have access to data. The first step in building such networks is the planning stage.

Planning for Windows Server 2003 is as easy as installing it. It doesn't have the same security holes that its predecessor Windows 2000 had. Windows Server 2003 also doesn't have Internet Information Services (IIS) installed by default. Even though there are changes between Windows 2000 and Windows Server 2003, they are not radically different from each other. For example, the installation is the same—just pop in the CD and configure the computer's basic input/output system (BIOS) to boot from the CD.

Windows Server 2003 can be upgraded from several previous operating systems. You can upgrade from the following server operating systems:

- Windows NT 4.0 Server with Service Pack 5
- Windows NT 4.0 Terminal Server Edition with Service Pack 5
- Windows 2000 Server

Windows Server 2003 is a networking operating system that is designed for networks. Windows Server 2003 can run on a local area network (LAN) or can be part of a wide area network (WAN). Server 2003 has four components for networking:

- *Client*—Makes requests for resources
- *Service*—Responds to requests
- *Protocol*—Defines the communication language
- *Adapter*—Is the driver for the network card

The Network Driver Interface Specification (NDIS) was created by Microsoft and 3Com to help developers with device drivers. Before this specification was defined, developers had to write code for every adapter to work with every protocol. With this specification, developers write code to this standard, which is the same standard to which hardware manufactures build their devices too.

The Transport Driver Interface (TDI) is a layer that applications talk to when clients and services are trying to access resources. TDI emulates NetBIOS and WinSock.

Windows Server 2003 supports four major protocols that can be used for communication on a network. The four major protocols are IPv4, IPv6, IPX/SPX, and AppleTalk.

Once Windows Server 2003 is installed, there is a limited amount of services installed along with the operating system. Because Windows Server 2003 is a networking operating system, there are many more services that can be added after the installation to better fit the network environment it resides in. In addition, domain controllers have even more services then member servers, and most of them are used to help with authentication.

When planning for Windows Server 2003, an administrator must decide which of the four editions he or she must install. If an administrator needs to have a low-cost Web server, then Web Edition is the right choice. Web Edition supports IIS and load balancing, but cannot be a domain controller.

Microsoft recommends that Standard Edition be used for departmental file and print servers. Standard Edition supports all the same software components as Web Edition.

For large enterprises that need high availability, Enterprise Edition is the route to go. It supports all the software components as Standard Edition and adds support for metadirectory services, 64-bit processing, Non-Uniform Memory Access (NUMA), and 8-node clusters.

The final edition is the Datacenter Edition, which is used for mission-critical applications.

Windows Server 2003 has services that can be used only by newer clients, which are those that run Windows 2000 and later operating systems (OSs). Server Message Block (SMB) signing is used by all Windows Server 2003 domain controllers to ensure that the communication between clients and servers is legitimate. If there are clients in the network that are older than Windows 2000, then the Active Directory will need to be installed so that the clients can use SMB signing as well. Secure channels are used when trust relationships are being used and Windows Server 2003 used them by default. Windows NT supports secure channels, but only after Service Pack 4 has been installed.

Planning makes all the difference when considering a Windows Server 2003 network infrastructure. The first step is to select a team that includes members from different departments within an organization. There also needs to be a defined project manager to ensure that resources are available to complete the project. Goals must be set for all members to see and be obtainable. It helps considerably if there is documentation of the current environment. Documentation needs to be created for the new plan, and it needs to stay current. Objectives and tasks will be assigned to teams to ensure that goals are completed. New technologies will also need to be tested out in a safe environment that is not connected to the production environment. The final step is to roll out the solution that was planned, scoped, and tested to the production environment.

CHAPTER 2 SUMMARY

Transmission Control Protocol/Internet Protocol (TCP/IP) is the most commonly used protocol today. Knowledge of TCP/IP is critical for planning, managing, and troubleshooting a Windows Server 2003 network infrastructure. In fact, Windows Server 2003 requires on it for several key services.

TCP/IP is used by most vendors for their primary networking communication protocol. TCP/IP is not controlled by any one organization. Without TCP/IP, access to the Internet would be impossible. Protocols such as Hypertext Transfer Protocol (HTTP), File Transfer Protocol (FTP), Simple Mail Transfer Protocol (SMTP), and Domain Name System (DNS) all rely on a TCP/IP infrastructure. Windows Server 2003 can use other protocols but always comes installed with TCP/IP by default and services such as Active Directory rely on it.

All computers on a TCP/IP network will have a unique Internet Protocol (IP) address. This address is similar to a street address, there can only be one computer with a specific address just as there is only one house on a street with a specific address. IP addresses are formatted into an octet separated by periods and it looks to the user like 10.15.1.9. Each octet is an 8-bit number with the entire IP address equaling a 32-bit number.

There are several fields that can be configured when configuring IP addressing info for Windows Server 2003. The first option is the IP address, which is used to identify the host. Each IP address consists of two parts, a network portion and a host portion. The network portion can be compared to a street address and the host portion can be compared to the actual house number on that street. Each computer will also have a subnet mask configured that defines which part of the IP address is the network ID and which part is the host ID. An IP address and subnet mask are required for every host on a TCP/IP network. The default subnet mask always begins with a 255 and plays a critical role in identifying to which network the current computer belongs.

Computers that need to communicate outside of their network need to have a default gateway configured. The default gateway is the doorway out of the computers current network and is usually a router. Routers can be either hardware or software based but need to have at least two network cards configured with two different networks.

There are three classes of IP addresses used to address hosts on networks. They are Class A, B, and C. Classes D and E are not used for clients that communicate on a local area network (LAN). The following chart shows where each address falls:

Class	First Octet	Default Mask	# of Hosts per Network
Class A	1–127	255.0.0.0 or /8	16,777,214
Class B	128–191	255.255.0.0 or /16	64,534
Class C	192–223	255.255.255.0 or /24	254

Within the IP addresses in the preceding chart are private addresses that can be used on private networks. The following chart shows each private IP address range:

Class	IP Address	Network ID	Directed Broadcast
Class A	10.0.0.0/8	10.0.0.0	10.255.255.255
Class B	172.16.0.0/16	172.16.0.0	172.16.255.255
Class C	192.168.0.0/24	192.168.0.0	192.168.1.255

Note that any IP address starting with 127 will be reserved for the loopback address. This is a special address that is used to troubleshoot the TCP/IP stack.

TCP/IP has several protocols that make up the TCP/IP suite. DNS is one that provides name resolution within a TCP/IP network. Without name resolution, we would have to

C

remember every computer's IP address. DNS works with fully qualified domain names (FQDNs) which are commonly known as host names. The Windows Internet Naming Service (WINS) is also a name resolution service that resolves IP addresses to computer friendly names. WINS is primarily used to perform name resolution for older Microsoft clients and some applications. The Dynamic Host Configuration Protocol (DHCP) is a service that allows servers to assign IP addresses that are configured to for dynamic IP addresses. This can be a time saver on larger networks where you would otherwise have to go and configure the IP address on each computer.

TCP/IP is structured so that every component has a task and is responsible for part of the entire communication process. The TCP/IP architecture has four layers and can be closely related to the industry standard Open Systems Interconnection (OSI) model.

The first layer is known as the Application layer. This is where you will find many of the most common and not so common application protocols that are used on the Internet. Protocols such as HTTP, FTP, Telnet and the e-mail protocols SMTP, POP3, and IMAP4. This layer matches up with the Application, Presentation, and Session layers of the OSI model.

The second layer is the Transport layer. The Transport layer is responsible for breaking down the file in communication into more bite-size packet chunks. Each service or application runs on a port that the Transport layer uses. TCP and User Datagram Protocol (UDP) are used at this layer to help define whether the communication should be connection oriented (TCP) or connectionless (UDP). TCP services are more reliable than UDP services. The Transport layer matches up with the Transport layer on the OSI model.

The third layer is known as the Internet layer. This layer is responsible for protocols that specialize in specific areas. IP is used for logically addressing each packet coming from the Transport layer. Routing Information Protocol (RIP) and Open Shortest Path First (OSPF) are dynamic routing protocols that help define where packets should go from one network to the next. Internet Control Message Protocol (ICMP) is used to send messages from host to host and is common when testing communication. Internet Group Management Protocol (IGMP) is used to manage multicast groups. Address Resolution Protocol (ARP) is the protocol that is used to convert IP addresses to physical medial access control (MAC) addresses. The Internet layer matches up with the Network layer on the OSI model.

The final layer is known as the Network Interface layer. This layer is responsible for all of the physical connections such as network cards, wiring, hubs, and Institute of Electrical and Electronic Engineers (IEEE) protocols. The Network Interface layer matches up with the Data Link and Physical layer on the OSI model.

CHAPTER 3 SUMMARY

Planning network data flow allows you to identify and eliminate bottlenecks. If these bottlenecks are discovered early enough, you may have to tweak your design to ensure the best possible performance. Once the network has been designed and implemented, it is critical to monitor the existing network data flow to maintain performance.

Unicast packets are the most common packets in networks. Unicast packets are addressed to a single computer on a network using any of the three ranges available to Internet Protocol (IP) addresses. These are the same type of packets that are used for the Internet or some of the traffic on a local network. Because unicast packets know exactly where they are going, hubs, switches, and routers will pass this traffic along.

Broadcast packets are addressed to all computers on a local network. The packet itself is addressed to the 255.255.255.255 IP address. It stays on the local network because routers do not usually forward these types of packets across networks. Network performance can be decreased if there are too many broadcasts.

Multicast packets are addressed to a group of computers using a Class D address range. Multicast packets offer networks better performance than broadcasts because only computers in that multicast group will process this traffic. Imaging software, such as Ghost, uses multicasts to deploy operating systems to computers.

Ethernet is the most common networking technology used in local area networks (LANs) today. Ethernet has become so popular because of its low cost and potential for high performance. Collisions, collision domains, and transmission modes can affect an Ethernet network.

Ethernet uses Carrier Sense Multiple Access/Collision Detection (CSMA/CD) to allow computers to send data on a network. Computers will listen to the network before they communicate to ensure that when they do send data, there will not be a collision on the network. Networks that use hubs drastically increase the amount of collisions that exist on a network.

Collision domains are the area in which a collision can occur. As you add computers to a collision domain, the chance for collisions increases. Switches and routers can be used to buffer and retransmit packets, thus creating new collision domains.

Transmission modes determine how data will be sent over the network. Ethernet networks transmit data in half-duplex or in full-duplex. Half-duplex allows a computer to send or receive data but not both at the same time. Full-duplex allows computers to send and receive at the maximum throughput allowed.

Data flow can also be affected by the type of media Ethernet is using. The most common media type in networks is twisted-pair. Twisted-pair allows for data transmission up to 1 Gbps for a maximum of 100 meters. Fiber optic can transmit data at speeds up to 10 Gpbs of a distance of 2 kilometers. Coaxial is an older standard that can reach 10 Mbps.

Whichever type of network connection you are using, you will have to plug into some type of device. It will probably be either a hub or a switch. Hubs are considered physical layer devices. When a packet is transmitted across a hub, each port except the one that sent it picks that packet up and processes that information. This can be very inefficient and cause lots of collisions. When hubs send traffic, that traffic is sent as signals. The more hubs you have connected together, the more latency you have, and the more your performance goes down.

A switch provides benefits over a hub because each port is its own collision domain. This can drastically improve network data flow. Switches work at the Data Link layer of the OSI model, which means they work with media access control (MAC) addresses and not IP addresses. The one downside to that is that a packet would not know where to go if it was outside of the switch. Routers, on the other hand, work at the Network layer of the OSI model and are responsible for routing traffic. Routers maintain a routing table that dictates where traffic needs to be routed.

Once a network has been designed and implemented, you will want to monitor that network to detect any problems such as latency. The obvious solution to fix network data flow would be to upgrade the media type to allow for faster communication.

Protocol analyzers can be used to capture network traffic as it goes across the network. These tools can be helpful when inspecting specific packets.

Cable testers test the different types of media to see if the cables are in working condition. Cable testers are media specific.

Windows Server 2003 comes with Task Manager, which allows you to monitor resources such as the central processing unit (CPU), memory, and network traffic. The Performance snap-in is used to log performance counters on many of the different resources of Windows Server 2003. This tool is an excellent choice when creating a baseline of performance to compare against over time.

There are several tweaks that can be done to servers or clients to optimize network performance. The first of those settings would be to configure the binding settings for protocols and network cards. If multiple protocols are installed, you can change the order in which the network card will send out data based on the protocol.

Another option you can use when optimizing performance is to uninstall any protocols that are not currently being used in the network. The maximum transmission unit (MTU) is a setting that Windows Server 2003 uses to control the size of Transmission Control Protocol/Internet Protocol (TCP/IP) packets. The default size is 1,500 bytes on an Ethernet network.

Windows Server 2003 has built-in command-line tools that can help when troubleshooting network problems, as follows:

- *Ping*—Used to test network connectivity of remote hosts
- *Tracert*—Traces the path of routers that packets travel from host to host
- *Pathping*—Performs the same task as Tracert except it pings each router 100 times by default
- *Nbtstat*—Used to troubleshoot NetBIOS over TCP/IP problems
- *Netstat*—Displays TCP connection information
- *Ipconfig*—Displays TCP/IP configuration information
- *Nslookup*—Used to query DNS servers to ensure configuration

Chapter 4 Summary

Routing is essential for medium to large networks. As networks grow, routers will need to be placed to divide larger networks into smaller networks. Using routers will allow for better traffic control and less network congestion. The new networks that are created are called subnets.

Subnets include hosts that use Internet Protocol (IP) addresses to communicate. IP addresses are expressed in dotted decimal notation. An example of how an IP address is displayed to users is 172.16.200.50. Computers see IP addresses as a 32-bit number displayed in binary. Binary works only with ones and zeros. If a bit has a 0, it is turned off, and that bit is not counted; however, if the bit is a 1, then it is considered on and should be counted. Scientific calculators such as the one included with the operating system are great for changing numbers into their binary format.

Subnet masks are also 32-bit numbers that are used to define which portion of the host's IP address is reserved for the network and which portion is reserved for the host. An example of a dotted decimal subnet mask is 255.0.0.0. The process used by computers to find out which portion belongs to the network ID is called ANDing. This process compares the computer's IP address in binary against the subnet mask in binary. If both digits have a 1, then the value is 1. If the digits are 0 and 0, or 1 and 0, then the value is 0. The process of ANDing gives us our computer's network ID. The remaining bits are designated as the host ID.

We create subnets to reduce the size of networks. By reducing the size of networks, our collisions will be decreased. Collisions are reduced because there is less traffic on the network to collide with other traffic. Subnets also reduce broadcasts because broadcasts are normally not forwarded across routers. Routers can also be configured to pass or block certain traffic. This capability gives you much greater control over network traffic.

Supernetting is used when the range of addresses you have configured for a subnet has run out. Supernetting is the complete opposite of subnetting in that supernetting takes many smaller subnets and makes them one large network. This can be used to reduce network routing complexity.

Windows Server 2003 can be configured as a network router and can route several protocols including Transmission Control Protocol/Internet Protocol (TCP/IP) and AppleTalk. Companies may implement a windows router to save costs because all they would need to do is ensure that the server has two network cards. No additional software is needed to configure a windows router. Routing is part of the Routing and Remote Access Service (RRAS). When a packet enters a router, the router checks its route table, which lists all known routes to that router. A router can be configured to use static routes that an administrator inputs or dynamic routes from a routing protocol.

Windows Server 2003 routers support two different types of dynamic routing protocols:

- Routing Information Protocol (RIP)
- Open Shortest Path First (OSPF)

C

If RIP is going to be used, there will be no configuration necessary. Once installed, RIP routers advertise their routes every 30 seconds and have a maximum of 15 hops before a destination becomes unreachable. There are options to further customize how RIP operates; for example, you can configure which interface on the router will use RIP. You can also set which version of RIP is going to be used and if it is going to broadcast its routes.

OSPF is by far a much more complex routing protocol to configure. OSPF routers do not broadcast out their routers every 30 seconds; instead, they will communicate with other routers only when a change has occurred.

Some routes may be separated by slow dial-up connections. These types of connections are normally turned off until data is ready to send over that route. This is called a demand-dial connection. Windows routers can be configured to use demand-dial connections for Point-to-Point Protocol over Ethernet (PPPoE), Point-to-Point Tunneling Protocol (PPTP), and Layer Two Tunneling Protocol (L2TP).

Like most portions of RRAS, there is a wizard that steps you through the creation of a demand-dial connection. The demand-dial interface has several properties that can be configured once installed. For example, you can set the idle time before hanging up, specify specific hours that you want the demand-dial connection to work, and create filters to determine which type of traffic is going to be used by this connection.

Switches normally work at Layer 3 of the OSI model, which is the Data Link layer. This layer uses media access control (MAC) addresses to send and receive data. Some switches have the capability to also work at Layer 3 of the OSI model, which is the Network layer. These switches are called Layer 3 switches. A common feature of these switches is the ability to create Virtual LANs (VLAN). Each VLAN is used as a broadcast domain and the switch is now responsible for routing traffic between VLANs. VLANs are commonly created and associated with their ports on the physical switch.

Companies usually use private IP addresses for their private network and then use one or more public IP addresses for Internet connectivity. Network address translation (NAT) can be used to translate the private IP addresses into the public IP addresses. This is very similar to what a proxy server does except NAT does not need clients to be configured like a proxy server. NAT is an option included with RRAS that can be easily configured. When a private address gets NAT, NAT will remove the original source IP address and port number and translate it into the public address that NAT has been configured to use. NAT servers need to have two interfaces and one must be configured as private and the other as public. NAT can also be used to issue out private addresses for clients that are configured to receive their IP address automatically.

The Internet Connection Sharing (ICS) feature is very similar to NAT except that the configuration cannot be changed. ICS always uses the addresses from 192.168.0.2 to 192.168.0.254. ICS is configured from the network card and not RRAS.

Windows Server 2003 has a built-in firewall called the Internet Connection Firewall (ICF). This is a basic firewall that performs stateful packet filters. ICF is normally configured only on an interface that is connected directly to the Internet and is enabled from the Advanced properties of that connection. ICF can be configured to allow specific services to pass through and has a default list of common services and the ability to add custom services. ICF can also be configured to block the use of Internet Control Message Protocol (ICMP) packets that are used in the ping command.

Having a secure and reliable connection to the Internet can be easily achieved through the built-in options of Windows Server 2003. With any type of network connection, a good amount of time should be dedicated to planning the network and the services that are going to be used.

CHAPTER 5 SUMMARY

Dynamic Host Configuration Protocol (DHCP) is a service that runs on Windows Server 2003 and that is used to configure Transmission Control Protocol/Internet Protocol (TCP/IP). You must learn how to properly plan, configure, and troubleshoot DHCP to successfully manage the service.

DHCP can save time when configuring TCP/IP settings because it configures these settings automatically. The other alternative would be for someone to go around to each workstation and configure them manually. DHCP is the default setup for workstations but it can always be checked by viewing the TCP/IP properties. If the Obtain an IP address automatically option is selected, then the workstation will use DHCP.

Client computers configured to use DHCP lease the Internet Protocol (IP) address granted by the DHCP server. The DHCP client communicates with the DHCP server to obtain the TCP/IP settings. There are four packets transmitted between the client and server:

- The first packet is a DHCPDISCOVER; this packet sends out a broadcast request for a DHCP assigned address. The media access control (MAC) address is included in this packet and is the only way a DHCP server will be able to communicate with the client.

- The second packet is a DHCPOFFER from the DHCP server to the client. The DHCP server sends this offer to the MAC address that was included in the discover packet. The offer contains DHCP lease information such as IP address, subnet mask, and any other setting that was configured at the DHCP server.

- The client will then send a DHCPREQUEST packet back to the DHCP server to indicate that they would like that offer.

- Once the DHCP server acknowledges that packet, it sends a DHCPACK to the client confirming that the address can be leased to the client.

Because DHCP addresses are just leases, they will expire at some time. The default to renew a DHCP address is at 50 percent and the client will send a DHCPREQUEST packet to the DHCP server to renew that address. If all goes well, the DHCP server will send a DHCPACK acknowledging the client's renewal. If all doesn't go so well, then the client tries the request again at 87.5 percent and again at 100 percent.

Small networks with a single network are easy to plan for DHCP. DHCP is a broadcast-based service, so most routers will not forward it across to other networks. When DHCP is going to be used in a routed environment, there needs to be some form of a relay agent to pass along that broadcast request to the appropriate DHCP server. DHCP relay agents can be installed on a Windows Server 2003 router or a hardware router.

Fault tolerance should be considered in case a server hosting the DHCP service fails. Because DHCP servers are not designed to communicate with each other, a plan needs to exist to provide fault tolerance. One form of fault tolerance is to have a hot spare DHCP server. This server is configured identically to the production DHCP server but is offline waiting to be turned on in case of an emergency. If multiple DHCP servers are used, they can have overlapping ranges but would not have those ranges activated. Microsoft uses an 80/20 rule when configuring such a situation: 80 percent of the addresses on a DHCP server will be for the local DHCP server and 20 percent will be for a remote DHCP server's range. Some recommendations allow for more of a 75/25 rule as well. Clustering can also be configured so that if a DHCP server fails, the service will fail over to another server in the cluster. Clustering is an option only if the DHCP server is installed on a Windows Server 2003 Enterprise or Datacenter Edition.

DHCP can be installed from the networking components in the Add/Remove Windows Components of the Add or Remove programs applet in the Control Panel. Once a DHCP server is installed in an Active Directory domain, it must be authorized within Active Directory before it starts issuing addresses. Whoever authorizes the DHCP server must be a member of the Enterprise Admin group.

Configuring DHCP starts with creating the scope. A scope is where you define a range of IP addresses for the DHCP server to lease out to clients. Each scope must have a name, a range of IP addresses, a subnet mask, and a lease duration. All other choices are optional in the DHCP scope. Exclusions of IP addresses in the range that was configured can be set up to ensure that an IP address is not assigned to a client.

DHCP has two other types of scopes that can be created: superscopes and multicast scopes. Superscopes allow the combination of multiple DHCP scopes into one large scope. Superscopes are often created because the network grew too large for the existing network. Multicast scopes are used to deliver addresses to clients that use an application that requires it. Multicast addresses are used by the Class D range, which is from 224.0.0.0 to 239.255.255.255.

DHCP can hand out specific IP addresses to specific clients. This is called a DHCP reservation. Reservations use the clients MAC address to identify if the client has been reserved an IP address or if it should be granted one randomly out of the scope.

DHCP can configure additional options for clients. Such options include default gateway, DNS, and WINS. DHCP can also differentiate between clients in a scope.

Vendor classes are based on the operating system that is being used, and user classes are based on how the client is connected to the network.

You can back up the DHCP server database through the DHCP Management snap-in. Your action will back up the dhcp.mdb database. DHCP backs up every 60 minutes by default, but this can also be done manually.

If DHCP information on leases is not showing up correctly, it may be necessary to reconcile the DHCP scope to synchronize the information. You can also view statistics that are tracked automatically by the DHCP server.

When troubleshooting DHCP, you should enable DHCP audit logging. This logs detailed information about your DHCP server.

Conflict detection is a great feature of DHCP that will ping the IP address it is about to lease to see if someone has assigned that address statically.

You also can configure where the DHCP database and log files are stored through the Advanced properties. Like most services in Windows Server 2003, DHCP can be configured to work on all or some of the network cards. This action is done through binding.

CHAPTER 6 SUMMARY

Windows Internet Naming Service (WINS) is a NetBIOS name resolution service that allows clients and servers to communicate on a network using computer names instead of Internet Protocol (IP) addresses. WINS is required for clients that are pre-Windows 2000 so that they can log on to a domain controller.

Clients use a specific method to resolve names when using NetBIOS name resolution. It is possible to change the order by editing the registry, but is not very common. The four methods and their order are as follows:

1. NetBIOS name cache
2. WINS
3. Broadcast
4. LMHOSTS

Client computers cache all names that they communicate to help speed up communication. Entries are stored in the NetBIOS name cache for 10 minutes by default. To view a workstation's current NetBIOS name cache, open the Command Prompt window and type nbtstat –c.

WINS is a service that can run on Windows Server 2003 and provide NetBIOS name resolution. Clients will need to have their Server 2003 uses to control the size of (TCP/IP) settings configured to use a WINS server.

Broadcast can be used to resolve NetBIOS names, but it is not a very efficient method. Clients broadcast names with which they are trying to communicate, which in turn causes excessive network traffic.

The LMHOSTS file is a last resort for NetBIOS name resolution. It is a file that must be modified manually with static entries that resolve names to IP addresses. LMHOSTS files are used only by Microsoft operating systems and can be very difficult to maintain.

Choosing a NetBIOS name resolution method depends a lot on the size of the network. In a small single subnet, network broadcasts would work to resolve all names but would limit bandwidth. Larger multisubneted networks would need to use either WINS or LMHOSTS files to resolve all names. LMHOSTS files are not recommended for large networks because they must be configured locally on each workstation.

WINS can work in conjunction with Dynamic Host Configuration Protocol (DHCP) to be configured on all clients. If a network has clients that cannot be configured for WINS, then it maybe necessary for a WINS proxy to be installed. A WINS proxy can be configured by modifying the registry on a Windows Server 2003. Non-WINS clients would then broadcast out the name they are trying to communicate with and the WINS proxy would forward that request to the WINS server.

WINS is Microsoft's NetBIOS name server. It stores names in the WINS database and each name also has a corresponding service tied to it such as file sharing. WINS performs four common tasks:

- Name registration
- Name renewal
- Name release
- Name query

Clients that are configured to use WINS register their name when they boot up. The request is sent directly to the WINS server's IP address. If the name is available, the WINS server will lease the name to the client. If the name is already taken, the WINS server will send a challenge to the existing host to see if it is still in use.

Each name that is leased has a Time to Live (TTL) assigned to it. When that TTL reaches 50 percent, the client will attempt to renew the registration. If the client cannot contact the WINS server and the TTL expires, then the client is not able to renew its NetBIOS name.

When a computer is shut down properly, it will send a request to the WINS server and release its name. At this point, another computer could come online with that name and register it in the WINS database.

If a computer wants to communicate with another using NetBIOS names, then it will use a name query. The computer will contact the WINS server for the IP address of the computer it is trying to contact. If the name exists in the database, the client can successfully communicate with the server.

WINS can be installed from the Add or Remove Programs applet in the Control Panel. It can be installed on a Windows Server 2003 server. Some companies will have more than one WINS server to provide fault tolerance if the other WINS server should fail. When multiple

WINS servers are present, the clients must know about both and have them configured as primary and secondary WINS servers.

Even though a single WINS server can handle thousands of clients, having multiple WINS servers provides fault tolerance. All the WINS servers need to have replication set up on them to communicate with their replication partners. WINS replication partners can be set up in three different ways:

- Push
- Pull
- Push/Pull

Push replication is when a WINS server pushes out its records to the WINS server's replication partners. Push replication is triggered by how many records have changed and the amount of records needed for push replication that can be configured. Pull replication is initiated by a WINS server based on a specified amount of time. When that time is reached, the WINS server will pull WINS information from its replication partner. WINS servers can also be configured to use both Push/Pull. By configuring Push/Pull replication, you can ensure that nothing is missed.

The WINS server's Properties allow you to manage the service to a more granular degree. The General tab allows you to change the location of the backup and also how often the WINS statistics are refreshed. The Interval tab allows you to configure when names expire and/or are deleted from the WINS database. The Database Verification tab allows you to verify the constancy of your WINS server. The Advanced tab configures logging options, burst handling, and where the database is stored.

Not all records in the WINS database are dynamically registered. You may have certain types of clients that are not WINS clients that you would like registered in the WINS database. UNIX clients or servers are a great example of this. UNIX is not known for using NetBIOS names, but you can manually input the name of the UNIX machine so that the other Microsoft Windows clients can access the UNIX machine by its NetBIOS name.

Chapter 7 Summary

Domain Name System (DNS) is one of the most important services in networks today. Not only does DNS provide host name resolution, but also it is required for Active Directory domains. To work effectively, DNS needs to be planned appropriately.

Windows Server 2003 performs host name resolution with the following four steps:

1. *Host name*—Server checks whether the requested name is its own name.
2. *HOSTS file*—Server checks the local HOSTS file for the name.
3. *DNS cache*—Server checks the local DNS cache.
4. *DNS server*—The request is sent to a DNS server.

A host file is a text document that lists Internet Protocol (IP) addresses and host names. The only entry in the hosts file is the loopback address at 127.0.0.1. If a line starts with a #, then it is ignored when the hosts file is processed.

DNS servers are used primarily to resolve host names to IP addresses. This process is called a forward lookup. A client requesting a name that is stored on the same DNS server is a very quick and easy process. The client queries the DNS server for the name and the DNS server responds back with the IP address. If that name is not on the DNS server, DNS root servers are used. There are 13 root servers and they are used to direct requests to top-level DNS servers such as the .com and .net DNS servers.

The process that occurs between your client request and the other DNS servers is called a recursive lookup. This is where the local DNS server attempts to resolve the name by contacting other DNS servers. The local DNS server may contact as few as three DNS server and it could be even more, depending on the design. This process is relatively fast.

Top-level domains are represented by either a country code or category. Under these top-level domains are domain names that can be leased from a registrar.

DNS does more then forward lookups; it also has the ability to do reverse lookups. A reverse lookup occurs when DNS can resolve an IP address to a host name. Many different applications from Web servers to mail servers take advantage of reverse lookups.

DNS servers maintain a database of records. There are many different types of records, as follows:

- *Record abbreviation*—Record name
- *A*—Host record
- *MX*—Mail eXchanger
- *CANME*—Canonical name
- *NS*—Name Server
- *SOA*—Start of Authority
- *SRV*—Service record
- *AAAA*—IPv6 host
- *PTR*—Pointer record

Microsoft is not the only company that creates DNS servers. UNIX/Linux servers can run their own DNS software called Berkeley Internet Name Domain (BIND). This implementation of DNS works with Windows clients and supports a lot of the same features that Microsoft's own DNS supports.

When planning DNS, it is important to plan external and internal namespaces. While these names can be the same, for security, you may want to differentiate them. If your company already shares its internal and external namespace, you will find that it will be easier for users to understand the entire process. The downside is that there may be more administration that needs to be done.

One method of maintaining the same namespace is to use a delegated subdomain. A delegated subdomain is its own domain namespace that falls under the same namespace as the external namespace.

The easiest method for administration is to completely separate the namespace. However, by doing this, users may be confused because the name used internally may be something new to them.

DNS can be installed from the Add or Remove Programs applet in the Control Panel. DNS can also be installed directly from the Active Directory Installation wizard. By installing DNS this way, you are also configuring it to work with Active Directory from the start.

Once DNS is installed, a zone will need to be created. A zone is a namespace for which the DNS server is authoritative. All the records in this zone are under the control of the DNS server. A primary zone is the first one created, and that DNS server is the only server that has the ability to read and write to the zone. Secondary zone are created for DNS servers to provide fault tolerance. These DNS servers have a read only copy of the DNS zone. They can also help with query traffic. There can be only one primary server, but you can have multiple secondary servers for a zone.

Microsoft's DNS server has the ability to create a special zone type just for Active Directory. Active Directory Integrated zones require that DNS be installed on a domain controller. The following are the three major benefits of Active Directory Integrated zones:

- Automatic backup of zone information because it is stored in Active Directory
- Multimaster replication, which allows for all DNS servers to read and write to the database
- Increased security by allowing only dynamic updates to authorized users of the domain

Active Directory Integrated zones use a special application partition to store their DNS information. Active Directory Integrated zones can be stored in three locations:

- In all DNS servers in the Active Directory forest
- In all DNS servers in the Active Directory domain
- In all servers specified in the scope of an application partition directory partition

Stub zones are a new type of zone that Windows Server 2003 can host. Stub zones are used as a shortcut to using root hint DNS servers for name resolution. These types of zones can save time when resolving common names from a DNS server.

Active Directory relies so much on DNS because of the use of SRV records. SRV records are registrations of services from Active Directory domain controllers (DCs). These DCs register service records common with Active Directory, such as Kerberos and LDAP. Clients need to know where these servers are so that they can log on to the domain. These records can be created manually, but it is recommended that you configure dynamic DNS to do the work for you.

Dynamic DNS will register all the SRV records for your domain controllers and also register client names in the DNS database. Windows 2000 and later operating systems (OSs) know how to use dynamic DNS. Older clients will need the help of Dynamic Host Configuration Protocol (DHCP) to update their records in DNS. DHCP will not only lease an IP address to the client, but also will contact the DNS server and notify DNS of the IP address and name that the DHCP server just leased.

DNS can also be integrated with WINS to perform a similar function as dynamic DNS. This was developed before DNS was dynamic and can be used only with Microsoft DNS servers because it uses a non-standard zone. This special zone would be contacted if the requested resource was not in the DNS zone.

CHAPTER 8 SUMMARY

Most networks today use Domain Name System (DNS), often as their sole means of name resolution. DNS is popular because it is the method used to resolve names on the Internet. Anyone who has ever surfed the Internet has used a DNS server. DNS translates a domain name to an Internet Protocol (IP) address and provides the IP address to the requestor. This allows a Web browser to find a particular Web site. Domain names make it much easier for end users to find network resources because they can rely on the friendly domain name, instead of the 32-bit IP address.

The DNS structure is created around zones, which are areas of authority over which the DNS server presides. When a zone is created on a DNS server, that server is responsible for all of the DNS namespace below that DNS name.

To reduce the load of a single server, you can delegate authority for a subdomain to another DNS server. In addition, you can create a caching-only DNS server. This server stores only recently requested DNS information. When a client requests a DNS lookup from the server, it does the lookup, and then stores the result for a set period of time.

The DNS server service performs recursive queries by default. A recursive query occurs when the DNS server performs the lookup queries on behalf of the client. You can disable the recursive capability of the DNS server, which causes the client to perform the queries to resolve a DNS name.

DNS servers can also be configured as forwarding-only DNS servers. This configuration causes the DNS server to either resolve the query using its locally hosted zone files or, if the query can not be resolved this way, forwarding the request to another DNS server. This is a common configuration when there is only one Internet connection. A conditional forwarder is similar; however, it only forwards requests that belong to certain domains.

Because a DNS server contains records identifying all of the IP resources in the network, it is a prime target of attackers gaining reconnaissance on a network. DNS is also critical for the proper functioning of Active Directory. Corrupted DNS records prevent workstations from locating network resources and logging into Active Directory.

Other security concerns relate to dynamic DNS and zone replication. DNS data contains vital information regarding network resources and their location. An unauthorized zone transfer is the transfer of DNS data to an unauthorized client. This can result in DNS information becoming available to unauthorized people. The default DNS configuration allows zone transfers from any IP address, which is insecure.

Along with security settings, it is important to manage the server for optimal performance. Aging and scavenging are parameters that can be set to improve the performance of DNS. They allow DNS records created by dynamic DNS to be removed if they are not updated, which keeps DNS records current.

You can control the interfaces on which the DNS server listens. By default, the DNS service listens on all IP addresses that are bound to the server on which it is running. However, you can also configure DNS to respond only to those certain IP addresses that are bound to the server.

Troubleshooting DNS is done through several tools. The DNS server has a query test it can run. It enables you to perform a simple query or a recursive query manually, or on a scheduled interval, and lets you know whether the query succeeded or failed.

Another useful utility is nslookup. This tool is used to query the DNS server for records. Nslookup allows you to specify a server and query it for DNS responses. You can then examine the returned information for accuracy or other issues.

Two other utilities are DNSLint and DNSCmd. DNSLint allows you to confirm zone configuration and verify Active Directory records. DNSCmd allows you to view the status of a DNS server, as well as configure zones and records. It can also be scripted, allowing you to implement changes on many servers effectively.

DNS servers are also able to log information, which assists in troubleshooting complex problems. Event logging logs errors, warnings, and related information. When using debug logging, additional information is stored as well. Debug logging includes packet direction and the protocol uses, as well as the packet contents and type.

DNS is one of the critical services that an administrator running Active Directory must manage. It is crucial, as it allows clients to find resources on the network. If DNS is not configured properly, then clients can have login problems, Group Policy issues may arise, and a large set of problems may crop up which will not be resolved until DNS is running again.

CHAPTER 9 SUMMARY

Networks are in such overwhelming use today because of our need to communicate. Certificate services are present because we need to be able to communicate securely, verify identities, and ensure that important data is not altered or tampered with in transit. Certificate services provide us these features. Certificate services and cryptography can be implemented on several different levels to secure different aspects of network communication.

Cryptography meets security needs in four different areas:

- *Confidentiality*—Protects information from unauthorized disclosure
- *Integrity*—Ensures that the data sent and the data received are identical
- *Nonrepudiation*—Provides a method to ensure the sender cannot deny ownership of the action
- *Authentication*—Verifies the identity of the sender as authentic

Some of these objectives are met by using encryption. Encryption methods can be broken down into three different categories. The three general encryption types are:

- Symmetrical
- Asymmetrical
- Hash

Symmetric encryption is a quick method of encryption, using a single key to both encrypt and decrypt the data. If user A uses a key to encrypt the data, then, with the same key, user B can decrypt the data. In contrast is asymmetric encryption. This method of encryption uses two keys, one to encrypt the data, called the public key, and one to decrypt the data, called the private key. The public key is known to all; the private key must be protected by the user or service using it. This ensures that no one but the holder of the private key can decrypt the data.

The third type of encryption is hash encryption. This differs from the other two methods. Hash encryption is one-way; it is most often used to verify data integrity. An algorithm takes the data and produces a single key. This is a unique value that can be used to identify the data. Different data produces different hash values, so comparisons between hash values can be used to indicate modified data.

Encryption has three common uses: to encrypt e-mail, to ensure data integrity, and to secure communications with Secure Sockets Layer (SSL). E-mail, by default, is sent in clear text, which can result in the unwanted disclosure of information. Using public and private keys allows senders and recipients to exchange messages securely.

Closely related is the concept of a digital signature. This is a hash value attached to the message. It can be used to ensure that the contents of the message have not been altered and to ensure the identity of the sender. It cannot be used to protect the data, however.

SSL is used to ensure that information transmitted to Web sites is done so securely. It encrypts the traffic at the Transport layer so that it is invisible to any applications. It ensures that sensitive information is protected and not disclosed.

All of these capabilities can be carried out through Certificate Services. Certificate Services is Microsoft's Public-key Infrastructure (PKI) system, which is a service designed to create and manage public keys, private keys, and certificates. There are four components to a PKI: certificates, a certificate authority (CA), a certificate revocation list (CRL), and certificate-enabled applications.

The first component is the actual certificate, which is a standards based component. It is defined by the X.509 standard. A certificates field includes the subject (or user name), serial number, validity period, public key, issuer name, and issuer signature.

The next component is the actual CA. This is the server responsible for issuing certifications to users, computers, and applications that request it.

Sometimes, however, a certificate is issued in error. In this instance, it needs to be revoked. There may also be other reasons to revoke a certificate before its normal expiration date. One reason might be the termination of a user. In these cases, the invalid certificate is published to the CRL, which is a list of certificates issued by the CA that are no longer valid.

There are two installation choices for your certificate server in Windows Server 2003, Enterprise, and Stand-alone. An enterprise CA is for organizations running Active Directory. It is Active-Directory integrated. In contrast is a stand-alone CA. It does not need Active Directory and cannot issue certificates automatically to Active Directory objects, such as user accounts. All requests for a certificate must be approved by an administrator.

The structure of servers installed in your PKI infrastructure is your certificate hierarchy. The starting point of the hierarchy is the root CA. Below it are subordinate CAs that received their certificate from the root and that can then in turn issue certificates.

Because the service is complex and critical, it is recommended that you back it up on a regular basis. It is backed up by default by backing up the system state data.

Management of certificate services includes planning for methods to achieve the primary tasks for administering a PKI. These include issuing, renewing, and revoking templates; managing the CRL; importing and exporting certificates; and mapping accounts to certificates.

To make this easier, Microsoft has implemented a Certificate Services Web page that can be used to request certificates for both enterprise and stand-alone implementations. Users can use the Certificate Request Wizard and the server can be set up for both automatic or manual issuance of a certificate.

Smart cards are also supported, and your CA can also be set up to issue smart card certificates. This aids in the implementation of smart card authentication in your network. You can set up a smart card enrollment station designed to allow configuration of smart cards. This will be a workstation with a smart card reader attached.

If certificates are used for user identification, they will need to be mapped to a user account. This can be done in Active Directory Users and Computers. When you right click a user account, the Name Mappings option allows you to set up certificate mappings as your organization requires.

Certificates can be easily implemented and can be used to ensure confidentiality, integrity, and authenticity of network communications. Windows Server 2003 can be used to provide certificate services for both your internal company and external customers. It is a full-featured way to ensure security in your organization.

CHAPTER 10 SUMMARY

The security of network communications today can not be understated. It is important to be able to securely pass information between hosts of a network. IP Security (IPSec) is a tool in Windows Server 2003 that can prevent typical malicious attacks against a network.

Typical Internet Protocol (IP) communication has no security. This allows several attacks:

- *Packet sniffing*—Using software called a packet sniffer, attackers can view the content of data traversing the network.

- *Data replay*—Using the data captured with a packet sniffer, attackers can replay the data in an attempt to establish illegitimate communication with a remote target.

- *Data modification*—Before replaying the data, the attacker may be able to modify the data.

- *Address spoofing*—By modifying the source address of a packet, the attacker can attempt to bypass firewalls or hide the true source of data.

IPSec is a standard that is designed to secure IP-based communication. It works at the Network layer, so it is able to encrypt communications seamlessly, without modifications to any networked applications. This raises the compatibility level of IPSec and allows it to be widely implemented.

IPSec is not supported on all operating systems. Microsoft implemented IPSec support in Windows 2000 operating systems and later. Older Microsoft clients do not support IPSec.

Other IPSec issues to be aware of include the overhead created by its use. Packets must be encrypted, which means there is a central processing unit (CPU) load for using IPSec.

IPSec components include Authentication Headers (AH) and Encapsulating Security Payload (ESP). AH mode enforces authentication, as the name implies, and includes a digital signature. ESP mode includes the AH features, and in addition, it encrypts the data packet. When IPSec occurs between two networks, it is referred to as tunnel mode. IPSec between two hosts is referred to as transport mode.

To begin IPSec communication, a key must be exchanged between the hosts. This is accomplished through a protocol called Internet Key Exchange (IKE). It is used to negotiate security parameters.

IPSec communications can be implemented in one of three methods: a preshared key, certificates, or Kerberos. A preshared key is the simplest to implement, and it involves providing the correct key at each endpoint. Certificates can be used for authentication as well. Kerberos is implemented with Windows 2000, XP, and Server 2003, and Kerberos can also be used to authenticate the parties in IPSec communication as well.

IPSec policies are administrator tools designed to further control the conditions under which IPSec communication is used. It controls the authentication, network connections, and IPSec mode governed by the use of IPSec. The three default policies are:

- Server (Request Security)
- Client (Respond Only)
- Secure Server (Require Security)

The preceding policies use Kerberos authentication by default, which results in easy Active Directory integration.

IPSec policies consist of IPSec rules. Rules include an IP filter list, which are the protocols affected by the rule. The filter action indicates how the traffic is handled, and whether or not it is allowed or denied. Authentication methods, such as Kerberos, are also a part of the policy, as well as a tunnel endpoint and a connection type.

Data integrity confirms that the information communicated has not been altered. There are two algorithms to ensure data integrity: Secure Hash Algorithm (SHA) and message-digest algorithm (MD5.)

To ensure that the information hasn't been viewed by a third party in transit, two algorithms can be used for ESP data encryption: Digital Encryption Standard (DES) and Triple Data Encryption Standard (3DES).

To troubleshoot communication, there are several utilities that can be used. The most common IPSec troubleshooting tools and utilities are:

- Ping
- IPSec Security Monitor
- Event Viewer
- Resultant Set of Policy
- Netsh
- Oakley logs
- Network Monitor

By using these utilities, you can verify that IPSec is properly implemented in your network. IPSec can enhance the security in your network by protecting sensitive data. IPSec can ensure that data is protected and kept confidential, while thwarting attacks such as replay attacks.

C

CHAPTER 11 SUMMARY

Network access from remote locations is an ever increasingly popular way to boost productivity and stay in touch with remote employees. As salespeople travel and employees telecommute, remote access to the corporate network can help boost a company's bottom line. To access the corporate network, typically, one of two methods is used. The two types of remote access commonly used are dial-up and virtual private network (VPN).

The method of access that has been around the longest is dial-up access, which uses a modem. It is slow by today's standards; however, in remote locations, it is often the only means of connecting to a corporate network. There are many locations where high-speed Internet access is unavailable.

The Routing and Remote Access Service (RRAS) provides dial-up services for Windows Server 2003. It is installed, but not enabled by default. It supports protocols such as Point-to-Point Protocol (PPP) and Serial Line Internet Protocol (SLIP). It also supports such features as multilink. Multilink allows multiple inbound dial-up connections from a single computer to be bound together into a single virtual connection that has higher bandwidth. This allows faster communication.

More commonly today, people use the Internet and make a VPN connection to the main office. A VPN uses an existing network connection over a public network to create a tunnel to securely transmit private information. Encryption keeps the information secure over the insecure public network.

As with a dial-up server, a VPN server is enabled using the RRAS Setup Wizard. The wizard is typically the simplest, most error-free way of setting up the server, but it can be run only if the service is disabled.

Two protocols are commonly used to create a VPN connection: Point-to-Point Tunneling Protocol (PPTP) and Layer Two Tunneling Protocol (L2TP). PPTP is the older of the two protocols and enjoys wide support. PPTP's main advantage over L2TP is its ability to work seamlessly with Network Address Translation (NAT). NAT is increasingly used as a popular method to share an Internet connection. PPTP uses Microsoft Point-to-Point Encryption (MPPE) protocol to encrypt data, and encryption is a part of PPTP; thus, it requires no extra configuration.

The other common VPN protocol in use is L2TP. However, it provides only for the tunneling of data, not the encryption. If encryption is necessary, then L2TP must work with an encrypting protocol such as IPSec. This is the most common solution for encrypting L2TP traffic.

An authentication method must be designated for either protocol. To ensure only authorized users are accessing the network, any of the following can be used for dial-up and VPN connections:

- *No Authentication*—This method does not authenticate the user, and access is permitted regardless of the username and password supplied.

- *Password Authentication Protocol (PAP)*—PAP is insecure and transmits passwords in clear text. It is not recommended and disabled by default.

- *Shiva Password Authentication Protocol (SPAP)*—SPAP uses reversible encryption to transmit passwords. It is preferable over PAP, but it is still not a recommended way of authentication; however, it is included for backward compatibility.

- *Challenge Handshake Authentication Protocol (CHAP)*—CHAP is more secure, as the password is not transmitted; instead, a password hash is sent over the network. However, passwords in AD must be stored using reversible encryption, which is a security risk.

- *Microsoft Challenge Handshake Authentication Protocol (MS-CHAP)*—MS-CHAP improves over CHAP by dropping the reversible encryption storage requirement, and it doesn't transmit passwords in clear text.

- *Microsoft Challenge Handshake Authentication Protocol version 2 (MS-CHAPv2)*—This enhanced version of MS-CHAP increases the security of MS-CHAP by no longer supporting older, less-secure authentication mechanisms, such as LAN Manager. It also provides mutual authentication.

- *Extensible Authentication Protocol (EAP)*—EAP is used as an authentication system for newer technologies, such as smart cards.

Remote access policies (RAPs) govern remote access connections. They determine whether or not a connection is allowed. To use RAPs effectively, you must understand:

- Remote access policy components

- Remote access policy evaluation

- Default remote access policies

Components of RAPs include conditions, remote access permissions, and a profile. Conditions are the requirements for a remote access policy to apply to a connection. There are a variety of conditions, including the authentication type, day and time, calling station ID, and the called station ID. Conditions allow an administrator to control access to the server. Based on the condition, permissions can be applied. Permissions consist of either a denial or a granting of remote access connections. The final part of the components is the profile, which are the policy settings applied to the connection once the conditions and permissions have been applied.

C

Windows Server 2003 supports Remote Access Dial-In User Service (RADIUS). RADIUS is designed to support large distributed networks. There are two required server roles with RADIUS:

- RADIUS client
- RADIUS server

The RADIUS client is responsible for accepting authentication information for hosts trying to connect to the remote access server, and passing this information to the RADIUS server. The RADIUS server is responsible for the actual authentication of the host based on the information provided by the RADIUS client. Windows Server 2003 can fulfill both roles.

A third role is that of RADIUS Proxy. The proxy is designed to benefit organizations with multiple RADIUS servers, and it acts as an intermediary between the clients and the servers.

Connectivity issues are often configuration problems. A misconfiguration of the end user's settings is the most common cause of problems. These are the issues that typically need to be checked:

- *Incorrect phone numbers and IP addresses*—It is vital that users enter the correct phone number or IP address for the connection. An incorrect entry will almost always fail. You can use the Connection Manager Administration Kit (CMAK) to help minimize configuration problems.

- *Incorrect authentication settings*—The client, server, and policies need to have the authentication settings set properly to allow proper authentication.

- *Incorrectly configured remote access policies*—It is important to review your policies to ensure they are performing as expected, which should include testing the policies.

- *Name resolution is not configured*—A failure to access LAN hosts by Domain Name System (DNS) name indicates that the connection does not have proper name resolution settings.

- *Clients receive incorrect IP options*—Confirm the DNS and Windows Internet Naming Service (WINS) settings that the client is issued by the interface on the RA server.

- *The remote access server (RAS) leases 10 IP addresses from Dynamic Host Configuration Protocol (DHCP) at startup*—RRAS does this by default if it is configured to hand out addresses using DHCP.

- *User accounts in Active Directory seem to be locked out at random*—When Internet Authentication Service (IAS) functions as a RADIUS server, Active Directory is used to authenticate accounts.

In addition, hardware problems can also be the culprit. They are less common, but still possible issues. Troubleshooting these issues includes the following tips:

- Check that all hardware used is on the Hardware Compatibility List (HCL) issued by Microsoft.

- Use the ping utility to ensure connectivity to the IP address and to other Internet hosts to ensure connectivity.

- Attempt to connect to a different RAS to ensure your hardware is functioning.

- Ensure the physical connection and network cards are functioning properly.

- Ensure you are using supported hardware. RAS supports analog modems, Integrated Services Digital Network (ISDN), X.25, Frame Relay, Asynchronous Transfer Mode (ATM), cable modems, and digital subscriber line (DSL) modems.

Secure remote access improves productivity and allows remote workers to stay in touch. This increased communication can make workers more effective. However, it is important to maintain security during this process, and the tools in Windows Server 2003, such as RADIUS, IPSec, and MPPE, permit that. Thus, workers can work away from the office and maintain security.

CHAPTER 12 SUMMARY

As a network administrator, it is important to keep your servers running and available to provide services to users. Scalability is an important consideration as well. Windows Server 2003 performs well in both availability and scalability. Administrator's can take action to increase the stability, availability, and scalability of Windows as well.

When a server fails, it is no longer able to provide services. Typically, this is an expensive outage as well, as services are no longer available, which often means work cannot be performed. Administrators must make decisions and value judgments, deciding if the cost of a solution to improve uptime is worth the potential cost of a loss caused by an outage. Some of the things that can cause a server or service to fail include hardware failures, network failures, administrator mistakes, operating system crashes, and application crashes.

Different actions can be undertaken to improve server availability. Options available include the following:

- Installing redundant hardware components, such as hard drives and power supplies.

- Implementing an uninterruptible power supply (UPS) in case of a power failure.

- Installing a backup power generator for longer power outages.

- Setting up redundant network paths to move data around failed network components.

- Using documented methods for tasks to improve standardization.

- Documenting the network configuration of your network and servers.

- Regularly patching operating systems and applications to prevent crashes and fix security issues.

- Using clustering to implement server clusters and network load balancing.

Windows Server 2003 supports Network Load Balancing (NLB). This feature distributes the load between multiple servers. It also senses failed servers and redistributes the traffic load accordingly.

Applications can also play a role. They can be broken into two categories: stateful and stateless. The server must store information regarding the client accessing the server for stateful applications, such as a shopping cart at an e-commerce site. A stateless application isn't required to do so.

Server clusters allow you to create high availability in your environment. If a service fails on a clustered server, another server can provide the service. The four most common configurations that Windows supports are:

- *Active/passive*—This mode has two nodes where one is providing services and the other is on standby until a failure in the active node.

- *N+I failover*—This is similar to the active/passive mode; however, multiple servers are providing services, and the N nodes, and the I nodes are passive and take over if an N node fails.

- *Active/active*—This cluster mode has no passive nodes, and a service on a failed server moves to another active server, which may result in the overloading of a server.

- *Single-node virtual server*—This model does not have failover capability. There is a single node often used for migration purposes so that services can be provided seamlessly during a transition.

Applications must be cluster-aware to take advantage of clustering features. Windows Server services and applications that are cluster-aware include:

- Distributed File System (DFS)

- Dynamic Host Configuration Protocol (DHCP)

- Windows Internet Naming Service (WINS)

- Microsoft Exchange Server

- Microsoft SQL Server

Not all applications are cluster aware, and there is a risk of data loss with applications of this sort running in a cluster.

Clusters provide high availability by implementing the following features:

- Shared disks
- Quorum resource
- Cluster communication
- Resource groups
- Failover and failback
- Virtual servers

Shared disks are a typical requirement for clusters and allow data to be shared by all servers in the cluster. Quorum resources are disk resources used to store configuration information regarding the cluster itself. Cluster communication allows all nodes in the cluster to be in constant communication using a heartbeat packet, which is a User Datagram Protocol (UDP) unicast or multicast packet with availability information for a node.

Resource groups are logical groupings of the resources required for an application or service to run. They can be Internet Protocol (IP) addresses, printers, disk partitions, services, and applications. Failover is the ability of a resource group on a node to fail over to another node. Failback occurs after failover, and it is the restoration of the service to the original failed node once the failed node has been restored.

Virtual servers appear to be a single Windows Server 2003 system to a client; however, it is actually representative of the cluster itself.

Network load balancing also has software requirements. To be suitable for NLB, applications need to adhere to the following:

- Transmission Control Protocol (TCP) or UDP must be used by the application.
- When clients modify data, that data must be synchronized between hosts in the NLB cluster or stored in a central location.
- Session state information, if used, must be stored on client computers or stored in a central location. Otherwise, affinity must be configured.
- The application must not bind to a computer name.
- The applications must not keep files open continually for writing.

Scalability and availability are critical in a network environment. They ensure that employees can continue to work, customers can continue to shop, and business can continue uninterrupted. Scalability allows for the growth of the business to support a higher demand on the services the network provides. Both of these are enhanced by Windows Server 2003, including NLB and clustering.

CHAPTER 13 SUMMARY

Security takes on several aspects in today's computing environment. Administrators must consider network security; however, the physical security of the environment cannot be overlooked either. Consideration to both enhances the overall security of a network.

There are two main types of security: physical security and network security. Physical security entails securing the physical environment, including access to computing equipment. This security is often overlooked. Network security refers to network-based solutions to enhance the security of data and resources on the network. Tools for increasing network security include:

- Authentication
- Internet Protocol Security (IPSec)
- Firewalls

Authentication is the first aspect of network security. Authentication verifies the identity of a user attempting to access the network and its resources. It is the primary tool in network security.

IPSec is a second tool to enforce security. IPSec allows the encryption of data passing over the network. This obscures sensitive data from being discovered by attacks, such as packet sniffing. IPSec also authenticates computers to further enhance the level of security on the network.

Another tool to control the flow of data on the network is the firewall. Firewalls can limit the traffic that is allowed on the network by controlling from where the traffic may come and where it may go.

Network design is also important. Network design typically includes such features as a demilitarized zone (DMZ). A DMZ is an Internet-accessible subnet between the Internet and a private network where publicly accessible resources should be located.

Stored data on the network must be protected as well. Data security can be accomplished through a variety of mechanisms, such as:

- New Technology File System (NTFS) permissions
- Share permissions
- Auditing
- Encrypting File System (EFS)

NTFS permissions are used to secure access to data stored on hard drives. Network users can only access data to which they have been granted access. Share permissions work when data is being accessed over the network and also limit access to users that have been granted it.

Auditing is a tool that allows you to track the actions of users on the network. Auditing gives information regarding object access, logins, privilege use, and other information regarding security on the network.

EFS encrypts files that are stored on NTFS partitions. It does not protect data in transit, but is designed so that a user can add an additional level of security beyond NTFS to ensure confidential data is not easily recovered by unauthorized users.

The role of the computer is a security consideration as well. Best practices for servers include adhering to the following recommendations:

- Disable unnecessary services.

- Limit access to the minimum required for users to perform their jobs.

- Use separate administrator accounts for different staff.

- Allow packets to necessary TCP and UDP ports only.

Different servers also have different security needs. Domain controllers, for instance, should be protected from external networks. Web servers, however, typically require more external access so they are typically DMZ candidates. However, they should be hardened and have unnecessary services disabled. Database servers should also be protected because they contain sensitive data. Keeping them on the internal network protected by a firewall is usually preferred.

Wireless networks require special considerations. Wireless networks are increasingly more common. Wired Equivalent Privacy (WEP) is a protocol designed to increase the level of security on wireless networks. It is not foolproof, however, and it is a good idea to include other security mechanisms as well, such as media access control (MAC) address filtering.

Security templates are an administrator's tool, which can allow uniform implementation of policy. They should be implemented along with a baseline, which is a secure minimum standard to which all PCs should conform.

In addition to modifying the rights granted to various workstations, administrators must also keep their systems up to date through patching. Microsoft offers several methods to accomplish this goal:

- Windows Update

- Automatic Updates

- Software Update Services

- Microsoft Baseline Security Analyzer

- Hfnetchk

Security is one of an administrator's most important tasks. To maintain a secure computing environment, administrators must be vigilant regarding the physical and network security in their realm of responsibility. To ensure security is maintained, administrators must take a proactive approach, including monitoring and assigning proper privilege levels and maintaining a secure operating system by keeping patches and service packs up to date.

C

CHAPTER 14 SUMMARY

Data is at the center of our need for network communication. As a driving force behind our needs for networks, data becomes highly valuable. Therefore, data must be protected. An administrator's failure to protect and back up data, or to secure data from prying eyes, can result in severe repercussions, financial losses, and public embarrassment.

The backup processes centers around file backup and recovery. Regardless of your data fault tolerance methods, at some point, disaster may strike and a full restore from backup media may be required.

Windows Server 2003 includes the Backup utility. It is not as full featured as some third-party utilities, because it cannot back up open files. However, it does have many scheduling features and can back up to several different media types.

There are three different primary backup options when backing up data. They all work off of the archive bit. It is turned on if a file has changed, and it is set to off after certain backup types. Each of the following backup methods uses and affects the archive bit of a file in a different way:

- Full
- Incremental
- Differential

A full backup backs up all of the selected files on the computer. This backup type is typically done on a regular basis and allows you to fully restore all files backed up.

An incremental backup backs up all the files that have changes since the last backup. It saves space using this method because it is typically much smaller than a full backup.

A differential backup backs up all the files that have changed since the last full backup. This backup method results in quicker restores because only the full backup and the last differential are needed. For incremental restores, the last full backup and all subsequent incremental backups are required.

In addition to regular backups, it is recommended that the system state data be backed up regularly. This backs up the registry, COM+ Class Registration, boot files, and system files. In addition, the Certificate Services Database is included if Certificate Services is installed. On domain controllers, Active Directory and the Sysvol folder are backed up, and IIS servers also back up the IIS metabase.

Volume Shadow Copy is a new feature of Windows 2003 designed to allow end users to back up their data. It creates a library of file versions as they are created so that end users can restore a file to a specific point in time, if necessary.

Disaster can strike from many different angles. Device driver rollback is a feature to revert to an older driver instead of a newly installed driver that may be causing problems. Safe mode is another recovery feature. When a server will no longer boot up properly, you can start in safe mode loading a minimal set of drivers. This can resolve many issues and allow you to correct irregularities that prevent the server from loading properly.

Last Known Good Configuration is also available as a startup option. It allows you to revert to an older copy of portions of the registry that may have been corrupted. It can fix errors in the registry as long as the user hasn't logged back in since the changes were made.

Introduced in Windows 2000, the Recovery Console is a command-line interface for Windows. It allows you to correct errors, move files around, and manage services. When safe mode will not start or is insufficient to resolve the issue, the Recovery Console provides another avenue to resolve problems.

Terminal Services gives administrators a way to allow users to connect remotely to the server to run applications. It allows the processing and central processing unit (CPU) load to be processed by the server instead of the end-user workstation. This allows end users to run more intensive applications than they may be able to run on their desktops.

Remote Assistance allows help desk personnel to remotely connect and view or interact with an end user's desktop. This can make it simpler for the help desk personnel or administrator to troubleshoot problems and provide guidance for end users.

Windows Server 2003 includes a solution for imaging called Remote Installation Services (RIS). A number of third-party imaging solutions, such as Norton Ghost, are also available. RIS allows the quick installation of an operating system and applications on computers over the network using the RIS Server. The RIS service must be installed on the server, and the clients must have a network bootable floppy or have a PXE-compliant network card.

Windows Server 2003 includes several features designed to make disaster recovery an easier process. To be successful, you must be familiar with the tools available to you. The process starts with a good backup plan, and Windows built-in Backup utility can be a versatile tool to create backups. Windows includes several recovery features such as the recovery console and last known good configuration. Finally, to aid in bringing machines back up rapidly, remote installation services can be used to quickly deploy full desktop images.

Practice Exam

70-293 Planning and Maintaining a Microsoft Windows Server 2003 Network Infrastructure

Name:_____

Date:_____

1. Which of the following versions of Windows Server 2003 supports network load balancing? (Choose all that apply.)

   a. Windows Server 2003 Web Edition
   b. Windows Server 2003 Standard Edition
   c. Windows Server 2003 Enterprise Edition
   d. Windows Server 2003 Datacenter Edition

2. What is the maximum number of Itanium processors supported by Windows Server 2003 Datacenter Edition?

   a. 4
   b. 8
   c. 32
   d. 64
   e. unlimited

3. Which of the following operating systems natively supports SMB signing? (Choose all that apply.)

   a. Windows 95
   b. Windows 98
   c. Windows 2000
   d. Windows XP
   e. Windows NT Service Pack 2

4. You are upgrading a Novell network to Windows Server 2003. Which protocols will support Active Directory? (Choose all that apply.)

   a. TCP/IP
   b. IPX/SPX
   c. AppleTalk
   d. NetBEUI

5. Which of the following statements regarding UDP is incorrect? (Choose all that apply.)

   a. UDP is connectionless.
   b. UDP uses sliding windows to send packets.
   c. UDP is commonly used for streaming audio.
   d. UDP resends lost packets if no ACK is sent.

6. Which protocol is used to send IP error messages?

   a. IGMP
   b. ICMP
   c. TCP
   d. UDP

7. Which protocol is used to resolve IP address to MAC addresses?

   a. ARP
   b. ARPA
   c. IGMP
   d. DNS

8. Which IEEE standard defines Token Ring?
   a. 802.2
   b. 802.3
   c. 802.5
   d. 802.11

9. Which of the following is an example of a local broadcast? (Choose all that apply.)
   a. 255.255.255.255
   b. 10.255.255.255
   c. 192.168.255.255
   d. 192.168.12.255

10. Which IP range is used for multicast packets?
    a. 10.x.x.x
    b. 172.31.x.x
    c. 192.168.x.x
    d. 169.254.x.x
    e. 224.x.x.x

11. At which layer of the OSI model does a hub operate?
    a. Physical
    b. Data link
    c. Network
    d. Transport

12. A switch divides network traffic into separate collision domains based on
    _____ .
    a. the IP address
    b. the MAC address
    c. the physical port address
    d. all of the above

13. What is the default MTU size in Windows Server 2003?
    a. 512 bytes
    b. 1000 bytes
    c. 1500 bytes
    d. 2048 bytes

14. Which of the following utilities can be used to list TCP connections on the local computer?
    a. TRACERT
    b. NBTSTAT
    c. NETSTAT
    d. IPCONFIG

15. **What is the maximum number of hops supported by RIP?**
    a. 8
    b. 10
    c. 15
    d. 16
    e. 24
    f. unlimited

16. **Which of the following statements regarding OSPF is incorrect?**
    a. OSPF sends updates to the routing table every 30 seconds.
    b. OSPF routing is based on cost.
    c. OSPF uses link-state routing.
    d. OSPF is not available in Windows Server 2003 64-bit versions.

17. **What type of switch can be used to create VLANs?**
    a. Layer 2
    b. Layer 3
    c. Layer 5
    d. None of the above are correct; you must use a router.

18. **Which of the following Internet Connection Sharing configuration settings *cannot* be changed from the default setting? (Choose all that apply.)**
    a. the option for the internal network connection's IP address
    b. the option for the internal network's default subnet mask
    c. the option for the DHCP scope
    d. the option for disabling DNS proxy

19. **You want to install Internet Connection Firewall on your Windows Server 2003 server. How will stateful firewall filter packets?**
    a. Rules are created based on incoming ports.
    b. Rules are created based on incoming and outgoing ports.
    c. Each incoming packet's header is examined for content.
    d. Rules are created to allow responses to outgoing traffic.

20. **To help troubleshoot ICF connections, you have enabled logging. What is the name of the ICF log file that you must use?**
    a. PFIREWALL.LOG
    b. ICF.LOG
    c. ICFIREWALL.LOG
    d. LOGGING.TXT

21. **You need to configure different DHCP options based on client properties. On what characteristic can scope options be based? (Choose all that apply.)**
    a. workstation vendor
    b. operating system version
    c. time of day
    d. connection type

22. **What is the maximum number of WINS servers that can be configured on the WINS tab in TCP/IP properties on a Windows Server 2003 member server?**

    a. 2
    b. 6
    c. 10
    d. 12
    e. unlimited

23. **On what is a push WINS replication based?**

    a. time interval
    b. number of changes
    c. size of changes
    d. time of day

24. **You are concerned about security regarding null sessions. Which operating system does *not* allow NetBIOS over TCP/IP null sessions? (Choose all that apply.)**

    a. Windows 9x
    b. Windows NT
    c. Windows 2000
    d. Windows XP
    e. Windows Server 2003

25. **Which DNS record contains the configuration information for the domain?**

    a. SOA
    b. NS
    c. PTR
    d. CNAME
    e. MX
    f. AAAA

26. **You have chosen to store DNS zone information in the domain directory partition in Active Directory. To what servers is the DNS information replicated?**

    a. to all DNS servers in the forest
    b. to all DNS servers in the domain
    c. only to DNS servers specified in the scope
    d. only to DNS servers that do not function as domain controllers

27. **Which operating systems support updating dynamic DNS records? (Choose all that apply.)**

    a. Windows 9x
    b. Windows NT
    c. Windows 2000
    d. Windows XP
    e. Windows Server 2003

28. **What occurs during an iterative DNS lookup?**
    a. The DNS server checks its own records and responds accordingly.
    b. The DNS server checks its own records first. If the information is not found, the query is forwarded to another DNS server.
    c. The DNS server automatically forwards the query to another DNS server identified by an NS record.
    d. The DNS server forwards the query to a root server on the Internet.

29. **What type of DNS zone can be used to configure the Windows Server 2003 DNS server as a conditional forwarder?**
    a. stub zone
    b. cache-only
    c. reverse lookup
    d. iterative lookup

30. **You are troubleshooting DNS functionality using DNSLint. What is the proper command syntax to test e-mail functionality?**
    a. dnslint /d
    b. dnslint /c
    c. dnslint /v /r
    d. dnslint /t /ql

31. **You need to use the DNSCmd utility to configure DNS servers. What MSI file contains the DNSCmd tool?**
    a. DNSCMD.MSI
    b. SUPPORT.MSI
    c. SUPTOOLS.MSI
    d. ADMINPAK.MSI
    e. DNSMGMT.MSI

32. **You have been attempting to optimize DNS on a Windows Server 2003 domain controller and inadvertently rendered DNS inoperable. You have selected Reset to Default on the Advanced tab of the DNS server. Which of the following settings is now enabled by default? (Choose all that apply.)**
    a. Round robin DNS
    b. Automatic scavenging of stale records
    c. Netmask ordering
    d. BIND secondaries
    e. Disable recursion

33. **What protocol supported by Windows Server 2003 allows DNS servers to send UDP packets larger than 512 bytes?**
    a. EMDNS
    b. EDNSP
    c. EAP
    d. EDNSO

34. **At what level of the OSI model does SSL operate?**
    a. Transport
    b. Session
    c. Presentation
    d. Application
    e. Physical

35. **Which of the following statements regarding stand-alone certificate authorities is correct? (Choose all that apply.)**
    a. A stand-alone CA can use certificate templates.
    b. A stand-alone CA cannot be integrated into Active Directory.
    c. A stand-alone CA automatically issues certificates.
    d. A stand-alone CA cannot issue certificates for smart card authentication.

36. **You want to enable autoenrollment of certificates on the Windows Server 2003 domain controller to eliminate user intervention. Which client operating system will support autoenrollment? (Choose all that apply.)**
    a. Windows 9x
    b. Windows NT
    c. Windows 2000
    d. Windows XP

37. **How often do clients download a new version of the Certificate Revocation List (CRL)?**
    a. every 6 hours
    b. every 24 hours
    c. every 3 days
    d. every 7 days
    e. every 10 days

38. **You are upgrading Rebecca's workstation to a new laptop. You need to export Rebecca's private key to install it on her new laptop. Which format must you use to export her key?**
    a. PKCS #12
    b. PKCS #7
    c. Base-64 encoded X.509
    d. DER encoded X.509
    e. any of the above

39. **Smart cards can be used to authenticate which type of connection? (Choose all that apply.)**
    a. network logons
    b. VPN connections
    c. Terminal Server connections
    d. Remote Desktop connections

40. To improve availability, you want to implement a server cluster for a custom-written network application. You are concerned about the clustering of the application because the network runs multiple LAN protocols. Which packet type is supported by a server cluster for applications? (Choose all that apply.)

   a. TCP
   b. UDP
   c. IPX
   d. NETBEUI
   e. AppleTalk

41. You want to implement an N+I failover server cluster to provide fault tolerance and load balancing of your Web servers. What is the maximum number of nodes supported?

   a. 4
   b. 8
   c. 16
   d. 32
   e. 64

42. Which of the following services is *not* cluster aware?

   a. DNS
   b. WINS
   c. DHCP
   d. RRAS
   e. all of the above
   f. none of the above

43. What type of affinity is enabled by default for network load balancing?

   a. None
   b. Single
   c. Multiple
   d. Class C

44. To secure LDAP traffic, you wish to implement SSL. To do so, what port do you need to open on the firewall for LDAP SSL traffic?

   a. 137
   b. 464
   c. 636
   d. 3268

45. You are performing a security audit on all workstations in your organization. You want to use the Microsoft Baseline Security Analyzer (MBSA) to verify security updates. Which of the following operating systems does MBSA support? (Choose all that apply.)

   a. Windows 95
   b. Windows 98
   c. Windows NT 4.0
   d. Windows 2000
   e. Windows XP

46. Which of the following statements regarding RIS flat images is correct? (Choose all that apply.)
    a. Flat images contain a fully installed operating system.
    b. Flat images contain a scripted installation of the operating system.
    c. Flat images do not contain applications.
    d. Flat images can be installed only on computers with similar hardware.

47. You need to prestage RIS clients to automatically install selected RIS images using the computer's GUID. However, some of the workstations do support PXE Boot ROM and must be started using the remote boot floppy. On what is the GUID based for non-PXE clients?
    a. computer name
    b. MAC address of the network card
    c. IP address
    d. DNS name of the computer

48. What command is used to remove all computer-specific settings from a computer before a third-party imaging utility is used?
    a. SYSPREP
    b. SETMGR
    c. RIPREP
    d. RBFG

49. You want to install RIS on a Windows Server 2003 member server. Which of the following is a requirement for installing RIS? (Choose all that apply.)
    a. RIS must be installed on a separate hard drive.
    b. RIS must be installed on an NTFS partition.
    c. RIS cannot be installed on the boot partition.
    d. RIS cannot be installed on the system partition.

50. Which service is *not* required for RIS to function?
    a. DNS
    b. DHCP
    c. Active Directory
    d. WINS

Glossary

802.11 — A standard for wireless communication created by the Institute of Electrical and Electronics Engineers (IEEE). The most common variant of wireless LAN is 802.11b.

802.11a — A not very common standard for wireless networks that is not backward compatible with 802.11b.

802.11b — A common standard for wireless networks that operates at 11 Mbps.

802.11g — A common standard for wireless networks that operates at 54 Mbps and is backward compatible with 802.11b.

802.1X — An authentication protocol that can be used with 802.11 networks to verify user identity before allowing a connection to the wireless network.

access control list (ACL)

access point (AP) — A device much like a hub or switch to which wireless clients can connect.

ACK bit — A bit used in TCP communication to indicate that a packet is an acknowledgment of a previous packet.

active/active server cluster — A cluster configuration in which all nodes provide services.

Active Directory — A directory service for Windows 2000 Server and Windows Server 2003 that stores information about network resources.

Active Directory client — The software for Windows 9x and Windows NT clients to let them use some Active Directory services, such as sites.

Active Directory integrated zone — A DNS zone in which DNS information is stored in Active Directory and supports multimaster updates and increased security.

Active Directory Service Interfaces (ADSI) — The interfaces used by programmers to access Active Directory. ADSI can also be used by administrators to manage Active Directory via scripts.

active/passive server cluster — A server cluster with one active node and one passive node. Services fail over from the active node to the passive node.

adapter — The networking component that represents the network interface card and driver.

Address Resolution Protocol (ARP) — A protocol used by hosts to find the physical MAC address of another host with a particular IP address.

address spoofing — The act of falsifying the source IP address in an IP packet, usually for malicious purposes.

affinity — The process for keeping a conversation between a client and server from being load-balanced. All requests from one client are directed to one host in the NLB cluster.

aging and scavenging — A feature of the Windows Server 2003 DNS server that deletes Dynamic DNS records after they have not been refreshed for a period of time.

algorithm — A mathematical formula used to process data for encryption or decryption.

AppleTalk — A protocol that is used when communicating with Apple Macintosh computers.

application directory partitions — The partitions that store information about objects that is replicated to a set of defined domain controllers within the same forest.

Application layer — The layer of the TCP/IP architecture that provides access to network resources.

asymmetric encryption — An encryption method that uses two different keys. When one key is used to encrypt, the other key must be used to decrypt.

Authentication Headers (AH) mode — The IPSec mode that performs authentication and ensures data integrity on the entire IP packet, including the headers.

automated system recovery (ASR) backup — A complete system backup that also creates a floppy disk that is used during the disaster recovery process.

Automatic Private IP Addressing (APIPA) — A feature of newer Windows operating systems that automatically generates an IP address on the 169.254.X.X network when a DHCP server cannot be contacted.

Automatic Updates — A Windows service that make the process of downloading and installing hotfixes automatic.

availability — The percentage of time that a server, service, or application is functioning properly.

backbone — A central communication point on a network that handles most of the data traffic.

backplane — The internal data processing area of a switch. This operates at a much faster speed than the individual ports to allow multiple conversations to pass through the switch at once.

Backup — A utility included with Windows Server 2003 that can back up and restore files and system state data.

Bandwidth Allocation Protocol (BAP) — A protocol used to dynamically control the number of phone lines multilink uses based on bandwidth utilization.

baseline security template — A security template that contains a set of security settings that define the minimum security settings that must be applied to a particular computer.

Berkeley Internet Name Domain (BIND) — A UNIX-based implementation of the Domain Name System created by the University of California at Berkeley.

binary — A base-two numbering system. There are only two valid values for each digit: 0 and 1.

binding — The process of configuring a network adapter to use a protocol. In Windows Server 2003, bindings are controlled by NDIS.

bit — A single binary digit.

Bluetooth — A short-range wireless communication protocol.

bottleneck — A point in the communication process that is slower than the others. Eliminating a bottleneck speeds up a process.

bridge — A network component that controls the movement of packets between network segments based on MAC addresses.

broadcast — A packet that is addressed to all computers on a network. A broadcast for the local network is addressed to 255.255.255.255.

burst handling — A process used by a WINS server that cannot write name registrations to the WINS database fast enough to keep pace with the number of registrations. The WINS server ceases verifying that the names are not in use before sending out successful name registration requests with a short TTL.

Cache time-out — The interval that defines how long other DNS servers and DNS clients cache records resolved through WINS. This is independent of the cache value used for other DNS records.

caching-only DNS server — A DNS server that is not responsible for any zones. It is used only to cache lookups as they occur to increase the speed of lookup times.

Carrier Sense Multiple Access/Collision Detection (CSMA/CD) — The access method used by Ethernet networks to decide which computer can communicate on the network and when.

certificates — A certificate for PKI that is a combination of public and private keys that can be used to encrypt or digitally sign information.

certificate hierarchy — The structure of trusted certification authorities consisting of a single root CA and possibly subordinate CAs.

Certificate Request Wizard — A wizard used to request certificates from an enterprise certification authority.

Certificate Revocation List (CRL) — A list of certificates that have been revoked before their expiration date.

Certificate Services — A service installed on Windows Server 2003 that allows it to act as a certification authority.

certificate templates — A template used by enterprise certification authorities to issue certificates with certain characteristics.

certification authority (CA) — A server that issues certificates.

Challenge Handshake Authentication Protocol (CHAP) — An authentication method that encrypts passwords using a one-way hash, but requires that passwords in Active Directory be stored using reversible encryption.

ciphertext — The data that has been encrypted.

classful routing — An older style of routing in which routing table entries would be based on Class A, B, and C networks with default subnet masks.

classless inter-domain routing (CIDR) — An addressing scheme that uses a defined number of bits for the subnet mask rather than relying on default lengths based on address classes. The number of bits in the network ID is defined by /*XX* after the IP address. *XX* is the number of bits.

client — A networking component that is installed on computers requesting network services. Client software communicates with a corresponding service.

Cluster — A command-line utility to manage server clusters.

Cluster Administrator — A GUI utility to manage server clusters.

cluster-aware applications — The applications that understand clustering and can take advantage of the clustering API.

cluster-unaware applications — The applications that have not been written to use cluster services.

clustering — The process of combining a group of computers to coordinate the provision of services. When one computer in a cluster fails, others take over its services.

coaxial — An older type of cabling that used a single conducting core to transmit data. The cabling for cable TV is a type of coaxial cable.

collision — The result of two computers transmitting data on a CSMA/CD network at the same time.

collision domain — The area of a network in which a collision can occur when two computers communicate. Each port of a switch or router is a separate collision domain.

Common Gateway Interface (CGI) — A vendor-neutral mechanism used to pass information from a Web page to an application running on a Web server.

Common Language Runtime (CLR) — A common component that runs code developed for the .NET Framework regardless of the language in which it is written.

Compatws.inf — A template that weakens the default security to allow legacy applications to run under Windows Server 2003.

COM port — The Windows term for a serial port in a computer.

conditional forwarder — A DNS server that uses forwarders based on the domain name being resolved. It uses forwarders for some domains, but not others.

conditions — The criteria in a remote access policy, or a connection request policy, that must be met for the policy to be applied.

connectionless — A term used to describe a protocol that does not establish a communication channel before sending data.

Connection Manager Administration Kit (CMAK) — A utility that can be used to configure dial-up and VPN connections on client computers.

connection-oriented — A term used to describe a protocol that verifies the existence of a host and agrees on terms of communication before sending data.

connection request policy — A policy used by IAS to determine whether a request is authenticated locally or passed on to a RADIUS server. Such policies are composed of conditions and a profile.

cost — In routing, a configurable value assigned to a packet being forwarded through a router interface.

cryptographic service provider (CSP) — The software or hardware that provides cryptographic services.

cryptography — The process of encrypting and decrypting messages and files using an algorithm.

data encryption standard (DES) — An algorithm for data encryption defined by the U.S. government in 1977 that uses a 56-bit key.

data modification — The process of modifying the contents of packets that have been captured with a packet sniffer before resending them on the network.

data replay — The process of resending packets that have been previously captured with a packet sniffer.

data security — The process of controlling access to data by ensuring that only authorized users are able to access data.

DC Security.inf — A template that is applied automatically whenever a Windows 2000 or Windows Server 2003 member server is promoted to a domain controller. It maintains settings for Active Directory security.

debug logging — The process of logging additional DNS-related events or messages for troubleshooting purposes.

decryption — The process of making encrypted data readable.

default gateway — A dedicated hardware device or computer on a network that is responsible for moving packets from one IP network to another. This is another term for IP router.

delegate authority — The process of specifying a different DNS server as authoritative for a subdomain. This is done by dividing the DNS namespace among multiple DNS servers.

delegated subdomain — A subdomain for which the authority for management has been assigned to a dif-

ferent DNS server than the one that is authoritative for the main domain. For example, a UNIX server may be authoritative for the external domain used by a company, but a Windows DNS server is responsible for handling the internal subdomain that holds the records for Active Directory.

demand-dial — A dial-up/VPN/PPPoE connection that is only activated when required to move network traffic.

demand-dial filters — The rules that limit the types of traffic that can trigger the activation of a demand-dial connection.

demilitarized zone (DMZ) — An Internet-accessible subnet between the Internet and a private network that is protected by firewalls.

device driver rollback — An option to restore a previously installed device driver.

DHCPACK — A packet sent from a DHCP server to a client when a renewal attempt or DHCP lease is successful.

DHCP allocator — A simplified DHCP service that can be used by NAT and ICS.

DHCPDISCOVER — The first packet in the DHCP lease process. This packet is broadcast on the local network to find a DHCP server.

DHCPINFORM — A DHCP packet sent by Windows 2000 and newer remote access clients to retrieve IP configuration options from a DHCP server.

DHCPNAK — A packet sent from a DHCP server to a client when it denies a renewal attempt.

DHCPOFFER — The second packet in the DHCP lease process. This packet is a broadcast from the DHCP server to the client with an offered lease.

DHCPRELEASE — A packet sent from a DHCP client to a DHCP server to indicate it is no longer using a leased IP address.

DHCPREQUEST — The third packet in the DHCP lease process. This packet is a broadcast from the DHCP client indicating which DHCPOFFER has been chosen.

dial-out hours — A limit for demand-dial connections that allows connections only during certain time periods.

distance-vector routing — Any routing algorithm based on simple hop calculation. RIP is the most common example.

dial-up — The connectivity between two computers using modems and a phone line.

differential backups — A backup of all files that have changed since a full backup. The archive attribute of backed up files is unaffected.

digital signature — A process using a cryptographic algorithm that ensures data integrity and nonrepudiation.

directed broadcast — A broadcast packet that can be routed to a particular network. The address is composed on the network address with all of the host bits set to 1.

Distributed File System (DFS) — A service that makes file shares stored on multiple servers appear as a single logical structure for users. It can also replicate content between servers for fault tolerance.

domain name — The portion of a DNS namespace that can be registered and controlled by an organization or individual.

Domain Name System (DNS) — A service used by clients running TCP/IP to resolve host names to IP addresses. Active Directory uses DNS to store service location information.

DNSCmd — A command-line utility for viewing and managing DNS information on Windows Server 2003.

DNSLint — An advanced utility for DNS troubleshooting that generates reports in HTML format.

DNS namespace — The portion of DNS for which a server or organization is responsible. For example, a domain name that can be registered is a DNS namespace.

DNS proxy — A service that accepts DNS requests from clients and forwards them on to a DNS server.

DNS zone — The part of the domain namespace for which a DNS server is authoritative. Commonly referred to as a "zone."

DnsUpdateProxy — A group used when multiple DHCP servers will be performing secure Dynamic DNS updates. Updates performed by members of this group have no security permissions assigned.

domain controller — A server running Windows 2000 Server or Windows Server 2003 that holds a copy of the Active Directory information for a domain.

domain directory partition — A partition that stores information about objects in a specific domain that is replicated to all domain controllers in the domain.

Domain Name System (DNS) — A service used by clients running TCP/IP to resolve host names to IP addresses. Active Directory uses DNS to store service location information.

Dynamic DNS — A system in which DNS records are automatically updated by the client or a DHCP server.

Dynamic Host Configuration Protocol (DHCP) — A service used by the Windows operating system to automatically assign IP addressing information to clients.

dynamic routing — The process by which routing tables are automatically generated by routers based on communication with other routers.

Encapsulating Security Payload (ESP) mode — The IPSec mode that performs authentication, data integrity, and encryption on the data portion of an IP packet. Integrity of IP headers is not performed.

encryption — The process of rendering data unreadable by applying an algorithm.

enrollment agent — A user authorized to request certificates for other users. An enrollment agent loads certificates onto smart cards for users.

Enterprise Admins — A default group in Active Directory with administrative rights for the entire forest.

enterprise certification authority — A certification authority that integrates with Active Directory, and can issue certificates without administrator intervention.

event logging — The logging of status messages in an event log. This logging is less detailed than debug logging.

exclusion — An IP address or range of IP addresses within a scope that are not leased to clients.

Extensible Authentication Protocol (EAP) — An authentication system that uses EAP types as plug-in authentication modules. This is used for smart cards.

Extensible Markup Language (XML) — A simple text-based mechanism to define content. It uses tags similar to HTML, but unlike HTML, developers can define their own tags.

Extension Mechanisms for DNS (EDNS0) — A new protocol for DNS that allows DNS servers to send query responses in UDP packets larger than 512 bytes.

external DNS — The DNS namespace that is used to hold records for Internet accessible resources.

extinction interval — The period of time that unused records exist in the WINS database before being marked as extinct.

extinction timeout — The period of time that extinct records exist in the WINS database before being removed.

failback — The process whereby a resource group migrates back to its original node after failover has occurred.

failover — The process whereby a resource group migrates from a failed node to a new node.

fails over — The process of a service stopping on one member of a cluster and starting on another.

fiber-optic — A type of cabling that uses glass fiber for a conducting core. This type of cabling is very difficult to tap into.

File Transfer Protocol (FTP) — A protocol that is used on the Internet to transfer files. By default, it uses TCP ports 20 and 21.

flat image — An image for RIS that performs a scripted installation of an operating system.

forwarding-only DNS server — A DNS server that uses forwarders when attempting to resolve DNS queries, but does not use the root servers on the Internet.

forward lookup — The process of resolving a domain name to an IP address.

forward lookup zone — A zone that holds records used for forward lookups. The primary record types contained in these zones are A records, MX records, and SRV records.

full backup — A backup of all data that turns off the archive attribute on each file that is backed up.

full-duplex — A transmission mode in which a computer can send and receive data at the same time.

fully qualified domain name (FQDN) — The combination of a host name and domain name that completely describes the name of a computer within the global DNS system.

globally unique identifier (GUID) — A unique identifier embedded in a PXE boot ROM.

graphical user interface (GUI) — A user interface for an operating system that supports graphics in addition to characters.

Group Policy — An Active Directory-based mechanism to apply centrally defined configuration information out to client computers.

Group Policy Objects (GPOs)

half-duplex — A transmission mode in which a computer can transmit or receive data, but not both at the same time.

hash encryption — A type of one-way encryption that cannot be decrypted. It is used to store information such as passwords and to create checksums.

hash value — A summary of the data being encrypted using hash encryption.

heartbeat packets — The packets sent between nodes in a cluster to confirm that all nodes are still operational.

Hfnetchk — An older command-line utility used to verify patch levels on Windows clients and servers. The functionality of this utility is now in MBSA.

Hisecdc.inf — A template that can be incrementally applied after the secure templates have been applied. It must be applied only to domain controllers.

Hisecweb.inf — A Security Configuration Manager template that configures a basic Windows 2000 system-wide policy to support a machine's use as a secure Web server.

Hisecws.inf — A template that can be incrementally applied after the secure templates have been applied. It is used for workstations of servers.

hops — In routing, a packet being forwarded by a single router.

host ID — The portion of an IP address that uniquely identifies a computer on an IP network.

host name — The name of a computer using the TCP/IP protocol.

hosts — A local text file used to resolve fully qualified domain names to IP addresses.

hotfixes — The small patches to fix security and stability problems that are considered too severe to wait for the next service pack.

hubs — A device that propagates all packets that receive it. Hubs operate at the Physical layer of the OSI model and forward packets to all ports except the one on which they received the packets.

Hypertext Transfer Protocol (HTTP) — The protocol used by Web browsers and Web servers. By default, it uses TCP port 80.

Ignore-User-Dialin-Properties — An attribute that can be configured in the profile of a remote access policy that prevents processing of the dial-in properties of a user object in Active Directory.

incremental backup — A backup of files that have changed since the previous incremental backup or previous full backup. The archive attribute is turned off on all files that are backed up.

incremental zone transfer — The process of updating only modified DNS records from a primary DNS server to a secondary DNS server.

Institute of Electrical and Electronics Engineers (IEEE) — The organization responsible for maintaining many Physical layer protocols used in networks, including Ethernet and Token Ring.

internal DNS — The DNS namespace that is used to hold records for internal resources that are not accessible from the Internet.

Internet service provider (ISP) — A company that sells Internet access.

Internet Authentication Service (IAS) — The Microsoft implementation of a RADIUS server. It allows distributed authentication for remote access clients.

Internet Connection Sharing (ICS) — An automated way to configure DHCP, NAT, and DNS proxy to share a single IP address and configuration information from an ISP.

Internet Connection Firewall (ICF) — A stateful packet filter that can be used to protect servers connected to the Internet.

Internet Control Messaging Protocol (ICMP) — The protocol used by routers and hosts to send Internet protocol error messages.

Internet Group Management Protocol (IGMP) — The protocol used by routers to track the membership in multicast groups.

Internet Information Services (IIS) — A popular suite of Internet services that includes a Web server and FTP server.

Internet Key Exchange (IKE) — A protocol used by IPSec to negotiate security parameters, perform authentication, and ensure the secure exchange of encryption keys.

Internet layer — The layer of the TCP/IP architecture that is responsible for logical addressing and routing.

Internet Message Access Protocol version 4 (IMAP4) — A protocol used to retrieve e-mail messages from an e-mail server. It is more flexible than POP3 for managing message storage.

Internet Protocol version 4 (IPv4) — The version of the Internet Protocol (IP) that is used on the Internet. It is the IP part of TCP/IP.

Internet Protocol version 6 (IPv6) — An updated version of Internet Protocol that uses 128-bit addresses and provides many new features.

Internet Server Application Program Interface (ISAPI) — A programmer interface defined by Microsoft for passing information from Web pages to programs running on a Web server.

Internetwork Packet eXchange/Sequenced Packet eXchange (IPX/SPX) — The protocol required to communicate with servers running Novell NetWare 4 and earlier.

IP filter list — A list of IP protocols that are affected by a rule in an IPSec policy.

IPSec filter action — The setting that defines what is done to traffic that matches an IP filter list in an IPSec rule.

IPSec policies — The sets of rules that define how packets are treated by IPSec. An IPSec policy must be applied to be in use.

IPSec rules — The combination of an IP filter list and an IPSec filter action.

IPSec Security Monitor — An MMC snap-in that allows the monitoring of IPSec security associations and configurations.

IP Security (IPSec) — A service used with IPv4 to prevent eavesdropping on communication and to prevent data from being modified in transit.

Itanium — A 64-bit processor family manufactured by Intel.

Kerberos — An authentication mechanism used to verify the validity of user information when Windows 2000 and newer clients log on to Active Directory.

key — A number, usually large, to prevent it from being guessed, used in combination with an algorithm to encrypt data.

LAN protocol — A networking protocol required to communicate over a LAN, or over a remote access connection. The same LAN protocol that is used by clients on the LAN must be used by dial-up and VPN clients to access LAN resources remotely.

Last known good configuration — A startup option used for troubleshooting that restores the part of the registry responsible for service and device driver configuration.

latency — The time lag between a network device receiving a signal and sending it out again.

Layer Two Tunneling Protocol (L2TP) — A protocol that places packets inside an L2TP packet to move them across an IP-based network. This can be used to move IPX or AppleTalk packets through a network that is not configured to support them.

lease — The length of time a DHCP client computer is allowed to use IP address information from the DHCP server.

Lightweight Directory Access Protocol (LDAP) — A protocol used to look up directory information from a server.

Link Control Protocol (LCP) — An extension to PPP that allows the use of enhancements such as callback.

link-state routing — A routing algorithm in which routers use a configurable cost metric to build a picture of the entire network. OSPF is the most common example.

Linux — An open source operating system that is very similar to UNIX.

LMHOSTS — A static text file located on the hard drive of NetBIOS clients that is used to resolve NetBIOS names to IP addresses.

load balancing — The act of two or more computers sharing a single IP address to provide a service to clients. The load balanced computers share the responsibility of providing the service.

Local Address Table (LAT) — Used by proxy devices; it contains local internal addresses and must be correctly configured.

local area network (LAN) — A computer network that is contained within a single building. A LAN usually has a minimum speed of 10 Mbps.

local broadcast — A broadcast packet addressed to the IP address 255.255.255.255. This is received by all computers on the local network.

Local Security Settings snap-in — Used to apply security settings directly to a computer.

Lookup time-out — The time a DNS server waits for a WINS server to respond before returning an error to the requesting client.

loopback — Any IP address that begins with 127.X.X.X. These addresses represent the local host.

mappings — An entry in the NAT table maintained by the NAT router that provides correlation between the original source IP address and port number and the port number used on the external interface of the NAT router.

Maximum Transmission Unit (MTU) — The largest size of packet that Windows Server 2003 will create. By default, this is defined by the network architecture being used. The default MTU for Ethernet is 1,500 bytes.

member server — A Windows server that is part of a domain but is not a domain controller.

Message Digest 5 (MD5) — A hashing algorithm that produces a 128-bit message digest.

Metadirectory Services — A service in Windows that synchronizes Active Directory content with other directories and databases.

Microsoft Baseline Security Analyzer (MBSA) — A tool that can be used to verify security updates and security settings on a wide variety of Microsoft operating systems and applications.

Microsoft Challenge Handshake Authentication Protocol (MS-CHAP) — An enhancement to CHAP that allows Active Directory passwords to be stored using nonreversible encryption.

Microsoft Challenge Handshake Authentication Protocol version 2 (MS-CHAPv2) — An authentication method that adds computer authentication and several other enhancements to MS-CHAP. This is the preferred authentication protocol for most remote access connections.

mobile users — The users who move from one location to another outside of the local network. They require remote access to use network resources.

modem pool — A group of modems connected to a remote access dial-up server. In high-volume situations, it is implemented as specialized hardware.

modems — The hardware devices that enable computers to communicate over a phone line. They convert digital signals from a computer to analog signals that can travel over a phone line, and then back to digital format.

multicast — A packet that is addressed to a specific group of computers rather than a single computer. Multicast addresses range from 224.0.0.0 to 239.255. 255.255.

multicast scope — A range of multicast IP addresses that are handed out to applications that request them.

multilink — A system for dial-up connections that allows multiple phone lines to be treated as a single logical unit to increase connection speeds.

N+I failover server cluster — A variation of an active/passive server cluster in which multiple passive nodes wait for services to fail over from multiple active nodes.

name query request — A packet from a WINS client to a WINS server requesting the resolution of a NetBIOS name to an IP address.

name query response — A packet from a WINS server to a WINS client in response to a name query request. If the request is successful, this contains the IP address for the NetBIOS name in the original request.

name refresh request — A packet from a WINS client to a WINS server requesting that the registration for a NetBIOS name be renewed.

name refresh response — A packet from a WINS server to a WINS client in response to a name refresh request. If the response is successful, the TTL of the client lease is extended.

name registration request — A packet generated by a WINS client and sent to a WINS server requesting to register the NetBIOS name and IP address.

name registration response — A packet generated by a WINS server in response to a name registration request from a WINS client. The response can be successful or negative.

name release request — A packet sent from a WINS client to a WINS server when the WINS client shuts down.

name release response — A packet from a WINS server to a WINS client in response to a name release request. This packet contains the NetBIOS name being released and a TTL of zero.

nbtstat — A command to view the contents of the NetBIOS name cache.

NetBIOS name cache — The location in which the results of Windows client NetBIOS name resolutions are stored for 10 minutes. The storage of these resolutions increases network performance by reducing the number of name resolutions on the network.

NetBIOS name server — A server that holds a centralized repository of NetBIOS name information. The Microsoft implementation of a NetBIOS name server is WINS.

netlogon — A service that controls user authentication, Active Directory replication, and Dynamic DNS updates for domain controllers.

Netscape Server Application Program Interface (NSAPI) — A programmer interface defined by Netscape to pass information from Web pages to applications running on a Web server.

NetWare — A network operating system from Novell that traditionally uses the IPX/SPX protocol.

Network Address Translation (NAT) — A service that allows multiple computers to access the Internet by sharing a single public IP address.

Network Basic Input/Output System (NetBIOS) — An older interface used by programmers to access network resources.

network bridging — A feature that combines two network cards in a server as a single, logical network. This can be used to combine two different media types, such as UTP and coaxial cabling.

Network Driver Interface Specification (NDIS) — An interface for developers that resides between protocols and adapters. It controls the bindings between protocols and adapters.

network ID — The portion of an IP address that designates the network on which a computer resides. This is defined by the subnet mask.

Network Interface layer — The layer of the TCP/IP architecture that controls placing packets on the physical network media.

Network Load Balancing (NLB) — A service that distributes client requests among multiple servers with the same application installed.

Network Load Balancing Manager — A GUI utility for managing NLB clusters.

Network Monitor — Used to look at traffic types and trends. It can help you revisit and adjust services running on the network to improve performance, extrapolate future need based on current trends, and schedule certain traffic generating activities for off-peak hours.

network monitor tool — A limited network monitor that can capture traffic flowing through an interface on the local computer only.

network operating system (NOS) — An operating system that is optimized to act as a server rather than a client.

network security — The process of controlling access to network resources through a computer network.

Nlb — A command-line utility for managing NLB clusters.

NLB driver — The driver that intercepts TCP/IP traffic on an NLB cluster host and applies port rules.

nonrecursive DNS server — A DNS server that looks only at zones stored locally when attempting to resolve DNS queries.

Non-Uniform Memory Access (NUMA) — A memory architecture for servers with multiple processors. It adds a third level of cache memory on motherboards.

Nslookup — A command prompt-based utility for troubleshooting DNS.

octet — A group of eight bits. An IP address is composed of four octets, with each expressed as a decimal number.

Open Shortest Path First (OSPF) — A link-state routing protocol that calculates paths based on a configurable metric called cost. Changes to the routing table are advertised only when they occur.

Open Shortest Path First (OSPF) — A protocol that is used by routers to share information about known networks and calculate the best path through an internetwork. OSPF calculates routes based on user-definable cost values.

Open Systems Interconnection (OSI) reference model — An industry standard that is used as a reference point to compare different networking technologies and protocols.

packet sniffer — The software used to view (capture) all packets that are traveling on a network.

packets — A packet is a single unit of data sent from one computer to another. It contains a source address, destination address, data, and error-checking information.

Password Authentication Protocol (PAP) — An authentication method that transmits passwords in clear text.

Path MTU Discovery (P-MTU-D) — A process used by servers to determine the largest MTU supported by all networks between the server and a remote host. This is done to eliminate packet fragmentation.

persistent connections — A connection that is created once and maintained over time for data transfer. This reduces communication overhead by reducing the number of packets used to establish connections over time.

personal identification number (PIN) — An alphanumeric password that is required to decrypt the contents of a smart card.

physical security — The process of controlling physical access to the computing devices on your network.

Ping — A utility used to test connectivity by sending an ICMP Echo packet.

Point-to-Point Protocol over Ethernet (PPPoE) — A protocol used for authentication and traffic control on high-speed Internet connections such as DSL.

Point-to-Point Protocol (PPP) — The most common remote access protocol used for dial-up connections. It supports the use of TCP/IP, IPX/SPX, and AppleTalk for remote access.

Point-to-Point Tunneling Protocol (PPTP) — A protocol that can be used to provide VPN connectivity between a Windows client and VPN server. PPTP is supported by Windows 95 and later.

poison-reverse processing — An option for RIP routing in which a router advertises a route as unreachable on the interface from which it was learned.

port — A TCP port or UDP port is used by Transport layer protocols to direct network information to the proper service.

port rules — The rules that define how traffic is to be load-balanced among the hosts in an NLB cluster.

Post Office Protocol version 3 (POP3) — A protocol that is used to retrieve e-mail messages from an e-mail server.

Pre-Boot eXecution Environment (PXE) boot ROM — A ROM on a network card that allows a computer to boot and run directly from the network without using a local operating system.

preshared key — An IPSec authentication method in which each device is preconfigured with a string of text.

primary WINS server — The first WINS server that a WINS client is configured to use.

primary zone — A zone that is authoritative for the specific DNS zone. Updates can only be made in the primary zone. There is only one primary zone per domain name.

private key — The key in asymmetric encryption that is seen only by the user to which it is issued.

profile — The part of a remote access policy, or connection request policy, that contains settings that are applied to the connection.

project manager — The leader of a project team who ensures a project is completed on time and on budget.

promiscuous mode — A network card mode in which all packets are passed up the protocol stack regardless of the destination MAC address.

protocol — The language that two computers use to communicate on a network. Two computers must use the same protocol to communicate.

proxy server — A server that can be used to control and speed up access to the Internet. It also allows multiple computers to access the Internet through a single IP address.

public key — The key in asymmetric encryption that is freely distributed to other users.

Public Key Infrastructure (PKI) — A system to create and manage public keys, private keys, and certificates.

pull replication — The replication between two WINS servers triggered by a defined amount of time passing.

push replication — The replication between two WINS servers triggered by a defined number of changes in the WINS database.

quorum resource — A special disk resource used by the server cluster to store configuration information and arbitrate which node owns the cluster.

RADIUS client — A server or device that passes authentication requests to a RADIUS proxy or RADIUS server. Most commonly, these are RASs.

RADIUS proxy — An intelligent server that acts as an intermediary between RADIUS clients and RADIUS servers. This server decides which RADIUS server should be used to authenticate a request.

RADIUS server — A server in the RADIUS process that accepts and authorizes authentication requests from RADIUS clients and RADIUS proxies.

RAID5 — A disk storage system that spreads data across multiple hard drives and adds parity information. A single disk in a RAID5 set can fail with no loss of data.

Recovery Console — A command-line interface that can be used to access system settings and files when Windows cannot be started properly.

recursive lookup — A DNS query that is resolved through other DNS servers until the requested information is located.

registrar — A company accredited by ICANN who has the right to distribute and register domain names.

remote access — The ability to access network resources from a location away from the physical network. Connections can be made using dial-up or VPN connections.

remote access permission — The part of a remote access policy that defines whether the policy denies remote access or grants remote access.

remote access policies — The policies configured on RASs to control how remote access connections are created. They are composed of conditions, remote access permissions, and a profile.

remote access protocols — A protocol that is required for dial-up remote access. PPP is the most common remote access protocol.

Remote Assistance — A system that allows users to request assistance from support staff via e-mail, Microsoft Instant Messenger, or a file. It allows support staff to view or take remote control of a remote system.

Remote Authentication Dial-In User Service (RADIUS) — A service that allows RASs (RADIUS clients) to delegate responsibility for authentication to a central server (RADIUS server).

Remote Boot Floppy Generator (rbfg.exe) — A utility that is used to create a bootable floppy disk that emulates a PXE boot ROM.

Remote Desktop — A method to remote manage Windows Server 2003. When Remote Desktop is used, an administrator or other authorized user can view the server desktop from a workstation and run applications.

Remote Desktop Connection — A client utility that connects to a server running Terminal Services.

Remote Desktop for Administration — A remote administration solution for servers that allows two administrators at a time to connect via Terminal Services.

Remote Desktops snap-in — A client utility that connects to multiple terminal servers at the same time.

Remote Installation Services (RIS) — A service included with Windows Server 2003 that can be used to image Windows Server 2003, Windows XP, and Windows 2000 computers.

Remote RADIUS server groups — The groupings of RADIUS servers to which IAS forwards connection requests when acting as a RADIUS proxy. Load balancing and fault tolerance can be configured.

renewal interval — The TTL handed out to WINS clients when they register NetBIOS names.

replication partners — Two WINS servers that synchronize information in their databases.

Request for Comment (RFC) — A submission to the Internet Engineering Task Force that is evaluated for use as part of the TCP/IP protocol suite.

reservation — A DHCP IP address that is leased only to a computer with a specific MAC address.

resource groups — The logical groupings of resources that fail over as a single unit.

Resultant Set of Policy (RSoP) snap-in — An MMC snap-in that is used to troubleshoot the implementation of Group Policies.

reverse lookup — The process of resolving an IP address to a domain name.

reverse lookup zone — A zone that contains records used for reverse lookups. The primary record type in these zones is PTR records.

RIPrep image — An image for RIS that includes a fully installed operating system and applications.

rogue services — The unauthorized services that may have been installed by an administrator or a hacker.

root certification authority — The first CA in the certificate hierarchy. Clients trusting this CA trust certificates issued by this CA and all subordinate CAs.

root hints — The list of root servers that is used by DNS servers to perform forward lookups on the Internet.

root servers — A group of 13 DNS servers on the Internet that are authoritative for the top-level domain names, such as .com, .edu, and .org.

round robin DNS — The process of creating multiple IP addresses for a specific host name for fault tolerance and load balancing.

ROUTE PRINT — A command-line utility used to view the contents of a routing table.

router — A network device that moves packets from one network to another. TCP/IP, IPX/SPX, and AppleTalk can be routed.

routers — The network devices that operate at the Network layer of the OSI model and control packet movement based on IP addresses. Routers maintain a list of IP networks, not individual hosts.

Routing and Remote Access Service (RRAS) — The Windows Server 2003 service that is responsible for controlling routing, dial-up, and VPN connections.

Routing Information Protocol (RIP) — A protocol used by routers to exchange routing table information and determine the best path through an internetwork based on the number of hops.

routing table — A list of IP networks maintained by a router. Routers use this table to look up where packets should be forwarded.

safe mode — A startup option for troubleshooting that loads a minimal set of drivers.

scalability — The ability to expand the capacity of a server or application.

scaling out — The process of adding capacity by adding additional servers.

scaling up — The process of adding additional capacity to a single server.

scope creep — A term that refers to the expansion of a project beyond its original goals.

Secedit — A command-line utility that can be used to analyze and configure client computers by using security templates.

secondary WINS server — A WINS server that is used by a WINS client when it is unable to contact the primary WINS server.

secondary zone — A DNS zone that stores a read-only copy of the DNS information from a primary zone. There can be multiple secondary zones.

secure channels — The communication channels used by Windows NT/2000/XP/2003 computers that are members of a domain.

secure dynamic updates — The process of controlling Dynamic DNS updates based on Active Directory permissions. These are available only for Active Directory-integrated zones.

Secure Hash Algorithm (SHA1) — A hashing algorithm that produces a 160-bit message digest.

Secure Sockets Layer (SSL) — A Transport Layer protocol that encrypts data communication between a client and service. Both the client and service must be written to support SSL.

security association (SA) — The security terms negotiated between two hosts using IPSec.

Security Configuration and Analysis snap-in — A snap-in that can be used to analyze and configure client computers by using security templates.

security template — A group of security settings that can be applied to a server or client computer.

Serial Line Internet Protocol (SLIP) — An older remote access protocol that only supports using TCP/IP as a LAN protocol. It is used by Windows Server 2003 only when acting as a client.

server clusters — The groups of servers that provide highly available services with the ability to fail over from one server in the cluster to another.

Server Message Block (SMB) — The protocol used by Windows servers for file and printer sharing.

service — A networking component that provides information to network clients. Each service communicates with corresponding client software.

service pack — A collection of patches for the Windows operating system.

Services for Macintosh — A service that allows Macintosh clients to access file and print services on Windows servers.

scope — A range of addresses that are leased by a DHCP server.

shared disks — The storage that is accessible to all nodes in a cluster.

Shiva Password Authentication Protocol (SPAP) — An authentication method that uses reversible encryption when transmitting passwords.

Simple Object Access Protocol (SOAP) — A standardized XML-based mechanism to access Web services using HTTP, SMTP, and MIME.

Simple Mail Transfer Protocol (SMTP) — A protocol used by e-mail clients to send messages to e-mail servers. It uses TCP port 25.

single node virtual server — A type of cluster with only one node that is used to consolidate multiple servers without reconfiguring clients.

sliding window — A process used in the TCP protocol to track which packets have been received by the destination host.

SYN bit — A bit used in TCP communication to indicate a request to start a communication session.

smart card — A physical device about the size of a credit card that contains a certificate that can be used to identify users. It can also hold additional information about users.

smart card certificate enrollment station — A computer that is used to configure smart cards for users.

smart card reader — A device used to read smart cards. It can be an internal or external device.

SMB signing — A mechanism to ensure that SMB packets are not tampered with while in transit on the network.

smurf attack — An attack in which ping request packets with a false source IP address are sent to a directed broadcast address. All hosts that receive the directed broadcast respond by sending a ping reply to the false source IP address, resulting in a denial of service attack on the false source IP address.

Software Update Services (SUS) — A service for Windows 2000 Server and Windows Server 2003 that automatically downloads the latest hotfixes and service packs from Windows Update and makes them available to other computers on the LAN.

split-horizon processing — An option for RIP routing in which a router is not advertised back on the same interface from which it was learned to prevent routing loops.

stand-alone certification authority — A certification authority that does not integrate with Active Directory, and requires an administrator to approve certificate requests.

stand-alone server — A Windows server that is not a member of a domain.

star topology — A physical network layout in which one central location is connected to several satellite locations.

start of authority (SOA) — A DNS record that defines which DNS server is authoritative for that particular domain and defines the characteristics for the zone.

stateful applications — An application that tracks ongoing information about a client session.

stateful firewall — A firewall that tracks TCP connections to allow response packets to return automatically without configuring a rule.

static routes — An entry in a routing table that is permanently added by an administrator.

static routing — The process by which routing tables are maintained manually by an administrator. Windows 2003 also has the ability to build static routes with an automated process called auto-static updates.

stateless application — An application that does not track ongoing information about a user session.

static mapping — An entry manually placed in the WINS database. These are normally created for servers providing NetBIOS services that are unable to use WINS.

stripe set — A storage system in which data is evenly spread among hard drives with no parity information. If any disk in a stripe set fails, all data is lost.

stub zone — A DNS zone that stores only the NS records for a particular zone. When a client requests a DNS lookup, the request is then forwarded to the DNS server specified by the NS records.

subnet mask — A string of 32 bits that is used to define which portion of an IP address is the host ID and which part is the network ID.

subnetting — A process by which a single large network is subdivided into smaller networks to control traffic flow.

subordinate certification authority — A certification authority that has been authorized by a root CA or another subordinate CA.

supernetting — The process of combining several smaller networks into a single large network by taking bits from the network ID and making them part of the host ID.

superscope — A logical grouping of scopes that is used to service network segments with more than one subnet in use.

switches — A network device that operates at the Data Link layer of the OSI model and control the movement of packets based on MAC addresses. Switches propagate broadcasts, but control unicast packets.

symmetric encryption — Encryption that uses the same key to encrypt and decrypt data.

Sysprep — A utility that is used to prepare computers to be imaged with third-party imaging software.

system state data — The set of data that includes the registry, COM+ Class Registration database, boot files, system files, Certificate Services Database, Active Directory Database, Sysvol folder, and the IIS metabase. It cannot be backed up across the network using Backup.

Telnet — A protocol used to access remotely a command-line interface on UNIX and Linux servers.

terminal server — A system that allows many users to view a remote desktop on a server. This is normally used to provide access to a line of business applications. Each user gets their own version of the desktop.

Terminal Services — A remote access solution that lets users connect to and run applications on a remote computer.

throughput — The actual amount of data that can be transmitted on a network rather than the theoretical data-carrying capacity.

timed lease — An IP address and set of configuration options given to a client computer from a DHCP server for a limited period of time.

Time to Live (TTL) — A parameter of IP packets used to ensure that if a packet becomes trapped in a router loop, it will expire. Each hop through a router reduces TTL by one.

tombstoned — The term used to describe a WINS record that has been marked for deletion from all WINS servers. The tombstoned status is replicated among all WINS servers.

top-level domain (TLD) — The broadest category of names in the DNS hierarchy under which all domain names fit. Some top-level domains include .com, .edu, and .gov.

topology — The physical layout of the network and how signals travel on the network.

Transmission Control Protocol (TCP) — A connection-oriented and reliable Transport layer protocol that is part of the TCP/IP protocol suite.

Transmission Control Protocol/Internet Protocol (TCP/IP) — A suite of protocols that allows interconnected networks to communicate with one another. It is the most common protocol in Windows networking and must be used to access the Internet.

Transport Driver Interface (TDI) — A software layer that exists between client or service software and protocols. Clients and services use this layer to access network resources.

Transport layer — The layer of the TCP/IP architecture that breaks messages into smaller packets and tracks their delivery.

transport mode — The IPSec mode used when two hosts create a security association directly between them.

triple data encryption standard (3DES) — A data encryption algorithm that uses three 56-bit keys in three rounds to give an effective key length of 168 bits.

trusted root certification authorities — A CA from which a client or application accepts certificates.

tunnel endpoint — The other end of the tunnel with the local host (in tunnel mode).

tunnel mode — The IPSec mode used when two routers encapsulate all traffic transferred between two or more networks.

twisted-pair — A type of cable that is composed of pairs of wires, with each pair twisted together. The most common variety of twisted pair cabling is Category 5 Enhanced, which has four twisted pairs.

unauthorized zone transfers — A zone transfer requested and obtained by an unauthorized server or person.

unicast — A packet addressed to a single IP host.

Universal Description, Discovery and Integration (UDDI) — A worldwide database of businesses and the Web services that they offer.

User class — An identifier from the DHCP client that is sent as part of the DHCP lease process. This can be set manually by the administrator on workstations.

User Datagram Protocol (UDP) — A connectionless, unreliable Transport layer protocol used in the TCP/IP protocol suite.

v.90 — A standard for modems that allows downloads at 56 Kbps and uploads at 33.6 Kbps.

v.92 — A standard for modems that allows downloads at 56 Kbps and uploads at 48 Kbps.

Vendor class — An identifier from the DHCP client that is sent as part of the DHCP lease process. This is based on the operating system in use.

verification interval — The period of time a WINS server waits before validating a record that has been replicated from another WINS server.

virtual IP address — The IP address on which cluster resources are available.

virtual LAN (VLAN) — A broadcast domain created by a switch based on subnets, protocols, MAC addresses, or switch ports.

virtual private network (VPN) — The encrypted communications across a public network such as the Internet. This is less expensive than implementing private lines for connectivity.

virtual server — The representation of the cluster service on the network.

volume shadow copy — A service that takes a snapshot of files at a particular point in time, even if they are open.

Web services — The platform-independent services that are available across the Internet or an IP network.

Web Services Description Language (WSDL) — A standardized, XML-formatted mechanism to describe Web services. WSDL is used by UDDI to describe available services.

Web Distributed Authoring and Versioning (WebDAV) — A protocol that allows documents to be shared using HTTP.

wide area network (WAN) — A network consisting of more than one physical location. Connec-tivity between physical locations is usually slower than 10 Mbps.

Windows Internet Naming Service (WINS) — A service used to resolve NetBIOS names to IP addresses as well as to store NetBIOS service information.

Windows Media Services — A service that provides streaming audio and video to clients.

Windows Sockets (WinSock) — A programming interface used by developers to access TCP/IP-based services.

Windows Sockets Direct (WinSock Direct) — An extension of the WinSock programming interface that allows developers to access resources on a system area network.

Windows Update — A Web site maintained by Microsoft to allow administrators and users to find out which updates are available for their systems and install them.

WINS proxy — A service that forwards local broadcast NetBIOS requests to a WINS server. This is implemented for NetBIOS clients that are unable to use WINS.

Wired Equivalent Privacy (WEP) — A protocol that is part of the 802.11 wireless network standards that is responsible for encrypting data transferred on the wireless network.

X.509 — A standard for certificates that was created by the International Telecommunication Union–Telecom-munication (ITU-T).

zone transfer — The process of updating DNS records from a primary DNS server to a secondary DNS server.

Index

Microsoft® Windows® Server 2003 Enterprise Edition 180-Day Evaluation

The software included in this kit is intended for evaluation and deployment planning purposes only. If you plan to install the software on your primary machine, it is recommended that you back up your existing data prior to installation.

System requirements

To use Microsoft Windows Server 2003 Enterprise Edition, you need:

- Computer with 550 MHz or higher processor clock speed recommended; 133 MHz minimum required; Intel Pentium/Celeron family, or AMD K6/Athlon/Duron family, or compatible processor (Windows Server 2003 Enterprise Edition supports up to eight CPUs on one server)
- 256 MB of RAM or higher recommended; 128 MB minimum required (maximum 32 GB of RAM)
- 1.25 to 2 GB of available hard-disk space*
- CD-ROM or DVD-ROM drive
- Super VGA (800 × 600) or higher-resolution monitor recommended; VGA or hardware that supports console redirection required
- Keyboard and Microsoft Mouse or compatible pointing device, or hardware that supports console redirection

Additional items or services required to use certain Windows Server 2003 Enterprise Edition features:

- For Internet access:
  - Some Internet functionality may require Internet access, a Microsoft Passport account, and payment of a separate fee to a service provider; local and/or long-distance telephone toll charges may apply
  - High-speed modem or broadband Internet connection
- For networking:
  - Network adapter appropriate for the type of local-area, wide-area, wireless, or home network to which you wish to connect, and access to an appropriate network infrastructure; access to third-party networks may require additional charges

Note: To ensure that your applications and hardware are Windows Server 2003–ready, be sure to visit **www.microsoft.com/windowsserver2003**.

* Actual requirements will vary based on your system configuration and the applications and features you choose to install. Additional available hard-disk space may be required if you are installing over a network. For more information, please see **www.microsoft.com/windowsserver2003**.

Uninstall instructions

This time-limited release of Microsoft Windows Server 2003 Enterprise Edition will expire 180 days after installation. If you decide to discontinue the use of this software, you will need to reinstall your original operating system. You may need to reformat your drive.